The Complete Book of
GARDENING

The Complete Book of
GARDENING

All You Need to Know About

LAWNS · TREES · FLOWERS · SHRUBS · GROUND COVERS
VEGETABLES · HERBS · FRUITS, NUTS & BERRIES
SOILS & FERTILIZERS · CLIMATE · SELECTING PLANTS
PLANNING A GARDEN · CONTAINER GARDENING
and much more!

By Richard Ray, Derek Fell and Michael MacCaskey

ORACLE BOOKS

Published by Oracle Books
A division of HPBooks, Inc.
P.O. Box 5367
Tucson, Arizona 85703
©1987 HPBooks, Inc.
Printed in U.S.A.
1st Printing

Library of Congress Cataloging-in-Publication Data

Ray, Richard.
   The complete book of gardening.

   Bibliography: p.
   Includes index.
   1. Gardening I. Fell, Derek. II. MacCaskey, Michael.
III. Title.
SB453.R33   1987   635   86-62455
ISBN 0-89586-515-7

CONTENTS

INTRODUCTION

It has often been said that plants are essential to our lives. They are the source of most of our clothing and shelter, and directly or indirectly provide all of our food. Less often considered is that plants soothe our spirits as well. Flower colors and fragrances stimulate and please our senses. The textures, forms and shades of green foliage are usually taken for granted.

Beyond the gratification of merely having plants present in our environment, great satisfaction can be derived from growing and caring for them—the practice of gardening.

A successful garden does not have to contain a wide variety of plants. Some of the most beautiful gardens consist of only a few kinds of plants, well-chosen to fit their surroundings, and arranged attractively. Gardener-writer Charles A. Lewis states, "The importance of gardens lies not in the flowers or vegetables produced, but in the personal benefits experienced by gardeners pursuing the process of gardening. Gardening teaches patience and observation—time is required for a seed to germinate or a fruit to ripen. Gardens connect us to the greater rhythms of nature—and ourselves."

The size or magnificence of the garden is irrelevant. If gardening space is limited, you can utilize multipurpose plants, such as a semidwarf apple tree that provides beauty, shade and fruit. There are dwarf and compact forms of many popular plants that can be fitted to small gardens. Container gardens also offer many possibilities where space is limited.

No matter what kind of garden you envision, success depends on raising *healthy plants*. This is the primary focus of this book.

No book can answer all of your gardening questions, but this one will teach you all of the basic cultural practices involved in growing plants. It will help you select plants best adapted to your area, provide the best possible conditions for growing them and care for them once they're planted. This book also directs you to those around you who can respond to your immediate questions—nursery personnel, landscape professionals, agricultural extension agents and others.

The only way to truly learn about growing plants is to grow them. To be a successful gardener requires the awareness of plants that comes with careful and frequent observation of their growth under the conditions in *your garden*. No rules or instructions cover every situation. This book will help you be more sensitive to your own plants and effectively respond to their needs as they grow. In this continuing process lies much of the enjoyment of gardening. If you are a beginner, use this book to guide you through your first efforts. No matter how much gardening experience you have, you'll find this a valuable reference book for realizing your garden plans and solving your gardening problems.

PLANT REQUIREMENTS

The first step toward creating a successful garden is understanding how plants grow and what they need in order to grow. The following is an overview of the basic requirements essential to plant growth. Specific information on how to

Gardening doesn't always require a lot of space. This small apartment garden consists mostly of container plants, which can be easily transported should their owners decide to move.

provide these requirements is organized by topic in the chapters that follow. The essentials of plant growth are:

● Soil, in which roots can anchor and air can circulate.
● Adequate water.
● Air temperature that is neither too hot nor too cold.
● Plant nutrients present in soil and air.
● Adequate light.

All of these factors work in concert to determine whether or not a certain plant will grow in a given location.

SOIL

Soil supplies water, air, nutrients and physical support to plants. A soil's ability to supply these elements depends on its physical and chemical characteristics, how they are determined and how they can be changed to produce healthier plants.

WATER

Water is essential to plants in several ways. It provides hydrogen and oxygen required by the plant to produce food. It regulates temperature by the process of *transpiration,* described on the facing page. It acts as a medium for transporting nutrients from the soil to all parts of the plant. As water percolates through the soil, it draws air to the plant roots.

Different plants need different amounts of water. The reasons are usually related to the environment in which the plant evolved. Root systems of some arid-climate clovers extend 6 to 12 feet into the soil. They are highly drought tolerant. Conversely, the root system of celery, a plant native to swamps, is shallow and requires frequent and abundant watering. Although the root systems of many drought-tolerant cacti and succulents are also shallow, these plants have the ability to store water in stems and leaves, thereby enabling them to endure long, dry periods.

The amount of water available to plants depends as much on the soil as it does on rainfall or the gardener's hose. The amount of water that soaks into the soil, the ease with which it soaks in and the amount the soil can hold all depend on soil texture and structure. Water enters clay soils slowly and sand soils quickly. Clay soils and soils high in organic matter hold the most water longest. Sand soils hold the least amount for the shortest period of time. One of the gardener's goals is to provide a soil structure that drains well, yet retains enough water to meet the plant's growing requirements.

More important than number of plants in garden is whether or not plants are healthy, as illustrated in this garden with its well-manicured lawn and carefully pruned shrubs.

Water in the air around the plant (humidity) affects, among other things, how fast water moves through the plant, called the *transpiration rate*. The type of plant and the amount of water in the soil determine the degree of influence humidity has on the transpiration rate.

Even with plenty of soil moisture, some plants wilt if humidity is too low—moisture is drawn from the plant's leaves into the air faster than the root system can replace it. This is one of the reasons why many plants adapted to arid climates have small or narrow leaves to expose the least amount of leaf surface possible to the air. Others have succulent, water-storing leaves, or hairy, gray leaves that help reduce transpiration. On the other hand, large, fleshy leaves usually indicate that the plant evolved in a shady or humid environment where a fast transpiration rate is necessary to the plant's survival. So humidity has some effect on the kind of plants you can grow in your garden.

AIR
Air supplies two elements essential to plant growth—carbon and oxygen. Plants require air circulation both above and below ground. Roots absorb oxygen and give off carbon dioxide, just as animals do by breathing.

In heavy, compacted or clay soils, the space between soil particles, called *pore space,* is small. When air in the soil is inadequate, as is common in heavy soils, or in soils where all pore space is filled with water, the roots of most plants will die. When roots begin to die, the leaves of the plant wilt, often prompting the gardener to give the plant even more water—which kills it that much faster. Soils with a crusted surface also restrict air circulation, as does soil that is compacted by repeated foot or vehicle traffic.

Air circulation above ground is also necessary for healthy plant growth. Lack of air circulation under moist conditions reduces water evaporation, promoting fungal diseases and mildew. Too much circulation of dry air, such as on a hot, windy day, can dry plants out.

TEMPERATURE
More than any other element of climate, temperature determines which plants will grow where. Temperature directly influences the rate of internal plant processes. The fastest growth occurs at the upper temperature limit that the particular plant tolerates.

Perhaps the most crucial temperature for gardeners is the freezing point of water, 32F (0C). Growing-season length, planting time for warm-season plants, and harvest time are all determined by the spring and fall occurrence of this temperature. Minimum winter temperature, as defined by the United States Department of Agriculture (USDA), determines which perennial plants you can grow in a given region.

Low temperatures just above freezing will often retard plant growth or prevent seed germination. The ideal temperature for plant growth is different for different plants. Seeds of cool-season plants—cabbage, onions and peas, for example—germinate at soil temperatures as low as 40F (4C). Seeds of warm-season plants, such as Bermudagrass, beans, corn, African violets and melons, will not germinate until soil temperatures reach about 60F (16C).

Temperature also affects the quality and maturity rate of many crops and has an influence on the kinds of pests and diseases likely to be troublesome.

PLANT NUTRIENTS

There are 16 elements necessary for plant growth. The plant receives three of these—carbon, hydrogen and oxygen—from air and water. The other 13 elements are received from the soil. They are: *nitrogen, potassium, calcium, magnesium, phosphorus, sulfur, iron, copper, manganese, zinc, molybdenum, boron* and *chlorine*. These elements are absorbed from moisture in the soil. Nitrogen, phosphorus and potassium are used by plants in the greatest amounts, so these three *primary nutrients* are the ones that must be replenished most frequently. The *secondary nutrients*, magnesium, sulfur and calcium, are used by plants to a lesser extent, and are usually added only when the plant shows a deficiency. The remaining nutrients, called *trace elements,* are used by plants only in minute amounts and are usually present in the soil in sufficient quantities.

Plants grow best when nutrients are present in a steady, uniform supply. Slow-growing, long-lived plants such as trees and shrubs are more adaptable than fast-growing, short-lived plants to changes in nutrient levels in the soil. They can suffer a deficiency then fully recover once the nutrient is supplied. This is why you usually wait for a sign of nutrient need before fertilizing a tree or shrub. Fast-growing, short-lived plants—annuals and most vegetables, for instance—never fully recover from an early-season nutrient deficiency. This is why you add fertilizer to the soil before planting and then at least once again during growth.

LIGHT

All green plants use sunlight, carbon dioxide and water to make food. This process is known as *photosynthesis.* The food—starch or sugar—is utilized by the plant to grow. In photosynthesis, the chlorophyll in green plants uses light energy to break water down into hydrogen and oxygen. The hydrogen then combines with carbon dioxide the plant takes in from the atmosphere to form the sugars that serve as food. The oxygen from the water is released into the atmosphere.

Light—the intensity and duration of it—affects all phases of plant growth. For instance, the intensity of light a plant receives affects its growing habit. As a rule, leaves distribute themselves so that each one receives the maximum amount of light and shades the others least. Plants in too little light become tall and spindly. Abundant light results in shorter, bushier plants. Some plants require a specific amount of light to maintain good growth. Others adapt to some degree of shade or full sun.

The duration of light is one way plants have adapted themselves to the changing seasons. For example, short days and long nights trigger the bloom of chrysanthemum flowers. Other plants respond in opposite ways and some plants are not affected by light duration at all.

OTHER PLANT NEEDS

Plants also need a growing environment that is relatively free of pests, diseases and competition from weeds. Many garden plants also require periodic pruning to maintain healthy growth or an attractive appearance.

As opposed to plants that grow in the wild, practically all plants bred for garden use require help from the gardener to survive and remain healthy—watering, fertilizing, pest and disease control, pruning, weeding and other gardening practices described in this book. The commitment to plant care does involve work, but the better you understand plant requirements, the easier and more enjoyable that work will become.

HOW A PLANT WORKS

At right is a simplified illustration of how a plant uses soil, water and sunlight to grow. It also shows how the component parts of roots, stems and leaves function in the growing process.

1. Water and soil nutrients (in solution form) are absorbed through tiny *root hairs,* which are located in the root-hair zone just behind rapidly growing root tips.

2. The water and nutrients are then conducted up through the roots, main stem and branches through a porous tissue called *xylem,* located beneath the bark or cambium layer of the stem.

3. The xylem tissue in individual leaf stems *(petioles)* transfers the water and nutrients to leaves. Water and nutrients are conducted to flowers and fruit in a similar manner.

4. Water and nutrients are conducted through leaf veins and absorbed by leaf cells, where they are converted to a form usable by the plant, as described below. Excess moisture is transferred to the leaf surface through small pores called *stomatas,* where it evaporates in the form of water vapor. Called *transpiration,* this process works somewhat like a human's perspiration to cool the plant. This process also releases oxygen into the air.

5, 6. Within each individual plant cell occurs the process of *photosynthesis*—the utilization of the sun's energy to convert inorganic plant nutrients into sugar (food) used for plant growth. *Chloroplasts* are microscopic bodies within plant cells (6) where photosynthesis occurs. They are also what give plants their green color. Several other complex chemical processes occur within plant cells to direct the plant's growth habits, determined by genetic information contained within each cell's nucleus.

7, 8. Buds are the points where all new plant growth starts. The *terminal bud* (7) is the growing point of the main stem or trunk. Terminal buds also occur at the growing tips of side branches. *Lateral buds* (8) on the main stem develop into side branches, leaves or flowers, depending on the plant. On many plants, side branches also develop lateral buds. The positions of various types of buds on the main stem and side branches determine the plant's eventual size and shape.

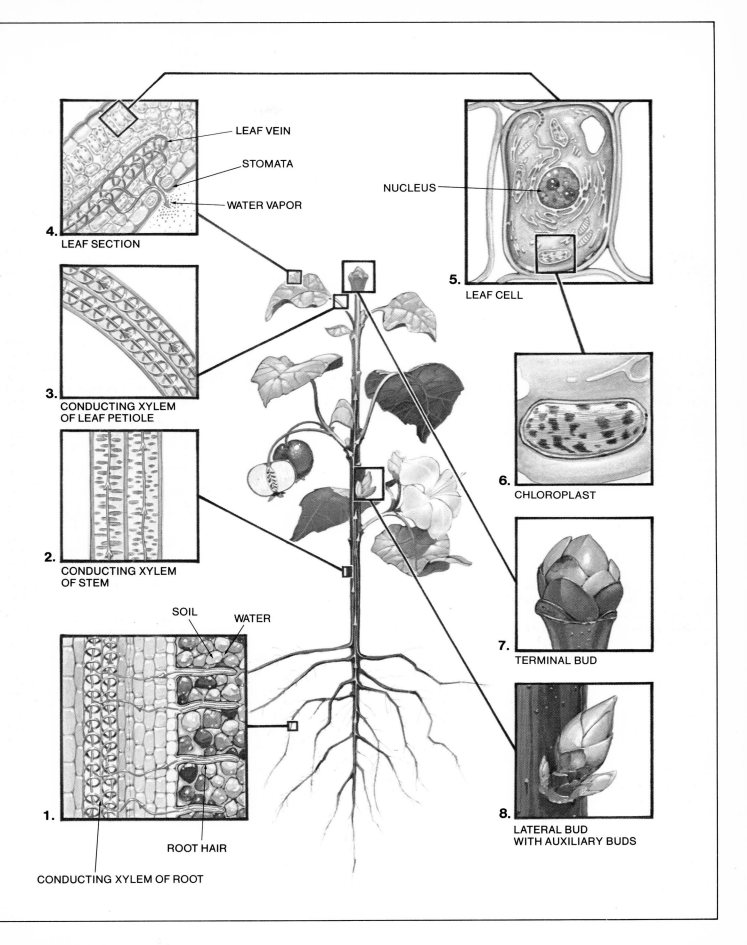

4. LEAF SECTION

LEAF VEIN

STOMATA

WATER VAPOR

3. CONDUCTING XYLEM OF LEAF PETIOLE

2. CONDUCTING XYLEM OF STEM

NUCLEUS

5. LEAF CELL

6. CHLOROPLAST

7. TERMINAL BUD

8. LATERAL BUD WITH AUXILIARY BUDS

SOIL

WATER

ROOT HAIR

1. CONDUCTING XYLEM OF ROOT

CLIMATE

Climate affects practically every aspect of gardening. At its gentle best, climate silently guides our gardening. The gradual warming of soil each spring determines when we plant warm-season plants. A bean seed, for example, will surely rot if planted too early when soil is too cold. At other times, climate forces us to take quick action to protect an important plant on a chilly night from an imminent frost. Our climates directly affect planting times and plant care, so it behooves any gardener to understand some climate fundamentals.

There are three basic elements of climate—*temperature, available sunshine* and *water* in the form of precipitation and humidity. The interrelationship of these three elements determines a region's climate throughout the year and what will grow where.

TEMPERATURE
This is the most influential element of climate in determining whether or not a certain type of plant will grow in your garden. Temperature affects all plant processes by controlling the rate of their internal reactions. Especially important are the expected winter minimum temperature in your area and the seasonal average time of first and last frosts.

Generally, growth begins at a certain temperature, then proceeds at a faster and faster rate until an upper limit is reached. When temperatures are either too low or too high, growth slows or stops. There are low and high temperature extremes that destroy plants outright.

The period in which temperatures are conducive to plant growth is called the *growing season*. It is the time between the last frost in spring and the first frost in winter. When the growing season ends, annual flowers and vegetables die and perennial plants begin their dormant period.

Certain *critical* or *cardinal temperatures* have been determined for a number of plants. These temperatures include the minimum, optimum and maximum temperatures for plant growth, as well as minimum and maximum lethal temperatures. As you might imagine, determining all of these temperatures is a com-

plicated process, and they have been worked out for relatively few plants. For instance, most plants have several different sets of critical temperatures for each of their growth stages. Usually, the optimum temperature for seed germination of a plant is lower than the optimum temperature for its vegetative growth.

Annual vegetables and flowers are classified as either *cool season* or *warm season*. Most cool-season plants need a minimum soil temperature of approximately 40F (4C) to germinate and an equivalent air temperature to sustain growth. Warm-season plants require temperatures some 10 degrees higher, or at least 50F (10C), to begin and sustain growth. Most perennial plants native to tropical areas are damaged by temperatures that approach freezing. A pepper plant or African violet is damaged by temperatures that fall much below 40F (4C).

Bolting—This is the premature development of a seed stalk of a biennial herb or vegetable such as celery, parsley or cilantro. Bolting frustrates beginner

Left: Late spring frost can destroy an entire fruit crop by killing blossoms. It can also kill newly emerging seedlings. Understanding your climate will enable you to help protect plants from such events. Polyethylene sheeting shown here is one form of frost protection.

Above: Simple unheated greenhouse can be used to start bedding plants early or protect cold-sensitive container plants. Surrounding hedge keeps greenhouse cool during summer months.

CLIMATE ELEMENTS

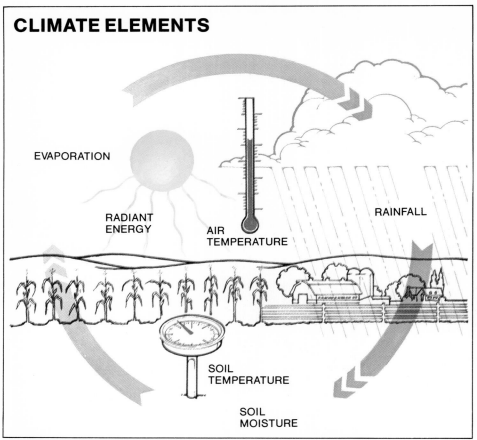

EVAPORATION

RADIANT ENERGY

AIR TEMPERATURE

RAINFALL

SOIL TEMPERATURE

SOIL MOISTURE

Successful gardening depends on being in tune with constant weather cycles in your area. This drawing illustrates how various weather elements work together to recycle water naturally available to plants. Amount of rainfall and when it occurs, as well as air and soil temperature, determine how much supplemental water must be given to plants.

and expert alike. If you have ever tucked a promising celery transplant into the garden only to watch it rush to seed and die a few weeks later, you know about bolting. In this case, it happens when cool temperatures due to an unseasonably cool spring occur shortly after planting. The plant is conditioned to develop a seed stalk after exposure to the winter following a season of growth. In effect, cool weather after planting replaces winter, the entire growth cycle is compressed and the plant is useless.

Some varieties of lettuce react in an opposite way. While prevailing temperatures are cool, about 50F to 60F (10C to 16C), the edible lettuce "heads" develop. When temperatures are warm, 70F to 80F (21C to 27C), flower stalks devel-

op rapidly at the expense of heads.

There is still more to the bolting story—some plants are triggered into flower development by a change in day length.

Cold Temperatures—The freezing point of water (32F/0C) is perhaps the most familiar critical temperature. The spring and fall occurrence of this temperature establishes the length of the growing season, the planting time of warm-season annuals and the harvest time of many crops.

Equally significant is the minimum temperature of winter. The ability to adapt to temperatures below freezing varies tremendously among different kinds of plants. This ability is referred to as a plant's *hardiness*. More than any

other element of climate, this determines which plants are perennial and where. The United States Department of Agriculture (USDA) plant hardiness zone map on the facing page shows the average annual minimum temperatures in various parts of the United States and Canada. It is the most common garden climate map currently in use.

Plants are damaged by cold when ice crystals form between cells. This damage occurs due to excessive cold during winter, early-spring or late-fall frosts, or to drought because both soil water and the root system are frozen and cannot absorb water. Plants are also damaged by alternate freezing and thawing of soil (soil heaving) and by the weight of snow or ice breaking branches.

The minimum winter temperature at which a plant is damaged is not a hard and fast thing. Many factors are involved. Plants with adequate nutrient and water supplies are more tolerant of cold than identical plants not so supplied.

Duration of cold is another factor. Some plants may be able to tolerate 25F (4C) for 10 minutes, but not for 1 hour. Likewise, the rate of temperature fall can damage an otherwise cold-hardy plant. Rapidly falling temperatures can cause the bark of trees and shrubs to split apart, sometimes resulting in the death of the plant.

The time of the year cold temperature occurs is also important. If it is very early or late in the season, the plant may be less resistant than if the same or lower temperature occurred in midwinter. Also, plants protected by a mulch or blanket of snow will survive colder winters better than plants that aren't.

Most cold-temperature damage happens in spring. That is when we try to get a jump on the season by setting out tender transplants early, or when seedlings are just emerging from the soil. Also, leaf and flower buds of perennial flowers, vines, shrubs and trees are just beginning to expand. This is the reason crops of early flowering fruit trees, such as apricots, so often fail in late-frost climates where the tree itself is winter-hardy. Spring and fall frosts are most common on clear, still nights when there are no clouds to limit heat loss and no wind to prevent an air inversion.

Frost—There are two basic kinds of frosts. *Air-mass frost* results from the occurence of a cold air mass with a temperature less than 32F (0C). *Radiation*

PLANT HARDINESS ZONE MAP

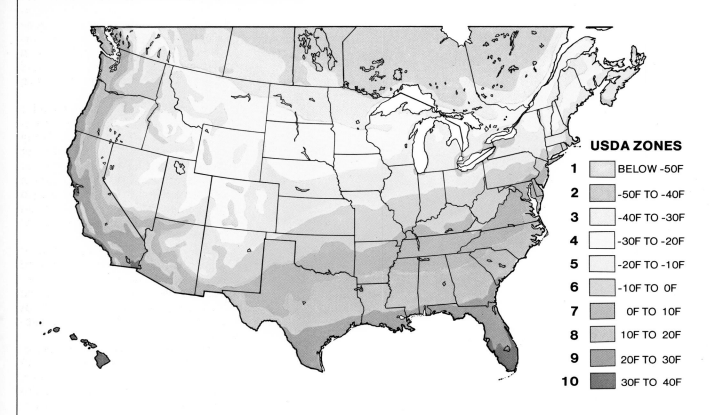

USDA ZONES

1		BELOW -50F
2		-50F TO -40F
3		-40F TO -30F
4		-30F TO -20F
5		-20F TO -10F
6		-10F TO 0F
7		0F TO 10F
8		10F TO 20F
9		20F TO 30F
10		30F TO 40F

UNITED STATES DEPARTMENT OF AGRICULTURE

This map shows average minimum winter temperature in various parts of United States and portions of Canada. Use it as a general guide to determine which perennial plants can be grown in your area. The USDA zone system is often used to indicate cold-hardiness of many perennial plants. For example, if a plant is said to be hardy to Zone 4, it can usually be expected to survive a minimum temperature between -30F to -20F. However, other factors, such as wind, sun, snow and frosts—and when these occur—also determine if a plant will survive the winter in any given location. Also, because North America has a complex climate—microclimates and variations in weather patterns from one year to the next cannot be accurately mapped—use this map as a guide only. You can get more specific information from your local weather service, county or university extension services and local nurseries.

frost results when plants quickly lose much more heat than they are absorbing until they reach the temperature of 32F (0C). Air-mass frosts are more likely to occur during winter and they threaten primarily half-hardy plants. Radiation frosts occur in fall or spring and threaten plants not yet fully dormant or at early, tender stages of growth.

There are variations within the two main frost types, determined by how frost affects the plant. A *white frost* or *hoarfrost* occurs when dew that has formed on a cooling leaf reaches 32F

(0C). If dew does not form before the freezing temperature is reached, it is called a *dryfreeze*, or more appropriately for gardeners, a *black frost,* because there is no visible sign of frost until damaged plant tissues blacken.

A *killing freeze* is the kind that cuts the growing season short. A *hard freeze* is a freeze that kills seasonal vegetation and freezes the ground surface solid. Heavy ice forms on the surfaces of small bodies of water, such as puddles and water containers. A *light freeze* occurs when the surface temperature of the air drops to

below freezing for a short time so that only the most tender plants are damaged.

Gardeners can do much to reduce the chances of losing plants or crops to cold winters or spring frosts. Where you plant—*site selection*—makes a significant difference. For instance, choose a wind- and overhead-protected location for a plant that is only marginally hardy. Also, south slopes and sandy soils trap more heat faster in spring. You could safely plant a vegetable garden there weeks earlier than you could on a north slope or in clay soil.

FROST

THERMAL BELTS

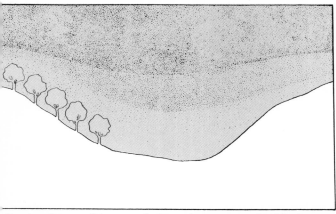

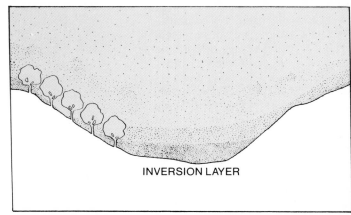

INVERSION LAYER

In the drawings on this page, darker colors represent colder temperatures. Under normal conditions, air temperatures decrease with height, as shown at left. With an *inversion layer,* cold air is trapped below a layer of warm air. This creates warmer-than-usual *thermal belts* on hillsides above low spots. Thermal belts can be ideal planting areas for plants that would normally be damaged by colder air in lower areas.

RADIATION FROST

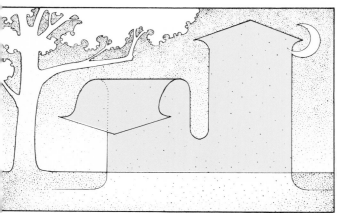

Heat from the sun is stored in soil during the day. At night, heat radiates back into the atmosphere. If the soil loses so much heat that it becomes colder than surrounding air, a radiation frost can occur. Objects such as trees, patio roofs or house-roof overhangs can trap radiating heat and often prevent frosts in localized areas.

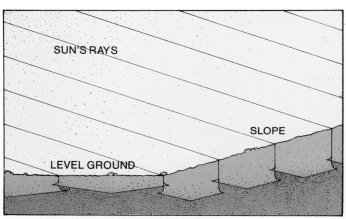

SUN'S RAYS

SLOPE

LEVEL GROUND

A south-facing slope receives more of sun's heat than does level ground, so radiation frosts are less likely to occur in this location. Similarly, west-facing slopes receive more sun during afternoon, so soil is warmer just before nightfall.

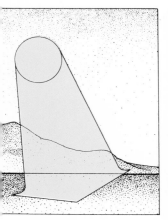
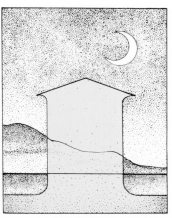

Radiation frosts are most common when night skies are clear and air is still. These conditions allow for maximum radiation of soil warmth back into atmosphere.

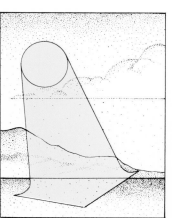
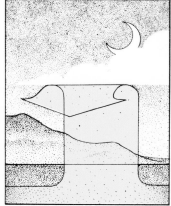

Cloudy nighttime skies trap soil heat radiating into atmosphere. Radiation frosts are less likely under these conditions.

Heating lamps or gasoline lanterns situated near the base of a shrub or tree are often enough to protect it from spring frosts. A plastic sheet held above the tree by long poles, by itself or in combination with a heat source, provides protection.

The way you take care of your plants has a great effect on their chances of surviving a cold winter. Raking a loose mulch of peat moss, straw, sawdust, wood shavings or leaves over the crowns of strawberries, roses and perennials will help prevent winter freeze and heaving damage. Heaving is the expansion and contraction of soil caused by alternate freezing and thawing. It damages plants by disturbing roots. In severe cases, smaller plants can be pushed out of the ground.

As previously mentioned, plants well supplied with adequate food and water will be much more cold-hardy than those that are not. Avoid heavy summer pruning and gradually reduce the amount of nitrogen fertilizer and water supplied in fall to slow growth and stimulate accumulation of food.

Innovative gardeners have discovered many methods to protect plants from untimely spring frosts by starting plants earlier, thus gaining a month or so on the growing season. There is more than pride to win from starting early—early crops are more likely to escape pest damage. Plastic sheets or wax paper draped or stretched over frames create mini-greenhouses in the garden. Minimum temperatures under such a tent are commonly warmer by 5F to 8F (-15C to -13C), which is often more than enough to make the difference. Of course, daytime temperatures under a plastic tent may rapidly become too high, so venting is often required.

Wind—This amplifies cold and has a drying effect on soil and plants. Plastic shelters are equally useful for wind protection. Seedlings and transplants will grow into vastly superior plants if protected from prevailing winds. Wood shingles are convenient for this purpose. Many commercial products are also available.

High Temperatures—Most common garden plants essentially stop growing at temperatures above 95F (35C). Among other things, high temperatures determine the quality and maturity rate of fruits and vegetables, and the kinds of pests likely to be a problem.

High temperatures restrict plants in other ways. In warm-winter climates, winters do not provide many deciduous fruit trees with enough cold to complete their physiological rest period. For instance, most peach varieties need between 600 and 900 hours of winter temperatures between 32F and 45F (0C and 7C). Fewer hours of cold result in *delayed foliation,* or weak growth, in spring. Luckily for gardeners in such climates, special *low-chill* varieties of

Row cover made from translucent corrugated fiberglass panel protects tomato transplants from frost. Panel allows soil to heat during day, retains heat at night.

Raised bed in greenhouse is convenient for starting large numbers of seedlings or for growing cold-tender plants out of season.

AVERAGE GROWING-SEASON LENGTH

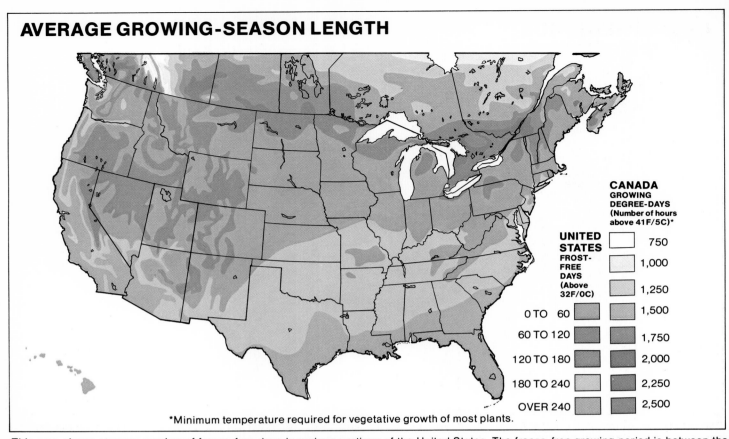

UNITED STATES FROST-FREE DAYS (Above 32F/0C)	CANADA GROWING DEGREE-DAYS (Number of hours above 41F/5C)*
	750
	1,000
	1,250
0 TO 60	1,500
60 TO 120	1,750
120 TO 180	2,000
180 TO 240	2,250
OVER 240	2,500

*Minimum temperature required for vegetative growth of most plants.

This map shows average number of freeze-free days in various portions of the United States. The freeze-free growing period is between the dates of the last 32F (0C) temperature in spring and the first 32F (0C) temperature in autumn, and is usually referred to as the *growing season*. The Canadian weather service uses a different scale to measure length of growing season: *Annual total growing degree-days above 41F (5C)*. The numbers on the map indicate the sum of the number of degrees above 41F (5C) accumulated over the growing season. The higher the number, the longer the growing season.

most deciduous fruit trees are available.

Pests are often more abundant when summer and winter temperatures are high. There are two reasons: First, most insects and disease organisms reproduce faster in high temperatures. Second, relatively warm winters allow more pests to survive. A really cold Minnesota winter does gardeners there more good than any pesticide used in summer.

SEASON LENGTH

The number of days between frosts determines the length of the growing season. This is important to know when planning what and how much you can grow. The maps above and at right, *Average Growing-Season Length, Last Spring Frost* and *First Fall Frost* show the variations. Growing seasons are as short as 60 freeze-free days in the coldest climates and as long as 330 or more in the mildest ones. Knowing your season length gives meaning to the information on a packet of bean seeds. When the packet says, "55 days," and your grow-

ing season is 200 days long, you can roughly figure three complete crop cycles are possible, providing temperatures remain within a favorable range. If your growing season is only 60 days long, you know you will have to work quickly to plant and harvest one crop.

In northern gardens where growing seasons are usually shortest, the sun shines longer during that time than it does farther south. All other things being equal, beans that require 55 days to mature at middle latitudes will grow faster in northern ones, sometimes needing as few as 45 days to mature. Conversely, frostless regions in middle latitudes are generally coastal areas with cool summers. The same beans there may require 70 days to mature.

SUNSHINE

Gardeners benefit by an understanding of three of the many ways sunlight influences plant growth. They are: *percent possible sunshine, light intensity*

and *light duration*.

Percent Possible Sunshine—The sun is the energy source plants use to grow. Percent possible sunshine shows us how much of this basic energy is available in our climate. *Possible sunshine* is the total number of hours of sunlight a location can receive annually in the absence of clouds. *Percent possible sunshine* is the actual amount of sunshine compared to the possible sunshine.

Possible sunshine is figured on the basis of latitude. At the equator, the earth can receive 4,420 hours of sunlight annually; at 25°N, the latitude of the Florida Keys, 4,449 hours; at 49°N, the western U.S.-Canadian border, 4,486 hours. In the continental United States, the longest day—sunrise to sunset—is 16 hours and 13 minutes at 49°N and occurs about June 21. The shortest day, about December 21, occurs at the same latitude and is 8 hours and 13 minutes.

Although northern climates have longer periods of possible sunshine during the growing season, this does not

LAST SPRING FROST

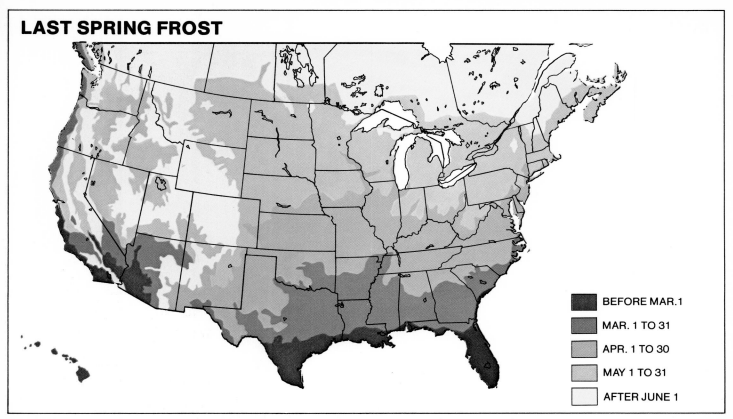

■	BEFORE MAR. 1
■	MAR. 1 TO 31
■	APR. 1 TO 30
■	MAY 1 TO 31
□	AFTER JUNE 1

This map shows average dates of last spring frost in various parts of United States and portions of Canada. Use it in conjunction with local observations to determine safe planting times.

FIRST FALL FROST

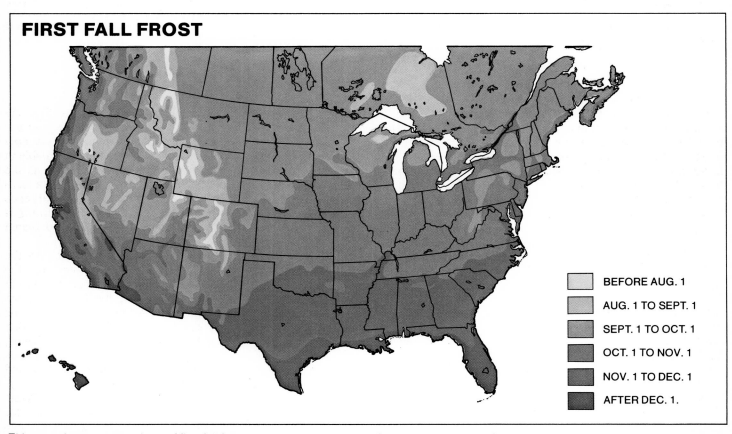

□	BEFORE AUG. 1
■	AUG. 1 TO SEPT. 1
■	SEPT. 1 TO OCT. 1
■	OCT. 1 TO NOV. 1
■	NOV. 1 TO DEC. 1
■	AFTER DEC. 1.

This map shows average dates of first fall frost in various parts of United States and portions of Canada. Use it in conjunction with local observations to determine planting and harvesting times for annual crops. For more precise information, contact local weather service or extension agent.

SUNSHINE

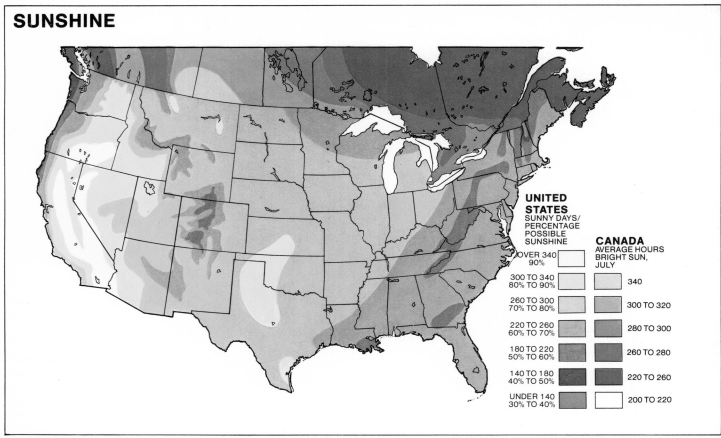

This map shows average number of sunny days and average (mean) percentage possible sunshine in various parts of United States. It also shows the number of hours of bright sunlight during month of July in portions of Canada.

UNITED STATES
SUNNY DAYS/
PERCENTAGE
POSSIBLE
SUNSHINE

OVER 340
90%

300 TO 340
80% TO 90%

260 TO 300
70% TO 80%

220 TO 260
60% TO 70%

180 TO 220
50% TO 60%

140 TO 180
40% TO 50%

UNDER 140
30% TO 40%

CANADA
AVERAGE HOURS
BRIGHT SUN,
JULY

340

300 TO 320

280 TO 300

260 TO 280

220 TO 260

200 TO 220

necessarily mean all northern regions receive more actual sunshine than southern ones. For example, coastal areas of the Pacific Northwest receive less sunshine than the Southwest desert due to overcast.

The map above shows seven regions of roughly equal sunshine. Most of the United States receives some 300 hours of sunshine a month through summer. It is along the foggy Washington coast that the least summer sun reaches gardens, followed closely by sections of the Appalachians. The greatest monthly hours of sunshine, usually more than 400 hours a month (90% possible sunshine), occur in the San Joaquin and lower Sacramento valleys of California during June, July and August. These valleys are highly productive agricultural areas.

Here is an example of how percent possible sunshine affects plant growth: An early ripening tomato is said to require 45 days between setting out as a transplant and the first ripe fruit. But experiments in western Washington— 40% to 50% possible sunshine— showed such a tomato grown there requires twice as many days to produce fruit. Although this difference in growth rate cannot be entirely attributed to less light—the cool temperatures of western Washington are also a factor—it does prove that the amount of available sunshine has a substantial effect on the growth rate of plants and maturation of crops.

Light Intensity—Light intensity is the actual amount of light falling on a surface at any given time. Naturally, this is quite variable. Intensity varies with seasons, latitude, overcast, pollution, and shade cast by trees or buildings. One measurement of light intensity is in units called *footcandles*. A footcandle (F.C.) is defined as the density of light striking the inner surface of a sphere with all surface area 1 foot away from a standardized, 1-candle-power light source.

A clear, desert day at noon may measure 12,000 F.C. while at the same moment in western Washington, light intensity measures 1,500 F.C. Light intensity in a typical, well-lighted home will measure between 50 and 300 F.C.

There is tremendous variation in the ability of different plants to utilize light. Many of our house plants evolved in heavily shaded jungle environments, which is why they can tolerate the low light levels of a house interior. There are also a number of outdoor plants that can tolerate low light levels.

Individual leaves of most plants can utilize only about 1,200 F.C. of light. But because of the way leaves are arranged on the plant to shade each other, most outdoor plants respond to a maximum of about 4,000 F.C.

Plants respond in several ways when light intensity is too low. Perhaps the first thing you will notice is they appear stretched out, with fewer, thinner leaves spaced farther apart. Seedlings grown in

SEASONS OF THE YEAR

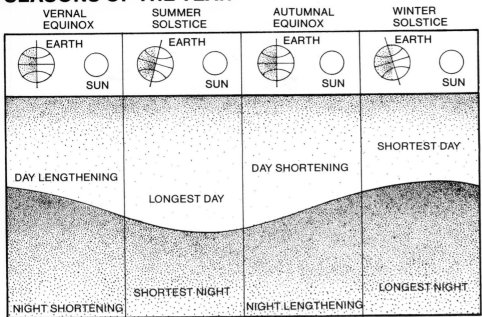

VERNAL EQUINOX	SUMMER SOLSTICE	AUTUMNAL EQUINOX	WINTER SOLSTICE
EARTH SUN	EARTH SUN	EARTH SUN	EARTH SUN

DAY LENGTHENING

DAY SHORTENING

SHORTEST DAY

LONGEST DAY

LONGEST NIGHT

SHORTEST NIGHT

NIGHT SHORTENING

NIGHT LENGTHENING

Relationship of earth's axis to orbital plane of sun causes change in seasons and variation in day length. These changes set planting and harvesting timetables for many plants, including most vegetables.

low light are yellowish-looking, with spindly stems and long internodes, a condition known as *etiolation*. Leaves of plants grown in low light are not only thinner, but more succulent and darker green. Most plants situated in low light will grow slowly at best. A longer duration of exposure to light helps compensate for low light intensity.

Adjust plants slowly from one condition of light to another. A house plant such as weeping fig (*Ficus benjamina*) can adapt to either low or high levels of light. But make the shift incremental, gradually increasing or decreasing the amount of light. Leaves adapted to low light will burn if the plant is abruptly moved into strong light. Leaves adapted to high light will fall off if abruptly moved to shade—shocking the gardener as well as the plant—to be replaced with low-light leaves.

Light Duration—Duration of light, or number of daylight hours, is the guide many plants use to coordinate themselves with the seasons. The processes of flowering, bulbing, forming tubers and other shifts in plant efforts are linked to this reliable clock. The response of a

plant to a particular day length (daylight hours) is called *photoperiodism.*

Chrysanthemums and poinsettias are well-known plants with specific responses to day length. They are called *short-day* plants. This means they respond to a day length shorter than a certain maximum. The shorter days of fall trigger blooming. Growers can speed blooming by covering plants to shorten their day length, or delay blooming by exposing them to artificial light to increase their day length. For details, see *How to Rebloom a Poinsettia* at right.

Spinach and onions are good examples of *long-day* plants. Spinach begins to develop a flower stalk when exposed to relatively long days. High temperatures also stimulate spinach flowering at the expense of edible leaves. When days are a certain length, spinach will flower no matter what size the plant is. Gardeners who plant spinach in late spring are much less likely to harvest a crop than those who plant when days are short in early spring or in fall.

Day neutral plants are not affected by day length. These are usually tropical plants accustomed to relatively un-

changing day length. African violet is an example.

Onions form bulbs when days are longer than a certain minimum number of hours. There are specific varieties of onions for northern and southern climates. For instance, Bermuda onions grow during the winter in the South and begin bulbing when days reach approximately 11 hours long. They are ready to harvest in early summer. In the North, onions cannot be planted until spring. By that time, days are already long enough for the southern onion to bulb. Northern onion varieties bulb when days reach 15 hours or more in length, approximately mid-June. They are ready to harvest in fall.

WATER

Water, in the form of precipitation (rainfall) and humidity, is the third critical element of climate. Usually, there is either too much or too little of it.

Water is essential to plants in more than one way. Water is an essential plant nutrient, contributing hydrogen, which is essential to the process of photosynthesis. Water is also a solvent and carrier of the sugars manufactured in plant leaves and of mineral nutrients from the soil. And not least of all, the water that plants consume works like an air conditioner to cool the plant.

HOW TO REBLOOM A POINSETTIA

Most people treat poinsettias as annual plants, disposing of them after they bloom. They are, in fact, tender perennials that will bloom year after year under the right conditions.

After Christmas, keep the plant near a sunny window to maintain best possible growth. Water and fertilize as you would any house plant. As soon as temperatures permit, move plant outdoors, gradually adjusting it to full sun.

Begin rebloom in early November by keeping the plant in a room where only natural daylight enters. Do not expose plant to artificial light at night because as little as a few minutes of interrupted darkness will delay the flowering process. It is also possible to induce flowering by covering the entire plant at sunset with a lightproof box, then removing the box at sunrise. Any special treatment can be stopped as soon as the flower bracts show color.

RAINFALL

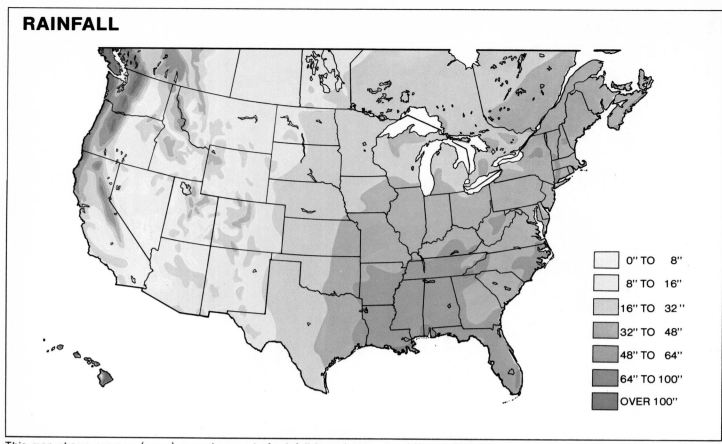

Legend:
- 0" TO 8"
- 8" TO 16"
- 16" TO 32"
- 32" TO 48"
- 48" TO 64"
- 64" TO 100"
- OVER 100"

This map shows average (mean) annual amount of rainfall in various parts of United States and portions of Canada. In most parts of the country, rainfall contributes relatively little water to garden plants during growing season. However, it does have a great influence on kinds of plants you can grow in your area, as described in text below.

Gardeners must work with the amount of water naturally available from rain and the particular requirements of the plants they wish to grow. In most areas, the water provided by rainfall during the growing season is not enough to support most garden plants, so supplemental water is needed. In a few areas of the country, however, rainfall provides *too much* water for many kinds of plants. See the rainfall map above.

When rain comes is also important. An untimely rain can damage certain plants and crops. Rainfall and the high humidity that usually accompanies it are associated with several plant diseases. Scab disease of apples and crabapples is virtually unknown where the growing season is dry, but is a fact of life where it is wet. The rose disease known as *black spot* and the potato disease known as *potato blight* are similarly stimulated by moisture. Nearly ripe, high-sugar fruits such as cherries and tomatoes often

crack after a rain. Rainfall patterns differ throughout the country, some regions receiving most of their rain in summer, others in winter. These kinds of distinctions are discussed in the following text on ecosystems.

ECOSYSTEMS

So far, we have discussed individually the three major elements of climate—temperature, sunlight and rainfall. Now let's look at how *all three* factors of climate come together in an area to produce a particular climate region, or *ecosystem*. The plant and animal life of a certain region can tell us much about the climate.

Temperature is not the only factor that determines whether or not a plant will survive in a given area. A few examples comparing the southeastern and southwestern United States demonstrate this point. Most garden reference books include a USDA rating for plants,

encouraging the misconception that a Zone-9 plant will grow anywhere that zone occurs. But the rating means the plant is only cold-hardy in that zone, not that it can be successfully grown in all parts of it. The plant may be completely unreliable in one part or another due to a myriad of other factors—distribution of rainfall, available sunlight, soil characteristics, regional pest problems and so on.

One example is the junipers. They are fully hardy to the expected minimum temperatures of Zone 9 but are prone to root rot when exposed to the heavy summer rainfall of the Southeast. Another example is English holly. Like many other hollies, it thrives in the Southeast but suffers and rarely lives long in the same Zone 9 of the Southwest.

The United States and southern Canada include three major types of ecosystems—forest, grassland and desert. There are subcategories of each,

ECOSYSTEMS

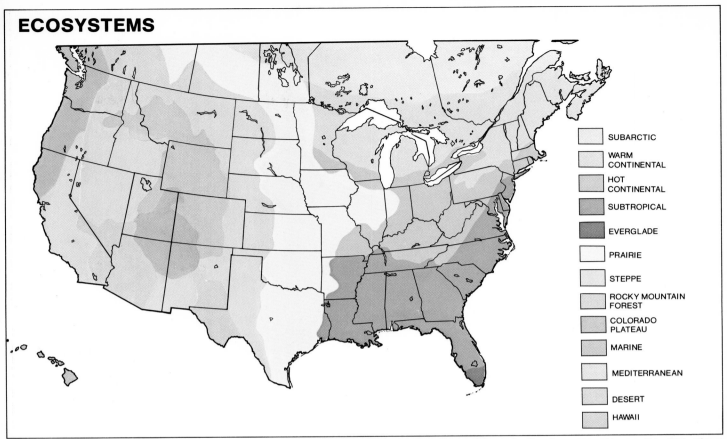

This map shows major climatic regions, called *ecosystems,* of United States and portions of Canada. Smaller ecosystems exist within these, depending on altitude, terrain, soil and climatic conditions. Observing natural vegetation in your ecosystem will give you a clue to kinds of garden plants that will do well where you live.

which appear on the map above and are described here:

Warm Continental—The climate here is generally noted by its warm, humid summers. There are 4 to 8 months of temperatures that exceed 50F (10C). There is no dry season, although most rainfall comes in summer. The natural vegetation is forest, primarily hemlock and several types of conifers that include red and white pine, spruce and fir. Deciduous trees include birches, beech, maple, basswood and the oaks. Soils tend to lack calcium, potassium and magnesium, and they are generally acid.

Hot Continental—The climate here is characteristically humid with hot summers. In the warmer regions, the frost-free growing season is 5 to 6 months long. In colder regions, growing seasons are 3 to 5 months long. In the northern portions, the dominant vegetation is forest. Trees include oaks, hickories, beech, maples, ashes, basswoods, black locust, yellow poplar and walnut. Soils are usually rich with humus.

Subtropical—Winters here are never really cold, and hot summers are humid.

Rainfall comes any time of year but mostly in summer. Thunderstorms are common and hurricanes occur. Soils tend to be wet, acidic, and low in major plant nutrients. The Southeastern forest is a mix of conifers and hardwoods. It includes many kinds of pine, red cedar, gums, oaks, hickories and bald cypress.

Everglades—This is a tropical climate with most rainfall occurring during summer. The average annual temperature is approximately 73F (23C). Cypress forests are extensive and mangrove is widespread along the eastern and southern coasts. Mahogany, redbay and palmettos are found growing on *hammocks*—areas raised above surrounding, wetter land.

Prairie—The prairie is a vast, largely treeless area, variable in temperature and generally low in rainfall. The part bordering the eastern forests was once covered with tall grasses, but is now planted with corn and other crops. Most of the 20 to 40 inches of rainfall that comes to the prairie occurs in the early part of the growing season, the reason trees are rare except in valleys and other

land depressions. Soils are among the most productive of any. Wind erosion is a potential problem.

Steppe—Winters are cold and dry and summers warm to hot. The frost-free growing season ranges between 100 days in the north to more than 200 days in Texas. Summertime evaporation exceeds rainfall. Vegetation is shortgrass prairie—now planted with wheat—and semidesert. Soils tend to be salty and low in humus.

Rocky Mountain Forest—Climate is similar to semiarid steppe. Most rainfall is in winter and much of that comes as snow. Engelmann spruce grow at the upper elevations. Ponderosa pine and Douglas fir dominate at medium elevations, aspen or lodgepole pine at lower ones.

Colorado Plateau—The climate is characterized by cold winters. Summer days are usually hot, but nights are cool. Rainfall ranges between 10 and 20 inches each year, mostly in winter but occasionally with summer thundershowers. Sagebrush is abundant as are several kinds of cacti and yucca. Annual and

Map Legend:
- SUBARCTIC
- WARM CONTINENTAL
- HOT CONTINENTAL
- SUBTROPICAL
- EVERGLADE
- PRAIRIE
- STEPPE
- ROCKY MOUNTAIN FOREST
- COLORADO PLATEAU
- MARINE
- MEDITERRANEAN
- DESERT
- HAWAII

perennial flowers appear during the summer rainy periods. Cottonwood trees grow along streams. At higher elevations, there is pinon pine, juniper, ponderosa pine, lodgepole pine and aspen.

Desert—These are areas of extreme drought coupled with extremely high air and soil temperatures. Temperature variation between day and night is also extreme. Average annual rainfall is 4 to 8 inches. Various kinds of cacti grow in some areas, as do trees such as palo verde, ironwood, mesquite and smoke trees. Shrubs include creosote bush, saltbush and desert broom. Other areas are comprised of shifting sand dunes and support no plants. Soils are low in humus and tend to be salty and generally alkaline. Deposits of calcium carbonate (caliche) are common.

Mediterranean—This is the transition zone between the dry West Coast desert and the wet, northern West Coast. The climate is characterized by cool, wet winters and hot, dry summers. Occurrence of a wet winter followed by a dry summer produces a distinctive natural vegetation of hardleaved evergreen trees and shrubs able to withstand 2 to 4 months of drought and high temperatures. Typical trees are California live oak, tanbark oak, bay laurel and madrone. Chamise, toyon and manzanita are typical shrubs.

Marine—The climate here is temperate, rainy and humid with frequent cloud cover. Summers are relatively cool and winters are mild. Rainfall is abundant throughout the year but primarily in winter. The natural vegetation is conifer forests. Here you'll find magnificent stands of Douglas fir, red cedar and spruce. Western hemlock and Sitka spruce populate the Olympic National Forest. Grand fir, silver fir and Alaska cedar occur. Coast redwoods dominate the fog belt along the coast of northwestern California—a few of these are over 300 feet tall.

Hawaii—The climate is tropical, and due to the surrounding ocean and persistent northeast trade winds, virtually unchanging. The average January temperature is about 70F (21C)—in July it is slightly warmer. Rainfall varies between 20 and 200 inches a year, being heaviest on the northeast, windward side of the islands and lightest on the southwest, leeward slopes.

Subarctic—Extremely low winter temperatures prohibit the growth of most traditional garden plants unless grown in

PHENOLOGY

Phenology is a little known branch of climate and weather observation. The word is pronounced *fen-ALL-o-gee,* and is derived from the Greek word *phaino,* which means to show or appear. The idea is simple enough: Use events such as the flowering of particularly reliable plants as *indicators* of a season's progress. For instance, yellow-flowering forsythia *(Forsythia intermedia)* is a good indicator of the arrival of early spring, and common lilac *(Syringa vulgaris),* of spring.

These phenological observations have some practical advantages over typical weather service records, and in any case, are a useful supplement. For example, the location of the station that records local weather records has a slightly different climate than your own backyard. The difference may not be much—a few degrees of temperature one way or another, or slightly more or less rainfall. But these small differences can be significant when determining when to do certain garden activities, such as spring planting. Perhaps more important, a signal event—once we know what to look for—in our own yard confirms seasonal changes in a more immediate, personal way. "Plant your beans when the elm leaves are as big as a penny," the oldtimers say.

Unfortunately, there is not much published on the subject of phenology. One source is the book *Phenology and Seasonality Modeling* by Helmut Leith, published by Springer-Verlag, New York, NY. If phenology interests you, begin keeping track of events in your own yard so you can gradually build your own record. Also, you need other gardeners to correlate your information with. A garden club could adapt phenology as a project.

In a sense, phenology is to meteorology what herbal remedies are to modern medicine—most of the information you're likely to find is in folklore. The following rhymes and sayings are examples:

January
A summerish January, a winterish spring
January warm, the Lord have mercy! (1)

February
When gnats dance in February,
The husbandman becomes a beggar. (1)

March
The first day of spring is one thing, and the first spring day is another. The difference between them is sometimes as great as a month. (2)

April
If it thunders on All Fool's Day
It brings good crops of corn and hay. (1)

May
A wet May
Makes a big load of hay.
A cold May is kindly
And fills the barn finely.
Let all thy joys be as the month of May. (1)

June
A cold and wet June spoils the rest of the year. (1)

July
In this month is St. Swithin's Day,
On which if that it rain they say,
Full forty days after it will
More or less some rain distill. (3)

August
August? Beware of hurricanes you must. (4)

September
By all these lovely tokens
September days are here,
With the summer's best of weather
And autumn's best of cheer. (5)

October
October gave a party;
The leaves by hundreds came:
The ashes, oaks and maples,
And those of every name. (6)

November
If All Saints' Day (Nov. 1) will bring out winter, St. Matin's Day (Nov. 11) will bring out Indian summer.(1)

December
Barnaby bright, Barnaby bright,
The longest day and the shortest night;
Lucy light, Lucy light,
The shortest day and the longest night. (4)
(Barnabas' Day is the summer solstice, St. Lucy's
Day is the winter solstice.)

1. Old English proverbs from Richard Inwards, *Weather Lore,* 1898.
2. Henry Van Dyke, *Fisherman's Luck.*
3. *Poor Robin's Almanac,* 1967.
4. Unknown origin.
5. "September" by Helen Hunt Jackson.
6. George Cooper, "October Party."

a heated greenhouse. There are few gardeners living in these regions.

ALTERING CLIMATE

Most of us live where the climate is pleasant in some respects and uncomfortable in others. Perhaps you live where it is too windy, too dry, too humid, too cool or too hot. In your house you can rely on a heater, air-conditioner or other device to maintain comfort. But you can also modify the climate outside the house.

Microclimates—These occur in small areas affected by changes in terrain or by large physical objects such as buildings or trees. Such changes or objects cause the climate immediately around them to be slightly different from the overall climate of an area. For example, a planting bed beneath a white, south-facing wall will be warmer than the surrounding garden.

Consider existing microclimates in your yard and how you can take advantage of them. You may be able to grow plants that otherwise might not do well in your area. Or, you can create microclimates to suit the kinds of plants you want to grow. Plants themselves can be used to create microclimates, such as using a tall hedge to deflect wind, or a large tree for shade.

Here are some ways to use landscape structures and plantings to create desirable microclimates around your house.

In cool-summer areas, such as near the seacoast, you can increase the warmth around your house by utilizing stone, brick or some similar material for outdoor paving. Compared to wood decking or bare soil, these materials absorb more heat during the day and hold it longer into the night. Similarly, a heavy stone or block wall can be situated where it can absorb the maximum amount of afternoon sun.

Where chilly winds are a problem, plant a windbreak of dense-growing shrubs or low trees, situated to divert the wind. If you would like more breeze or more air circulation, prune trees and shrubs to allow more air movement through them, perhaps installing sprinklers near the shrubbery to take full advantage of evaporative cooling.

For outdoor cooling, few structural devices are superior to a 40-foot shade tree. If you already have such a tree, you can design your outdoor living area to take best advantage of it. If your property doesn't have a substantial shade tree in the right location, consider planting a fast-growing tree with a broad, dense canopy. Deciduous trees planted on the south or west side of the house will shade it during summer, yet allow maximum sunlight to enter during the cold season. Lawns, ground covers and any shade-giving structures also help cool outdoor areas.

Tall hedges and trees are one of best methods for creating microclimates within a yard. Here, hedges and trees create protected area for swimmers, offering shade, wind control and privacy.

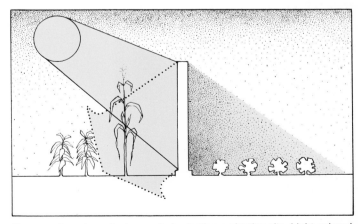

Exposure is an important aspect of selecting a planting site. Light-colored, south-facing walls reflect heat and light on soil and plants nearby. North-facing exposures receive more cooling shade. East-facing exposures are generally cooler than west-facing exposures because they receive shade during the hottest part of the day.

HELPING PLANTS THROUGH CLIMATE EXTREMES

As is usually true with anything that causes trouble in life, damage to plants from climate extremes can usually be traced to a combination of factors rather than just one influence.

Cold—Winter damage in cold northern or high-elevation climates is often caused by a combination of one or several of the following factors—wind, low temperatures, lack of soil moisture and sunlight. On a sunny or windy winter day, many evergreen plants will lose moisture through their foliage. If the ground is frozen, roots will not be able to replace the water lost. This condition is known as *physiological drought*—there's plenty of water in the ground but the plant's roots can't absorb it. Leaves, twigs and even entire branches can become desiccated and die.

Frost cracks or splits in bark occur when the west or south side of a tree trunk is warmed by winter sun. Cells on the exposed side of the tree are tricked into becoming less hardy. When the sun goes down and temperatures drop, these cells are killed and the bark cracks or splits. If severe enough, such damage can kill all the above-ground parts of a tree.

To avoid winter injury, make sure there is ample soil moisture available to plants before the ground freezes in fall. Spraying plants with anti-transpirants can also be effective in preventing winter damage. To minimize frost cracks and bark splits, paint trunks with white latex paint to help reflect warm sunlight. Light-colored tree wraps also help. With any type of winter damage, whether from frost or desiccation, wait until new growth has begun in spring before you prune out dead wood. The extent of actual damage will be more apparent at that time.

Heat—In hot, dry areas such as the deserts of California and Arizona, climate factors and growing conditions combine to pose threats similar to winter cold. High temperatures and strong winds dry out plants regardless of how much water is available in the soil. Intense light can heat bark, foliage and fruit to lethal levels. Bleached-out foliage, damaged fruit and cracked bark are common in these areas.

The first step in avoiding these problems is to choose plants well adapted to hot climates. Also, select planting locations carefully. A spot sheltered from strong winds and the hottest afternoon sun is often the key to success with less-tolerant plants.

Painting tree trunks and branches with white latex paint will help prevent sunburn. This protection is particularly important with newly planted or recently pruned trees.

Container Plants—Plants growing in containers are particularly susceptible to climate extremes. Plant roots are usually less hardy than the branches and foliage. Luckily, open soil provides the perfect insulation from the coldest temperatures. Container plants have both the roots and tops exposed and are often killed at temperatures that will not harm the same plant grown in open soil. One of the easiest way to protect container plants in winter is to group them together and cover the pots with a thick mulch. Individual plants can be tipped on their side and covered with mulch.

Plants grown in porous clay pots are highly susceptible to drying out because of the increased evaporation through the sides of the container. Small clay pots may need watering more than once a day in hot, windy weather.

Containers made of dark materials, such as black plastic, can get so hot on sunny days that they can actually kill roots growing inside. Nurseries often group dark colored containers together so they shade each other. Placing a small pot inside a larger one also works. Conversely, dark-colored pots keep roots warmer in winter, and may speed seed germination in early spring.

Painting tree trunk with white interior latex paint protects trunk from sunburn during summer and frost cracks during winter.

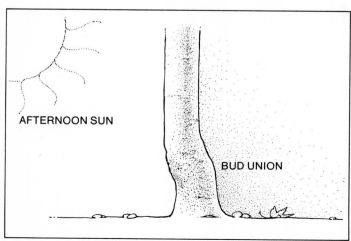

Bud union on young trees is more sensitive to sunburn than trunk. Plant so bud union faces away from hot afternoon sun.

COLD-PROTECTION DEVICES

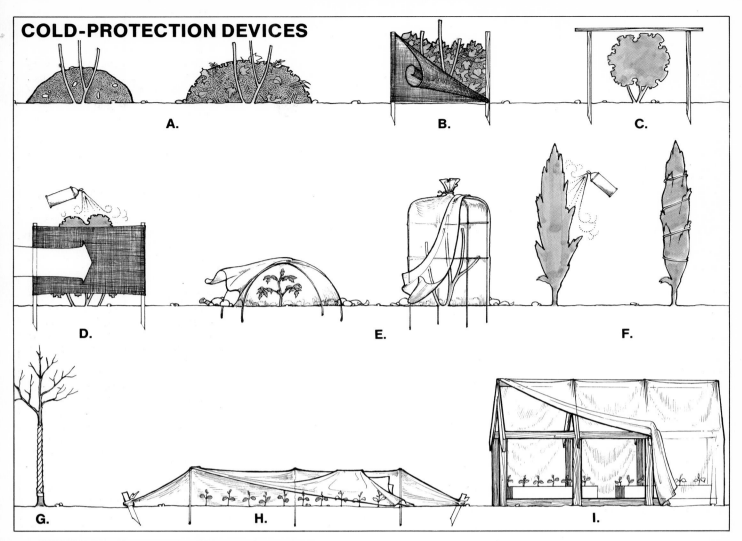

A.   B.   C.

D.   E.   F.

G.   H.   I.

Here are some methods of protecting plants against cold winter temperatures and late spring frosts:

A. Layer of mulch acts as insulation from coldest air temperatures. Exposed branches may be damaged but roots and buds below mulch will grow the following spring.

B. Wooden frame surrounded by burlap or cloth permits a deeper mulch to protect taller plants.

C. Covered frame traps heat radiating from soil and provides frost protection.

D. Winter winds desiccate plants, increasing chance of cold damage. Windbreaks and anti-transpirants are effective protective measures.

E. Wire frames covered with clear plastic can prevent frost damage to small or large plants and help you get an early start in areas with short growing seasons. The covers also act as mini-greenhouses, trapping heat and speeding growth.

F. Strong winds can increase chances of winter damage. Use anti-transpirants and secure loose branches of evergreens to minimize damage.

G. Wrap trunks of young trees with burlap or commercially available tree wraps to prevent bark cracking and winter damage.

H. A temporary row cover of wire hoops covered with clear plastic is used to protect newly emerging seedlings from late spring frosts.

I. Simple unheated greenhouse with clear-plastic cover is used to start large numbers of seedlings or provide frost protection for outdoor container plants.

Wood shingles make good shading devices for individual plants. Cool-season crops such as lettuce are particularly sensitive to hot sun.

Altering Climate

Few climates cannot be improved. Manipulating the *microclimates,* small climates around your property, within your general climate zone, can make both your outdoor and indoor living areas more comfortable. Using microclimates to your advantage also saves money by reducing heating and cooling bills. Air movement, solar radiation, humidity and air temperatures are factors you can alter with hedges, screens and espaliers. The first step is to decide your needs so you can manage climate elements to your benefit.

If you examine your property carefully, you will notice outdoor areas that would be more livable if they were warmer, cooler or sheltered from winds. Use the planting tricks described in the following pages to insulate, cast shade, provide wind protection, create breezeways or add humidity. Supplement, modify or remove existing plantings that do not suit your needs.

WINDBREAKS
Properly planned and positioned windbreaks can cut winter heating bills by as much as 30%. Windbreaks may be a hedge, a single row of trees or shrubs or an elaborate combination of plants calculated according to formula. The latter is called a *shelterbelt.*

Most people want wind to flow over their houses so that outdoor areas are sheltered. Use a simple, semicircular hedge to extend a house wall and create a sheltered spot. Use the opposite principle—trapping winds—to stir breezes in hot, still air. Thin screens can be used to shelter outdoor areas while allowing some mild wind to enter windows of buildings for increased air circulation.

It may not be possible to plant a windbreak without casting shade where it is not wanted. In many areas, shade is desirable. Common sense is important in planning.

Winter gales and summer breezes usually originate from different sources. Determine the direction of the prevailing wind and sunshine in each season. Existing plantings, adjacent buildings and the slope of the land affect airflow patterns. Cold air flows downhill on still nights.

Most winds blow predictably from the same direction during winter seasons or storms. Windbreaks are positioned perpendicular to the prevailing wind. There is a calm area just behind the break. Just beyond this is an area of shelter called the *wake* that receives some turbulence or moving air. Wind force gradually returns to normal as it moves beyond the wake.

Length of the calm and wake areas depends on windbreak height and density. Sparse plants allow more wind through, but the wake extends for a greater distance behind the break. With dense plants, the calm area just behind the break extends a distance approximately equal to twice the height of the windbreak. The sheltered area extends a distance approximately equal to 10 to 15 times the height of the break.

Dense, evergreen plants with almost vertical sides placed perpendicular to the wind make the most effective windbreak. Foliage must reach the ground or wind speed can increase as air is forced down through the bottom of the break in a funnel effect. Plant low, dense shrubs in front of thin windbreaks to bolster them.

Baffle Hedge

A baffle hedge is a group of hedges planted together to provide the screening effect of a typical hedge. Because they are planted at a 45° angle, their shade pattern is reduced. Plants grown near them receive plenty of sunlight. A baffle hedge can be used to screen vegetable gardens from view, while protecting vegetable plants from wind.

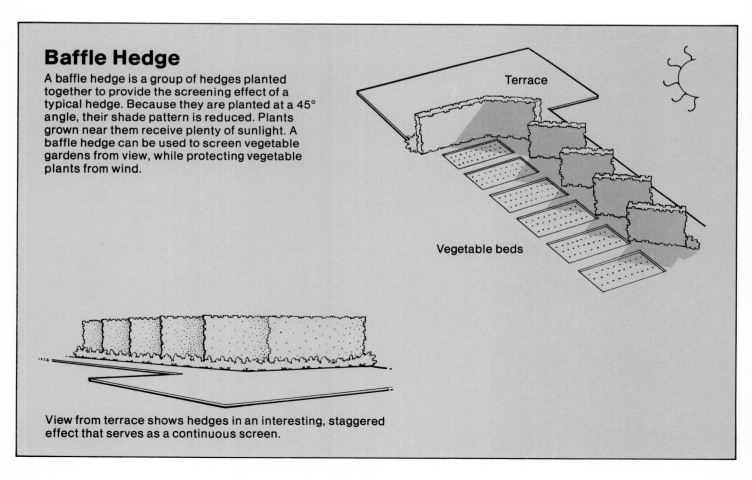

Terrace

Vegetable beds

View from terrace shows hedges in an interesting, staggered effect that serves as a continuous screen.

Deciduous species and sparse evergreens, or plantings with gaps between plants, also make useful windbreaks. They produce less turbulence, and their effectiveness increases as wind velocity increases.

In urban areas where tall buildings send wind rushing through canyonlike avenues, it is often impossible to predict wind direction. Gardens in such areas must be enclosed for protection. Use plants in boxes or other containers on roof gardens and balconies to create sheltered areas. Unfortunately, many species that do well rooted in the earth suffer when exposed to the constant, harsh, drying winds found high above street level. Choose tough, compact varieties.

SHADING

When planning windbreaks, hedges and screens, consider what a solid line of tall plants will do to the amount of sunlight reaching the windows of your home and outdoor areas. What will the shade patterns be?

If shade is not wanted in an area, locate the hedge or screen at a distance

Bamboo is fast growing, and serves as a suitable windbreak where adapted. Use *clumping* species instead of *running* species to avoid invasive spreading.

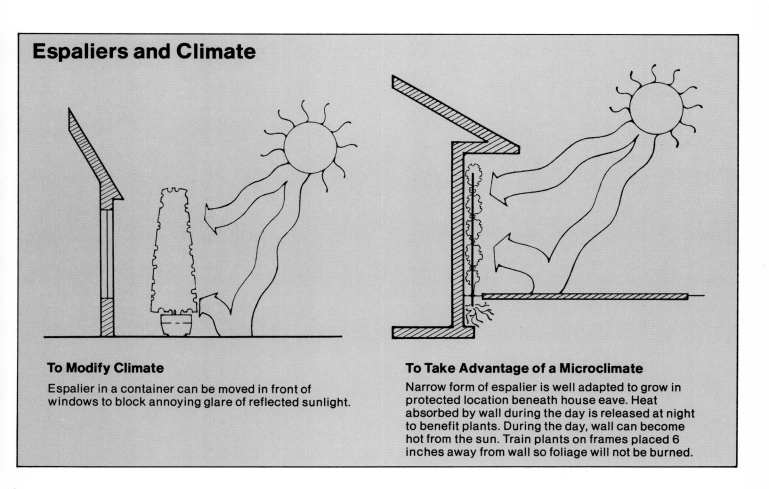

Espaliers and Climate

To Modify Climate
Espalier in a container can be moved in front of windows to block annoying glare of reflected sunlight.

To Take Advantage of a Microclimate
Narrow form of espalier is well adapted to grow in protected location beneath house eave. Heat absorbed by wall during the day is released at night to benefit plants. During the day, wall can become hot from the sun. Train plants on frames placed 6 inches away from wall so foliage will not be burned.

equal to twice the expected mature height of plant. For example, if the mature height is 15 feet, place plants 30 feet away from the area. You can also control hedge height by planting plants that naturally stay low or by regular pruning.

COOLING

Use hedges, screens and espaliers to reduce summer cooling costs. Cooling is achieved through shading, blocking reflected heat, channeling breezes, lowering air temperature and insulating.

The shady side of a line of plants is distinctly cooler than the sunny side. This is because the sun's rays are blocked, and plants are absorbing moisture from the air and releasing it. This is the process known as *evapo-transpiration*.

A living wall is more effective in cooling dry air than a wood or canvas shade. Put this principle to work on the south and west sides of buildings where the sun's heat is most intense. In humid climates, the cooling effect of added moisture is minimal, but shade and breezes are always welcome.

Use loose, deciduous species to block summer sun. When plants drop their leaves in fall, the winter sun is able to penetrate to add its warmth. Choose plants with sparse or dense foliage to regulate the penetration of sun or wind.

Rows of plants can be used to block the wind or channel it for cooling purposes. Use hedges and screens to capture breezes and funnel them where they are needed. A shady tunnel lowers the air temperature. Position a plant tunnel to take advantage of the prevailing breezes, and the cooler air can be directed to a patio or terrace. One word of caution: Be sure to funnel summer breezes, not cold winter winds.

To make a tunnel, plant two rows of hedges or screens. Shear the sides or prune out the inside branches of the screens. Allow foliage to meet overhead, or plant two rows of canopy-shaped trees to form the ceiling. You can also use espaliers on a pergola framework for a fruiting tunnel. Use these dramatic features as an approach to an entry, and the cool air can be channeled directly inside your home.

Allees and *pleached allees* are two ancient landscape forms that can be used for cooling purposes. An allee is parallel rows of trees traditionally used to direct views, but allees can be positioned to channel breezes.

Pleaching is a grafting method. Branches from separate trees are interwoven until their tissues have bonded and grown together. Pleach allees along their length and overhead to form tunnels.

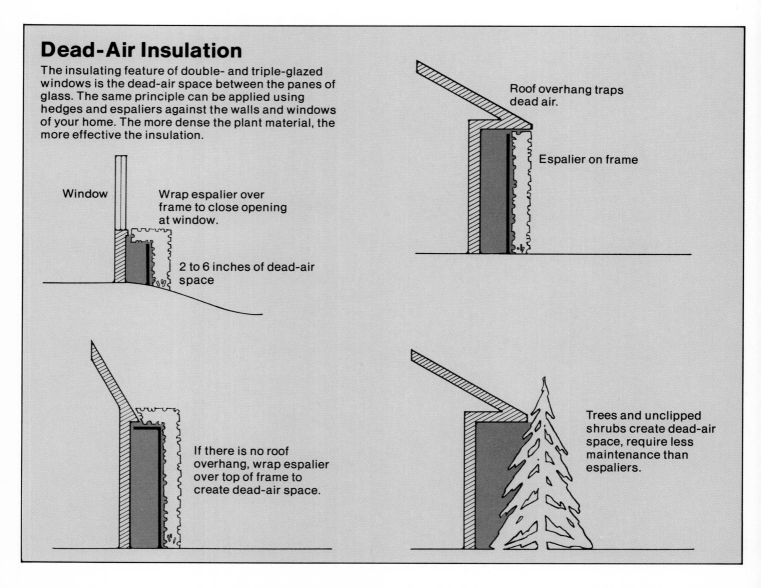

Dead-Air Insulation

The insulating feature of double- and triple-glazed windows is the dead-air space between the panes of glass. The same principle can be applied using hedges and espaliers against the walls and windows of your home. The more dense the plant material, the more effective the insulation.

Window

Wrap espalier over frame to close opening at window.

2 to 6 inches of dead-air space

If there is no roof overhang, wrap espalier over top of frame to create dead-air space.

Roof overhang traps dead air.

Espalier on frame

Trees and unclipped shrubs create dead-air space, require less maintenance than espaliers.

PLANTS FOR WINDBREAKS

Any hedge or screen provides wind protection. These plants are for persistent, harsh wind conditions.

Acer ginnala ....Amur maple
Calocedrus decurrens .... California incense cedar
Caragana arborescens ..... Siberian pea tree
Ceratonia siliqua ....Carob
Chamaecyparis lawsoniana .... Port Orford cedar
Cotoneaster lucidus .... Hedge cotoneaster
Cupressocyparis leylandii Cupressocyparis
Cupressus glabra .... Arizona cypress
Cupressus sempervirens
'Stricta' .... Italian cypress
Dodonea viscosa ....Hopbush
Elaeagnus angustifolia ....Russian olive
Elaeagnus pungens .... Silverberry
Escallonia rubra .... Escallonia
Eucalyptus ....Eucalyptus species
Juniperus .... Juniper
Ligustrum lucidum .... Glossy privet
Ligustrum texanum .... Waxleaf privet
Lonicera korolkowii
'Zabeli' ....Zabel's honeysuckle
Lonicera tatarica .... Tatarian honeysuckle

Nerium oleander .... Oleander
Philadelphus x virginalis ....Mock orange
Picea abies ....Norway spruce
Picea glauca .... White spruce
Pinus eldarica ....Mondell pine
Pinus nigra .... Austrian pine
Pittosporum .... Pittosporum species
Populus alba 'Bolleana' ....Bolleana poplar
Populus nigra 'Italica' ....Lombardy poplar
Populus simonii 'Fastigiata' ....Pyramidal Simon poplar
Prunus caroliniana .... Cherry laurel
Prunus ilicifolia ....Hollyleaf cherry
Prunus laurocerasus ....Laurel cherry
Prunus lusitanica ....Portugal laurel
Prunus maritima ....Beach plum
Pseudotsuga menziesii .... Douglas fir
Punica granatum .... Pomegranate
Pyracantha .... Pyracantha
Rhamnus alaternus ....Italian buckthorn
Rhamnus frangula
'Columnaris' ....Tallhedge buckthorn
Sequoia sempervirens ....Coast redwood
Syringa x chinensis ....Chinese lilac
Syringa vulgaris ....Lilac
Tamarix aphylla .... Tamarisk
Thuja occidentalis .... American arborvitae
Tilia cordata .... Littleleaf linden

An *allée*, a walk or passage created by rows of closely spaced trees, creates a cool, shady tunnel. Use allées to direct views or funnel cooling breezes.

Windbreaks and Shelters

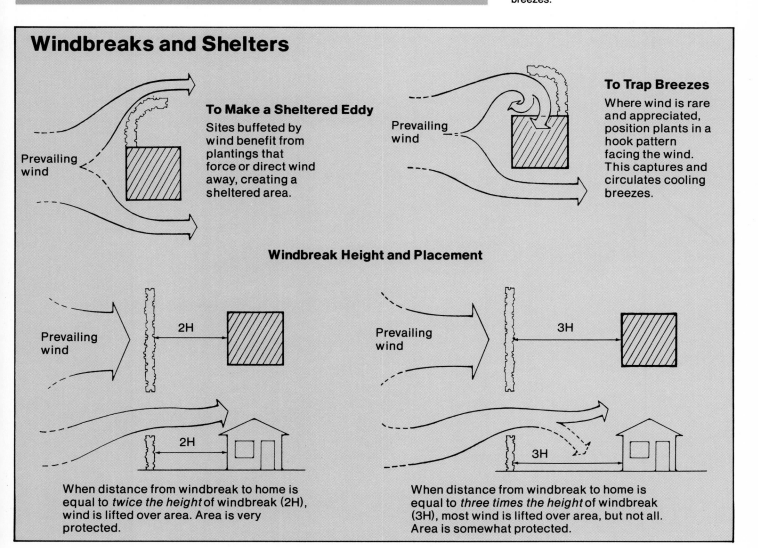

To Make a Sheltered Eddy
Sites buffeted by wind benefit from plantings that force or direct wind away, creating a sheltered area.

To Trap Breezes
Where wind is rare and appreciated, position plants in a hook pattern facing the wind. This captures and circulates cooling breezes.

Windbreak Height and Placement

Prevailing wind — 2H

Prevailing wind — 3H

When distance from windbreak to home is equal to *twice the height* of windbreak (2H), wind is lifted over area. Area is very protected.

When distance from windbreak to home is equal to *three times the height* of windbreak (3H), most wind is lifted over area, but not all. Area is somewhat protected.

If you live in a hot, arid climate, you can adapt a trick used by the Moors in their 16-century Spanish gardens. They cut windows in garden walls to permit cooling breezes to enter. The breezes distribute sprays of moisture from fountains in the garden. Glimpses of the desert outside heighten the sense of the cool oasis inside. Similarly, windows can be cut in hedges to create the same effect.

Instead of using fountains, place a sprinkler between the prevailing breeze and a loose screen or hedge to create a similar air-conditioning effect. With planning, you can use this sprinkler trick for watering a vegetable plot on one side of a hedge while cooling a patio on the other side.

HEAT CONTROL

Espaliers or hedges placed directly against walls are excellent for heat control. They dramatically reduce temperatures by absorbing solar radiation and reflected heat, while cooling through evapo-transpiration. Vines are usually suggested for these purposes, but their rampant growth can be difficult to control. Many vines cover windows, cause damage to wood and mortar surfaces and invade indoors. Espaliers and wall hedges are far better choices. Plant deciduous species. They drop their leaves in fall to allow winter sun to warm walls. Plant evergreen species for surprisingly effective insulation.

Boxed plants can be positioned to shield windows and walls from solar and reflected heat gain.

INSULATION

The space between the walls of buildings and plants loses and gains heat slowly, preventing substantial heat loss and gain indoors. Set evergreen hedges or espaliers on frames close to walls to create a few inches of "dead-air" insulation. This affects home heating and cooling requirements.

Roof overhangs help to trap dead air. Trees and shrubs should clear the overhang. Or, follow a regular pruning program. Where there is no overhang, wrap espaliers over the top of their frames or train hedge branches back to trap dead air. Seal openings at windows and corners to prevent dead air from escaping. Wrap espaliers around the end of their frames or train hedge branches back.

COLD-AIR DRAINAGE

Cold air flows downhill on still nights. It drains down slopes into low spots and valleys like water running off

PLANTS FOR INSULATION

The key to using dead-air space to insulate your home is keeping plants under control. Sheared, espaliered and naturally compact, evergreen plants are the most effective subjects. Here are some of the best.

Needled Evergreens

Cupressocyparis leylandii	Leyland cypress
Cupressus	Cypress species
Juniperus	Juniper species
Picea	Spruce species
Pinus strobus	White pine
Taxus	Yew species
Thuja	Arborvitae species
Tsuga canadensis	Canadian hemlock

Broadleaf Evergreens

Berberis	Barberry
Buxus sempervirens	English box
Camellia japonica	Camellia species
Carissa grandiflora	Natal plum
Cocculus laurifolius	Cocculus
Elaeagnus pungens	Silverberry
Escallonia rubra	Escallonia
Euonymus kiautschovica 'Manhattan'	Euonymus
Ilex	Holly evergreen species
Laurus nobilis	Grecian laurel
Ligustrum japonicum	Waxleaf privet
Ligustrum lucidum	Glossy privet
Osmanthus fragrans	Sweet osmanthus
Osmanthus heterophyllus	False holly
Pittosporum tenuifolium	Black-stemmed pittosporum
Podocarpus gracilior	Podocarpus fern pine
Podocarpus macrophyllus	Yew pine
Prunus caroliniana	Carolina cherry
Pyracantha	Pyracantha
Rhamnus alaternus	Italian buckthorn
Syzygium paniculatum	Eugenia
Viburnum tinus	Viburnum
Xylosma congestum	Shiny xylosma

Evergreen Espaliers

Camellia	Camellia species
Citrus	Citrus
Eriobotrya japonica	Loquat
Ilex	Holly species
Magnolia grandiflora	Southern magnolia
Podocarpus gracilior	Podocarpus fern pine
Pyracantha	Pyracantha
Pyrus kawakamii	Evergreen pear
Rosa banksiae	Lady Banks' rose
Rosmarinus officinalis 'Tuscan Blue'	Rosemary
Taxus	Yew species

Hedgewall of *Cocculus* is used for heat control by shading and insulating this window.

after a storm. If your house is situated on a slope, you can obstruct or divert cold-air flow around houses and outdoor living areas with hedges and screens. Damming is not as effective as diverting, but diverting usually requires more space. Dense, evergreen plants are most effective. Low hedges divert cold air as effectively as tall hedges.

People who live in hot climates can position hedge or screen obstructions on the downslope of their dwellings. This traps the cold-air flow for cooling purposes. There should not be diverters upslope. Loose, deciduous plants are best so cold air can pass through unimpeded during winter months.

SHELTERBELTS AND SNOWCATCHES

Shelterbelts and snowcatches are special screens for large-scale properties. Shelterbelts are windbreaks consisting of numerous rows of trees and shrubs. They protect farms, livestock, agricultural soils and highways. Snow-catches are planted in conjunction with shelterbelts to trap windblown snow. They also serve as substitutes for snow-fences along highways and at ski resorts. Check with your local cooperative extension agent for planting recommendations.

Snowcatch Design—Wind deposits snow particles where turbulence occurs, such as in front of and behind wind-breaks. Density and height of snowcatch has an effect on how the snow is deposited. The most efficient snowcatch is short in stature and 50% permeable. Deciduous shrub species are usually recommended for snowcatches.

To make a snowcatch, plant two staggered rows close together 40 to 60 feet in front of windbreaks. Species native to your area are recommended.

Shelterbelt Design—A shelterbelt should last at least 70 years and provide food and cover for wildlife. It should also serve as a windbreak, reducing home heating costs by as much as 30%.

Position shelterbelts perpendicular to the prevailing winter wind. Use fast-growing, deciduous plants to provide protection until evergreen species are established. Shelterbelts often consist of 8 to 10 rows of trees and shrubs. They should face the wind in the following order: snowcatch shrubs, 40 to 60 feet open space, deciduous trees in rows, evergreen trees in rows, protected area. There is evidence that a dense, vertical block is more effective than rows that slope up like a peaked roof.

Space rows far enough apart to allow maintenance and cultivating equipment to pass through. Stagger rows. Space evergreen trees far enough apart within rows to prevent crowding when ultimate size is reached. Use shrubs to fill in gaps at tree bases. Remove deciduous rows as necessary as evergreen trees mature.

PLANTS FOR SNOWCATCHES

Berberis .... Berberis
Caragana .... Dwarf peashrubs
Elaeagnus angustifolia .... Russian olive
Lonicera korolkowii
 'Zabeli' .... Zabel's honeysuckle
Lonicera tatarica .... Tatarian honeysuckle
Prunus .... Some deciduous species
Rosa multiflora .... Japanese rose
Rosa rugosa .... Rugosa rose
Salix purpurea .... Purple-osier willow
Salix purpurea 'Gracilis' .... Dwarf blue
                                                    arctic willow
Syringa .... Lilac
Viburnum ..... Viburnum—deciduous species

PLANTS FOR SHELTERBELTS

Acer ginnala .... Amur maple
Caragana arborescens ..... Siberian pea tree
Elaeagnus angustifolia .... Russian olive
Lonicera korolkowii 'Zabeli' .... Zabel's
                                                    honeysuckle
Lonicera tatarica .... Tatarian honeysuckle
Picea abies .... Norway spruce
Picea glauca .... White spruce
Populus nigra 'Italica .... Lombardy poplar
Populus alba 'Bolleana' .... Bolleana poplar
Populus simonii 'Fastigiata' .... Pyramidal
                                                    Simon's poplar
Prunus .... Deciduous species
Pseudotsuga menziesii .... Douglas fir
Rosa multiflora .... Japanese rose
Rosa rugosa .... Rugosa rose
Salix purpurea .... Purple-osier willow
Syringa .... Lilac
Viburnum ..... Viburnum—deciduous species

Acer ginnala, amur maple, can be used in a shelterbelt design planting.

PLANNING YOUR GARDEN

Winter is the best time to plan your displays of flowering annuals. Seed catalogs generally arrive soon after the holidays, and stores begin to set out their seed-packet displays. Planning early, before spring arrives, allows you time to decide what to plant and where.

The first decision you should make is whether to grow plants from seeds, or wait until planting time and buy ready-grown transplants. Growing your own plants from seeds gives you greatest freedom of choice. Major seed catalogs offer up to 2,000 varieties of flowers. This compares to about 50 varieties of transplants from a well-stocked garden center.

If you plan to raise plants from seeds purchased from a mail-order catalog, order before February 15. If you live in a mild-climate area, order earlier. You must provide sufficient time for seeds of slow-growing plants such as begonias and coleus to grow to transplant-size for early flowering. As a bonus, many mail-order seed suppliers give discounts for early orders.

PLAN ON PAPER

To help you decide the number of plants and type of plants—sun-loving or shade-loving for example—make a plan of your outdoor planting areas. Graph paper is commonly used, with one square on the graph equal to one square foot of actual garden space.

Draw beds, borders and gardens to scale, using colored felt pens to represent groups of plants. You can then count the squares within the colored areas to determine number of plants needed. For most flowering annuals, figure on planting one plant for every square foot—the same as the squares in your graph-paper plan. Some spreading kinds need more space, and some edging plants can be planted more closely.

Make a list of the different annuals you need to match your planting plans. Decide which you wish to start from seeds and which you plan to buy as ready-grown transplants. Many gardeners prefer to start large-seed, quick-growing varieties such as marigolds, zinnias, dahlias and calendulas. They buy ready-grown transplants of slow-growing, fine-seed kinds such as begonias, impatiens and coleus from a garden center.

Use your list to decide when to start seeds indoors and when to sow those that can be planted directly in the garden. For example, coleus and begonia seeds should be planted indoors 10 to 12 weeks before your last frost date. They will then have enough time to become decent-size transplants. Marigolds and asters require only 4 to 6 weeks to reach transplant size. Nasturtiums, poppies and sweet peas can be sown directly in the garden as soon as soil can be worked in spring.

Left: Landscape at Filoli Estate, Woodside, California, has spectacular displays of flowering annuals. 'Yellow Sun' zinnias combine with cosmos, phlox and white nicotiana in massed bed. Above: Border planting features tall orange calendulas, dwarf blue ageratum, blue lobelia, white wax begonias, white alyssum, dwarf French marigolds and mixed zinnias.

Principles of Color

Like an artist daubing a canvas with bold or subtle strokes of paint, you can use flowers and foliage to paint your landscape. Many principles of color that apply to art also apply to flower gardening.

It's easier to select colors for harmony or contrast if you know how to use a color wheel such as the one shown below. The wheel is divided into *cool* and *warm* hues, or "pure" colors using three *primary* colors—red, yellow and blue. Cool colors such as blue, green and violet are subdued. Warm colors such as red, yellow and orange tend to catch the eye more easily.

The primary colors are the source of all other colors. Primary colors cannot be made by mixing other colors together. A primary color mixed with another primary color makes a *secondary* color. For example, red and yellow make orange, yellow and blue make green and blue and red make violet. When mixed with black, gray or white, tints, shades and tones are created.

Color groupings of flowers can be *harmonious* or *contrasting. Hues* are particular shades of colors. Hues in any neighboring group on the color wheel are harmonious or *analogous.* You can create *complementary* contrasts by selecting colors at opposite sides of the color wheel. These complementary colors produce the most dramatic companion plantings in beds and borders.

Examples of effective combinations using complementary color contrasts include springblooming, orange Siberian wallflowers and blue forget-me-nots. Try yellow French marigolds and violet petunias in midsummer. Red impatiens and green coleus are good combinations in late summer.

The concept of coordinating cool and warm colors can be applied to the different seasons of the year. For example, annuals with white and blue flowers are most appealing if they bloom in early summer—when these colors naturally predominate. Follow these with vibrant yellow and red flowers timed to bloom in midsummer. They will come into their best bloom at this time, and are most effective at reflecting the increased sunlight.

Planting *monochromatic* theme gardens—those using a single color—is an effective way to use annuals. All-white, all-blue, all-gold and all-pink are just a few examples. Photos of these kinds of plantings can be seen throughout this book.

"Rainbow" plantings of several colors are probably most widely used when seeking a brilliant mixture of colors. Many seed companies offer inexpensive mixtures of popular, long-lasting annuals. However, a more spectacular effect can be produced by planting a mixed border of separate colors.

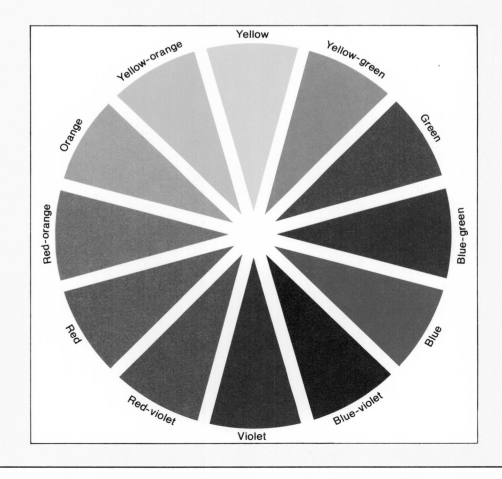

SUCCESSION PLANTING

If you want continual color from early spring to fall frosts, you might have to plant more than one kind of annual in a particular location. For example, Siberian wallflowers, forget-me-nots and pansies bloom prolifically in spring yet are often exhausted by summer. They can be replaced with heat-tolerant plants such as zinnias and marigolds to finish the season. Similarly, beds of petunias that flower poorly after midsummer can be removed and replanted with chrysanthemums or scarlet sage for fall displays.

PLANTING DESIGNS

The scope of your flower garden is often dictated by the amount of land available. In small back yards, borders can be planted along fences, hedges or walls. In larger spaces, consider planting *island beds*. These are areas planted within a lawn or ground-cover planting. Island beds allow plants to be seen from all sides. Plants are also easy to reach so weeding and watering is easier. An open, well-ventilated, evenly lighted location tends to produce the best flowering displays.

If space is restricted, grow flowering vines against walls and fences. Plant in containers for bright spots of color in entryways and on porches, decks and patios.

BEDS AND BORDERS

Flower beds are most effective when located at the edge of a lawn, alongside the house or as islands of color in a lawn. Located on either side of a driveway, a border makes an attractive ribbon of color leading to the house.

Stake out the area of your proposed bed with string and stakes. Use a spade to make a crisp, clean border at the edge of the lawn. In the center of the bed, mound soil so it is several inches above the surrounding surface, sloping at the edges. This displays the flowers better and allows excess water to drain away. When a border is made alongside a fence or wall, soil can be made higher at the back, sloping slightly forward.

After plants are in position, you may want to lay down a decorative mulch of pine bark or coco bean hulls. It will help discourage weeds and is more attractive than the bare earth.

When selecting annuals, you should have some idea which plants can be grown successfully in your region. Visit local parks and botanical gardens. Make note of the good gardens in your neighborhood. These will help give you ideas you can copy or improve for your own garden.

With beds of annuals, it is best to keep the design simple. Avoid creating a hodgepodge of unrelated heights and colors. Check the seed-packet description so you will know whether a variety is tall, intermediate or dwarf in height. You can then plant them correctly so tall plants do not obstruct your view of shorter plants. Although plant mixtures can be effective, it's best to plant separate colors when combining different flower classes in the same bed.

Beds and borders planted in shades of a single color can be especially effective. For example, consider planting an all-white garden using plants with silver foliage and white flowers, or a striking, all-blue garden.

Island Beds—Square, rectangular, round or kidney-shape island beds are viewed from all directions. They look best if completely edged with a low-growing annual such as ageratum, portulaca or alyssum. A short, evergreen hedge such as dwarf boxwood, dwarf barberry or germander also makes an effective edging. For simplicity, the center of the island bed can be planted with a single color or mixture of one variety. If a bed of mixed annuals is desired, place tall varieties in the center, intermediate-height varieties next, and dwarf varieties around the edge. This way no plant blocks the view or shades another plant.

Island beds are usually located in sunny locations, surrounded by open lawn. They can be shaded by high trees or by a tree located in the middle of the bed. This way the bed forms a "collar" around the tree.

Borders—The only difference between a bed and a border is that borders usually have a solid backdrop such as a hedge, fence or wall. They are generally of one or two types: sunny borders facing east or south and shady borders facing north or west.

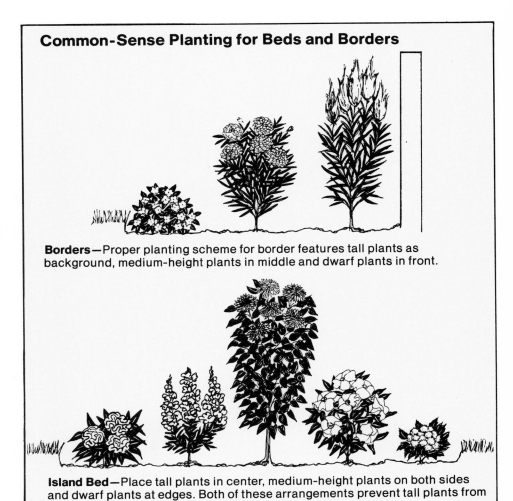

Common-Sense Planting for Beds and Borders

Borders—Proper planting scheme for border features tall plants as background, medium-height plants in middle and dwarf plants in front.

Island Bed—Place tall plants in center, medium-height plants on both sides and dwarf plants at edges. Both of these arrangements prevent tall plants from growing up to obstruct your view of other lower-growing plants.

Designs for a Cutting Garden

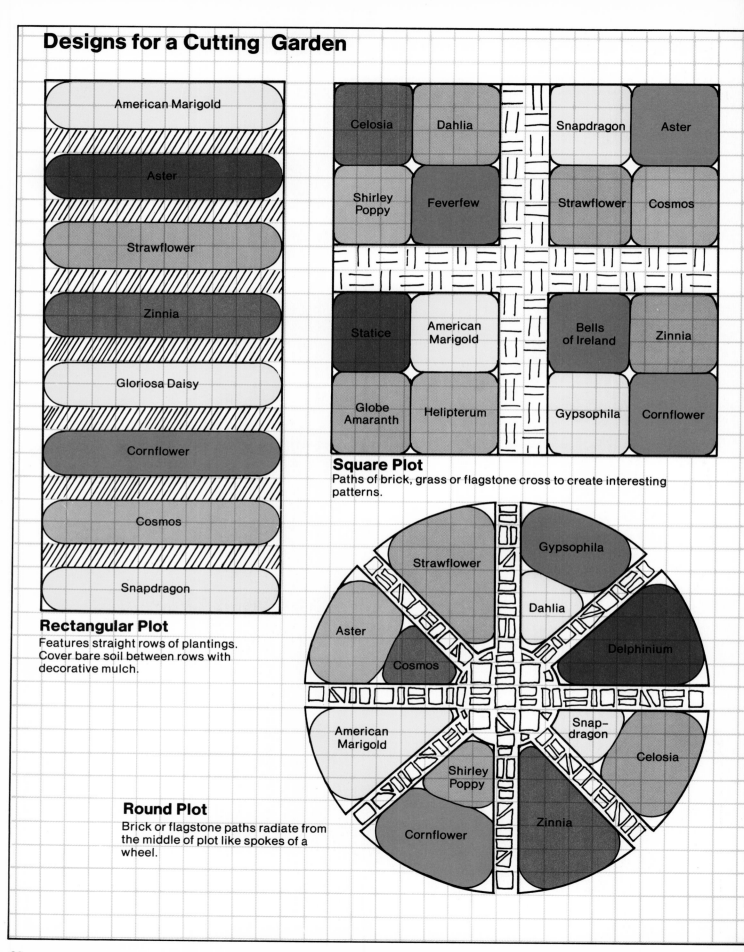

American Marigold

Aster

Strawflower

Zinnia

Gloriosa Daisy

Cornflower

Cosmos

Snapdragon

Rectangular Plot
Features straight rows of plantings.
Cover bare soil between rows with
decorative mulch.

Celosia **Dahlia**

Snapdragon **Aster**

Shirley Poppy **Feverfew**

Strawflower **Cosmos**

Statice **American Marigold**

Bells of Ireland **Zinnia**

Globe Amaranth **Helipterum**

Gypsophila **Cornflower**

Square Plot
Paths of brick, grass or flagstone cross to create interesting
patterns.

Strawflower

Gypsophila

Dahlia

Aster

Cosmos

Delphinium

American Marigold

Snap-dragon

Shirley Poppy

Celosia

Cornflower

Zinnia

Round Plot
Brick or flagstone paths radiate from
the middle of plot like spokes of a
wheel.

Designs for Beds and Borders

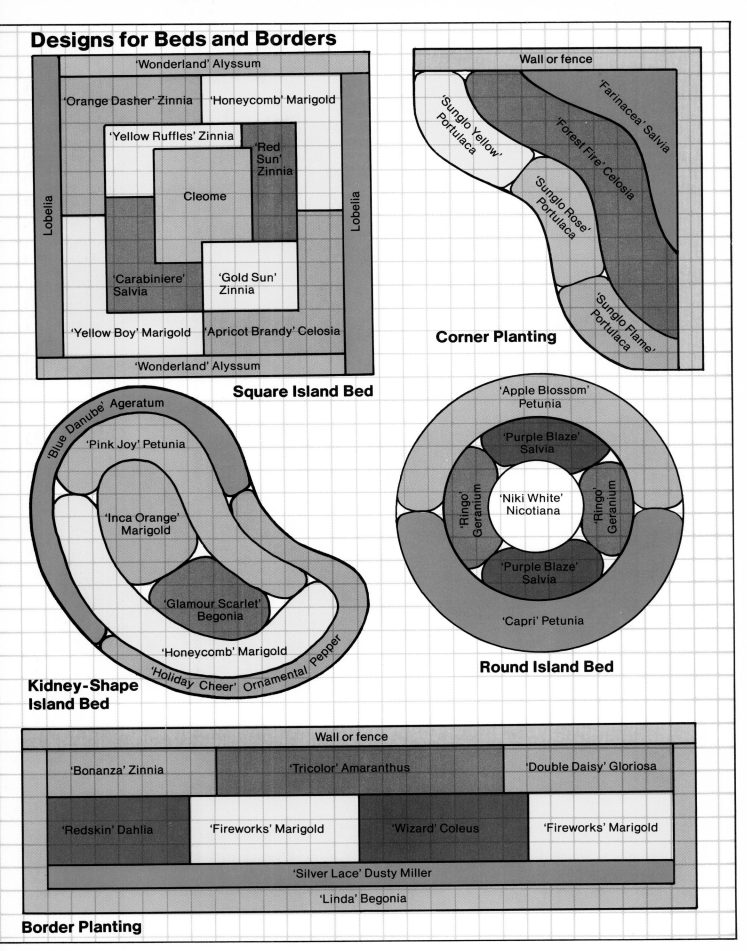

'Wonderland' Alyssum

'Orange Dasher' Zinnia

'Honeycomb' Marigold

'Yellow Ruffles' Zinnia

'Red Sun' Zinnia

Cleome

Lobelia

Lobelia

'Carabiniere' Salvia

'Gold Sun' Zinnia

'Yellow Boy' Marigold

'Apricot Brandy' Celosia

'Wonderland' Alyssum

Square Island Bed

Wall or fence

'Sunglo Yellow' Portulaca

'Farinacea' Salvia

'Forest Fire' Celosia

'Sunglo Rose' Portulaca

'Sunglo Flame' Portulaca

Corner Planting

'Blue Danube' Ageratum

'Pink Joy' Petunia

'Inca Orange' Marigold

'Glamour Scarlet' Begonia

'Honeycomb' Marigold

'Holiday Cheer' Ornamental Pepper

Kidney-Shape Island Bed

'Apple Blossom' Petunia

'Purple Blaze' Salvia

'Ringo' Geranium

'Niki White' Nicotiana

'Ringo' Geranium

'Purple Blaze' Salvia

'Capri' Petunia

Round Island Bed

Wall or fence

'Bonanza' Zinnia

'Tricolor' Amaranthus

'Double Daisy' Gloriosa

'Redskin' Dahlia

'Fireworks' Marigold

'Wizard' Coleus

'Fireworks' Marigold

'Silver Lace' Dusty Miller

'Linda' Begonia

Border Planting

Like island beds, borders can be planted with a single variety in one color or a mixture. An edging around the border is generally desirable. It serves as a frame for the planting. Dwarf annuals or dwarf evergreen plants clipped to make a low hedge can form the frame.

Position tallest plants at the rear against the backdrop. Intermediate-height plants should be placed next, with dwarf varieties planted in front. All plants will be displayed in full view and no plant will shade another.

Corner Plantings—These generally form a triangle. The leading side can be straight but looks more natural if it curves. Corner plantings are especially effective if soil is terraced. Use lumber, stone or railroad ties to form the terraces. This allows dwarf annuals to be used on different levels to create uniform "steps" of color. Unless they face due south, corner plantings are likely to be shady.

CUTTING GARDENS

These are gardens designed primarily for utility. Annuals are planted so they can be "harvested" and brought indoors so you can enjoy their beauty. Each group of plants should be attractive for display purposes and accessible for cutting.

The first and simplest plan is a rectangular plot featuring straight rows with pathways between—just like a traditional vegetable plot. To keep pathways from becoming muddy, cover with an organic mulch such as pine needles, straw, grass clippings or wood chips. For decorative appeal, frame the entire area with a white picket fence or dwarf evergreen hedge.

The square or rectangular plot features planting squares within the garden. Paths cross to provide easy access to planting areas. Paths can be bare soil but are more attractive and clean when covered with an organic mulch. For even greater decorative appeal, plant grass pathways. They should be at least as wide as your mower will cut. Or install a gravel, rock or brick path. To enhance each planting square, frame with dwarf edging plants or dwarf evergreens such as boxwood to create a low hedge. This creates what the French call a *parterre*, a garden separated by paths.

All the planting area can be enclosed in a regular hedge or picket fence. A trellised arbor at the entrance decorated with vining annuals makes a spectacular and inviting entry.

The round cutting garden is laid out like a wagonwheel. Spokes of the wheel form narrow pathways with spaces between, creating pie-shape beds. For a decorative touch, pathways can be covered with flagstone or gravel. The circumference of the circle can be planted with dwarf boxwood. By enclosing each pie-shape bed with a low boxwood hedge, you can create a *parterre* garden.

SELECTING A SITE

Consider several factors before choosing a planting site. These include amounts of sun and shade, heat and reflected light, winds and soil condition. Make note of these on your graph-paper plan.

Sunlight and Shade—Amount of available sunlight is the most important factor when choosing a location for your annuals. Most flowering annuals do best in full sun—a minimum of 7 hours is required for good flower production. Some, such as portulaca and gazanias, close their flowers on cloudy days.

When choosing a location, avoid shady sites. Relatively few flowering annuals do well in shade. Select a site that receives plenty of sun. For sun-loving annuals, do not plant in a location that is shaded during noon hours. If shadows from a tall building or tree block the sun during midday, it may be better to choose shade-tolerant plants for the location. This is true even if the site

Pink wax begonias with bronze foliage and dusty miller with silvery foliage produce an unusual but striking combination.

Sunny border does double-duty as cutting garden. Yellow gloriosa daisies and red, dahlia-flower zinnias have long stems. Dwarf, compact, triploid hybrid marigolds and white grandiflora petunias provide lower level of color at edges of border.

receives 7 hours sunlight daily.

Keep in mind that plants recommended for shaded areas perform best in a *partially* or *lightly* shaded area. In deep shade or locations that do not receive any direct sun, even shade-tolerant plants may come under stress and fail to flower.

A gardener once planted some impatiens and coleus in a raised planter under a dense maple tree. They performed poorly. He selectively pruned a few tree limbs from the tree's interior. It didn't hurt the appearance of the tree, but greatly increased the amount of light reaching the planter. Soon after, both impatiens and coleus began to thrive.

Heat—Temperature is the second most important factor for plant adaptation. Most flowering annuals can be classified as *cool-season* or *warm-season* plants. Warm-season plants generally thrive in heat if they are irrigated. Cool-season plants burn up if temperatures get too high. In hot-summer areas, you can grow many desirable cool-season plants if you time plantings so they mature during cool weather.

Some plants don't mind the heat as long as their roots are cool. One way to reduce temperatures in a hot, dry location is to add lots of organic matter to the soil. Leaf mold, peat moss or garden compost are good soil amendments. Organic matter in the soil significantly increases its moisture-holding capacity. Adding a light covering of organic mulch helps reduce evaporation of moisture and cools the soil even more.

Deeply dug soils are also cooler than shallow soils. For sweet peas, dig a trench and fill it with good soil. Roots penetrate deep and remain cool.

An experience a gardener had growing Shirley poppies is an example of putting this practice to work. He never had much success growing these plants. Just as they came into flower, the hot, summer sun would burn them up. One year he made a raised bed for a planting of the poppies. He added large quantities of compost to the soil for moisture retention. He installed drip irrigation and covered the soil surface with a mulch of pine needles. The drip irrigation combined with the mulch kept the soil moist and cool. The results were fantastic. He had displays of Shirley poppies like never seen before.

Reflected Light and Heat—Locations with insufficient light or heat can sometimes be modified by reflecting heat and light toward plants. Painting a dark wall white increases the amount of reflected heat and light. Surrounding a shaded planter with white landscape stone reflects light upward to plants.

Reflected heat and light can be a detriment. In hot-summer areas, planting against a south or west wall may be too much for certain plants. In desert regions, plants do best with some afternoon shade in summer months.

Shelter and Protection—Flowers exposed to the drying effects of summer winds can suffer rapid moisture loss. Warm-season plants exposed to cool winds can be damaged. Many annuals with tall, brittle stems will topple over in high winds or stems may break. If your planting area is exposed to winds, a windbreak may be necessary. A row of evergreen shrubs or trees is more effective than a solid fence or wall. When wind hits a solid barrier it flows over and down with severe force. A windbreak of evergreen shrubs or trees filters the force of the wind and dissipates it.

Protection from animals is also important. A stray dog can destroy a flower bed. Rabbits, quail and deer enjoy the tender transplants of many annuals. You may need to concentrate your plantings in a special area, fencing it in to keep animal pests away.

Soil Drainage—Most flowering annuals require good soil drainage. Both air and moisture are needed in the root zone for health and growth. How well the soil drains depends on its composition. Clay soil tends to drain slowly. Sandy soil drains rapidly. Both can be improved with the addition of large quantities of organic matter such as peat moss, compost and leaf mold.

In certain regions, soil drainage may be so poor that the soil is constantly waterlogged. In these conditions, plants are doomed to fail. Ditches lined with drainage tiles can be installed to channel excess water away. This can become costly or impractical. As an alternative, consider building a raised planting bed on a foundation of crushed stones.

SELECTING ANNUALS

Annuals comprise a diverse group of plants, with wide applications around the home and garden. Plants are available that grow 3 to 4 inches high, suitable as ground covers. Annual vines grow to 10 feet long, useful for decorating walls or as screening. Most annuals prefer sun but some tolerate shade. In recent years, annuals for shady locations have greatly increased in popularity. Impatiens, one of the best shade-adapted plants, is a top-selling bedding plant for this reason.

Flowering *height* is important, as well as *color*. Red is the favorite of seed buyers, closely followed by yellow, orange, pink and white. Blue is an uncommon flower color because it is the color of the sky. Most flowers contrast with the sky so they will be seen by pollinating insects. Green flowers are even more scarce because green is the common color of leaves and stems. Brown and black are extremely rare.

All white, all blue, all red and pink and all yellow and orange are popular color schemes for beds and borders. Unusual flower colors such as brown, green and black have poor display value, but are in great demand among flower arrangers.

Most annuals adapt to various kinds of soils and grow acceptably without much fertilizer. However, heat and drought tolerance are important considerations when selecting plants. Where conditions are hot and dry it is unwise to plant cool, moisture-loving plants.

BULBS IN THE LANDSCAPE

Many of the basics of landscape design apply to the bulb garden. The primary purpose is to bring all garden elements together in a way that is pleasing to the eye. The garden should include interesting accents, with a common element or unifying theme.

Depending on how bulbs are grouped and the supporting landscape materials and architecture, a garden can project many moods. For example, one daffodil enthusiast may want a formal garden. He could divide an area into equal squares and edge them with a finely trimmed hedge. A piece of sculpture would provide a focal point at the center of the garden where the squares converge. The daffodils, many of them rare, could be planted and labeled in groups within the squares.

Using the same daffodil varieties, another bulb enthusiast may wish to take an informal approach. The daffodils could be planted in labeled drifts in a small, natural meadow, using stones and weathered logs to complement the natural theme. What a difference from the formal garden!

THE IMPORTANCE OF PLANNING

Whether you want to design a formal or informal garden, or add some simple bulb plantings to your existing garden, it is important to begin with a plan. A plan can be as simple as a rough sketch on the back of an envelope, or measured to exact specifications on graph paper.

Certain obvious factors limit what you can do. The most important include garden space, and available time and money. In addition to these major factors, you need to consider the following:

Climate—Narrow your selection of bulbs to those that will do well in your particular climate. Although many bulbs are adaptable, certain bulbs naturally grow better in certain types of climates. Bulb growers in cold-winter areas have a different group of bulbs to select from than those in mild-winter areas.

Garden Location—Observe the nature of the proposed garden site. Does the location receive full sun, light shade or full shade? Are there trees nearby that will compete for light? *Endymion, Clivia,* lily-of-the-valley, *Fritillaria* and *Cyclamen* are well adapted to light shade. *Crocus* and *Ixia* need the warmth of full sun to bloom. Does the soil drain well, and is it of sufficient quality? If not, soil amendments may have to be added.

Color—Selecting bulb color is a personal choice, depending on the effect you want to create. Consider how various colors combine. White or blue goes with anything, and pastels are forgiving colors. But you might find a brilliant orange next to a strong magenta a bit overwhelming. It doesn't hurt to experiment. Grouping color opposites, such as blues with oranges and purples with yellows, intensifies the colors in your garden. If you are planning certain color combinations, keep in mind that there are early, midseason and late varieties of tulips, daffodils, hyacinths, *Irises* and *Crocus.* You must match up the seasons to successfully coordinate your color scheme.

Opposite Page: Red and white flowers of *Hippeastrum* are perfect complement to brick walk. Left: 'Gudoshnik' tulip typically has great color variation from flower to flower. Plant them in groups to accent their subtle variations.

Groups of the same color are most often more effective than mixing several colors. This is especially true when plantings are viewed from a distance. For example, grouping yellow daffodils of the same variety is more natural and pleasing than different colors and sizes. Likewise, *Ranunculus* provides a more effective show of color if the colors are separated into groups.

Timing—Generally, a garden can be planned to bloom in one of two ways: It can produce an outstanding show of color for a short period, with bulbs scheduled to bloom all at one time. Or, by planting a selection of bulbs with early, midseason and late bloom times, you can have color throughout the year. Either schedule requires careful planning. It is extremely helpful to keep records of the bloom dates of your bulbs. The weather may change the actual date of blooms from year to year, but the time relationship between different bulb types remains the same.

Height—Learn the mature height of bulbs before you plant. A tall-growing bulb can be planted in the foreground for variety, but low-growing bulbs planted behind them will be hidden from view. Don't assume that all bulbs of one species are the same general height—most range from high to low. For example, *Agapanthus* grows from 1-1/2 feet to 5 feet high, depending on the named variety. Kaufmanniana tulips grow to 5 inches high, but cottage tulips reach 30 inches high. The mature height of bulbs is usually given in mail-order catalogs, or at retail outlets where bulbs are sold.

It is best to plant early blooming bulbs toward the rear of a flower bed or border. Daffodils invariably bloom before tulips. If daffodils are planted in the foreground, you will have to look past their spent flowers when tulips begin to bloom.

Relationships—This is a difficult concept to explain, but certain plants and landscape materials look "right" when planted together. Generally, it is a matter of blending texture, form and color into a pleasing combination. For example, formal, precise plant forms do not look at home in a woodland situation. Likewise, a formal, contained garden will not welcome a bulb that spreads and naturalizes rapidly. Study gardens that appeal to you. If you look closely enough, you will see factors that unify the different bulbs, plants and materials.

Landscape planting features rich color combinations, including violet-colored fairy primrose, *Primula malacoides,* against earth-toned wall. Bright-purple pansies in front contrast nicely with white tulips, their white repeated by candytuft ground cover in center.

This garden combines many kinds of bulbs for an attractive, casual effect. White border is candytuft, *Iberis sempervirens.* Yellow flowers in foreground are *Freesia.* Golden flowers at left front are *Narcissus bulbocodium.* Blue anemone link clumps of daffodils at left rear, and Dutch hyacinths, right center.

KEEPING RECORDS

Keeping accurate records of planting and bloom dates is necessary to repeat a star performance, or adjust a planting so it will be more attractive the following year. As mentioned, the actual bloom dates may not fall on the same calendar day each year, but the timetable between the different bulb types remains constant. Also keep notes of the bulbs that bloom at the same time in your neighborhood.

SAMPLE PLANS AND LISTS

Two plans are supplied: one for mild climates and one for cold climates. If planted as shown, these gardens require little maintenance and are long-lived. If you happen to have the area to accommodate dimensions of the sample plan—perfect! If not, it is simple to adjust the size, and adapt the plan and plants.

BULBS WITH BEDDING PLANTS AND GROUND COVERS

Many bulb growers plant compatible bedding plants or ground covers over a bulb planting. *Overplanting* bulbs is simple to do. First, plant the bulbs. Then rake the area smooth and plant seeds or bedding plants of ground covers over the same area.

Bedding plants are often placed over bulbs for additional color and contrast. Imagine pink tulips with blue forget-me-nots, or white Dutch iris with yellow violias.

Planting over bulbs also prolongs color. After the bulbs finish, summer annuals such as petunias begin to bloom, blending one season of color into the next. As soon as summer annuals become available, plant them between bulbs to prolong the life of a colorful border. Star performers include ageratum, marigolds and asters. They hide the dying leaves of the bulbs as they grow.

Bedding plants and ground covers having neutral-colored flowers are usually best combined with brightly colored bulbs. However, don't be afraid to try pink tulips with purple pansies. But, avoid a white-flowered ground cover if your bulbs have white flowers. White daffodils with white alyssum do neither any service. The same is true of planting yellow daffodils with yellow English primroses. White and yellow daffodils are much more effective with contrasting blue violas or pansies.

Bedding plants or ground covers should be a single color, not a mix. Various colors of violas or pansies call more attention to themselves than to the flowering bulbs.

Ground Covers—Many bulbs are happy to rise through an established ground cover of violets, *Ajuga*, *Vinca minor* or English ivy. The height relationship between the ground cover and bulb flower is important. As a rule, the ground cover should be no more than half the height of the bulb flower. *Freesias, Sparaxis* and *Tritonia* thrive under a border of candytuft. *Crocus,* on the other hand, suffocates under any but the lowest ground covers. It does well in lawns as long as the first mowing is made after foliage has matured.

A ground cover supports bulb stems and protects flowers from mud splashed by rain or sprinklers. An overplanting of ground cover also acts as a mulch to cool soil temperatures. For example, lilies thrive with shallow-rooted ferns at their base, shading the soil.

Babiana stricta is delicate and low growing—perfect for viewing close up, such as between stepping-stones.

A expanse of color can be created with large beds, such as these 'Renown' tulips.

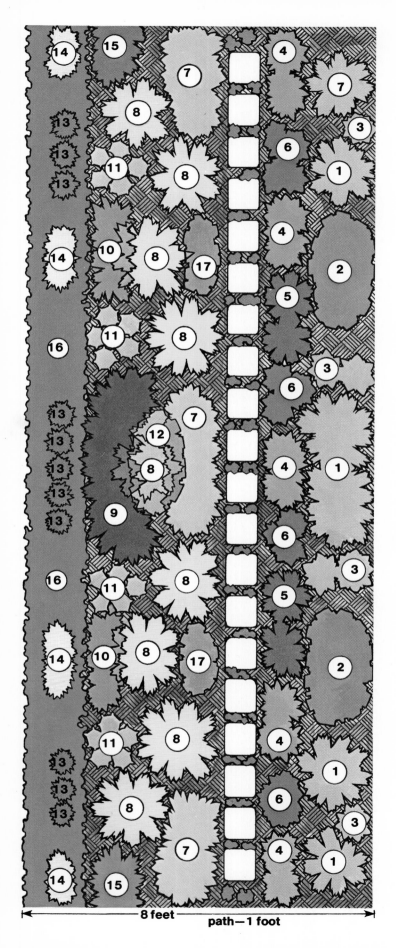

Plan for Mild-Climate Bulb Garden

If you live in a mild-climate region, you have the opportunity to grow color plants the year round. Annuals make an attractive, colorful display, but take a lot of time. Bulbs are excellent for easy-care color. After they are planted, they return year after year. Many have evergreen foliage, adding to their landscape value. These include *Agapanthus, Hemerocallis, Canna* and *Cliva.*

The plan at left includes many plants with varied bloom periods to provide color through the whole year. The numerals following the plant names are recommended numbers of plants for the best effect. Adjust the number of plants to fit your own situation.

1. Tall, dark *Agapanthus:* 2
2. Pink or white *Crinum:* 2
3. White or dark-pink *Amaryllis belladonna:* 2
4. Tall, yellow, bearded iris: 1 or 2
5. Dwarf blue *Agapanthus:* 2
6. *Lycoris africana:* 4 or 5
7. Dutch iris 'Wedgewood': 1 dozen
8. Deciduous *Hemerocallis:* 1
9. Daffodil 'February Gold': 2 dozen
10. Daffodil paper-white: 1 dozen
11. *Nerine bowdenii:* 5
12. Daffodil 'Professor Einstein': 1 dozen
13. *Lycoris radiata:* 3 to 5
14. Yellow *Freesias:* 1 dozen
15. Daffodil 'Soleil d'Or': 1 dozen
16. Ground cover: *Iberis sempervirens*
17. Dutch iris 'Blue Ribbon': 1 dozen

Plant *Oxalis* 'Grand Duchess' between pathway steppingstones.

Bloom Sequence

Spring
Daffodils
Dutch iris
Freesias
Oxalis 'Grand Duchess'

Early Summer
Hemerocallis
Agapanthus
Bearded iris

Summer
Hemerocallis

Late Summer and Fall
Crinum
Amaryllis belladonna
Lycoris

Christmas
Paper-white daffodil
Nerine
Oxalis 'Grand Duchess'

8 feet   path—1 foot

Plan for Cold-Climate Bulb Garden

After a winter of gray and white, gardeners in cold-climate regions have the chance to enjoy a tremendous display of spring-blooming bulbs. Many bulbs have waited for the cold weather to pass before bursting into bloom, creating a riot of color. Blooms of daffodils, tulips, *Crocus* and others are a firm affirmation that winter has ended.

Many mild-climate bulbs can be planted after danger of frost has passed. They must be dug and stored after bloom and before fall frost.

The plan at right features bulbs with varied bloom periods for color through most of the year. The numerals following the plant names are recommended numbers of plants for the best effect. Adjust the number of plants to fit your own situation.

1. *Eremurus robustus:* 1
2. *Lilium auratum:* 3
3. Tall bearded *Iris,* your favorite color: 3
4. *Galtonia candicans:* 1
5. *Lilium speciosum:* 5
6. *Lilium,* Bellingham Hybrid: 3
7. Deciduous *Hemerocallis:* 2
8. Tall perennial tulips: 1 dozen
9. *Fritillaria imperialis:* 2
10. *Chionodoxa luciliae:* 4 dozen
11. *Eranthis hyemalis:* 4 dozen
12. Low botanical tulips, *Tulipa kaufmanniana* or *T. fosterana:* 1 dozen
13. Daffodils planted around *Hemerocallis:* 1 or 2 dozen
14. *Crocus speciosus:* 1 dozen
15. Ground cover: *Vinca minor* or *Iberis sempervirens*

Plant *Muscari, Eranthis* and *Crocus* species between pathway steppingstones.

Bloom Sequence

Early Spring
Eranthis
Chionodoxa
Botanical tulips

Spring
Daffodils
Tulips
Fritillaria
Muscari
Crocus
Eremurus

Early Summer
Hemerocallis
Lilium Bellingham Hybrid
Bearded iris

Late Summer and Fall
Galtonia
Lilium speciosum
Lilium auratum

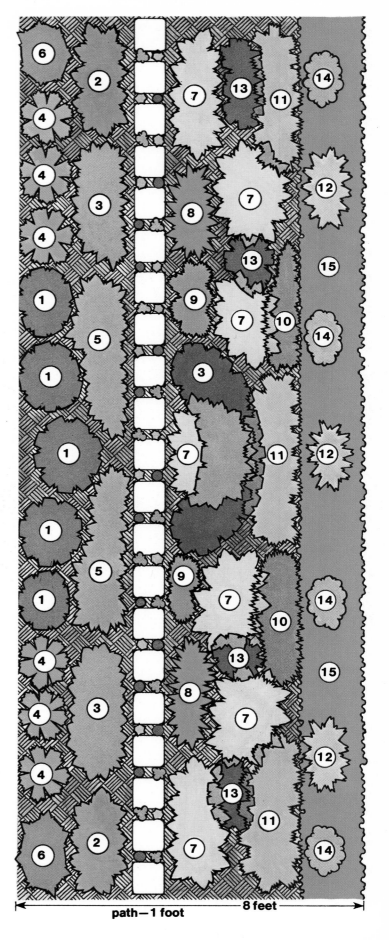

path—1 foot   8 feet

THE GARDEN FLOOR

Every garden has a floor. It may be nonliving such as brick, wood decking, cement paving or a mulch of tree bark, pine needles or gravel. It may be a grass lawn or ground cover. Many garden floors are a combination of the two.

Each kind of ground cover has advantages and disadvantages. Paving materials are the most expensive to install but are the best surfaces for patios and walkways. They last for many years and require little maintenance except for an occasional cleaning.

Lawns usually require the most maintenance, which varies according to grass type. For most grasses, regular watering, mowing and fertilizing are in order. Lawns are generally adapted to most soils and situations. Green grass is a pleasing, complementary color and one of the softest, most resilient surfaces for play.

If lawns are generally adapted, ground covers are specialists. There is a ground cover for nearly every landscape use, but few for every situation. Ground covers also range from high maintenance to low maintenance, depending on the plant and the situation. Many demand little care once they are established.

Mulches, too, are quite varied. If installed properly, they can be maintenance-free for many years. Organic mulches decompose to benefit the soil. Some kinds must be replaced periodically, because they tend to be washed or knocked out of their boundaries.

A matter of function—Deciding which ground covering plant or material to use as the floor of your garden is an essential part of landscaping. The garden floor is usually the most extensive feature of a home landscape, helping to establish its character.

Whether starting from scratch or upgrading an existing landscape, consider the function you want a ground cover to fill. In some cases, decking can perform the same duties as a living ground cover. The same is true for brick and concrete paving. But if you have a slope to protect, plants are by far the best choice. Consider, too, the natural beauty of plants versus inert materials. Plants are frequently the best possible option.

The garden floor may be grass, rock, wood or any other material that appropriately serves its function. This lawn is Kentucky bluegrass. Pebble rocks imitates a stream bed.

Lawn or Ground Cover?

A lawn of Kentucky bluegrass, rye-grass or bermuda grass has a place in nearly every landscape. No other ground cover plant is as readily planted, maintained and enjoyed. A grass lawn is unsurpassed as a recreational surface, whether in a football stadium or in a child's yard. The color, texture and evenly cropped height of a grass lawn complement, enlarge and enhance the landscape.

But large expanses of grass lawn can be expensive and difficult to maintain—especially in these days of water shortages. The large, rolling grass lawn as an American institution and status symbol is giving way to more practical, economical alternatives. The smaller lawns or sections of grass integrated with other ground covers.

Instead of *only* lawn, you need to be aware of the many ground cover options. Along with the nonliving ground covers mentioned before, there are hundreds of low, spreading plants that cover the ground effectively and economically.

Here are a few ideas to help you select the floor for your landscape:

● Alter patterns and planting areas of older landscapes to create different moods and capture a unique quality. Fine-textured, low surfaces such as grass lawns lend a sense of spaciousness to the landscape.

● Consider the effects of various colors. Light yellow-green is bold. Medium green and blue-green are more discreet. Large expanses of bright flower colors attract the eye.

● Complex patterns and coarse textures reduce the sense of space. They may become distracting and irritating. Aim for simplicity.

Precisely clipped driveway border of boxwood is complemented by equally meticulous lawn. Regular maintenance is required, and the effect is formal.

Informality and much less maintenance generally characterize gardens that feature ground covers. This ground cover is *Pachysandra terminalis.*

Choosing a Lawn or Ground Cover

Making the final choice of one plant over another can be the most agonizing part of landscaping. Consider your experience and the information in this book, plus all the advice you can collect from friends, neighbors and local nurserymen.

It is a good idea to make notes of what plants you have, need or want. Putting thoughts in writing will help crystalize your objectives. It is then easy to compare your data with plant descriptions and landscape plans. To give you some idea of how this process might occur, here are some notes made by a gardener living in Pasadena, California.

Lawn areas for play do not have to be large to be effective. Dichondra is sometimes difficult to maintain in large plantings, but works well as a soft, safe outdoor surface on a small scale.

One Gardener's Notes

Maximum and minimum temperatures—Called local nursery and airport. Minimum around 27F (−3C). Maximum rarely to 113F (44C).

Recommended lawn grasses—Warm-season grasses include bermuda, zoysia and dichondra. Ryegrasses are the best cool-season grasses.

Water—Summer drought is certain with occasional winter drought. Nurseryman says local water is "salty."

Soil—Fairly heavy clay type. Hard to work. Lawn will need organic amendment.

Outdoor spaces needed—Need fenced play yard for children. Some space for vegetables and fruit trees.

Full sun areas—Front yard faces south, gets most of sun. Perhaps vegetables should go here.

Shade areas—Heavy shade under trees in back yard. No grass there. Entire back yard faces north.

Slope areas—East side of lot is steep slope. Need ground cover for erosion control.

Garden maintenance—Vacations and business require a landscape that has some degree of self-sufficiency.

SOME CHOICES

After comparing notes with available plants and other data, the Pasadena gardener made these selections:

● Plant dichondra in back yard. This grass takes shade and thrives on high heat.

● Campanula, ferns or liriopope should grow in shade of deciduous tree.

● Remove weeds and control slope erosion with *Convolvulus cneorum* and *Cistus* species shrubs, surrounded by African daisies or Baccharis pilularis. For more color, plant one of the small varieties of ice plant. Install permanent drip watering system with automatic timer.

Low-Maintenance Landscapes

Ground covers other than grass have traditionally been associated with low maintenance. This assumption needs some clarification. In specialized situations, a ground cover planting my be low maintenance from the beginning. Seeding native grasses on a hillside is an example. But ground covers usually demand regular care the first few years, with particular attention paid to weed control. Gradually, maintenance diminishes, but only after careful attention in the beginning.

Here are some specifics to keep in mind if a low-maintenance landscape is your goal:

Reduce lawn size—Reducing the size of lawn increases its visual impact. Smaller lawns become more of an accent and less anonymous. Your efforts to maintain a beautiful lawn are concentrated over a smaller area, making an attractive lawn more attainable.

Confine lawn to specific areas— Small, numerous patches of grass, each requiring watering, mowing and edging, are very time consuming. Usually, lawns of this type happen by accident. Without planning, your landscape soon becomes dominated by grass.

Make lawn accessible—Do not surround lawn completely with shrubs or flower beds. Lawns should be used for play and recreation. Design lawn areas so you can get mower to and from them easily. Avoid having to carry a heavy mower from front to back yard.

Use ground cover alternatives— Ground covers exist for every situation around your home. Some will serve in place of a lawn. They are most useful in heavy shade, on steep slopes and in excessively wet or dry soils where grass will not grow.

Install a mowing strip—A firm, narrow edging at the right height guides the mower's wheels and reduces the amount of time it takes to hand trim. See illustration at right.

Consider installing a drip irrigation system, low-precipitation spray heads and an automatic clock—Consult a professional irrigation specialist for advice if landscape is complicated, or if a slope or hillside is involved. Quality counts when installing an irrigation system. A cut-rate system will often cost you more over a period of time due to failure of materials and inefficient, wasteful watering.

Improve soil, if necessary—Choose plants that will thrive in the existing soil, or thoroughly amend soil to accommodate the plants you want. Plants forced to struggle where not adapted are less attractive, grow more slowly and are more prone to problems.

Learn how to water—Many troubles result from poor watering habits. Get to know the specific needs of the plants in your landscape. When you water, be certain to wet soil to the depth of the roots. Wait for first signs of water stress—drooping, wilting, lackluster leaves—before watering again.

Use a mulch—Mulch around new ground cover plantings in summer to prevent infestations of wees, cool the soil and save water through reduced evaporation. Winter mulches protect plants from cold and prevent damage caused by alternate freezing and thawing of the soil.

Garden with the natural rhythms of the seasons—Time feeding, mowing, watering and pruning to seasonal cycles—not calendar dates. Feed lawns in fall when roots will store energy. Increase mowing frequency when grass is growing fastest.

Create wide tree basins—Surround lawn trees with a wide circle of mulch or ground cover. The tree is relieved of competition from grass, aided by mulch and protected from mower damage. At the same time, lawn area is reduced. Thin, weedy lawn in dense shade of tree is also eliminated.

Make comfortable paths—Where easy flow of pedestrian traffic is important, paths should be wide enough for two people to walk abreast. Be practical—determine width of utility paths by measuring distance between wheelbarrow handles.

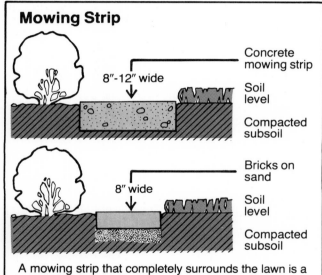

Mowing Strip

8"-12" wide

Concrete mowing strip

Soil level

Compacted subsoil

8" wide

Bricks on sand

Soil level

Compacted subsoil

A mowing strip that completely surrounds the lawn is a standard feature of low-maintenance landscapes. Consider installing sprinkler heads down center of concrete strip. Heads are protected from edger or mower damage and trimming is eliminated. Place sleeve of 2-inch-diameter plastic pipe around heads to depth of concrete.

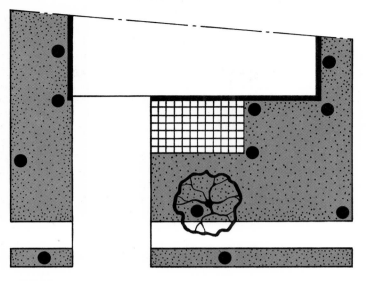

High, Medium and Low Maintenance

High Maintenance

A black spot ● indicates problem areas in this typical garden design. The lawn between the sidewalk and street is difficult to mow and water. Numerous stops and starts slow mowing. The tree in the lawn needs special protection from the mower, necessitating hand trimming. Edges along the house and property line must also be trimmed by hand.

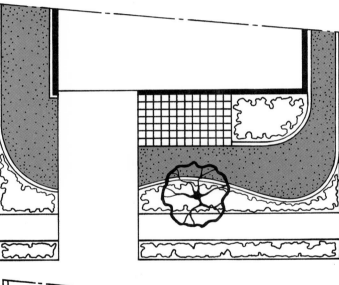

Medium Maintenance

A combination of lawn and ground cover makes mowing and watering jobs easier. Sweeping curves and a mowing strip speed mowing. Problem areas of lawn are reduced. Ground cover is used around the tree, at the entry and in the strip between sidewalk and street.

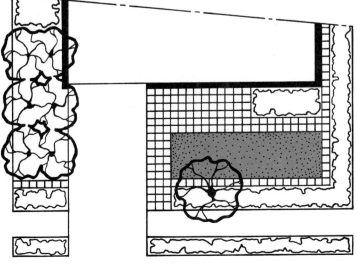

Low Maintenance

Mowing this lawn is now easy. Lawn area is reduced and bordered by a mowing strip. Ground covers fill odd spots. Side lawn area has been replaced by a small orchard of dwarf fruit trees.

Alternatives

Many gardeners are experimenting with ground covers that are distinctly different from traditional plantings. Low maintenance and water and energy conservation characterize each. Here are five that might interest you.

ROCKSCAPING

Landscaping with rock, or *rockscaping*, has many practical virtues. A rockscape is best and most commonly used to *reduce* lawn and ground cover areas, not eliminate them. When properly planned, a rockscape is attractive and requires little maintenance. A rockscape is especially appropriate with natural settings and Spanish or western architecture. In the desert Southwest, a rockscape can connect your home to the natural landscape. Realize, however, that even a rockscape is not completely maintenance-free. If not installed properly, it could require more weeding and raking maintenance than a lawn. To ensure success, follow these steps.

1. Eliminate all perennial weeds and grass in the area to be covered with rock. These include nutgrass, Bermudagrass, Johnsongrass and ground morning glory. If necessary, use glphosate herbicide or a soil fumigant.

2. Level and roll all surfaces to be covered until firm. Position any large boulders you intend to use at this time. Spread and level 1 inch of sharp, 20 grit concrete sand over soil. Sand is necessary—it acts as a cushion for the plastic cover to come. Without sand, gravel will cut through the plastic, allowing weed growth.

3. Cover sand with black plastic that is at least 4 millimeters thick. Be sure to overlap edges sufficiently or weeds will grow through. Lay rocks at the corners to hold in place until gravel is spread. Cut 2-foot-diameter holes in plastic for plants.

4. Spread a 4-inch layer of 1-inch-diameter gravel over the plastic for a "ground cover." This size gravel has a texture and effect similar to low-growing, connecting plants.

5. Spread 4 inches of pea gravel or finely decomposed granite rock, 5/8-inch diameter or less, over the plastic in the "lawn" area. Rock this size has a visual texture similar to a grass lawn.

6. Bury steppingstones or boards in the rock for walkways. Without some kind of pathway, you'll eventually ruin your shoes walking over the crushed rock.

Most landscapes look best with a combination of ground covers. Curving lines of rock mulch for tree basin is attractive, accents the grass lawn and benefits tree's health.

Design principles—Effective design using rocks in the landscape is the same as designing with plants: You want an attractive landscape using compatible materials placed in a natural way. Here are some tips:

● Situate boulders and large stones where you would typically place shrubs and hedges.

● Use fewer sizes of stones in a rockscape than you would different kinds of plants in a landscape.

● Bury one-fourth to one-third of large rocks below soil surface. This is how they would be found in nature.

● Position large sedimentary stones on a horizontal plane for accent.

● Use rock and gravel of similar texture or related origin. Avoid combining volcanic rock with granite or stream-bed rock.

● Use pea gravel to simulate the effect of lawn.

● Use 1-inch-diameter gravel or washed pebbles for ground cover effect.

● Use 2- to 4-inch stones for low border effect.

● Red and black volcanic rock combine well.

● Use native or adapted plants to accent rockscape.

● Use sedums and bulbs around large boulders.

MULCHES OF BARK OR WOOD CHIPS

A wide variety of organic mulches is available and varies by locality. All are beneficial in many ways. They reduce water evaporation, modify soil temperatures and help control weeks. Some of the best organic mulches include bark and wood products.

Fir bark pebbles or chunks are very attractive. They are rich, reddish brown when first placed in the garden, gradually aging to a pleasing gray. Garden centers offer many grades of fir bark in bags. If a large quantity is needed, you will save money by buying through a supplier of bulk garden materials. Many companies will sell materials by the yard or by the pickup truckload.

Shredded bark has the same rich color as fir bark but is variable in size and shape. Tree chips are irregular in shape and come in many colors. In many areas, tree chips are available at nominal cost

Carefully placed stream-bed rocks accent shape and emphasize character of mature oak. Moisture, which can cause disease, does not accumulate around tree's crown. Adjacent planting of ivy is blocked from spreading to, and up, tree.

Where lawn is difficult to grow, such as under and around trees and driveway borders, a mulch or live ground cover is a good alternative.

from the city maintenance department or private tree care companies.

These kinds of ground covers are very effective in natural, low-maintenance landscapes. They act as a forest floor. The primary disadvantage is need of replenishment. Every year or two, fresh bark must be added to compensate for the amount that decomposes or washes away. Bark must be bordered or confined to prevent excessive loss from water runoff or pedestrian traffic.

If weeds are a problem, a bark cover is best applied in a 3- to 4-inch layer. To cover 1,000 square feet to this depth requires 10 cubic yards. Where weeds are not a major problem or where slow-growing ground cover plants will eventually fill in an area, a layer 1 to 2 inches thick will be sufficient. You can reduce cost by using the least-expensive mulch for the bottom layer, covering this with a thin layer of the most attractive material.

NATIVE MOSS

Native mosses are outstanding, low-maintenance ground covers and lawn substitutes. But these are not plants you buy at the nursery. Rather, you encour-age them where they grow naturally. A moss lawn requires moist, well-drained acid soil, preferably with some clay. It does well in shade, such as on a north-facing slope.

David Benner, a horticulturist who lives in New Hope, Pennsylvania, has experimented with a lawn of native moss for the last dozen years. He reports:

"I have found moss to be an outstanding lawn substitute. My moss lawn is now 12 years old and has never been mowed, fertilized or sprayed. If given moisture, it is green all year. During extended drought, it browns but does not die. It becomes green all year.

"I simply encouraged the moss at the expense of my former grass lawn. Grass prefers a soil pH of 6.5, whereas moss prefers a pH of 5.5 or less. Instead of liming to raise the pH to encourage grass, I applied 4 pounds of soil sulfur per 100 square feet. Within a few months, the soil pH had dropped from 6.5 to about 5, and the moss began to thrive. Over the next three or four years, the grass continued to give way to the moss until the lawn turned entirely to moss.

"Moss can be transplanted. Try it in the early spring when the weather is cool and the soil is moist. Most important, leave no air spaces between soil and transplanted clumps of moss. You must sprinkle them frequently the next several weeks until they are established.

"Moss lawns need very little care until fall. Leaves falling on moss from deciduous trees must be removed before winter. If leaves are not removed, the moss will rot and die. I will wait until after the first hard freeze. The moss is frozen to the ground and less likely pulled loose by a rake.

"The only maintenance is occasional weeding. Dandelion, thistle, oxalis and veronica are sometimes problems. I try to pull them out by the roots before they set seed.

"One interesting advantage of a moss lawn is that it is an ideal germination medium for all kinds of rare and normally hard-to-grow wildflowers. Right now I have seedlings of *Shortia galacifolia* as well as seedling rhododendrons, azaleas, *Pieris, Leucothoe, Chrysogonum, Lobelia* and *Houstonia.*"

PRAIRIE GRASS

Just a century ago, a huge sea of prairie grass covered most of the arid Midwest and the northern section of the United States. The sight must have been impressive to the pioneers. On the plains of the Illinois, Des Moines and Wabash rivers, the prairie stretched as far as the eye could see. Full height in the fall was an incredible 10 to 12 feet.

There are three basic kinds of natural prairie grass. *Shortgrass prairie* is mostly western wheatgrass, buffalograss and blue grama. It survives on as little as 20 inches of rain a year. *Midgrass prairie* of the Dakotas, Nebraska, Kansas and Oklahoma produces 1-1/2 to 2-foot-tall side oats grama, split beard bluestem, little bluestem, needle-and-thread, prairie propseed and others with about 30 inches of rain. *Tallgrass prairie* thrives the farthest east where rainfall averages 40 inches or more a year. Grasses there include big bluestem, switchgrass and Indiangrass.

Prairie grass is one of the most outstanding landscape features of North America. However, most stands were gradually sacrificed to farming over the last century. Now many architects, designers, ecologists and gardeners are re-establishing prairie grass for low-maintenance landscapes. Where the setting is appropriate, prairie grass is attractive, interesting and maintenance-free once established.

Bark mulch covers soil between conifers to reduce weeds, cool soil and conserve water. Bark gradually decomposes and improves soil. Replenish mulch each spring by spreading one-third of the quantity originally required.

Seed or plants of prairie grass are commercially available. Obtaining seed from a commercial source is advised. The supplier will also provide good advice for planting your particular site. It is important that you plant seed adapted to your climate and soil area. Consult your local county agricultural adviser or the Soil Conservation Service for further help.

Establishing prairie grass requires effort and patience. Allow three seasons—the first for preparing the seedbed, the second for planting and the third for watching prairie grass takeoff.

First season:

Prepare soil—Make seedbed reasonable weed-free by repeated tilling at monthly intervals through the season. Fertilizer and amendment are not necessary. Roll until soil is packed fairly hard.

Seed—A typical mix includes three kinds of grasses and six flowering plants. Fast-growing grasses such as needlegrass, Junegrass, Canadian wild rye, bee balm, yellow coneflower and black-eyed Susan are often included in mixes. Use big bluestem, Indiangrass or switchgrass in moist, heavy soil. Rely on side oats grama, needle-and-thread, western wheatgrass and Junegrass in dry, sandy soil.

Second season:

Planting—Sow in spring. Mix tiny grass seed with sand for easier spreading. Sow flower seed in bunches so new plants will not be overrun by faster-growing grass. Cover with 3/8-inch layer of soil or mulch. Roll to ensure good seed-to-soil contact. Start some flower seed in flats for later use as fill-in transplants.

Mow—Mow first and second month planting with a rotary mower set to cut 4 to 8 inches high. Mowing retards growth of fastest-growing weeds and plants and encourages slower-growing prairie grasses.

Patience—Prairie grass plants show little above-ground activity the first year. Deep and strong root systems are developing underground.

Fill-in—Transplant plants grown from flats or nursery-grown plants to thin areas. Plant prairie flowers in clumps.

Third season:

Mow—Mow 2 to 3 inches high with rotary mower early in spring. No mowing required thereafter.

Enjoy—Growth will be fast and strong from now on. Your own landscape of prairie grass will give you some idea of the texture and beauty of America's prairie 200 years ago.

Thymus pseudolanuginosus, woolly thyme, is one of the best ground cover herbs. It grows low—usually less than 1 inch high. It spreads fast, is cold hardy and drought tolerant.

HERB LAWN

Herbs such as creeping thyme, chamomile and yarrow make the toughest, most traffic-resistant ground covers. Make a lawn using one or all three of these. Adding seed of legume such as white clover or birdsfood trefoil makes a wonderful, wild, grow-what-will lawn.

Herb lawns need mowing, weeding, watering and fertilizing just aw typical grass lawns, but less of each. Their fragrance and texture is also a pleasure.

A lawn of creeping thyme (*Thymus praecox arcticus*) is extremely beautiful. It is hardy and tolerant, but also needs regular weeding. Even when a planting of thyme is completely filled in, grassy weeds invade easily. Best way to start a thyme lawn is with plugs planted about 12 inches apart.

Chamomile (*Chamaemelum* species) is the tradtional English lawn substitute.

Plant perennial Roman chamomile, not the taller, annual chamomile used for tea. Roman chamomile can be kept low by mowing with a reel mower, and is fairly resistant to weed invasions. Start with plugs planted 12 inches apart.

Yarrow (*Achillea* species) is particularly tolerant of drought and infertile soil, even compared to other herbs. There are several species. *Achillea tomentosa* is the common, low ornamental. Some recommend *A. millefolium* for use as a lawn. It is well adapted as a lawn, evidenced by the vigor with which it invades and overtakes some grass lawns. Nurseries sell yarrow in 1-gallon containers. Set these large clumps about 18 inches apart.

Before planting, prepare the soil by making it as weed-free as possible. Sow legume seed after planting herbs, then mulch and water.

HEDGES, SCREENS AND ESPALIERS

Hedges, screens and espaliers are the basic, *practical plants* of the landscape. Planted in the right location, they reduce heating and cooling costs, and increase privacy and outdoor space. Edible hedges, screens and espaliers perform triple duty, supplying beauty, landscape function and fresh produce.

On a large scale, hedgerow and screen plantings provide cover to wildlife. Barrier plants can often be substituted for fences wherever practical on large properties for increased security. On a small scale, property owners in residental areas can plant screens and hedges in a common effort to screen eyesores or channel breezes. Such unified plantings create a real sense of elegance and harmony, and regional identity is achieved.

Some hedges and screens produce flowers. Some are deciduous after a brilliant burst of fall color. Some make thorny barriers. Screens are excellent for gardeners who want minimum maintenance, or a natural effect. Espalier is a surprisingly efficient training method that dates back centuries.

CHEAPER THAN FENCES

Walls and fences provide privacy, protection and wind control, but plants do these things at less cost. Plants do require a period of time before they are able to serve their purpose, but substantial results are usually obtained within three years.

Growing plants is a rewarding experience in other ways. It is satisfying to watch seedlings increase in size and beauty each year, while also increasing the value of your property. And the natural qualities of seasonal change, leaf texture, flower color and fragrance cannot be duplicated by human-built objects.

Opposite Page: Home landscape features a narrow hedge of *Taxus* species, yew. It functions as a privacy screen and as a backdrop for mixed shrubbery inside. Left: Same location as at left but from a streetside view. Hedge and retaining wall with a feathery base of *Picea,* spruce, gives a softer effect than a solid screen of tall foliage.

Hedges

A hedge is a neat, living wall, usually composed of one kind of plant for a simple, pleasing effect. Shearing produces elegant formality but is by no means necessary. Informal hedges consist of plants that grow in a natural form, requiring only periodic shaping. Hedges form part of the garden framework by defining edges and spaces. They also give a sense of movement to paths by transforming flat, two-dimensional lines of direction into functional channels.

Hedges are categorized by size. *Borders* fall below the knee. They edge flowerbeds and paths. *Low hedges* are knee- to waist-high. They keep people in or out of areas by serving as visual or actual barriers. *Medium hedges* are waist- to chest-high. They provide privacy for seated people and form true barriers. They also make excellent backdrops for flowers and sculpture when dark-green, fine-textured foliage is used. *Tall hedges*—6 to 8 feet high—provide privacy and enclosure, and make suitable backdrops. *Informal* tall hedges move into the screen category.

Large-scale *hedgewalls* reach stately proportions from 8 to 50 feet high or more. They are used for grand architectural effects and complete privacy. Plants that have the potential to last for centuries are the best choice if large-scale hedgewalls or stately effects are desired.

Hedgerow describes a line of plants or a large-scale installation of mixed varieties. Hedgerows have been used in Great Britain since the Middle Ages to define field ownership lines and contain livestock. Hedgerows form complex ecological relationships with the land and give regional identity to the landscapes where they appear. They may or may not be pruned.

Precisely shaped hedge of *Buxus microphylla* var. *japonica,* Japanese boxwood, creates an interesting pattern.

A border planting of *Nandina domestica* 'Nana', dwarf nandina, helps prevent shortcuts across walkway.

Manicured hedge of *Thuja* species frames driveway and makes an impressive entry.

Spacious landscape allows for spectacular use of low hedges and tall hedgewall of *Taxus x media,* intermediate yew.

Medium-size hedge and juniper ground cover serve as an evergreen buffer zone between house and street.

Closely sheared hedgewall makes front yard private and helps to reduce noise slightly from nearby street traffic.

Screens

Anything that blocks a view is a screen. Chain-link fence covered with vines or espaliers, and hedges six feet or more high are screens. In this book, however, a *screen* is defined as a row of tall plants in their natural form.

Screens perform many of the same functions as tall hedges but are generally broader and take up more space. They also have fewer maintenance requirements. Screens composed of unclipped, low-branching trees or shrubs require only periodic shaping. They are always suitable for a casual, natural effect, and have great flower and fruit potential. Screens are usually less expensive than hedges because individual plants are spaced farther apart.

Natural forms of plants vary. *Fastigiate* plants, those that are tall and narrow, are quite useful for screens. They take little space and require no shaping. *Columnar* plants, which are slightly wider, also make excellent screens. Columnar and fastigiate forms do not always have branches at their base, so planting shrubs may be necessary to make a solid screen. If space is not at a premium, use round, arching and pyramidal plants for their flowers, fruit or low-maintenance requirements. Deciduous plants allow for maximum penetration of winter sun.

A canopy tree is a screen in an umbrella form. Widespreading branches block views of tall buildings and elevated highways overhead, while providing a sense of enclosure. Canopies also block the view of people looking down into private gardens. Deciduous trees out of leaf provide a light, twiggy canopy, and most winter sun penetrates to help warm your home.

Screens are typically used to conceal unattractive views, such as highways, business signs or telephone wires. They also work well to offset crowded effects of suburbanization. Houses, condominiums and gardens can be blended with the regional landscape by screening with native plants.

Screens with regular gaps lend a different quality to a landscape than a solid line of plants. A rhythm is created, especially when tall, narrow trees are used. People can catch glimpses in or out of a garden scene. Widely spaced plantings are still effective as windbreaks.

Similarly, a curtain or *scrim* of delicate greenery serves as a partial veil to create interest in the view. Use these curtains of plant material when screening is necessary, but when some light and air penetration is desired.

Ilex 'Foster's No. 2' is excellent for large-scale screening.

Plants in wooden containers are movable screens. Here they substitute for railing along edge of raised deck.

Many screens provide colorful displays of flowers or fruit. *Ilex cornuta* 'D'Or' produces large, yellow berries in abundance.

Tall bamboo screen provides shade to cool patio and house. Plants at base are *Nandina domestica,* nandina.

Hibiscus rosa-sinensis, tropical hibiscus, produces large, colorful flowers if plants are not sheared.

Azaleas create a mass of color, and serve as a low, protective screen on this slope.

Espaliers

Espalier—pronounced *ess-PAL-yeah* or *ess-PAL-yer*—is an ancient method of training plants to grow flat against a support. You may wonder why anyone would want to shape plants into unnatural forms. But espaliers have many advantages. Most important, they save space. This feature alone makes them worth growing, especially in today's smaller gardens. More leaf surface captures light for higher and more efficient fruit yield. Heat radiated from a south wall permits growth of flowering shrubs or fruit in marginal climate areas. The small stature of espaliers makes them easy to protect against frost damage or marauding birds. Espaliers are well suited to windy sites because they are supported. In humid climates, their open form tends to reduce mildew problems.

Espaliers are vinelike, but lack a vine's rampant and sometimes destructive growth. They can be used to reduce home heating and cooling bills by insulating the walls they are trained against.

Espaliers create a dramatic and decorative architectural effect. In essence, they are living, sculptural forms in tailored, formal, natural or informal patterns. The most basic form is the *cordon,* a single, straight stem, with many, shortened side shoots. Hedge effects are obtained by staking single cordons in rows or by training multiple cordons along wires.

Espaliers have many uses. They make excellent screens on trellises or wire supports. A container-grown espalier on a frame makes a handy, space-saving, movable screen. Espaliers soften blank stretches of wall or chain-link fence. They make living, space-saving fences. Cordon fences are both ornamental and productive when fruit trees are used. A *Belgian fence* is a special lattice pattern that makes an attractive espalier screen. Border espaliers are often used to edge paths and vegetable plots.

A simple way to get started with espaliers is to buy them pretrained from the nursery. Early shaping that is critical to the plant's form is done by specialists. This makes it easy for today's gardener to adapt ancient espalier principles to produce fruit on balconies, rooftops and small, city lots. By growing espaliers, it is possible and practical to raise miniorchards without sacrificing outdoor gardening and living space.

Formal apple espalier trained as a horizontal T is gorgeous in spring and productive in fall. Major limbs have been carefully pruned to produce maximum amounts of fruit.

Formal espalier is a pear formed in a Verrier palmette pattern. This traditional form originated centuries ago.

Informal pyracantha espalier decorates a wall. These are spring flowers; berries will follow in fall.

Espalier-fence of 'Golden Delicious' apples. It provides tasty fruit, and adds beauty and privacy to the landscape.

An Inside Look

It is sometimes difficult to understand the value of hedges, screens and espaliers. Much of their usefulness is their *utility*—screening and dividing to increase privacy and livability. To best show this aspect, we took a bird's-eye vantage point to photograph some exceptional examples of hedges and screens in use.

Right: From the street, passers-by can only imagine what lies behind this massive, evergreen screen. Dark-green foliage shows off ornately designed fence. For a look inside the screen, see photos below.

Below: High above ground level, the camera looks into an expansive, secluded landscape. The double rows of evergreens perform their screening function well.

Below right: Inside, it's a flower-lover's world. The same evergreens that served as streetside screens are excellent backdrops for flowering annuals and perennials.

Above: Hedge of *Prunus laurocerasus,* English laurel, was planted to extend code-imposed fence height. Impatiens add a bright row of color.

Above right: Beyond this gate is a courtyard, formed by fence-hedge combination. It creates a transition zone between public street and private home.

Right: Inside, the garden courtyard is quiet and private, with a formal yet relaxed feeling. Views of neighboring houses and street traffic are screened out. Dark-green hedge is a nice backdrop for flowers.

67

Below: The owners of this home wanted a pool, but the best exposure to the sun was in the front yard, which faced a busy street. A pool was installed and enclosed by an evergreen hedge and bamboo screen. Seldom used previously, area is now private for swimming and sunbathing. Inside, sunbathers see only leafy greenery.

Right: Streetside view of home reveals nothing of the pool inside. Stone retaining wall, wooden fence and evergreens combine nicely as a privacy screen, yet are not obtrusive.

Above: This home is located at a busy city intersection. Tall, dense screen helps reduce street noise slightly, but more importantly, it blocks views of passing automobiles and tall busses.

Right: Without a tall screen, front yard would not be a desirable place to spend time.

TREES & SHRUBS
IN THE LANDSCAPE

Of all plants, trees and shrubs are the most prominent in a landscape. They are the most permanent, the least demanding of care, and they establish a sense of place and design better than all other plants.

Well-planned landscapes use a combination of *needleleaf evergreens, broadleaf evergreens* and *deciduous trees and shrubs* in varying proportions. Needleleaf evergreens establish a greater sense of permanence than other plants, not only because of their stature, but also because of their cold tolerance. Landscape architects often refer to evergreens as the *bones* of a garden. Planted as skyline and lawn accents, windbreaks, screens and hedges, or borders and edging, evergreens can delineate garden space or create permanent *outdoor rooms* and provide dominant highlights. Apart from a brighter leaf color in spring, their appearance changes little from one season to the next.

Because evergreens make especially good background plants, they are usually the first plants to be fitted into a landscape plan.

Deciduous trees and shrubs, on the other hand, are constantly changing with the seasons. Certain deciduous trees can even provide four seasons of dramatic color changes—such as lovely flowers in spring, lush greenery in summer, brilliant leaf coloring in fall and an artistic branch silhouette through winter.

Trees are the most influential design elements in a garden. For instance, palms instantly suggest a tropical climate. A small garden hedged in by tall evergreens becomes a secret garden—a refuge from the pressures of civilization.

DESIGNING WITH
TREES AND SHRUBS

The placement of trees and shrubs in a garden is based on a relatively few basic design principles. In some cases, a tree or shrub is planted so its branches partially conceal a structural feature—such as a wall or fence—or drape over it as an embellishment. In other cases, trees and shrubs serve as a background to bring into relief special foreground features—such as a boulder, sculpture or a planting highlight.

The best gardens avoid symmetrical placement of trees and shrubs, except where an avenue, hedge or grove is desired. In informal plantings, trees and shrubs should never be planted in straight lines, but *staggered.* Trees and shrubs intended to form hedges, avenues or sentinels should be planted at precise distances, in lines.

When trees and shrubs are grouped together in numbers, it is best to use different species that will contrast pleasingly with each other, unless the intent is to create a natural woodland or grove of predominantly one type of tree—such as oaks, pines or tulip poplars.

Contrasts of form and line are especially important—for example, an open, irregular-branching tree such as a rugged pine or a drooping willow in contrast to the dense, smooth contours of mounded azaleas shaped by shearing. Contrasts in leaf size and color are also desirable.

Taller trees should be employed in the background. Unless a windbreak or curtain effect is desired, deciduous trees are best employed as background plants because of their wintry, bare silhouetted aspect that can be admired from a distance. An exception is made with flowering deciduous trees such as cherries and crabapples because of their profuse blossoming, which is best admired close up.

Clipped or sheared broadleaf evergreen shrubs, such as azaleas, hollies and boxwood, can be used as foreground features to contrast with background trees that present a rugged appearance. These mounded shrubs can form cushions, like clumps of moss, to soften a landscape. Mound-shaped shrubs can also be planted on a slope, towering one above the other, to give the appearance of gently rolling hills.

Often, a single specimen of an especially beautiful or interesting tree or shrub is featured as an accent or focal point in the garden. It is usually positioned so it does not compete with other plants for visual attention.

Left and Above: Azaleas make excellent understory plants for woodlands and groves. They prefer light shade and acid soil.

Authentic Japanese gardens rely heavily on evergreen trees and shrubs—the complete opposite of a traditional English garden, where deciduous trees often predominate.

A favorite practice in Oriental gardens is to highlight a *lone tree*—such as a pine, willow or plum—on a promontory or earth mound. The tree itself can be surgically shaped to simulate weathered trees found in the wild. Limbs are removed between prominent scaffold branches and remaining limbs bent and shaped with wires and splints until they assume wild, rather than cultivated, forms. In other instances, special weeping forms—such as hemlocks and cedars—are placed to represent cascades, fountains and torrents.

THE ORIENTAL INFLUENCE

In Oriental gardens it is a general rule that four-fifths of the vegetation should be *evergreens*, with a heavy emphasis on conifers, rhododendrons, camellias and bamboo. A few deciduous flowering trees—notably cherries, crabapples and wisteria—and a few deciduous shade trees—notably oaks, maples, ginkgo and willows—are used principally for their fall coloring or texture. However, the somewhat somber Oriental style is not to everyone's taste. In the English style of landscaping, this emphasis is often completely reversed to achieve a totally different, but no less pleasing, result—one that is more airy and informal. Whatever ethnic style is preferred, this comparison does serve to show that in garden design a boldness and clarity of purpose is needed from the very outset to determine the choice of plants.

Trees, Stone and Water—It is the Japanese who believe that only three elements are essential to create a beautiful garden. They are *stone, water* and *trees*.

Stone is a symbol of endurance, power and permanence. It brings to the garden an aura of rugged grandeur. Ancient Japanese landscapers would scour the mountains for rocks and boulders with interesting colors, shapes and textures. Some the size of grand pianos would be dug from the forest floor because just a nub of exposed stone revealed to the finder that something visually exciting lay hidden there. Others would be raised from river beds or hauled out of rock falls—moved by armies of men and mules, the rocks themselves carefully wrapped in quilts to protect their flawless texture or some delicate plant growing on them, such as a fern or a clump of moss. In the mind's eye, stones can conjure up visions of craggy peaks and windswept rocky islands, of dry water courses and pebble beaches.

Water is the *music* of nature—splashing, gurgling, trickling. Water is also a mirror, reflecting the moon, vistas and highlights—doubling the visual impact of its surroundings. Water is cool and fluid—a reminder that all life on earth originated there. In a still pool it can be dark as night or flashing with the silver and golden images of fish. Cascading over rocks or arching out from a bamboo spout, water can twinkle with a thousand flashing lights. The shapes of rocks and trees are contorted in its reflection. Still water is level. There is a mystery to water—unknown creatures can lurk in its depths.

Trees are the life of a garden. Their presence is soothing to the senses. They provide more color, more gradations of texture and more structure to a garden than rocks or water combined. Color comes not only from blossoms, but also from leaves, berries, bark and branches. Trees introduce texture from the size, shape and arrangement of leaves, from the density and configuration of twigs and from the patterns of bark. Structure is evident in the lines of a tree—a pencil-straight trunk or a multitude of stems. The horizontal spread or the weeping effect of its branches are other visual delights associated with structure. The earth, with its stones and water, is a canvas. The trees are brush strokes.

Apart from blossoms of a few kinds of trees and shrubs—notably cherry, camellias and azaleas—flowers are noticeably absent from Japanese gardens. A discreet clump of water lilies to embellish a pool of water, and an occasional clump of iris, admired more for its swordlike leaves, are virtually the only flowering perennial plants found in traditional Japanese gardens. If a delphinium or a marigold raised its head, it would be pounced upon and eradicated as a weed. When conducting a private tour of the Katsura Imperial Garden, in Kyoto, the guide announced that visitors had come at the perfect time—summer—because then the garden could be admired for its enduring beauty without the distraction of spring flowers or fall foliage.

The Japanese philosophy of garden design is an extreme example of tree worship, but most other garden styles also hold woody plants in high regard. The Italians and the French with their emphasis on grandeur and formality of design and the English with their liking for natural landscapes, have developed special uses for trees as part of a garden's overall design.

THE EUROPEAN INFLUENCE

One of the most important design concepts used in the European style of landscaping is the *vista*, whereby trees help to establish a beautiful view. The French and Italians do it with avenues of trees in parallel lines. The most famous French avenues, called *allees,* are on level ground, but the outstanding Italian examples are more often seen on hillsides where steps may descend a slope to give the illusion of greater distance. Usually, a large sculpture or an ornate structure such as a fountain is sited at the end as a focal point.

English-style vistas are more natural, often cutting through natural woodland and with a view of a free-form lake in the distance. To emulate these European concepts of landscaping it is not necessary to own large, parklike estates. The principles can be applied to the smallest home garden, using smaller trees and compact shrubs to delineate a narrow or short vista.

This is the antithesis of traditional Oriental styles, where winding paths and zig-zag bridges are used to create *stroll gardens,* with twists and turns at every opportunity to make maximum use of confined areas and provide surprises around every corner.

In modern times, neither style need be exclusive of the other. In fact, there are many fine American gardens that borrow tree and shrub planting ideas from both European and Oriental cultures.

Beautiful harmony between evergreens and deciduous trees at Dumbarton Oaks Garden in Washington, D.C. Spire-shaped cedars frame a vista where fall coloring of billowing native deciduous trees provides a focal point.

Beautiful rock garden uses mostly evergreen conifers to enhance brighter colors of alpine plants and perennials, such as the pink *Astilbe* in foreground.

American linden (*Tilia americana*) has an attractive rounded, pyramidal habit.

'Pendula' is a lovely weeping form of deodar cedar (*Cedrus deodara albrea*).

GROWTH HABIT

The term *growth habit* refers to the height, spread, growth rate and outline of a tree or shrub. Because these characteristics are highly variable among different kinds of trees and shrubs, it is important to consider them when making design decisions in a landscape. Growth habit is not only variable from species to species, but also within a single species where mutations have been used by horticulturists in developing new varieties.

When you see the towering, spirelike growth habit of a standard Canadian hemlock and compare it to the low, billowing, weeping features of the mutant variety 'Sargent's' weeping hemlock, it's hard to believe they are the same species. Whereas the standard Canadian hemlock is limited to mundane uses in the garden, such as for a windbreak or hedge, the weeping form is invaluable as a sophisticated lawn highlight or accent plant.

The drawing on the facing page shows some of the basic growth habits of trees and shrubs, which are described here.

Columnar trees are mostly evergreens with a dense foliage cover. Width is more-or-less equal from the base of the tree to its crown. The top is usually blunt or rounded. American arborvitae, Irish yew, podocarpus and Italian cypress are the best examples of columnar trees. They are used for vertical highlights—to delineate an avenue or create tall screens and windbreaks—and singly as exclamation points in the landscape. Columnar trees are also good in pairs at entryways and as sentinels at the corners of a building.

Fastigate trees are mostly deciduous. They have branches that point upward, sometimes in a spiral form, and usually a tapered top. Lombardy poplar trees are a good example. The fastigate English oak is effective as a foundation plant against a tall building, as a landscape highlight similar to columnar trees, and especially as a skyline tree.

Pyramidal trees are mostly evergreen, though some deciduous trees form a distinct pyramid shape—notably the pin oak. Pyramidal trees have wide, spreading lower branches that often sweep the ground, but the top tapers to a definite point. This is a classical shape immensely popular as a lawn highlight and for decorating with lights at Christmas. Evergreen forms such as deodar cedar, Norway spruce and Colorado blue spruce also make sturdy windbreaks.

Spirelike trees are mostly evergreens with wide-spreading lower branches that quickly slant up to a long, slender point. A particularly beautiful spirelike tree is the mature Norfolk Island pine, looking like a gigantic feather pointing skyward. They are magnificent skyline trees, and it is a pity they can be grown outdoors only in mild-winter locations close to the ocean. For colder regions, Douglas fir and the deciduous dawn redwood make beautiful spires, and are valued for lining long driveways and as lawn highlights.

Conical trees are shaped like spinning tops or squat pyramids. They are generally slow-growing evergreens that are dwarf mutations of standard trees, particularly hemlock, yew and spruce. Dwarf forms are popular for rock gardens.

Weeping or pendant trees bring a softness to the landscape. Weeping willow and weeping cherry are the best examples. Branches first grow upright, then arch and descend downward. Weeping trees are especially effective when planted at the edge of ponds so the water surface reflects their weeping outline and the hanging branches can touch the surface as though flowing into the water like a waterfall. They also make wonderful skyline trees. Some weeping varieties are grafted onto the trunk of a closely related plant to provide a pedestal on which to display the weeping form.

Cascading trees are more umbrella-

BASIC TREE SHAPES

WEEPING (WEEPING WILLOW)

CASCADING (SARGENT'S HEMLOCK)

FOUNTAIN (SAGO PALM)

ROUNDED CROWN (ASH)

OPEN CROWN (SCOTCH PINE)

SPREADING CROWN (ENGLISH WALNUT)

CONTORTED (CORKSCREW WILLOW)

COLUMNAR (ARBORVITAE)

FASTIGATE (POPLAR)

PYRAMID (WHITE PINE)

SPIRE (DOUGLAS FIR)

CONE (YEW)

BASIC SHRUB SHAPES

GLOBULAR (BOXWOOD)

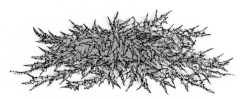

PROSTRATE (HORIZONTAL JUNIPER)

MULTI-STEMMED (FORSYTHIA)

VINING (WISTERIA)

file to resist wind and avoid the possibility of the tree falling on the house in the event of a storm. They are perfect trees from which to hang a swing.

Contorted trees have twigs and branches that twist and curl like the coils of a snake. The corkscrew willow and contorted form of hazel are the best-known examples. The contorted hazel is especially admired in foundation plantings where its tortuous, bare branches can be admired against a wall or screen during winter. The corkscrew willow grows tall and can make a dramatic skyline tree.

Multi-stemmed trees do not form a single main trunk. They sprout a cluster of main stems like shrubs. Usually, this cluster of stems can be thinned out by pruning to leave one main stem for the plant to be grown as a single-stemmed tree. Lilacs are good examples of multi-stemmed woody plants where the terms *tree* and *shrub* become interchangeable. In their juvenile years, lilacs are considered shrubs, but with age they are often referred to as trees.

In their natural state, multi-stemmed trees are good for creating a hedge, or in mixed-shrub borders and foundation plantings. For an especially artistic effect, the thicket of stems can be thinned out, stripped of lower side branches, and the dense overhead canopy shaped to form an umbrella or mushroom. This sculptural pruning is especially popular with camellias and European olives, so distant landscape features can be seen through boldly defined lines formed by the multiple trunks.

Another special effect possible with multi-stemmed trees and large shrubs is to form a *tunnel*. Planted on either side of a rustic path, large multi-stemmed shrubs, such as rhododendrons and camellias, can be encouraged to arch their upper branches to meet and form a leafy canopy. When flowers appear in summer, the spent petals drop like confetti to carpet the path.

Globular shrubs are round in shape and popular for foundation plantings. They are often referred to as *meat balls* when used in formal gardens. When rounded shrubs like boxwood and azaleas are heavily sheared to present a smooth outline, they have a soothing effect, like mounds of moss on a stream bank. Globular forms are extremely popular in Oriental gardens and rock gardens, arranged in informal groups of different heights to resemble a landscape of rolling hills.

like than weeping trees, though the terms are often used interchangeably. Cascading forms of catalpa, hemlock—particularly the Sargent's weeping hemlock—and mulberry are good examples, as are weeping crabapple and weeping cherry. All make excellent lawn highlights. *Pleaching* is a favorite pruning technique with cascading trees. The main trunk is *topped,* with few main scaffold branches left as stubs, to produce clusters of cascading whips.

Fountain-shaped trees and shrubs create an exploding fountain effect from outward-arching canes or fronds. Forsythia, fetterbush *(Leucothoe)* and Lady Banks roses have long, whiplike branches that do this. They are especially admired for their wintry outline where snow and ice can coat their limbs to sparkle in the sunlight. Plant them as informal hedges or highlights in odd corners. Used singly, they are best planted against a background of evergreens so the fountain effect can be

emphasized. In frost-free areas, juvenile Sago palms and tree ferns create a more tropical fountain effect.

Rounded-crown trees with straight, single trunks are perhaps everyone's image of the classic tree. Many deciduous trees grow this way, including beeches, ash, maples and many oaks. All are perfect as skyline trees, lawn highlights, shade trees, street trees and woodlots.

Open-crown trees have an irregular outline and sparse scaffold branches. Usually, this occurs on older trees. For example, Scotch pine, which begins its life pyramid-shaped, will shed branches as it ages. The gaps between the main side branches become greater and the tree opens up, often presenting a rugged, weathered silhouette to the landscape.

Spreading-crown trees are best for shade. Silk trees, Southern live oak and English walnut are excellent examples. Long, sinuous lower branches radiate out like the spokes of a wheel or arch elegantly. The crown presents a low pro-

Prostrate shrubs make effective ground covers for both decoration and erosion control. Many have branches that sweep across the ground, rooting along their length and suffocating all weed growth. Horizontal juniper species are the most frequently used prostrate shrubs for ground covers.

Vining shrubs come in many different forms. Some, like wisteria, will climb by twining—these will strangle a young tree if they get hold of it. Others, like trumpet vine, use clinging roots. Care should be taken to match the vine to its intended support. For example, honeysuckle is better used to cover an arbor than to decorate a tree. Virginia creeper is preferred for climbing up stone because of its clinging ability. Cherokee roses and jasmine are safer for garlanding trees. Many kinds of woody vines can be planted to serve as ground covers, such as English ivy.

TREES AND SHRUBS
FOR DIFFERENT PURPOSES

Trees and shrubs are planted in the home landscape for both esthetic and practical reasons. Here are some of the uses for trees and shrubs:

Shade—Cooling shade is probably the most desirable reason for planting trees. A deck or patio may benefit from the shade of a spreading tree. When planting for shade, consider whether you need dense shade or light shade. Trees such as acacias, mimosa and honeylocust have delicate leaves that allow sufficient light to penetrate so that grass will grow right up to the trunk. Under the deeper shade of cedars, oaks and maples, grass may have to give way to a more shade-tolerant ground cover such as ivy, vinca or pachysandra.

When planting for shade, also consider whether or not the tree is messy, and if this trait is acceptable for the location you've chosen. For example, female ginkgos will drop unpleasant-smelling fruits, and the prickly nut cases of Chinese chestnuts can be a nuisance near heavily-used outdoor areas. Walnuts and fruiting varieties of mulberry are similarly messy. These trees would be poor choices around decks, patios, concrete driveways and swimming pools.

Ornamental Flowers—Few hardy trees and shrubs are *perpetual flowering*. This term refers to trees and shrubs that bloom over a long period of time during spring and summer. Those that are perpetual flowering—such as glossy abelia—tend to produce small blos-

European olive is an excellent example of a multi-stemmed tree.

English boxwood *(Buxus sempervirens)* is pruned to globular form. Because of its small leaves and slow growth rate, boxwood is excellent for formal hedges and topiary subjects.

Raised deck allows striking pink blossoms of flowering crabapple *(Malus* species) to be admired close up.

soms. The exotic tropical hibiscus *(Hibiscus rosea-sinensis)* and bougainvillea are glorious exceptions for frost-free areas. Usually, woody plants have a brief period of bloom at a particular time of year. Amelanchiers and witchhazels are among the earliest to flower in spring, while camellias and franklinias are usually the last to flower in fall.

The prima donnas among hardy flowering trees and shrubs—magnolias, azaleas, rhododendrons, cherries, crabapples and dogwoods—squeeze their spectacular flowering displays into a brief 6-week period in spring. So it takes careful planning to achieve a continuous flowering display beyond spring, either by planting late-blooming varieties or summer-blooming trees and shrubs. Crape myrtle, silk tree, golden rain tree and pagoda tree are examples of summer-flowering trees. Good summer-flowering shrubs include oleander, hy-

drangeas, smoke tree and bottlebrush buckeye. Some flowering trees, such as hawthorns and crabapples, provide color twice—with flowers in spring and fruit in fall. A number of flowering trees and shrubs have the additional appeal of fragrance, such as lilac, jasmine, gardenia and many deciduous azaleas.

Ornamental Leaves—Though flowers can be fleeting, *perpetual color* is possible by choosing trees and shrubs with colorful leaves. 'Crimson King' maple and 'Thundercloud' plum, for example, are two of many trees with permanent bronze foliage. Colorado blue spruce has bluish needles. The selection among shrubs is even more extensive—golden barberry with golden yellow leaves, and 'Red Tips' photinia with shiny red leaves are two examples. Gray and silver are also common leaf colors besides the many gradations of green.

When fall coloring is considered, the

color variation is even more extensive. Bright yellow, scarlet-red and deep maroon are common leaf colors among many native deciduous trees during fall.

Leaves also have ornamental value according to their shape. The fernlike leaves of staghorn sumac and the lacy leaves of Japanese cutleaf maples are especially attractive, aside from their beautiful fall coloring.

Ornamental Bark—The trunks of many trees are decorative because of colorful or textured bark. The paperbark maple is a prized lawn specimen because of its handsome, light-brown peeling bark. Similarly, the canoe birch is admired for its smooth, paper-white bark and contrasting black color bands. Deeply fissured bark can be an attractive feature—such as the basket-weave pattern of a black locust. Among shrubs with decorative bark, the red-twig dogwood is especially popular for coloring winter landscapes.

Trunks of trees can be straight as pencils—as in tulip or poplar trees—or twisted and gnarled. In some situations, English hawthorns are valued for their gnarled trunk and scaly bark. Observed against a stone wall or a wintry sunset, they can be appealing in their grotesqueness.

Because shrubs tend to be bushy, those with interesting trunks usually need lower branch pruning to reveal the trunk pattern, or, in the case of deciduous shrubs, are best admired in winter after the leaves have fallen. The evergreen English yews have beautiful red trunks revealed by lower branch pruning. Yellow-twig dogwood is strikingly beautiful after leaf fall.

Ornamental Roots—Though roots are normally hidden from view, those of many trees can be highly decorative, especially among trees with a natural tendency to form roots above ground. Beech trees in particular have decorative surface roots, extending a great distance from the trunk. Roots growing along a slope can be worn by footsteps to create natural stairways. Also, soil erosion from wind and rain can expose surface roots.

Ornamental Fruit—Many trees and shrubs produce decorative fruit after the flowers fade. Many have the added advantage of attracting songbirds. Those that produce red, orange and yellow fleshy fruits are especially appealing, though blue, black and even white fruits are not uncommon. Fruits that persist on the tree after the leaves have fallen are valuable for winter color, such as those

American beech spreads a decorative network of roots over soil surface. To heighten ornamental effect, tiny blue Siberian squill have been planted among roots.

Handsome silver, orange and black bark patterns are strong decorative feature of Austrian pine *(Pinus nigra).*

Multicolored Japanese maples are backlighted by sun in early spring. As colorful as any flowers, these leaves all turn brilliant orange in fall.

of hawthorns, winterberry and berberis. *Caution:* Some ornamental berries are poisonous and should be avoided where children might be tempted to pick and eat them. Bittersweet and yew are potentially the most dangerous.

Some fruit-producing trees can be messy and undesirable for high-traffic areas. As mentioned, the female ginkgo produces malodorous, plumlike fruits. Black walnuts drop hard, oily nuts that are best kept clear of driveways. The most desirable trees with ornamental fruits are those that hold their fruit on the tree a long time and eventually are eaten by birds. Hawthorns and sarvistrees are good examples.

Shrubs As Ground Covers—Shrubby, ground-hugging plants have distinct advantages over grass. They never need mowing, can crowd out weeds more effectively than grass and require less care. Dense plantings of low shrubs make effective ground covers on slopes to prevent soil erosion. Horizontal junipers work well on dry, sunny slopes where grass would burn up, while low-growing forms of azaleas can work well in shade.

Additional shrubs to use as ground covers include berberis, cotoneaster, winter creeper, euonymus, heathers, English ivy, dwarf hollies and honeysuckle.

Evergreen windbreak of blue spruce and white spruce is more effective at cushioning force of winds than a wall or fence.

Hedges—Some trees and many shrubs make good formal hedges. Plants like boxwood, holly and hemlock have dense, evergreen growth that can be severely pruned to create clean, straight lines and an impenetrable thicket of branches. Small-leaved shrubs make better formal hedges than large-leaved shrubs. Billowing plants such as spirea and forsythia lend a more informal effect and produce beautiful flowers in the bargain. Hedges can mark a property line, form corridors or create screens. They can form straight lines and gentle curves. Columnar evergreens such as American arborvitae make excellent tall hedges. Dwarf boxwood and dwarf berberis can be used to create *parterres*.

Windbreaks—Trees and large shrubs make far more effective windbreaks than solid fences or walls. Whereas a strong wind can hit a solid wall and jump over it with equal or greater force, the branches of trees and shrubs cushion the force of the wind, dissipating it. Tall, dense needleleaf evergreens such as spruce and pines are favored trees for windbreaks. Among broadleaf evergreens, holly makes a good windbreak. In coastal gardens where protection from salt spray is also important, salt-tolerant plants are vital—such as Japanese black pine, Atlas cedar, Monterey cypress and Russian olive.

Foundation Plantings—Tidy, mixed-shrub borders against the house, with an occasional tree used as a highlight, are highly useful design features—they can enhance the desirable architectural features of a house and hide undesirable features. However, a common mistake among new homeowners is to cram beds around the house foundation with a "horticultural zoo" of shrubs and trees, leaving the perimeter of the property bare and forlorn.

Beware of cluttered, overgrown foundation plantings. They can give a house a reclusive, suffocated appearance. The wrong plant in a foundation planting can quickly become untidy and overgrown, cutting light from windows. Desirable architectural features can become hidden and underground wiring and drains interfered with. Frequent pruning will be required to keep shrubs and trees from growing against the house itself. It's better to confine large, fast-growing shrubs and billowing trees to island beds on the lawn and to borders edging the property.

Foundation borders should contain a balance of needleleaf evergreens and broadleaf evergreens, plus an occasional deciduous tree or shrub for maximum interest. Because architectural lines generally run horizontal and vertical, a blend of upright and spreading plants is desired to soften the vast expanses of wall. Upright yews, pittosporum and arborvitae are good for planting at corners and entryways. Dwarf mounded plants, such as Japanese holly and azaleas, are good to locate under windowsills.

Shade tolerance should be considered along north-facing walls, heat and sun tolerance along south- or west-facing walls. Also, excessive soil alkalinity due to lime leaching from a masonry foundation or walls can sometimes be a problem.

When selecting and placing foundation plantings, plan for their ultimate mature size and allow enough space for them to reach their mature height and spread without interfering with the house structure or nearby walkways. Slow-growing plants are best, particularly those that withstand severe annual pruning. Above all, avoid any trees and shrubs that have a tendency to *sucker*, such as Lombardy poplar, tree of heaven and sumacs.

Rough Woodland—Lord Lionel de Rothschild, head of the famous banking family—and an eminent rhododendron breeder—once lectured a group of horticulturists, and said: "Every garden, no matter how small, should have its two acres of rough woodland." He himself lived on a vast estate called Exbury, in the South of England, and thought of gardens in terms of hundreds of acres, rather than hundreds of square feet, like most of us do. However, the advice does serve to illustrate the point that rough woodland—an uncared-for wilderness of mostly native trees—can be a conscious and desirable element of garden design, just as a meadow of wildflowers can be.

A source of firewood and wildlife shelter, rough woodland has a natural, informal, carefree beauty that can be a pleasant contrast from the formality of parkland and garden rooms, especially when threaded with winding paths. Rough woodland need not be an untended jungle of weedy trees choked with vines. Glades, glens and clearings can be made to expose the best native species or to introduce some desirable foreign kinds. Pines and deciduous trees with large leaves are particularly desirable for rough woodland because they carpet the ground with a thick layer of mulch and leaf mold that can effectively smother excessive weed growth and keep the woodland floor clean.

Though 2 acres is certainly the most desirable size for a woodlot and wildlife refuge, even 1/2 acre of rough woodland can provide a haven for birds and small wildlife, and offer a moderate amount of firewood.

Groves—Even if you don't have room for 1/2 acre of rough woodland, the effect can be achieved on a much smaller scale by planting a grove of trees. For example, a small grove of just a dozen trees, randomly planted, need not occupy more than a few hundred square feet at the edge of a lawn to provide a cool, peaceful retreat. A bench circling a trunk, or a hammock strung between two stout trees, can provide a peaceful spot for reading or contemplation. Pines, oaks, maples and tulip poplars are good trees for planting in groves because the cover from their fallen leaves will deter weeds. After the trees have grown to a desirable height, the lower branches should be pruned off to make it easy to walk among the trees.

Orchards—Orchards are groves of trees that produce fruit or nuts and are best planted with equal spacing between them to allow maximum air circulation and access by bees for maximum yields. Even spacing also facilitates harvesting, pruning, spraying and other special care that food-producing trees demand. Trees for home orchards are best planted in staggered rows, forming a diamond pattern. Apples, cherries and English walnuts make particularly fine ornamental orchards. Apples and cherries are highly ornamental in spring when covered with white blossoms, and English walnuts have a dense, spreading crown that forms a cool, green leaf canopy.

Woodland garden of deciduous trees underplanted with evergreens creates pleasant contrast of colors in fall around a clearing with picnic table.

Even a small fruit orchard (100 x 100 feet) can accommodate a good assortment of favorite fruits, such as apples, pears, peaches apricots and plums. However, many nut trees grow large before they begin bearing, such as walnuts, pecans, hickory and butternuts, so planting more than two kinds might be impractical.

For extra ornamental effect, fruit trees can be underplanted with shade-tolerant shrubs such as azaleas. If you do this, make sure shrubs don't interfere with tree care and harvesting.

Where space is limited, dwarf fruit trees can be chosen to make an orchard. For extra decorative appeal, the dwarf trees can be criss-crossed with miniature hedges of dwarf boxwood, dwarf barberry or similar edging plants.

Skyline Trees—Trees visible against the sky, on a hill, at the edge of a property or distant landscape are known as *skyline trees*. These trees help define the skyline of a particular area. Few natural landscape features add character to a location better than skyline trees. Tall, gnarled conifers with open branches, weeping willows with arching boughs and Southern live oaks festooned with wisps of Spanish moss can present a magnificent silhouette to admire against sunrises and sunsets or against monotone winter skies and seascapes.

Perhaps the most familiar effect from skyline trees is the *lone tree*—a single specimen perched on a cliff edge or crowning a hilltop. It is a symbol of survival, defying the elements. Perhaps the most famous example is a single gnarled Monterey cypress clinging to a rocky promontory overlooking the Pacific Ocean near Carmel, California. Named the "Lone Cypress," it has often been referred to as "the most photographed tree in the world."

A line of trees on the skyline can be equally picturesque. In the New York Finger Lakes region, Lombardy poplars cresting the slopes of vineyards help create an aura suggestive of the Italian or French countryside. A riverbank billowing with weeping willows conjures up visions of the English countryside. A mild-climate resort with an avenue of tall palms is transformed into an image of tropical splendor. A line of Japanese black pines lends an Oriental look and spirelike Italian cypresses a Mediterranean appearance.

Street Trees—In much the same way that skyline trees can lend a distinctive feel or look to an area, so can street trees. An avenue of Southern live oaks draped in Spanish moss identifies many Southern towns, while an avenue of sugar maples is the trademark of many New England communities. Fort Myers, on the Gulf Coast of Florida, has an avenue of royal palms 3 miles long.

It must be realized, however, that a street in a quiet country town and one in a busy, bustling, industrialized metropolis are completely different environments. Also, coastal and inland locations differ in the amount of salt-tolerance needed. Salt tolerance should also be considered in areas where salt is used to control ice on streets during winter. Where pollution is a problem, the choice becomes limited to trees noted for surviving noxious fumes, soot and grime. The London plane tree and Bradford pear are examples of pollution-tolerant trees.

In addition to the above considerations, street trees planted in planting strips between the street and sidewalk should have non-invasive root systems that won't tear up paving or interfere with underground utilities. The tree must be the right shape and size for the space to which it will be fitted—it should not interfere with overhead wires, parking, traffic (both vehicular and pedestrian) or street lighting, nor block street signs.

Topiary—Pronounced *TOE-pee-air-ee,* the word describes what many experts believe to be the most challenging of all horticultural endeavors. It is the art of training plants into special shapes. The shapes can be highly realistic—recognizable as animals, humans and other whimsical animated objects—or they can be abstract as spirals, pyramids and other geometric shapes. The work is especially challenging because the outlines must be clean and well-defined to

TOPIARY

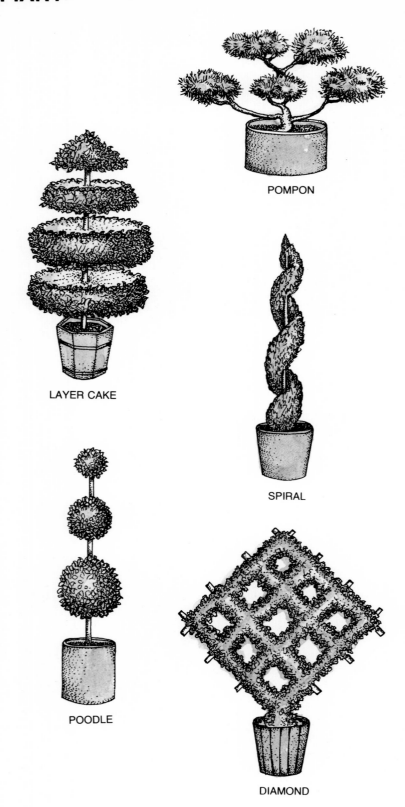

POMPON

LAYER CAKE

SPIRAL

POODLE

DIAMOND

Shown here are several standard topiary forms. Topiary can be trained to geometric shapes such as those shown here, or can represent natural or whimsical figures such as the fox chase pictured on the facing page.

Horse and rider chase a pack of hounds across a lawn at Ladew Topiary Garden in Monkton, Maryland. Plants used are Hick's Japanese yew.

Eastern white pine *(Pinus strobus)* is favorite subject for bonsai training.

look good, requiring special skill in pruning and constant attention. Outdoor topiaries are demanding of space, plants need good care to maintain dense growth, and the work of shaping is labor intensive.

Few plants make good topiaries. The main need is for slow, dense, evergreen growth. Japanese yew, Canadian hemlock and English boxwood are the preferred choices for Northern gardens. Pittosporum and creeping fig are the popular choices for Southern gardens.

There are three ways to create topiary. The old-fashioned way is to shape plants into free-standing units. A bushy shrub is shaped with shears, similar to a sculptor chopping away at a block of stone. The more modern method is to grow plants over preshaped metal frames that serve as pruning guides as the foliage grows to cover them. The third method is more often used for *table-top topiaries*. A shape made of Styrofoam or tightly packed sphagnum moss is kept moist for roots of vines to cover the surface—especially vines of English ivy and creeping fig. Roots from the creeper penetrate the mold and the surface is hidden by a thin, dense covering of leaves. These table-top topiaries are the easiest to grow. They can be planted quickly and the shape covered within a

matter of months, whereas topiaries planted as free-standing units, or through frames, can take years to reach a decent size.

The best examples of outdoor topiary work in America can be seen at Ladew Gardens in Monkton, Maryland; Green Animals in Portsmouth, Rhode Island; and Disneyworld in Florida. The photo above depicts an especially elaborate design at the Ladew Gardens of a horse and rider jumping a fence in pursuit of five hounds and a fox, all clipped out of Japanese yew grown around metal frames. During a trip to England, the garden's founder Harvey S. Ladew saw the topiary foxhunting scene along the top of a hedge. Though he copied the design, he made the figures more animated—and improved on the original—by planting them across his front lawn.

Bonsai—Pronounced *Bone-SIGH*, this is the Oriental art of dwarfing and shaping trees in shallow pots known as *bonsai dishes*. Contrary to popular belief, bonsai was not invented by the Japanese. Nature produced the first bonsai trees. Miniature trees and trees with gnarled trunks with sparse foliage are found in many mountainous areas of the world where rocky conditions restrict normal growth by confining root systems, while

wind, rain, ice and salt spray bend trunks and branches into dramatic and beautiful shapes.

The Chinese are credited with being the first to recognize the special beauty of their dwarf tree forms, and centuries ago began collecting specimens from the wild, digging them up and transferring them to pots. The Japanese are credited with being the first to discover that the same dwarfing and twisted effects can be created artificially by special training techniques, involving judicious pruning of trees and roots, use of wire to direct branches and restricting the roots to a small container.

One way to create a bonsai tree is to start it from seed and deliberately stunt its growth in a shallow, confined container. Another, more widespread practice is to prune young trees down to miniature size and sculpt them into interesting forms.

The least successful method is to actually dig a tree up from the wild—it can take 5 to 15 years to *condition* a wild bonsai before it will grow in a container and the survival rate is low.

Evergreen trees such as spruce, juniper, pine and cedar are the easiest to start with. Shrubs such as azaleas and camellias are also popular bonsai subjects.

Espaliered firethorn *(Pyracantha coccinea)* trained against bare wall to soften expanse of garish brick.

This intricate horticultural maze planted from English boxwood is a half-size replica of the one at Hampton Court, England. It proves the superb quality of boxwood as a hedge.

Espalier—Pronounced *es-PAL-yay* or *es-PAL-yer,* this is the art of training trees and shrubs to a single plane, either against flat, vertical surfaces like walls, or along wires or wooden frames. Those grown horizontally along wires or wooden railings are called *cordons,* for their resemblance to ropes. There are many advantages to this form of training, but the two main ones are for decorative value and to save space.

Plants chosen for espaliers are mostly those with attractive flowers or fruits for which training can heighten the decorative appearance. Camellias, firethorn, pears, plums, apples, peaches, nectarines and figs are especially popular because of their pliable branches, which make them easy to train. However, English ivy, Japanese yew and podocarpus are also espaliered because of their evergreen qualities.

A typical espalier is shown in the photo at left. The secret to success is *pruning* and *training.* Although a full-size apple tree may naturally grow 20 feet high with upright branches in its natural state, it can be heavily pruned to keep it dwarf, and the upright-growing branches can be bent at right angles and secured in position with string. The training is best done with young branches called *whips* because they are generally slender and pliable. Dwarf fruit trees cost more than standard sizes, but they are generally easier to keep low.

Espaliers are a great way to save space because they grow flat against a wall or frame. When grown against a wall, care should be taken to match the proper plant with the wall. For example, apples thrive in full sun, but pears will tolerate light shade. Brick walls and wood fences are better than stucco walls for espaliers because plants grown against stucco walls are susceptible to sunscald and damage from high temperatures. On stucco walls, dense evergreens such as ivy and yew have the best chance for survival.

A much higher success rate, especially with apples and pears, can be achieved by growing the espaliers along low wooden railings to edge a lawn area or vegetable plot, where free air circulation and stable temperatures help increase fruit yields.

Many nurseries and garden centers sell ready-trained espaliers already growing on a trellis in a container. These are also available by mail order from Henry Leuthardt Nurseries, Montauk Highway, East Moriches, New York

11940. The owner, Mr. Leuthardt, has been growing espaliers for 50 years.

Parterres and Mazes—The French word *parterre* (pronounced *PAH-t-air*) in its literal sense means "along the ground" and describes patterns formed by low hedges, usually along a vista. Parterres are popular in both France and England. They are laid out on flat ground so they can be observed from a tower or hill. In some instances, a special mound is made from which to observe the patterns more effectively.

The first parterres were simple designs cut out of turf to reveal white limestone soil. Most had religious symbolism. As they became incorporated into gardens, parterres became more elaborate, in the form of scrolls and flourishes, accentuated by hedges and colored gravel.

The *maze* was developed out of a desire to add a touch of humor. Reproduced at left is a plan of the famous Tudor maze at Hampton Court, England. A life-size replica is made from English holly at the Governor's Palace, Colonial Williamsburg. However, a much better copy is in the privately owned garden of Deerfield, in Rydal, Pennsylvania. Made of English boxwood, it is a half-size replica, created by first making the outlines with string, then digging away the turf to form planting beds.

Though English boxwood is the best choice for mazes and parterres, it grows extremely slow, at only 1 inch a year. For this reason, other plants are more often used, including holly, yew, hemlock, beech and—in the South—podocarpus. The Deerfield maze is kept sheared to a height of 4 feet because it seems esthetically pleasing at exactly that height. Children can get thoroughly lost along its leafy corridors, while adults can peer over its hedges to find the middle with little hesitation.

The maze concept has also been used to spell out words. At the Hershey Chocolate Factory, in Hershey, Pennsylvania, the words *Hershey Cocoa* are spelled out in immense block letters across a sloping lawn in front of the factory. Appropriately, the words are planted in *Berberis atropurpurea*, which is the color of chocolate when observed from a distance.

Pleaching—The word *pleach* is derived from the French and Latin words meaning "to weave." In horticulture, the term is used to describe a hedge or double line of trees that have their branches in-

Beautiful arbor of pleached apple trees in a restored colonial garden at Eleutherian Mills, near Wilmington, Delaware.

tertwined to form a leafy tunnel, arbor or a covered avenue. Beech and hornbeam are especially favored for creating pleached arbors and avenues. Their branches are pliable and easily woven. They tolerate severe pruning and can be kept shrublike or trained to a stout, single trunk. To create a pleached arbor, a metal or wooden frame is first constructed and the chosen trees planted around the outside.

There are some fine examples of pleached arbors at Colonial Williamsburg. At Old Westbury Gardens, Long Island, there is a pleached tunnel created from Canadian hemlock. It is so dark and eerie it is called *The Ghost Walk*. In this instance, the plants are free-standing, with no frames for support.

Another kind of pleaching requires no frames. Trees are planted along an avenue. The top growth is allowed to intermingle its branches and the trunks are trimmed of all lower branches so they look like pillars or posts. When a sufficient canopy has developed, the top is usually sheared square so that from a distance it looks like a hedge on stilts.

When this kind of pleaching forms a circle around a lawn or fountain, it is called a *rondel* or an *ellipse*. A fine example of a pleached avenue can be seen at Longwood Gardens, Pennsylvania, and a beautiful ellipse can be seen at Dumbarton Oaks, Washington, D.C.

Pollarding—This is the practice of consistently pruning back the main branches (scaffold limbs) on a tree to a single growing point so they produce a flush of new growth. Sometimes all main branches are drastically lopped off right to the crown, and other times several large branches are cut back to mere stumps of varying lengths, each stump producing a top-knot of foliage. This style of pollarding is known as a *poodle cut*.

The practice of pollarding is popular with willows, catalpas, sycamores and similar vigorous trees that have a tendency to sprout a multitude of new branches and leaves from the stumps. Pollarded trees are effective in formal gardens as lawn highlights, street trees, and when paired on either side of gates and entryways.

Burning bush *(Euonymus alatus)* grows shrublike when young, as shown here, but eventually becomes a handsome small tree.

SHRUBS INTO TREES
AND TREES INTO SHRUBS

Many plants defined as *shrubs* can become trees—either by virtue of age and maturity or by deliberate training. Alternatively, many plants familiar to us as *trees* can become shrublike—either by accidental damage to the leader or by selective pruning. A large number of shrubs will naturally become treelike with age—hollies, burning bush, camellias, boxwood and rhododendrons are familiar examples. Lilacs, viburnums, privets, hydrangeas and azaleas are good examples of shrubs that have a tendency to be multi-stemmed but can, by selective pruning to form a single stem, be trained into a tree form over a period of years. This selective pruning includes the constant removal of any side branches and *suckers* to maintain one strong main trunk. When choosing shrubs from a nursery, it's often possible to buy one that already has its tree form started with a definite main trunk.

Shrubs with potential for training into trees must be pruned with care. Sometimes, pruning a shrub to a single trunk must be done over a period of years, nudging the plant gradually toward taking on a tree form, because excessive removal of branches at any one time

could weaken and kill it. When the main trunk thickens and the crown fills out to form a definite overhead canopy, side branches can be removed entirely.

Many times, the removal of side branches will stimulate a shrub into *suckering,* whereby whiplike stems sprout from the roots in an effort to regain a shrublike appearance. These fleshy shoots are best cut off as soon as they emerge, before they have a chance to become woody and drain the main trunk of energy.

Conversely, it is sometimes desirable to encourage a tree to grow shrublike. This is generally done in the tree's juvenile stage by pruning out the *central leader* (main trunk) and keeping it pruned at a set height. Yews, Russian olives and pittosporum make effective hedges when the central leader is not allowed to dominate.

To encourage multiple-trunk growth on older trees, the crown must be *topped.* The main trunk is drastically cut down from the top, usually by means of a chain saw, by as much as a third—or even half—of its original height.

Some trees can be cut down right to the ground because they will sucker profusely from the roots. Examples are poplars, sassafras and magnolias.

LANDSCAPING A
BARE LOT

The photograph at right shows a new house on a bare lot. It is typical of tens of thousands of homes built every year in the suburbs and country on square or rectangular lots. The drawing at right shows what can be accomplished within a few years with plantings of trees and shrubs. In addition to creating a beautiful living environment, the relatively small investment in plantings has significantly increased property value.

First, notice how ground covers (A) at the front of the property cut down on mowing and add texture to a dry slope. Here, horizontal junipers or ivy would work well.

A formal hedge (B) runs along the south side of the property on either side of the entrance gateway. This could be yew, holly or boxwood for slow growth and a sharp outline. An informal, unpruned hedge (C) extends along the south boundary line. Forsythia, spirea or azalea might be good choices here. These hedges provide privacy and serve as a barrier against animals and intruders. In the corner where the hedges meet, a flowering tree (D) spreads its branches overhead. A cherry, dogwood, crabapple or magnolia would be perfect here.

Midway along the informal hedge is an arbor (E) to break up the monotony of architectural lines and bare expanse of house siding. A flowering vine—such as clematis or climbing rose—is trained to cover it.

The driveway to the house is lined with pyramidal evergreens as an avenue or *allée* (F) to create a natural corridor for embellishment. These also help screen the paving from other areas of the garden.

Close to the house are foundation plantings (G)—mostly needleleaf and broadleaf evergreens. Some are spire-shaped and others clipped as spheres. They help soften the expanse of bare walls. An espalier (H) is trained against the south wall for a special sophisticated effect, and again to soften the severe architectural lines of the house siding.

The east side of the house has three rectangular flower beds bordered with low hedges (I) to create a simple parterre garden. The large bed has a topiary centerpiece (J) to provide a highlight. The edging could be dwarf boxwood. A brick path separating the flower beds leads to a vine-covered pergola (K), creating a transition from the formal flower garden to a more informal area containing a mixed-shrub border (L). The vine covering the pergola could be wisteria, trumpet creeper or climbing roses.

Though the mixed-shrub border could contain any number of choice flowering shrubs, the main kinds represented here are azaleas and rhododendrons. In the northeast corner is a small rock garden (M), featuring a collection of dwarf evergreens.

Beyond the shrub border are some skyline trees (N)—large specimens of weeping willow, cedar and pine—though buying specimens of significant size may be beyond the means of most homeowners because of high cost.

In the northwest corner is a shade tree (O) with a swing and a paved area for seats and outdoor dining. A maple or oak would be perfect here. A topiary juniper (P) given a "poodle cut" stands in a container for decorative value. A semicircle of unpruned hydrangeas, viburnum or lilacs provide privacy (Q). On a deck overlooking the back lawn, is a containerized bonsai on a table for

LANDSCAPING A BARE LOT

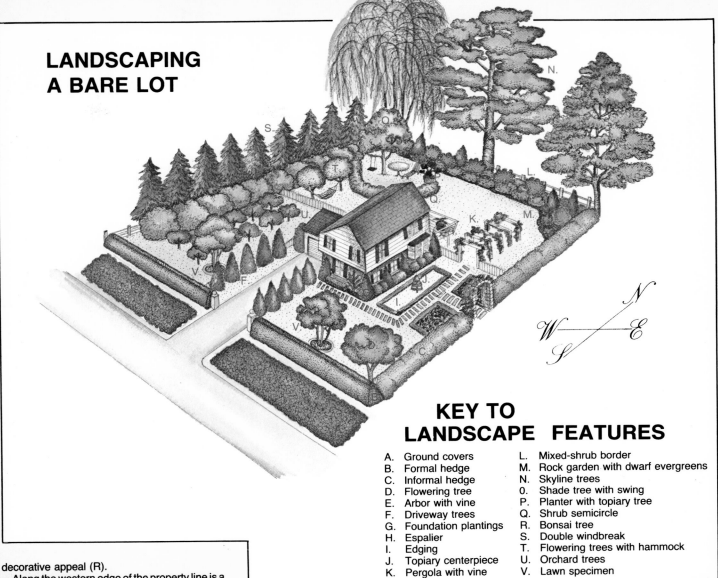

KEY TO LANDSCAPE FEATURES

A. Ground covers
B. Formal hedge
C. Informal hedge
D. Flowering tree
E. Arbor with vine
F. Driveway trees
G. Foundation plantings
H. Espalier
I. Edging
J. Topiary centerpiece
K. Pergola with vine

L. Mixed-shrub border
M. Rock garden with dwarf evergreens
N. Skyline trees
0. Shade tree with swing
P. Planter with topiary tree
Q. Shrub semicircle
R. Bonsai tree
S. Double windbreak
T. Flowering trees with hammock
U. Orchard trees
V. Lawn specimen

decorative appeal (R).

Along the western edge of the property line is a double row of trees to act as a windbreak (S). Most prevailing winds in North America come from the west, hence the positioning of this landscape feature. The background trees are evergreens—perhaps blue spruce, while the foreground trees might be gray-foliaged Russian olives for an appealing color combination, in addition to dense habit for screening qualities.

The lawn area running parallel to the windbreak is divided by a fence. On the north side of the fence are two flowering trees (T), such as hawthorns, cherries or crabapples, with a hammock slung between them. On the south side of the fence is an orchard (U) planted with dwarf fruit trees—pairs of apples, peaches, pears, cherries, apricots and plums, each pair representing different varieties to ensure good pollination and maximum fruit set.

The front lawns feature a matching pair of white birch (V) as handsome lawn specimens, each underplanted with a circle of ivy or pachysandra to act as a shade-loving ground cover.

The plants shown in this design are not elaborate, and with the exception of the skyline trees, are within the scope of any homeowner to purchase and plant without the help of a landscape architect. Moreover, the plants suggested in this particular design are easily changed to suit special climatic situations.

House on bare lot is typical of thousands of new homes built every year.

VEGETABLES

The time to begin thinking about which vegetables to plant is when the mail order seed and nursery catalogs become available. In parts of the South and West, this can be as early as September. In other parts of the United States, the catalogs are normally available in January. These colorful dream books, filled with beautiful pictures, try to seduce us into ordering dozens of seed packets and plants. But it is essential to *plan* your garden before you send in your order for plants and seeds. Without thinking ahead, you may buy too much of one vegetable and not enough of another. Or you may completely forget one of your favorites.

WHERE TO PLANT?

The first step to planning your garden is choosing a good location. Important considerations include:

Sunlight—Sunlight is the most impor-tant factor for a successful garden location. As a general rule, vegetables require a minimum of seven hours of full sun to produce worthwhile crops. Most fruit-producing vegetables—tomatoes, squash, peppers—need almost a full day of sun. Root crops and leaf crops can get by with less. Sunlight is essential because vegetables obtain a good part of their food supply through a process known as *photosynthesis*. Photosynthesis occurs when sunlight shines on leaf cells containing water and *chlorophyll*—the green you see in a leaf. Photosynthesis allows the leaf to produce carbohydrates, which the plant uses to make sugars and starches, essential for its survival.

If you have no choice and must plant in an area that receives less-than-ideal sunlight, try growing early maturing varieties. They generally produce with less sun and lower temperatures.

When considering garden placement, note the shadows of nearby walls, trees and buildings. Also keep the seasonal patterns of the sun in mind. In midsummer when the sun is high, shade from a tall object may not be cast on the garden. But in the latter part of the growing season the sun appears lower in the sky. Shadows lengthen and reach your garden. The reduced sunlight can bring production to an abrupt halt, even though many more weeks of frost-free growing conditions may remain.

Avoid a garden site that is shaded during noonday hours, when sunlight is brightest. If shadows from a building or a tree shade the garden during mid-day, it will significantly reduce crop yields. Years ago a gardener planted a vegetable garden in a sunny spot, but a tall cherry tree cast shade over the garden for about an hour at noon. Although the garden received an average of seven hours sun-

Opposite Page: A well-planned garden makes best use of available space. Dual rows of pole beans will soon cover this twine trellis. Left: 12x20' plot features wide, raised planting beds. Pine-needle mulch prevents most weed growth.

light each day, loss of the bright noon light prevented success with melons and other fruiting vegetables. Another location—an open meadow area—was prepared to grow these vegetables. Leaf vegetables, which generally require less sunlight, grow in the shaded garden.

Plant your garden so rows run north to south rather than east to west. This way, plants receive more even exposure to the sun. Place taller plants and trellises to the north so they will not shade shorter plants.

Reflected Light and Heat—If a location has insufficient heat or light because it is shaded, you may be able to correct it by reflecting heat and light toward plants. For example, painting a dark wall white increases the amount of reflected light and heat onto plants. Clear plastic or aluminum foil spread over the soil also reflects light and heat onto plants. Actually, it is light *intensity* rather than direct sunlight that affects the growth of plants. In desert areas, you might want to *avoid* reflected heat so vegetable plants will not be overheated.

Soil Drainage—Vegetables, like most plants, require good soil drainage. Both air and water are necessary in the root zone for plant growth. How well the soil drains depends on its composition. Clay soils have a tendency to drain slowly; sandy soils drain rapidly. Both can be improved with the addition of large quantities of peat moss, ground bark, compost or other organic material.

Low spots tend to retain water. Ditches lined with drainage tile can be installed to channel excess water away. If this is too costly or can't be done, plant your garden elsewhere, or build a raised planting bed.

Shelter and Protection—Vegetables exposed to the drying effects of summer winds can suffer from serious moisture loss. Exposure to cool winds can create problems for warm-season crops such as melons, tomatoes and peppers. If your vegetable garden is exposed to such winds, consider planting a windbreak. A row of shrubs or trees is more effective than a solid fence or wall. When wind hits a solid barrier, it flows over and down with severe force. A windbreak of evergreens, shrubs or trees filters the force of the wind and dissipates it.

A special consideration is protection from animal pests. You may have to build a sturdy fence around your garden to keep rabbits, raccoons, deer and other animals out.

Proximity to the House—Try to locate the garden near the house. This makes it convenient to slip out the door at mealtime to gather a few crisp parsley leaves for a garnish, or some salad fixings. Locating your garden close to the house also means that it will be near a water faucet.

Toxic Trees—Certain plants can be harmful to vegetable plants located nearby. Black-walnut trees give off a toxin through their roots that can poison the soil and prevent growth of many vegetables, particularly tomatoes. For this reason, do not add black-walnut leaves to compost or use them as a mulch.

Although not as toxic as black walnuts, pine trees can also inhibit growth of other plants, oozing a sticky resin from branches, cones and roots. Fallen, dried pine needles, however, are generally safe to use as a mulch.

Sunflower roots produce a growth inhibitor that effectively reduces competition from weeds. This inhibitor can also slow the growth of nearby vegetables.

SIZE OF GARDEN: SMALL, MEDIUM OR LARGE?

The size of your garden is often dictated by the amount of available land. Many modern homes are built on small lots so there is often little choice. Surprisingly, a common mistake for beginners is planting a garden that is *too big*. It is fairly simple to plant a large area, but maintaining it is another matter. Seeds and plants start out small, but before long you can be overwhelmed with weeding, watering, fertilizing and harvesting. If you fall behind in any of these tasks, especially weeding, the garden is headed for disaster.

When deciding garden size, realistically consider how much time you are willing to spend and the resources you have available. A small, well-cared-for garden yields much more than a large, neglected garden. If you have a friend or spouse who is willing to share some of the responsibilities, you can plant a larger area. Your partner will be more help if you involve him or her in deciding which vegetables to grow and how much to plant!

When planning garden space, you should have some idea of potential yields. Generally, seed packets are based on planting a 15-foot row. In most situations, a 15-foot row will supply enough fresh vegetables to feed a family of three. This is true of peas, beans, carrots, beets, onions, tomatoes, cucumbers, melons, peppers, cabbage, lettuce and most other vegetables.

Landscaped garden produces an abundant crop of vegetables and is an attractive, pleasant place to spend some time. Its owner, Mrs. Harriet Heaney of Philadelphia, uses a net to capture cabbage white butterflies *before* they lay their eggs.

Herbs such as parsley, garlic and thyme need much less space because a little goes a long way. If herbs are used mostly for kitchen flavorings, a 5-foot row is plenty.

At the other extreme, sweet corn and asparagus require a lot of space. To feed a family of three adequately, you will need to plant a 15-foot row for each person—a total of 45 feet.

Length of row also depends on whether you want quantities for canning or freezing. If you plan to store vegetables in these ways, add approximately 15 more feet of row. These recommendations are based on planting a single row. By growing a wide, matted row or a wide, block planting, a shorter row may be in order.

PLAN ON PAPER

After you have decided on the location of your garden, mark down the dimensions of the area you wish to plant. Graph paper is especially good for this purpose. You can lay out your plan using each square to equal a given unit of measurement. A common ratio is one square equals one foot of space. Mark off the plan into planting rows using the *straight-row system, wide-row system, block-planting system* or a combination of all three. Your plan will give you a good idea of how many vegetables you have room for.

Review the vegetables you want to grow. Decide which crops you want to start from seed and which you prefer to buy as ready-grown transplants. Separate vegetables into annuals and perennials, allocating permanent locations for perennials such as asparagus, rhubarb and horseradish. Separate the vegetables again into cold-hardy varieties and cold-tender varieties. Divide your garden into two parts—one to plant early in the season with cold-hardy vegetables, and the other to plant later in the season with cold-tender crops.

In deciding where to plant varieties, place tall kinds such as pole beans, corn and tomatoes at the north end of the garden. This way they will not shade lower-growing vegetables such as bush beans and lettuce.

The following two pages show sample plans of small, medium and large garden layouts. Each makes use of traditional, rectangular plots and single, straight planting rows. Popular vegetables are included in the samples, but simply substitute your own choices where desired.

Large-scale garden at Longwood Gardens in Pennsylvania features vegetables in traditional single rows. Wide spacing between rows allows room for a power tiller for cultivation and weed control.

Raised beds—planting beds with soil above ground level—make efficient small gardens. All of the soil area can be planted and the garden is neat and easy to care for.

Sample Garden Layouts

Small garden. When planting a small garden—15x26' or smaller—your goal should be to produce maximum yields from minimum space. A limited amount of garden room forces you to be selective in the amount and kinds of vegetables grown. Avoid the temptation to grow corn or melons—they take up too much room.

The easiest-to-grow, most productive vegetables are illustrated in this sample. Bush-type cucumbers could be substituted in place of peppers. Among summer squash varieties, zucchini types are the most productive. Yellow crookneck varieties are also popular. A 15-foot row of tomatoes—5 or 6 plants—can produce up to 150 pounds of fruit. Supporting them with stakes or wire cages saves space. Snap beans are the second most-productive crop after tomatoes, so two rows are worthwhile. One row can be planted with green snap beans, the other with yellow wax beans or bush romano beans. Lettuce is an extremely useful and early crop. One row in the sample garden is devoted to looseleaf lettuce such as 'Oak Leaf'. It matures within 50 days. The other row is planted with a head lettuce such as 'Buttercrunch', which requires an additional 20 days to mature.

Small Garden—15x26'

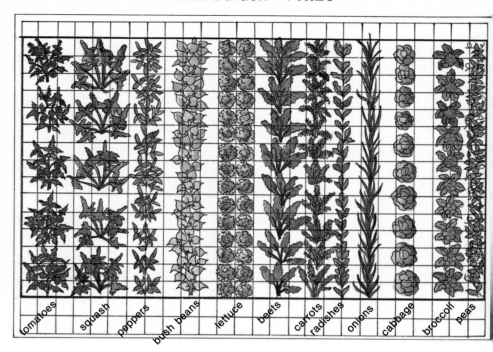

tomatoes · squash · peppers · bush beans · lettuce · beets · carrots · radishes · onions · cabbage · broccoli · peas

One square equals one foot

Medium Garden—20x35'

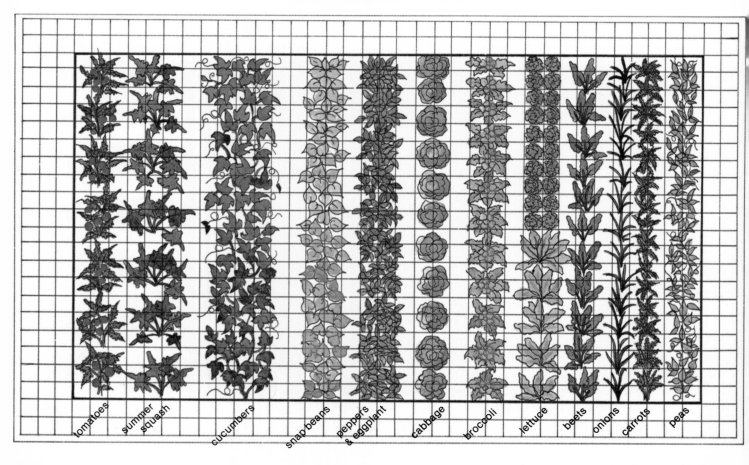

tomatoes · summer squash · cucumbers · snap beans · peppers & eggplant · cabbage · broccoli · lettuce · beets · onions · carrots · peas

Medium garden. Even if you have a garden that is 20x35', you also need to be selective in the kinds of vegetables grown. Corn and melons have been left out of the sample plan deliberately. These crops occupy too much space for the amount of yield.

Cabbage, broccoli, cauliflower and garden peas are included. Garden peas can be trained up chicken wire for support. Broccoli and cauliflower can share a 20-foot row. Broccoli can be planted in spring to mature in early summer, with cauliflower planted in its place after harvesting to mature in fall. Similarly, when the garden peas are finished bearing in midsummer, vines can be pulled up and the row planted with a fall-maturing vegetable such as brussels sprouts.

Large garden. The beauty of a large garden

is the space available to grow favorites such as melons, winter squash and sweet corn. These vegetables demand a lot of room for worthwhile quantities, but they reward us with special tastes!

This garden features *perennial vegetables* such as asparagus, rhubarb and perennial herbs. These are crops that overwinter and remain productive for more than one year.

Large gardens are best sectioned into planting squares. This makes it easy to tend the rows of vegetables. Walkways are wide enough to allow you to take a wheelbarrow or cart into the garden for harvest or clean-up. You may wish to allow additional spacing between rows of vegetables if you plan to use a power tiller to cultivate the soil during the growing season.

Use each planting square to group plants that require similar care and growing conditions. Also practice *rotation planting,* which is moving the groups—except perennials—to a new bed each year. This may reduce the possibility of diseases.

Maximum productivity in any garden, no matter what size, can be accomplished by *double cropping* snap beans, radishes, beets, carrots and lettuce. This means making one planting in spring to mature by early summer, and a second planting in mid-summer—after the first planting has been harvested—to mature in fall.

Succession planting, planting crops a few weeks apart instead of all at once, extends the harvest. Instead of picking all crops at one time, the harvest is staggered over several weeks.

Large Garden—30x34'

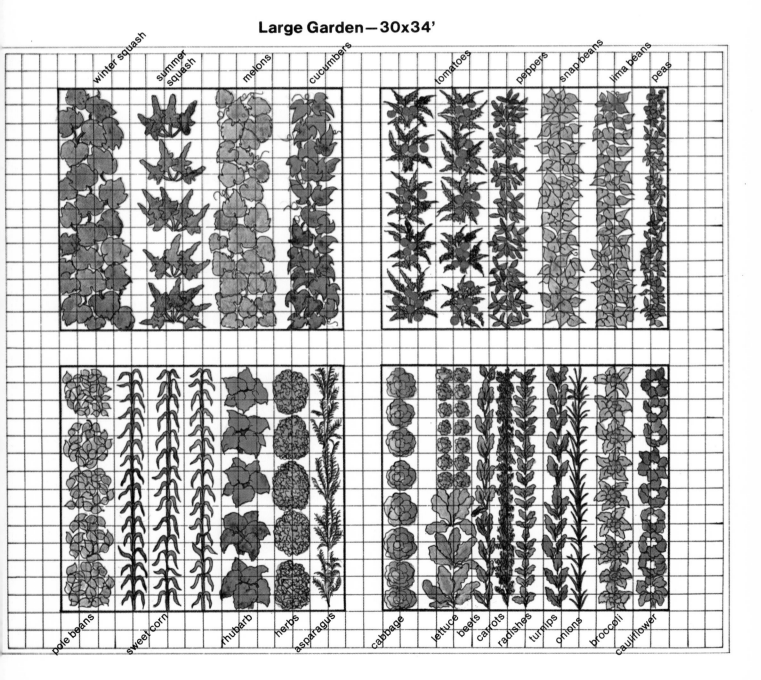

'Shiro' Japanese plum.

FRUIT GARDENING

Fruit gardeners in the western United States share an activity that is both rich in tradition and refreshingly new. Many of their gardening techniques are centuries old, handed down from Spanish missionaries who were the first to realize the exciting potential of western climates, soils and waters. The great migration of easterners who followed these missionaries found the West full of opportunity but remarkably different from their homeland. Many of their time-honored horticultural practices had to be altered. Western fruit growing became a science of its own, constantly more exciting and ever more localized.

Today, from the arid Southwest to the moist Pacific Northwest, commercial orchards and home gardens produce an incredible amount of fruit. No place in the world supports such a variety and abundance. The West truly is the Mecca of the fruit grower.

As thousands of Western gardeners can attest, growing fruit at home can be very satisfying. Can you think of anything more flavorful than a peach or apple picked at peak ripeness from a tree in your own back yard? There's special satisfaction in knowing that you've chosen one of the finest-tasting varieties and nurtured it faithfully from a young tree to bearing age. Nothing from the supermarket tastes as fresh or pleases the palate as fruit you've grown yourself.

LET YOUR GARDEN DO MORE FOR YOU

Taste isn't the only pleasure in fruit gardening. Many fruit plants are as beautiful as they are bountiful. Spring blossoms of apricots and plums are as colorful and fragrant as any ornamental. Cooling shade from a pecan or walnut tree is as pleasant as the best ash or sycamore. It makes sense to take advantage of these ornamental edibles. Why not grow versatile, attractive plants that give you an abundant harvest?

This is all part of a new philosophy in gardening: *Let your garden do more for you.* Realize the potential of your garden space or landscape. With proper planning and selection, anyone can grow practical, productive, fruit-bearing trees or plants. The idea of gardening efficiency is an underlying philosophy in this book. Information contained here will help you plan and establish a more beautiful, rewarding and productive garden—no matter where you live in the West.

TRIED AND PROVEN INFORMATION

Material in this section has its inspiration in the pioneering work of Reid M. Brooks and Claron O. Hesse. Their understanding of western climates and appreciation of the needs of the home gardener provide the foundation for much of the information available on growing fruit in the West.

This section also benefits greatly from the work of hundreds of university experts, breeders and extension agents. They have expanded our knowledge of horticulture and helped home gardeners achieve success. Progressive nurseries have also contributed much to the home fruit grower by offering plants that produce fruit of superior quality and flavor. Without the willingness of breeders, agents and nurseries to share the most up-to-date information on varietal introduction, cultural practices and climate adaptation, this section would not have been possible.

IMPORTANCE OF ADAPTATION

Westerners can grow such a wonderful range of fruit because there are so many different climates. However, each fruit has its own climatic requirements. Each area of the West will not be able to grow all the fruit described in these pages. Choosing fruit types and varieties that are adapted to your area is the first step in successful fruit culture. This is an important consideration and a major point of emphasis throughout this section.

Left: Nothing surpasses the juicy flavor of fruit fresh from the tree. Stand back and enjoy.

STARTING SEEDS AND PLANTING

Seeds of annuals come in a variety of shapes and sizes. For example, it takes 1,500,000 begonia seeds to equal 1 ounce. Seeds are so tiny they resemble dust particles. It seems impossible that something as beautiful as a begonia could grow from such tiny, insignificant specks. On the other side of the scale, an ounce of nasturtiums requires only about 175 seeds. They are as large as peas and easy to handle.

The many kinds of annuals represent a wide variety of methods for starting seeds and planting, with no single system suitable for all plants.

Some seeds, like begonias, need light to germinate. They should be *surface-sown*—barely pressed into the soil surface—and not covered. Nasturtiums, however, represent a large group of seeds that require total darkness for germination. They should be covered with soil to approximately three times their width.

Germination—the process of seeds sprouting roots and leaves—is stimulated by various conditions, depending on the requirements of individual varieties. All seeds need adequate *moisture,* suitable *temperature* and *air* (oxygen). Moisture is necessary to soften the seed coat and allow the *embryo*—the undeveloped plant—to grow. Correct temperature is necessary to break dormancy. Air is essential for seeds and seedlings to live. If the soil is poorly drained or compacted, seeds will die from suffocation.

SEEDS OR TRANSPLANT?

The tendency is to use transplants for most plantings of annuals. You can grow transplants from seeds or buy them from a garden center ready to plant. Even annuals that generally transplant poorly—zinnias for example—are being transplanted. Certain methods of growing transplants, such as peat pots and peat pellets, reduce root disturbance and transplant shock.

Large-area plantings devoted to naturalizing or ground covers are usually planted from seeds sown directly in place. In these instances, transplanting seedlings is too time-consuming or expensive.

Even though transplants are readily available from garden centers as bedding plants, there are many good reasons to start your own from seeds. Selection of bedding plants is limited, and most an-

Left: Seedlings of flowering annuals in greenhouse were started from seeds. Flats are divided into eight compartments each. When seedlings are large enough to handle, they are transferred to individual pots to grow to transplant size. Above: Geranium transplants in a "six-pack" are ready for planting.

nuals are not offered for sale until plants are in bloom. This helps sell them more quickly. But blooming transplants generally do not perform as well and as long as plants that are transplanted "green," before flowering.

STANDARD OR HYBRID?

Annuals are available in *standard* and *hybrid* forms. Hybrids cost more, or fewer seeds are included in each packet compared to standards. Standard varieties are sometimes called *open pollinated* because they are mass-produced through pollination by bees and wind. Hybrids require careful, *controlled pollination*—tedious hand pollination between selected parent plants. These plants are usually different species that are sexually compatible.

The word hybrid comes from the Latin word, *hybrida,* meaning the offspring of a wild boar and a domestic sow. A more familiar animal hybrid is the mule—a cross between a jackass, male donkey, and a mare—female horse. The mule is stronger and more useful than either parent. As with most hybrids, the mule is sterile and cannot reproduce itself. To create more mules the original cross must be repeated.

Seeds of plant hybrids are produced in a similar way. To make more seeds you must make the original cross. That's why you should not save seeds from hybrid flowers—the seeds will either be sterile or produce inferior plants.

If you have any doubts about the superiority of hybrids over standard varieties, visit a trial garden and compare performances. Hybrid wax begonias or triploid hybrid marigolds are good examples. A hybrid not only has more flowers per plant, it has stamina to bloom all season right up to fall frost.

The Making of a Hybrid—The main advantage of a hybrid is its vigor, a quality called *heterosis.* This results in increased size, improved disease resistance, earliness, heat or cold tolerance and other desirable characteristics.

Hybrid flowers are usually grown in greenhouses so that insects can be kept away from flowers. Insects may introduce pollen from other plants, which can ruin a hybrid cross. The sequence of photographs at right show the making of a *triploid* hybrid marigold—a plant made by crossing a French marigold, the male parent, with an American marigold, the female parent. A triploid has three sets of chromosomes and outstanding vigor.

The Making of a Hybrid

1. Male parent, a French marigold, is crossed with female parent shown at right.

2. Female parent, an American marigold, is male-sterile and has only female parts. It cannot pollinate itself, which would ruin cross.

3. After cross, mature seeds form under petals. Seeds are harvested and cleaned before being packaged for sale.

4. Result of the cross is triploid hybrid 'Copper Canyon'. These hybrids are sterile and unable to set viable seeds, but plants bloom profusely.

Picture 1 shows the male parent, French marigold *Tagetes patula*. Pollen from this flower is crossed with the female parent. Picture 2 shows the female parent, American marigold *Tagetes erecta*. The flower has no outer petals because it is "male sterile." Possessing only female parts, it cannot pollinate itself to ruin the cross. In creating other hybrids, the male parts must be removed by hand. Occasionally, male-sterile flowers such as these are found as mutations, helping make the hybridizer's job much easier.

Picture 3 shows the mature seeds formed under the faded petals of the female parent. Seeds are harvested, dried and cleaned to remove chaff and placed into seed packets.

Picture 4 shows the resulting triploid hybrid variety 'Copper Canyon' in full flower. Triploid hybrids are sterile and unable to set viable seeds. They put all their energy into flower production, blooming early and continually until fall frost.

SEED PACKETS, PELLETS AND TAPES

New ways to plant seeds, such as seed pellets and seed tapes, are introduced frequently. But no one has come up with a more efficient system than the traditional seed packet.

Seed tapes are said to make thinning easier for small-seeded flowers like petunias and pansies. Tapes have seeds bound into transparent biodegradable material, pre-spaced at regular intervals. The material dissolves quickly after it comes into contact with moisture. Seed tapes are more expensive than conventional seed packets and you get fewer seeds. If germination is not high, you will end up with gaps in your plantings.

Pelleted seeds are the least gimmicky of the alternative seed-sowing systems. The pellet is a harmless clay coating around small seeds that makes them larger and easier to handle when planting. Coating dissolves on contact with moisture, and seeds germinate unhindered.

The biggest boon in recent years has been the introduction of foil packaging, creating a moisture-proof packet. Moisture deteriorates seeds quickly, and traditional paper packets offer little protection. Seeds lose viability quickly during periods of high humidity. Moisture-proof packets keep seeds in harvest-fresh condition until seal is broken.

When you buy seeds at the nursery or they arrive in the mail from a mail-order catalog, store them in a cool, dry place indoors until it is time to plant.

SEED RACK OR MAIL ORDER?

Flower seeds are readily available in seed racks at retail outlets, in nurseries, home centers and supermarkets. Or you can order them by mail through seed catalogs. Rack displays in local stores have the advantage of convenience. It's easy to visit your local store and make selections, using the color pictures and descriptions on the seed packet as a guide. But shopping the rack has its shortcomings. Selections are usually limited to only popular kinds of annuals, with an emphasis on standard, well-established varieties rather than hybrids. And if you delay making your purchases late in the season you may end up shopping from a picked-over rack.

Ordering by mail is more bother, and it takes time to receive your order. But you do have the advantage of a much larger selection, with many new varieties and hybrids. If you plan ahead, the delay in receiving your seeds should not make a difference to your planting schedule.

Some of the best flower-seed catalogs available to gardeners in the United States and Canada are listed in this section. Some of these are European companies, but their catalog and seeds are available to you. You'll receive a special sheet giving instructions on how to order. These foreign catalogs generally offer large selections, with emphasis on certain classes of annuals that are not commonly found in North-American catalogs.

SAVING YOUR OWN SEEDS

Most flowering annuals will set seeds after flowering. Unless the plants are hybrids, seeds can be saved to produce beautiful flowering displays the following year. Seeds saved from *F-1 hybrids*—first generation hybrids—produce inferior results the second season.

If you want to save seeds, take some precautions to ensure success. To maintain viability, seeds should be kept *cool* and *dry*. Place seeds in packets in a wide-mouth jar that can be sealed with a tight-fitting lid. Put 2 heaping tablespoons of powdered milk in a paper envelope and place inside jar. Seal jar and store in vegetable bin of your refrigerator until you are ready to plant seeds.

The powdered milk will absorb moisture from air inside jar, keeping seeds dry. This method should also be used to store seeds left over from purchased packets.

How long seeds last depends on seed type and storage conditions. High temperatures and high humidity deteriorate seeds rapidly. Delphinium seeds are naturally short-lived and germination is usually poor after only 1 year. However, sweet peas can stay viable for several years.

If you don't know the condition of stored seeds, it is a good idea to test their viability before you plant them. Select 10 seeds and lay them on a moist paper towel. Roll up towel and place inside a plastic bag in a warm location. The plastic bag prevents towel from drying out too quickly. After 10 to 14 days, count seeds that have germinated. If 2 out of 10 have sprouted, this indicates 20% germination rate—not good. If 5 out of 10 sprout, this shows 50% germination—acceptable. Keep the germination test results in mind when you sow seeds to compensate for the lower-than-normal germination rate.

Saving seeds from your own flowers for use the following season will not always produce as good a display as buying fresh seeds from the original seed company. Seedsmen maintain the purity of a strain by selecting special stock seed plants. These are usually plants that possess uniformity of height, color and flower size. If a mixture is involved it may contain a special balance of colors. Production fields are usually isolated to prevent cross-pollination from other strains. Also, seedsmen inspect their production fields before plants have a chance to set seeds. If *rogues*—those too tall, too short or wrong color—appear, they are pulled and destroyed.

If you grow a strain of annual where the resulting crop is uneven, the seedsman has probably done a poor job of "roguing." Gardeners have seen as much as 1/3 of a crop discarded to maintain quality. Hybrid seeds saved from a home-garden crop can quickly revert to their original wild forms if strict, quality-control methods are not followed.

BULB BASICS

Bulbs are ideal beginner's plants. Most contain enough stored food to provide for a season's growth, needing only moisture, warmth and light to grow. With minimum care, bulbs will succeed almost anywhere.

Even though bulbs are forgiving, it makes sense to learn their cultural requirements. The following section on bulb basics will acquaint you with the fundamentals of bulb growth and care. Understanding them will increase your pleasure of gardening with bulbs.

BUYING BULBS

One of the best places to purchase bulbs is at your nursery or garden center. You can inspect the bulbs, purchasing only the best ones. Nursery personnel can be a big help, providing information on bulb selection and care.

In the store, each bin of bulbs usually has a picture of the bulb in flower. The pictures are fairly accurate. If an exact picture is not available, a substitute variety might be used in its place. When the name of the variety is *printed* on the picture, it is most often accurate. If the name is *pasted* or *written* on the picture, it is likely to be a similar substitute.

Bulbs labeled as *mixed* are sometimes available at a discount. Pictures of mixed bulbs may have little relation to what is actually in the mix. Mixed bulbs may be made up of varieties that the supplier has in excess, or varieties that have lost their labels. If you are particular about the bulbs you want to grow, the savings may not be worthwhile.

LOOK BEFORE YOU BUY

Bulbs vary in size and quality, so examine them before you buy. Generally, the larger the bulb, the better the results at bloom time. Choose firm bulbs. With a few exceptions, soft, mushy bulbs indicate damage from rot fungus or insects. Bulbs missing their *tunics*—thin, outer coverings— may be dried out and will not bloom. They are usually lighter in weight than fresh bulbs. Avoid lily bulbs that are wilted and soft. This probably means they are dehydrated. Choose firm, moist bulbs. Do not buy any bulbs infested with insects.

All bulb types do not become available at the same time, so it may be necessary to make several trips to the nursery to get the freshest stock. For example, madonna lilies may arrive at the end of August, and tulips at the beginning of October. Oregon-grown daffodils do not arrive at the store the same time as those grown in Holland.

When bulbs go "on sale," it usually signals the end of the planting season, and retailers want to close out their stocks. Bulbs purchased at this time should be examined closely.

Opposite Page: Many kinds of bulbs are available from local nurseries or mail-order suppliers. Most bulbs should be stored in a cool, dry place until planting time. Some, such as lilies, should be kept moist until they are planted. Left: Bulb planting tool makes it easy to dig individual planting holes.

MAIL-ORDER SUPPLIERS

In addition to local sources, you can order bulbs from mail-order catalogs. These suppliers generally have a larger selection than retail nurseries. If you want to specialize in growing lilies, daffodils or *Iris*, for example, ordering by mail is a must. Many varieties are available only in these catalogs. Specialty catalogs that feature one group of bulbs usually contain the newest bulbs and novelties.

Mail-order bulbs are usually mailed so they will arrive at the proper planting time for your area. This is a big advantage when purchasing lilies, which should not be out of the ground any longer than necessary.

When you receive bulbs in the mail, open and examine packages immediately. Check for signs of damage. If the bulbs are injured, contact the company.

HORTICULTURAL SOCIETIES

An excellent way of acquiring bulbs is to go to sales sponsored by local horticultural societies. Members often donate their extra bulbs to the society to raise money. Many of these bulbs are not available from commercial sources, giving you an opportunity to grow out-of-the-ordinary bulbs. Check for such sales listed in your newspaper, in garden publications and on nursery bulletin boards.

MISTAKEN IDENTITY

Gardeners may buy the same type of bulb two years in a row and discover at bloom time that they have two different bulbs. This is an exasperating experience that seems to occur most often with tulips. One reason for this mix-up is the complicated distribution network of certain bulbs. A grower in Holland sells bulbs to a wholesaler in Holland, who sells them to a distributor in the United States. This person in turn sells them to a nursery, which finally sells them to you. In passing through so many hands, the labels can be switched.

If you order bulbs from a mail-order source that specializes in a certain type of bulb, you can be almost certain that you will receive what you ordered.

Sometimes the bulb in the garden does not resemble the emerald-green daffodil or cobalt-blue *Gladiolus* shown in the catalog. Occasionally, it is the photograph or printed matter that is inaccurate. In addition, various cultural conditions affect flower color. For example, a green flower can fade to yellow in full sun.

Tips for Buying Bulbs

Bulb	Comments
Achimenes	Small and brittle. Handle roots carefully.
Alstroemeria	Sometimes available growing in 1-gallon cans. Takes 3 to 4 years before flowers are produced from plants grown from seeds.
Amaryllis belladonna	Plant in fall when in bloom so growth cycle is not interrupted. If dug or planted any other time, bloom cycle can be set back for years.
Anemone	Bulbs vary greatly in shape. European bulbs look like dried raisins. United States bulbs are shaped like cones. With European bulbs, it is difficult to determine which end goes up or down. Plant sideways to be safe. Large bulbs are not necessarily the best. Select smaller, younger bulbs.
Canna	Usually tough. They are reliable performers unless they dry out.
Colchicum	Avoid soft spots, an indication of damage or rot.
Cyclamen	Check for small bumps from the tuber—new growth appears from these. These bumps are easily broken off. Without them, it takes bulb a year to recover.
Dahlia	Tubers should be firm and connected to a stem bud. If not, the tuberous root is worthless.
Endymion	Soft, fleshy bulb, unlike other bulbs.
Freesia	Bulbs have netted tunic, which should be held close to the corm.
Gladiolus	Quality determined by depth of bulb, not width. A small, thick bulb is superior to a large, flat bulb.
Hippeastrum	Large bulbs produce two or more spikes of flowers.
Hyacinthus	Carefully graded by size. The larger the bulb, the larger the flower spike. The largest, called *exhibition,* are often grown to be used in pots and hyacinth jars, but second-size bulbs make a respectable showing. They are usually grown in large beds. Handling bulbs may cause skin irritation. Keep away from eyes.
Hemerocallis	Daylily roots do not last long out of the ground, so plant or replant as soon as possible. Often available blooming in 1-gallon cans.
Iris	Large rhizomes accept a lot of abuse. For bulbous iris, look for firm, unwrinkled bulbs. Wrinkling can be a sign of drying out.
Lilium	Bulbs should be firm and moist, not shriveled. Bulbs should have roots intact. Lilies never go completely dormant, so plant bulbs as soon as possible.
Narcissus	Daffodils can be judged by the size of the bulb within their own group. Depending on species, bulbs can range from 1/2 inch to 5 inches wide. Avoid bulbs with soft, mushy spots, especially if near the basal plate. Lightweight bulbs are dried out and should be discarded.
Polianthes	With tuberose, it is commonly advised to buy them when green shoots begin to show. I believe green shoots are unnecessary.
Ranunculus	Bulb size does not determine size or quality of flower, but definitely influences the number of blooms.
Tulipa	Bulb should have brown, protective coating. Bulb without coating tends to dry out. Avoid tulips showing green shoots. They have probably been in the store a long time and are sending up what should be spring growth, but roots are not developed.
Zantedeschia	Select firm bulbs. Avoid those with soft spots, whether bulbs are common white, pink, or yellow.

VEGETABLE SEED STARTING AND PLANTING

Seeds come in all different shapes and sizes, from tiny celery seeds that blow away if you breathe on them, to lima bean seeds that are large and easy to handle. Some seeds, like peas and corn, have seed coats that soften quickly on contact with moisture. Others, like okra, have extremely hard seeds. They should be soaked in lukewarm water 12 hours before planting. It adds up to a wide variety, with no one planting system suitable for all seeds.

Germination—the process of seeds sprouting roots and leaves—is one of the great miracles of nature. For most seeds, three conditions must be met before germination occurs: *adequate moisture, suitable temperature* and *air* (oxygen). Moisture is necessary to soften the seed coat and allow the *embryo,* the undeveloped plant, to expand and grow. Suitable temperature is needed to break dormancy. Some vegetable seeds like lettuce and spinach germinate at a temperature as low as 40F (5C). Tomatoes and peppers require at least 60F (16C) and higher before they germinate. Air is

required for seeds to live. If the soil is waterlogged for an extended period, seeds will die. For this reason, it is best to start seeds in a potting mix that drains well to allow air to enter the soil.

Some vegetables have special germination requirements. *Light* is required for celery, lettuce and endive. When you sow seeds of these plants, press them lightly into the soil, and mist often to keep them moist. Onion and amaranth germinate best in *darkness.* If you start seeds indoors, place them in a cupboard or closet out of light.

SEED OR TRANSPLANT?

Some gardeners sow only easy-to-handle seeds directly in the garden, and buy inexpensive transplants of other vegetables from the nursery. But there are good reasons to start almost all of your vegetables from seed. Selection of ready-grown transplants is limited to a few popular varieties. For example, you'll be lucky to choose from three kinds of tomatoes. 'Big Boy' hybrid, 'Rutgers' and 'Beefsteak' are commonly

available at nurseries. Among peppers, the choice may be between two—'California Wonder' and 'Bell Boy' hybrid.

You may have trouble finding the vegetables you want, when you want to plant. Consider too, that it often takes years before transplants of new varieties become available to garden centers. Some excellent varieties never become available as transplants. A bonus of starting your own seeds is the satisfaction you experience knowing you are fully responsible for a crop from seed to harvest.

STANDARD OR HYBRID?

Vegetables are available in *standard* and *hybrid* forms. Sometimes standard varieties are called *open pollinated* because they are mass produced through pollination by bees and wind. Hybrids require *controlled pollination*—careful hand pollination between selected parent plants, usually different species that are sexually compatible.

Above: Indoor-started lettuce seedlings emerge from a flat.

The word hybrid comes from the Latin word, *hybrida,* meaning offspring of a wild boar and a domestic sow. A more familiar animal hybrid is the mule—a cross between a jackass (male donkey) and a mare (female horse). The mule is stronger and more useful than either parent. As with most hybrids, the mule is sterile and cannot reproduce itself. To create more mules, the original cross must be repeated. Seeds from plant hybrids are produced in a similar way. To make more seeds, you must make the original cross. A good example of a hybrid is seedless watermelon.

The main advantage of a hybrid is its vigor, a quality called *heterosis.* This results in higher yields, increased size, improved disease resistance, earliness, heat or cold tolerance, improved nutritional value and other desirable characteristics.

Disease resistance has become such an important part of hybridizing that names of hybrid varieties often carry the initials of diseases or pests they are resistant to. An example is the tomato hybrid 'Supersteak VFN'. The "V" means it resists *verticillium* wilt, the "F" means it resists *fusarium* wilt, the "N" indicates resistance to *nematode* pests. Gardeners in hot, humid areas should look for such varieties.

SEED PACKETS, PELLETS AND TAPES

Almost every year there seems to be a new way to plant seeds. *Seed pellets, seed tapes* and other methods are said to make seed starting easier and more reliable. It can be difficult to sow tiny seeds such as carrots, but even these seeds can be planted properly by hand. You get better value with a seed packet because it contains many more seeds at less cost compared to seed tapes and other systems.

Seed packets have been significantly improved with the introduction of foil packaging. They are moisture-proof and keep seeds fresher longer. Some seeds deteriorate quickly and the traditional paper packet may allow seeds to lose viability. Under controlled conditions, seeds in moisture-proof packets maintain high germination until the seal is broken.

Pelleted seeds are probably the least gimmicky of the alternative seed-sowing systems. The pellet is a clay coating around small seeds that makes them larger and easier to handle. The coating dissolves on contact with moisture, and

the seed germinates unhindered. Pelleted seeds tend to look like they have been manufactured, which might bother the gardening purist. But they do make it easier to sow small-seed vegetables such as carrots and lettuce.

Seed tapes are seeds bound into a transparent, biodegradable material, prespaced at regular distances. The material dissolves quickly after it comes in contact with moisture. Seed tapes save time with thinning, but they have some disadvantages. They are more expensive than conventional seeds from packets. And, if you don't get a high rate of germination, you will probably end up with wide gaps between plants. The tapes can also be a nuisance to plant. Because they are usually packed folded with sharp corners, they buckle out of the soil when you stretch the tape in the furrow.

SEED RACK OR MAIL ORDER?

Vegetable seeds are available in seed racks at retail outlets, or by mail order through seed catalogs. The advantage of rack displays in local stores is convenience. It is easy to go down to the nearest garden supply store and make your selections. The kind of vegetables and varieties offered depends on the type of store. Usually, garden centers carry more than one brand and offer the best selection.

Seed companies strongly represented in retail stores do not usually produce

mail order catalogs. The largest of these are Northrup King of Minneapolis, Minnesota; Ferry Morse of Fulton, Kentucky; Asgrow of Kalamazoo, Michigan; Vaughans of Downers Grove, Illinois; and Fredonia of Fredonia, New York.

Rack displays offer a basic selection of traditional, established varieties. Occasionally, some hybrids are offered. If you plan to buy your seeds from these displays, it pays to shop early. Toward the end of the season, the rack is not refilled as often because the seed company must take back unsold seeds.

The big advantage of ordering your seeds through a mail order catalog is the huge selection available. Compared to 100 or 200 varieties normally offered in a large rack display, a major vegetable seed catalog will offer up to 2,000 varieties. There will also be a heavier concentration of hybrid varieties than in the rack displays.

Seed catalogs number in the hundreds. Some are filled with color pictures and mailed to millions of gardeners. Others are specialized, appealing to the interests of a few thousand gardeners. Large or small, printed in color or on mimeographed sheets, each year's catalogs offer far more than simple variety listings. Each catalog strives to establish an individual identity and personality. Along with variety listings, descriptions and pictures, you will often find valuable cultural hints.

Shopping from a rack at your garden supply store is the handiest and most economical way to buy seeds. Seeds from mail order catalogs take a little more time and effort to obtain, but the added selection can be worth it.

Seed Catalogs

AGWAY INC.
Box 4933
Syracuse, NY 13221
Color catalog with many exclusive vegetable varieties developed by the company's own breeders. Catalog free.

APPLEWOOD SEED COMPANY
Box 10761—Edgemont Station
Golden, CO 80401
Seeds for herbs, sprouts and wildflowers. Catalog free.

BURGESS SEED & PLANT CO.
905 Four Seasons Road
Bloomington, IL 61701
Fine selection of vegetable seeds. Many unusual seeds exclusive to this established company. Catalog free.

W. ATLEE BURPEE
300 Park Avenue
Warminster, PA 18974
Wide selection of vegetables, many developed by the company's own breeding program. Free catalog features flowers, bulbs, nursery stock and garden aids.

COMSTOCK, FERRE & CO.
263 Main Street
Wethersfield, CT 06109
Illustrated catalog lists old and new varieties of vegetables and flowers. Extensive list of herbs. Catalog free.

J.A. DEMONCHAUX CO.
827 N. Kansas Ave., PO Box 8330
Topeka, KS 66608
French gourmet vegetables. Catalog 50¢.

DOMINION SEED HOUSE
Georgetown
Ontario, Canada L7G4A2
An excellent selection of vegetable seeds for Canada. Will ship only in Canada. Catalog free.

EXOTICA SEED CO.
1742 Laurel Canyon Boulevard
Los Angeles, CA 90046
Rare and hard-to-get seeds from around the world. Catalog $2.

FARMER SEED & NURSERY CO.
818 N.W. Fourth Street
Faribault, MN 55021
Vegetable seeds, including midget varieties. Northern-grown nursery stock. Garden aids. Color catalog free.

HENRY FIELD SEED & NURSERY CO.
407 Sycamore Street
Shenandoah, IA 51602
Beautiful, full-color catalog offers a wide selection of vegetable and flower seeds, nursery stock and garden supplies. Catalog free.

GURNEY SEED & NURSERY CO.
Yankton, SD 57079
One of America's largest seed and nursery catalogs. Extensive selection of vegetable seeds, plus nursery stock and garden aids. Catalog free.

JOSEPH HARRIS CO.
Moreton Farm
Rochester, NY 14624
Exceptionally fine listing of vegetable seeds, many developed by the company's own breeders. Catalog free.

THE CHARLES C. HART SEED CO.
Main & Hart Streets
Wethersfield, CT 06109
Fine assortment of vegetable and herb seeds. Catalog free.

H.G. HASTINGS CO.
Box 4274
Atlanta, GA 30302
Assortment of vegetable seeds and nursery stock, especially suitable for Southern gardens. Catalog free.

JOHNNY'S SELECTED SEEDS
Box 100
Albion, ME 04910
Vegetable, herb and farm seeds. Specializing in early, hardy varieties for the North. Catalog free.

J.W. JUNG SEED CO.
Randolph, WI 53956
Vegetable and flower seeds, nursery stock, fruit trees and gardening supplies. Catalog free.

OROL LEDDEN & SONS
Center Street
Sewell, NJ 08080
Large selection of vegetable seeds. Seedsmen since 1904. Catalog free.

MASON PLANT FARMS
Box 270
Reklow, TX 75784
Certified vegetable plants. Catalog free.

EARL MAY SEED & NURSERY CO.
Shenandoah, IA 51603
Vegetable seeds and nursery stock in a colorful catalog. Catalog free.

McLAUGHLINS SEEDS
Box 550 SP
Mead, WA 99021
Reliable vegetable seed supplier serving mostly West Coast gardeners. Catalog 50¢.

MELLINGERS, INC.
North Lima, OH 44452
Extensive listing of seeds, plants, organic plant foods and pest controls. Catalog free.

NICHOLS GARDEN NURSERY
1190 North Pacific Highway
Albany, OR 97321
Extensive listing of herb and vegetable seeds. Good source for many unusual and early maturing varieties. Catalog free.

L.L. OLDS SEED COMPANY
2901 Packers Avenue, PO Box 7790
Madison, WI 53707
Assortment of vegetable and flower seeds, nursery stock, lawn seeds and garden aids. Catalog free.

GEORGE W. PARK SEED, INC.
Greenwood, SC 29647
Recognized as flower seed specialists. Vegetable seed selection is also extensive. Color catalog free.

PIEDMONT PLANT FARMS
Box 424
Albany, GA 31703
Established supplier of field-grown vegetable plants. Free color catalog features many popular varieties.

SEEDWAY, INC.
Hall, NY 14463
Formerly Robson's Seeds. Vegetable varieties especially suited for Northeast conditions. Specialists in hybrid sweet corn. Catalog free.

R.H. SHUMWAY
628 Cedar Street
Rockford, IL 61101
Catalog is a blend of newly developed varieties and many established varieties. Source for plants, bulbs, shrubs and fruit trees. Catalog free.

STOKES SEEDS INC.
Box 548
Buffalo, NY 14240
Excellent selection of vegetables. Lots of growing tips. Catalog free.

THOMPSON & MORGAN
Box 100
Farmingdale, NJ 07727
Exclusive listings of vegetables, many rare and unusual. Useful nutrition and flavor charts. Catalog free.

OTIS S. TWILLEY SEED CO.
Box 65
Trevose, PA 19047
Vegetable seed specialists with extensive selection. Catalog free.

VERMONT BEAN SEED COMPANY
11 Garden Lane
Bomoseen, VT 05732
Complete line of all types of vegetable seeds, specializing in hard-to-find types. Source for sprouting seeds. Catalog 25¢.

VESEY'S SEEDS LTD.
York, Prince Edward's Island
Canada COA 1PO
Specialists in flowers and vegetables for Northern areas with short seasons. Catalog free.

WYATT-QUARLES SEED CO.
331 S. Wilmington Street, Box 2131
Raleigh, NC 27602
Wide selection of vegetable seeds for Southern gardens. Catalog free.

ALL-AMERICA SELECTIONS

Seed companies offer dozens of new vegetable varieties each year. Some are slightly different from existing varieties; others offer substantial improvements. Because of the number of new varieties, it is not always easy to decide which are worthwhile. For this reason, the American garden seed industry founded All-America Selections—the national seed trials. Each year, many new varieties are tested in trial gardens representing every area of the United States. Judges from the seed industry and academic areas grow and evaluate the varieties in their own test plots. They then make awards of recognition—a bronze medal, silver medal or gold medal, according to merit.

All-America Selections does not test every variety. Introducing a variety to the marketplace takes time, and some breeders are anxious to introduce their best varieties. They bypass the sometimes long periods required—up to three years—to gain an award.

For a current list of All-America Award-winning vegetables, write: All-America Selections, Box 344, Sycamore, IL 60178.

SAVING YOUR OWN SEEDS

Many gardeners like to save seeds from their garden plants for use the next season. This may seem like a good idea, but saving seeds is not as advantageous as it may sound. Plants grown from seeds from your own garden may give unpredictable results. Seeds saved from *F1 hybrids,* first generation hybrids,

produce inferior results the second season. Saving seeds from standard varieties is also plagued with problems. Beets, chard, parsley, carrots, onions and celery are *biennials,* requiring two years before they flower and produce seeds.

Spinach, sweet corn, melons and cucumbers are pollinated by wind or insects. Cross-pollination can occur from a neighbor's garden or from other varieties in your own garden. Beet pollen, for example, can travel as far as two miles. This may cause your saved seeds to grow into something completely different than what you grew the previous year. Tomatoes, peppers and eggplant, which are considered self-pollinating, may give unpredictable results unless the varieties are isolated. Some vegetables such as lettuce and snap beans are also prone to carrying seed-borne diseases. This is especially true in the northeast United States and Canada.

Storing and Testing Leftover Seeds— Most seed companies are generous with the quantities of seeds they provide in their packets. You may find that after planting you have a lot of leftover seeds in opened packets. To maintain viability, seeds must be kept *cool and dry.*

To store seeds, place packets in a wide-mouth jar that can be sealed with a tight-fitting lid. Put 2 heaping tablespoons of powdered milk in a paper envelope, and place this in the jar. The powdered milk absorbs moisture from the air inside the jar, keeping the seeds dry. Seal the jar and store in the vegetable bin of your refrigerator. How long seeds last depends to a great extent on storage conditions. High temperatures and high humidity deteriorate seeds quickly and reduce the rate of germination.

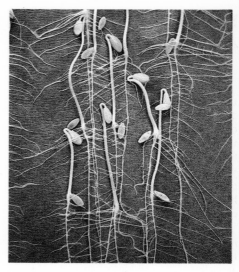

Viability of stored seeds can be checked by germinating them on a paper towel. See text for instructions.

To see if seeds are viable, select about 10 seeds and lay them on a moist paper towel. Put the towel inside a plastic bag and place in a warm location. The plastic bag prevents the paper towel from drying out too quickly. After 10 days, count the number of seeds that have germinated. If 2 out of 10 germinate, this indicates a 20% germination rate—not good. If 5 out of 10 sprout, this shows 50% germination—acceptable.

Even if you have seeds left over from last year's seed order, it is probably better to start with fresh seeds. Some seeds are long-lived under ideal conditions, but high humidity and other factors can cause rapid deterioration. Many gardeners advise not to save seeds, unless you have a variety that is unobtainable from normal sources.

A Close Look At Seeds

Seed form, color and size are interesting to compare. From left: watermelon, sunflower, squash and beet.

BUYING TREES AND SHRUBS

Trees and shrubs can be purchased from mail-order suppliers, local garden centers, nurseries and tree farms. Mail-order is generally the least expensive way to purchase plants, and it allows you to choose from a greater selection. But you must be careful to read the catalog description to understand what you are buying and only buy from reputable companies.

Young trees and shrubs are sold *bare-root, balled-and-burlapped* and *container grown.* Bare-root trees and shrubs are sold in a dormant state when the plant is not actively growing. The roots are usually packed in moist sawdust or moss. Mail-order trees and shrubs are generally sold this way because bare-root plants are lighter in weight so shipping costs are less. Some mail-order sources also offer seeds and unrooted cuttings—6- to 8-inch dormant sticks capable of rooting and leafing out when inserted into soil.

Plants sold through local retail outlets are generally balled-and-burlapped or container-growth. The sizes available are much larger than bare-root plants offered by mail. Bare-root stock is also available through most nurseries during the dormant season. Though the selection at local nurseries may be limited, you have the advantage of examining the tree or shrub before you buy it.

The best way to buy a tree or shrub is from a specialty nursery or tree farm. For instance, there are nurseries that specialize in dwarf conifers, others in azaleas and rhododendrons. Camellias and fuchsias are other popular specialty items, planted out in fields or under shade, ready for digging. If you want a weeping Norway spruce with a particular outline, or a red maple with a particular intensity of fall coloring, you can walk the rows, point to a plant you want, have it tagged and dug with a root ball for transporting to your property. This is the true connoisseur's method of selecting plants. It's also the most expensive. There is an increasing number of tree specialists who tour old estates and defunct arboretums to collect particularly fine tree specimens for resale. As much as $50,000 has been paid for a single tree, and another $10,000 paid to move it, with no guarantee of survival!

Selecting Healthy Plants—When buying bare-root stock by mail, you don't have the advantage of choosing what you get and must rely on the reputation of the mail-order company to send you a healthy plant. You almost always have the opportunity to send back plants you are not satisfied with and get a replacement or refund, but this can be a nuisance.

If you order plants by mail, immediately open the package when it arrives and examine the stems and roots of the plant. If a few small branches or roots are broken, they can be pruned away without harm to the plant. However, if the roots have signs of mildew or tiny fungus pustules, return the plant.

Buying bare-root stock from a local nursery allows you to pick and choose. The most important thing to look for is a vigorous root system. Scaffold branches should be well spaced, and buds should be plump, never shriveled and dry. Shriveled, dried-out buds that flake apart in your fingers indicate the plant may be too dehydrated to survive planting.

Because bare-root plants should be planted while dormant or when just breaking dormancy, avoid plants with leaves that have already sprouted. A few buds breaking dormancy and showing a little green is okay—and it tells you the plant is alive—but too much advanced leaf growth may already be placing the root system under excessive stress. If you have no choice but to accept a bare-root plant that is already green, prune away about one third of the branches before planting.

Sometimes bare-root stock is purchased to make economical mass plantings—a homeowner once purchased 10,000 bare-root azaleas by mail. Although this is an extreme example, with any large purchase it is best to make a temporary nursery bed to keep plants in until they are acclimatized and you know how many survivors you have to work with. Provide light shade until plants are more mature and ready for moving to permanent positions.

Determine if the plants you're buying are *seedling stock,* (seed-grown plants) *grafted stock* or a named variety grown *vegetatively* (such as cuttings). Seedling trees and shrubs are generally the least expensive, but can be variable in quality. If a tree or shrub has been grafted it will have a large swelling near the soil line, where the top of a special variety has been joined to the root system of a different variety or species noted for root hardiness. This swelling, called the *bud union* or *graft union,* should be located above the soil line of the container and it should be examined closely for strength.

Always check for rodent and deer damage. Deer damage is fairly obvious—the bark is usually shredded in long strips. Rodent damage is easily overlooked because it occurs close to the roots and might consist of a narrow band of bare wood girdling the trunk.

Plants sold in containers and balled-and-burlapped at garden centers are usually big enough to plant directly in the garden. In the case of flowering shrubs, they may already be flowering size, some in full bloom. Optimum planting times are determined by the kind of tree or shrub you've bought and the climate in which you live.

Always check the soil before taking home a containerized or balled-and-burlapped plant. Some nursery personnel are careless about watering. If soil is dust-dry, chances are the plant is already dehydrated and on the verge of dropping its leaves. Weeds growing in containers also indicate a lack of care. Feel the leaves to test if they are brittle. Look for good color—leaves should be a healthy green. There should be no curling, yellowing or blemishes such as browned tips or spots. Wilted leaves indicate that the plant is either dehydrated or diseased.

With needleleaf evergreens, look for signs of localized browning. Rub your hand over the needles. If they feel brittle and fall from the branches easily, don't buy the plant. Needles that shatter or drop at the touch of your hand indicate the tree may be on the verge of dehydration and will probably worsen after transplanting.

Check for pest damage, including chewed or discolored leaves. Examine the underside of leaves for signs of mites—detected by a lackluster appearance and presence of fine webs. To check mite damage on needleleaf evergreens, part the branches and look inside the canopy. Look for blisters on branches, leaves and trunk—signs of fungus infections. Small holes or gummy sap deposits on the trunk or branches are signs of borer infestation.

NURSERY CLOSEUP

Your local nursery is the single best garden-making resource. Each one is part display garden and part idea garden, part research center, part botanical garden. In addition to landscape plants, nurseries usually stock bulbs, seeds, soil amendments, fertilizers, tools and other garden supplies. Most nurseries welcome questions concerning gardening problems or suitable plants for specific areas.

Each nursery is different, reflecting the varying climates, communities and interests of the owners. But all nurseries have certain elements in common. Plants stocked are the most reliable for the region. Usually, a brief description including sun, soil and water requirements is either posted near each kind of plant, or appears on the plant's identification tag. Additional cultural information is available from the nursery staff.

Plants in the nursery are usually grouped according to habit and use—blocks of trees, shrubs for sun and for shade, ground covers, vegetables and herbs, bedding plants and tropicals. The drawing on the facing page shows a typical nursery layout. No other one will be exactly the same, but most share these features.

Your nursery mirrors the garden cycle in your area. Shopping tours—whether you buy or not—will familiarize you with the plants you need for a changing garden. Plants stocked vary with the seasons. For instance, bare-root roses and bare-root fruit trees come in late winter, bulbs in fall and many flowering plants in spring.

Choosing healthy plants is mostly a matter of common sense. Na-turally, you wouldn't choose a plant that is showing signs of stress or one that looks stunted or sickly when compared to its neighbors. Here are some specific signs to look for when inspecting plants at the nursery:

- **Leaf Color**—Plants that show yellowing or other discoloration in leaves might indicate poor drainage, fertilizer deficiency, insect damage or disease.
- **Bud Development**—Buds on dormant plants should be firm, moist and uniformly spaced. Scratch lightly into the bark to see that the cambium or growing layer is moist and green.
- **Uniformity of Growth**—Plants in any given group should be uniform in vigor and health.
- **Plant Spacing**—Nursery plants are ideally grown and displayed with sufficient spacing to permit good development of the individual plant. Plants spaced too closely in the row or block will be tall and spindly with little, if any, side branching. Shade trees grown too close together may be extremely high headed.
- **Soil**—Plants to be balled and burlapped must be grown in soil that will hold a firm ball. If possible, check these plants to make sure root balls are not broken or loose.
- **Weeds**—Plants growing in weedy containers indicate lack of care. Plants may be in poor vigor due to weed competition. Also, you don't want to introduce weeds into the new landscape.
- **Decay**—Inspect trees for spots of decayed tissue on the trunk and branches.
- **Sunscald or Sunburn**—Damage of either kind usually appears on the side of the trunk facing the southwest. Sunburn destroys the cambium layer under the bark and increases the plant's susceptibility to various pests and diseases.
- **Abrasions on Bark**—Fresh abrasions or scrapes from handling during delivery or at the nursery are reasons to avoid a plant.
- **Girdling Roots**—These are circling roots, usually close to the soil surface, caused by poor timing or procedures in transplanting. Girdling roots tend to encircle the growing trunk and may eventually kill the plant. Any size plant that has been kept in a container too long will become rootbound. Avoid plants that seem to have outgrown their containers.
- **Improper Pruning**—Stubs left by improper pruning cause dieback into the main trunk and are common entry points for pests and diseases.
- **Frost Damage**—Long, vertical splits can occur on the south and southwest sides of young and thin-barked trees. Frost cracks are also convenient openings for various insects and diseases.
- **Signs of Injury**—Check for wilted or dead leaves, dry buds, twig or branch dieback and sunken or discolored patches in bark or stems, as well as any recent physical damage to plant.
- **Diseases**—These can take many forms. Check for abnormal growth of leaves, twigs and fruits, discoloration of leaves and bark, and unusual discharges of sap through the bark.
- **Insects**—Check for insect eggs, and evidence of damage from insect feeding on leaves, twigs, buds or other plant parts. Examine trunks of trees for holes made by boring insects.

Adequate spacing in nursery row allows for good development of individual plants.

Plants growing in weedy containers indicate lack of care.

Check bark of trees for disease, sunburn and other signs of injury. Damage to this trunk was caused by tree borer.

TYPICAL NURSERY

KEY

1. **Garden trees:** Soften lines of buildings, provide shade, may also provide flowers.
2. **Fruit trees:** For orchard or landscaping. Usually grouped into deciduous fruits and citrus.
3. **Foliage shrubs:** Provide privacy, shape spaces, soften wind, control glare, act as barriers. Can be trained as hedges or used as accents or in groupings.
4. **Flowering shrubs:** Provide color, used as accents or foundation plantings.
5. **Roses:** Add color to garden, come in many forms, from miniatures to shrubs to climbing vines. Sold bare root in winter, in containers the rest of the year.
6. **Ground covers:** Carpet large areas, prevent erosion, add color, can be used instead of lawn.
7. **Vines:** Dress up walls and fences, cover trellises and arbors to provide shade, may also provide flowers or fruit.
8. **Bedding plants:** Used for fast and easy color. Includes flowering annuals and perennials. Available in cell packs and various-size containers.
9. **Vegetables and herbs:** Available as seedlings in cell packs and individual pots. Seeds also available.

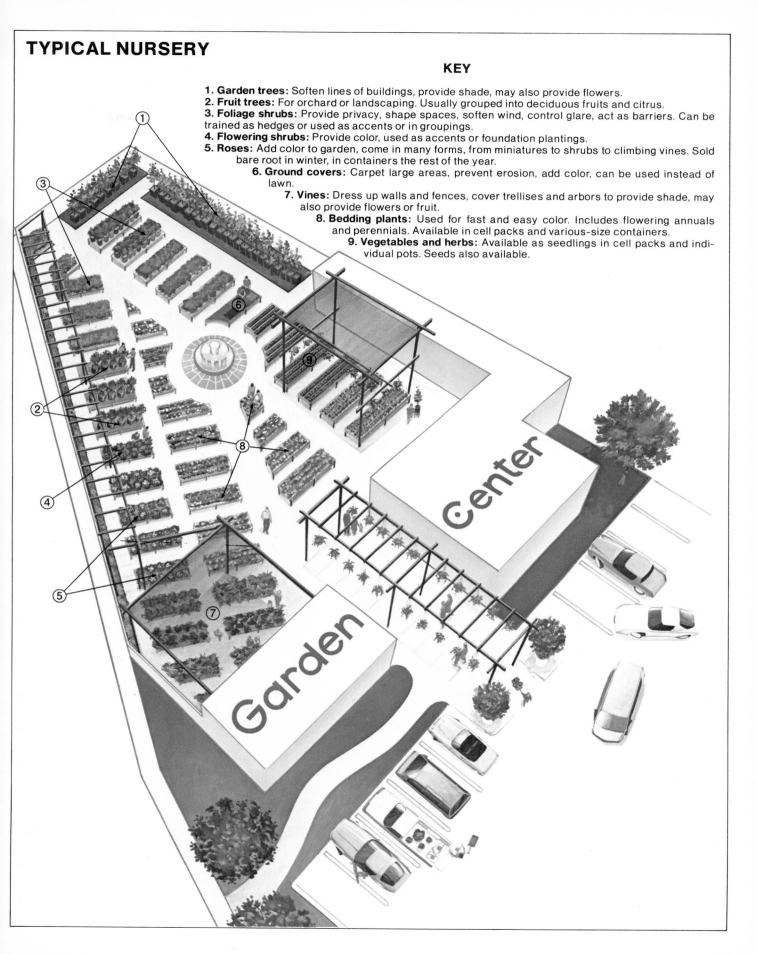

SOILS AND FERTILIZERS

Any good gardener is also a good scientist. Granted, most experienced gardeners may not consider themselves scientists, but anyone who successfully raises plants has a good knowledge of the ways in which plants, soil, fertilizer and water all work together. While you are reading this chapter, remember that these are not isolated subjects. Soil, nutrients and water, along with climate, all work in harmony to produce vital, thriving gardens. They form the foundation for understanding all types of gardening—from indoor plants to lawns.

Before you can know how much water or fertilizer to give a plant, or how to improve the soil, you need to know how these three factors work together and what effects each have on the other.

THE BASICS

To understand how soil, nutrients and water work together, you must look at the subject relative to a plant. In the simplest terms, soil provides a structure that permits roots to grow freely, anchoring the plant in place. In most areas—the exception being ones with extremely sandy soil—the soil also contains the nutrients needed to sustain plant growth. Water, from rain or irrigation, soaks into the small spaces between individual soil particles where it becomes available to plant roots. Through the process of *transpiration*—much like a human's perspiration—water is drawn up from the roots, through the plant, and released from the surface of its leaves. Because the water is lost to the atmos-

phere in this process, water in the soil must be more or less constantly replenished or the plant will wilt and eventually die of dehydration.

The small spaces between individual soil particles are an extremely important factor in any type of successful gardening. These spaces are where the roots of the plants receive the air, food and water they need to grow. And surprisingly, these small spaces—alternately filled with water, oxygen and nutrients held in a suspension of water—are hard to come by.

The two extreme soil types are clay and sand. Clay soils are made up of extremely small inorganic particles. Conversely, sandy soils are made up of comparatively large individual particles. Clay soils are often referred to as *heavy*,

---

Left: Roto-tiller makes easy work of cultivating large areas.

Above: Raised beds allow more complete control over soil conditions. Soil is easier to keep free of weeds, has better drainage and warms up faster in spring for earlier planting.

a term that can be misleading. Clay soils don't necessarily weigh more than sand soils, but they are denser and have a greater water-holding capacity.

In between these two extremes is the ideal soil type, called *loam*. It is also referred to as *loose* or *friable* soil. Loam soils contain both large and small particles, held together in small groups by a substance called *humus,* described below. When these groups, or aggregates, of different-size particles are held together by humus, they leave fairly stable air spaces in the soil. These spaces allow roots to grow freely, water to enter and room for oxygen after the water drains through—*all* of which are necessary for a healthy plant.

How do you get a soil like this? Some gardeners happen to be lucky enough to live in an area where loam is naturally present. The rest of us have to work at it. Whether you have clay or sandy soil, the key to creating a good soil is *humus,* a sticky excretion produced by microorganisms present in soil. Because there are millions of these microorganisms present in every tablespoon of soil, you may wonder what these creatures eat to produce the byproduct, humus. The answer is *organic matter*—and lots of it. Without a free supply of organic matter, the number of microorganisms present in the soil dwindles drastically, lessening the amount of humus produced. Without humus, the state of poor soil remains the same.

The organic matter may be peat moss, grass clippings, redwood compost, leaf mold, sawdust, manure or any of the other soil amendments illustrated on the facing page. One or more of these materials is commonly available at nurseries and garden centers. It doesn't really make that much difference what type of organic matter you add to the soil, as long as you add it.

In addition to producing humus, and thereby improving the quality of the soil, a thriving population of microorganisms has an important side benefit. Any organic matter (soil amendment), or organic fertilizer such as manure, bone meal, bloodmeal or fish emulsion, must be processed first by the microorganisms before it can be used by the plant. If the microorganism population is low, most of the nutrients from the organic fertilizer will be leached through the soil without ever benefitting the plant.

SOIL

Dealing with your garden soil can be as simple or complex as you care to make it. Much has been written recently on the subject of soil analysis, the results of which give you an accurate evaluation of the physical makeup of your soil, its mineral deficiencies or excesses, and its pH. While a battery of sophisticated soil tests aren't essential to a successful garden, there are several you may want to make. The most important tests are for pH and nutrient deficiencies. Most university or county extension services will test your soil for a nominal fee. You can also buy simple test kits at most nurseries and garden centers. Or you may prefer to take the advice of nursery personnel and gardeners familiar with soil conditions in your area.

If the plants in your garden are not growing as well as you think they should be, or if you're planting a new garden on bare land, you'll need to improve the soil. A soil improvement program can be divided into three main steps:

1. Improving the soil structure.
2. Providing correct nutrient levels.
3. Adjusting the soil pH, if necessary.

The materials needed to carry out such a program are readily available at nurseries and garden centers. These include soil conditioners used to improve soil structure and fertilizers to increase the nutrient levels in the soil. To adjust the pH level, you can use either lime or sulfur, depending on whether you need to increase or decrease the pH.

IMPROVING SOIL

Even those lucky enough to have naturally occurring loam soil should make yearly additions of organic matter to keep the soil in good shape. If your soil is too sandy or clayey, the following section tells you what soil conditioners you can use, when to use them and how to apply them.

WHAT TO ADD TO THE SOIL

Organic matter is available in many different forms. Peat moss, ground bark, sawdust and manure are almost universally available. Redwood soil conditioner, mushroom compost, cocoa bean, almond or rice hulls, and grape or apple pomace are usually available on a regional basis. You can buy organic matter in bags from nurseries and garden centers, or in bulk—sold by the cubic yard—from topsoil dealers. To find topsoil dealers, look under "topsoil" in the yellow pages of your telephone book.

Many studies have been conducted concerning the relative merits of different types of organic matter used as a soil conditioner. While it's true that some are better than others, *all* of them will have a beneficial effect on the soil. The only word of caution would be concerning fresh or non-composted manure, which may contain ammonia and salts in levels high enough to damage plant growth. The following is a brief overview of the

Compost pile is good source of organic matter for improving soil. Grass border improves appearance.

SOIL AMENDMENTS

Shown here are some of the more common soil amendments used to improve soil structure. Organic amendments such as bark and peat moss enrich soil by providing *humus*. Amendments such as manure also have value as a fertilizer, adding nitrogen to the soil. Sand is used to improve the structure of clay soils.

Peat moss has excellent water-holding ability and is good for sandy soils. Readily available but expensive.

Manure improves soil structure, also adds nitrogen to soil. Should be well-composted—fresh manure is high in salts, can burn plants.

Straw makes good surface mulch for weed control, can be dug into ground at end of season to enrich soil.

Sand is used along with organic amendments to improve structure of clay soils. Promotes drainage.

Leaf mold decomposes quickly in soil and is relatively short-lived, but adds important nutrients as well as improving soil structure.

Bark chips make good surface mulch, long-lasting soil conditioner.

Pine bark is one of several kinds of ground bark used as a soil conditioner.

Redwood sawdust is a popular soil conditioner in western states. Long-lasting.

COMPOST PILE

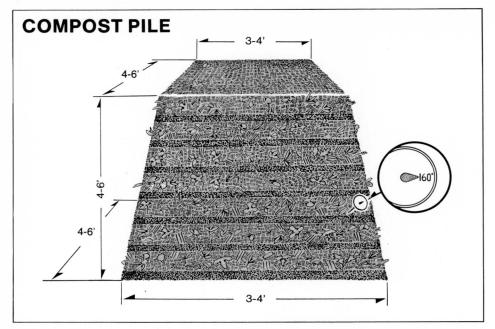

This drawing shows typical dimensions of compost pile. There must be sufficient mass in pile to keep heat at about 160F (72C). A 3'x3'x3' pile is minimum. High temperature promotes decomposition, kills any weed seeds, pests and disease organisms that could be transferred to plants.

properties of commonly available organic substances used as soil conditioners:

Ground Bark—The bark of various trees, including fir, are ground into an excellent, long-lasting soil conditioner. Usually available in bags or bulk.

Homemade Compost—If you have your own compost bin or pile and can produce it in large enough quantities, homemade compost is one of the best all-around soil conditioners.

Leaf Mold—A good, although comparatively expensive, soil conditioner. Somewhat short-lived in the soil, but adds nutrients in addition to conditioning soil.

Manure—Available from nurseries in bags or in bulk, or directly from the source—chicken ranches, dairies or feed lots. Usually inexpensive, but make sure it has been composted, or *well-rotted*. Fresh manure is dangerously high in salts and should not be used around plants or in seed beds. As a soil conditioner, manure is comparatively long-lasting, and has some fertilizer value. Best when used in combination with other types of soil conditioners.

Mushroom Compost—Sold in sacks but occasionally available in bulk. A byproduct of mushroom culture, this compost is usually a combination of manure and straw, and as such, should be thoroughly composted before using in the garden. Mushroom compost is a good, comparatively long-lasting conditioner, with some fertilizer value on its own.

Peat Moss—Widely available in bulk or bags. It is an excellent conditioner with superior water-holding ability, making it especially good for use in sandy soils. When incorporated into the soil in large amounts, peat moss will also create a soil structure that permits the high level of aeration demanded by a large group of plants such as azaleas, rhododendrons, camellias and others. Peat moss is a relatively expensive amendment.

Redwood Soil Conditioner—Made from redwood sawdust, this amendment is popular and widespread in the western states. The effects of redwood soil con-ditioner are long-lasting. Redwood by-products larger than sawdust can be used as mulch.

Sawdust—Various types of sawdust are often available in bulk form for garden use. They are usually comparatively inexpensive, but unless they have been "nitrogen-fortified," nitrogen will have to be added to keep the sawdust from robbing nitrogen from the soil as it breaks down.

Vermiculite and Perlite—These are considered soil amendments but instead of being organic, they are mineral elements. Vermiculite is mica which has been heated to the point where it puffs up, almost like popcorn. Perlite is pulverized volcanic stone. Both contribute no nutrients but are extremely light in weight and have a tendency to stay in the top layer of soil rather than sinking into lower layers. They are excellent for increasing the water and nutrient-holding capacity of sandy soils, and for increasing aeration in clay soils.

WHEN TO IMPROVE THE SOIL

You can add organic matter to your soil virtually any time during the year but some times are better than others. Obviously, adding organic matter to soil to benefit plants is only effective *before* you plant. Once a plant is in the ground, it is impossible to incorporate the organic matter into the soil without seriously damaging the roots of the plant.

One of the best times to do the job is early autumn, before rains or snow have begun. Apply the organic material of your choice in a thick (3 to 6 inch) layer over the area that you want to improve. It's a good idea to remove large weeds from the area before you cover it with the soil conditioner—smaller weeds will die from lack of sunlight.

Allow the organic material to stay in place through the winter. When spring rains have subsided, and the soil has dried out enough to cultivate easily, incorporate the organic matter into the soil using a tiller or shovel. Leaving the organic matter in place through the winter has two main benefits—first, it inhibits growth of weeds in early spring, and second, the effects of weather mellow the organic matter and it actually begins to compost right on the soil. If you live in a warm-winter area subject to high winds, do not use a light amendment such as peat moss as a surface dressing because it will probably be blown away from the area you're trying to amend.

The second best time to add organic matter to the soil is in spring, just prior to the beginning of the planting season. Wait until the soil has dried out enough to be workable, remove any weeds in the area and then incorporate the organic matter into the soil. This way, any plants planted at the beginning of the season will benefit from the improved soil.

HOW TO USE SOIL CONDITIONERS

To improve large areas of soil for a lawn, vegetable garden or flower bed, add organic material in an even layer over the top of the soil and then dig in with a tiller or shovel. If you are planting large individual trees or shrubs from 5- or 10-gallon containers, you need only improve the soil in the immediate vicinity of the planting hole.

Large Areas—For an organic material to work as a soil conditioner it has to be added in significant amounts. This is especially true for large areas. The basic rule of thumb is that one third of the final mix should be organic matter. For example, if you are planning to improve the soil to a depth of 9 inches, you should add 3 inches of organic matter to the top of the soil before mixing it in. If you want to improve the soil to a depth of 12 inches, you should incorporate a 4-inch layer of organic matter into the soil.

Depending on the size of the area to be improved, this usually calls for a large amount of organic matter. Before you get started, it's a good idea to measure the area and do a little calling around to find the best value in soil conditioners. Many bulk suppliers will deliver directly to your home. Although you will want to replenish the organic matter in the soil on a regular basis in smaller amounts, rest assured that this massive addition is a one-time-only proposition.

Once you've spread the organic material over the area in a fairly even layer, you will need to incorporate it into the soil to the desired depth. If it's a large area, a power tiller does the job in little time, with the least amount of strain—but just because it's not that much trouble, don't go over the area so many times that you create a fine, powdery mixture. Overtilling the soil to the point that it's powdery and completely free of clods will cause the soil to form a crust the first time water is applied. It's far better to err on the side of undertilling rather than overtilling. Clods the size of half-dollars are perfectly acceptable—they can be

Roto-tiller is best way to work organic matter into soil over a large area.

easily dispatched when you rake the area smooth.

Small Areas—If the area is smaller, or you want some challenging exercise, the same process can be done with a shovel with far less chance of overpulverizing the soil. Spread the organic matter on top of the soil in an even layer and start turning over the soil from one end of the plot to the other. Two passes, perpendicular to each other, will be necessary to achieve a good mix.

Single Planting Holes—This procedure will work for any tree or shrub you might plant. First, dig a hole roughly twice as large as the root ball or the can from which you are taking the plant. Put the dirt from the hole in a pile, add roughly the same amount of organic matter to it and mix together.

Take the plant from the can and check to see how much improved soil you must add back to the hole to have the root ball at the same level as the surrounding soil. Add the soil back to the hole and wet thoroughly to settle. Set the plant in the hole to see if the top of the root ball is at

the surrounding soil level. If it is still a little low, add more of the improved soil to bring it up to the correct level.

Once you've added enough improved soil to the bottom of the hole, put the plant in place, and start adding soil around the root ball, tamping lightly with your hand or shovel handle as you go. After you have filled the hole, use the extra improved soil to make a small berm around the newly planted tree or shrub for a watering basin. The basin should be about the same circumference as the original hole. Water thoroughly. If the soil settles below the level of the surrounding soil, add more improved soil to bring it up to grade, and add water to settle the soil.

Special Method for Vegetable Row Crops—If you are planning an especially large vegetable garden and don't want to go to the effort of improving the soil in the entire area, you can compromise and improve only that soil where the plants are going to grow. The easiest way to accomplish this is to dig a trench, 8 to 10 inches deep and approximately 6 to 8 inches wide, and as long as you intend the row to be. Add organic matter, roughly 50% of the total volume of the soil taken out of the trench, to the soil taken from the trench and mix thoroughly. Put the improved soil back in the trench and water thoroughly. Seeds will germinate with far greater success in this mixture, and plants will get off to a much quicker start, compared to those planted in unimproved soil.

A variation of this method can be used for vegetable transplants, such as tomatoes and squash plants, using the same procedure as described for large areas.

SOIL pH

Soils in different parts of the country have different pH levels. If you're not quite sure what pH is, and why it is important to plants, don't worry. The following explanation tells you all you need to know.

The degree of acidity or alkalinity of a soil is designated by the term pH. The pH scale ranges from 0 to 14. At pH 7.0 the soil is neutral. As the values go downward from pH 7.0, the acidity increases. Conversely, as the values go upward from 7.0, the alkalinity increases. Although many plants have rather specific soil pH requirements, the best growth for a wide range of plants occurs when the pH of the soil is approximately 6.5.

CHANGING SOIL pH

To raise pH: Here are the approximate amounts of ground limestone (dolomite) needed to raise pH (increase alkalinity) of various soils to 6.5 from various lower levels. 6.5 is considered ideal for most plants.

POUNDS OF GROUND LIMESTONE PER 1,000 SQUARE FEET*

Change in pH	Sand	Sandy Loam	Loam	Silt Loam	Clay
4.0 to 6.5	60	115	161	193	230
4.5 to 6.5	51	96	133	161	193
5.0 to 6.5	41	78	106	129	152
5.5 to 6.5	28	60	78	92	106
6.0 to 6.5	14	32	41	51	55

*In southern and coastal states, reduce amounts by approximately one half.

To lower pH: Here are approximate amounts of soil sulfur to lower pH (increase acidity) of various soils to 6.5 from various higher levels.

POUNDS OF SULFUR PER 1,000 SQUARE FEET

Change in pH	Sand	Loam	Clay
8.5 to 6.5	46	57	69
8.0 to 6.5	28	34	46
7.5 to 6.5	11	18	23
7.0 to 6.5	2	4	7

The pH of a soil affects plant growth because it has a distinct effect on the availablity of nutrients.

You can test the pH of your own soil using a simple pH test kit available from nurseries, garden centers and mail-order scientific supply houses.

Acid Soil—If you find that your particular soil is too acidic, you will want to add lime to it. How much you add depends on how acidic the soil is. Lime is a compound of calcium, and it comes in several different forms. One of the most popular forms is *dolomitic limestone,* because it adds magnesium at the same time it reduces the acidity of the soil. Refer to the above chart for the amount to add to your soil to bring it into a pH range suitable for the plants you want to grow. The best time to add lime is in autumn or spring, at the same time you add the organic matter to improve the soil structure.

Alkaline Soil—If you find your soil is too alkaline, a common problem in warm, dry areas with limited rainfall, you can bring the pH into a more acceptable range with the addition of sulfur, gypsum or lime-sulfur. All are commonly available at nurseries and garden centers. These materials are best added in the spring or any time you are adding organic material to the soil. Refer to the above chart for the amount to add to bring your soil into a pH range suitable for the plants you want to grow.

SHALLOW SOILS

Shallow soils present a real problem to gardeners, especially in some areas of the West and Southwest. You can tell that you have shallow soil if you dig a hole for a tree or shrub and you hit a seemingly impenetrable layer known as *hardpan.* If hardpan occurs within the first 18 inches, you have shallow soil.

Although you may be able to grow annual vegetables and flowers, and some perennials, the vast majority of trees and shrubs will not be able to survive in shallow soil. Some gardeners discover that the hardpan layer is actually quite thin. You can test this yourself using an earth auger, available at most large nurseries and garden centers. Once you encounter the hardpan, use the earth auger to bore through it. If you find that the hardpan is less than 12 inches thick,

trees and shrubs will probably grow satisfactorily as long as you bore a hole through the hardpan in each planting hole before planting. If the hardpan is thicker than 12 inches, you'll probably have to garden in raised beds or containers, or change the garden site.

RAISED BEDS

Gardening in raised beds has become the preferred method of vegetable and flower gardening for many people— even for those without the problem of shallow soil. Perhaps the best thing about raised beds is that they can be made any size or shape, as deep as you like, and can be filled with whatever type of soil mixture you desire.

The sides of a raised bed may be built of railroad ties, bricks, 2x4s or 2x6s, or a low rock wall. How tall you make the sides depends on what types of crops you intend to grow. Deep-rooted root crops such as carrots or turnips require 10 to 12 inches of loose soil. Most other types of garden crops will make do in a raised bed with sides 6 to 8 inches tall, provided their roots can penetrate through into the natural layer of soil beneath the raised bed.

Soil in raised beds is much easier to keep free of weeds and debris. It almost always has better drainage qualities, it warms up faster in spring for earlier planting, and it gives a look of order to the garden.

In some respects a raised bed is like a gigantic, open-bottom container. As such, it needs to be filled with a lightweight soil mix that is easy and relatively inexpensive to make in large quantities. The following instructions for making a lightweight soil mix can be used both in containers or raised beds.

Lightweight Soil Mix—Over the years many different formulas or "recipes" have been developed for soil mixes. One of the most successful is equal parts fine sand, peat moss and ground bark. Do *not* use beach sand because of its high salt content. Add to this a complete dry fertilizer, such as a 5-10-10 formula, and some ground limestone in the amounts recommended on the package. The standard proportions for a large quantity (1 cubic yard) are 9 cubic feet each of sand, peat moss and ground bark, 5 pounds of complete fertilizer and 7 pounds of ground limestone.

Start the mix by dampening the peat moss. Combine in one big pile the dampened peat moss, sand and ground bark, and sprinkle the fertilizer and limestone on top. Shovel the mix from this pile into a new pile beside it, one shovelful at a time. Repeat this "pile building" process two more times, and the ingredients should be thoroughly mixed.

ORGANIC MULCHES

Many gardeners are confused by the difference between an organic soil conditioner or amendment and a *mulch*. The confusion stems from the fact that any organic soil conditioner can also be used as a mulch—the difference is not in the material, but how it is used. A soil conditioner is mixed into the soil, while a mulch is applied in a layer on top of the soil.

A 2- to 3-inch layer of an organic mulch is practically a panacea for all sorts of common garden woes. A mulch helps preserve the good structure of a soil by preventing a hard crust from forming on the soil surface. It keeps a majority of weeds from ever sprouting, and the few that do make it through are much easier to pull. A mulch conserves moisture and keeps the moisture level in the soil constant. Lastly, it keeps soil temperature cool and conducive to healthy root growth.

The best time to apply an organic mulch is in autumn after the garden has been cleaned of weeds and debris, or in spring after the soil has had a chance to warm up and dry out a bit. Good gardeners will apply a 3-inch layer of organic mulch in the autumn, then incorporate it lightly into the soil the following spring, adding an inch or so to the top of the soil to replenish the mulch. This highly recommended practice keeps the soil microorganisms well fed and the garden virtually weed-free.

Inorganic Mulches—Inorganic materials such as gravel, decorative rock and black plastic sheeting are sometimes referred to as *inorganic mulches,* because they serve many of the same purposes as an organic mulch. The difference is that they do not decompose in the soil, nor do they provide any nutritional value to plants. Gravel and rock are usually used as a more permanent form of mulch.

Black plastic is used primarily for weed control. It also absorbs heat, warming the soil and is thus sometimes used to get a head start on the growing season for warm-season crops. For this reason, it should not be used around plantings in hot climates. Because black plastic is unsightly, it's often covered with another mulch, such as gravel or bark chips.

MULCH COVERAGE

Here are the numbers of 2-cubic-foot sacks and cubic yards of mulch needed to cover various-size areas at various thicknesses.

Area in Square Feet	Mulch Thickness					
	1/8"	1/4"	1/2"	1"	2"	3"
	2-Cubic-Foot Sacks					
25	.125	.25	.5	1	2	3
50	.25	.5	1	2	4	6
100	.5	1	2	4	8	12
200	1	2	4	8	16	24
300	1.5	3	6	12	24	36
	Cubic Yards*					
1,000	.49	.8	1.5	3.1	6.25	9.4
2,000	.8	1.5	3.1	6.25	12.5	18.75
3,000	1.2	2.3	4.7	9.4	18.7	28
4,000	1.5	3.1	6.25	12.5	24	37.5
5,000	2	4	8	15.5	31.25	47

*13-1/2 sacks of 2 cubic feet equal 1 cubic yard (27 cubic feet).

Here are the numbers of cubic feet and cubic yards of mulch required to cover 1,000 square feet of area at various depths; also the number of cubic yards required to cover 1 acre at these depths.

Depth in Inches	Cubic Feet per 1,000 Square Feet	Cubic Yards per 1,000 Square Feet	Cubic Yards per Acre
1/8	10.53	0.39	17
1/4	21	0.78	34
3/8	30.5	1.17	51
1/2	42	1.56	68
5/8	52.5	1.95	85
3/4	63	2.34	102
1	84	3.12	136
2	168	6.24	272

PEAT MOSS COVERAGE

Here are the number of square feet covered by standard-size bales of compressed peat moss at various depths.

	COVERAGE IN SQUARE FEET	
Depth in Inches	4.0 Cubic Foot Compressed Bale*	5.6 Cubic Foot Compressed Bale*
1/4	345	480
1/2	172	240
1	86	120
2	43	60
3	28	40
4	21	30
6	14	20

*When loosened, compressed peat moss expands approximately 1.8 times its original volume.

USING PLASTIC MULCH FOR VEGETABLE GARDEN

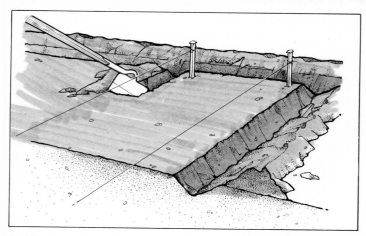

1. After preparing soil, establish straight planting rows with stakes and string. Dig furrows 6 to 8 inches deep. Plastic should be about 12 to 16 inches wider than width of planting row.

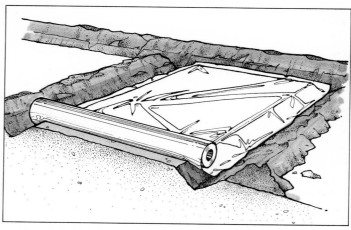

2. Unroll plastic over planting row so edges overlap into furrows.

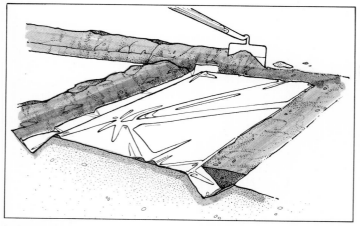

3. Backfill furrows with dirt to hold plastic in place.

4. Dig watering furrows just outside edges of plastic sheet as shown. Use hoe or shovel to punch an "X" at each plant location, then plant seedlings through cuts in plastic.

Pine needles make an attractive mulch in this bed of azaleas.

FERTILIZERS

In ideal situations, the soil naturally supplies plants with all the nutrients they need for healthy growth. Unfortunately, there are many soils where this is not the case, especially in gardens where plants are closely spaced. One example is lawns, where hundreds of thousands of individual grass plants are growing in extremely close proximity to one another, all competing for the same nutrients. Another example is container-grown plants, where nutrients in the soil are eventually leached out by repeated waterings.

There are cases where the nature of the soil itself keeps certain nutrients from being made available to the plant, or where the plant has special requirements, such as acid-loving plants like azaleas, camellias and rhododendrons, that must be met with a unique fertilizer. There are also plants, such as most of the annual vegetable crops, roses, and many citrus trees, that are naturally "heavy feeders," requiring a helping hand from the gardener.

PLANT NUTRIENTS

Before reviewing fertilizers in general, it is important to know a little about how a plant feeds itself. There are 16 nutrients necessary for plant growth. The plant gets three of these—carbon, hydrogen and oxygen—from air and water, the other 13 nutrients from the soil. All 16 nutrients are essential to plant growth. Three of these—nitrogen, phosphorus, and potassium—are called the *primary nutrients* because they are the ones that most often need replenishing and in the greatest amounts. The *secondary nutrients,* magnesium, calcium and sulfur, are added less frequently because most soils contain adequate amounts of these elements. The remaining nutrients, called *trace elements* or *micronutrients,* are required by plants only in minute amounts and rarely have to be added to the soil.

Primary Nutrients—Nitrogen is the most important nutrient in any plant food. It is the ingredient that stimulates new growth and the ingredient usually in shortest supply in soils. Plants use it up quickly and it is rapidly leached from the soil by watering.

Nitrogen is used by plants only when they are growing—during the dormant season, the plant has no use for it. Applied at the wrong time, nitrogen can trigger tender new plant growth during periods of harsh, cold weather. So when you apply a fertilizer, remember that you want to help a plant grow during the period that it naturally wants to grow, which is usually from spring through early autumn.

The other two primary elements are phosphorus and potassium (potash). Both are used by plants to a much lesser degree than nitrogen, but more so than the trace elements.

Trace Elements—In addition to the primary and secondary nutrients, plants require minute amounts of the *trace elements,* also called *micronutrients.* Most soils contain sufficient quantities of these nutrients, but in some soils (notably alkaline ones) some of these nutrients may be "locked-up" in the form of insoluble compounds, making them unavailable to plants. Alkaline soils are often deficient in soluble iron and manganese. Acidifying the soil with sulfur, iron sulfate or ammonium sulfate "releases" these nutrients, making them available to plants.

Most complete fertilizers contain a correct portion of trace elements. Some trace elements are sold individually, but you should not use them unless a plant shows a deficiency. An oversupply of certain trace elements can be toxic to plants. Apply trace elements on their own only if they are specifically recommended to correct a condition diagnosed by your agricultural extension agent or local nursery.

FERTILIZER CHOICES

A quick look at the fertilizer section of any good-sized nursery or garden center reveals a bewildering array of general fertilizers and an even more confusing selection of specialty products. The following information should help simplify your choices and guide you to the products you really need.

Manufacturers of mixed commercial fertilizers are required by law to state on the container the guaranteed content of primary nutrients. When a fertilizer contains all three of these nutrients it is considered a *complete* fertilizer. These three nutrients are used by plants in large amounts and are likely to be deficient in the soil in varying amounts. When you buy a fertilizer, you generally buy it for its content of these materials.

The primary nutrient content of a fertilizer mixture is indicated by its *grade*—a series of three numbers separated by dashes, usually highly visible on some part of the label. The numbers show the percentage of nitrogen, phosphorus and potassium, in that order, contained in the mixture. For example, a mixture with the grade 5-10-5 contains by weight 5% total nitrogen, 10% available phosphorus and 5% soluble potash.

The relative proportions of primary nutrients in a fertilizer mixture determine the suitability of the mixture for specific soils and plants. For example, lawn fertilizers are usually highest in

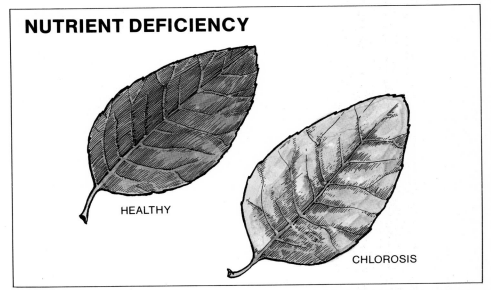

NUTRIENT DEFICIENCY

HEALTHY

CHLOROSIS

Yellowing of leaf tissue between leaf veins usually indicates a deficiency in iron or, less often, zinc. Called *chlorosis,* this condition usually appears on newest growth first. Iron chlorosis is common in alkaline soils. Overall yellowing of older leaves often indicates nitrogen deficiency.

119

FERTILIZER APPLICATION RATES

Here are number of pounds of various-percentage nitrogen fertilizers required to equal 1 pound of actual nitrogen per 1,000 square feet for various-size areas.

Percentage Nitrogen	COVERAGE IN SQUARE FEET					
	500	1,000	1,500	2,000	3,000	1 acre
	POUNDS FERTILIZER					
40%	1.3	2.5	3.8	5	7.6	109
36%	1.4	2.75	4	5.5	8.5	121
30%	1.7	3.5	5	6.6	10	145
25%	2	4	6	8	12	180
20%	2.5	5	7.5	10	15	218
15%	3.3	6.6	10	13	20	308
10%	5	10	15	20	30	436
7%	7	14	21.5	29	43	622
6%	8.5	17	25.5	34	51	726
5%	10	20	30	40	60	870
2%	25	50	75	100	150	2,178

Here are recommended amounts of some soluble dry fertilizers added to water to make nutrient solutions*.

Nutrient	Material	Amount
Nitrogen, Sulfur	Ammonium sulfate	2-3 lbs./100 gal.
Nitrogen	Sodium nitrate	1 oz./gal.
Nitrogen, Calcium	Calcium nitrate	1.5 oz./gal.
Nitrogen, Potassium	Potassium nitrate	1.5 oz./gal.
Nitrogen	Ammonium nitrate	.25 oz./gal.
Nitrogen, Phosphorus	Monoammonium phosphate	1.5 oz./gal.
Potassium, Sulfur	Potassium sulfate	.25 oz./gal.
Magnesium, Sulfur	Magnesium sulfate	1 lb./100 gal.
Iron	Ferrous sulfate	3 lbs/100 gal.

*Adapted from O'Rourke, Louisiana State University.

Here are amounts of soluble dry fertilizers added to water to make foliar sprays to supply nutrients*

Nutrient	Material	Amount	Application
Nitrogen	Urea	.5 lb./100 gal.	Weekly until leaves green
Iron	Ferrous sulfate	.5 oz./gal.	Weekly until leaves green
Manganese	Manganese sulfate	8 oz./100 gal.	Cautiously

*Adapted from O'Rourke, Louisiana State University.

nitrogen—the nutrient used most by lawns. Fertilizers for use on vegetables are usually highest in their proportion of phosphorus for healthy root growth. It may be wasteful, and even harmful, to use the wrong type of fertilizer. Uses for general-purpose fertilizers are customarily listed on the labels, along with recommended amounts for each kind of plant. Always follow the label directions carefully.

Specialty Fertilizers—Some fertilizers are manufactured in grades suitable for use on a specific type of plant. These include fertilizers for tomatoes, lawns, orchids, house plants, acid-loving plants, citrus and avocado, roses and others. While excellent for use on the plants for which they are intended, these are often more expensive than general formulations. Before you buy a specialty fertilizer, ask whether a more general fertilizer—one you may already have on hand—would work just as well.

The Best Deal—As a rule, fertilizers with the same relative proportions of primary nutrients can be used interchangeably. Although fertilizers may be labeled different grades, the nutrient proportions may be the same. For example, 5-10-5 and 6-12-6 are both composed of 1 part nitrogen, 2 parts phosphorus and 1 part potash, but the 6-12-6 contains the higher percentage of these nutrients. It usually is only necessary to alter the rate of application so that the desired amounts of primary nutrients are applied to the area being fed.

Frequently, the price per pound of the *nutrients* in fertilizers containing a high percentage of nutrients may be lower than the price per pound of nutrients in fertilizers containing a lower ratio of percentages. For example, 1 pound of 10-20-10 fertilizer contains the same amount of nutrients as 2 pounds of 5-10-5, yet an 80-pound bag of 10-20-10 may cost only 1/3 more than an 80 pound bag of 5-10-5. For the greatest economy, buy fertilizer for its weight of nutrients per dollar, not for its total weight.

ORGANIC VS. CHEMICAL FERTILIZERS

There has long been a debate over the relative merits of organic versus chemical fertilizers. Actually, a plant cannot tell the difference from the nitrogen contained in fish emulsion, for example, and the nitrogen contained in a manufactured chemical fertilizer. But the plant's reaction to the nutrients is only part of the story.

Generally speaking, organic fertilizers, such as composted manure, activated sewage sludge, cottonseed meal, blood meal and fish emulsion, benefit the soil as well as the plant. The organic material that contains the nutrients also provides the microorganisms in the soil with the materials they need to be active. As a rule, chemical fertilizers are beneficial to the plant only. But the nutrients found in organic formulations are usually much lower in percentages than those in manufactured chemical products. And nutrients in organic fertilizers usually are slower to act.

Most serious gardeners favor a combination of organic and chemical fertilizers—the organic for long-term, light feedings that benefit the soil, and chemical formulations for faster-acting results. In the long run, this is a wise practice.

FERTILIZER FORMS

Commercial fertilizers come in dry or liquid forms. Dry fertilizers may be granules, pellets or powder. The granulated or pelleted forms are the easiest to apply, which can be done using a spreader, and neither blow around as freely nor cake as readily as powdered forms. Dry fertilizers are favored for such wide-area large applications as lawns or ground covers.

Liquid, concentrated fertilizers can be mixed with water and applied with a hose-end sprayer or a liquid proportioner through a drip-irrigation system or sprinkler, or by hand in a bucket or watering can. Being liquid, these fertilizers go to work right away—they do not need additional water to carry nutrients into the root zone. Liquid fertilizers are favored by container gardeners—both indoors and out.

Slow-release fertilizers are available in capsules, spikes and pelleted forms in such a way that their nutrients are available over a long period of time, somewhat like a time-release cold capsule. These products can be a boon, especially for container gardeners who find it hard to remember when to feed their plants. Most of these products last for 3 to 6 months, eliminating the need for frequent feedings.

COMBINATION PRODUCTS

Fertilizer-insecticides and fertilizer-weed killers are generally designed for use on lawns. The USDA has this to say regarding these combination products: "One problem with such combinations is that chemicals are being applied that would normally be used less frequently or not at all. In some instances, fertilizers containing pre-emergence crabgrass herbicides are applied in the fall when, in fact, the herbicide should be applied in the spring. Some fertilizer-herbicide combinations injure or kill trees or shrubs when applied to grass under them. Pushing a fertilizer spreader back and forth under a tree or shrub often results in applying much more than the recommended rate of material.

"Another problem is the concentration of the ingredients. There is no way of adjusting the rate of application for different uses. Combination fertilizer and broadleaf-weed herbicides are often applied when broadleaf weeds are not present in the lawn. Also, there is a tendency to apply fertilizer with a broadleaf weed killer in the summer when cool-season grasses should not be fertilized."

DRY-FERTILIZER SPREADERS

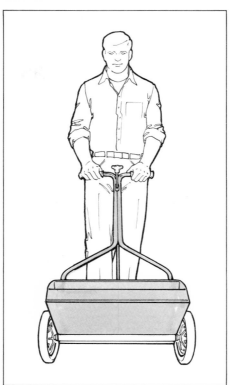

1. Drop spreaders apply accurate amounts of fertilizer to lawns in 18-inch-wide bands. Usually hold more material than other types of spreaders. Preferred if using fertilizer-herbicide combination products.

2. Broadcast spreaders distribute material in bands up to 16 feet wide. Best for large lawns.

3. Hand-held broadcast spreaders are inexpensive but must be refilled often. Good for use on flower beds, ground covers and uneven terrain.

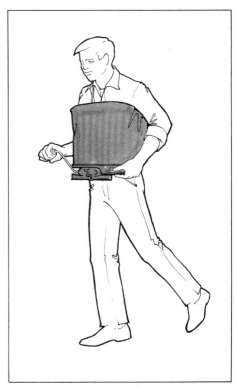

4. Carry-along broadcast spreaders hold more fertilizer than hand-held spreaders and are ideal for feeding large lawns, flower beds, ground covers and uneven areas.

Siphon attachment mixes liquid fertilizer with water at faucet connection, which allows fertilizer to be applied through drip systems, various kinds of sprinklers or other hose-end watering devices.

Root feeder applies fertilizer directly to root zone of trees and large shrubs.

"Homeowners should be aware of these problems and considerations when purchasing and applying fertilizer-insecticide or herbicide combinations. Usually, fertilizers and pesticides are best applied separately."

That may well be the case for combination products for lawn use, but the ones designed for use around roses can be particularly helpful to the home gardener. There are several combination products—fertilizer with systemic insecticide, fertilizer with weed killer, or fertilizer with both insecticide and weed killer—that are both easy to use and very effective. It is extremely important when you use any combination product that you read and follow the label directions explicitly, especially with regard to rates of application and timing.

NON-NITROGEN FERTILIZERS

Fertilizers containing no nitrogen are usually sold as *bloom or fruit enhancers* and they do improve both flower and fruit production when used correctly. Apply them in late autumn through early spring. The phosphorus and potash promote healthy root development and increase the plant's abilities to withstand the rigors of winter. But remember that these are not complete fertilizers, and they are generally meant to be used during the dormant season only. When warm weather arrives in spring, it's time to switch to a complete fertilizer containing nitrogen.

WHAT TO DO WHEN YOU'VE APPLIED TOO MUCH

Nothing is worse than finding out after you've applied a fertilizer that you've applied too much. Although most organic forms of fertilizer are slightly more forgiving when it comes to overfertilization, both organic and chemical formulations will quickly burn or kill a plant or lawn if the concentrations are high enough.

About the only thing you can do is try to leach the nutrients through the soil with repeated heavy waterings. This is particularly effective with plants in containers where it is relatively simple to turn a hose on low and let it completely leach the fertilizer out the drain hole. In garden situations, the chances for leaching successfully are less but it may keep plants from dying completely. This is why it is extremely important to read and understand all label directions and precautions *before* you apply any fertilizer.

PLANTING A LAWN

The following pages detail the fundamentals of planting a lawn with seed, sod, stolons and sprigs. The method you choose and the sequence of operations you follow will vary with site, grass type and your own judgment. But the basics are the same.

Should you plant seed, sod, stolons or sprigs? Seed is least expensive, and more kinds of grasses, custom blends and mixes are available. If you choose to start your lawn with seed, use the highest-quality seed available. The label should show that it contains "0" crop and "0" weed seed. Buying bargain-basement seed saves a few dollars initially, but promises a future of weed pulling and eventual renovation.

The exact mix of seed you plant may be designed for beauty, or practical quality such as tolerance of shade, drought or wear. Seed mixes also vary by climate region. But rather than attempt a technical analysis that accounts for all these factors, the best advice is to rely on a reputable, high-quality seed company.

Sod produces a finished lawn as soon as it is installed. But surprising to some, a sod lawn requires the same degree of soil preparation and frequent watering as a seed law the first few months. Quality of sod, sprigs and plugs is equally important. However, the lawns from which these come are usually grown locally under controlled conditions. Quality is normally very high.

Many southern grasses—notably hybrid Bermudas, centipede and zoysia—are planted by *sprigs,* individual stems or pieces of stems.

Keep in mind that sod, sprigs and plugs are living plants and plant parts. Plant as soon as they are delivered and keep them watered after they are planted—just as with a new seed lawn.

Use the preceding chapter on Lawns to help determine the best grass for you. Plant at the most favorable time of year. Early fall is best for cool-season lawns from seed and bentgrass sprigs. Late spring is the best time to plant seed, sod and plugs or warm-season grasses.

Rich, loose, weed-free soil can make the difference between a beautiful, easy-care lawn and a mediocre-troublesome one. But given an ideal soil, lawns are more robust, more vigorous, less demanding and easier to maintain.

If the planting area is prepared beforehand, sod lawns are easy to install. Pallets of sod were delivered to this site about one hour ago and the job will be complete, including cleanup, in another hour.

PREPARE SOIL

The appearance of your lawn and how you care for it largely depends on soil quality. Lawns will grow only as well as the roots grow. For this reason, well-prepared soil is an important key to a healthy, attractive lawn. You can follow many different procedures in preparing the soil for a lawn planting. Here are the essentials.

TEST SOIL

Fertilizers, lime, sulfur and gypsum frequently are recommended additions to new lawns. But they are not always necessary. If added incorrectly without directives provided by a soil test, they might be wasted or cause harm. The only sure way to know if nutrients and soil pH are correct is by a *soil test*.

With the exceptions of California and Illinois, your nearest county extension office or state university will provide soil sample containers, information and soil analysis. In California and Illinois, look in the Yellow Pages for "Soil Testing Laboratories."

When you collect soil for a test, gather it from various parts of the area to be planted. The laboratory test will then represent the general soil condition of the site. Collect soil by taking small cores of soil from five locations for each sampling area.

Each area of a home lot should be sampled separately. For example, the front lawn area will be one sample, the back lawn area another, and so on. Areas in shade should be sampled separately from sunny areas. Slopes should be sampled separately from low spots.

A soil coring tube is the easiest way to collect samples. When pushed into damp soil, this tube pulls a 3/4-inch-wide and 12-inch-long plug of soil. Place the middle 2 or 3 inches of soil plug in a bucket. You can also take a sample with a trowel or shovel as long as soil is collected from a depth of 4 to 6 inches. Be sure the trowel or shovel is clean and does not have chemicals or other residues that might affect the sample.

Mix the soil samples from the five locations in a bucket. Place 1 or 2 cups of this mixed soil in the container provided by the laboratory.

CLEAN AND GRADE SOIL

Remove all debris, including large stones, roots, stumps and construction materials. Do not bury debris under the future lawn.

Eliminate any perennial weedy grasses such as quackgrass, Bermudagrass and creeping bentgrass. Spray with glyphosate herbicide when weeds are actively growing. Water weeds before spraying. Wait 7 to 10 days before removing weeds to be sure they are completely dead.

If extensive grading is necessary, scrape away and retain topsoil. Eliminate low areas that may become basins for standing water. Contour soil surface so water will run off. A slight, 1 percent grade sloping away from buildings is recommended. Steeper grades make lawn establishment and maintenance more difficult. Contours can be used to add interest and blend with natural or created landscape features.

Redistribute topsoil after rough grade is established. Allow soil to settle before planting. Uneven settling around buildings and over water and sewer trenches is common. Several deep waterings will aid settling.

AMEND SOIL

Poor soil is a major cause of lawn problems. The only time soil can be significantly improved is before planting. Improving soil under an existing lawn is possible but it is a gradual and difficult process.

If the composition of your soil is largely clay or sand, mix organic material—composted sawdust, fir or redwood bark or peat moss—into the top 4 to 6 inches. Water a day or two before finishing the soil preparation. This will help eliminate large, hard clods.

Fertilizer—Phosphorus and potassium applications should be based on soil test information. As a rule, do not apply more than 2 pounds of actual nitrogen per 1,000 square feet before seeding or sodding. If a soil test is not possible, the general recommendation calls for 15 to 20 pounds of 10-10-10 fertilizer per 1,000 square feet. Thoroughly mix the fertilizer into the soil.

Lime—Use lime only if the soil test indicates the pH is below 6.0. Excessive lime causes problems, especially in sandy soil. Thoroughly incorporate ground limestone into the top 4 to 6 inches of soil during one of the initial cultivations.

Sulfur—If soil pH is above 7.5, lower it by applying elemental sulfur.

Gypsum—This amendment is often recommended to improve clay soils. But gypsum definitely does not loosen heavy clay soils unless sodium content is excessive. Benefits are negligible unless addition is specifically recommended by a soil test laboratory. Use gypsum if soil is high in "exchangable sodium percentage," which means it is high in sodium salt. Gypsum is also recommended if pH is acceptable and either calcium or sulfate is low.

PREPARE SEEDBED AND ELIMINATE WEEDS

Level, roll and rake the weed-free seedbed before planting. Use a roller half-filled with water to firm seedbed. Rollers are available from nurseries and rental yards. Your footsteps will indicate the proper firmness. If steps leave an impression more than 1/2 inch deep, roll again. Rolling will also reveal those slightly high or low areas that need further leveling.

If you plan to install an underground sprinkler system, do so at this stage.

If sod is your choice, planting can follow immediately after final preparation of soil. Be sure that all perennial weeds are controlled. Soil level should be 1/2 to 1 inch below final grade, to accommodate sod thickness.

Adjusting pH

To raise pH to 6.5, apply ground limestone

| if pH is | Pounds to apply per 1,000 square feet | |
	Sandy Soil	Clay Soil
5.5-5.9	25-50	50-100
5.0-5.5	50-100	75-150
4.5-5.0	75-150	100-200

To lower pH to 6.5, apply elemental sulfur

| if pH is | Pounds to apply per 1,000 square feet | |
	Sandy Soil	Clay Soil
7.5	10-25	20-25
8.0	25-35	35-50
8.5	35-50	40-50

Adding Soil Amendment

Cubic yards of material to apply

| Square feet of area | Amendment thickness over area | | |
	2 inches *1/4 by volume	3 inches 1/3 by volume	4 inches 1/2 by volume
250	1.56	2.34	3.12
500	3.12	4.68	6.24
1,000	6.24	9.36	12.48
1,500	9.36	14.04	18.72

*Assuming the amendment is tilled into soil to 8-inch depth.

If weeds are present and you plan to sow seed or plant sprigs, stolons or plugs, make another effort to control weeds now. You have already cleaned the lawn area of existing perennial weeds and grasses. Now you must reduce the number of weed seeds waiting on the surface. Once you plant and begin watering, the weeds will germinate and compete with your lawn grass. Sod covers these weed seeds and prevents their growth.

There are three ways to reduce the number of weeds at this time: *fumigation, pre-emergent herbicides* and *fallowing.* Fumigation is an involved process using potent chemicals, and is best performed by landscape maintenance professionals. Consider if you anticipate a particularly severe weed problem.

An alternative is to use a pre-emergent herbicide. Many kinds are compatible with newly planted plugs. A few might be used with newly planted stolons and sprigs—check labels, cooperative extension agents and manufacturers. Siduron, which is sold under the trade name Tupersan, prevents the growth of many weeds such as crabgrass and Ber-

mudagrass without affecting the grass seed that you sow. Do not use it on newly seeded Bermudagrass or bentgrass lawns. Siduron is also recommended when reseeding renovated lawns.

Fallowing is the third alternative. Basically, this means to wait out the weeds. This will take 6 weeks at least, sometimes longer. Water the prepared seedbed just as if seed is sown. In a few days, weed growth appears. Eliminate them with a spray of cacodylic acid herbicide. Repeat this cycle until no new weed growth appears after you water. Rather than using herbicide, you can lightly cultivate to eliminate weeds. However, each time soil surface is disturbed, previously buried weed seeds are brought to the surface. More time is then required to make the bed relatively weed-free.

SOWING SEED

Early fall is the best time to establish a cool-season lawn from seed. Early spring is an acceptable alternative, but cool, often excessively wet soil and severe competition from annual weeds are significant problems. Late spring is the

best time to establish a warm-season lawn from seed. Midsummer plantings are more difficult with either type because of high temperatures, lack of rainfall and weed competition.

Sow seed at the recommended rate. Evenly sow one half of the total amount in one direction and the remaining half in the crisscross direction. Use a spinning, *centrifugal* spreader for large areas, or the more comon and more controllable *drop* spreader for moderate-size lawns. After seeding, rake very lightly with a stiff, narrow-pronged rake. You do not want to move seed, just cover it slightly. An alternative to raking soil over seed is to cover the seedbed with a mulch or peat moss, composted fir bark or similar light organic material. Mulch should not be more than 1/4 inch thick. Finally, lightly roll mulch and seed with a roller *half-filled* with water to ensure good contact between seed and soil.

Watering—Perhaps the most important step to a new lawn from seed is regular watering. If soil is very dry, water deeply before planting. The soil surface must be kept moist at all times after planting.

ANNUALS

Flowering annuals are synonymous with dramatic garden color, and it is no wonder. No other plants will give you more color over a longer period at less cost than flowering annuals. The vibrant pinks of petunias, the shimmering reds of zinnias and the glowing yellows of marigolds equal the most colorful tulips. As a bonus, annuals put on a far-longer flowering display, lasting for weeks or even months.

On a per-plant basis, annuals are less expensive than perennials or flowering bulbs. One daffodil bulb, blooming for about 10 days each year, costs approximately 50¢. A packet of marigold seeds for the same money can produce more than 100 plants, flowering non-stop for 100 days or more. You can see why annuals have such universal appeal.

ANNUALS, BIENNIALS, PERENNIALS

Technically, *annuals* are a large group of plants that complete their life cycles in a single growing season. An annual germinates, flowers, sets seeds and dies with the first frost. In nature, plants grow from these seeds that remain dormant until conditions are right for germination. When light, temperature, moisture and other factors are correct for the particular annual, the life cycle begins all over again.

Because they must complete their life cycle in a single season, flowers of most annuals are bright and colorful. The colorful flowers attract the attention of pollinating insects, to help ensure a good crop of seeds for the next cycle of life.

A few *biennials*—plants needing two seasons to produce flowers and then die—can be grown to bloom the first year. The trick is to start seeds early in the year so they have enough time to mature and flower. Some of these, such as foxglove 'Foxy' and sweet William 'Wee Willie', have been specially bred to possess this first-season quality.

A few *perennials*—plants that require two seasons to flower and live year after year—can be grown to flower as annuals. One example is gloriosa daisy. Seeds started early in the season will flower the first year. Plants then perform as hardy perennials thereafter, flowering year after year.

ANNUALS IN THE LANDSCAPE

Annuals are such a diverse group of plants they can be used in many ways. Because they have varied cultural requirements, certain annuals do better in certain climates or locations. Some prefer cool conditions, producing the best blooms either early or late during the growing season. Pansies, sweet peas and snapdragons are representative of this group. Other annuals bloom more spectacularly during warm, sunny periods. Many of these originate from desert areas. Marigolds, zinnias and portulacas are examples of heat-lovers. Some annuals, such as impatiens and begonias, prefer shade but the majority do best in

Left: Beautiful flower border features 'First Lady' marigolds, cactus-flower zinnias and 'St. John's Fire' scarlet sage. Above: Silver-gray of 'Silver Lace' dusty miller creates striking divider between beds of petunias and American marigolds.

A garden of annuals can take many forms. Left: Large-scale planting of different annuals is as colorful as any garden. Above: View of 'Irish Eyes' gloriosa daisy shows striking simplicity.

an open, sunny location.

Annuals can be used to create beautiful, temporary ground covers. Others make spectacular hanging baskets—striking in entryways. Some are best adapted to containers as greenhouse plants, or planted in tubs for placement on decks and patios. Certain ones are valued for drying to make dried arrangements. Some thrive in dry walls and rock gardens. Some annuals are suitable for cutting to make spectacular fresh-flower arrangements. In fact, a *cutting garden*—a rectangular plot of annuals resembling a vegetable garden—is becoming a popular feature among homeowners.

Many kinds of annuals are used as *bedding plants*. This is a term used frequently in the book. It refers to annuals commonly planted in flower beds and borders along walks and paths. Petunias,

impatiens and marigolds are the most popular in the group. They are widely available as transplants from garden centers.

Annuals also play an important role in wildflower or naturalistic landscapes. Meadows, banks, hillsides and roadsides sparkle when planted with coreopsis, gaillardias, poppies, godetias and larkspur.

ABOUT THIS SECTION

The following pages provide a complete guide to growing annuals successfully. Emphasis has been placed on 10 important factors:

1. Selection of a Good Site—Some annuals tolerate shade but most do best with full sun. A location receiving full sun allows you to plant the widest selection and most colorful kinds of annuals.

If you have no choice and some of your garden is in partial shade, grow impatiens. It is the best annual for shade.

2. Garden Layout and Design—Beds, borders and cutting gardens are the most popular ways to grow flowering annuals. Also, there are many outstanding public display gardens and test gardens you can visit. These are great places for ideas. Use them to make your planting plans and variety selections. Many of these gardens are All-America display gardens, where recent award winners can be seen and evaluated.

If space is at a premium, consider container plantings.

3. Principles of Color—Like an artist, the gardener uses the colors of flowers and foliage to paint and accent the landscape. Use a color wheel to guide you in making color selections.

4. Recommended Varieties—Strong-

Annuals are popular for creating wildflower meadows. Field of annual calliopsis and Queen-Anne's lace was established in one season.

A single color can be dramatic. This is a seed-production field of French marigolds near Lompoc, California. The same effect can be achieved on a smaller scale in the home landscape.

'Springtime' verbena creates a multicolor carpet in this island bed.

ly consider *hybrids* and those that have won awards in the All-America Selections, the national seed trials.

5. Soil Preparation—Soil quality is not as necessary as it is for growing vegetables, but good soil will increase your flower-garden success. Testing soil, adding amendments and increasing soil fertility will ensure best results for most annuals.

6. Seeds, Plants and Supplies— After investing time, materials and effort in locating, planning and preparing your garden, you should plant quality seeds or transplants. This is usually the least expensive part of your entire investment. Learn how to buy quality transplants. Purchase seeds from reputable companies, either from a seed rack or mail-order catalog.

7. When and How to Plant—Annuals can be grouped into two categories: *har-dy annuals* that tolerate mild frosts, and *tender annuals* that are damaged by frost. Also, knowing whether a plant is a *cool-season* annual or a *warm-season* annual is helpful.

8. Irrigation—Some annuals are drought resistant. Regular amounts of water ensure earliest flowers, largest flower size and prolific bloom over a longer period. Drip irrigation as a watering method is becoming more popular.

9. Weed Control—Weeds can dampen your enthusiasm for gardening faster than anything. Mulching is a simple method of weed control. Decorative mulches will not detract from the beauty of your flower garden.

10. Pest and Disease Control—Prevention is the best method of pest and disease control. Keeping your garden clean avoids most problems. Being alert for early signs of trouble is important.

Plant and Flower Forms

Most annuals are available in dwarf and tall forms, and sizes in between. The illustration below compares relative sizes of a tall gloriosa daisy, left, to a dwarf variety.

Single flower, top right, means the flower has a single layer of petals. This is 'Golden Daisy' gloriosa daisy.

Double flower, second right, has more than one layer of petals. If the multilayers of petals form a complete globe, the flower is *fully double.* If the flower forms a partial globe, it is a *semidouble.* This fully double variety is 'Double Gold' gloriosa daisy.

Bicolor flower, third right, has two distinct color patterns in the petals. This 'Pinwheel' gloriosa daisy has a mahogany-color zone around a dark *eye,* or center, creating a beautiful contrast to the yellow petal tips.

Star flower, fourth right, is created if a bicolor flower has bands meeting at the center. This is 'Star Joy' petunia.

Picotee flower, fifth right, is a bicolor with contrasting petal edges. This is 'Red Picotee' petunia, winner of an All-America award.

Annuals Selection Guide

Annuals for Beds and Borders

An annual bed is usually an island of soil—either square, round, rectangular or kidney shape— surrounded by paving or lawn. An annual border is usually a long, narrow strip—either straight or free-form—backed by a wall, fence or hedge.

The most important considerations when planning beds and borders are *height* and *color*.

The following flowering annuals are noted for long-lasting displays in beds and borders under a wide range of conditions. Those marked with an asterisk are widely available as bedding plants from garden centers.

*Begonia, Wax	Nicotiana
Cleome	*Pansy
Celosia	Pepper, Ornamental
Chrysanthemum	*Petunia
*Coleus	*Portulaca
*Dahlia	*Snapdragon
*Dusty miller	*Salvia
*Geranium	Torenia (Wishbone flower)
Gloriosa daisy	Verbena
*Impatiens	Viola
*Lobelia	Vinca
*Marigold	*Zinnia
Nasturtium	

'Inca Orange' marigold edged with dusty miller makes a magnificent border.

Annuals for Cutting

By choosing the right varieties, annuals planted in beds and borders can be used for cutting fresh flowers. Certain kinds are stimulated into producing more blooms the more they are cut. These are called *cut-and-come-again.* It's not always easy to step into formal beds and borders to cut flowers without causing damage. It makes sense to have a special cutting garden in a separate section of the garden.

Those plants marked with an asterisk are cut-and-come-again varieties.

*Ageratum	*Larkspur
*Aster	Lavatera
Arcotis	*Marigold
Bells of Ireland	Mignonette
Calliopsis	Penstemon
*Calendula	Phlox
*Carnation	*Poppy, Iceland
*Celosia	Salpiglossis
*Chrysanthemum	*Scabiosa
Cleome	Schizanthus
Columbine	*Shasta daisy
*Cornflower	*Snapdragon
*Cosmos	Statice
*Cynoglossum	Stocks
*Dahlia	*Strawflower
Delphinium	Sunflower
Dianthus	Sweet pea
Feverfew	Sweet William
Foxglove	Tidy tips
*Gaillardia	Tigridia
Gerbera	*Tithonia
*Gloriosa daisy	Venidium
*Gypsophila	Verbena
Helipterum	Wallflower, Siberian
Hunnemannia (Mexican tulip poppy)	Xeranthemum
	*Zinnia

Annuals for Edging

A flower bed or border featuring tall annuals looks best with a well-defined edge. This can be created by low-growing flowering annuals, which fill in the base of the planting with color. Even low beds and borders used to create a carpet effect generally look better framed with colorful edging plants.

Listed below are some good, low-growing plants for edging. Those marked with an asterisk are extremely compact and especially desirable for this use.

*Ageratum	*Pansy
*Alyssum	*Pepper, Ornamental
Anchusa (Dwarf types)	Petunia
Aster (Dwarf border types)	Phacelia
*Begonia, Wax (Dwarf types)	Phlox (Dwarf types)
Browallia (Dwarf types)	Portulaca
Candytuft	*Sanvitalia
Cuphia (Cigar plant)	Schizanthus
*Dahlberg daisy	*Snapdragon (Miniature kinds)
*Dianthus	Sweet William (Dwarf kinds)
*Dusty miller	Torenia
*Felicia (Dwarf types)	Vinca
*Forget-me-not	*Viola
Gazania	Zinnia (Miniature kinds)
Impatiens (Dwarf types)	
Kale, Ornamental	
Linaria	
Livingstone daisy	
*Lobelia	
*Marigold, French (Dwarf types)	
*Marigold, Signet	
Mimulus	
*Nemesia	
Nemophila	
*Nierembergia	

Shade-Loving Annuals

There are many kinds of shade—light shade, deep shade, low shade, high shade, shade with moist soil, shade with dry soil, morning shade, afternoon shade and others. The worst kinds of shade are deep shade and shade with dry soils. Annuals recommended for shade generally do not tolerate these difficult conditions. Dense shade can sometimes be improved by pruning tree branches to allow more penetration of sunlight.

Impatiens are by far the most popular flowering annual for shade. The best shade is a moist, partially shaded area, either from high, light leaf cover or from a few hours of morning or afternoon shade.

In the following, annuals most tolerant of shade are noted with an asterisk.

Anchusa	Nicotiana
*Begonia	Primula
Browallia	Salvia splendens (Scarlet
Canterbury bells	sage)
*Coleus	Thunbergia (Black-eyed
*Impatiens	Susan vine)
Lobelia	*Torenia (Wishbone flower)
*Mimulus (Monkey flower)	Viola
Forget-me-not	
Nemophila (Baby blue-eyes)	

'Futura' impatiens add bright spot of color in the shade.

Annuals for Dry Places and Rock Gardens

Exposed, dry slopes and expanses of flat, open ground are common problem areas around a home. Lawn grasses and perennial ground covers are the first plants to consider for these sites. But many flowering annuals—most from desert areas of Mexico, South America and South Africa—can be used to create a dramatic color scheme. Problem dry areas can be found along the south-facing wall of a house, edging of a driveway, edge of a retaining wall and along property lines. A particular problem spot is where the soil meets hot pavement.

The best rock gardens rely heavily on three natural elements—*plants, rocks* and *water*. If water is unavailable, plants and rocks can work well together. Usually rock gardens feature perennials and flowering bulbs as the main plantings. These remain in permanent positions from year to year. Annuals are added in clumps and pockets for extra color. Particularly effective are ground-hugging annuals, and those that form bushy, compact clumps.

If possible, locate rock gardens on slopes. Good drainage is essential. In choosing rocks for the garden, use those prevalent locally to give your garden a more natural appearance.

Prepare the site before setting stones into place. Dig over the original soil and remove weed roots and other obstructions. Move in some good topsoil and grade the site. You may need to use railroad ties to create a retaining wall.

Begin laying rocks at the lowest level. Try to create natural ridges and outcrops. Place flat-top rocks where they can be used for steppingstones to gain access to different parts of the garden. Group rocks into natural-looking clusters to create bluffs. Place broadest-side facing down and set it firmly in soil. Stones that wobble when stepped on can cause injury.

The following plants are "survivors." They do well in dry places and are especially suited for growing in rock gardens and along dry walls. Many are at home planted with dwarf evergreens and perennials. Varieties with asterisks are specially recommended for rock gardens and dry walls.

Amaranthus	Kochia (Burning bush)
*Arctotis	*Marigold
Brachycome	*Mesembryanthemum
*California poppy	(Livingstone daisy)
*Calliopsis	Morning glory (Dwarf kinds)
*Candytuft	*Nasturtium
Cornflower	Petunia
*Dahlberg daisy	Phlox
*Dianthus	*Polygonum (Knotweed)
*Dimorphotheca	*Portulaca
*Dusty miller (especially	Salvia (Scarlet sage)
cineraria)	*Sanvitalia (Creeping
Euphorbia marginata	zinnia)
(Snow-on-the-mountain)	Tidy tips
Four o'clock	Tithonia (Mexican
Gaillardia	sunflower)
*Gazania	Venidium
Globe amaranth	*Verbena
(Gomphrena)	*Vinca
Gloriosa daisy	Zinnia (Dwarf kinds)
Grasses, Ornamental	
*Gypsophila	

Annuals for Naturalizing and Wildflower Plantings

Many annuals are native to North America. Because they reseed themselves freely, they are suitable for planting in open meadows, along slopes for erosion control and in vacant lots. Some types tolerate shade and can be planted in woodland. Many non-natives will adapt and naturalize.

When planting mixtures, it's best to plant at least 75% native plants. Choose plants adapted to your particular climate. Some seed companies sell special mixtures with local conditions in mind. For example, a Western wildflower mixture might contain godetias, scarlet flax, cornflowers, Shirley poppies, wild larkspur, California poppies and other native species. A Southern wildflower mixture might be made up of cosmos, calliopsis, gaillardias and black-eyed Susans. Mountain mixtures, desert mixtures and shade mixtures are also available.

Wildflower mixtures generally contain plants of different vigor. Sometimes a particular species dominates and crowds out the other wildflowers after the first year. Most commercial mixtures contain some perennial species. The annuals provide instant color. If a mixture effect is desired each year, it is often better to dig the planting area each spring and reseed exclusively with annuals. The best wildflower meadows are planted this way.

Sow seeds of mixtures alone or with non-spreading clump grasses such as blue fescue or chewing fescue. Plant at the rate of 1/2 pound of grass seed per 1,000 square feet—20 to 25 pounds per acre. The fescue grass grows quickly and helps to stabilize the soil. An appropriate planting rate for most wildflower mixtures is 4 ounces per 1,000 square feet—4 to 7 pounds per acre.

Pasture grasses—bluegrass, bromegrass, crested wheatgrass and annual ryegrass—will dominate and crowd out your wildflowers. Such grasses are planted where only a green ground cover is desired.

On steep slopes and in sandy, non-irrigated areas, add a layer of coarse gravel or 1- to 2-inch lava rock before sowing. These materials help control erosion and keep soil moist. Till soil and apply rock. Then broadcast seeds and soak thoroughly with water. Seeds will sprout in crevices where they are in contact with moist soil.

Do not fertilize wildflower plantings unless soil is extremely poor. Fertilizers generally encourage excessive weed and grass growth at the expense of wildflower plants. Provide adequate moisture and recommended seeding rates for wildflowers. This allows wildflowers to germinate rapidly and compete with seeds and grasses, crowding them out.

Plants in this list marked with an asterisk * are *warm-season* annuals. They do well where summers are hot. Others are *cool-season* annuals that do best in most coastal locations and wherever summers are cool. Most reseed and overwinter in locations where the ground does not freeze.

Alyssum
Brachycome (Swan River daisy)
Calendula
*Calliopsis
Chrysanthemum carinatum
Chrysanthemum coronarium
Clarkia
Cornflower
*Cosmos
Daisy, Shasta
Dimorphotheca (African daisy)
Forget-me-not
*Four o'clock
Foxglove
*Gaillardia
*Gazania
Gilia tricolor (Bird's eyes)
*Gloriosa daisy
Godetia
Gypsophila (Baby's breath)
Hunnemannia (Mexican tulip poppy)
Larkspur, Rocket
*Lavatera
Linaria
Nasturtium
Nemophila
Pennisetum ruppelii (Ornamental grass)
Phacelia
Phlox drummondii
Poppy, California
Poppy, Iceland
Poppy, Shirley
*Salvia farinacea
Scarlet flax
*Sunflower
Tidy tips
Wallflower

Dry slope is planted with annual statice. Rock border helps reduce soil erosion.

California poppies are popular in Western wildflower mixes.

Annuals for Ground Covers

Many locations exist around the home where a carpet effect is desired. Annual ground covers can be used to cover a slope, edge a driveway and frame a flower bed. The following are especially useful as flowering ground covers. Those that last the longest are noted with an asterisk.

African daisy
  (Dimorphotheca)
Cuphea (Cigar flower)
*Dahlberg daisy
Dianthus barbatus (Sweet
  William)
Dianthus chinensis (China
  pinks)
Gazania
Livingstone daisy

*Nasturtium
Phlox
*Polygonum capitatum
  (Knotweed)
*Portulaca
*Sanvitalia (Creeping
  zinnia)
*Vinca
*Zinnia angustifolia

'Fordhook Finest' annual phlox makes a spectacular, flowering ground cover for cool, sunny locations.

Annuals for Moist Soils

No flowering annual can tolerate constantly wet roots like waterlilies and other "aquatic" plants. Some can be grown in moist soil such as at the edge of ponds, lakes and stream banks. The best are marked with an asterisk.

Cleome (Spider plant)
Euphorbia marginata
  (Snow-on-the-mountain)
*Forget-me-not
*Mignonette
Mimulus (Monkey flower)

Nasturtium
*Primula
Ricinus (Castor bean
  plant)
Vinca
Viola

Annuals for Indoors

Any flowering annual suited for growth indoors in a greenhouse or sunroom is known as a *pot plant.* Some do well only in a sheltered indoor environment. Others grow well outdoors and indoors. When fall frost dates approach, it's possible to dig up some of your outdoor plants and transfer them to pots for flowers indoors. It may take a little grooming to make them presentable, but it is usually worth it. Plants marked with an asterisk below can be treated this way. To prepare them for an extended life indoors, follow this step-by-step procedure.

1. Select bushy, compact plants. These can be dug before frost, placed in pots, trimmed a bit and taken indoors.
2. If plants are tall and straggly, you can often take *stem cuttings.* This is possible with impatiens, coleus, geraniums and wax begonias. Using a sharp knife, remove a non-flowering shoot with 6 inches of stem. Dip the base in rooting hormone and plant in moist potting soil.
3. You can revive straggly plants for indoor flowering —especially petunias and wax begonias—by pruning away top growth to within 3 inches of stem. Prune roots so you have a rootball that will fit comfortably into a 5-inch pot. Add about 1 inch of new potting soil, surrounding the original rootball. Water and fertilize every 2 weeks with liquid house-plant fertilizer.

*Begonia, Wax
*Browallia
Calceolaria
Calendula
Candytuft
Carnation
*Chrysanthemum
Cineraria
*Coleus
*Cuphea
Felicia
Forget-me-not
*Geranium
Gerbera
Heliotrope
*Impatiens
*Lobelia
Marigold

Mesembryanthemum
  (Livingstone daisies)
*Nasturtium
Pansy
*Pepper, Ornamental
*Petunia
Primula
Salpiglossis
Salvia
Schizanthus
Snapdragon
*Solanum, Ornamental
Stocks
*Thunbergia
*Torenia
*Vinca
*Viola

Annuals for Fragrance

An unfortunate side effect of plant breeding has been the loss of fragrance in many modern varieties. Modern sweet peas, for example, are fragrant but do not have the strong fragrance of old-fashion varieties. To correct the situation, some seedsmen now offer special collections of old-fashion varieties noted for intense fragrance.

Although sweet peas are the most popular flowers grown for fragrance, carnations, mignonette, sweet William and stocks are other favorites. Strongly fragrant annuals are noted with an asterisk.

Brachycome (Swan River
  daisy)
*Carnation
Four o'clock
*Heliotrope
*Mignonette
Nasturtium
Nicotiana
*Night-blooming stocks

Petunia
Primula
Siberian wallflower
Snapdragon
*Stocks
Sweet alyssum
*Sweet pea
Sweet sultan
*Sweet William

Annual Vines

Climbing plants are often needed to decorate a bare wall. If surfaces are smooth, a trellis may be necessary for vines to climb. Vines are also popular for covering fences—especially chain-link and split-rail—or to cover unsightly utility poles. Those with an asterisk in the following list produce thick foliage cover, sufficient to create a screen for privacy. Morning glories are the most popular, all-purpose, flowering vine.

Canary creeper
*Cypress vine
Geranium (Vining, ivy-leaf)
*Gourds, Ornamental
Hyacinth bean
*Moonflower

*Morning glory
Nasturtium (Tall kinds)
Sweet pea
*Thunbergia (Black-eyed Susan vine)

'Heavenly Blue' Morning glory is North America's most popular flowering vine.

Annuals For Dried Arrangements

Dried-flower arrangements can be expensive to buy in flower shops and gift stores. Quality-made arrangements retain their colors for years.

Using special commercial drying agents such as silica gel, it's possible to dry any flowering annual. In addition, some plants can be preserved simply by *air drying*, hanging them upside down in bunches in a cool, dry, dark place. These have papery petals and are called *everlasting* flowers. The most popular are strawflowers.

To preserve flowers by using a drying agent, follow these steps:
1. Cut flowers on a dry, sunny day when they are in peak bloom. Avoid flowers that are wilted or blemished.
2. Exclude light during drying process because it fades petal colors quickly.
3. Place flowers face down in deep bowl filled with *drying agent*. A drying agent can be any dry, absorbent powder, but silica gel works best. Flowers on spikes can be placed horizontally. Cover flowers with more drying agent, filling in all contours until flower is completely covered.
4. How long to dry depends on the variety. Usually the process is complete in 4 to 6 days. Depth of color and natural petal formation depends on how fast moisture is removed.

Pressed Flowers—Making floral prints with pressed flowers is also fun. Place flowers between pages of blotting paper. Insert them in a flower press or between the pages of a heavy book. Leave there for up to 7 days until dry. Flowers with flat faces such as violas, pansies, daisies and calliopsis are good subjects. Gently lift dried flowers from blotting paper and arrange them on cards for framing. Stick them in place with glue.

Flowers marked with an asterisk can be air-dried. Others require use of a drying agent.

Aster
*Bells of Ireland
Blue-lace flower
Calendula
*Celosia, Crested
*Chinese lantern
Chrysanthemum
Cornflower
Cosmos
Dahlia
Daisy, Shasta
*Globe amaranth
Gloriosa daisy

*Gourds, Ornamental
*Grasses, Ornamental
Gypsophila
Larkspur
Marigold
Pansy
*Statice
*Star flower (Scabiosa stellata)
*Strawflowers (Helichrysum)
Sweet sultan
Tahoka daisy

Strawflowers are the most popular annuals for dried arrangements.

Mail-Order Seed Catalogs

Agway Inc.
Box 4933
Syracuse, NY 13221
Color catalog with basic selection of annuals. Catalog free.

Applewood Seed Co.
Box 10761, Edgemont Station
Golden, CO 80401
Specialists in seeds for wildflower plantings. Catalog free.

W. Atlee Burpee
300 Park Ave.
Warminster, PA 18974
Extensive selection of annuals, many developed by the company's own plant-breeding program. Burpee also maintains trial gardens for testing and evaluating new varieties, including an All-America trial garden. Catalog free.

Comstock Ferre & Co.
263 Main St.
Wethersfield, CT 06109
Color catalog lists old and new annuals. Company also maintains trial gardens for testing and evaluating new varieties, including an All-America trial garden. Catalog free.

Dominion Seed House
115 Guelph St.
Georgetown, Ontario
Canada L7G 4A2
Good selection of annuals for Canada. Free full-color catalog available to Canadian gardeners only. Dominion maintains trial gardens for evaluating new varieties.

Farmer Seed & Nursery Co.
818 N.W. Fourth St.
Faribault, MN 55021
Good selection of flower seeds. Full-color catalog free.

Henry Field Seed & Nursery Co.
407 Sycamore St.
Shenandoah, IA 51602
Beautiful, full-color catalog offers an extensive listing of annuals. Catalog free.

Gurney Seed & Nursery Co.
Yankton, SD 57079
One of America's largest seed and nursery catalogs. Extensive list of annuals. Catalog free.

Jackson & Perkins
Box 1028
Medford, OR 97501
Beautiful, full-color catalog featuring good selection of annuals. Catalog free.

Joseph Harris Co.
Moreton Farm
Rochester, NY 14624
Excellent listing of annuals, many developed by the company's own breeders. Company maintains trial gardens for testing and evaluating new varieties, including an All-America trial garden. Full-color catalog is free.

The Charles Hart Seed Co.
Main & Hart Streets
Wethersfield, CT 06109
Good selection. Catalog free.

H.G. Hastings Co.
Box 4274
Atlanta, GA 30302
Assortment of annuals especially suited for Southern gardeners. Full-color catalog free.

Inter-State Nurseries
Hamburg, IA 51640
Full-color catalog features good selection of annuals. Catalog free.

J.W. Jung Seed Co.
Randolph, WI 53956
Full-color catalog features basic selection of annuals. Catalog free.

Johnny's Selected Seeds
Albion, ME 04910
Good selection of annuals for Northeast gardens.

Laval Seeds Inc.
3505 Boul St. Martin
Chomedey Laval
Quebec, Canada H7V 2T3
Quality seed house serving Canadian gardeners. Catalog free.

Orol Ledden & Sons
Center St.
Sewell, NJ 08080
Good selection. Catalog free.

Earl May Seed & Nursery Co.
Shenandoah, IA 51603
Full-color catalog featuring good selection of flowering annuals. Maintains trial gardens for testing and evaluating new varieties, including an All-America trial garden. Catalog free.

McLaughlins Seeds
Box 550
Mead, WA 99021
Flower-seed supplier serving mostly West-Coast gardeners. Catalog free.

Mellingers Inc.
North Lima, OH 44452
Good listing of annuals. Catalog free.

L. L. Olds Seed Co.
2901 Packers Ave.
Madison, WI 53707
Colorful catalog features good selection of quality annuals. Catalog free.

George W. Park Seed Inc.
Greenwood, SC 29647
Flower-seed specialists. Full-color catalog features extensive list of annuals. Company maintains trial gardens for evaluating new varieties, including an All-America trial garden. Catalog free.

W.H. Perron & Co. Ltd.
515 Labelle Blvd.
Chomedey Laval
Quebec, Canada H7V 2T3
Colorful catalog offers an excellent selection of annuals for Canadian gardens. Company maintains extensive trial gardens for evaluating new varieties, including an All-America trial garden. Catalog free.

Seedway Inc.
Hall, NY 14463
Formerly Robson's Seeds. Flowering annuals are especially selected for the Northeast. Full-color catalog free.

R.H. Shumway
628 Cedar St.
Rockford, IL 61101
Full-color catalog offers good selection of annuals, both newly developed and established. Catalog free.

Stokes Seeds Inc.
Box 548
Buffalo, NY 14240
This colorful catalog features an excellent selection of annuals, many that are difficult to obtain elsewhere. Company maintains trial gardens for testing new varieties, including an All-America trial garden. Catalog free. Canadian gardeners should write to:
Box 10, St. Catharines, Ontario, Canada.
L2R 6R6

Suttons Seeds
Hele Road
Torquay, Devon, England
Suttons does not have a mailing address in the United States or Canada, but they will supply free color catalog upon request. Company maintains trial gardens for evaluating new varieties.

T & T Seeds Ltd.
120 Lombard Ave.
Winnipeg, Manitoba, Canada R3B 3A9
Good selection of annuals for Canadian gardens. Catalog free.

Thompson & Morgan
Box 100
Farmingdale, NJ 07727
Full-color catalog claims to feature the most extensive listing of flower seeds in the world. Established company is headquartered in England, sold seeds to Charles Darwin. Catalog free.

Otis S. Twilley Seed Co.
Box 65
Trevose, PA 19047
Full-color catalog offering an excellent selection of flower seeds. Company maintains trial gardens for testing new varieties, including an All-America trial garden. Catalog free.

Wyatt-Quarles Seed Co.
331 S. Wilmington St.
Raleigh, NC 27602
Good selection of flower seeds for Southern gardeners. Catalog free.

STARTING WITH SEEDS—INDOORS AND OUTDOORS

When growing annuals from seeds, you have two options. Start seeds indoors to gain healthy transplants, or sow seeds directly in the garden. Sometimes you can do both with annuals such as marigolds, asters, zinnias and gloriosa daisies. These plants germinate outdoors readily when sown directly in the garden. And early flowering is possible if seeds are started indoors early in the season.

Sometimes there is a definite advantage to starting seeds indoors, or sowing them directly outdoors. For example, seeds of impatiens, begonias and lobelia are tiny and grow slowly in the seedling stage. They do best grown under controlled conditions indoors. Others, such as poppies, nigella and scarlet flax, don't do well when transplanted. They are best sown directly where you want plants to grow. Another group—polygonum, cornflowers and dahlberg daisies— tolerate crowding and transplanting is tedious. They, too, are best sown directly in the garden.

SEED-STARTING BASICS

If you choose to start seeds indoors, be sure to provide the following conditions necessary for successful germination.

Regular Moisture—One of the biggest problems with growing seeds indoors is maintaining moisture. Seeds grown in small peat pots and soil blocks lose moisture rapidly. If germinating seeds or seedlings are allowed to become dry— even for only a few hours—they will probably wilt and die. Begonias, coleus, nigella, celosias, primulas and stocks are particularly sensitive to drying.

When watering seeds in seed trays, apply water in a fine mist from a mister. Or add water to a tray placed below the seed-starting medium. Pouring water directly on the soil surface disturbs seeds and hinders germination. To prevent rapid moisture loss, enclose trays or pots of newly planted seeds in a clear plastic bag. The bag slows evaporation and keeps the soil moist.

Scarifying—Some seeds have a tough seed coat and require moisture over a period of time to soften it so water can penetrate. *Scarifying* is a technique where the seed coat is chipped or sanded so moisture can penetrate more freely. Use a razor blade to nick a small portion of the seed coat, or use a nail file to cut into the hard coating. Scarifying is most often used on large-seeded annuals such as morning glories, hibiscus and sweet peas.

Another way to achieve water penetration for hard-coated seeds is to soak them in a glass of lukewarm water overnight. By morning, seeds should have swelled to twice their original size. If not, leave them to soak another day.

Best Temperature—Seeds require a predetermined, best temperature range in which to germinate. This temperature varies from annual to annual. Nemesias and schizanthus, for example, are sensitive to temperatures above 65F (17C). Coleus, impatiens and begonias are sensitive to temperatures below 70F (21C).

Pre-chilling—Some seeds germinate better by chilling them to break dormancy. Columbine, viola and delphiniums germinate more reliably if placed in the vegetable bin of a refrigerator for 3 weeks before planting.

Proper Light—Some seeds, usually large-seeded annuals such as sweet peas and morning glories, prefer total darkness in which to germinate. Seeds should be completely covered with soil. Seeds of most annuals, however, germinate better with exposure to light. These include mostly small-seeded varieties. For those annuals that require exposure to light, surface-sow seeds and gently press them into soil. Seeds should be anchored but above soil level. Larger seeds requiring light can be lightly covered with a fine layer of soil to anchor them.

Inadequate light after seeds germinate is a major reason for poor-quality transplants. Young seedlings often become spindly and "stretch" when not given sufficient light. Seedlings should be exposed to about 12 hours of sunlight each day.

Here is an example of materials you'll need to grow plants from seeds: peat pots, milk cartons, plastic trays, seeds, potting soil, peat pellets, fungicide and spray bottle.

If you grow transplants on a windowsill, raise pots to the level of the windowpane. Consider placing an aluminum-foil reflector on the dark side of seedlings so light will bounce back to increase illumination.

Where indoor lighting is poor, consider purchasing an artificial-light unit. Fluorescent lights are generally recommended. Fixtures and tubes can often be purchased in department and hardware stores. Many growers use a combination of *warm-white* and *cool-white* tubes, which supply plants with proper light rays for growth.

You can purchase plant-growth or wide-spectrum tubes, manufactured especially for growing plants. Mail-order catalogs usually offer them for sale.

Plant lights, which simulate daylight, can be set on timers to turn on and off automatically. Placing lights about 6 inches above seedlings helps keep them stocky and prevents stretching. Grown under artificial lights, plants need about 16 hours of light per day.

Disease Prevention—The biggest cause of poor germination is *damping-off* disease. It attacks seedlings at the soil surface, causing them to fall over and die. Damping-off is caused by a fungus present in unsterilized soil, dirty pots and unclean seeds. Overwatering, poor ventilation, poor light and high temperatures encourage the disease. It attacks seeds sown indoors and outdoors but is most destructive on indoor sowings. Germinating seeds are often killed before emerging through soil.

Prevent damping-off by using new or clean seed-starting pots and sterile potting soil. Spray surface of potting soil with a fungicide such as captan or benomyl before you plant.

MATERIALS FOR STARTING SEEDS INDOORS

No single seed-starting system suits all situations. Generally, indoor methods can be classified as *one-step* or *two-step*. A one-step method is best for large seeds such as nasturtiums and sweet peas. You simply plant a few seeds in a pot filled with potting soil. You can then thin seedlings to leave one healthy specimen. When seedling reaches sufficient size, you plant it directly in the garden.

With the two-step method, seeds are first sown in a tray or flat filled with potting soil. When large enough to handle, they are separated and transferred to individual pots—usually 2-1/2-inch

size. They grow in these pots until they reach transplant size. Seeds of begonias, impatiens and coleus are best planted this way. Geraniums are sometimes transferred a third time to a larger pot—usually 4 inches in diameter—before seedlings are ready for transplanting.

Following are descriptions of popular materials and methods used to start seeds indoors.

Peat pots are small, round or square containers made of peat, an organic material. They are filled with potting soil, and seeds are planted in them. Plant roots are able to grow through the pot, which gradually decomposes after it is planted in soil. Transplanting is achieved without disturbing roots.

To prevent pot from restricting root growth after it is transplanted, gently remove pot bottom just before planting. This gives the root system greater freedom to grow into the soil. When planting these pots be sure top edge is set *below* soil surface, or it will act as a wick and draw moisture away from roots.

With small seeds it's better to use peat pots in a two-step operation. Start seeds in a tray, then transplant to the peat pot after they have sprouted and are large enough to handle.

Peat pellets are made of compressed peat that expands to seven times its volume when moisture is added. Peat pellets are a popular seed-starting product for large-seeded annuals. Two kinds are available.

Jiffy-7 peat pellets expand to 1-3/4 inches in diameter and 2-1/8 inches high. Netting holds the peat together, and there is a depression in the top of each pellet for seeds. At transplant time the entire pellet can be planted in the garden without bothering the seedling. It is a good idea to remove the netting before planting, or it may restrict plant growth.

Jiffy-9 does not have netting and is slightly smaller and less expensive. Peat is held together by an invisible binding agent. Some believe it is superior to the Jiffy-7 because roots have complete freedom to grow once the pellet has been planted.

Both types are excellent for starting large-seeded annuals in a one-step operation. They can also be used for small seeds. Asters, marigolds, pansies, petunias and zinnias are annuals that do well started in peat pellets.

Fiber blocks and cubes, like Jiffy pellets, have a depression in the top for seeds. They are light, clean and easy to

use. Roots penetrate the block freely. After seedlings grow to transplant size, the whole block can be planted without root disturbance.

Cell packs are small planting trays sectioned into four or six compartments. You fill them with potting soil and plant medium and large seeds. Cell packs are also used for planting small-seeded annuals in a two-step method.

Peat, wood or plastic seed trays are used to start small, fine seeds such as begonias, petunias and coleus. The usual method is to fill planters with sterile potting soil. Make several furrows with a flat edge, then sow seeds thinly along furrows. Keep soil moist with a fine spray. When seedlings develop their first set of true leaves, transfer to individual containers.

Household containers that are normally thrown away every day are excellent alternatives to manufactured products. The quart-size paper milk carton is, in my estimation, one of the best transplant containers for large-seeded annuals. Because of the size of the container, the rootball will be several times larger at transplant time than the rootball started in a peat pot. Because the plant is well established when planted, it flowers earlier.

Use your imagination to seek out other seed-starting containers. Paper and Styrofoam cups and the plastic bottoms of 1-liter soft drink containers work well. You can also use deep-dish plastic containers such as those used for holding dips, whipped butter and cheese spreads. These make excellent seed-starting trays.

Soil mixes are commonly used to fill peat pots, cell packs and other containers for seed starting. Regular garden topsoil is a poor growing medium for indoor-started seedlings. *Soilless mixes and substitutes* or *potting mixes*—combinations of sterile materials such as peat moss, vermiculite and perlite—are much better. They are lightweight, free from disease, and have better aeration and moisture retention than topsoil. Several ready-mixed brands are available from garden centers, including Jiffy Mix, Pro-Mix, RediEarth, Super Soil and Starting Formula.

DIRECT SEEDING OUTDOORS

A common mistake many gardeners make is planting seeds too deep. Most small and medium-size seeds of annuals need exposure to light to germinate. It is better to sow these on the soil surface

Starting Seeds Indoors
One-Step Method

1. Moisten peat pellets to expand them. Large seeds such as nasturtiums are best planted in peat pellets.

2. When pellets are fully expanded, plant one seed in each pellet. Push seed into depression in center of pellet. Pinch sides to cover seed.

3. A few weeks after planting—time varies from annual to annual—seedling is ready to plant. You can plant the peat pot with netting intact, but it is better to remove it.

Two-Step Method

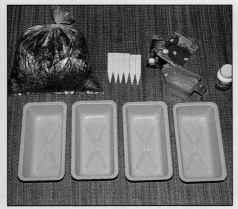

1. Materials needed for two-step method: plastic seed trays, bag of potting soil, labels, seeds, water and benomyl fungicide to prevent damping-off.

2. Throughly moisten potting soil before planting. This is easiest to do when soil is in bag. Squeeze bag so moisture is absorbed evenly into soil.

3. Fill seed trays with soil to about 1/2 inch from top of tray. If you have several trays, plant one annual or one variety in each tray.

4. Sow seeds on soil surface. Many seeds need light to germinate and can be pressed lightly into soil. See individual descriptions. Spray soil surface with benomyl.

5. Seedlings as they appear several days later. Be sure to provide seedlings with several hours of bright, indirect light after they emerge from soil.

6. Using a sharp pencil or similar object, lift seedlings from tray and transplant into larger container. Grow them in this container until they reach transplant size.

and press gently to anchor them.

Before you plant seeds outdoors, determine which tolerate frost in the seedling stage and which are tender and susceptible to frost damage. Don't plant seeds of tender annuals until all danger of frost has passed.

When planting groups of annuals in a mixed bed or border, use a stick or tool handle to outline a planting section for each variety. Then scatter seeds thinly within each designated area.

Unless rain is predicted, water immediately after planting. Even drought-resistant annuals require plenty of moisture to germinate and grow from seedling stage.

If heavy rains threaten to cause erosion of the planting bed, cover seeded areas with a light layer of mulch such as straw, hay or pine needles. Mulching will also help retain soil moisture so the seed bed will not dry out as quickly.

After seedlings are established, thinning may be necessary. Some annuals such as alyssum, portulaca and California poppies tolerate crowding. Others such as marigolds and zinnias do best when thinned so each plant has adequate room to grow.

DIRECT-SEEDING TIPS
● Never walk on garden soil before or after planting. Heavy footprints compact soil and ruin a well-prepared seedbed. Use paths between rows or walk on planks.

● When fertilizing planting bed at time of planting, do not use high-nitrogen, fast-acting fertilizers. They may burn tender seedlings. After applying fertilizer, wait 7 to 10 days before planting. Or apply a timed-release fertilizer at time of planting.

● A hand trowel is one of the best tools for creating seed furrows or planting holes. If you want a shallow, narrow furrow for small seeds, use the pointed tip of the trowel. To make a deep, wide furrow for larger seeds, press trowel in deeper, or dig out a few scoops of soil to set transplants in place.

● Do not use the entire seed packet in one sowing. Save some seeds to fill in bare spots after the planting comes up, and to stagger flowering times.

● Firm soil over planted seeds with your foot or back of a spade. Don't compress soil too much. Press just enough to eliminate air pockets.

● A strainer is handy for planting small seeds. To use, first spread seeds evenly on soil surface. Fill strainer with fine garden topsoil. Shake it over seeds until they are covered with about 1/4 inch of soil. Large stones, weed roots and other debris are left behind in strainer.

TRANSPLANTING
Plants grown indoors and transplanted to the garden should be handled with care. Treat them like eggs. Rough handling can shock plants, and they will grow poorly or die.

Hardening-off—Before moving transplants from a warm, comfortable indoor environment to the cool or windy outdoors, they should be *hardened-off*. This means to gradually acclimate them to their new home. Even cold-hardy plants such as sweet peas and dianthus should be given a gradual transition period from an indoor environment to the outdoors. Hardening-off is most important with tender plants such as impatiens, begonias and petunias.

Transplants should be planted when conditions are cool, such as on cloudy days or in late afternoon. After planting, do not let the soil dry out. You will probably have to water every day, maybe twice a day in warm weather. Place water directly on the soil around the root area. If sunlight is intense, protect seedlings with some sort of shade the first few days after planting.

A simple way to harden-off plants is to expose them to increasing amounts of cold or sunlight, depending on the weather. For example, place plants in the sun for an hour the first day, and gradually increase the exposure for about a week until plants can accept a full day of sun.

Water transplants before you plant them. Moisture helps the rootball ease out of the container or six-pack and lessens transplant shock. If the transplant is in a plastic pot, you may need to run a knife around the rim between soil and pot. Rootball will then come free without disturbing roots. The more original potting soil you can plant, the better transplants will grow.

Placing transplants in a *cold frame* is the best way to get them adjusted to the outdoors. A cold frame is usually a wooden compartment set outdoors, sometimes partially below ground level. It has a covering of glass or plastic. The frame is left open during the day and closed at night. Normally transplants remain in a cold frame for 10 days. The best cold frames have an automatic vent opener that is activated by the sun. Information on solar-powered vent openers can be obtained by writing: Bramen Co. Inc., Box 70, Salem, MA 01970; or Dalen Products Inc., 201 Sherlake Drive, Knoxville, TN 37922.

If you don't want to invest in a cold frame, improvise with a wooden crate covered with a sheet of glass. Or place plants outdoors during the day and cover them with a sheet of plastic at night. Anchor sides with bricks or stones. Do not let the plastic touch plants.

BEDDING PLANTS
A garden center is a popular place to buy annuals. It's so easy to stop by at planting time and pick out your favorite ready-grown transplants, or *bedding plants*. Generally sold in "six-packs" or small containers, plants are often in bloom so it's easy to plant effective color schemes. The bedding-plant industry, which supplies garden centers with transplants, has been one of the fastest-growing segments in gardening.

After reading about a dazzling new hybrid flower in your local newspaper, don't expect to find it as a ready-grown transplant at your garden center. The bedding-plant industry prefers to satisfy the demand for established plants rather than create a demand for new varieties. Space at garden centers is limited. Usually the most popular, best-selling annuals are offered for sale.

Ten classes of annuals provide the majority of bedding-plant sales:

Geraniums	Scarlet sage
Petunias	Coleus
Marigolds	Ageratum
Impatiens	Celosia
Begonias	Zinnias

With the exception of petunias, bedding-plant outlets usually do not offer more than four or five varieties in each class.

TRANSPLANTING TIPS
Be aware that the quality of plants can vary enormously. Following are some points to watch for:

● Buy stocky, compact plants that have healthy green color. Avoid tall, lanky specimens that have yellow leaves and appear to be stretched. Their spindly growth is a sign of stress—usually caused by crowding, inadequate light or infrequent watering. Never judge a plant by its height. Quality transplants are short with thick stems and have side branches close to the base.

● Ask nursery personnel if plants

Planting a Garden

1. Select site in sunny, well-drained location. Lay out according to plan. Stakes and string are helpful for cutting gardens.

2. Remove sod or weeds if present. Shake topsoil from roots. After removing sod, take soil sample for a soil test.

3. Most garden soil requires addition of organic matter. Spread 3 to 6 inches of amendment over area to be planted.

4. Use a spade or power tiller to mix topsoil and amendment. Dig down about 12 inches.

5. Use a rake to level soil surface. Remove stones and pieces of weeds or grass roots. Watch for larvae of insect pests.

6. Scatter fertilizer over soil. Lime or sulfur may be required to adjust soil pH. Rake into top few inches of soil. Wait about 10 days before you sow seeds or set out transplants.

7. Use a hand fork or similar tool to loosen soil prior to planting.

8. Sprinkle seeds evenly in wide row. Most annuals germinate best when exposed to light. Read seed packet for instructions.

9. Thin seedlings to prevent overcrowding. For the earliest blooms, start seeds indoors or buy ready-to-plant transplants at your nursery.

have been *hardened-off*—gradually acclimated from greenhouse to outdoors. If not, plants may sustain severe shock if transplanted immediately to your garden.

• Buy "green." Resist the temptation to buy plants already in flower. A young plant that hasn't blossomed generally puts on a better flowering display. This is especially true of zinnias, scarlet sage and celosias. Marigolds and petunias will flower longer and more profusely if transplanted before plants reach flowering stage.

• If you've decided on petunias, choose the small-flower *multifloras* over the large-flower *grandifloras*. The small ones live longer, produce more flowers and make a more colorful display. They also recover from rain more quickly.

• Examine the undersides of leaves for signs of pests. If you find colonies of aphids, mealy bugs or whiteflies, do not buy plants. Plants may die later of wilt disease even if you completely eradicate pests before transplanting.

'Orange Jubilee' marigold was transplanted while in full flower. Weeks later, growth is uneven, flowers are few and plant looks tired.

This 'Orange Jubilee' was transplanted while green. Weeks later, growth is sturdy, vigorous and flowers are plentiful. Plant has potential to bloom for several more weeks.

Flower garden in full bloom was planted with seeds sown directly in garden, and with seedlings transplanted from six-packs and small pots.

Pine-bark chips are among the most decorative mulches to use for flower beds.

CARING FOR ANNUALS

Regular watering and weeding are the two most important maintenance chores after seeds or plants are in the soil. *Mulching*—putting a covering of material over the soil—helps conserve moisture and reduces the amount of weeding.

Another important part of caring for your garden is pest and disease control. Information on identifying and treating problem pests are discussed in the following pages.

WATERING

Water is the key to growth of all plants. In addition to supplying life-giving moisture, water dissolves nutrients so they can be absorbed by plant roots. Plants grow rapidly when moisture is plentiful, but become subject to both moisture and nutrient stress when water is scarce.

Water is also the key to seed germination. It softens the seed coat and swells the seed embryo to stimulate growth.

The most common mistake when watering flowers is failing to provide enough on a regular basis. Although many annuals are drought tolerant, sur-viving without water for extended periods, plants need water regularly to flower well.

Too much water can be detrimental. Constantly wet soil prevents air from reaching the root zone. If soil is wet for prolonged periods, it creates a stagnant condition that rots plant roots. Fungus diseases are more prevalent when foliage and soil are constantly wet.

Good soil drainage is essential. To improve a poorly drained site, you can install drainage tile to channel the water away. Or you can build a *raised bed*. A raised bed elevates the garden soil above the surrounding level so water drains freely. You may want to support the sides with railroad ties, lumber or stones.

WHEN TO WATER

Seeds and Transplants—When small seeds are planted directly in the garden, water every day if it doesn't rain. These seeds are planted close to the soil surface and are more susceptible to drying out than large-seeded annuals. Moisture is also important immediately following germination.

When transplants are set in the garden, water immediately and keep soil moist until plants are established. Transplanted seedlings often sustain root damage and need regular moisture for a couple of weeks to recover from transplant shock. If the temperature is warm when you set out your transplants, supply some kind of temporary shade until they become adapted.

Established Plants—As soon as a plant begins to wilt, it needs water immediately or it will die. Lack of moisture shows itself in different ways, depending on the plant and its sensitivity to moisture stress.

Do not wait until plants show symptoms of water need. Check the garden soil regularly—every day if temperatures are warm—and supply plants with water in their root zone. An easy way to check moisture content of garden soil is to grab a handful and squeeze it. If particles cling together, soil has adequate moisture. If particles separate and feel dry, like sand, soil needs moisture.

A frequent question asked about watering is, "What time of day is best?" If possible, water in early morning. Watering at this time means less loss through evaporation and from wind.

MOISTURE-HOLDING CAPACITY OF SOIL

Different types of soil have varied capacities for holding moisture in the plant's root zone. Clay soils are prone to waterlogging. Sandy soils allow moisture to drain away too rapidly. The best kind of garden soil is a loam soil. Its composition is somewhere between sand and clay. A loam soil drains well, yet the spaces between soil particles retain water long enough to supply plant roots.

WAYS TO WATER

Irrigation methods that supply water in steady, regular amounts are desirable. Common methods for flowers are hand-held garden hoses, lawn sprinklers and drip-irrigation systems that apply moisture slowly for long periods directly to the root zone.

Hand irrigation is tedious and the least effective means of watering. It seems as if you are applying more water than you actually are. Usually only the top few inches of soil are getting moisture. If you have the time and patience to wet soil thoroughly to the root zone, hand irrigation is an acceptable way to water. Using an extension wand, which attaches to the end of the hose, makes hand watering easier and applies water in a rainlike spray.

Lawn sprinklers are an improvement over hand watering. They can be set in place to water as long as necessary, soaking the soil. But sprinklers can waste water through evaporation on hot days. In climates with humid summers they can promote disease. Fungus infestations such as powdery mildew and botrytis are encouraged if sprinkler systems soak foliage, creating a wet, humid environment around plants.

Drip irrigation is a system of hoses that lie across soil close to plant roots, either on top of soil or buried out of sight. Depending on design, drip hoses are usually attached to a garden hose, which is attached to an outdoor faucet. The drip hose oozes moisture through micropores along the hose wall, or drips moisture from *emitters,* tiny holes spaced at regular intervals along the hose. *Spaghetti* emitters have long, flexible tubes coming from a main hose. At the end of each flexible tube is a type of valve that drips moisture. Spaghetti emitters are probably best suited for watering individual plants in containers.

The biggest benefit of drip irrigation is that you can water the whole garden regularly by a single turn of the faucet.

Plants receive regular moisture, and are not subjected to water stress. The basics of watering correctly still apply— putting sufficient amounts of water in the root zone.

Economically, drip-irrigation systems make sense. They save water due to less waste—as much as 30% compared to other methods. Because plants make continuous, rapid growth, they begin to flower early and flower profusely.

Drip irrigation is especially effective when installed under black plastic. This not only protects the hoses from damage, it reduces evaporation.

For a small area, it is sufficient to place drip hose up and down the rows with one end connected to a water spigot. With 1/2-inch diameter hose and emitters spaced 2 feet apart, and with average water pressure, water should be able to travel about 250 feet on level ground from your water spigot. This can be doubled to 500 feet if two hoses are connected to the spigot by a Y valve.

To irrigate large gardens, you may have to consider a more sophisticated set-up. Such a system might involve lateral hoses connected to a larger line, called a *header* line, fitted with a water-pressure regulator. Some systems can incorporate a special fertilizer unit that injects soluble fertilizer into water. Plants are fed automatically while they are being irrigated.

Water Correctly

The illustration at right shows what happens when a plant is given frequent, shallow waterings. Roots grow where there is water—in the upper soil surface. During periods of warm, windy weather or if an irrigation is missed, the plant is unable to absorb the water it needs. The plant at far right is given deep, regular waterings. The roots penetrate deeply into the soil so they have a greater reservoir of water and nutrients to draw upon.

Planting a Weed-Free Garden

Using black plastic for weed control and drip-irrigation hose for watering is an easy-care way to grow annuals. Weeding and watering chores are reduced considerably and plants flower continually.

To make a weed-free, drip-irrigated garden, dig a rectangular plot 17 feet wide by 30 feet long. Make 10 raised beds 2 feet wide by 15 feet long. Leave room for 1-foot-wide walkways between raised beds. Lay continuous length of drip-irrigation hose down middle of each bed. Hose should go from one row to the next.

Next, cover beds with lengths of 3-foot-wide strips of black plastic. Look for plastic that is 4 mils thick. Anchor edges with soil. Lay down straw between beds to reduce weed growth and to provide a mud-free walkway.

Space plants 12 inches apart in double rows through the black plastic. Cut an X in plastic for each transplant. Take care not to damage drip hose in middle of bed. Attach drip hose to outdoor faucet. Turn on faucet whenever garden needs watering.

Drip-irrigation hose, connections and instructions are available as a kit called *Derek Fell's Automatic Garden*. For more information, write International Irrigation Systems, 1555 Third Avenue, Niagara Falls, NY 14304.

If you don't have access to a well or water spigot, a gravity-feed system can be used. Place a water barrel several feet above the soil level and run a drip hose from its base.

Drip systems vary in cost and quality. To decide which system is best for you, look for advertisements in garden magazines. Send for their descriptive material and study it. Many retail garden centers carry drip-irrigation supplies that you can examine in the store.

Some drip-irrigation companies will help you design a system if you send them a plan of your garden with your order. Many have a specification sheet at the front of their supply catalog.

One of the least-expensive systems is Irrigro, consisting of white, plastic hose with tiny pores. The pores allow droplets of water to ooze through the sides. A source of Irrigro hose is International Irrigation Systems, 1555 Third Avenue, Niagara Falls, NY 14304.

Polyflex hose has emitters spaced at 18-inch or 24-inch intervals. Water drips from the emitters and saturates soil in a wide circle. For more information on Polyflex hose, write to Submatic Irrigation Systems, Box 246, Lubbock, TX 79408.

WEEDING

In a short time, unchecked weed growth can turn an attractive flower bed into a jungle. Weeds not only compete with your flowers for moisture and nutrients, they also block sunlight. It is easy to become discouraged when weeds claim your garden. The best way to combat them is to keep them from getting ahead.

When you do the initial soil preparation of your garden, remove all pieces of weed roots that you see. The smallest piece of plantain or dandelion root can grow into a full-size weed. Avoid walking on newly cultivated soil. The surface compaction helps many weed seeds to germinate.

A few minutes spent pulling young weeds at the end of each day is far more sensible than trying to catch up on a week of neglect. This is especially true in midsummer when weeds grow fast. If you kill weeds when they are immature, they will not have a chance to set seeds for a new crop. Some gardeners use every good rain as a signal. They go outside immediately after the rain has ceased. Weeds are easy to pull while the ground is wet and yielding.

Use a mulch between rows to reduce weed germination and growth. If installed correctly at the beginning of the gardening season, a mulch is the easiest way to control weeds.

Even when you use a mulch, some weeds are persistent enough to break through. Two tools are excellent for hand weeding—a hoe for weeding between plants and a hand fork for scratching out weeds. If you use one of these tools to remove weeds, try to cultivate the soil to a shallow depth—about 1-1/2 inches. Digging deeper tends to bring up a new crop of weed seeds that will germinate in the upper soil surface.

When using a hoe or hand cultivator, take care not to disturb roots of adjacent annuals. For example, dandelion roots are long and tapering. When pulled, they come up without disturbing adjacent soil area. Plantain roots spread. Yanking them out can unseat nearby plants.

Wear gloves when removing weeds by hand. Some cause skin irritations. Try to remove weeds with roots intact. If the stem breaks above ground and the

root remains in the soil, the weed will grow back.

Herbicidal Weedkillers—These are chemicals that are sprinkled or sprayed on flower beds prior to planting. They work by preventing the germination of weed seeds. There is usually a waiting period after applying them before you can plant. Follow label directions carefully.

MULCHING

A *mulch* is a covering over garden soil. It is a popular form of weed control and supplies many other important benefits.

● It reduces weed growth by cutting off light to germinating weed seeds. Weeds that germinate are easy to pull from a mulch.

● It conserves moisture by reducing surface evaporation.

● It modifies soil temperatures by cooling or warming soil. Organic mulches tend to cool soil. Plastic mulches tend to warm it.

Drops of water ooze slowly from tiny pores in drip-irrigation hose. Water is supplied slowly and directly to root zone of plants so there is less waste through evaporation. Various kinds of drip systems are available, including those with *emitters*—tiny valves—set at regular spaces along hose.

A drip hose is placed in garden, which will supply plants with all water needs. Here hose is placed up and down a series of narrow raised beds.

• It reduces soil erosion and preserves good soil structure and nutrient levels.

• It reduces risk of disease by keeping foliage of annuals away from bare soil.

As mentioned, organic mulches such as wood chips and pine needles tend to cool soil. Inorganic mulches such as black plastic tend to warm soil. In areas with hot, dry summers, black plastic may overheat soil, but plastic can be covered with organic mulch for a weed-free garden. Drip irrigation works well in conjunction with black plastic to provide regular amounts of water, which also helps reduce soil temperature.

Black plastic is the best barrier against weeds. It is usually desirable to cover the plastic with a decorative organic mulch to maintain an attractive appearance. Some of the best decorative mulches include bark chips and ground bark, hay and straw, leaf mold, pine needles, coco bean hulls, licorice root and peat moss. These all have a natural appearance. They will eventually decompose to add their organic matter to the soil.

A disadvantage of mulches is that they can be great hiding places for snails and slugs. These pests are most prolific during rainy weather. If they are a problem, use a slug bait or pick them off plants with a gloved hand.

DEAD-HEADING

Removing dead flowers is called *dead-heading*. It is an important practice that should be followed regularly. Otherwise, annuals direct their energy into seed formation and stop flowering. Removing spent flowers before they form seeds maintains attractive floral displays. At the same time, this stimulates the plant into producing more flowers.

STAKING PLANTS

Certain types of tall-growing annuals may need staking to keep them erect. Larkspur, delphiniums, tall snapdragons and tall sunflowers have brittle stems that are easily damaged by wind. The best material for staking is bamboo stakes, which are readily available from garden and home-improvement centers. When tying stems to stakes it's best to use a twist-tie rather than string. String has a tendency to cut into stems. Twist-ties are easily looped into a figure-8. The stem goes through one loop and the stake occupies the other. This allows stake and stem to stand parallel.

Circular flower bed planted with wax begonias is kept free of weeds with an attractive mulch of pine bark. Area beyond garden is covered with decorative rock mulch.

Dead-heading means removing spent flower heads before they have a chance to set seeds, which drains the plant's energy. By removing spent flowers, plants are stimulated to produce more blooms.

PESTS AND DISEASES

Problems caused by pests and diseases among flowering annuals are not nearly as severe as with edible crops. After flowers pass the seedling stage, few serious problems occur.

The best pest and disease control is *prevention*. Keep your garden clean and do a major clean-up at the end of each season. Remove and destroy all garden debris.

Large animal pests such as stray dogs, deer, rabbits and groundhogs can be kept out by fencing your garden. Birds such as pheasants and quail like young transplants. It may be necessary to make portable cages from chicken wire and cover young plants until they pass the tender, succulent stage.

Before you implement a pest-control program, decide which pests and diseases present potential dangers. If you are new to an area or a beginning gardener, ask neighborhood gardeners, nursery personnel and county agents which pests and diseases are common.

CONTROLS: THE CHOICES

In deciding how to combat pests and diseases, you have two choices— *chemical controls* and *organic controls*. Most flower parts are not usually consumed by humans, so most gardeners do not mind using chemical controls. Many insecticides are specially formulated for use on ornamentals but are not approved for use on vegetables. There are some exceptions. Nasturtiums, for example, are sometimes used in salads. If you know you will be using flower parts for culinary use, avoid using chemical sprays altogether.

It's impractical and expensive to buy, store and use a multitude of insecticides—either organic or chemical. Most home gardeners prefer to use all-purpose controls that take care of most insects or most diseases. Some recommend the use of a *pyrethrum-base* insecticide as an organic control for insects. It is a general-purpose, contact poison derived from a South-African daisy. It is short-lived, so it must be used at regular intervals and after every rain.

Pyrethrum is applied as a liquid spray or powder. It controls a wide range of insect pests, especially leaf hoppers, aphids and whiteflies. Pyrethrum leaves

Gardener uses knapsack sprayer to apply herbicidal weedkiller in paths between rows of annuals.

no poisonous residues in the soil.

Soaps can be used to control many pests, especially those with soft bodies, such as aphids and mealy bugs. A solution of liquid dishsoap—1 teaspoon to 1 gallon of water—can be used. Frequent applications are usually required. Because dishsoaps can vary greatly from one brand to another, it is a good idea to test-spray a few plants before spraying your entire planting.

Commercially available insecticidal soaps contain certain fatty acids that are known to be potent to pests. A commonly available brand is Safer Agro-Chem Insecticidal Soap.

An effective, all-purpose chemical control is *Orthene*. It is specially formulated for protecting ornamental plants and is not approved for edible kinds. Suitable alternatives to Orthene are Sevin or diazinon.

Certain insects—notably slugs, snails and Japanese beetles—can be so destructive they require *specific* controls. A Japanese beetle trap uses a sex attractant to lure insects into a disposable bag. Slugs and snails can be killed with

poisonous baits sprinkled among plants. Or use a mulch of cedar bark, which has been found effective in repelling slugs and snails from gardens.

Contact and Systemic—With both insect pests and fungus diseases you have a choice of using *contact* or *systemic* poisons.

A contact poison is sprayed or dusted directly on plants. Contact controls are washed off by rain. It is difficult to apply them under leaf surfaces and into densely foliaged areas.

Systemic controls are generally the most effective means of protection. A systemic is applied to the root zone. The plant absorbs it and distributes it to roots, leaves and stems. When a pest attacks the plant, the systemic goes to work and attacks the pest. Systemic controls protect plants for a longer period than contact controls. Bonide is a popular systemic insecticide effective against thrips, mites, aphids, whiteflies and other hard-to-control sucking insects.

DISEASES

Although annuals are relatively disease-free, certain plants are susceptible to particular diseases. Snapdragons and hollyhocks, for example, are prone to rust disease. Zinnias tend to be attacked by alternaria and powdery mildew. Asters are attacked by wilt and yellows disease.

Fortunately, plant breeders have been able to breed disease resistance into many of the more popular flower groups. Gardeners can now choose varieties of rust-resistant snapdragons, mildew-resistant zinnias, wilt-resistant asters and others.

Keeping your garden clean is an important part of disease prevention. Disease organisms will overwinter on dead leaves and stems, infecting your garden in spring and summer.

Air pollution is not a disease but produces diseaselike symptoms. It can cause unsightly blemishes on flowering annuals, with some classes more susceptible than others. Petunias—especially white and pale-pink grandifloras—are extremely sensitive to pollution. Resistant varieties are now being developed.

Avoid air-pollution damage by planting resistant varieties and locate flower beds away from roadsides and driveways.

Insect Pests

APHIDS are tiny, sucking insects that form large colonies on plant stems and leaf undersides. Colors are green, red, black or white. Aphids suck plant juices and produce a sticky substance called *honeydew,* formed by their excrement. Infested plants turn yellow, lose leaves and become stunted. Aphids are also carriers of disease.
Control: Effective chemical controls are malathion, diazinon or bonide. Organic controls include washing stems and leaves with insecticidal soap or spraying them with pyrethrum or nicotine sulfate. Ladybugs and lacewing larvae are natural enemies.

CUCUMBER BEETLES are 1/4 inch long, yellow-green with stripes or spots. They usually cluster around crowns of tender plants and among blossoms, chewing leaves, stems and flowers. They are carriers of disease.
Control: Apply Sevin or diazinon as a chemical control. Pyrethrum is an effective organic control.

COLORADO POTATO BEETLES are 3/8 inch long, yellow with black stripes. The equally destructive larvae are reddish, hump-backed and resemble grubs. They chew all tender plant parts.
Control: Sevin, diazinon and malathion are effective chemical controls. Pyrethrum is an effective organic insecticide.

CUTWORMS are black, brown or gray grubs, 1/2 inch to 1-1/2 inches long. They spend the day curled up in soil. They emerge at night to chew on plant stems at soil line, causing plants to fall over.
Control: The most common chemical control is a soil drench of diazinon applied in the early evening when grubs are most active. Transplants can also be protected by a paper or metal collar. Use bottomless paper cups slit along one side and wrap around plant stems. Bury tip of cup in soil.

JAPANESE BEETLES are 1/2 inch long, shiny, coppery brown with metallic-green shoulders. When disturbed, they fly off suddenly, emitting a whirring sound. Larvae resemble white cutworms. They overwinter in lawn. Adults eat leaves and flowers of many plants.
Control: Malathion and Sevin are effective chemical controls. The best organic control is a Japanese beetle trap using a sex hormone to attract male beetles.

LEAF HOPPERS are 1/8-inch-long, grasshopperlike insects, usually green. They sit on leaves then hop abruptly into the air. Leaf hoppers are especially troublesome in fall, sucking plant juices and transmitting disease such as aster yellows.
Control: Apply Sevin, diazinon or malathion as chemical controls. Dust plants with pyrethrum to control organically.

MEALY BUGS are white insects that cluster around tender plant parts, resembling bits of cotton. They suck juices from plants.
Control: Malathion is an effective chemical control. Washing stems with insecticidal soap or dabbing their bodies with rubbing alcohol are organic alternatives.

MITES are spiderlike pests only 1/50 inch long. They are yellow, green or red. They spin fine, silvery webs among leaves and stems. Mites suck plant juices, causing leaves to curl and wilt.
Control: The miticide dicofol is most effective. It must be administered early in the season. After mites are established they are difficult to eradicate. Diazinon and malathion sprays used regularly offer some control. The systemic insecticide, Bonide, is also effective. Spraying with water helps some. Ladybugs are natural predators of mites.

NEMATODES are microscopic worms that live in soil and attack plant roots, causing swellings called *galls.* Plants become stunted and turn yellow.

Aphids prefer to colonize vegetable plants, but will attack annuals, introducing diseases.

Cutworms were exposed while digging a flower bed for planting. Soil drenches containing diazinon are common means of control.

Mealy bugs will attack the tender stems of many flowering annuals. If infestations are minor, dislodge these pests with jets of water from the garden hose.

Control: Chemical controls such as soil drenches are generally ineffective. Soil fumigation using Vapam is best. Applied in liquid solution to soil, it releases a gas, destroying weed seeds and soil fungi in addition to nematodes. This is best done by a pest-control company. An organic control is French marigolds planted as a cover crop for 1 year. Studies have shown they help repel nematodes.

STEM BORERS are the caterpillar stage of a moth that lays its eggs at the base of plants. Larvae bore their way into stems. Borers are white, about 1 inch long. They leave holes and a sawdustlike material called *frass* where they enter plant. They are difficult to control because they are hidden inside stems. Plants wilt as larvae bore deeper.
Control: Some control is possible using malathion. The most effective control is endosulfan, trade name Thiodan. To control organically, use pyrethrum or rotenone. Garlic- pepper sprays help repel the egg-laying moth.

SLUGS AND SNAILS are similar pests. Snails have a shell they can retract into when threatened. Both are most active during wet weather and at night. They emerge from hiding places to chew tender plant parts.
Control: Slug bait sprinkled among plants is an effective chemical control. To control organically, use a mulch of cedar bark, which is repellent to slugs and snails. Or hand-pick them with gloved hand and destroy them.

THRIPS are tiny, threadlike, winged insects that suck plant juices. You can spot them on plants using a magnifying glass. They are pale yellow when immature, turning to a tan-brownish color as adults. Symptoms of their damage are white streaks on leaves and flowers. Edges of leaves sometimes turn brown.
Control: If these pests are discovered, spray with malathion solution every 5 to 7 days until signs of thrips and damage are no longer evident. Also spray soil surface around plant to kill *nymphs*—the immature stage of this pest. Remove spent blossoms regularly to prevent infestations.

WHITEFLIES are small, sucking insects with white bodies covered with powder. They fly up in a cloud like flakes of snow when disturbed.
Control: Diazinon and malathion are chemical controls. Also effective is the systemic Bonide. Washing stems with an insecticidal soap is an organic control. Ladybugs are natural predators of whiteflies.

Diseases

ALTERNARIA is a fungus disease that causes severe leaf spots and patches on a number of annuals, particularly zinnias and geraniums. Leaf spots and patches are usually light brown with a lighter-color center. Spots spread to cover leaves, which wither and die.
Control: Regular rainfall or frequent overhead irrigation such as from sprinklers helps spread the disease. Spray plants with wettable sulfur or copper-base fungicide. To control organically, pick off and destroy infected leaves. Do not save seeds from your own plants because they can spread infection the following season.

BOTRYTIS is a widespread fungus disease that attacks leaves, stems and flowers. It shows itself most noticeably in flower heads, especially those of geraniums. Center of flower becomes mushy and blackened. When the disease infects leaves and stems, plant tissue blackens and enlarges rapidly.
Control: Abundant rainfall or frequent overhead irrigation encourages spread of disease. Sprays of benomyl, zineb and captan are effective. Without these fungicides, control is difficult. Remove infected plants. Provide space between plants for circulation.

Presence of mites on this hollyhock plant is indicated by curling leaf edges.

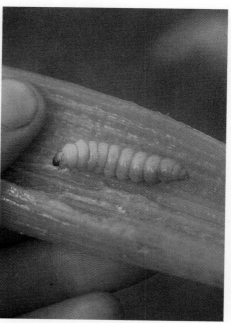
Stem borers come in many sizes. They attack numerous kinds of annuals, including zinnias and marigolds. This is squash-vine borer.

Botrytis disease on geranium plant is identified by mushy, black flower centers and brown patches on leaves.

DAMPING-OFF disease is most troublesome on seedlings grown indoors, but is a common cause of seedling death outdoors. Seedlings are attacked at soil line and fall over and die. The fungus is present in unsterilized soil, and can be transmitted by dirty pots. Tiny seedlings such as impatiens and begonias are particularly susceptible.
Control: Use only sterile potting soil and sterilize pots. The most effective control is to spray the soil surface with benomyl. Avoid waterlogged soil and provide seedlings with optimum light and temperature to help them resist the disease.

POWDERY MILDEW is a widespread fungus disease that thrives in wet weather and attacks a wide variety of flowering annuals. It is most prevalent on zinnias. Grayish-white, powdery patches appear on leaf surfaces, especially following periods of rainfall and high humidity. Plants turn brown, shrivel and die.
Control: Avoid irrigating with overhead sprinklers. Dust or spray plants with sulfur-base fungicides or dinocap, trade name Karathane. Benomyl is also effective in controlling the disease. As an organic control, grow mildew-resistant varieties. Clean the garden thoroughly in winter, destroying all infected plants.

RUST is a destructive fungus disease that commonly affects hollyhocks and snapdragons. It shows itself as orange or brown powdery pustules on leaves or stems—particularly the undersides. If infestations are severe, plants can die.
Control: Avoid overhead sprinkling. High humidity and periods of high rainfall promote the disease. Remove and destroy infected leaves as soon as they are noticed. Spray plants with sulfur, captan or zineb. Among certain flower classes, notably snapdragons, rust-resistant varieties can be planted. When pruning infected plant parts, disinfect shears after each cut by dipping in a solution of 50% bleach and water. Discard infected plant parts.

WILT is a name for numerous bacterial and fungus diseases that cause the plant to wilt. The most serious disease commonly called *wilt* is fusarium wilt. Its principal target is asters. Afflicted plants suddenly become limp, droop, turn brown and die. Sometimes part of plant will show symptoms. The plant may appear to recover briefly, but the entire plant usually dies.
Control: Plant wilt-resistant varieties. Spray soil with benomyl. Certain plants such as dahlias and cosmos are more susceptible to *bacterial* wilt.

In these instances, the most effective prevention is to control insects, which are largely responsible for spreading the disease.

YELLOWS disease affects mostly asters, but also attacks marigolds, chrysanthemums and other flowering annuals. It is often called *aster yellows.* A microplasmalike organism is responsible for the disease, but leaf hoppers are the primary cause of its spread. First evidence is a yellowing of growing tips, especially around a flower bud. Stunted plants, deformed blooms and an abnormal number of side shoots are further symptoms. Affected plants do not generally wilt or die, but remain unsightly. See photo below.
Control: Destroy infected plants. Spray healthy plants with malathion to control leaf hoppers. Or spray with rotenone-pyrethrum organic insecticide.

Powdery mildew infests zinnia leaf. Zinnias resistant to this disease are available.

Rust disease on hollyhock shows orange-brown pustules that burst and spread spores.

Aster yellows attacked these marigolds. Deformed flowers and sickly yellow leaves identify this disease, which is often spread by leaf hoppers.

GALLERY OF GARDEN ANNUALS

The following encyclopedia includes 18 familiar and not-so-familiar flowering annuals. They are arranged alphabetically by common names used by the majority of North-American seedsmen. In some instances the botanical name is also the common name, such as *Delphinium* and *Impatiens*.

Each class of annual is shown in one or more photographs including several large "portraits." Many were grown in my own garden. When possible, a close-up and garden landscape scene are shown to present both *flower form* and *plant habit*.

HARDY OR TENDER

In the first paragraph of the descriptions, each annual is identified as *hardy* or *tender*. This is an important distinction. A hardy annual withstands some frost and can be planted several weeks before the last expected frost date in your area. A tender annual is susceptible to frost and should not be planted until all danger of frost has passed.

COOL SEASON OR WARM SEASON

In addition to classifying annuals as hardy and tender, many of the descriptions state whether the plant flowers best during cool or warm periods of the growing season. They are termed *cool season* or *warm season*. This is important in regions with warm summers. Cool-season annuals must be planted so they mature in the cool weather of early summer or fall. Some cool-weather annuals—nemesias, cinerarias, calceolarias and schizanthus—are not practical to grow in many regions of North America, except coastal areas and the Pacific Northwest. They need a long, cool, summer season to perform well.

The midsummer heat common to most of North America burns them up.

HEIGHT AND SIZE

Where heights and sizes are supplied with descriptions, the standard is to state mature height at time of flowering. In conditions such as excessive rainfall and high soil fertility, dwarf varieties may grow much higher than usual. Conversely, if soil fertility is poor and regular moisture is not available, plants will not grow to their expected mature size.

VARIETY RECOMMENDATIONS

Descriptions give recommended varieties with reasons why they are superior. Realize that new varieties are continually being introduced. Be alert for new sizes, flower colors and improvements by visiting local arboretums and display gardens and by reading garden publications.

Left: Nasturtiums grown for seed production create a kaleidoscope of color. This field is located near Lompoc, California, flower-seed capital of the world. Above: Dark-purple rocket larkspur is striking in contrast to orange and yellow flowers in background.

When you're ready to plant, don't expect to find each annual or the recommended varieties as transplants at your local garden center. The bedding-plant industry that supplies local garden centers does 90% of its business in just five classes of annuals—petunias, impatiens, geraniums, marigolds and pansies. Within these classes, variety selection is limited. Local seed racks are also poor sources for recommended varieties. Seeds available are largely confined to old, established, standard varieties.

Recommended varieties are usually widely available from flower-seed catalogs. By sending away for three or four catalogs—most are free—you should have no difficulty purchasing recommended varieties.

AWARD-WINNERS

When reading plant labels, scanning mail-order seed catalogs or searching seed racks, it is sometimes difficult to decide which varieties are best. Major classes such as petunias, marigolds and zinnias can be especially confusing.

Several award systems have been organized to help identify outstanding varieties. The three most important are the *All-America Selections, Fleuroselect*—the European seed trials—and the award system of the *Royal Horticultural Society* in England.

All-America Selections was organized in 1932 by the American seed trade. Each year it makes awards of recognition to outstanding new varieties. New flowers are planted in test gardens located in every climatic region of the United States and Canada. Judges at each location evaluate the newcomers alongside plantings of existing, similar varieties, comparing performances. Judges are drawn equally from academic circles and the seed trade. They score points for each variety according to its performance in their test garden. The points are added. By averaging the scores, a committee decides the winners. Awards are Gold Medals, Silver Medals and Bronze Medals.

Winners are those that usually do well in most parts of North America. A network of display gardens allows the public to see current and recent award-winning varieties.

Fleuroselect is the European equivalent of All-America Selections. Founded in 1970, it also evaluates new varieties and makes awards of recognition based on plant performance. Trial gardens are lo-

cated as far north as Finland and as far south as southern Italy.

A unique aspect of Fleuroselect is its recognition of "novelty" plants. Even if a new variety fails to win an award, the organization may feel it is different enough to rate recognition. Thus the plant is announced as a novelty.

The Royal Horticultural Society was founded in 1804. Its award system grants First-Class Certificates, Awards of Merit and Honorable Mentions for outstanding plants.

The RHS award system differs significantly from Fleuroselect and All-America Selections. Its testing system is open to *all* cultivated varieties, not just new ones. With few exceptions, only certain groups of plants are chosen for testing in a given year. All plants are tested in one location—at the society's headquarters near Wisley (Surrey). If marigolds or scarlet sage are tested one year, they may not be tested again for another 20 years. Exceptions are sweet peas and delphiniums. They are so popular in England that the RHS tests them every year.

SEED FACTS

Under the heading *How To Grow,* information is given concerning seed germination. Care has been taken to give number of days to germination, as well as optimum temperature range and other factors that may influence germination. These would include exposure to light, need for darkness, pre-chilling, pre-soaking and other special factors. This information has been gained from my personal experience of growing from seeds every annual described here. It has also been verified with the *Journal of Seed Technology,* published by the Association of Official Seed Analysts, a group that establishes official seed germination standards for government and industry.

Many gardeners prefer to grow medium-size and large-seeded varieties from seeds, and buy nursery transplants of fine-seeded varieties. Fine seeds are more difficult to grow. Seeds need careful misting and close attention to light requirements. It also takes a long time for seedlings to reach transplant size.

All-America trial gardens like this are located in every climatic area of the United States. Entries are submitted by plant breeders from around the world, hoping to gain an All-America award.

ASTER, CHINA
Callistephus chinensis

China asters are magnificent, tender annuals native to China. They would be more popular in North America if plants were not so susceptible to several common diseases. Plants grow 6 inches to 3 feet high, depending on variety, spreading 12 to 15 inches wide. The fluffy, mostly double, chrysanthemum-type flowers can measure up to 7 inches across. Color range is extensive, including white, yellow, pink, red and blue. Under cool conditions, plants flower continually from summer to fall frost.

Recommended Varieties—'Giant Perfection', mixed colors, 2 feet high, grows upright as narrow bunches of loosely double, 4-inch flowers. Long stems are excellent for cutting. 'Powderpuff Super Bouquet', mixed colors, 2 feet high, has double flowers with creamy yellow centers. The entire plant can be cut and presented as an instant bouquet. Dwarf varieties are suitable as bedding plants. 'Dwarf Queen' strain is especially attractive, growing 10 to 12 inches high in a mound shape. Large double flowers come in red, white, blue and pink.

How to Grow—Asters do not transplant well. Sow seeds directly in the garden after all danger of frost has passed. Cover with 1/4 inch of fine soil. For earliest flowers, start seeds indoors in peat pots 6 weeks before last frost date. Avoid root disturbance as much as possible when transplanting or plants may wilt. Germination takes 4 to 10 days at 60F to 70F (16C to 21C) soil temperature. Space dwarf varieties 6 inches apart. Space tall varieties 12 to 18 inches apart.

Avoid planting China asters in the same location where asters grew previously. This reduces risk of wilt disease. Rotate planting site each year. Plant in full sun, in loose, fertile, well-drained soil. Keep soil moist.

The two most serious problems with asters are fusarium wilt and aster yellows. Fusarium wilt is caused by a fungus. Young seedlings stricken with the disease topple over suddenly and die. Older specimens that are afflicted may remain stunted or become lopsided. Yellowing of leaves and collapse of the entire plant may follow. Sometimes the disease does not show itself until plants are ready to bloom. To control, grow only wilt-resistant varieties.

Aster yellows disease is caused by a microorganism that attacks several other plants but is especially destructive to asters. The microorganism responsible is spread by leaf hoppers. Controlling these insect pests reduces risk of infection. Sevin chemical spray or pyrethrum organic spray are effective against leaf hoppers. Pull up and destroy plants known to be affected with aster yellows to prevent its spread.

Uses—Tall kinds are excellent for cutting and create beautiful flower arrangements. China asters are widely grown in greenhouses to provide cut flowers during winter months. Dwarf varieties are commonly used as edging for beds and borders.

Scarlet 'Powderpuff Super Bouquet' China aster.

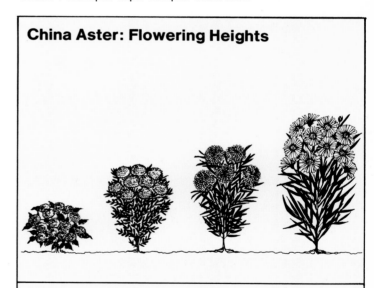

China Aster: Flowering Heights

1 foot	1-1/2 feet	2 feet	2-1/2 feet
'Color Carpet'	'Early Charm'	'Crego'	'American Beauty'
'Dwarf Border'	'Pompon'	'Duchess'	'American Branching'
'Dwarf Queen'		'Early Bird'	'California Giant'
'Dwarf Spider'		'Fluffy Ruffles'	'Ostrich Plume'
'Mini-Lady'		'Giant Perfection'	'Super Giants'
'Mumsters'		'Perfection'	'Totem Poles'
'Pinocchio'		'Princess'	
'Red Mount'		'Powderpuff Super Bouquet'	
'Star Flowered'		'Unicum'	

CALENDULA
Calendula officinalis

This is a hardy annual growing 1 to 2 feet high, spreading 1 to 2 feet wide. Another common name is pot marigold. Flowers are usually yellow, orange and apricot. Most are double, 3 to 4 inches across, closely resembling chrysanthemums. Plants bloom from spring to fall during cool weather. Leaves have a pleasant, spicy fragrance. Native to the Mediterranean.

Recommended Varieties—'Pacific Beauty', 2 feet high, mixed colors, is the most popular for bedding and cutting. 'Gypsy Festival', 1 foot high, is a free-flowering dwarf mixture with contrasting dark centers. 'Mandarin', 2 feet high, is a vigorous orange hybrid.

How to Grow—Easy to grow from seeds sown directly in the garden. Plant seeds 4 to 6 weeks before your last frost date in spring. Seeds germinate in 4 to 10 days at 70F (21C). Cover with 1/4 inch of soil and thin plants to stand 12 to 15 inches apart. In mild areas sow seeds in August through September for blooms at Christmas. In areas with snow cover during winter, seeds can be sown in September. Plants will make strong growth then remain dormant during cold weather to bloom early in the spring. Plants prefer full sun and tolerate poor soil if drainage is good. Irrigate during dry spells.

Young plants are susceptible to damage from slugs and snails. Leaves are susceptible to mildew.

Uses—Excellent for beds and borders. Good for cutting. Popular as a container plant during winter in a cool greenhouse.

Calendula is commonly used by herbalists. The slightly bitter leaves and flowers are added to salads. In addition, a dye can be made from the flowers.

'Mandarin' calendula is a vigorous grower and bloomer.

DELPHINIUM
Delphinium elatum

Delphiniums are actually hardy perennials. True annual kinds are known as *larkspur*. However, some perennial strains can be treated as annuals to bloom the first year from seeds sown indoors. Delphiniums tolerate mild frosts but are sensitive to freezing.

Plants produce tall flower spikes up to 6 feet high and spread 2 feet wide. Colors include white, blue, purple and pink. Individual florets measure up to 2-1/2 inches across. At the center of each floret is a ring of smaller petals known as a *bee*. These decorative bees are usually white or black in contrast to the floret. Native to Siberia.

In addition to tall species—*Delphinium elatum*—seedsmen offer *D. belladonna*. Plants are bushy, growing up to 2-1/2 feet high, producing a loose cluster of flowers. Both species generally flower for several weeks during cool weather in early summer or fall.

Recommended Varieties—'Pacific Giants', 6 feet high, are the most popular tall type. They are available in a mixture in a beautiful assortment of colors. 'Blue Fountains', 3 feet high, is a good, earlier-flowering mixture classified as a dwarf. 'Blue Heaven', 3 feet high, is a selection of 'Blue Fountains'. It produces flowers that are sky-blue with a white bee—the most appealing color combination in delphiniums.

How to Grow—Delphinium seeds do not stay viable long after harvest. Fresh seeds are essential for good germination. Seeds are often harvested and packaged before they can be *vernalized*—winter chilled. To ensure that dormancy is broken, store seeds in the refrigerator for 24 hours before planting. Germination takes 8 to 18 days at 70F to 85F (21C to 30C) soil temperature.

Space plants 1-1/2 to 2 feet apart in full sun. Plant in fertile loam or fertile, sandy soil with plenty of organic matter mixed in. Keep soil moist and feed every 2 weeks with diluted liquid fertilizer. Delphiniums flower spectacularly during cool, sunny weather, but expire rapidly when summer days turn hot and humid.

Where summers are hot and winters are severe, tall types should be started in a cold frame or greenhouse in September of the year prior to flowering. Protect plants in cold frames until spring and transplant when the soil warms. Plant will flower in early summer. Some dwarf varieties such as 'Blue Fountains' can be started indoors 10 to 12 weeks before planting outdoors. They are transplanted in early spring to bloom in early summer. Similarly, 'Connecticut Yankees' can be started from seeds 10 weeks before time to plant outdoors to produce flowers the first year.

Slugs and snails are pests of delphiniums. Control with slug bait or pick by hand. Thrips are another common pest. Control by using a systemic insecticide such as Di-Syston. The most common plant disease affecting delphiniums is aster yellows, also known as *stunt* and *witch's brooms*. Symptoms are yellowing of new growth. It can be spread by leaf hoppers. Control leaf hoppers with sprays of Sevin or malathion. Pyrethrum is an organic alternative.

Uses—Tall delphiniums are best used as a background in mixed flower beds and borders. Dwarf kinds are best as bedding plants. Both are valued for cutting to make fresh-flower arrangements.

'Summer Skies' delphinium displays huge, light-blue flower spikes and dark "bees" at petal centers.

'Pacific Giant' delphiniums are valued as cut flowers and for flower arrangements.

'Mardi Gras' gerbera is a special early flowering strain. Yellow is just one of many colors in the mixture.

Gilia, or bird's eyes, is a California wildflower that grows best in cool, sunny conditions.

GERBERA
Gerbera jamesoni

Gerbera is also known as *Transvaal daisy* for the region of South Africa where it grows wild. This tender perennial is usually grown as a tender annual. Large, daisylike blooms measure up to 5 inches across. They appear on long, strong stems above a rosette of leaves that grow close to the ground. Colors include yellow, orange, white, pink, red and salmon. Flowers appear continually during summer. Plants grow 15 inches high and spread 12 inches wide.

Recommended Varieties—'Florist's Strain' is a popular mixture. 'Mardi Gras' flowers weeks earlier. Both produce single flowers. No variety will produce 100% double flowers, but 'Fantasia' produces up to 75% double, crested flowers.

How to Grow—For flowers outdoors, start seeds indoors 10 weeks before last frost date. Plant after all danger of frost has passed. Barely cover seeds with soil because they need light to germinate. Sow only fresh seeds, because they do not store well. Seeds germinate in 5 to 10 days at 70F to 85F (21C to 30C) soil temperature.

To bring plant to flower indoors, they will need 14 to 18 weeks of continuous growth. Germinate seeds in flats or seed trays and transfer to individual 6-inch pots when large enough to handle. Fill pots with a mixture of 1/3 sand, 1/3 peat or leaf mold and 1/3 sterile topsoil. Feed every 2 weeks with a diluted liquid fertilizer. Maintain night temperatures as close as possible to 50F to 55F (10C to 13C).

Space plants 12 inches apart in full sun in fertile loam soil. Water during dry spells. Gerberas tolerate daytime heat and prefer cool nights. Without cool nights, flowering will stop.

Control slugs and snails by using slug bait or pick them off by hand. Mites can be a serious problem indoors. Spray with dicofol or wash plants with an insecticidal soap.

Uses—Usually grown as cut flowers in a cool greenhouse. Popular for beds and borders.

GILIA
Gilia tricolor

Commonly known as *bird's eyes,* this California wildflower is a hardy annual that requires cool, sunny conditions to grow well. Flowers are small, borne in clusters. They are white with pink tips to the petals and have black centers. Plants grow to 2 feet high and spread 6 inches wide. Flowers appear for several weeks in early summer.

Recommended Varieties—Not sold by variety name.

How to Grow—Sow seeds directly in the garden as soon as soil has warmed in spring. Germination takes 8 days at 60F (16C) soil temperature. Seeds are sensitive to temperatures above 70F (21C).

Space plants 6 inches apart in full sun. Plants tolerate a wide range of soil conditions—even poor soils—but prefer loam or sandy soil. Water regularly during dry spells. Plants cannot tolerate heat or drought and do best in cool regions such as coastal California and the Pacific Northwest. Generally free of pests and diseases.

Uses—Usually grown in beds and borders of mixed annuals and in wildflower plantings.

HOLLYHOCK
Alcea rosea

Sown early in the season, hollyhocks will flower the first year. Botanically they are hardy perennials, and usually come up each year. They are tall-growing plants with large blooms up to 4 inches across. They appear on flower spikes that can grow to 10 feet high, spreading 2 to 3 feet wide. Plant breeders have produced some dwarf types that are grown mostly as annuals. Colors include white, yellow, pink, crimson and red. Flowers can be single, semidouble or fully double. Fully double forms resemble a powder puff. It is these varieties that are most available. Native to China.

Recommended Varieties—'Summer Carnival', mixed colors, grows to 5 feet high. It won an All-America award for its earliness and superb color range. 'Majorette', mixed colors, also won an All-America award for its smaller size—2-1/2 feet. 'Chater's Giants' grow to 10 feet high. All are fully double forms.

How to Grow—For blooms the first year, start seeds indoors 6 to 8 weeks before last frost date. Barely cover seeds with soil because they need light to germinate. Germination takes 5 to 18 days at 70F to 85F (21C to 30C) soil temperature. Soaking seeds overnight speeds germination. Set out seedlings after all danger of frost has passed.

Space plants 12 inches apart in full sun. Plants prefer a deep, fertile loam soil and plenty of moisture. They are heavy feeders and benefit from applications of liquid fertilizer at flowering time. Although newer dwarf varieties are perennial, they are generally weak and usually fail after the first season. Taller varieties will self-sow, but volunteers of double-flower types will revert back to single-flower form.

The worst problem with hollyhocks is rust disease, identified by brown pustules on undersides of leaves. Dusting plants with sulfur or spraying with zineb offers some control. It is best to destroy severely infected plants. Anthracnose is another destructive disease, identified by black blotches on stems and leaves. Control with sprays of Bordeaux mixture. Prune and destroy infected plant parts in fall.

Uses—Tall forms are an old-fashion favorite, useful as background highlight in borders or as temporary screen. Dwarf forms can be used in beds and borders for summer displays.

'Chater's Giants' hollyhock has attractive, double, pompon-type blooms.

Flowers of 'Loveliness' lavatera have a satinlike sheen. Plants are heat resistant.

LAVATERA
Lavatera trimestris

Lavatera, also known as *tree mallow,* is a hardy annual native to the Mediterranean. It closely resembles the wild mallows widely distributed throughout North America. Flowers are large, prolific and eye-catching in shimmering white or pink, up to 4 inches across. They appear from midsummer to fall frost. Plants grow 3 to 4 feet high and spread 2 feet wide. Leaves are shaped like maple leaves.

Recommended Varieties—'Loveliness' is the most widely available. 'Tanagra' has larger flowers. It won a Fleuroselect award in 1973.

How to Grow—Lavatera dislikes transplanting. Sow seeds directly in the garden after all danger of frost has passed. Plant 1/4 inch deep. Germination takes 7 to 21 days at 70F (21C). Soak seeds in water overnight or file seed coat to aid penetration of moisture.

Space plants 1 to 2 feet apart in sandy soil. Water is necessary only after soil becomes dry. Like most members of the mallow family, plants are highly susceptible to rust disease. Brown pustules on undersides of leaves are signs of rust. In susceptible areas, dust with a sulfur-based fungicide. Remove and destroy rust-infected leaves as soon as they are noticed.

Uses—Accent plant in mixed beds and borders. Also effective as a background because of their height. Flowers are edible and are useful for cutting.

LINARIA
Linaria maroccana

These hardy annuals are also called *toadflax.* Dainty, snapdragonlike flowers closely resemble wild snapdragons known as *butter and eggs,* common to waysides in North America. Colors include white, yellow, pink, red, purple, blue and many bicolors. Flowers last several weeks during summer. Plants grow 8 to 12 inches high and spread 6 inches wide. Native to Morocco.

Recommended Varieties—'Fairy Bouquet' won an All-America award for its compact growth habit and multitude of bright colors.

How to Grow—Sow seeds outdoors as soon as soil can be worked in spring. Or start seeds indoors 6 weeks before time to plant outdoors. Germination takes 8 days at 60F (16C) soil temperature. Chilling seeds for 3 days at 40F (5C)—about the temperature in the vegetable bin of the refrigerator—encourages maximum germination.

Space plants 6 inches apart in full sun. Soil should be sandy and fertile. Water regularly. Plants flower best during cool, sunny weather. Generally free of pests and diseases.

Uses—Low, edging plant for beds and borders. Popular in rock gardens. Sometimes grown as container plant in greenhouse during winter.

'Fairy Bouquet' linaria won an All-America award for its extensive color range. Flowers resemble miniature snapdragons.

MIMULUS
Mimulus hybridus

Mimulus is also known as *monkey flower* because the velvety, freckled flower design resembles a monkey's face. It is a tender annual. Recently developed cultivated hybrid varieties are mostly dwarf, mound-shape plants. They are available in a rich range of colors, including red, yellow, orange and white. Many of the funnel-shape flowers have exotic, spotted patterns with contrasting colors. Plants grow 12 inches high and spread 12 inches wide. Flowers appear continually during cool weather. Native to Chile.

Recommended Varieties—'Velvet' hybrid is an American strain. Flowers are predominately red and yellow shades.

How to Grow—Start seeds indoors 10 weeks before last frost date. Germination takes 14 days at 60F (15C) soil temperature. Exposure to light aids germination.

Space plants 6 inches apart in full sun or light shade. Soil should be cool and moist, preferably enriched with plenty of organic matter. Plants cease to flower in hot weather. Pick faded flowers to promote continual bloom.

Uses—Bedding plant in moist, shaded locations and around the perimeter of ponds or garden pools. Suitable for container plantings in tubs and window boxes.

MOONFLOWER
Ipomoea alba

These tender annuals are fast-growing vines that need a strong trellis or fencing for support. Moonflowers resemble large, white, morning glories but bloom at night all summer. Flowers begin to open in the late afternoon and remain open until midmorning of the following day. The 6-inch flowers are pollinated by night-flying moths. Plants grow to 15 feet high and have large, decorative, heart-shape leaves. Native to the tropics of South America.

Recommended Varieties—Not normally sold by variety name.

How to Grow—Seeds have an extremely hard coat. To speed germination, soak seeds overnight in lukewarm water or notch seed coat with file to allow moisture penetration. Seeds may be sown outdoors after all danger of frost has passed. Or start seeds indoors 4 weeks before last frost date. Cover with 1 inch of soil. Germination takes 10 days at 70F to 85F (21C to 30C) soil temperature.

Space plants 12 inches apart in full sun. Loose, fertile, sandy soil suits them best. Overwatering can encourage too much leaf growth at expense of flowers, especially if soil is high in nitrogen. Sturdy support for heavy vines is essential.

New transplants should be protected from slugs and snails. Use slug bait or remove pests by hand. Japanese beetles can cause damage. Control with Sevin chemical spray or traps.

Uses—Climbs around porch or other structure close to the house. Locate so flowers can be highlighted by moonlight. Makes a thick, luxurious screen.

Mimulus, or monkey flower, has been hybridized to make them more heat tolerant and suitable to grow as early summer bedding plants.

Moonflower is a spectacular vining annual. Flowers open in late afternoon and last until the following morning.

Nemophila, or baby blue eyes, is a California wildflower commonly used to edge beds and borders.

NEMOPHILA
Nemophila menziesii

This hardy annual is a California wildflower also known as *baby blue eyes*. It is valued for its ability to produce masses of delicate, cup-shape, sky-blue flowers under cool, sunny conditions. Neat, compact, mounded plants grow 9 inches high and spread 9 inches wide.

Recommended Varieties—Not normally sold by variety name.

How to Grow—Sow seeds outdoors as soon as soil warms in early spring. Or start seeds indoors 6 weeks before time to plant outdoors. Germination takes 5 to 10 days at 60F (16C) soil temperature. Seeds are sensitive to temperatures above 70F (21C).

Space plants 6 inches apart in full sun. Nemophila tolerates a wide range of soil conditions, even poor soil. Keep soil moist during dry spells. Plants readily self-seed and are rarely troubled by pests or diseases.

Uses—Excellent for edging beds and borders and for naturalizing along waysides and in wildflower meadows.

NICOTIANA
Nicotiana alata

Nicotiana is also known as *flowering tobacco*. These tender annuals have been grown for many years, but old, traditional varieties had many shortcomings. Flowers would close in the afternoon, and plants would grow tall and weedy to 3 feet high. Recently, plant breeders have introduced improved hybrids that are semidwarf, growing 1-1/2 feet high. Flowers grow to 2 inches across and remain open all day. Flowering continues through summer, matching petunias for sheer brilliance. Colors include white, lime-green, yellow, pink, red and purple. Petals have a shimmer to them that intensifies the color impact. Native to South America.

Recommended Varieties—'Niki' series of semidwarf hybrids is outstanding, particularly 'Niki Red', winner of an All-America award. Other separate colors are available, including an eye-catching white.

Among non-hybrid types, 'Lime Green', an unusual pale green, is popular with flower arrangers. This old-fashion favorite has been surpassed by 'Really Green', a selection from 'Lime Green'. It grows to 30 inches high and has the deepest green available.

How to Grow—Start seeds indoors 6 to 8 weeks before last frost date. Plant after all danger of frost has passed. Light aids germination so press seeds into soil surface just enough to anchor them. Keep seeds moist with a fine spray. Germination takes 5 to 12 days at 70F to 85F (21C to 30C) soil temperature.

Space plants 12 inches apart in full sun. Soil should be fertile, well-drained loam. Plants tolerate dry spells but prefer regular water.

A few virus and fungus diseases cause leaf blemishes, but they are rarely serious enough to affect flowering display. Several kinds of beetles are attracted to nicotiana, including Colorado potato beetle, flea beetle and cucumber beetle. These can be controlled with Sevin chemical spray or pyrethrum organic spray.

Uses—Excellent as summer bedding plants in beds and borders.

'Niki Red' nicotiana, rear, creates a stunning background for French marigold 'Queen Sophia' and verbena 'Sangria'. This planting is part of an All-America display garden.

PEPPER, ORNAMENTAL
Capsicum annuum

Ornamental peppers are tender annuals. Although flowers are usually small and insignificant, they are quickly followed by beautiful yellow, orange and red fruit. Most fruit are cone shape, round or sharply tapered. Plants grow 9 to 12 inches high and spread 9 to 12 inches wide. Native to South America.

Recommended Varieties—'Holiday Cheer', 8 inches high, won an All-America award for its unique, round fruit. 'Fiesta', 9 inches high, produces an abundance of colorful, slender, tapered fruit.

How to Grow—Start seeds indoors 8 to 10 weeks before last frost date. Cover seeds with 1/4 inch of fine soil. Germination occurs in 6 to 14 days at 70F to 85F (21C to 30C) soil temperature. Plant seedlings after all danger of frost has passed. Plants started from seeds in July will have colorful fruit by Christmas for indoor decoration.

Space plants 9 inches apart in full sun. Soil should be fertile loam. Keep soil moist. Feed plants every 2 weeks with a liquid fertilizer after plants begin to flower. Because fruit are exceedingly hot, plants are generally free of pests and diseases.

Uses—Edging beds and borders. Christmas peppers are often grown in pots for sale at Christmas.

PERILLA
Perilla frutescens

Perilla is a tender annual commonly grown for its colorful, purple leaves that resemble coleus. Plants grow to 3 feet high and spread 2 feet wide. Native to India.

Recommended Varieties—Not normally sold by variety name. Sometimes sold as beefsteak plant.

How to Grow—Sow seeds outdoors after all danger of frost has passed. Or sow seeds indoors 5 to 6 weeks before last frost date. Germination takes 15 to 20 days at 70F to 85F (21C to 30C) soil temperature. Do not cover seeds because they need light to germinate. Take care not to disturb roots when transplanting.

Space plants 15 inches apart in full sun. Plants tolerate wide range of soil conditions. Provide with regular water. Plants may need staking in rich, fertile soils. Control height by pinching out growing tip. Plants are generally free of pests and diseases.

Uses—Background to create contrast for more brightly colored annuals such as marigolds, petunias and zinnias.

'Holiday Cheer' ornamental pepper won an All-America award for its value as a colorful bedding plant.

Close-up of perilla shows its shiny, textured, bronze-color leaves.

Mass planting of annual phlox covers an enormous flower bed near Orlando, Florida.

Selection of pimpernel blossoms shows main assortment of colors.

PHLOX

Phlox drummondi

Annual phlox is a hardy, heat-resistant, summer-flowering annual. Flowers are single, borne in clusters on compact, mound-shape plants. Colors include white, blue, red, pink and lavender. Some are bicolor with white stars in the center. Petal tips can be smooth or fringed. Plants grow 8 to 15 inches high and spread 8 inches wide. Native to Texas.

Recommended Varieties—'Twinkle', mixed colors, 8 inches high, won an All-America award for its exotic, pointed petals and beautiful, star patterns. 'Dwarf Beauty' is a compact, free-flowering mixture, with plain-edge petals, growing to 8 inches high.

How to Grow—Sow seeds outdoors in spring as soon as soil can be worked. Cover seeds with 1/8 inch of fine soil. Seedlings are hardy and will tolerate mild frosts. For earlier flowers, start seeds indoors 6 to 8 weeks before time to plant outdoors. Keep seed tray in total darkness until seedlings emerge. Germination takes 6 to 15 days at 55F to 65F (13C to 19C) soil temperature. When thinning seedlings don't discard smallest or weakest plants. These generally produce the best colors.

Space plants 12 inches apart in full sun in fertile, loose soil. Water regularly during dry spells. Feed plants with a diluted liquid plant food when flower buds appear. Pick faded flowers to encourage continual bloom.

Potential insect pests include beetles, phlox plant bug, mites and nematodes. The beetles and phlox plant bug can be controlled by Sevin or malathion chemical spray or rotenone-pyrethrum organic spray. Control mites with dicofol or wash plants with insecticidal soap. To control nematodes, sterilize soil by fumigation. This is best done by a professional exterminating company.

Several fungus diseases such as powdery mildew can infect plants. Benomyl can reduce infestations.

Uses—Massed plantings in beds and borders. Popular as edging and in rock gardens. Valued as cut flower by flower arrangers.

PIMPERNEL

Anagallis linifolia

These are tender perennials usually grown as tender annuals. Pimpernel are large-flower cousins of the scarlet pimpernel, a weed common throughout North America. Colors include blue, purple and red. Plants grow 12 inches high and spread 6 inches wide. Flowers are produced during summer under cool, sunny conditions. Native to the Mediterranean.

Recommended Varieties—Not normally sold by variety name. Sometimes the mixture is sold as grandiflora.

How to Grow—Sow seeds directly in the garden after all danger of frost has passed. Lightly cover seeds with fine soil because light aids germination. Or start seeds indoors 6 to 8 weeks before last frost date. Germination takes 10 to 21 days at 60F (16C) soil temperature. Seeds are sensitive to temperatures above 60F (16C).

Space plants 6 inches apart in full sun. Plants prefer cool, loam soil. Water regularly during dry spells. Generally free of pests and diseases.

Uses—Edging beds and borders. Planted as clumps in rock gardens. Does best in cool regions.

SHASTA DAISY
Chrysanthemum maximum

Shasta daisies are hardy perennials, flowering the second season when grown from seeds. Special, early flowering dwarf kinds are becoming available. They can be grown as hardy annuals, flowering the first year from seeds sown indoors early in the season. Flowers of annual types are smaller than perennial varieties, and there are not yet any double flowers. Flowers are pure-white with yellow centers, measuring up to 2-1/2 inches across. Plants grow 12 inches high and spread 12 inches wide. Flowers bloom continually all summer. Native to Europe.

Recommended Varieties—'Silver Princess', also listed as 'Miss Muffet', grows as a beautiful mound of leaves just 12 inches high, with many flowers held on strong, wiry stems.

How to Grow—Seedlings tolerate mild frosts if they are hardened-off. Start seeds indoors 8 weeks before time to plant outdoors. Transplanting can occur several weeks before the last frost date. Do not cover seeds with soil because they need light for germination. Germination takes 10 to 14 days at 70F to 75F (21C to 24C) soil temperature.

Space plants 12 inches apart in full sun in fertile loam soil. Keep soil moist and feed with liquid fertilizer at time of flowering to obtain largest flowers and longest bloom. Generally free of pests and diseases.

Uses—Mixed beds and borders, particularly for edging. Valued by flower arrangers for cutting.

'Silver Princess' Shasta daisy is a special dwarf variety that creates a cushion of flowers.

SHOO-FLY PLANT
Nicandra physaloides

This tender annual received its name because its blue flowers are repellent to insects. Flowers resemble miniature morning glories and are followed by yellow, lantern-like seed cases. These cases can be dried and used in flower arrangements. Plants grow 2 to 3 feet high and spread 2 feet wide. Native to Peru.

Recommended Varieties—Not sold by variety name.

How to Grow—Start seeds indoors 8 to 10 weeks before last frost date. Plant after all danger of frost has passed. Germination occurs in 15 to 20 days at 70F to 85F (21C to 30C) soil temperature.

Space plants 12 inches apart in full sun. Plant in fertile, well-drained garden soil. Water regularly during dry spells. Flowering is enhanced by feeding plants monthly with a diluted liquid fertilizer. Generally free of pests and diseases.

Uses—Mostly used as a curiosity in mixed beds and borders. Also grown as winter-flowering container plant in greenhouses. Decorative seed cases are used in dried arrangements.

Shoo-fly plant is grown mostly as a curiosity because of its trait of repelling insects.

BULBS

Mention the word bulbs to someone, and what images come to mind? *Color* is often mentioned, usually in the form of tulip beds, blended together like a brilliant rainbow. *Spring,* with its spirit of renewal, is also associated with bulbs. For many gardeners, the brilliant sungold yellow of a daffodil, more than any other flower, announces that spring has arrived.

This chapter is intended to introduce you to the magical group of plants known as *bulbs.* It is fascinating to plant a bulb, enjoy its bloom and have it disappear, knowing it will reappear. Most bulbs live for years, and it is fun to anticipate their annual return.

Bulbs are easy to grow and care for. For best results, you should know which ones are best suited to your tastes and climate, and details of their culture.

Adventurous gardeners are in for many exciting surprises when they experiment with some of the lesser-known bulbs. Although such experimentation is not always successful, gardeners have had a great deal of fun growing out-of-the-ordinary bulbs.

BULBS IN THE PAST

Before written history, about 1500 B.C., fresco paintings of *Crocus,* lilies and *Iris* were used to decorate the walls of the palace of Knossos, Crete. Garden designs that include bulbs have been found among the hieroglyphics of ancient Egypt. Persian sultans of the 15th and 16th centuries sent emissaries throughout the Near East to scout for tulips and other bulbs. In 1593, the Austrian ambassador to Turkey brought the first tulips to Europe. "Tulipmania" soon followed. During this period, speculation by the Dutch sent bulb prices to astronomical heights. It wasn't unusual for a single bulb of a new tulip variety to cost more than $5,000!

Since that time, Holland has been commonly associated with bulbs. The Dutch, more than any other people, have elevated bulb growing to an art. By seeking out new species and through extensive hybridizing, they have enhanced the vigor and beauty of bulbs.

BULBS ARE ADAPTABLE

Most bulbs are adapted to regions that have cold winters or seasonally dry conditions when dormancy is required. The majority of bulbs prefer dry, well-drained soil during dormancy. This often occurs shortly after flowering. Some, such as *Lilium* species, never become completely dormant. They should not be allowed to dry out completely.

Many variations exist among the different kinds of bulbs. This diversity is what makes bulbs such fascinating garden subjects. This chapter will help you learn the "personalities" of the different kinds of bulbs, common and unusual, helping to ensure successful bulb culture year after year.

Left: Fresh spring blooms of 'Big Chief' tulips brighten this garden scene. Above: 'Spellbinder' daffodils, aglow with afternoon sun, cast their spell on a young admirer.

Bulbs are Bold

Most bulbs appear above ground only when conditions are favorable to their growth. As a result, they may spend half to three-quarters of their life beneath the ground. Because their above-ground life is often short, they compensate by producing brilliant displays of colorful or fragrant flowers. These unique characteristics have made bulbs popular throughout the world.

The Dutch Bulb Growers Association sponsors Keukenhof, a 60-acre park devoted exclusively to the display of spring bulbs. Open only six weeks each year during April, May or June, depending on the weather, it is a spellbinding sight. Lawns, lakes, trees, fountains and sculptures are featured with the bulb plantings. Areas of the park are informal, with paths wandering among trees. Other sections are spectacular, with expansive plantings of bulbs in full bloom. After the brilliant spring show, the park is closed and plans are made for the following year.

Above: Colorful tulips welcome spring at Old Westbury Gardens, Long Island, New York.

Right: 'King Alfred' was introduced in the early 1900s, and quickly became the premier daffodil. As with all daffodils, it is a superb bulb for containers.

Above Left: 'Professor Einstein' is one of many popular daffodils.

Left: Keukenhof Gardens, Holland, is open to the public only six weeks out of the year. During this time, thousands visit the gardens daily, awed by the spectacular displays of spring-blooming bulbs.

Bulbs and Their Origins

Bulbs can be found all over the world. Probably the greatest number come from South Africa. The long, dry, summer weather has forced plants to retreat into life-preserving bulb forms. *Gladiolus* is the most widely grown, but *Freesia, Sparaxis, Tritonia, Ixia, Babiana, Lachenalia, Amaryllis, Clivia, Agapanthus* and many others are from there.

In Asia Minor, winters are exceedingly cold and summers are hot. Tulips have adapted to these conditions. Without cold, top growth begins before roots are able to develop sufficiently to support the plant. During the heat of summer, the bud is formed. *Tulipa clusiana* and *T. saxatilis* are among the few species that can thrive in mild-winter areas. Hyacinths prefer areas with similar conditions, but their close relative, *Muscari*, grape hyacinth, is well adapted to a wide range of climates.

From the western Mediterranean, Portugal, Spain and North Africa, come most of the *Narcissus* species. A few are native to England. Poeticus *Narcissus* come from the mountains of southern Europe. The Tazettas, a special group that produces foliage in the fall, grow in mild-winter areas that extend as far east as Japan.

Crocus also hails from around the Mediterranean. Certain species have adapted to other locales. *C. vernus*, from the Alps, requires cold to do well. *C. goulimyi* from Sparta and *C. imperati* from Naples have adapted to milder climates.

In most parts of the Northern Hemisphere, some species of *Iris* are native. Surprisingly, none are native to the Southern Hemisphere. The largest number come from the Mediterranean and from Asia Minor. *Iris x germanica* var. *florentina* became the symbol of the city of Florence. *I. pseudacorus*, the yellow water iris, was the emblem of Louis VII. It was stylized into the *Fleur-De-Lis*, the armorial emblem of the French royal family. *Iris germanica*, the bearded iris and its many hybrids, is probably the most widely grown.

Several *Irises* are natives of North America, such as the Louisiana iris and the Pacific Coast iris. *Irises* are also found in the Orient and Siberia. The tall, bulbous iris comes from North Africa, Spain and France. The early blooming dwarfs are from the eastern Mediterranean and Asia Minor.

The biggest contribution of bulbs from Asia are the many superb lilies. *Lilium auratum*, the gold-banded lily, *L. speciosum rubrum* with its pink shades and dots and *L. longiflorum*, the Easter lily, are from Japan. *L. regale*, the regal lily, is from Tibet. Many fine lilies also come from North America, Europe and Asia Minor.

Lycoris, from the mild areas of the Orient, is the counterpart to *Nerine* of South Africa. Both have similar, handsome flowers and are often confused with each other.

North and South America have all classes of bulbs: *true bulbs, corms, rhizomes, tubers* and *tuberous roots*. Rhizomes, tubers and tuberous roots are most numerous. They include favorites such as *Cannas, Dahlias*, tuberous begonias and *Caladiums*.

Hippeastrum are from South America. Botanists have separated them from the *Amaryllis* of South Africa. Dutch amaryllis were developed from *Hippeastrum*, and have managed to keep their now-incorrect name.

One genus, the legendary *Paramongaia* of Peru, is rare and seen only in a few botanical gardens. It resembles a large, fragrant, oversize daffodil.

According to modern-day bulb explorers, many bulbs remain to be discovered, especially in regions of South America and Russia.

Trillium grandiflorum, commonly known as *wake robin,* is native to North America. It requires moist, forestlike conditions.

Alstroemeria species and hybrids are tuberous-rooted plants native to South America. They make unusually long-lasting cut flowers, and come in a range of bright colors.

Tigridia pavonia is a summer-blooming bulb from Mexico. Large, showy flowers last only one day, but many flowers are produced over a long period.

Bulbous oxalis are found throughout the world, but the best garden kinds come from South America and South Africa. Most are deciduous and reliable plants in mild climates. In cold-climate areas, they make attractive house plants.

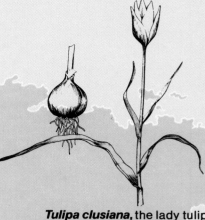

Narcissus, common daffodil, is planted more than any other bulb. Most are native to Portugal, Spain and England. Some are native to areas around the Mediterranean. The family is large—daffodils are adapted to almost every climate.

Anthericum is a fine bulb for Eastern gardens. Native to European Alps, it is a distant relative of the common house plant known as *spider plant, Chlorophytum comosum.*

Tulipa clusiana, the lady tulip, is a charming, informal species tulip. A Mediterranean native, it is one of the few tulips that grows well in southern California. It spreads by *droopers,* small bulbs that form at the root tip.

Crocus is native to the Mediterranean region. Flowers truly announce the beginning of spring: Without sufficient warmth from the sun, flowers cannot open.

Muscari is native to the Mediterranean region. It is a rampant naturalizer, sometimes to the extent that it becomes a weed. Its flowers are rich, deep blue—the best to combine with yellow daffodils.

Gladiolus is a large group of corms from South Africa. The most common hybrid comes in a wide range of sizes and colors.

Zantedeschia, the well-known calla lily, is native to South Africa. It is easy to grow in mild climates and is an adaptable house plant.

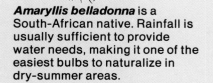

Amaryllis belladonna is a South-African native. Rainfall is usually sufficient to provide water needs, making it one of the easiest bulbs to naturalize in dry-summer areas.

171

Bulb Selection Guide

Bulbs for Containers

Any bulb can be grown in a container for at least one season. Tulips, hyacinths, *Narcissus*, *Crocus* and Easter lilies are favorites. Because of their naturally extensive root systems, they seldom flower well year after year. Rhizomatous bulbs such as bearded iris and *Canna* grow horizontally and quickly push to the side of the container.

Some bulbs thrive under crowded conditions. They can remain in the same pot for years. Eventually, they have to be separated and repotted. The best include:

Agapanthus
Clivia
Eucharis
Eucomis
Freesia
Haemanthus
Hippeastrum
Hymenocallis
Ipheion
Ixia maculata
Lapeirousia
Muscari
Nerine
Oxalis
Pancratium
Sparaxis
Tritonia
Urginea
Velthemia

Muscari armeniacum

Bulbs for Fragrance

Many bulbs produce some fragrance. The following have a strong and pleasant scent.

Acidanthera bicolor
Amaryllis belladonna
Chlidanthus fragrans
Convallaria majalis
Crinum americanum
Crinum moorei
Eucharis amazonica
Freesia refracta
Gladiolus tristis
Hyacinthus orientalis
Hymenocallis species
Iris x germanica var. florentina
Leucocoryne ixioides
Lilium species, especially trumpets
  and bowl shaped
Lycoris squamigera
Narcissus jonquilla
Narcissus tazetta
Pancratium
Polianthes tuberosa

Bulbs that Naturalize

If conditions are ideal for growth most bulbs *naturalize*—grow and multiply on their own. Some are especially suited to naturalizing because they are long-lived, or because they multiply rapidly. Naturalized bulbs require little care after they are established.

*Agapanthus
Allium
*Amaryllis
Anemone
Belamcanda
Brodiaea
*Chasmanthe
Chionodoxa
Crocus
Cyclamen
Endymion
Eranthis
*Freesia
Fritillaria
Galanthus
Gladiolus tristis
Hemerocallis
Hippeastrum
Ipheion
Iris
*Ixia
Leucojum
Lilium
Muscari
Narcissus
*Narcissus tazetta
*Oxalis
Scilla
*Sparaxis
*Tritonia
Tulipa clusiana
*Zantedeschia

*mild climates only

Bulbs for a Rock Garden

Vigorous-growing bulbs such as *Muscari* are not used in rock gardens because they eventually crowd out other bulbs.

Anemone
Babiana
Calochortus
Chionodoxa
Crocus
Cyclamen
Eranthus
Habranthus
Iris, small kinds
Lapeirousia
Narcissus
Oxalis
Rhodohypoxis
Sternbergia
Tritonia
Tulipa
Zephyranthes

Narcissus bulbocodium obesus

Bulbs for Hanging Baskets

Only a few bulbs have the trailing growth habit and long bloom period particularly adapted to hanging baskets. These include:

Achimenes
Begonia
Oxalis

Convallaria and *Freesias* can be planted in a hanging basket. A bonus is their delightful fragrance. However, their bloom period is relatively short.

Regional Favorites

Many bulbs are widely adapted. Others are best suited to certain climates. Here are some listings to guide your selections.

Cold Climates

Allium
Anthericum
Belamcanda
Bulbocodium
Chionodoxa
Convallaria
Crocus
Eranthis
Galanthus
Hemerocallis
Iris reticulata
Leucojum
Lilium Bellingham hybrids
Muscari
Puschkinia
Scilla
Tulipa

Warm and Humid Climates

Achimenes
Agapanthus
Amaryllis
Caladium
Canna
Clivia
Colocasia
Crinum
Dietes
Eucharis
Gloriosa
Habranthus
Hemerocallis
Hippeastrum
Hymenocallis
Pancratium
Polianthes
Sauromatum
Zantedeschia
Zephyranthes

Mild Climates

Agapanthus
Allium
Amaryllis
Anemone
Babiana
Brunsvigia
Bulbinella
Canna
Chasmanthe
Clivia
Crinum
Crocosmia
Crocus—selected species
Dietes
Endymion
Freesia
Gladiolus
Gloriosa
Habranthus
Haemanthus
Hemerocallis
Hippeastrum
Hymenocallis

Ipheion
Iris
Ixia
Lachenalea
Lapeirousia
Leucojum
Lycoris
Muscari
Narcissus
Nerine
Ornithogalum
Oxalis
Ranunculus
Scilla
Sparaxis
Sprekelia
Tritonia
Tulbaghia
Tulipa—selected species
Watsonia
Zantedeschia
Zephyranthes

Desert Climates

Amaryllis
Brodiaea
Calochortus
Canna
Habranthus
Hemerocallis
Ipheion
Iris
Milla
Oxalis
Ranunculus
Sparaxis
Tulbaghia
Tulipa species
Zephyranthes

Bulbinella species

Ground Covers for Overplanting

Many ground covers complement bulbs. They act as a living mulch, moderating temperatures and conserving moisture. They help keep down mud splashes from rain and irrigation. Choose a ground cover that will be no more than half the height of the bulb flower. Examples are:

Arabis
Arenaria
Aubrieta
Aurinia
Campanula
Cerastium
Chamaemelum
Cotula
Cymbalaria
Erodium
Ferns, low kinds
Galium
Geranium
Hedera helix
Herniaria
Iberis
Lamiastrum

Lamium
Laurentia
Lobelia
Lobularia
Lysimachia
Mazus
Mentha
Myosotis
Omphalodes
Phyla
Potentilla
Sedum
Soleirolia
Thymus
Vancouveria
Veronica
Vinca minor

Bulbs for Special Cultural Conditions

These bulbs are adapted to some of the more common problems of shade, moist soil, and acid or alkaline soil.

Shade

Achimenes
Anemone
Anthericum
Begonia
Clivia
Convallaria
Cyclamen
Endymion
Erythronium
Eucharis
Fritillaria
Galanthus
Muscari
Scilla
Trillium
Zantedeschia

Acid Soil

Allium moly
Convallaria
Endymion
Eranthis
Erythronium
Galanthus
Leucojum
Lilium auratum
Lilium canadense
Lilium superbum
Narcissus cyclamineus
Oxalis
Puschkinia
Scilla
Trillium
Tulipa
Zephyranthes

Moist Soil

Caladium
Camassia
Canna
Colocasia
Convallaria
Eranthis
Hemerocallis
Iris, some species
Zantedeschia

Alkaline Soil

Allium
Amaryllis
Anemone
Brodiaea
Cyclamen
Iris
Narcissus
Nerine
Ornithogalum

Canna species

173

Bulbs by Mail

A wide selection of bulbs may be available from your local nursery, but sometimes you may not be able to find exactly what you need. Or, you may want to specialize in certain kinds of unusual bulbs. If this is the case, mail-order suppliers are dependable sources. Listed here are general and specialty suppliers of bulbs. Specialists are often the only source for rare bulbs.

General Suppliers

Breck's Dutch Bulbs
6523 N. Galena Road
Peoria, IL 61632
Catalog free.

Burpee Seed Co.
231 Burpee Building
Warminster, PA 18991
Catalog free.

DeJager Bulbs, Inc.
188 Asbury St. Dept. HPB
South Hamilton, MA 01982
Catalog free.

Dutch Gardens, Inc.
Box 400
Montvale, NJ 07645

International Growers Exchange
Box 397-P
East Farmington, MI 48024
Catalog $3.00.

John Scheepers
63 Wall St.
New York, NY 10005
Catalog free.

Mary Mattison Van Schaik
Cavendish, VT 05142
Catalog 50¢.

Messelaar Bulb Co.
Box 269
Ipswich, MA 01938
Catalog free.

Park Seed Co.
459 Cokesbury Road
Greenwood, SC 29647
Catalog free.

Quality Dutch Bulbs, Inc.
Dept. B
52 Lake Drive
Hillsdale, NJ 07642
Catalog free.

Wayside Gardens
503 Garden Lane
Hodges, SC 29695
Catalog $1.00.

White Flower Farm
Litchfield, CT 06759
Catalog $5.00.

Dahlia Specialists

Almand's Dahlia Gardens
2541 West Ave. 133
San Leandro, CA 94577

Blue Dahlia Gardens
G. Kenneth Furrer
San Jose, IL 62682

Forest View Gardens
Route 3, Box 136
Fairmont, WV 26554

Ruschmohr Dahlia Gardens,
H. Dewey Mohr, Prop.,
38 Vincent St. Box 884
Rockville Centre, NY 11571

White Dahlia Gardens
2480 S.E. Creighton Ave.
Milwaukie, OR 97222

Daylily Specialists

Cordon Bleu Farms
418 Buena Creek Road
San Marcus, CA 92069

Gilbert Wild & Son
1110 Joplin St.
Sarcoxie, MO 64862
Catalog $2.00.

Lee Bristol Nursery
Sherman, CT 06784
Send long, self-addressed, stamped envelope for catalog.

Louisiana Nursery
Route 7, Box 43
Opelousas, LA 70570

Seawright Gardens
134 Indian Hill
Carlisle, MA 01741
Catalog $1.00.

Tranquil Lake Nursery
45 River St.
Rehoboth, MA 02769
Catalog 25¢.

Gladiolus Specialists

Baldridge Glads
Sidney L. Baldridge
1729 19th Ave.
Greeley, CO 80631

Coastal Bulb Farm
John Ooosterwyk
Box 97
Hamstead, NC 28443

Flad's Glads
2109 Cliff Court
Madison, WI 53713

Gladside Gardens
Corys M. Heselton
61 Main St.
Northfield, MA 01360
Also carry *Dahlias* and tropical bulbs.

Kingfisher Glads
Sam N. Fisher
11345 Moreno Ave.
Lakeside, CA 92040

Noweta Gardens, Inc.
900 Whitewater Ave.
St. Charles, MN 55972

Pleasant Valley Glads
Gary Adams
163 Senator Ave.
Agawam, MA 01001

Valley Stream Farm
D.R. Woudstra
Orano, Ontario, Canada
LOB 1MO

Iris Specialists

Alpenflora Gardens
17985 40th Ave.
Surrey (Cloverdale) B.C.
Canada V3S 4N8
Good selection of Pacific Coast Natives.

Bay View Gardens
1201 Bay St.
Santa Cruz, CA 95060
Many species iris. Catalog $1.00.

Borbeleta Gardens
10078 154th Ave.
Elk River, MN 55330
Siberian iris only.

Cooley's Gardens
Box 126
301 S. James St.
Silverton, OR 97381
Tall bearded iris.
Catalog $2.00, deductible from first order.

Cordon Bleu Farms
418 Buena Creek Road
San Marcus, CA 92069

Louisiana Nursery
Route 7, Box 43
Opelousas, LA 70570
Louisiana iris.

Melrose Gardens
309 Best Road South
Stockton, CA. 95206
Catalog $1.00.

Schreiner's Gardens
3625 Quinby Road, NE
Salem, OR 97303
Many varieties. Color catalog $2.00.

David B. Sindt - Irises
1331 West Cornellia
Chicago, IL 60657
Pumilas and small-bearded iris.
Catalog on request.

Thompson and Morgan
Box 100
Farmingdale, NJ 07727
Iris seeds.

Tranquil Lake Nursery
45 River St.
Rehoboth, MA 02769
Catalog 25¢.

Vagabond Gardens
11115 Bodega Highway
Sebastopol, CA 95472
Bearded, Siberian, Louisiana and Pacific-Coast hybrids. Reblooming irises. Catalog $1.00.

Gilbert Wild & Son
Box 338
Sarcoxie, MO 64882
Color catalog $2.00.

Lily Specialists

Rex Lilies
Box 774
Port Townsend, WA 98368

Strahm's Lilies
Box 2216
Harbor, OR 97415
Color catalog 50¢.

Narcissus Specialists

Blom's Daffodils
Leavesden, Watford
Hertfordshire, England
Color catalog.

Carncairn Daffodils
Carncairn Lodge, Broughshane
Ballymena BT43-7HF
County Antrim, Northern Ireland
Free catalog.

John Lea
Dunley Hall, Stourport on Severn
Worcestershire, England
Descriptive list available.

Grant E. Mitsch Novelty Daffodils
Box 218
Hubbard, OR 97032
Specialists in pinks and species hybrids.
Color catalog $2.50, deductible from first order.

P & G Phillips
P.O. Box 177
Otorohanga, New Zealand
Many Southern Hemisphere hybrids.

Rathowden
Knowehead, Dergmoney, Omagh
County Tyrone, Northern Ireland
Many show favorites. Color catalog available.

River's Edge Farm
Rt. 3, Box 228A
Gloucester, VA 23061

Mrs. J. Abel Smith
Orchard House, Letty Green
Near Hertford, England
Pinks specialist. Descriptive list available.

Nerine

Nerine Nurseries
Welland, Worcestershire
WR 13 6LN, England
Catalog $2.00.

PLANTING BULBS

Too often, bulbs are thought to grow and bloom regardless of how they are planted. Although this is true to a certain extent, you can increase your success by supplying bulbs with good growing conditions.

EXAMINE BULBS

Before you plant, look bulbs over closely to determine their quality. Soft bulbs or those showing signs of rot should be discarded. If a particularly rare or valuable bulb shows damage, you might be able to save it by removing the bad spot with a sharp knife. Dust with sulfur or a fungicide to help prevent spread of disease. Bulbs that are lightweight are usually dehydrated or dead, and should be discarded. Lilies without protective covers often have dehydrated scales. You may be able to save them by placing them between wet towels or damp peat moss until the scales plump up again. *Anemones* that are overly dry may also benefit from this treatment.

PREPARE SOIL

Most bulbs prefer a soil that is not too acid. Any soil that has a pH 6.0 or below should be adjusted. It is a good idea to test the soil of a new planting area tested. Home test kits are available that will tell you the soil's pH. To be absolutely accurate, a laboratory soil test interpreted by an expert is best. State universities in all states except California and Illinois perform soil tests for a fee. Look in the white pages of your phone book under "county extension agent," "cooperative extension service," or contact your state university to determine the soil-testing laboratory nearest you. In California and Illinois, consult the Yellow Pages of your phone book for a listing of private soil-testing laboratories.

You can adjust the soil pH yourself by adding lime to the soil, but the trick is to know how much to add. You can add small amounts, testing soil after each application until the proper pH level was obtained.

In some areas, particularly in the Southwest, soil that is highly alkaline—having a pH of 9.0 and above—can be a problem. Alkaline soil can be adjusted by adding sulfur. Follow package directions closely.

Soak the soil two or three days before planting to make the soil easier to work. When the soil is moist but not muddy, turn it over and break up the clods. It is important that the soil drain well. Most bulbs rot if they sit in soggy soil too long. A heavy clay soil, which tends to drain slowly, can be improved by working in organic matter such as compost, peat moss or leaf mold. Organic materials added to sandy soil help retain moisture and nutrients in the root zone. Do not mix animal manures that are high in nitrogen into the soil. They may burn the bulbs.

Add superphosphate after organic matter has been mixed into the soil. Follow soil test recommendations or directions on package label. Work it into the future root zone of the bulbs. Unlike nitrogen, superphosphate takes a long time to move downward to the root zone, so do not apply it on the soil surface. After all materials have been added, rake the soil level. You are now ready to plant.

How Deep to Plant Bulbs?
As a general rule, plant bulbs at a depth equal to twice the height of the bulb. In heavy clay soil, plant slightly closer to the surface. Plant bulbs in containers as shallow as possible to allow maximum room for root growth. Bulbs that remain in the ground for more than a season will adjust, gradually moving to their preferred depth.

PLANTING

Before you plant bulbs, you should make some sort of plan. Use a stick or stakes and string to mark lines where each group of bulbs is to be located. For natural-looking plantings, you can toss the bulbs on the ground and plant them where they fall. This avoids even, unnatural spacing. The biggest concentration of bulbs should be at the center of a group. This mimics the appearance of bulbs that multiply naturally in the wild.

Bulbs can be planted two different ways. One method is often used for large, formal beds. Remove the soil to an even depth. The bulbs can be placed an equal distance apart and covered with the proper amount of soil. This assures that bulbs of the same variety are planted at the same depth. They will bloom at the same time with stems of equal length.

A second method is to dig individual holes for each bulb with a trowel or other tool. If the ground is loose and well prepared, you can use a bulb planter. This is a conical-shaped device that looks like a tin can open at both ends, with a handle on the top. When pressed into the soil and pulled out, the bulb planter brings the soil with it, creating a hole. The bulb is placed in the hole and the soil is returned. Another device used in turf plantings is a short cylinder at the end of a pole. When pushed into the ground, it cuts out a circle of turf that can be replaced after the bulb is planted. See photo 1 below.

After planting bulbs, rake some fertilizer into the soil. Select a complete fertilizer low in nitrogen, such as a 5-5-5 or 5-10-10. *Complete* means that the major nutrients—nitrogen, phosphorus and potassium—are included. Follow the instructions on the fertilizer label.

1. Bulb planting tool makes individual planting holes. Markings are used as a depth gage. Recommended planting depth of bulb means to bottom of hole, not top of bulb. If planting depth for bulb is 6 inches, make hole 6 inches deep. Long-lived bulbs will eventually adjust to their preferred depth, which varies according to soil composition.

2. Place bulbs in individual holes. Growing tip should face up. If you can't identify the growing tip, place bulb on its side and it will adjust on its own. Check to be sure there are no air pockets beneath bulbs.

3. Water thoroughly and deeply to settle the soil after planting. Water requirements for newly planted bulbs vary considerably, depending on the bulb, the season planted and climate.

4. Add a layer of organic mulch to reduce evaporation of soil moisture, moderate temperatures and deter weeds. Many mulches are available. Or consider overplanting with a ground cover for a colorful, living mulch.

Be sure to label the location and identity of your bulbs. If you don't, you may accidently injure them while digging in the bed at a later date, or plant over them. Plastic or metal labels last longer than wood. Mark with waterproof pens or pencils.

BULBS HAVE VARIED PLANTING DEPTHS

The fact that different bulbs are planted at various depths may seem odd when you consider that all bulbs originate from seeds dropped on the earth's surface. But over the years, bulb growers have found that tulips and daffodils planted near the surface break up into bunches of small bulbs. This is good for reproduction of the species, but not for the following year's bloom. Tall growers such as *Gladiolus* and lilies need the extra support of deep planting to hold them upright. Even then, they often require stakes for supports. *Lilium candidum* is one exception. It should be planted near the soil surface.

The general rule is to plant large bulbs at a depth equal to twice the depth of the bulb, and small bulbs slightly deeper than twice their depth. Bulbs in marginally cold areas benefit from slightly deeper planting to escape below-freezing temperatures. Bulbs in light, sandy soils should be planted a little deeper than normally recommended, and a little shallower in heavy clay soils.

Some bulbs have *contractile* roots that pull the bulb down to the natural desired depth. The beautiful *Leucocoryne*, glory-of-the-sun, has not learned when to cease its downward journey! A rock or piece of broken crockery can be placed under the bulb to halt its continuous descent.

The trench method of planting bulbs is often used for tulips and hyacinths. Remove soil to recommended depth. Level bottom of trench and place bulbs in trench. Bulbs planted at the same depth bloom at the same time and grow to the same maximum height.

Cover trench-planted bulbs with soil. Add soil carefully so that bulbs are not dislodged from their spots when first layer of soil is added.

If plants will need staking, drive stake into the ground at planting time. This is commonly recommended for *Dahlias*. The tuberous roots extend some distance to the sides and can be damaged if stakes are driven into ground after planting.

Gophers, mice, squirrels and chipmunks love tulips, *Crocus* and *Gladiolus* but ignore daffodils. Bulbs susceptible to rodent damage can be protected by encircling the bulbs in chicken wire.

Early Spring Blooming

Anemone x fulgens
Bulbinella floribunda
Chionodoxa, all species
Crocus biflorus
Crocus chrysanthus
Crocus flavus
Crocus sieberi
Crocus angustifolius
Crocus tomasinianus
Cyclamen coum coum
Eranthis hyemalis
Galanthus nivalis
Iris danfordiae
Iris reticulata
Lachenalia pendula
Narcissus, some species
Tulipa, some species

Spring Blooming

Allium aflatunense
Allium karataviense
Allium neapolitanum
Allium triquetrum
Anemone appenina
Anemone coronaria
Anthericum liliago
Babiana, all species
Calochortus albus
Chasmanthe aethiopica
Clivia, all species
Convallaria majalis
Crocus aureus
Crocus kotschyanus
Crocus oliveieri
Crocus vernus
Crocus, Dutch hybrids
Cyclamen coum
Cyclamen hybrids
Cyclamen repandum
Dietes bicolor
Dietes vegeta
Eremurus, all species
Erythronium species
Eucharis grandiflora
Eucomis bicolor
Freesia, all species
Fritillaria meleagris
Galanthus elwesii
Gladiolus x colvillei
Gladiolus tristis
Hippeastrum
Hyacinthus
Hymenocallis caroliniana
Ipheion uniflorum
Iris cristata
Iris douglasiana
Iris, Dutch hybrids
Iris foetidissima
Iris innominata
Iris orientalis, Spurias
Iris, Regeliocyclus hybrids
Iris sibirica
Iris tectorum

Iris unguicularis
Ixiolirion tataricum
Lachenalia pearsonii
Lachenalia tricolor
Lapeirousia laxa
Leucocoryne ixiodes
Leucojum aestivum
Leucojum vernum
Lilium pumilum
Moraea pavonia
Muscari, all species
Narcissus asturiensis
Narcissus bulbocodium
Narcissus cyclamineus
Narcissus hybrids
Narcissus jonquilla
Narcissus poeticus
Narcissus pseudonarcissus
Narcissus tazetta
Narcissus triandrus
Ornithogalum arabicum
Ornithogalum thyrsoides
Oxalis adenophylla
Oxalis bowiei
Oxalis pes-caprae
Oxalis purpurea 'Grand Duchess'
Puschkinia scilloides
Ranunculus asiaticus
Rhodohypoxis baurii
Scilla peruviana
Scilla siberica
Sparaxis tricolor
Sternbergia fischerana
Streptanthera cuprea
Trillium, all species
Triteleia—see *Brodiaea*
Tritonia crocata
Tulipa garden hybrids
Veltheimia capensis
Watsonia garden hybrids
Zantedeschia aethiopica

Late Spring Blooming

Allium aflatunense
Allium karataviense
Allium moly
Allium neapolitanum
Allium triquetrum
Alophia pulchella
Anthericum liliago
Calochortus albus
Clivia nobilis
Dietes bicolor
Dietes iridiodes
Eucharis grandiflora
Fritillaria imperalis
Gladiolus recurvus
Hemerocallis garden hybrids
Hyacinthus orientalis
Iris douglasiana
Iris foetidissima
Iris innominata
Iris x germanica, bearded
Iris, Louisiana group
Leucojum aestivum
Lilium pumilum
Moraea villosa
Muscari comosa
Narcissus poeticus
Oxalis adenophylla
Oxalis bowiei

Plant in Early Spring

Achimenes
Agapanthus
x Amarcrinum
Begonia
Bletilla striata
Chasmanthe aethiopica
Chlidanthus fragrans
Clivia
x Crinodonna
Dietes

Eucharis grandiflora
Sinningia
Sprekelia formosissima
Tulbaghia

Plant in Spring

Achimenes
Acidanthera bicolor
Agapanthus, all species
Alstroemeria, all species
x Amarcrinum
Begonia tuberous kinds
Belamcanda chinensis
Bessera elegans
Bletilla striata
Bulbinella floribunda
Caladium x hortulanum
Canna, all species
Chlidanthus fragrans
Clivia
Colocasia esculenta
x Crinodonna
Crinum, all species
Cyclamen hederifolium
Dahlia garden hybrids
Dietes bicolor
Dietes iridoides
Eucharis grandiflora
Galtonia candicans
Gladiolus alatus
Gladiolus byzantinus
Gladiolus carinatus
Gladiolus caryophyllaceus
Gladiolus hybrids
Gladiolus natalensis
Gloriosa rothschildiana
Habranthus, all species
Haemanthus, all species
Hemerocallis, all species and hybrids
Homeria breyniana
Hyacinthus orientalis
Hymenocallis amancaes
Hymenocallis x festalis
Hymenocallis narcissiflora
Iris x germanica, bearded
Leucojum autumnale
Lilium auratum
Lilium davidii
Lilium henryi
Lilium lancifolium
Lilium longiflorum
Lilium pardalinum
Lilium regale
Lilium speciosum
Lilium superbum
Milla biflora
Polianthes tuberosa
Sauromatum guttatum
Sinningia
Smithiantha
Tigridia pavonia
Tulbaghia fragrans
Tulbaghia violacea
Vallota speciosa
Zantedeshia, all species
Zephyranthes, all species

SUMMER

Early Summer Blooming

Allium aflatunense
Allium karataviense
Allium moly
Allium neapolitanum
Allium triquetrum
Alophia pulchella
Alstroemeria, all species
Anthericum liliago
Calochortus, all species
Camassia, all species
Dietes iridiodes
Dietes tricolor
Eucharis grandiflora
Hemerocallis species and hybrids
Iris douglasiana
Iris foetidissima
Iris innominata
Ixia maculata
Ixia viridiflora
Leucojum aestivum
Lilium pumilum
Moraea villosa
Muscari comosa
Narcissus poeticus
Oxalis adenophylla
Oxalis bowiei
Sauromatum guttatum
Zantedeschia, all species
Zephyranthes atamasco

Summer Blooming

Achimenes
Acidanthera bicolor
Agapanthus
Allium caeruleum
Allium christophii
Allium giganteum
x Amarcrinum
Begonia, tuberous kinds
Belamcanda chinensis
Bessera elegans
Brodiaea, all species
Caladium x hortulanum
Canna garden hybrids

Chlidanthus fragrans
Colocasia esculenta
x Crinodonna
Crinum, all species
Crocosmia, all species
Dahlia garden hybrids
Dietes bicolor
Dietes iridiodes
Eucomis bicolor
Galtonia candicans
Gladiolus alatus
Gladiolus byzantinus
Gladiolus carinatus
Gladiolus caryophyllaceus
Gladiolus hybrids
Gladiolus liliaceus
Gladiolus natalensis
Gloriosa rothschildiana
Habranthus, all species
Haemanthus coccineus
Haemanthus katharinae
Homeria breyniana
Hymenocallis amancaes
Hymenocallis x festalis
Hymenocallis narcissiflora
Iris kaempferi
Iris xiphioides
Lilium, many species
Lycoris radiata
Milla biflora
Sinningia hybrids
Smithiantha hybrids
Sprekelia formosissima
Tigridia pavonia
Tulbaghia violacea
Zephyranthes grandiflora

Late Summer Blooming

Achimenes
Acidanthera bicolor
Amaryllis belladonna
Begonia, tuberous kinds
Brunsvigia josephinae
Canna hybrids
Crinum species
Crocosmia, all species

Dahlia garden hybrids
Dietes bicolor
Dietes iridiodes
Galtonia candicans
Gladiolus alatus
Gladiolus natalensis
Haemanthus albiflos
Lilium auratum
Lilium lancifolium
Lilium speciosum
Lycoris radiata
Polianthes tuberosa
Urginea maritima
Vallota speciosa
Watsonia beatricus
Zephyranthes candida
Zephyranthes tubiflora

Plant in Early Summer

Agapanthus
x Amarcrinum
Clivia
x Crinodonna
Cyclamen hederifolium
Dietes bicolor
Dietes iridiodes
Eucharis grandiflora
Tulbaghia violacea

Plant In Summer

Agapanthus africanus
x Amarcrinum
Brunsvigia josephinae
Clivia
Colchicum, all species
Crocus goulimyi
Crocus longiflorus
Crocus nievus
Crocus sativus
Crocus speciosus
Cyclamen coum coum
Dietes bicolor
Dietes iridiodes
Eucharis grandiflora
Iris cristata
Iris douglasiana
Iris foetidissima
Iris innominata
Iris sibirica
Iris tectorum
Lycoris africana
Lycoris radiata
Moraea polystachya
Nerine species
Tulbaghia fragrans
Tulbaghia violacea
Urginea maritima

Plant In Late Summer

Agapanthus africanus
Amaryllis belladonna
Clivia
x Crinodonna
Dietes bicolor
Dietes iridoides
Eucharis grandiflora
Tulbaghia fragrans

Early Fall Blooming

Achimenes
Acidanthera bicolor
Amaryllis belladonna
Begonia x tuberhybrida
Brunsvigia josephinae
Canna hybrids
Crinum, all species
Crocosmia, all species
Dahlia hybrids
Dietes bicolor
Galtonia candicans
Gladiolus alatus
Gladiolus natalensis
Haemanthus albiflos
Lilium auratum
Lilium lancifolium
Lilium speciosum
Lycoris africanus
Polianthes tuberosa
Urginea maritima
Vallota speciosa
Zephyranthes candida
Zephyranthes tubiflora

Fall Blooming

Achimenes
Acidanthera bicolor
Amaryllis belladonna
Begonia x tuberhybrida
Canna hybrids
Colchicum, all species
Crocosmia, all species
Crocus goulimyi
Crocus longiflorus
Crocus niveus
Crocus sativus
Crocus speciosus
Cyclamen hederifolium
Cyclamen neapolitanum
Dahlia hybrids
Dietes bicolor
Dietes iridoides
Galtonia candicans
Gladiolus alatus
Gladiolus natalensis

Leucojum autumnale
Lilium auratum
Lilium lancifolium
Lilium speciosum
Lycoris africanus
Moraea polystachya
Narcissus viridiflorus
Nerine bowdenii
Nerine sardensis
Sternbergia lutea
Urginea maritima

Late Fall Blooming

Colchicum, all species
Crocus goulimyi
Crocus niveus
Dietes bicolor
Dietes iridiodes
Narcissus tazetta paper-white
Nerine bowdenii

Plant in Early Fall

Agapanthus, all species
Allium, all species
Alophia pulchella
x Amarcrinum
Amaryllis belladonna
Anemone, all species
Anthericum liliago
Babiana stricta
Brodiaea, all species
Calochortus, all species
Camassia, all species
Chionodoxa, all species
Clivia, all species
Convallaria majalis
x Crinodonna
Crocus angustifolius
Crocus aureus
Crocus biflorus
Crocus chrysanthus
Crocus flavus
Crocus imperati
Crocus kotschyanus
Crocus olivieri
Crocus sieberi
Crocus tomasinianus
Crocus vernus

Cyclamen coum coum
Cyclamen persicum
Cyclamen repandum
Dietes iridiodes
Endymion hispanica
Endymion hispanica
Eranthis, all species
Eremurus, all species
Erythronium, all species
Eucharis grandiflora
Freesia refracta
Fritillaria, all species
Galanthus, all species
Gladiolus x colvillei
Gladiolus liliaceus
Gladiolus recurvus
Gladiolus tristis
Hippeastrum species and hybrids
Homeria breyniana
Hyacinthus orientalis
Hymenocallis caroliniana
Ipheion uniflorum
Iris danfordiae
Iris, Dutch hybrids
Iris kaempferi
Iris, Louisiana group
Iris orientalis, Spurias
Iris, Regeliocyclus hybrids
Iris reticulata
Iris unguicularis
Iris xiphioides
Ixia, all species
Ixiolirion tataricum
Lachenalia, all species
Lapeirousia, all species
Leucocoryne ixiodes
Leucojum aestivum
Leucojum vernum
Lilium, most kinds
Lycoris africana
Milla biflora
Moraea villosa
Muscari, all species
Narcissus asturiensis
Narcissus hybrids
Narcissus poeticus
Narcissus tazetta
Ornithogalum arabicum
Ornithogalum thyrsoides
Oxalis, all species
Puschkinia scilloides
Ranunculus asiaticus
Rhodohypoxis baurii
Scilla peruviana
Scilla sibirica
Sparaxis
Sternbergia, all species
Streptanthera cuprea
Trillium, all species
Tritonia crocata
Tulbaghia fragrans
Tulbaghia violacea
Tulipa, all kinds
Veltheimia capensis
Watsonia, all species and hybrids
Zantedeshia aethiopica

Winter Blooming

Anemone blanda
Crocus angustifolius
Crocus biflorus
Crocus chrysanthus
Crocus flavus
Crocus imperati
Crocus niveus
Crocus sieberi
Crocus tomasinianus
Cyclamen coum coum
Cyclamen persicum
Eranthis hyemalis
Galanthus nivalis
Iris danfordiae
Iris reticulata
Narcissus minor
Narcissus tazetta

Narcissus tazetta paper-white
Oxalis hirta
Oxalis purpurea
Tulbaghia fragrans

Winter Blooming As House Plants

Convallaria majalis
Crocus species
Eucharis amazonica
Freesia refracta
Hippeastrum hybrids
Hyacinthus orientalis
Muscari armeniacum
Narcissus tazetta
Oxalis purpurea
Sinningia hybrids
Tulipa species and hybrids
Zantedeschia aethiopica

BULB CARE

Ample water is the most important requirement for bulb growth. In nature, bulbs in cold-winter areas receive moisture from melting snow. In mild or warm regions, bulbs receive heavy seasonal rains. Good soil drainage is necessary when bulbs are subjected to large amounts of water. Without fast drainage, water stagnates in the root zone. This can suffocate and kill the bulbs.

When watering bulbs, water should go deep into the soil—one foot deep is not too much. This promotes deep rooting. Frequent, light sprinklings do not do the job properly. The soil surface remains moist, which encourages viruses, fungi, snails and slugs. Because the water penetrates into the top few inches of soil, the roots stay near the surface. This makes them susceptible to drying out in periods of warm and windy weather.

Give bulbs a long, slow soak when flower buds first appear. Watering at this time means less water is needed when the bulb is in bloom. This avoids problems caused when water accumulates on the flowers, which makes the stems sag and bend. In nature, *Crocus* and tulips eliminate this problem by closing their blooms tightly on cloudy, rainy days.

Sprinklers that spray or shoot water can be damaging to blooms. Soaker hoses or flood irrigation are probably the most effective ways to water and do not damage blooms.

Water bulbs regularly while they are blooming, and for a short time after bloom. Water is necessary because bulbs are building up food reserves for the next year. Generally, water bulbs until the leaves begin to turn brown. This stage signals that bulbs are beginning to rest and enter dormancy. After bloom, some gardeners often give their bulbs a diluted solution of liquid fish-based fertilizer.

WEED CONTROL

Weeds steal nutrients and moisture away from bulb plants. They are also unsightly. Some may be so vigorous that they actually cover the bulb foliage and reduce the amount of available sunlight. Weeds also harbor pests such as slugs, snails and cutworms. The best practice is to pull or hoe weeds when they are small, before they can reseed and return tenfold.

Herbicides are tricky to use in a flower bed because of the diversity of plants. If

Tall-growing bulbs should be staked, especially if weather is likely to be windy or rainy. Tie plant to stakes in two locations so top will not snap off. A pencil-thick bamboo stake is plenty for *Gladiolus*. Use a heavy redwood stake for *Dahlia*.

weeds become a serious problem, weed seeds can be killed with *Vapam,* a soil fumigant, before preparing the bed for the following year.

GENERAL CARE

When cutting flowers for a bouquet or arrangement, leave as much of the foliage on the growing stem as possible. Leaves are important because they manufacture food that the bulb stores for future growth and flower production. If you remove too much foliage, the vigor of the bulb may be decreased the following year.

Snip off flowers as soon as they have passed their prime. Allowed to remain, the spent flowers form seeds, which takes a lot of the plant's energy. It is more important for the strength of the plant to go back to the bulb.

If flowering diminishes, it can be caused by overcrowding, or loss of sunlight due to the spreading branches of nearby shrubs and trees. This often occurs with mature bulb plantings. To eliminate this problem, dig, separate and replant bulbs.

Some bulbs such as daffodils accept moderate watering throughout the year. Others, such as certain *Ranunculus, Anemone* and *Calochortus* species, rot during summer heat if the surrounding soil remains damp.

FERTILIZER

Supplementary feeding is valuable. For most bulbs, phosphorous and potash are more important than nitrogen. By reading the numbers on a fertilizer label, you can determine the amounts of these three primary nutrients in the package. They are always listed in the same order: *nitrogen, phosphorus* and *potassium*. A 2-10-10 or a 5-10-10 ratio, low in nitrogen, is better for bulbs than one high in nitrogen, such as 10-5-5. If minor nutrients such as iron are included in the formula, so much the better. If your soil is deficient in nitrogen, the foliage of the bulbs will take on a pale, yellowish cast. In this case, use a fertilizer that is slightly higher in nitrogen.

The best time to apply fertilizer is when the shoots first appear. Moisten soil and rake fertilizer into the top few inches. Avoid getting dry fertilizer on the foliage, or it will damage the plant. After the bulbs finish blooming and are storing energy before going dormant, apply fertilizer a second time.

MULCH

A mulch is a covering of material over the ground. In addition to making the garden look neater, a mulch helps reduce the weed population. A layer of organic mulch helps keep the soil cool, retains moisture and eventually breaks down to improve the soil composition. When adding a mulch, don't apply a thin covering. A layer 3 to 4 inches deep is best in most situations.

One of the best mulches is screened compost. Others include grass clippings, ground bark products and leaf mold. Some mulches are by-products of agriculture, and are available only in certain areas. These would include cottonseed hulls, peanut hulls and grape pomace. Check locally with your county extension agent or your nurseryman for recommendations and availability.

An organic mulch over the root area of bulbs is beneficial. It looks attractive, reduces loss of soil moisture through evaporation and helps prevent weed growth.

As soon as flowers have passed their prime, snip them off. Flowers allowed to stay on the plant form seeds, which takes energy away from the bulb.

PESTS AND DISEASES

Most bulbs, corms, tubers and rhizomes are relatively free of pests and diseases, but problems do occur. Many can be eliminated or controlled by planting bulbs at the correct depth and providing them with proper care.

One of the most important things you can do is watch for the first signs of a pest attack. By discovering and treating problems early, the damage to your bulbs will be minimized. Read and follow all label directions carefully when using insecticide and fungicide products.

Keep in mind that *you* can be your bulb's worst enemy. Learn their cultural requirements, so that you don't plant sun-loving bulbs in the shade or vice versa. You can mistakenly shorten the life span of bulbs by removing the foliage before the bulb is able to store up strength for the next year. Or, you may unknowingly place a trowel or shovel through a bulb hidden underground.

ANIMAL PESTS

Gophers and mice frequently attack bulbs, both in the ground and in storage. One exception is daffodils, which are normally left alone. Keep such pests away from bulbs in the ground by lining planting holes with chicken wire. Follow the same procedure when storing bulbs. Line the storage area with chicken wire to keep out animal pests.

Birds and rabbits love the tender, new buds of *Ranunculus* and lilies as the buds emerge from the ground. Until they toughen, cover buds with plastic bird netting or chicken wire.

INSECT PESTS

Aphids damage plants by sucking plant juices, weakening the plant and distorting growth. Some transmit plant diseases in the process. Aphids multiply fast, so take action as soon as you spot them. Spray infested plants with a soap and water solution consisting of 1 teaspoon of dish soap per gallon of water. Or, spray with the chemical malathion. *Systemic insecticides,* which are absorbed by the plant, are effective and last longer. Aphids that inhabit the soil attack roots. Eliminate them by drenching the soil around bulbs with malathion.

Mealybugs are wingless insects that cover themselves with a sticky, cottony substance. They usually hide at the base

Spray for gladiolus thrips at the first sign of discolored foliage. Use a *systemic* pesticide—one that is absorbed by the plant. Systemic granules worked into soil at the base of plant are slow acting but effective.

of bulbs that have strap-shaped leaves. You may not notice mealybugs until you see distorted leaves, caused by their constant sucking. Control with a systemic insecticide or oil spray.

Mites can enter a bulb that has been bruised or damaged during digging or handling. They begin to parasitize the bulb during storage. Cyclamen mites colonize on the undersides of leaves, stunting growth and causing leaves to curl. The surest way to control them is with a miticide such as dicofol, sold under the trade name Kelthane.

Narcissus flies prefer *Narcissus* species but damage other bulbs. They attack *Hymenocallis*, laying their eggs on new

foliage during late spring and early summer. There are two species of these flies. The larger lays one egg; the smaller lays several. You may notice them buzzing over dying bulb foliage. Both look like small bees but they have two wings instead of four. They lay eggs in the center of the foliage. Eggs mature into grublike pests that crawl down into the bulb and eat it. Grubs may also tunnel into the soil to the bulb's basal plate and eat into the bulb from there.

Infected bulbs are soft and spongy. The grubs can be found inside. Dust the foliage with diazinon early in the season before the flies have a chance to lay their eggs.

Normally, it is best to discard infected bulbs. But if a bulb is especially valuable, the grubs can be killed by soaking the bulb in hot water 110F (43C) for one hour. This might damage the bulb, but is the only way to save it. You can only plant the bulb and wait.

Nematodes damage bulbs by attacking bulb roots. A severe infestation is difficult to eliminate. They are most prevalent in the warm South, where the lack of cold temperatures allows them to proliferate. Susceptible bulbs should be grown in pots in a sterile potting soil.

Slugs and snails can be dispatched by hand picking, traps or poison bait. It helps to keep the garden area clean of trash and debris, which are their hiding places. Snails love to climb the stems and nibble the flowers of daffodils and other members of the *Amaryllis* family. Their presence is easily spotted in early morning by their slimy trails on paths and sidewalks. If they aren't too numerous, snails and slugs can be hand-picked and destroyed. Or, use snail bait containing metaldehyde or mesurol. Apply bait just after a rain or watering when snails and slugs are most active.

Thrips can be devastating to the usually tough *Gladiolus,* especially those planted late in the season. Thrips hide in the forming leaves and in the buds. When infestations are heavy, buds and leaves look distorted and often have silvery markings. Control by using a systemic insecticide such as Orthene. Thrips also hibernate on the corms through the winter. Scatter naphthalene flakes over them while in storage, or soak in water 110F (43C) for 20 to 30 minutes.

It helps to check plants frequently for signs of pests and diseases. This gardener is using a magnifying glass to see if tiny thrips are damaging his *Gladiolus* blooms.

DISEASES

Mildew is a serious problem that plagues tuberous begonias, but it is one of the easiest diseases to prevent and control. Provide good air circulation and avoid watering plants at night so that foliage remains dry. Control mildew with a fungicide spray such as benlate as soon as you notice it.

Botrytis is a fungus disease identified by brown or gray spots that form on leaves. It can spread quickly. It kills bulbs gradually by sapping their strength. Lilies and tulips are especially susceptible to botrytis. It can spread to other bulbs of the same family, so remove and destroy diseased plants immediately.

Basal rot is usually the result of poor drainage or high heat. Eventually, the *basal plate*—the area from which the roots grow—is destroyed and the bulb becomes soft. In warm climates, basal rot of trumpet daffodils is common. Control by planting the bulbs deep, to 8 inches, so soil temperature around the bulb does not exceed 75F (24C).

Viruses can be identified by streaked flowers and foliage. Occasionally, leaves and stems are twisted and distorted. Some virus-infected plants are not seriously damaged and actually produce unusual yet attractive colorations. For example, a virus was the cause of "broken tulips." Broken tulips were considered rare and unusual during Holland's period of "Tulipmania." You can grow broken tulips, but do not plant them with regular tulips or the virus may be transferred.

In most cases, a virus can cause a serious disease that may eventually kill the bulb. If you discover a lily infected with a virus, destroy it immediately before it spreads to other plants.

Viruses are often carried from one plant to another by aphids. Control these pests to reduce problems from virus diseases.

Mosaic virus damages lilies and bulbous irises. It causes spotting, streaking and stunting of the flower stem. No cure is known.

PROPAGATING BULBS

Bulbs are normally propagated in one of two ways: by seeds, or by dividing and planting some part of the plant—bulb offset, corm bulbil—that is able to produce a new bulb.

SEPARATING BULBS

Many bulbs form new bulbs around the original. When they become so crowded that flowering starts to diminish, it is time to dig and separate them. For instance, daffodils form a large clump of bulbs after several years. When dug, the smaller bulbs normally fall away from the parent plant. If bulbs do not separate easily, use a sharp knife to separate them. Treat cuts with a fungicide to reduce the potential for insect or disease damage. Each new bulb must have a section of basal plate or it will not be able to grow.

DIVIDING BULBS

Division is used to increase the stock of rhizomes, tubers and tuberous roots. A clean, sharp knife is usually required to divide them because they do not fall apart as easily as true bulbs.

Dig rhizomes such as *Iris* and *Cannas* when they become overly crowded. Use the knife to divide the rhizomes. Leave two new rhizomes with their fan of leaves connected with an old rhizome. This helps ensure the best bloom the following year. Treat cuts with a fungicide. Allow them to dry and heal for one or two days before planting.

Daylilies can be dug and separated easily. Simply washing the soil away from the roots often separates the new plants. They should bloom with identical flowers the next year.

Tubers such as *Begonias* and *Cyclamen* can be divided as new growth begins. At that time, the location of buds on the tuber is most evident. This is important because each division requires a bud to grow. Dust cuts with a fungicide and replant after cuts have healed.

A tuberous root such as *Dahlia* must be connected to a living bud on the stem. The stem can be split with a knife. Often, buds are more apparent in the

Daffodils, shown above, tulips, lilies, *Amaryllis* and bulbous iris are usually increased by separating offsets. When mature, offsets should pull apart easily. Be sure each offset has a section of basal plate—roots develop from it.

Rhizomatous iris are divided after four or five seasons of growth. After flowering—usually midsummer—dig, divide and replant. For fastest multiplication, divide into single fans, each with a section of rhizome. For best bloom, retain two or three fans of leaves per rhizome.

Tuberous-rooted bulbs such as *Dahlias* are best divided in spring just before planting, and can also be divided in fall. Each divided section must have at least one bud. Buds are easiest to notice in spring, when they are beginning to grow.

Some lilies develop small bulbs, *bulbils,* in the leaf axils. Often, they develop into separate plants while still attached to the mother plant. Plant the small bulbs in flats of moistened potting soil before they fall to the ground.

spring just prior to planting.

BULBILS, BULBLETS AND CORMLETS

Bulbils are miniature bulbs that form in the leaf axils on the stems of certain lilies such as *Lilium tigrinum* and *L. bulbiferum*. They sometimes form a rudimentary leaf and root. When mature, they disengage easily from the stem, and can be planted the same as a bulb.

Bulblets are similar but they form at the base of the stem, often underground. They can be removed when the stem dries. Plant bulbils and bulblets one inch deep. They generally bloom in one to three years.

Corms such as *Gladiolus, Freesia* and *Ixia* produce a new corm on top of the old, which withers away. However, small, numerous *cormlets,* or miniature corms, can be found around the base of the new corm. Plant the same as regular corms. They generally bloom after one year.

BULB SCALES

The fleshy scales of lilies can be removed to form a new bulb at their base. They should be inserted into a mixture of sand and leaf mold, or laid flat on damp peat moss. Keep humidity high by covering the flat with a clear plastic bag. For best results, maintain a temperature as close as possible to 70F (21C).

LEAF CUTTINGS

This method is confined almost entirely to the *Gesneriads,* which include the popular *Sinningia* and *Gloxinia.* Detach a leaf with a small section of stalk. Insert it upright to the base of the leaf in a mixture of peat moss and sand. *Begonias* and *Cyclamen* can also be propagated this way. It is possible to propagate a few bulbs such as *Muscari, Lachenalia* and *Haemanthus* by leaf cuttings, but this is not a common practice.

STEM CUTTINGS

Some bulbs can be propagated by *stem cuttings.* Stems cut from tuberous begonias and *Achimenes* bloom the same year they are planted.

Corms such as *Crocus* and *Gladiolus* are useless after they have flowered, but a new corm forms on top of the old one. Pull off and discard the old corm. *Cormels,* small corms that form around the base of the new corm, can be planted.

Many lilies are easy to propagate. Remove individual scales from bulb. Dip scales in hormone rooting powder and place in moistened perlite, shown above or sand, peat moss or vermiculite. A bubil will form at each scale base.

Tuberous begonias, *Dahlias* and *Achimenes* develop new bulbs from stem cuttings. A hormone powder aids root development and helps prevent decay.

Gloxinias are propagated by leaf cuttings. Well-developed green leaves are removed from the bulb top and placed in the rooting media. Bury stem several inches below the surface.

SCOOPING AND SCORING

The hyacinth is probably the most difficult of all bulbs to propagate. Although it reproduces itself each year, it multiplies slowly, and has to be coaxed into increasing its numbers. One common propagation method is called *scooping*. Using a knife with a curved blade, remove the entire basal plate from the bulb, including the main sprout. The bulb then forms bulblets at the base of each scale. These can be removed and planted.

Scoring is also used to propagate hyacinths. Using a straight knife, make three complete cuts across the base. Each cut should go through the center of the basal plate. In the fall, the mother bulb, along with the bulblets, can be planted about 4 inches deep. In the spring, the bulblets send up a lot of leaves as the mother bulb withers away.

Scooped bulbs produce up to 60 bulbs but take five years before they reach blooming size. Scored bulbs produce about half as many but require three to four years to mature.

SEEDS

Most bulbs can be grown from seeds. It is simple to do. Allow bulbs to flower and produce seeds. When seeds are completely dry, you can remove them for planting. Seeds started from bulb species usually produce a plant similar to the parent, but slight differences in height, size or shape of flower and color sometimes occur. This is called *natural variation*. When man creates new bulbs from seeds by *hybridizing,* changes are more drastic. Bulbs with good plant form are deliberately crossed with similar bulbs of particularly good color. The hope is that among the seedlings, one having the best attributes of both parents will appear.

When bulbs are hybridized, seedlings of mixed parentage are produced. Present-day tulips, *Gladiolus* and *Iris* look little like their ancestral parents. When naturally pollinated seeds of these hybrid plants are grown, variations usually result. Occasionally, a plant of considerable interest is produced. But because the mother plant was a *selected hybrid*—most often the best of a group of seedlings—her progeny are seldom as attractive.

Hybridizing between species can cause bulbs to produce sterile seeds. The same thing occurs in the animal kingdom. When a mare (horse) is bred with a donkey, the offspring, a mule, is sterile.

Some of the beautiful show daffodils have reached the end of their evolution and are now producing sterile seeds.

To hybridize bulbs from seeds, you must do your own pollinating. To ensure production of many fertile seeds, select flowers of the same species. In general, the pollen from the male parent has more influence on the *color* of the flower. The female parent that produces the seeds has more influence on the *size* and *shape* of the flower. As an example, you may want to cross a pink daffodil with a white Triandrus daffodil, which has several flowers to a stem. The hope is that you will get a quality Triandrus with pink flowers.

After selecting flowers, it is necessary to protect them from outside pollination before you make your cross. Cover the immature blooms of the flowers you intend to cross with a paper bag and secure with a rubber band. This keeps insects from reaching them. Many bulbs are *self-fertile,* meaning they have the ability to polinate themselves. To prevent this, remove *anthers,* the male organ in the flower, as soon as they become evident.

To make the cross, remove the *anther* (male) of one flower and place its powdery pollen onto the *stigma* (female) of another flower. This is done by rubbing the anther onto the stigma. The best time to do this is when the stigma is sticky, which means it is receptive to the pollen. Look for glistening on the tip of the stigma.

After pollinating, cover flowers with paper bags to prevent insects from transferring any more pollen. Leave bags over flowers for several days. If your pollination is a success, seeds will form.

Harvest seeds after they are completly dry, then plant them in a soil mix in flats. Place the flats in a warm, sheltered location where they are protected from pests. Keep the soil mix moist until the seeds germinate. Water regularly until they can be transplanted to individual containers. When the seedlings reach sufficient size, they can be transplanted into the garden.

For the first three years, the immature bulb may produce only foliage. After this period, who knows what will happen?

A close-up look at a daffodil flower displays the *anthers,* the male organ of the flower, surrounding the *stigma,* the female organ.

STORING BULBS

Many bulbs are dug and stored while they are dormant to protect them from cold, heat or moisture. Most commonly, they are stored to protect them from freezing in the ground during winter.

In cold areas, evergreen bulbs such as *Cliva*, *Agapanthus* and *Crinum* need light and water during winter. It is best to grow these bulbs in containers and bring them indoors during cold periods. Some, such as *Cannas*, continue to bloom indoors for several months if given sufficient light and warmth.

The majority of bulbs that require storage are deciduous kinds that would otherwise freeze in the ground. They are dug and stored in a loose material such as vermiculite, sand, perlite or peat moss. There should be enough material to keep the bulbs from touching. This helps protect them from bruising one another and reduces the spread of disease.

Bulbs and corms that have a protective coating or hard shells, such as *Gladiolus*, *Crocosmia*, *Tigridia*, *Freesia*, *Achimenes* and *Hymenocallis*, should be stored in a completely dry location. *Gladiolus* and other South-African corms can be tied up in loosely knit sacks or old nylon stockings and hung in an area sheltered from frost. Plastic bags are not recommended unless holes are punched in them to allow for air circulation.

Succulent, thin-skinned bulbs such as the tubers and rhizomes of *Dahlia*, *Calla*, *Canna*, *Ornithogalum* and *Gloriosa* lilies benefit from occasional drops of water added to the storage medium. This helps prevent the bulbs from drying out.

Bulbs in containers can be stored by stacking pots away from freezing temperatures. This works well with small bulbs such as *Freesia*.

Do not divide or separate bulbs before storing. It could encourage drying out where the cut is made. It also provides easy entry for diseases.

Some bulbs require protection from a combination of warmth and moisture. Otherwise, they rot. These include *Ranunculus* and *Calochortus*. If grown in a container, they can be stored easily in a dry location. Bulbs planted in the ground should be dug and put in an open box. Store them in a dry, shady spot.

1. After leaves have died back at least halfway, bulbs are ready to lift for storage. Daffodils, shown above, can be replanted immediately, or stored until fall planting time.

2. Remove bulbs by gently tapping them from container. If digging bulbs from the ground, use a spading fork to lessen the chance of injuring bulbs.

3. Remove bulbs from soil. This is easiest to do when the soil is dry. Keep bulbs separate and label them if you are sorting more than one kind of bulb.

4. Remove dried leaves from bulbs, and discard those that are soft. Don't separate individual bulbs at this time. Bulbs separate more easily after they are dried, just before planting.

5. Dusting bulbs with fungicide and insecticide is not necessary, but is recommended if you have had prior infestations of pests.

6. Bulbs can be stored in a variety of ways. Different containers serve as holding bins during the dormant season. Here, they are kept in sand. Vermiculite or perlite can also be used.

ENCYCLOPEDIA OF BULBS

This encyclopedia describes many of the diverse plants known as *bulbs*. Even though they are a varied group, bulbs have much in common. By definition, all are adapted to endure unfavorable weather by storing food underground. This may be accomplished by the formation of bulbs, corms, rhizomes, tubers or tuberous roots.

In the following descriptions, the "vital statistics" that follow each bulb name provide much valuable information. Details are noted on bloom season and length, available colors, height, planting time and depth, and specific cultural requirements. Helpful information such as climate adaptation, design use and superior species for garden use are provided in the descriptive copy.

The vast majority of bulbs belong to one of three plant families: *Iridaceae, Iris; Amaryllidaceae, Amaryllis;* and *Liliaceae, Lily.* The lily family include *Allium, Lilium, Tulipa, Muscari* and *Trillium. Amaryllis, Narcissus* and *Nerine* belong to the *Amaryllis* family. *Crocus, Freesia, Gladiolus* and *Iris* are part of the *Iris* family.

Only three bulbs—*Dahlia imperialis, Eremurus robustus* and *Urginea maritima*—grow taller than 7 feet. No bulbs develop woody stems. Only one, *Gloriosa rothschildiana,* can be considered vinelike in its growth habit.

Bulb Names

Compared to most plant groups, bulbs comprise a wide array of botanical and common names. In this book, bulbs are listed alphabetically by their botanical name according to the standard horticultural reference, *Hortus Third.* Exceptions are *Dichelostemma* and *Triteleia,* which are found under *Brodiaea.* In the text, botanical names are shown in italics. In some cases the botanical name and common name are the same, such as *Iris, Dahlia* and *Gladiolus.* Note the sample below for a further explanation of botanical nomenclature.

Genus: Plants consisting of one or more species sharing many characteristics, usually flowers and fruit. Plural is *genera.*

Species: Plants with certain differences compared to other plants of the same genus. Characteristics normally continue from generation to generation. Variations in species that occur in nature are *varieties,* designated in this book as var.

Bessera elegans
Coral-drops
Family: Amaryllidaceae.

Family: Plants within a family share some general characteristics, but differ enough to be further categorized into genera.

Common Name

Hybrid crosses are sometimes made between different species or genera. It is designated by an "x." Example: *Begonia x tuberhybrida.*

Bulb flowers come in many forms, both common and unusual. Left: *Nerine* species. Above: *Lachenalia aloides.*

Bulbs and Climate

If you are looking for bulbs that are easy to grow, choose those that originate in climates similar to your own. For example, bulbs from England thrive in the Pacific Northwest and British Columbia. Bulbs native to the humid tropics thrive in Florida. Those from South Africa flourish in southern California.

Many bulbs can be grown successfully in climates differing from their native homes. This often requires special care, but some gardeners love to try something different and challenging. This ambition and curiosity is what makes gardeners grow tulips in southern California and *Gladiolus* in Nebraska. To be successful, tulips in California require preplanting chilling. They should be planted after the soil cools—normally after Thanksgiving. *Gladiolus* grown in Nebraska must be dug in the fall and stored away from freezing temperatures during the winter months.

Climate and latitude have a great effect on the bloom period of bulbs. It's possible for a person in San Diego to see his pampered tulips bloom and fade, then fly to Washington D.C. and see tulips at their prime. He could then fly to Holland and see the tulip season again. If he were a true tulip fanatic, he could then dash to Scotland for another show. The farther north, the later spring arrives, and with it, a corresponding period of bloom.

Year-to-year weather patterns also cause change. In a warm year, spring bulbs bloom earlier. When winter cold lingers on, they bloom later in the season.

MICROCLIMATES

Microclimates are small climates that exist within a larger climate. They can have a great influence on how well bulbs adapt to a certain area. Daffodils will bloom a week or two later on a cool, north slope than they will on a warm, south-facing slope.

You can increase your success by recognizing these climates, and using them to your advantage. Before you plant your bulbs, take a walk around your home. You will notice subtle differences in temperature and accumulation of moisture. The northern exposure of your home does not receive afternoon sunshine, so temperatures are cooler, and the ground is often more moist. Conversely, the south and west exposures are warmer and drier due to the additional sunshine they receive. Bulbs that thrive in full sun or those that require heat to bloom should be planted here. If you live in a cold-climate area, or in a coastal region where cloudy conditions reduce sunshine, it would be helpful to plant heat-loving bulbs against a south wall. Extra heat is released onto the bulb plant. Heat absorbed by the wall during the day is released at night to increase the temperature around plants.

In some areas, placement in the garden can make a great difference in how the bulb grows. Because cold air sinks and warm air rises, a garden on a hillside is warmer than one in the valley below. A few degrees can make a difference to plants. Similarly, large bodies of water such as oceans or lakes *increase* temperatures of the surrounding area in the winter, and *decrease* temperatures in the summer.

Climate Zones

Pacific Northwest—The climate of much of this region is ideal for commercial bulb culture. Many daffodil, *Iris* and lily growers are located here. *Dahlias* are grown, but roots must be dug and stored during winter. Even though *Gladiolus* and tuberous begonias do well, they also must be protected from cold weather.

For some bulbs, there is not enough summer heat in the Pacific Northwest. Without sufficient heat, tulips left in the ground in summer are unable to produce buds for the next year. It is necessary to utilize microclimates to the fullest to grow bulbs such as *Eucharis, Gloriosa* and *Polianthes,* which need heat while actively growing.

Southern California—Winter rains and arid summers makes this area perfect for most bulbs from South Africa. Problems arise with bulbs such as tulips that require a period of cold temperatures. Tuberous begonias are at their best close to the coast, but farther inland they become temperamental. Lily-of-the-valley is difficult to establish because it requires cold. Winter aconite, dwarf species of *Iris,* snowdrops and many *Crocus* also require cold. Trumpet daffodils, a joy in other areas, are subject to basal rot, which destroys the bulb when the soil temperature goes over 70F (21C). But the early blooming Tazetta daffodils thrive here.

Desert Areas—Bulbs that bloom in early spring, before high heat arrives, are best for hot-summer regions. *Ranunculus* thrives in desert regions but must be kept dry during the summer. Some of the unusual, South-African bulbs that are native to regions with dry summers do well here. Species tulips, which come from areas in Turkey with cold winters and long, hot, dry summers, may do well in some of the high-elevation deserts. Desert summers are usually too hot and arid for lilies, tuberous begonias and *Caladiums.* Conditions can be modified by planting under lath and by increasing humidity around plants.

The South—The Gulf Coast, from Texas to Florida, has the heat and humidity ideal for *Caladium, Crinum* and *Achimenes.* Louisiana iris thrives here, but bearded iris is subject to rot and fungus. Tropical *Cannas* are superb. The standard spring bulbs—tulips, daffodils, hyacinths and *Crocus*—thrive throughout much of the upper South.

Midwest and North—Farther north, the standard spring bulbs are easier to grow. Bulbs that bloom in the winter and early spring but cannot tolerate freezing, such as paper-white *Narcissus,* are grown as house plants. Cold-tender bulbs such as *Dahlias* and *Gladiolus* have to be dug in fall and stored in a protected location during the winter.

Cold Areas—Even in the coldest areas such as Zones 2 to 4, certain bulbs are easy to grow. Among those that are cold-hardy are: *Belamcanda, Bulbocodium, Camassia, Chionodoxa, Convallaria,* many *Crocus, Eranthis, Erythronium, Fritillaria, Galanthus* and *Tulipa.*

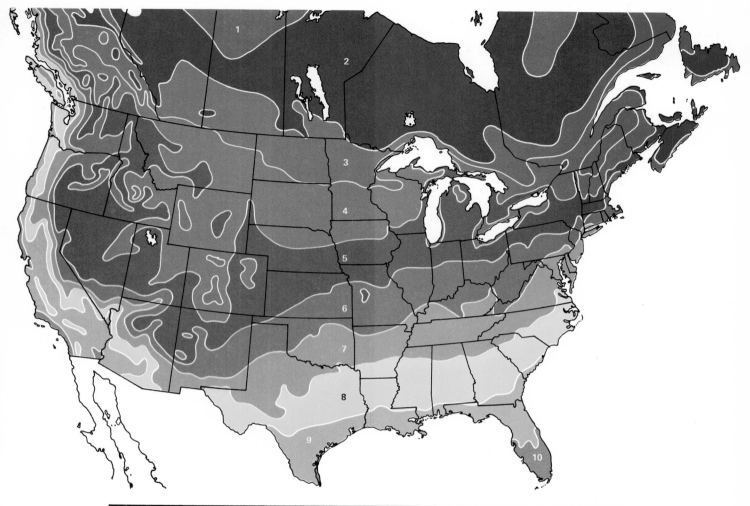

Hardiness Zones of the United States and Canada

	Zone 1	Below −50F (−45C)
	Zone 2	−50 to −40F (−45 to −40C)
	Zone 3	−40 to −30F (−40 to −35C)
	Zone 4	−30 to −20F (−35 to −29C)
	Zone 5	−20 to −10F (−29 to −24C)
	Zone 6	−10 to 0F (−24 to −18C)
	Zone 7	0 to 10F (−18 to −12C)
	Zone 8	10 to 20F (−12 to −7C)
	Zone 9	20 to 30F (−7 to −1C)
	Zone 10	30 to 40F (−1 to 5C)

Each of the bulb descriptions in the following pages contains recommended zone adaptations based on the hardiness zone map shown above, developed by the United States Department of Agriculture. To find out if a bulb will grow in your area, note which climate zone you live in, then refer to the bulb descriptions for the zone recommendation.

Climate zones and maps are based on average temperatures, and many small climates exist within a general climate zone. Because of these variables, it is possible that you can grow plants not rated for your zone. For the best information on bulbs and climate adaptation, consult your local county extension agent or nurseryman.

Alstroemeria ligtu

Alstroemeria ligtu

ALSTROEMERIA
Peruvian lily

Family: Alstroemeriaceae.
Native to: West coast of South America primarily.
Bulb type: Elongated, thickened roots.
Bloom season & length: Late spring for 5 weeks.
Colors: Orange, yellow, pink, red, lavender and white.
Height: 1 to 4 feet.
Planting time: Early spring.
Planting depth: Cover roots with 2 to 4 inches soil.
Soil: Rich, well-drained loam.
Water: Keep moist during growing season.
Fertilizer: Once with light application after shoots appear.
Spacing: 1 foot.
Exposure: Prefers filtered shade.
Propagation: Usually from seeds, but roots can be divided in spring.
Pests & diseases: Snails.
Storage: Leave in ground in Zones 6 to 10. In other zones grow in containers and bring inside during periods of cold weather.

This elegant and superior garden plant deserves wider recognition. It is adaptable to a number of climates, growing outdoors in Zones 6 to 10.

Alstroemeria produces thick, long, tuberous roots that look like fingers. Handle carefully because they are brittle. Plant in a rich, loamy, well-drained soil. Build a small cone in the planting hole and spread the roots gently out from the crown. Position the crown 2 inches below the soil surface. Planted in filtered shade, it grows and spreads indefinitely. The tall, stiff stems usually do not require staking.

Alstroemeria aurantiaca, A. ligtu and their hybrids are becoming staples of the florist trade. Each stem produces many flowers. They are pretty and among the longest-lasting cut flowers. Their common names Peruvian lily and lily-of-the-Incas refer to the lily shape of the 2-inch flowers.

Notable species are:

Alstroemeria ligtu and its hybrids are available in many colors. The color of the species is light pink with purple spots. White, dark pink, salmon, apricot and orange-red are also available. All have 2- to 3-foot-high stems and bloom over a long period. Those known as *Dutch hybrids* include some of the most popular kinds.

Alstroemeria pelegrina, lily-of-the-Incas, grows to 1 foot high. Its lilac flowers are splashed with purple, and are the same size as taller varieties.

Alstroemeria psittacina also grows low. Flowers are dark red tipped with green. Flowers are more tubular than other forms. Plant does well in light shade and spreads by seeds.

AMARYLLIS BELLADONNA
Naked lady

Family: Amaryllidaceae.
Native to: South Africa.
Bulb type: Bulb.
Bloom season & length: Late summer to fall for about 3 weeks.
Colors: Usually pink, but some varieties range from white to dark red.
Height: 2 to 3 feet.
Planting time: Midsummer to late summer.
Planting depth: Cover bulb with 2 inches of soil. Plant slightly deeper in cold climates.
Soil: No preference.
Water: Keep moist when in foliage.
Fertilizer: Not necessary in most soils.
Spacing: About 10 inches.
Exposure: Full sun or filtered shade.
Propagation: Divide bulbs in late summer or start from seeds.
Pests & diseases: None.
Storage: Leave in ground.

Amaryllis belladonna has many close relatives. *Brunsvigia, Hippeastrum, Lycoris, Sprekelia* and *Vallota* species are similar and occasionally confused with *Amaryllis*. At one time, all were classified as *Amaryllis*.

In late summer or fall, when the garden is lacking in flowers, these large, 4-inch bulbs send up a bare stem from the earth. Although bulbs produce foliage, the leaves dry out before the blooming period—thus their common name, "naked ladies." The 2-foot-high stem is topped by a cluster of large, light pink, fragrant trumpets. Plants live for years in mild-climate regions, multiplying into large clumps. Large clusters of bulbs eventually push their way out of the soil.

Plant with *Agapanthus* or Shasta daisies to mask the bareness of the stems. *Amaryllis* are tough enough to push their way up through a ground cover of English ivy.

Hybrids are superior to the original species. Trumpet-shaped flowers go all the way around the stem to form a loose umbel. Colors range from wine-red through shades of pink and rose to white. Most hybrids have a yellow center.

Plant grows in Zones 9 and 10 without care. It can be planted with the bulb barely covered. In Zones 5 to 8, plant in a warm, sunny location. Cover with at least 5 or 6 inches of soil to protect bulbs from frost. Plant grows in any soil that is not overly wet. *Amaryllis* do not do well after they are moved. They may require three or four years to bloom if moved when roots or leaves are actively growing. The best time to divide is in summer or when they are in bloom, before growth of new roots and leaves begins.

Amaryllis belladonna

Amaryllis belladonna 'Hybrid White'

Belamcanda chinensis

BELAMCANDA CHINENSIS
Blackberry lily

Family: Iridaceae.
Native to: China and Japan.
Bulb type: Rhizome.
Bloom season & length: Midsummer for 4 to 5 weeks.
Colors: Orange and yellow.
Height: About 30 inches.
Planting time: Spring.
Planting depth: Just below soil surface.
Soil: No preference.
Water: Keep moist during growing season.
Fertilizer: Not necessary.
Spacing: About 6 inches.
Exposure: Full sun.
Propagation: Divide in spring or fall or plant seeds.
Pests & diseases: Few.
Storage: Not usually required. Mulch north of Zone 6.

The blackberry lily is a little-known bulb from the Orient. It is related to the rhizomatous iris but resembles it only in foliage. It earned its common name from the clusters of shiny black seeds that form after flowering. Showy, 2-inch flowers appear on 2- to 3-foot-high stems during summer. Flower colors include pure yellow, orange and yellow, and orange and crimson. New hybrids and crosses are being developed that will increase the range of colors. Most important is the hybrid genus, *x Pardancanda*, which is available in a wide range of colors, including stripes and polka dots.

Blackberry lily grows as far north as Ohio, farther if plants are protected with a mulch during winter. Heat and drought tolerance are excellent.

Bessera elegans

BESSERA ELEGANS
Coral-drops

Family: Amaryllidaceae.
Native to: Mexico.
Bulb type: Corm.
Bloom season & length: Midsummer for several weeks.
Colors: Coral, red and purple.
Height: About 2 feet.
Planting time: Whenever available, usually in fall.
Planting depth: Cover with 4 inches of soil.
Soil: Rich and gritty.
Water: Regular during growing season.
Fertilizer: Light applications.
Spacing: About 10 inches.
Exposure: Full sun.
Propagation: Divide after leaves die to ground.
Pests & diseases: Snails and slugs.
Storage: Dig and store in regions where the ground freezes.

Coral-drops is an unusual bulb that produces drooping, scarlet buds on top of 2-foot-high stems. When buds open, they reveal a white center with conspicuous purple anthers. Each stem has 10 to 15 buds. The bulbs are attractive in groups and make interesting cut flowers.

Coral-drops is cold-hardy as far north as Zone 7. Use it as an attractive container plant that can be taken outdoors in late spring in colder areas.

Give plants a rich, gritty soil in full sun. Cover with 4 inches of soil. Keep well watered until foliage dies down. At that time dig, divide and replant.

BULBOCODIUM VERNUM
Spring meadow saffron

Family: Liliaceae.
Native to: Europe.
Bulb type: Corm.
Bloom season & length: Early spring for 2 to 3 weeks.
Colors: Lavender-pink.
Height: 4 inches.
Planting time: Early fall.
Planting depth: Cover with 3 inches of soil.
Soil: Well drained.
Water: Regular during growing season.
Fertilizer: Light dose at planting time.
Spacing: About 4 inches.
Exposure: Full sun.
Propagation: Cormels that form at base.
Pests & diseases: Few.
Storage: Not required.

This is one of the most reliable and useful bulbs in cold climates. It can be grown successfully as far north as Zone 3 in Canada. It adds its lavender-pink color in early spring. Flowers look like those of *Crocus*. When fully open, flowers look like stars.

Culture is simple. Plant about 3 inches deep and 4 inches apart in a sunny location. Soil should have good drainage. Dig every 2 to 3 years to separate and replant.

CALADIUM X HORTULANUM
Fancy-leafed caladium

Family: Araceae.
Native to: Tropical South America.
Bulb type: Tuber.
Bloom season & length: Attractive leaves are displayed all summer.
Colors: Leaves in combinations of green, white, pink and red.
Height: 12 to 15 inches.
Planting time: After last frost or start indoors.
Planting depth: Cover with 1 inch soil.
Soil: Rich loam is best.
Water: Ample supply at all times.
Fertilizer: Once per month with complete liquid fertilizer.
Spacing: 8 inches.
Exposure: Filtered shade.
Propagation: Divide tuber.
Pests & diseases: Snails and slugs.
Storage: Allow bulb to dry gradually, then store in warm, dry area.

These tubers from the tropical part of South America are a boon to gardeners in warm, humid climates. In Louisiana, they have naturalized on the levees, but *Caladiums* are grown throughout the United States and Canada for the brilliant leaf colors. In most areas, tubers must be dug in fall and kept dry and warm during the winter. As house plants, they need at least 75% humidity, warmth and bright light.

Their combinations of leaf colors—green, white, red and pink—seem endless. Some, such as the popular 'Candidum', are white with thin, green veins. At the other extreme is 'Postman Joyner', with dark-red leaves with a wide, green border. In between are 'Pink Cloud', and 'Miss Chicago', which has pink and white with green speckles clustered around the border.

Although these are shade plants, they need lots of bright, indirect light. Indoor locations are usually too dark. After a week or two, they begin to lose their color intensity, especially the pink and red kinds.

Caladium x hortulanum

Caladium x hortulanum

Habranthus robustus

A month before the last frost, start tubers indoors by pressing them into damp peat. When rooted, transfer to 4-inch pots. After soil warms in spring, set out as bedding plants or transplant into larger pots for the terrace or house. Rich, organic, well-drained soil is best. Feed once a month with liquid, organic fertilizer. Flowers resemble small calla lilies. Remove them because they sap strength from the plant. Leaves are fragile. They are damaged if whipped by wind and burn in direct, intense sun. Bait for snails and slugs.

In fall, allow tubers to dry, then dig and store in a warm, dry place. Don't stack tubers on top of one another. Store in a box filled with perlite or vermiculite. Tubers in containers can be stored dry during winter.

HABRANTHUS

Family: Amaryllidaceae.
Native to: North to South America.
Bulb type: True bulb.
Bloom season & length: Flowers appear after summer rains.
Colors: Red, pink and yellow.
Height: 6 to 9 inches.
Planting time: Spring.
Planting depth: 1/2 inch of soil over bulb.
Soil: Sandy loam.
Water: Periodically.
Fertilizer: Not necessary.
Spacing: 2 to 4 inches.
Exposure: Full sun to light shade.
Propagation: From offshoots and seeds.
Pests & diseases: Few. Watch for snails.
Storage: Store in pots until crowded.

Habranthus is a small group of true bulbs. Most species bloom in summer and fall. They are similar to *Zephyranthes,* but most have larger flowers. *Habranthus* can also be distinguished by its stamens, which are four distinctly different lengths. Upward or outfacing, solitary, funnel-shaped flowers appear on a short stem. Some kinds bloom with the foliage, some without. Often, first flowers appear before leaves. Later flowers appear after leaves have grown. Most are natives of South America. One, *Habranthus* var. *andersonii texanus,* is native to Texas. There it is called *rain lily* because it often blooms soon after a rain.

Habranthus andersonii has gold-yellow flowers on 6-inch stems. A coppery brown tint flushes the outside. Variety *texanus* is yellow on the outside and petals are more rounded. *H. robustus* has large, 3-inch, pale-pink flowers with deeper-colored veins and a green throat. Flowers appear in late summer before leaves appear.

In Zones 9 and 10, *Habranthus* is grown in a sunny location outdoors in well-drained soil. Plant with the neck of the bulb at soil surface, and leave it undisturbed to multiply. In other areas, *Habranthus* is an interesting pot plant, similar to *Amaryllis,* to which it is related. Plants do not need large pots. Plant a dozen bulbs in a 6-inch container.

HAEMANTHUS
Blood lily

Family: Amaryllidaceae.
Native to: Africa.
Bulb type: True bulb.
Bloom season & length: Summer or fall.
Colors: Red, coral or white.
Height: 6 inches to 2-1/2 feet.
Planting time: Spring after frost.
Planting depth: Just under soil surface.
Soil: Loamy with fast drainage.
Water: Ample during the growing season.
Fertilizer: Light application with a complete fertilizer when growth starts.
Spacing: 1 foot.
Exposure: Light, filtered shade.
Propagation: By offsets in spring.
Pests & diseases: Snails and mealybugs.
Storage: Store dry bulbs in their pots.

At least four dozen species of *Haemanthus* grow wild in central and southern Africa. Some are called *blood lilies* because of the red spots on the bulb. Others are called *paint brush* or *shaving brush* from the thickly set stamens in the flowers. Presently, three species are commonly available for home gardeners. They are quite distinct from one another.

Haemanthus albiflos is easiest to grow. It is evergreen and multiplies prolifically. Strap-shaped leaves are leathery and bordered with tiny, white hairs. Flowers appear in late summer, held above the foliage on 8- to 10-inch stems. Bracts around the flower are white, and the center is filled with many golden stamens. Grown closely together in a large low tub, they look similar to an exotic water lily.

Haemanthus coccineus is the most unusual species. Its flower appears in late summer without foliage on a 6-inch stem. The 3-inch-wide flowerheads are coral-red with typical, upright-protruding stamens. The scarlet bract underneath is wider than the umbel. After the flower dies, two leathery leaves grow from the bulb, spreading over the ground. The leaves grow to 6 inches wide and 2 feet long.

Haemanthus katharinae is the most beautiful of the group. It develops a large, completely round umbel of small, salmon-red, sometimes scarlet or pink flowers with bright yellow, protruding stamens on a 2-foot stem. Leaves are generally evergreen, but not leathery as with most *Haemanthus*. It is often grown in pots in cold areas, then brought inside during winter. A pot twice the size of the bulb is adequate.

All *Haemanthus* can be grown outdoors in Zones 9 and 10. They need fast drainage and a winter rest period. Most prefer filtered shade or optimum light indoors. A light application of fertilizer when plants are growing is beneficial. Plant bulbs with the neck at the soil surface. Watch for slugs and snails. Protect from frost.

Haemanthus katharinae

Haemanthus albiflos

Hippeastrum Dutch hybrid

HIPPEASTRUM
Dutch amaryllis

Family: Amaryllidaceae.
Native to: Mostly tropical America.
Bulb type: True bulb.
Bloom season & length: April to May for in-ground planting.
Colors: Red, pink, orange, salmon, white and striped.
Height: 2 feet.
Planting time: Fall, spring.
Planting depth: Just under soil surface.
Soil: Sandy loam.
Water: Frequently during growing season.
Fertilizer: Light applications of a house-plant fertilizer.
Spacing: 1 foot.
Exposure: Full sun or light shade.
Propagation: From offsets removed in fall before new growth appears.
Pests & diseases: Snails, mealybugs, narcissus fly and cutworm.
Storage: Dry, directly in their pots. Start watering about 5 weeks before flowering.

Common *Hippeastrum* is usually sold as Dutch hybrid amaryllis. It was developed from crosses of *Hippeastrum reginae, H. vittatum* and the hybrid *H. x johnsonii.* From these beginnings, outstanding varieties were developed.

Hippeastrum are sold by the tens of thousands before Thanksgiving—potted and ready to bloom indoors for Christmas and New Year. Colors are white, pink, orange, salmon, scarlet and dark red, including many variations and combinations. They grow 2 feet high and develop showy, 6-inch flowers.

Plant bulbs in pots 1 inch wider than the bulb. The top of the bulb should protrude out of the soil. Hold the bulb in the container with the roots pointing down. Add soil carefully. Soil should be loose with lots of humus and good drainage. Push soil down to firm it and eliminate air pockets. Keep soil slightly damp until growth begins. As it grows, gradually increase amount of water. Rotate pot so the stem does not lean toward light.

After blooming, Christmas bulbs can be saved for the following year. Cut off faded flowers and seed pods after bloom. Put the plant in filtered shade after danger of frost has passed. Apply a light dose of fertilizer and water regularly. Let it begin to dry out and rest by the first of August. Stalk and leaves eventually wither and disappear. This supplies a necessary dormant period. Begin the watering cycle again in the second week of November to have plants bloom again at Christmas time.

Hippeastrum are easy to grow outdoors in Zones 9 and 10. Bulbs grown in the ground generally bloom in May. Snails can be a serious problem, and will even eat the bulb.

Of the 70-odd species, only a few are commercially available, primarily because most people grow the immensely popular Dutch hybrids.

Hippeastrum

Hippeastrum Dutch hybrid

IPHEION UNIFLORUM
Spring star flower

Family: Amaryllidaceae.
Native to: Argentina and Uruguay.
Bulb type: True bulb.
Bloom season & length: Spring over a long period.
Colors: Pale to dark blue.
Height: 6 inches.
Planting time: Fall.
Planting depth: 1 inch of soil over bulb.
Soil: Not fussy.
Water: During the growing season.
Fertilizer: Not necessary.
Spacing: 1 inch.
Exposure: Full sun to light shade.
Propagation: Seeds and offsets.
Pests & diseases: None.
Storage: Not necessary. Can be grown in the same pot up to four years.

Ipheion uniflorum is a pretty but surprisingly tough bulb from South America. Because of its low growth habit, *Ipheion* is especially well suited for rock gardens, between steppingstones and as edgings. It has been previously classed as a *Brodiaea, Triteleia* and *Milla*.

The plant carries 1-inch, star-shaped flowers on a 6-inch stem above grasslike foliage. It blooms for months. Leaves smell like onions when bruised.

Ipheion can remain undisturbed for years in a container. Bulbs should be planted fairly close together for the best effect when plants are in bloom. The most-common variety has pale-blue flowers. The dark-blue variety was discovered mixed with other *Ipheion* in the Wisley Gardens outside London. It is named 'Wisley Blue', and is worth looking for.

Grow *Ipheion* outdoors in Zones 6 to 10. Plant with 1 to 2 inches of soil over the top of bulbs in almost any soil, except soggy soil. In cold, Northern areas, plant bulbs deeper than normal for frost protection. Bulbs are splendid indoors, and bloom a month earlier than those planted outdoors. Provide them with an exposure to a sunny window.

Ipheion uniflorum

Nerine hybrid

NERINE

Family: Amaryllidaceae.
Native to: South Africa.
Bulb type: True bulb.
Bloom season & length: Fall for several weeks.
Colors: Red, scarlet, pink, rose, mauve and white.
Height: 20 inches, but variable.
Planting time: Early fall.
Planting depth: Tip of neck at soil surface.
Soil: Fast drainage.
Water: Keep on dry side when dormant.
Fertilizer: Not necessary.
Spacing: 1 foot.
Exposure: Full sun or light shade.
Propagation: Bulbs form dense clumps and force their way out of the soil. Blooms best when crowded.
Pests & diseases: Few.
Storage: Store in pots.

Although *Nerine* species are rare, they are bound to become better known. One reason is the excellent keeping-quality of their flowers. Another reason is the cross-breeding work done by Edmund de Rothschild in England. There are many species and hybrids, but this book deals only with the two most important species.

Nerine bowdenii comes from the mountains of South Africa. It can be grown as far north as Zone 8. In its native habitat, it is watered heavily by summer rains and remains comparatively dry in winter. The home gardener should follow suit and water the same way. The pink flower cluster is borne on 15-inch stems.

Nerine sarniensis is from the lowlands of South Africa where it rains during winter and is dry during summer. It received its common name guernsey lily when the first bulbs shipped from Africa were cast adrift in a storm onto the isle of Guernsey. There they rooted and bloomed, and soon gained the attention of horticulturists.

It is less cold-hardy and grows only in Zones 9 and 10. It is the more exciting of the two species. Flowerheads are fuller with more protruding stamens. Petals are covered with an iridescent sheen that makes the flower look as though it had been sprinkled with gold or silver dust. Indoors, under artificial light, this quality is even more pronounced. Most of the hybridizing has been done with this species, resulting in shades of pink, orange, salmon, red, scarlet, mauve and white. Some have two-toned flowers.

According to some authorities, *Nerine* grows wild in some of the poorest soils in the world. For best results, soil should be sandy with good drainage. Plant bulbs with the top of the neck exposed. A small amount of fertilizer may be beneficial, but too much nitrogen keeps them from blooming. It used to be thought that they needed high summer heat to produce flowers, but this has been proven to be untrue.

Nerine blooms best when rootbound, so they make excellent pot plants. Divide or move them to a larger pot if overcrowded. In the ground, they form large clumps with exposed bulbs. They do not have to be separated except to increase plantings.

RHODOHYPOXIS BAURII

Family: Hypoxidaceae.
Native to: South Africa.
Bulb type: Cormlike rootstock.
Bloom season & length: Late spring to late summer.
Colors: Dark rose to white.
Height: 3 to 4 inches.
Planting time: Early spring.
Planting depth: 1/2 to 1 inch below soil surface.
Soil: Slightly acid sandy loam.
Water: During the growing season.
Fertilizer: Minimal amounts are required.
Spacing: 1 inch.
Exposure: Full sun to light shade.
Propagation: By division of rootstocks. Seeds.
Pests & diseases: Few.
Storage: Allow to dry in pot.

This small, attractive, South-African native, *Rhodohypoxis baurii*, was recently introduced to the bulb trade. It has many, star-shaped, 1-inch flowers held on stems just above ground level. Flowers appear in many shades from white to rose-pink. Foliage is hairy and grasslike.

Rhodohypoxis multiplies by offsets and self-sows its seeds. It is choice in rock gardens and between stepping-stones. Try it as an eye-catcher in a small bonsai pot. Blooms in early summer.

Plant in sandy loam, 1/2 inch to 1 inch below the surface. It does well in Zones 9 and 10, but has not been tested in other areas.

Rhodohypoxis baurii

SAUROMATUM GUTTATUM
Voodoo lily

Family: Araceae.
Native to: India.
Bulb type: Tuber.
Bloom season & length: Spring for a week. Also used as foliage plant.
Colors: Yellow, spotted.
Height: 2 to 3 feet.
Planting time: Spring after warm weather has arrived.
Planting depth: 1 inch over tuber.
Soil: Rich loam.
Water: Regular during the growing season.
Fertilizer: When flowers appear.
Spacing: 3 to 6 inches.
Exposure: Light shade.
Propagation: Offsets or seeds.
Pests & diseases: Few.
Storage: After foliage dies, dig and store dry until danger of frost has passed.

As the common name implies, this bulb is more of a curiosity than a traditional garden subject. *Sauromatum guttatum* forms a large, 5-inch bulb. Indoors, on a windowsill, it produces a flower that looks like a large, yellow-green calla dotted with dark-purple spots.

In mild climates, after bloom, plant bulb in the garden. It will soon produce leaves. The exotic-looking foliage is attractive, resembling a deeply cut, split-leaf philodendron with a squared-off end at the stem. Because of these distinctive leaves, it is an interesting container plant. Use a house-plant soil mix and keep soil damp while growing. Plants multiply from bulbs formed on top of the mother bulb near the soil surface.

Sauromatum guttatum

GROUND COVERS

What classifies a plant as *ground cover* is often a matter of opinion. Plants that are *perennial, evergreen, trailing* or *clumping,* and *grow to one foot high or less* are potentially useful as ground covers. But this book has less rigid definitions. The following pages include some low shrubs, many perennial border "rengrades," some flowing annuals and some herbs. The reason: If you choose a plant you like and it covers the ground, then it is a ground cover!

Ground covers are automatically associated with low maintenance—even neglect. Most require less time and upkeep than many plants, and certainly less than a lawn—*after they are established.* But until then, ground covers require considerable time, effort and expense—often equal to or greater than a lawn.

Few low-maintenance covers will become established and thrive on their own. Keep the following in mind to help insure success with your ground cover plantings.

● Choose a plant that is well adapted to your area. It should hve a reasonable chance of thriving in the particular situation. For example, don't plant a sun-loving plant in the shade, or vice versa.

● Learn the plant's cultural requirements and meet them.

● Improve the soil to help plants become established faster and grow better. Adding amendments to the soil is one of the best investments you can make to ease future maintenance.

● Water newly planted ground covers regularly. This is especially important the first weeks after planting. Even the most drought-tolerant native plants require supplemental water the first one or two seasons.

● Weeds ruin more ground cover plantings than anything else. Don't let them get a foothold. Rid the soil of weed seeds as much as possible before planting, use a mulch and utilize herbicides if necessary.

Words frequently used to describe ground cover functions apply here. This planting of *Pachysandra terminalis* **fills** the lower spaces, creating a **balanced, layered** effect. It **links** path to shrubs and **blends** different plantings together. It **cools,** serving as **living mulch,** and **controls,** keeping weeds to a minimum.

Ground Cover Selection Guide

EROSION CONTROL

Plants that root as they spread and cover the ground completely are used to control erosion on banks and slopes. Roots of the plants listed below grow deeply and strongly. Some measure of drought tolerance is necessary because water is difficult to apply to slopes. Plant in fall to allow time for establishment before summer heat. Mulch to control weeds and to further protect soil. Grasses provide the fastest cover for slope stabilization.

Abelia
Arctostaphylos
Arctotheca
Artemisia
Arundinaria
Atriplex
Baccharis
Ceanothus 'Point Reyes'
Centranthus
Cistus
Comptonia
Convolvulus
Coprosma
Coronilla
Cotoneaster
Drosanthemum
Eschscholzia
Euonymus

Grasses: Brome
Fescue
Orchardgrass
Rye
Grevillea
Heaths and heathers
Hedera
Hemerocallis
Hypericum
Juniperus
Lantana—trailing types
Lonicera
Lotus
Mahonia
Myoporum
Oenothera
Rosa
Rosmarinus
Vinca

Sedum dasyphyllum

SHADE TOLERANT

These plants are some of the most reliable for the different degrees of shade. Those marked with an asterisk tolerate a combination of shade and dry soil.

Aegopodium*
Anemone
Asarum
Asparagus*
Astilbe
Campanula
Cymbalaria
Euonymus
Ferns
Galium*
Hedera
Hosta*
Hypericum
Iris
Lamiastrum
Lamium
Laurentia

Liriope
Lysimachia
Mentha
Moss
Omphalodes
Ophiopogon
Pachysandra
Paxistima
Ranunculus
Ribes*
Sarcococca
Soleirolia
Taxus
Vancouveria
Vinca
Waldsteinia

DROUGHT TOLERANT

Drought tolerance is related to climate adaptation and healthy growth. Keep in mind that no plant is drought tolerant until established. Water deeply and infrequently after plants are established to promote drought tolerance. Plant roots are then forced to go deeply into the soil. If watering is shallow, roots stay near the surface and are more susceptible to water shortages.

Acacia
Achillea
African daisies
Arctostaphylos
Artemisia
Baccharis
Bamboo
Brooms
Ceanothus
Centranthus
Cistus
Convolvulus
Coprosma
Coronilla
Cotoneaster
Dalea
Eschscholzia

Grevillea
Hypericum
Iberis
Ice plants
Juniperus
Lantana
Myoporum
Oenothera
Phyla
Polygonum
Ribes
Rosmarinus
Sedum
Teucrium
Thymus
Verbena

POPULAR AND RELIABLE

Here are the most commonly planted ground covers. They are proven to be adaptable to most climates and are widely available.

Ajuga
Arctostaphylos
Cotoneaster
Euonymus
Hedera
Hemerocallis
Hosta
Hypericum
Iberis

Juniperus
Mahonia
Pachysandra
Potentilla
Rosa
Sedum
Thymus
Vinca

FIRE RETARDANT

Shape and growth habit are important when selecting a fire-retardant ground cover. For example, upright rosemary is not fire retardant but trailing rosemary is. Ground-hugging plants ignite less readily. Succulent plants that rapidly develop a cover several inches thick are ideal. Plants with high moisture or high salt content tend to be fire retardant.

Artemisia
Atriplex
Baccharis
Cephalophyllum 'Red Spike'
Cistus
Convolvulus
Delosperma 'Alba'
Gazania
Maleophora crocea
Myoporum
Phyla
Rosmarinus
Santolina
Sedum
Teucrium

BETWEEN STEPPINGSTONES

These are low creepers that will withstand footsteps now and then.

Armeria	Lobularia
Aubrieta	Mazus
Cerastium	Mentha
Chamaemelum	Phyla
Cotula	Sagina
Erodium	Soleirolia
Galium	Thymus
Hernaria	Veronica
Laurentia	

SHOWY FLOWERS

Many ground cover plants produce colorful flowers. By growing plants with different bloom periods for each season, you can have color the year-round.

African daisies	Hemerocallis
Agapanthus	Hosta
Astilbe	Iberis
Bougainvillea	Lantana
Campanula	Lobelia
Catharanthus	Lobularia
Centranthus	Lysimachia
Chrysanthemum	Myosotis
Convallaria	Oenothera
Convolvulus	Omphalodes
Dianthus	Phlox
Dyssodia	Rosa
Eschscholzia	Rosmarinus
Felicia	Spirea
Heaths and heathers	Trachelospermum
Helianthemum	Verbena

DRAPE AND TRAIL

Many of the best ground covers grow flat along the ground because they are pulled by gravity. The habit is accentuated if they grow over a wall or edge of a bank.

Arabis	Lamium
Arctostaphylos	Lantana
Asparagus	Lobelia
Baccharis	Lobularia
Bougainvillea	Lysimachia
Ceanothus	Myoporum
Cerastium	Osteospermum
Cotoneaster	Picea
Euonymus	Pinus
Felicia	Rosa
Gazania	Rosmarinus
Helianthemum	Santolina
Juniperus	Thymus

Vinca minor

LARGE AREAS

Two kinds of plants are listed here. Some, identified with an asterisk, will not stay confined to small areas. Give them a large area, or they will take it on their own. Others are manageable, but most effective in large-scale, mass plantings.

Acacia	Lantana
African daisies	Lonicera*
Baccharis	Lotus
Ceanothus	Myoporum
Comptonia*	Oenothera
Coronilla*	Pachysandra
Cotoneaster	Plumbago*
Euonymus*	Polygonum*
Forsythia	Prunus
Hedera	Rosa
Hemerocallis	Sedum
Hypericum*	Vinca
Juniperus	

Two species of *Thymus: T. praecox arcticus* flowers over layer of *T. pseudolanuginosus.*

BENEATH TREES AND SHRUBS

Plants that can grow in soil dominated by tree or shrub roots are among the most useful. Evergreen ground covers that grow several inches high such as *Vinca major* allow falling leaves to sift through, hiding the leaves.

Duchesnea	Ophiopogon
Epimedium	Pachysandra
Euonymus	Paxistima
Hedera	Polygonum
Hemerocallis	Ribes
Hypericum	Sarococca
Liriope	Vancouveria
Nandina	Vinca

SELF-SOWERS

Here are the carefree, easy-come, easy-go ground covers. Not for tidy perfectionists, they disappear with heat or cold. But they come back each season, sometimes in unexpected places. These plants might be considered weeds but for their appealing flowers or growth habit.

Aurinia	Felicia
Brooms	Geranium
Catharanthus	Lobelia
Centranthus	Lobularia
Chrysanthemum	Moss
Dimorphotheca	Myosotis
Dyssodia	Polygonum
Eschscholzia	Portulaca

POTENTIAL WEEDS

These plants are aggressive spreaders—perfect in some situations. But be aware of what you are planting. These plants have a reputation of being pests if they get out of control or if they grow too fast.

Aegopodium	Phalaris
Atriplex	Phyla
Aurundinaria	Polygonum
Coronilla	Ranunculus
Hypericum	Sagina
Lonicera	Veronica
Lysimachia	Vinca
Oenothera	

GROUND COVERS YOU NEED TO MOW

Many ground covers are best if mowed occasionally. The leafy carpet is more even and vigorous with young growth, and flower display is more dramatic. To mow these plants, use a rotary mower you can adjust to cut very high, or rent a weed mower. See plant descriptions for more details.

Achillea	Fragaria
Aegopodium	Hedera
African daisies	Hypericum
Arundinaria	Liriope
Aurinia	Lonicera
Baccharis	Phlox
Dianthus	Vinca
Euonymus	

BULB COVERS

These plants complement flowers or are simply used as a living mulch over the ground where bulbs are planted. Ground covers eliminate the mess of splashed soil when bulbs are watered, and cover the drying leaves of bulbs as they go dormant. Taller bulbs are usually combined with higher-growing ground covers. As a rule, ground cover should be half the height of flowering bulbs.

Arabis	Laurentia
Arenaria	Lobelia
Aubrieta	Lobularia
Aurinia	Lysimachia
Campanula	Mazus
Cerastium	Mentha
Chamaemelum	Myosotis
Cotula	Omphalodes
Cymbalaria	Phyla
Erodium	Potentilla
Galium	Sedum
Geranium	Soleirolia
Hedera	Thymus
Herniaria	Vancouveria
Iberis	Veronica
Juniperus	Vinca
Lamiastrum	Waldsteinia
Lamium	

REGIONAL FAVORITES

Some ground covers are popular and reliable in distinct regions of the United States. England is much like the Northwest, and Australia can be compared to the West.

North, Northeast and Eastern Canada

Arctostaphylos	Moss
Comptonia	Pachysandra
Coronilla	Paxistima
Euonymus	Picea
Forsythia	Pinus
Heaths and heathers	Potentilla
Hedera	Sedum
Juniperus	Vinca

Northwest and British Columbia

Arctostaphylos	Mahonia
Aubrieta	Moss
Aurinia	Oxalis
Broom	Paxistima
Gaultheria	Pernettya
Heaths and heathers	Picea
Hypericum	Pinus
Lysimachia	Prunus

Coastal Regions

Arctostaphylos	Heaths and heathers
Atriplex	Helianthemum
Baccharis	Hypericum
Carissa	Ice plants
Ceanothus	Juniperus
Cistus	Myoporum
Coprosma	Pittosporum
Fragaria	Ribes

Desert

Acacia	Lantana
African daisies	Oenothera
Atriplex	Phyla
Baccharis	Rosmarinus
Catharanthus	Santolina
Dalea	Verbena
Euonymus	Vinca
Grevillea	

West

Acacia	Eschscholzia
African daisies	Grevillea
Agapanthus	Myoporum
Arctostaphylos	Ribes
Baccharis	Rosmarinus
Ceanothus	Santolina
Convolvulus	Trachelospermum
Coprosma	

Mountain States

Arabis	Mahonia
Arctostaphylos	Phlox
Artemisia	Picea
Aubrieta	Rosa
Baccharis	Sedum
Cerastium	Thymus
Juniperus	Waldsteinia
Lysimachia	

South

Asarum	Ilex
Convallaria	Lamium
Euonymus	Liriope and Ophiopogon
Ferns	Pachysandra
Gardenia	Phlox
Hedera	Trachelospermum
Hosta	

Arctostaphylos hokkeri 'Wayside'

LAWN ALTERNATIVES TO WALK ON

No cover is as perfect for play as a grass lawn. But the ground covers listed here can be mowed and will tolerate considerable foot traffic.

Achillea	Mazus
Arenaria	Moss
Chamaemelum	Phyla
Cotula	Thymus
Laurentia	Veronica
Lotus	

Phlox subulata

GROUND COVER BASICS

SOIL

As with a lawn, the majority of ground covers prefer a fertile soil high in organic matter. Generally, soil preparation for lawns and ground covers is the same. The goal is to improve the soil in the root-zone area—the top 6 to 8 inches. The best way to do this is by adding organic matter. Add enough so that this top layer is one-third organic matter by volume. This means adding a 2- to 3-inch layer of an organic material such as sawdust, peat moss, ground bark, decomposed manure or compost over the soil, and working it in. "Raw," uncomposted organic material such as sawdust uses up nitrogen fertilizer when it decomposes. Add 1 to 2 pounds actual nitrogen per cubic yard of raw amendment.

Before you plant is the time to adjust the soil pH, which is determined by a soil test. Raise pH by adding ground or dolomitic limestone. Lower pH by adding sulfur.

If you do not test the soil, or a soil-test facility is unavailable, the general guide for preplant fertilizer calls for 1-1/2 to 2 pounds of 10-10-10 fertilizer per 100 square feet.

Sometimes improving the total soil area is neither necessary nor practical. If the area is exceedingly large or steep, complete soil amendment is not wise. Digging up and amending the soil could aggravate erosion problems. And, some native plants prefer unimproved, sandy soil instead of fertile soil high in organic matter.

When you plant wide-spreading shrubs such as *Ceanothus* or *Juniperus* species, amend the soil immediately surrounding the rootball, but do not add amendments to the entire area. Unless your soil is very sandy or heavy clay, it is best to fill the planting hole with the same soil that you took out. If you have a heavy clay or light, sandy soil, blend two parts native backfill soil with one part organic material such as compost, peat moss or shredded bark. If you are planting from containers, this 2:1 mix provides a transition between the usually lightweight container soil mix and native soil.

WEED CONTROL IN GROUND COVERS

Ground covers are not low-maintenance plants until they develop a dense, weed-choking cover of foliage. Until that time, it is possible to spend more time weeding your new ground cover planting than caring for a new lawn of comparable size. Depending on plant spacing and growth rate, this weed-battling period can last from a few weeks to a few years. After the planting establishes a cover, soil is shaded where weed seeds sprout and their growth is blocked. But even then, perennial weeds such as Bermudagrass, field bindweed and nutsedge might invade. That's why it is very good advice to asume that some kind of weed control will be necessary, both before and after planting.

Before Planting—Where tough perennial weeds are not a problem, the best method of preplant weed control is repeated cultivations. Turn soil and existing weeds under with shovel or power tiller. Water to germinate weed seeds brought to the surface by the cultivation, then turn soil under again. Repeat this cycle until few weeds appear.

A *nonselective herbicide* such as cacodylic acid can help with this process. Instead of repeat cultivations, spray new weed growth. This will save work and time because buried weed seeds are introduced to the surface with each cultivation.

Nonselective herbicides effective against both annual and perennial weeds are necessary if the planting area includes perennial weeds such as Bermudagrass, dallisgrass or Johnsongrass. Two applications of an herbicide such as glyphosate are necessary to rid an area of such weeds.

Soil fumigants might be necessary where the weed problem is severe. Fumigants kill perennial and annual weeds, germinating seeds and most dormant weed seeds. Two of the best fumigants for home gardeners to use are calcium cyanamide and metham. Both require a waiting period of 3 to 6 weeks before soil can be planted. Other fumigants are available, such as the highly toxic methyl bromide. Only professional weed control operators use it.

After Planting—Remember that a soil-shading ground cover is the best weed defense. Providing adequate water and nutrients for optimum growth will enable the ground cover to spread over the soil faster.

A thick layer of mulch aids growth of the ground cover and is one of the best methods of preventing weed invasion. A weed-free mulch shades the soil surface, preventing germination of weed seed waiting there. Weeds that do manage to grow through a mulch layer are easily pulled compared to weeds pulled from hard-packed soil.

Pre-emergent herbicides are great aids for control of summer and winter annual weeds. Apply pre-emergent herbicides just after planting and before weed seed germinate and begin growth. Remove sprouted or mature weeds in established plantings before applying the herbicide.

If you plan to use a pre-emergent herbicide after planting, set each plant deep enough to completely cover the root mass with soil. After planting and before applying the herbicide, water the planting area to settle the soil around the plants. Be certain to read the product label carefully to be sure it is safe to use around the ground cover you intend to plant.

Rainfall or a light watering is necessary to activate the pre-emergent herbicide chemical in the soil area where weed seeds germinate. On a newly planted slope, be careful that soil carrying herbicide does not run off onto lawn or other landscape plants.

PLANTING

Ground cover plants are available at the nursery in individual containers, in flats or in separate cells of plastic "6-paks." Containers are usually plastic or metal. Metal containers require cutting before you can plant them. They are awkward to cut at home, so let nursery personnel do it for you. But do not have containers cut unless you can plant that day. After cans are cut, plant roots dry quickly.

Arrange plants on the site in approximate planting positions. Make adjustments in spacing and position.

Set large, woody plants at the same soil level as they were in their containers. If soil is loose from tilling, set plants slightly higher to allow for some settling.

When to Plant—In general, early fall is the best time to plant ground covers.

Temperatures are moderate, rainfall is plentiful and weed competition is less severe than in summer. Soil temperature cools more gradually than the air, so root growth continues further into fall than you might expect. By spring, plants are partially established and can grow with maximum vigor.

If you live where the soil freezes, plant in fall or spring. If you choose fall, plant soon after summer heat has passed to allow maximum time for establishment before freezing weather arrives. Use a mulch to insulate soil. This will keep the soil warmer long into fall. A mulch will also prevent premature thawing of frozen soil in spring, which can damage plants.

Planting on a Slope—The degree of slope and threat of erosion determines the method of planting. In many cases, planting in a triangular or staggered fashion, firming small basins around each plant, will be adequate. A mulch of straw or shredded bark further protects soil.

Planting from Containers

1. Before planting, position plants in their containers to determine proper spacing. See chart, page 76.

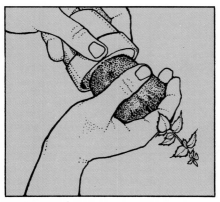

2. Remove plant by lightly tapping, pressing or turning the pot upside down until rootball is free.

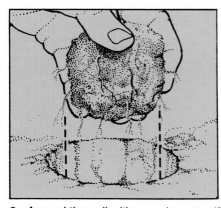

3. Amend the soil with organic matter if required. Make a hole large enough to accommodate rootball without bending roots.

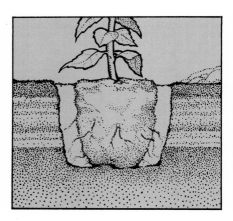

4. Set plant at or slightly above soil line to allow for some settling.

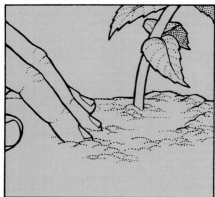

5. Firm soil around plant just enough for it to remain upright. Too much pressing compacts top few inches of soil.

6. Water plant to settle the soil. Protect from sun and wind until roots are firmly established.

SPACING GROUND COVERS

Close spacing of plants will normally cover an area faster than wider spacing. The expense and mature size of plants are limiting factors. Don't space plants too closely. Keep the plant's growth habit and spread in mind as you plan spacing. *Hedera, Hypericum, Vinca* and *Pachysandra* species are usually planted on 1-foot centers. Fast-spreaders such as *Arctotheca* and *Baccharis* species are spaced on 18- to 36-inch centers. Shrubby, spreading plants such as *Abelia, Carissa, Juniperus, Rosa* and others need at least 36 inches between plants. Some require even more. For example, some *Ceanothus* species grow best with 5 feet of space between plants.

Positioning plants in a triangular pattern rather than rectangular pattern is most efficient for covering the ground. Triangular-spaced plants are all one distance on-center, and a shorter distance between rows. The chart on this page shows distances between rows for various spacing and the number of plants required for 100, 500 and 1,000 square feet of coverage.

WATERING

All newly planted ground covers deserve attentive watering. New plants have limited root systems, and are stressed when transplanted. No matter where you live, regular supplemental water is usually necessary for at least the first two seasons. Many shallow-rooted ground covers need attention during periods of drought. Even some native plants require occasional watering during summer months.

Just as for lawns, water ground covers *thoroughly* and *efficiently*. Soil should be moistened to the depth roots are expected to grow. The best watering method is one that adequately meets the needs of the ground cover. It should also ignore the needs of nearby weeds, and prevent water from running into the gutter.

Hand watering with a hose works fine for small areas and plants with shallow roots. But even in small areas you should check for adequate water penetration. Sprinkler watering is sufficient for somewhat larger areas. Adequate irrigation of a very large area requires some kind of permanent sprinkler system.

An underground sprinkler system for ground covers is basically the same as for lawns. The main difference is in the height of the riser or pop-up. You need to account for the ultimate height of the mature ground cover.

If you are considering an underground system, seek the advice of an irrigation consultant. It is money well spent. This is especially true if you are planting on a slope. A slope adds complex variables requiring experience to understand.

Drip Watering—This important watering method is not practical for lawns or closely spaced ground covers such as *Hedera, Hypericum* or *Vinca*, but is ideal for larger, widely spaced plants. Drip systems apply water slowly and over a small area. Many types are available and most are relatively simply to install. Drip systems can also be automated just as any lawn sprinkler system.

If you live in an arid climate or where water is in short supply, seriously consider installing a drip watering system. You'll save water due to reduced evaporation and reduced runoff. Drip watering systems can save up to 25 percent of the normal water cost.

Drip watering systems are ideal for establishing native, drought-resistant ground covers on slopes. Most sprinklers apply water faster than the soil on a slope can absorb it, causing runoff and erosion. Watering by drip eliminates such problems.

It is most practical to install a simple, inexpensive system for watering native ground covers. After plants are able to live on natural rainfall and adjust to periods without water, remove or disconnect the system.

FERTILIZING

Ground cover plants have such varied nutrient needs that giving exact speci-

Number of Plants You Will Need

On-center spacing*	Distance between rows	Plants/square foot	Plants/100 square feet	Plants/500 square feet	Plants/1,000 square feet
6 inches	5 inches	5	461	2,080	4,610
8	7	3	260	1,300	2,600
10	9	2	166	830	1,660
12	10	1	115	575	1,150
15	13	1	74	369	738
18	15	1	52	256	512
24	21	—	29	145	290
30	26	—	19	93	185
36	30	—	13	64	128
4 feet	3½ feet	—	7	36	73
5	4	—	5	23	46
6	5	—	3	16	32
8	7	—	2	9	18
10	8	—	1	6	12
12	10	—	1	4	8

*Distance from center of one plant to center of adjacent plants.

fications is impossible. In general, ground covers need less fertilizer than laws. But to maintain an attractive cover, regular applications of fertilizer are necessary. As a general guide, apply between 2 and 4 pounds of actual nitrogen per 1,000 square feet per year. Use a complete fertilizer such as a 10-10-10. The best time to fertilize is in the early fall. Spring applications are also helpful with some plants. One or two summer applications of fertilizer may also be required, depending on soil fertility and plants used.

PROPAGATION

If you have a large area to cover with ground cover, or would like to use relatively expensive plants, propagating your own makes good sense. Or the planted area can gradually expand as the supply of plants increases.

Cuttings—This is the best way to propagate ground covers such as English ivy and euonymus. A cutting is a 3- to 6-inch long section of healthy growth. The best time to take cuttings varies with the plant. As a general rule, take cuttings after new growth is finished and before it has hardened. Determine this stage of growth by bending the stem or twig. If it can be bent 180 degrees without breaking, it is too soft. If it cannot be bent at all without breaking, it is either too hard or too thick.

Set cuttings in a flat filled with rooting medium composed of fast-draining potting soil. A mix with equal proportions of sand, peat moss and vermiculite works well. Maintain high humidity with a transparent cover of glass or plastic and be sure leaves receive adequate sunlight. It is a good practice to check the cuttings frequently, but allow 4 to 6 weeks for the first sign of root development.

Layering—This is the propagation method many ground cover plants use naturally. A stem grows over the top of the soil, and where moisture is adequate, roots develop. You can speed up this process by mounding soil over trailing stems. Rooted stems can be removed from parent plant and transplanted.

Division—This is a common method of increasing the number of ground cover plants. To divide plants, remove and replant side shoots or small plants from a large, established clump. Spring is typically the best time to divide ground covers. Liriope, star jasmine, periwinkle, daylily, ajuga and many others are commonly propagated this way.

One you establish an area with ground cover, there is generally an ample supply of small plants available for division. It is simple to remove them to extend the planting or bolster thin areas without harming the main planting bed.

Planting Ground Covers on a Slope

10°
Stones with sand
Boards and stakes
Up to 20°
Soil berm

Establishing a ground cover on a slope is challenging. Erosion destroys sections of new plantings and irrigation water washes soil. Make low, 1- to 2-foot high retaining walls of stone or concrete rubble supported with sand if slope is steep. Walls should span width of slope or position them in front of plants. Simple terraces strengthened by boards and stakes protect less-steep slope plantings. Plantings on slopes of 20 degrees and less are adequately served by soil berms that catch and hold water.

Jute netting was applied first, secured with heavy wire staples. Knife-cut holes permitted planting rooted cuttings of English ivy.

The slope at left 3 years later. Established ivy is attractive, suppresses weeds and protects slope.

EROSION CONTROL

Bare slopes are certain to erode. The impact of falling rain and water runoff soon creates gullies in the soil surface and washes topsoil away. Wind also erodes soil.

A complete cover of vigorously growing plants is one of the best ways to prevent erosion. But it is a challenge to establish a slope planting—bare slopes usually have little or no topsoil. In addition, subsoil is infertile and either rocky or heavy clay—subject to severe soil loss during periods of heavy rainfall. Protecting slopes from erosion involves three phases:

1. Diverting water away from slope with ditches and drain pipe.
2. Protecting soil with organic mulch or netting.
3. Planting and maintaining a ground cover.

Divert Water—Build a small ditch or dike at the top of the bare slope to channel runoff to a suitable safe point such as a storm drain or heavily vegetated area. Try to keep the runoff path nearly level.

If it must be steep, line path with concrete or rock or use corrugated pipe to carry water down steep slopes to a safe outlet.

Prevent water from flowing along one route on the slope. If soil is loose, cover potential gully area with plastic sheets overlapped like shingles. Overlapping is important: It prevents water from getting beneath and creating more severe problems. Anchor sheets with wire staples made of coathangers or with rocks. To plant, cut holes in plastic. Drip irrigation lines may be installed either below or on top of the plastic.

If slopes are steep, cut terraces to disperse the flow of water and trap the eroding soil. This will also make a better planting site. Terraces should be largest at the bottom of the slope where flow of water is greatest. A rough-graded surface is more erosion resistant than a smooth one.

There are "slope-stabilizing" chemicals available, but investigate them carefully before relying upon them. Some are of minimal value and may inhibit plant growth.

Apply a Mulch—Mulches are beneficial used alone or in combination with seed or small plants. A well-secured mulch shields bare soil from the force of sprinkler drops or raindrops, as well as protecting it from running water. It also protects grass seed and young plants. Common mulches for slopes include straw, hay, bark or coarse wood chips, jute netting, excelsior padding, large rocks and gravel.

Commercial landscaping firms can "plant" a slope with a spray of wood fiber and seeds—a process called *hydromulching*. A hydromulch of wood fiber alone without quickly germinating seed is better than nothing, but less effective on a steep slope than other mulches.

You can use weed-free alfalfa hay as a mulch to protect soil until plants are well established. Spread evenly over the surface in a layer about 2 inches deep. About 100 pounds is required to cover 1,000 square feet. Firm it into the soil by punching every few inches with a spade, or cover with staked-down netting of jute, plastic or wire.

Bark, shredded fir bark, pine needles or coarse wood chips are useful as mulches, especially if partially mixed into the soil surface. They can discourage weed growth if layered more than 1 inch thick. Because bark mulch is usually lightweight and larger than wood chips, it is more likely to blow or wash off the slope. Generally, both wood chips and bark mulch are less effective for erosion control than an equal weight of straw.

Fill small gullies that develop after a rain with additional mulch, or protect with overlapped plastic sheets or jute netting.

Rock mulches are not commonly used on slopes, but do make a rough, protective seedbed and reduce both wind and water erosion. Pea gravel is likely to wash away. Use 1-1/2- to 2-inch diameter rock or larger.

Netting—Jute or excelsior mats of netting are effective if properly anchored. These are sold in rolls by horticultural supply outlets. Secure them to the slope with wire staples. It is important that the mat maintains close contact with the soil surface. On rough surfaces where soil contact is lost, erosion can occur under the mat. Mats are more expensive than straw or hay but are convenient to install, longer lasting and more effective.

Plant a cover—If desirable plants are not encouraged, weeds will probably take up residence. In some cases you may be able to take advantage of natural weed growth to control erosion. You can mow weeds or kill them with contact herbicides without disturbing the soil.

Grasses are the No. 1 choice where a fast cover is needed. Annual grasses and unirrigated perennial grasses become dry in warm-summer areas and can create a fire hazard. However, even dead grass protects the slope from erosion.

Plant grasses in fall before the rainy season. Spread seed by hand or use a mechanical spreader. Use a 20-20-20 starter fertilizer to provide at least 2 pounds of actual nitrogen per 1,000 square feet.

In general, annual grasses become established faster than perennial grasses. In either case, watering before the rainy season will speed establishment. Also consider adding a legume such as rose clover or birdsfoot trefoil to grass plantings. Legumes supply nitrogen, which helps the grasses to grow, and provide a habitat for quail and other wildlife.

Check further with local nurseries and your county extension agent.

Preventing Erosion

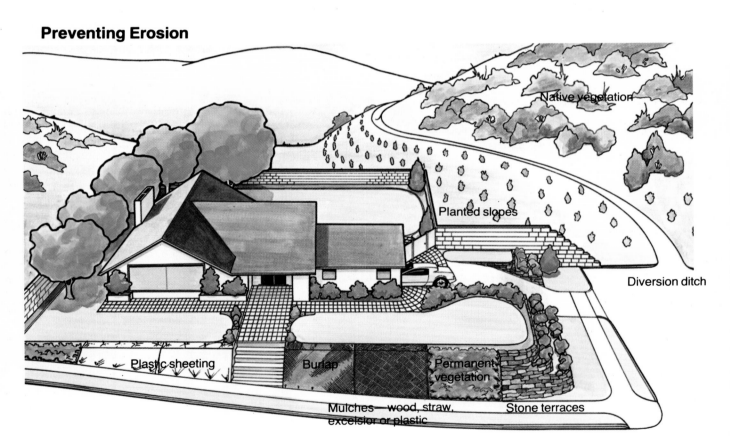

Specific needs of individual sites in potential erosion areas vary, but usually include at least one of these illustrated techniques. Temporary aids such as mulches, burlap and overlapping sheets of plastic normally last until a vegetative cover is complete. For more elaborate solutions such as diversion ditches and stone terraces, consult a qualified engineer or landscape architect.

Achillea tomentosa is a delicate-looking plant with bright flowers—perfect for small areas.

ENCYCLOPEDIA OF GROUND COVERS

All plants are listed alphabetically by their botanical name. Though perhaps unfamiliar at first, botanical names are by far the best way to avoid confusion. Occasionally, botanists differ regarding a plant's proper name. That's why this encyclopedia is cross-referenced throughout with both common names and botanical synonyms.

Planting and care information represents the combined knowledge of the authors, numerous consultants and ground cover nurseries. Basics such as distance between plants, notable pest problems and treatments, and low-temperature hardiness are also found here.

Welcome to the world of ground covers!

ABELIA GRANDIFLORA 'PROSTRATA'
Prostrate abelia

Prostrate abelia is a dwarf form of a well-known and deservedly popular shrub. Tough yet decorative, use it like 'Wheeler's Dwarf' pittosporum—massed for a solid cover on banks or in small groupings blended with other low ground covers. It has been used with much success on freeway banks and slopes.

Height is 1-1/2 to 2 feet and spread is to 4 feet. A *g.* 'Sherwoodii' grows slightly taller and wider. New leaves are glossy red then become bright green when mature. Flowes are bell shaped and small, but abundant throughout summer.

Planting and care—Plant from containers 3-1/2 feet apart for solid cover. Give full sun, regular water and fertilizer. Drought tolerant once established.

Hardy to 0F (-18C). Partially deciduous when exposed to cold temperatures.

ACACIA REDOLENS

This is a low, spreading member of the fast-growing, evergreen, heat- and drought-tolerant *Acacia* family. It is a fine choice for erosion control on dry banks.

Height usually remains below 2 feet, but spread is wide—to 15 feet. Long, narrow, golden green leaves form a dense carpet. Yellow flowers, which cause some people allergy problems, appear in early spring.

Planting and care—Full sun is most important requirement. Any well-drained soil is okay. Plant in fall, usually from 1-gallon containers. Water frequently first season. Drought tolerant once established. Although excellent for most Southwest gardens, it is not completely hardy. This prevents its use in colder areas of the high desert, such as Globe, Arizona and Albuquerque, New Mexico.

Hardy to about 20F (-7C).

ACHILLEA TOMENTOSA
Wooly yarrow

Woolly yarrow is an evergreen, hardy, sun-loving, easy-to-grow plant. Native to northern temperate areas. It is adapted to dry, exposed locations. It is not fussy about soil and is fire retardant.

This low-growing yarrow reaches 6 to 9 inches high, spreading about as wide. Fernlike leaves are light olive-green. Canary-yellow flowers are borne in flattish clusters. They completely cover foliage in spring.

Planting and care—Plants are available in a variety of sizes—1 gallon containers, flats or plastic packs. Space fast-spreading clumps 6 to 12 inches apart. Mow faded flowers with a rotary mower for repeat bloom. Divide clumps to propagate.

Hardy to -40F (-40C).

Aegopodium podagraria 'Variegatum' is a vigorous ground cover when grown in full sun. Clusters of white flowers produce large quantities of viable seed.

AEGOPODIUM PODAGRARIA 'VARIEGATUM'

Goutweed

Goutweed is an easy-to-grown plant for difficult situations. It is one of the few plants that thrive in dry, shaded soil.

Goutweed was popular with Victorian gardeners. They used it to edge flower borders, but usually discovered—as you might too—that it is not always a polite garden citizen. Because it spreads by both seeds and creeping roots, goutweed will eventually dominate any area where it is planted.

Plant is deciduous, grows 6 to 12 inches high and spreads indefinitely. Leaves are gray-green and have white edges. Parsleylike flowers appear in spring. Mow or clip them off before they mature to prevent or slow invasions of seedlings.

Planting and care—Some nurseries offer plants, usually in 1-gallon containers. More often, it is passed from neighbor-to-neighbor in shovel-dug clumps. Space clumps about 2 feet apart in full sun or part shade. Mow two or three times a season with a rotary mower set to cut as high as possible.

Plants die to the ground with first hard frost but roots are hardy to about -40F (-40C).

AGAPANTHUS

Lily-of-the-Nile

Agapanthus species are favorites of professional landscapers, but rarely considered ground covers. Plants can be used in many ways—as accents or border—and they excel in containers. They are complementary in color and texture when planted *en masse*, such as around a lawn.

Lilylike leaves are long and narrow. Flowers appear in ball-shaped clusters on straight stems that grow from base of plant. Peak flower display occurs in late spring and lasts as long as two months.

There are three species and five named forms of *Agapanthus*. Plants are usually blue or white, large or dwarf.

A. africanus produces blue flowers in spring and early summer on top of 1-1/2-foot stalks.

A. inapertus has deciduous leaves and deep blue flowers that hang from the top of large, 4-1/2-foot stalks.

Armeria maritima is colorful yet surprisingly drought tolerant.

ARMERIA MARITIMA
Common thrift

Common thrift is a neat and tidy evergreen plant, long favored for use in rock gardens. It also works well in front of borders, in contaners and between steppingstones.

Plant grows 3 to 6 inches high, forming a clump up to 18 inches wide. Gray-green leaves are narrow and grasslike but stiff. Dense, globular, 3/4-inch flowers are borne in profusion on top of 10-inch stems. They are typically pink but selected forms may be white, rose or red. Flowers are in bloom throughout spring, summer and fall in coastal areas. In other regions flowers are most abundant spring and fall.

The many *Armeria* species hybridize freely, resulting in many cultivated forms. Some of the more common are:
'Alba'—A small, choice form with pure white flowers.
'Brilliant'—Bright pink flowers.
'Laucheana'—Densely tufted, 6-inch plants. Flowers are intense rose-pink.
'Royal Rose'—Abundance of bright pink flowers on top of 15-inch stems.
'Vindictive'—Deep rose-red flowers.
Planting and care—Plants are available in flats, plastic packs or gallon containers. Fall is best planting time. Space plants 8 to 10 inches apart. Relatively poor, dry but well-drained soil is best. Rich, moist soil encourages root rot and generally causes plants to be short-lived. Full sun is necessary at the coast, but afternoon shade is fine, perhaps beneficial, elsewhere. To maintain plantings, remove faded flowers with a mower or clippers. Apply a balanced fertilizer such as 10-10-10 in the fall. Propagate by dividing plants in spring.

Hardy to -50F (-45C).

ARTEMISIA
Silver spreader, Angel's hair

Artemisia is a large and varied genus that includes many drought-tolerant, silvery gray plants. Two that serve particularly well as ground covers are *Artemisia caucasica*, commonly called silver spreader, and *A. schmidtiana*, angel's hair. They both make striking border or accent plants.

Silver spreader grows from 3 to 6 inches high and eventually forms a clump 2 feet wide. It came to nurseries and gardens via the University of California at Riverside and then Forest Fire Laboratory. It is fire resistant and a good choice for a bank cover around Southwest homes surrounded by flammable hillside growth.

Angel's hair grows 2 feet high and spreads 1 foot wide. Look for 'Silver Mound'. It is lower—6 to 12 inches high—and makes an interesting low border. Silver-white leaves are fern-like with a woolly texture, and are fragrant when crushed.

Planting and care—Plants are normally available in 1-gallon containers. Plant in fall in any well-drained soil. Space plants about 18 inches apart. Both species tolerate extremes of heat and drought. Once established, little or no water is needed in summer. Feel free to cut plants back severely in early spring if necessary to rejuvenate. New growth will cover plant by fall.

Silver spreader is hardy to -20F (-29C). Angel's hair is hardy to -10F (-24C).

Asarum caudatum grows best in shade and moist soil.

Asparagus densiflorus 'Sprengeri' drapes gracefully over a wall.

ASARUM
Wild ginger

Given the right conditions—heavy shade and moist, humus-rich soil—the gingers make beautiful, fast-spreading ground covers. Many species are available. Most are native to North America; one is native to Europe. Roots have a pungent quality, vaguely reminiscent of tropical, culinary ginger. In no other way are the plants related.

Plants form a mat 6 to 10 inches high with a similar spread. Green leaves are heart shaped, 2 to 7 inches across. Cold weather gives them a purple tint. Bell-shaped flowers are an unusual purple-brown color. They appear in spring but are hidden by leaves.

Commonly available species are:

Asarum canadense, Canadian wild ginger. Deciduous. Native to much of northeastern United States and Canada. Hardy to -34F (-40C).

A. caudatum, British Columbian wild ginger. Evergreen. Native to western Canada and south to California's Santa Cruz Mountains. Excellent under redwoods. Glossy green leaves. Attractive, high-quality ground cover. Hardy to 0F (-18C).

A. europaeum, European wild ginger. Evergreen. Spreads by underground runners. Hardy to -20F (-29C).

A. shuttleworthii 'Callaway'. Evergreen. Spreads by underground runners. Selected form of a southeastern native originating at Callaway Gardens, Pine Mountain, Georgia. Leaves are mottled, smaller than the species. Hardy to 0F (-18C).

Planting and care—Plant in spring from divisions or containers 8 to 15 inches apart. Water regularly through summer. Protect from slugs and snails.

ASPARAGUS DENSIFLORUS 'SPRENGERI'
Sprenger asparagus, Asparagus fern

Sprenger asparagus is a popular house plant. It also serves as an excellent, outdoor container plant and evergreen ground cover in mild-winter areas. It is especially suited to raised planters. Cut foliage is attractive in arrangements.

Growth habit is open and mounding to 2 feet high. Bright green leaves are needlelike and reach 3 to 5 feet long. New leaves project from a ground-level clump. Older plants produce small, white, 3/8-inch flowers in spring, followed by round, shiny, bright red berries in fall.

'Sprengeri Compacta' is lower growing, to 1-1/2 feet, and has more closely set leaves.

Planting and care—Plants are available in various sizes of containers. Fall is normally the best planting time, but anytime is okay. Space plants 1 to 2 feet apart, in full sun or some shade. No soil preference; plants also tolerate salty soil. Excellent drought tolerance after they are established. Plants do look more attractive with regular water and fertilizer.

Hardy to 25F (-4C).

Cotoneaster horizontalis

COTONEASTER
Cotoneaster

Cotoneasters are a large group of shrubs that include many low and spreading forms. Several make excellent ground covers. Most are hardy, tough and easy to grow. Most are natives of northern Asia, the Himalayas and Europe. Most have small shiny, thick, green leaves, small flowers in spring and red berries in fall. Stems do not have thorns.

C. adpressus praecox—Fishbone-pattern branches follow ground contours. Grows to about 18 inches high, spreading 5 to 6 feet wide. Leaves are oval, 1 inch long and closely set. They turn brilliant red in fall. Berries are 1/2 inch in diameter, bright red. Deciduous.

Hardy to -20F (-29C).

C. apiculatus 'Nana', dwarf cranberry cotoneaster— Large, red, cranberry-size fruit stay on plant all winter. Plant grows to 12 inches high, spreads 4 feet. Branches bend down at tips. Leaves are round with wavy margins, shiny, bright green on top, turning deep red in fall. Deciduous.

Hardy to -25 (-32C).

C. congestus—Grows 3 feet high but hugs the ground. Small, 1/4-inch leaves are round, dark green on top, white below. Berries are bright red, 1/4 inch in diameter. One of the most hardy, evergreen types. Recommended for the desert. Variety 'Likiang' is especially compact, low and attractive.

Hardy to 0F (-18C).

Cotoneaster microphyllus visually softens a mortarless stone wall.

Cotoneaster horizontalis displays fine, feathery texture and red berries. This one is a little taller than typical.

Cotoneaster dammeri drapes over a low planter wall.

C. dammeri, bearberry cotoneaster—Very low, wide spreading, cascading and evergreen. Often grows no more than 8 inches high. Rooting branches spread rapidly to 10 feet wide. Leaves are oval, 1 inch long. Berries are bright red and showy. Several varieties are available: 'Coral Beauty' has coral-colored berries. 'Lowfast' is 12 inches high and spreads 2 feet per season. It serves as an excellent bank cover. 'Royal Beauty' has deep red berries. 'Skogsholmen' grows 12 to 18 inches high. It has stiff branches and attractive spring flowers.

All are hardy to -10F (-24C).

C. horizontalis, rock cotoneaster—Popular, wide-spreading ground cover. Distinctive characteristic is pattern of secondary branches—all are on the same level and grow in a herringbone pattern. Plant grows 2 to 3 feet high and spreads 15 feet or more wide. Give it room: Don't plant where ends must be clipped. Leaves are 1/2 inch wide, round, glossy green on top, pale below. In fall, leaves turn orange for a brief time, then red before falling. Bright red berries remain on branches long after leaves fall. Subspecies *C. h. perpusillus* is lower and more compact. Dedicuous.

Hardy to -20F (-29C).

C. microphyllus, rockspray cotoneaster—Smallest leaves and finest texture of ground cover cotoneasters. Develops into dense, tangled mass of stiff branches. Maximum height is 2 to 3 feet. Spreads to 6 feet wide. Main branches trail and root. Evergreen leaves are small, dark green on top, gray and hairy below. Berries are rose-red, 1/4 inch in diameter. Three common varieties are: 'Cochleatus', more compact and prostrate than others. It is considered the best variety. 'Emerald Spray' features good fireblight resistance. *C. m. thymifolius* is compact with stiff, upright growth. Berries are smaller, borne in clusters.

Hardy to -10F (-24C).

Cotoneaster microphyllus, foreground, covers this steep slope.

221

Cotoneaster species make excellent low borders, but edges do not take shearing.

Cotoneaster dammeri spreads low, wide and fast.

C. salicifolius, willowleaf cotoneaster—is a tall, shrub cotoneaster with many low, spreading forms. 'Herbst-feuer' grows 6 inches high and spreads up to 8 feet. It is evergreen and becomes maroon-red in winter. Some catalogs list it as 'Autumn Fire'. 'Emerald Carpet' is compact with a dense growth habit and smaller leaves. It is semi-evergreen. Excellent under taller shrubs and draped over walls. 'Repens', occasionally listed as *C. s. repandens*, also has trailing, rooting branches. Grows 12 inches high and 6 to 8 feet wide. Leaves are dark green and 3 inches long. 'Scarlet Leader' is very low growing, to 6 inches high, and more dense. Good retaining wall and bank cover.

Hardy to -10F (-24C).

Planting and care—Plant cotoneaster in spring or fall. Many kinds are regularly stocked by nurseries, usually in 1-gallon containers.

Full sun and dry, average soil and best, but light shade and moist soil are acceptable. Prune with clippers to remove wayward branches—don't use hedge shears. Scale, red spider mite or lace bug may cause problems. They are easily controlled with soapy sprays, malathion or kelthane sprays.

Fireblight disease occasionally affects cotoneaster. Leaves wilt, look scorched and hang on branches. Prune infected branches, cutting back into at least 4 inches of healthy wood. Dip pruners into bleach to disinfect between cuts. Burn or dispose of diseased wood.

Polystichum acrostichoides

Polystichum species prefer bright light with moist soil.

Ferns

As you might expect, ferns used as ground covers are a varied lot. Some are hardy and adaptable; others are tender with more exacting requirements. All will lend that exotic fern character to adapted locations of your garden.

ADIANTUM PEDATUM

Five-finger fern

This is a delicate, particularly graceful fern, reaching 1 to 2 feet high and spreading as wide. Plant spreads by creeping rootstalks. Medium green leaflets rise from shiny, nearly black stalks. Roots are perennial and fronds essentially evergreen. Fronds will die-back during unfavorable growth periods.

Planting and care—Usually available in 1-gallon containers. Plant spring or early fall in loose, highly organic, moist, well-drained soil.

Hardy to -35F (-40C).

ATHYRIUM GOERINGIANUM 'PICTUM'

Japanese painted fern

This is the most colorful of the hardy ferns. Leaflets of the 9-inch long fronds are soft, dull green and have a metallic sheen. Stems and main veins are ruby-red, creating a dramatic contrast.

Plant grows about 15 inches high and makes a dense, weed-choking cover. It is deciduous.

Planting and care—Plant from 1-gallon containers, spring or fall. Grow in full sun or partial shade in moist, mulched soil. Does best in wind-sheltered locations.

Hardy to -35F (-40C).

CYRTOMIUM FALCATUM

Holly fern

Holly fern makes an attractive, evergreen, informal border along entryways or planted under camellias, rhododendrons and similar shrubs.

In some ways plant does not look like a typical fern. Thick, leathery, shiny green leaflets are 3 inches long and toothed, similar to holly leaves. Fronds are 2-1/2 feet or more long.

Planting and Care—Plant from 1-gallon containers, 1-1/2 feet apart in light shade. Moist, loose soil is best. Set plants slightly high—planting too deep may cause crown rot. Be generous with water.

Hardy to 25F (-4C).

DAVALLIA TRICHOMANOIDES

Squirrel's-foot fern

This is a cold-tender fern of limited use. But it is interesting and worthwhile in temperate gardens, where it thrives, making an excellent, evergreen ground cover. It is often thought of only as a house plant. Most striking are the brown, fuzzy rhizomes that creep over the soil surface. Dark green fronds are about 12 inches long and 6 inches wide at the widest point. Height is 6 to 8 inches. Plants spread to about 12 inches.

Planting and care—Easy to grow. Plant from containers in spring or fall. Any soil is acceptable. Plant in shaded, protected location. Water generously for best results.

Hardy to 30F (-1C).

Athyrium goeringianum 'Pictum' has unusual frond coloring.

Adiantum pedatum grows best with bright light, needing little or no direct sun.

DRYOPTERIS ERYTHROSORA
Autumn fern, Wood fern

The large group of *Dryopteris* species includes many, hardy native ferns. Autumn fern is a low-growing, spreading Asian import. It reaches 1-1/2 to 3 feet high and slowly spreads to about as wide with underground rhizomes.

When young fronds emerge, they are delicate looking and reddish. Later they become a rich, deep green.

Planting and care—Plant from containers as early in spring as soil can be worked. Grow in shade and moist, loose soil. Use a mulch and water frequently until established.

Hardy to -20F (-29C).

NEPHROLEPSIS CORDIFOLIA
Sword fern

These ferns often survive in neglected gardens, proof of their resilience. In adapted climates, sword ferns are easy to grow and spread with a vigor approaching invasiveness. Plant them around trees, in narrow beds or in any shaded, confined area.

Bright green fronds are 2 to 3 feet long and very upright. They spread by wiry, hairy rhizomes.

Planting and care—Plant from 1- or 5-gallon containers in shade in about any soil. Regular amounts of water are adequate. Drought tolerance is surprisingly good for a fern.

Hardy to 25F (-4C).

Dryopteris species are at home in woodland plantings, as shown above. Below, *Dryopteris* combine well with *Trachelospermum* and *Liriope muscari*.

POLYSTICHUM
Christmas fern, Western sword fern

Two species of these hardy, evergreen, North American natives make fine ground covers.

Polystichum acrostichoides, Christmas fern, grows 2 to 3 feet with an equal spread. It is very similar in appearance to Boston fern and often used as a house plant. Fronds are long lasting in indoor arrangements and are frequently available from florists. It prefers shade but will accept sun in moist soil.

Hardy to -35F (-40C).

P. munitum, western sword fern, is the large fern common to redwood forests of northern California. Shiny, dark green fronds may reach 2 to 5 feet in length. Spread is variable, but usually reaches about 3 feet. Individual plants produce up to 100 fronds. Plant in shade in moist soil high in organic matter.

Planting and care—Start with nursery plants—transplants rarely succeed. Grow in shade. Plants are self-sufficient once established.

Hardy to -25F (-32C).

RUMOHRA ADIANTIFORMIS
Leatherleaf fern

Deep green, finely divided fronds of leatherleaf fern look more delicate than they feel. They are surprisingly smooth and tough. They almost seem artificial. Leatherleaf fern tolerates more light and less water than most ferns. Plant grows 1 to 3 feet high in slow-spreading, evergreen clumps that eventually reach about 18 inches high. The durable, long-lasting fronds are florist's favorites. Some catalogs list this plant as *Polystichum capense* or *Aspidium capense*.

Planting and care—Plants are available in 1-gallon containers. Plant in shade and moist soil to establish.

Hardy to 25F (-4C).

LAWNS

A lawn has many virtues. Color, texture and feel of grass pleases the senses. Grass cools and freshens the air, traps dust and reduces glare. A neatly clipped and trimmed grass lawn lends a consistency and order to the landscape. Above all, there is no more versatile outdoor surface than a lawn. Lawn is relatively inexpensive, clean and safe for outdoor activities and tumbling children. No other ground cover possess these combination of utility and beauty.

GRASS SELECTION GUIDE

Lawn grasses are classified as either *cool season* or *warm season*. Cool-season grasses grow best during cool periods of spring and fall. Most are tolerant of cold winters, so are used in the northern latitudes. Cool-season grasses include Kentucky bluegrass, fine fescues, ryegrasses and bentgrasses.

Warm-season grasses grow best in areas with high summer temperatures. Most become dormant to some degree when temperatures drop below freezing. Most are killed by cold northern winters. Warm-season grasses grow best in areas with high summer temperatures. Most become dormant to some degree when temperatures drop below freezing. Most are killed by cold northern winters. Warm-season grasses include bahia, Bermuda, centipede, St. Augustine and zoysia.

About the grass descriptions—In the following section, each grass is pictured close-up and in the landscape. These photos give you some idea of texture, color and overall appearance of each grass. The accompanying map shows the area of the United States and Canada where each grass is best adapted. Keep in mind that these adaptation zones are general guides. Local conditions vary considerably. Also, many grasses do well beyond their typical range, though they may require pampering to grow well. Some gardeners want to grow a specific grass and are willing to provide the extra care necessary for it to thrive.

Relative tolerances to heat, cold, salt, disseases, pests, drought, shade and wear for each grass are indicated by the chart at the top of each description. These ratings, like the zones of adaptation, serve only as useful guides. Those listed primarily in the "high tolerance" column are the low-maintenance grasses. Those frequently rated "low" in tolerance will likely require extra care.

A "perfect" lawn, such as this one in Richardson, Texas, begins by choosing a well-adapted grass. This is 'Tifway' hybrid Bermuda.

LAWN REGIONS

The map below outlines the basic lawn grass zones of the United States and Canada. Use the map as a guide and compare it to descriptions of individual grasses and specific climate adaptations. Much lawn seed is sold as *mixes*—combinations of several grasses. These combine strengths and compensate for weaknesses. A typical mix of cool-season grasses includes Kentucky bluegrass, fine fescue and perennial rye. Perennial ryegrass combined with common Bermudagrass tolerate summer heat and stress and remains green in winter.

PACIFIC NORTHWEST AND COASTAL BRITISH COLUMBIA

Climate of this zone is generally cool and humid. This region is the center of cool-season grass-seed production. Adapted grasses are Kentucky bluegrass, fine fescue, bentgrass and ryegrasses.

SOUTHERN CALIFORNIA

Many kinds of grasses are planted in this zone. Common Bermudagrass, *Paspalum* species and zoysiagrass are low maintenance. Kentucky bluegrass, mixed with improved perennial ryegrass for disease resistance, is popular. Tall fescue is also grown here. Use annual and perennial ryegrass to overseed dormant Bermudagrass. mudagrass.

SOUTHWEST

Summer heat is intense here. Soils are dry and water is precious. Lawns are best planted small and oasislike. Common and improved Bermudagrass are best bets. Overseed them with ryegrass for winter. Zoysiagrass and St. Augustinegrass are options.

MOUNTAIN, NORTHERN GREAT PLAINS AND CANADIAN CENTRAL PLAINS

Climate is dry and semiarid. Rainfall varies between 10 and 25 inches annually. Daily temperature range is extremely wide. Kentucky bluegrass and fine fescues are most common. Hardy varieties of improved perennial ryegrass and tall fescue are sometimes used. Bermudagrass and zoysiagrass are occasionally planted in the southern part of the region. Use crested wheatgrass, buffalograss or blue grama for low-maintenance lawns.

GREAT LAKES, NORTHEASTERN STATES AND EASTERN CANADA

Rainfall is abundant, averaging up to 45 inches. Kentucky bluegrass, fine fescues and improved perennial ryegrasses are common and well adapted. Hardy Bermudagrasses and zoysiagrass are sometimes planted in coastal areas.

MOUNTAIN, PIEDMONT AND THE CENTRAL SOUTH

Climate is warm and humid with rainfall ranging between 40 and 70 inches per year. Bermudagrass and zoysiagrass are common. Tall fescue is well adapted. Kentucky bluegrass, fine fescues and perennial ryegrass are frequently grown. Use improved perennial or annual ryegrass over dormant Bermudagrass.

GULF COAST AND FLORIDA

Climate is tropical, with a year-round growing season. St. Augustinegrass is the most important lawn grass of Florida. Zoysiagrass is widely recommended. Bahiagrass, centipedegrass and tall fescue are commonly grown. Due to the longer growing season, all grasses need more mowing and more fertilizer.

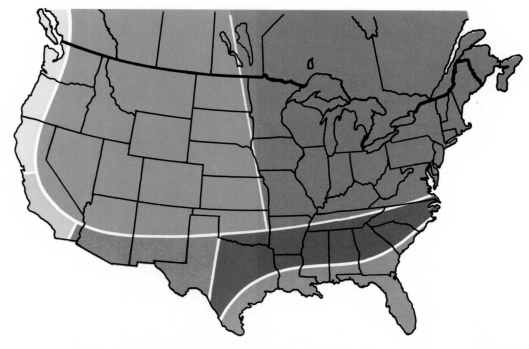

BAHIAGRASS
Paspalum notatum

To Plant: Sow 8 to 10 pounds of seed per 1,000 square feet in spring. Germinates in 20 to 40 days.
Water: Moderate
Fertilizer: 2 to 4 pounds actual nitrogen per 1,000 square feet per year.
Mowing: Frequent mowing required to remove seed-heads. Adjust rotary mower to about 2-1/2 inches high.

Bahiagrass was introduced to the United States from Brazil around 1913. It is well adapted to coastal areas from central North Carolina to eastern Texas, especially where soils are sandy and infertile. A coarse-textured grass, it spreads aggressively with short, thick rhizomes. Drought tolerance is above average, but bahiagrass is best where rainfall is abundant and evenly distributed throughout the year. Mole cricket is a common pest.

VARIETIES

'Argentine'—Leaves are more narrow than common bahiagrass but wider than 'Pensacola'. Medium cold tolerance. Sometimes used for home lawns.
'Paraguay'—Coarse texture, tough leaves. Used along roadsides for erosion control.
'Pensacola'—Narrow, upright leaves. Tolerant of low temperatures. Good response to fertilizer. Best bahiagrass for home lawns.

Bahiagrass

Bahiagrass
Areas of Optimum Adaptation

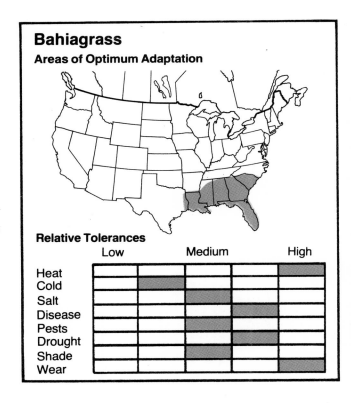

Relative Tolerances

	Low		Medium		High
Heat					■
Cold		■			
Salt			■		
Disease				■	
Pests			■		
Drought				■	
Shade			■		
Wear					■

Bahiagrass

Common bermudagrass

Common bermudagrass

BERMUDAGRASS, COMMON
Cynodon dactylon

To Plant: Sow 1 to 2 pounds of seed per 1,000 square feet. Germinates in 10 to 30 days.
Water: Moderate.
Fertilizer: 2 to 6 pounds of actual nitrogen per 1,000 square feet per year. Use higher rate for improved appearance and where growing season is long.
Mowing: Cut at 3/4 to 1-1/2 inches high with reel or rotary mower.

A tough, low-maintenance lawn that can be attractive if watered and fertilized regularly. Overseed with ryegrass or fine fescue for winter lawn. Control invasiveness with glyphosate chemical spray.

BERMUDAGRASS HYBRIDS AND VARIETIES
Cynodon species

To Plant: Use sod, plugs or sprigs. Seed of hybrid Bermudagrass is sterile. If you plant sprigs, spread 2 bushels per 1,000 square feet, late spring to midsummer.
Water: Moderate.
Fertilizer: Use 6 to 10 pounds actual nitrogen per 1,000 square feet per year. Use higher rates when maintenance is intensive and growing season is long. Use complete fertilizer with minor elements depending on soil conditions.
Mowing: Use reel mower adjusted to cut 1 inch high.

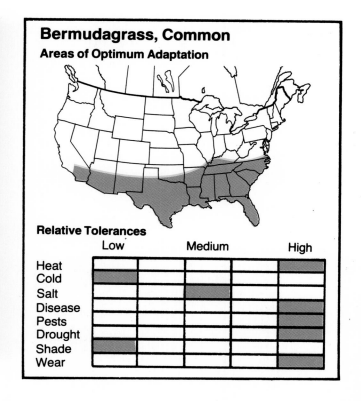

Bermudagrass, Common
Areas of Optimum Adaptation

Relative Tolerances

	Low		Medium		High	
Heat					▓	
Cold	▓					
Salt			▓			
Disease					▓	
Pests					▓	
Drought					▓	
Shade	▓					
Wear					▓	

Tif series Bermudagrass hybrids are dwarf and fine textured compared to common Bermudagrass. Some are used as substitutes for creeping bentgrass in the South.

HYBRIDS AND VARIETIES

'Midiron'—Dark green, medium texture. Vigorous. Excellent cold tolerance. Wears well in winter.
'Midway'—Dark green, medium texture. Excellent cold tolerance. Minimum thatch buildup.
'Pee Dee'—Dark green, medium texture. Good cold tolerance. Relatively high maintenance.
'Santa Ana'—Dark green, fine texture. Developed in southern California. Features short dormant season and high air-pollution tolerance. Very dense growing. Needs periodic thinning and dethatching.
'Sunturf'—Dark green, very fine texture. Good cold tolerance.
'Tifdwarf'—Dark green, fine texture. High maintenance. Tolerates exceptionally low mowing. Normally used for golf greens and lawn bowling—rarely for home lawns.
'Tifgreen'—Medium green, fine texture. One of the best for golf greens—accepts heavy wear and close, 1/8-inch cut.
'Tifway'—Dark green, fine texture. Best of the Tif series for home lawns. Does not require ultra-low mowing and generally needs less maintenance.

Hybrid bermudagrass

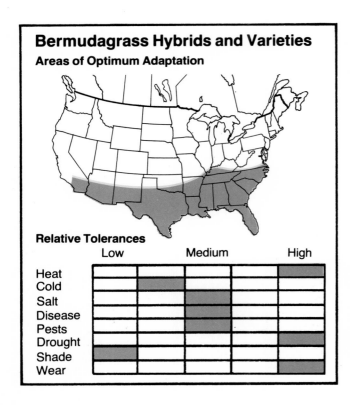

Bermudagrass Hybrids and Varieties
Areas of Optimum Adaptation

Relative Tolerances

	Low	Medium	High
Heat			■
Cold	■		
Salt		■	
Disease		■	
Pests		■	
Drought			■
Shade	■		
Wear			■

'Tifgreen' hybrid bermudagrass

231

BENTGRASS
Agrostis species

To Plant: Sow 1/2 to 1 pound per 1,000 square feet of 'Penncross', 'Emerald', 'Seaside' and 'Penneagle'. For 'Cohansey', 'Congressional' and 'Toronto', use 2 bushels of sprigs per 1,000 square feet. Seed germinates in 6 to 20 days.

Water: Needs large amount.

Fertilizer: 4 to 6 pounds of actual nitrogen per 1,000 square feet per year. Might require a complete fertilizer including minor elements, depending on soil conditions.

Mowing: Use reel mower adjusted to cut 1/4 inch to 1 inch high.

SPECIES AND VARIETIES

A. canina, Velvet bentgrass—Tolerant of low soil fertility. Aggressive if mowed close and often. High-quality lawn for home, bowling green or putting green. Sometimes used in seed mixes.

A. gigantea, Redtop—Prefers clay soils of low pH and low fertility. Rarely included in seed mixes because it tends to be short-lived and weedy.

A. stolonifera, Creeping bentgrass—High-quality lawn for putting or bowling greens. Mow low—1/4 inch—with a reel mower. Established by either seed or vegetative means. See varieties listed under "To Plant" above.

A. tenuis, Colonial bentgrass—Aggressive, usually dominant grass if planted in a mix. Varieties include 'Astoria', 'Exeter', 'Highland' and 'Holfior'.

Bentgrass

'Seaside' bentgrass

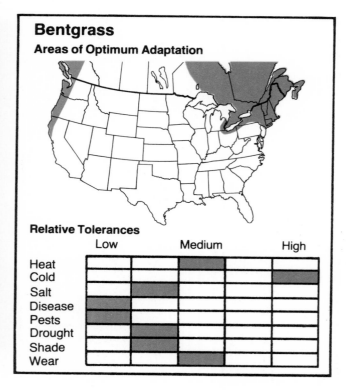

Bentgrass
Areas of Optimum Adaptation

Relative Tolerances

	Low		Medium		High
Heat			▨		
Cold					▨
Salt		▨			
Disease	▨				
Pests	▨				
Drought		▨			
Shade		▨			
Wear			▨		

CENTIPEDEGRASS
Eremochloa ophiurides

To Plant: Sow 1 to 2 pounds of 'Centi-Seed' per 1,000 square feet. Germinates in about 20 days. Requires two seasons to establish. Or spread 5 or 6 bushels of sprigs per 1,000 square feet.

Water: Medium.

Fertilizer: Provide 1 to 2 pounds actual nitrogen per 1,000 square feet per year. Use low, 12 to 15 percent nitrogen fertilizer. Apply phosphorus and potassium only during the dormant season.

Mowing: Cut 1 to 1-1/2 inches high with reel or rotary mower.

Centipedegrass was introduced to the United States from southern Asia in 1916. It is well adapted to infertile, acid soils common to many regions of the Southeast. It tolerates less cold than Bermudagrass, but more than St. Augustinegrass. Too much nitrogen promotes tender growth, which can be severely damaged by winter cold. Seedheads develop but are low and inconspicuous compared to Bermudagrass or bahiagrass. Not as fine textured as Bermudagrass so it will not develop a manicured look. Subject to iron chlorosis, especially after nitogren fertilization. Correct with iron sulfate.

'Oklawn' is the only variety available. Released by Oklahoma Agricultural Experiment Station in 1965, it features improved drought and cold tolerance compared to common centipedegrass.

Centipedegrass

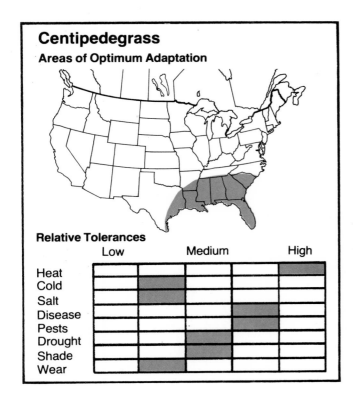

Centipedegrass
Areas of Optimum Adaptation

Relative Tolerances

	Low		Medium		High
Heat					
Cold		■			
Salt		■			
Disease				■	
Pests				■	
Drought			■		
Shade			■		
Wear		■			

Centipedegrass

FESCUE, FINE
Festuca rubra, F. longifolia

To Plant: Sow 5 pounds of seed per 1,000 square feet. Germinates in 7 to 14 days.
Water: Drought tolerant. Moderate.
Fertilizer: Low—1 to 3 pounds per 1,000 square feet per year. Dies out if overfertilized.
Mowing: Use reel or rotary mower adjusted to cut 2 inches high. Keep mower sharp. Hard fescues, *F. longifolia*, are relatively difficult to cut. Dull mowers shred leaf tips, giving lawn a brownish cast.

Three kinds of fine fescue are included here. Creeping red fescue and chewings fescue are subspecies of *F. rubra*. Red fescue spreads by underground runners called *rhizomes*. Chewings fescue is a clump-forming, nonspreading type. Hard fescue, *F. longifolia*, grows in clumps like chewing fescue, but has more heat and drought tolerance. In outward appearance, all three are virtually indistinguishable.

Fine fescues mix well with other grasses. They frequently comprise about 20 percent of a mix along with Kentucky bluegrass and improved perennial ryegrasses. In general, fine fescues add shade and drought tolerance to such a mix. Fine fescues are also useful for overseeding dormant Bermudagrass.

Creeping fescue

'Fortress' creeping fescue

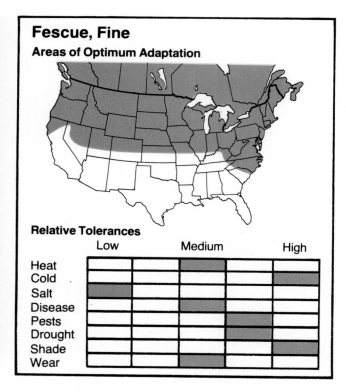

Fescue, Fine
Areas of Optimum Adaptation

Relative Tolerances

	Low		Medium		High
Heat			▓		
Cold					▓
Salt	▓				
Disease			▓		
Pests				▓	
Drought		▓			
Shade					▓
Wear			▓		

VARIETIES OF CHEWING FESCUE

'*Banner*'—Dark green. Tolerates low mowing. Disease resistant but occasionally susceptible to powdery mildew.
'*Highlight*'—Medium green, very fine texture. Very aggressive in mixtures. Tolerates low mowing.
'*Jamestown*'—Medium to dark green. Dense and vigorous. Tolerates low mowing. Susceptible to powdery mildew.
'*Shadow*'—Dark green. Dense and vigorous. Improved disease resistance. Resists powery mildew in shade.

VARIETIES OF CREEPING FESCUE

'*Dawson*'—Medium dark green, slender. Good for overseeding dormant Bermudagrass. Tolerates low mowing. Susceptible to dollar spot.
'*Fortress*'—Dark green color blends well with Kentucky bluegrass and improved perennial ryegrasses. Strong spreader. Resists powdery mildew and has relatively good heat tolerance.
'*Pennlawn*'—A blend of fescue types, but primarily red fescue. Dark green with dense growth habit. Commonly mixed with Kentucky bluegrasses and improved perennial ryegrasses. Most commonly available fine fescue.
'*Ruby*'—Dark green color. Medium texture and density.

VARIETIES OF HARD FESCUE

'*Scaldis*'—Medium dark green. Improved heat and drought tolerance. Low maintenance.
'*Waldina*'—Medium dark green. Improved disease, heat and drought tolerance.

Left, 'Alta' fescue. Right, creeping fescue.

FESCUE, TALL
Festuca arundinacea

To Plant: Sow 10 to 20 pounds of seed per 1,000 square feet. Seedlings are vigorous and fast growing. Germinates in 7 to 15 days.
Water: Moderate.
Fertilizer: 2 to 6 pounds of actual nitrogen per 1,000 square feet per year.
Mowing: Adjust rotary mower to cut about 2 inches high.

Tall fescue is a low-maintenance lawn grass. Most commercially available varieties were developed for forage qualities. Their utility has made them popular for home lawns in some areas. Generally, they do not perform well and make low-quality lawns. Tall fescue does not form a dense sod and tends to retreat into clumps, especially if not seeded at high rates. In many lawns, it is a coarse, fast-growing weed.

Despite these disadvantages, tall fescue is being used more frequently as a grass for home lawns. Several new "turf-type" tall fescues are available. They are new and have not yet been evaluated over the long term. But they promise to combine the heat, drought and wear tolerance and low-fertility requirements of forage types with other desirable characteristics. Look for varieties that have better color, finer texture, good mowing characteristics and improved disease resistance.

VARIETIES OF TURF-TYPE TALL FESCUE

'*Falcon*'—Medium dark green, medium leaf texture and turf density. Moderately low growing. Good heat and drought tolerance. Moderately resistant to leaf spot and brown patch.
'*Houndog*'—Medium dark green, medium leaf texture. Medium to low turf density. Semiprostrate growth habit. Good heat and drought tolerance. Moderate resistance to brown patch and *Helminthosporium* net blotch.
'*Olympic*'—Dark green, medium leaf texture and medium turf density. Somewhat lower growing than other varieties. Modern shade adaptation. Less prone to develop iron chlorosis. Improved resistance to crown rust and *Helminthosporium* net blotch. Moderate resistance to brown patch. Maintains good green color with low soil fertility.
'*Rebel*'—Medium dark green, medium leaf texture and medium turf density. Good heat and shade tolerance. Moderate resistance to *Helminthosporium* net blotch. Somewhat susceptible to brown patch. Persists well with close mowing compared to other varieties.

'Alta' fescue

'*Shannon*'—Medium dark green, medium to coarse leaf texture. Medium turf density. Slower vertical growth rate than other varieites. Good drought and shade tolerance. Improved cold tolerance compared to common tall fescues. Moderate resistance to brown patch and *Helminthosporium* net blotch. Good mowing qualities.

VARIETIES OF FORAGE-TYPE TALL FESCUE

'*Alta*'—Medium green, coarse leaf texture and medium to low turf density. Upright growth habit. Good drought tolerance, poor cold tolerance. Susceptible to *Helminthosporium* net blotch and brown patch.

'*Fawn*'—Light green, coarse texture and low turf density. Well adapted to heavy clay soils. Poor heat and cold tolerance. Very susceptible to *Helminthosporium* net blotch, brown patch and crown rust.

'*Goar*'—Medium green, medium to coarse texture and medium to low turf density. Upright growth habit. Improved heat tolerance, but poor cold tolerance. Tolerant of salinity and high pH. Susceptible to *Helminthosporium* net blotch and brown patch. Slow to establish.

'*Kentucky 31*'—Medium green, coarse texture, medium to low turf density. Slightly prostrate growth habit. Good heat tolerance but poor cold tolerance. Good shade tolerance. Susceptible to *Helminthosporium* net blotch. Well adapted to transition zone. Forms medium-textured turf under shaded conditions in warm, humid climates.

Tall fescue

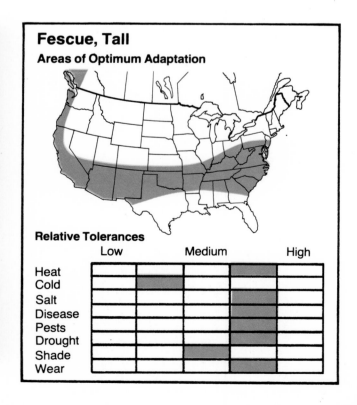

Fescue, Tall
Areas of Optimum Adaptation

Relative Tolerances

	Low		Medium		High
Heat				▨	
Cold		▨			
Salt				▨	
Disease				▨	
Pests				▨	
Drought				▨	
Shade			▨		
Wear				▨	

KENTUCKY BLUEGRASS
Poa pratensis

To Plant: Sow 1 to 2 pounds per 1,000 square feet. Germinates in 14 to 30 days. Commonly available as sod.
Water: Medium to large amount.
Fertilizer: Apply 4 to 6 pounds actual nitrogen per 1,000 square feet per year. Use a complete fertilizer including minor elements depending on soil conditions.
Mowing: Varieties differ, but few should be cut below 1-1/2 inches high. Dwarf, low-growing varieties can be cut as close as 3/4 inch. Common Kentucky bluegrass should be cut higher, approximately 2-1/2 inches.

Kentucky bluegrass is widely adapted, attractive and hardy. It is the most widely planted grass in northern latitudes. It is the standard of color, texture, feel and maintenance against which other grasses are measured. Plants spread by strong, underground rhizomes, ultimately forming a dense sod.

In most areas, Kentucky bluegrass requires supplemental irrigation to maintain healthy growth during periods of drought. Without irrigation, leaves brown and cease to grow. Growth resumes with rains or renewed irrigation.

VARIETIES

'Adelphi'—Dark green, medium texture. Dense and low growing. Very good low-temperature color. Greens up fast in spring. Resistant to leaf spot, stripe smut and *Fusarium* blight.

Kentucky bluegrass

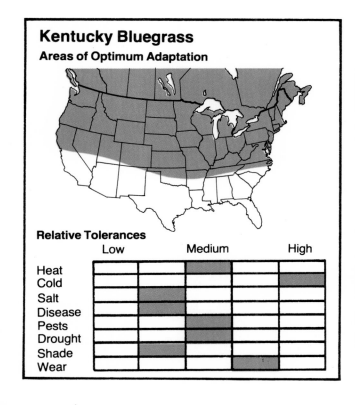

Kentucky Bluegrass
Areas of Optimum Adaptation

Relative Tolerances

	Low		Medium		High
Heat			▓		
Cold					▓
Salt		▓			
Disease		▓			
Pests			▓		
Drought			▓		
Shade		▓			
Wear			▓		

Kentucky bluegrass

Kentucky bluegrass

'America'—Dark green, fine texture. Dense and low growing. Slow vertical growth rate. Moderate shade tolerance. Resistant to leaf spot, stripe smut, striped rust and *Fusarium* blight. Tolerates low nitrogen levels.

'Aquilla'—Medium dark green, medium to fine texture. Dense and fairly low growing. Good low-temperature color and spring green-up. Accepts low nitrogen levels.

'Baron'—Dark green, medium to coarse texture. Dense and low growing. Good low-temperature color. Moderately slow to green up in spring. Good seedling vigor—establishes rapidly. Moderate resistance to leaf spot and stripe smut.

'Bensun' (A-34)—Medium green, medium texture. Very dense and low growing. Tolerant of shade and low mowing. Very aggressive and competitive. Good wear resistance and spring green-up. Resists stripe smut. Moderately resistant to leaf spot.

'Birka'—Dark green, medium to fine texture. Dense and low growing. Moderately slow to green up in spring. Moderately tolerant of shade and low mowing. Resistant to leaf spot, stripe smut and powdery mildew.

'Bonnieblue'—Medium dark green, medium texture. Dense and low growing. Excellent low-temperature color. Greens up quickly in spring. Establishes fairly fast. Tolerates low mowing. Resists leaf spot and stripe smut.

'Bristol'—Dark green, medium texture. Dense and low growing. Excellent low-temperature color. Greens up quickly in spring. Recommended for shady sites. Moderate tolerance of low mowing.

'Cheri'—Dark green, medium texture. Dense and low growing. Accepts low mowing. Fair color at low temperatures. Vigorous seedlings establish fast.

'Columbia'—Medium dark green, medium texture and density. Low growing. Excellent color at low temperatures. Greens up quickly in spring. Good heat tolerance. Establishes fast. Moderately tolerant of low mowing. Resists leaf spot, stripe smut and *Fusarium* blight.

'Eclipse'—Dark green, medium texture and density. Very low growing. Good low-temperature color and spring green-up. Excellent cold tolerance. Tolerant of heat, drought and shade.

'Enmundi'—Dark green, medium texture and density. Very low growing. Tolerant of heat, drought and low mowing. Limited seed availability.

'Fylking'—Dark green, medium to fine texture. Dense and low growing. Good low-temperature color and spring green-up. Tolerant of cold and drought. Establishes fast and accepts low mowing. Makes a strong sod. Resistant to leaf spot. Some resistance to stripe smut. Highly susceptible to *Fusarium* blight.

'Glade'—Dark green, medium texture. Dense and low growing. Moderately good color at low temperatures. Good for shady sites. Slow vertical shoot growth. Moderately competitive. Resistant to stripe smut and powdery mildew. Moderate resistance to leaf spot.

'Majestic'—Dark green, medium texture. Dense, low, semiprostrate growth habit. Excellent low-temperature color. Greens up quickly in spring. Establishes fast. Accepts low mowing. Good resistance to leaf spot. Moderate resistance to stripe smut.

Kentucky bluegrass

'Merion'—Dark green, medium to coarse texture. Dense and low growing. Relatively poor color at low temperatures. Slow to green up in spring. Cold and drought tolerant. Slow to establish from seed. Fast to root when planted as sod in summer. Resists leaf spot. Susceptible to stripe smut, powdery mildew and rust. Not recommended for shady sites.

'Nugget'—Dark green, medium to fine texture. Dense and low growing. Cold hardy but very poor color at low temperatures. Slow to green up in spring. Excellent shade tolerance—recommended for shady sites. Resists leaf spot and powdery mildew. Susceptible to dollar spot.

'Parade'—Medium dark green, medium texture and density. Low growing. Very good low-temperature color. Fast to green up in spring. Establishes fairly fast and wears well. Resists leaf spot, stripe smut and *Fusarium* blight.

'Plush'—Medium green, medium texture and density. Low growing. Good low-temperature color and spring green-up. Establishes fast, moderately aggressive. Wears well.

'Ram I'—Dark green, medium to fine texture. Dense and low growing. Resistant to powdery mildew. Slow vertical shoot growth rate.

'Rugby'—Medium dark green, medium texture. Dense and low growing. Good low-temperature color and spring green-up. Medium heat and drought tolerance. Establishes rapidly. Very tolerant of low mowing. Good disease resistance. Tolerant of low fertility.

'Scenic'—Dark green, medium texture and density. Low growing. Attractive color with low fertility. Drought tolerant. Spreads fast. Resists pink snow mold, snow scald, powery mildew and leaf spot diseases. Susceptible to stripe smut.

'Shasta'—Medium dark green, medium texture and density. Excellent resistance to stripe rust in Pacific Northwest and northern California. Resistant to leaf spot and stripe smut.

'Sydsport'—Medium dark green, medium texture. Dense and low growing. Fairly good spring green-up. Widely adapted variety. Establishes fast and wears well. Aggressive and competitive. Forms dense sod. Resistant to leaf spot, stripe smut, *Fusarium* blight and powdery mildew.

'Touchdown'—Medium green, medium to fine texture and density. Erect growth habit. Greens up fast in spring. Shade tolerance better than most. Aggressive and competitive. Tends to develop thatch. Resists leaf spot, stripe smut and powdery mildew. Very susceptible to stripe smut.

'Vantage'—Medium green, medium to fine texture and density. Erect growth habit. Excellent heat and drought tolerance and good spring green-up. Use for a low-maintenance lawn. Looks acceptable with little care, but is susceptible to stem rust.

'Victa'—Dark green, medium to coarse texture. Dense and low growing. Moderately slow to green up in spring. Establishes fast. Moderately resistant to leaf spot and stripe smut.

'Windsor'—Dark green, medium to fine texture. Fairly dense and low growing. Good spring green-up and medium cold tolerance. Looks and grows best with high levels of nitrogen. Moderately resistant to leaf spot. Susceptible to stripe smut.

Annual ryegrass

RYEGRASS, ANNUAL
Lolium multiflorum

To Plant: Sow 5 to 10 pounds of seed per 1,000 square feet. Apply heavier rates in poor soils where low germination is expected, or when dense, fine-textured winter lawn is desired. Germinates in 5 to 14 days.
Water: Medium.
Fertilizer: Grows best with moderate fertility. Provide approximately 4 pounds actual nitrogen per 1,000 square feet per year.
Mowing: About 1-1/2 to 2 inches high with reel or rotary mower.

Huge quantities of annual ryegrass are sown over winter-dormant lawns each fall. For a brief period—fall to late spring—they are an attractive alternative to a dormant, brown lawn. Individual plants that survive into the following season become coarse-textured, fast-growing, weedy clumps. Most overseeded annual ryegrass dies out with heat. To encourage the permanent, dormant lawn, mow ryegrass lawn low in late spring.

An improvement over annual ryegrass for winter overseeding is called *Oregon intermediate ryegrass*. Its botanical name is *Lolium x hybridum*. It was developed from a cross between a low-growing annual ryegrass and 'Manhattan' perennial ryegrass. Oregon intermediate ryegrass is much lower growing, more disease resistant and has better heat and cold tolerance than annual ryegrass.

Annual ryegrass

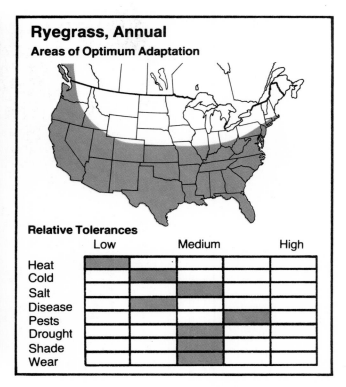

Ryegrass, Annual
Areas of Optimum Adaptation

Relative Tolerances

	Low		Medium		High
Heat	■				
Cold		■			
Salt			■		
Disease		■			
Pests				■	
Drought			■		
Shade			■		
Wear			■		

RYEGRASS, PERENNIAL
Lolium perenne

To Plant: Sow 5 to 10 pounds of seed per 1,000 square feet. In a mix, limit improved perennial ryegrasses to 20 percent by weight of mix. Germinates in 3 to 10 days.
Water: Medium.
Fertilizer: Apply 4 to 5 pounds actual nitrogen per 1,000 square feet per year.
Mowing: Cut 1-1/2 inches high. Some varieties will tolerate consistent mowing at 3/4 inch.

Common perennial ryegrass is short-lived and has poor heat tolerance. Leaves are very fibrous so they tear rather than cut cleanly. Common perennial ryegrass grows rapidly and vigorously, making a usable lawn in as little as three weeks. "Improved" or "turf-type" perennial ryegrasses are equally rapid growers. In addition, they are more disease resistant, more heat and cold tolerant, have better color and texture and live longer. Improved ryegrasses also mow more cleanly and easily.

VARIETIES OF PERENNIAL RYEGRASS

'Birdie'—Medium green, dense, fine texture. Good heat tolerance. Resists brown patch, usually resistant to crown rust. Mows cleanly.
'Blazer'—Moderately dark green, dense, fine texture. Moderately good heat and cold tolerance. Resists leafspot and brown patch. Good mowing quality.

'Citation'—Dark green, dense, fine texture. Heat tolerant. Resists brown patch and usually red thread disease. Mows well.
'Delray'—Medium dark green, dense, fine texture. Moderately good heat, cold and brown patch resistance.
'Derby'—Medium dark green, good texture and density. Medium heat and cold tolerance. Mows well and resists brown patch disease.
'Diplomat'—Medium dark green, very dense with fine texture. Medium heat and cold tolerance. Mows well and resists brown patch.
'Fiesta'—Moderately dark green, dense, fine texture. Moderately good heat and cold tolerance. Resists brown patch.
'Omega'—Medium dark green, dense, fine texture. Medium heat and cold tolerance. Mows well. Resists brown blight and brown patch.
'Pennant'—Moderately dark green, fine texture. Good heat and drought tolerance. Good brown patch and sod webworm resistance.
'Pennfine'—Medium dark green, dense, fine texture. Resists brown patch. Good mowing quality.
'Regal'—Dark green, dense, fine texture. Medium heat tolerance. Mows well. Resists brown patch.
'Yorktown II'—Dark green, fine texture. Very dense. Medium-to-good heat and cold tolerance. Mows very well. Resists brown patch and crown rust.

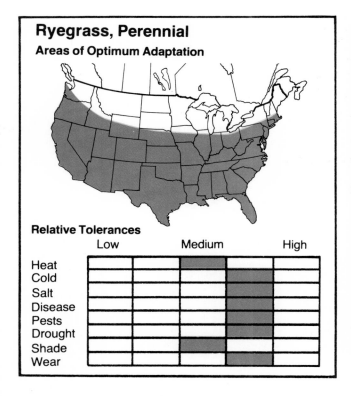

Ryegrass, Perennial
Areas of Optimum Adaptation

Relative Tolerances

	Low		Medium		High
Heat			■		
Cold				■	
Salt				■	
Disease				■	
Pests				■	
Drought				■	
Shade		■			
Wear				■	

'Derby' perennial ryegrass

'Bitter Blue' St. Augustinegrass

ST. AUGUSTINEGRASS
Stenotaphrum secundatum

To Plant: Frequently started with plugs planted on 12- to 18-inch centers. Widely available as sod.
Water: Large amount.
Fertilizer: Use 4 to 5 pounds actual nitrogen per 1,000 square feet per year. Use a complete fertilizer. May require minor elements if soil is depleted.
Mowing: Mow 1-1/2 to 2 inches high. Use a reel mower if possible. A rotary mower allows thatch to develop.

St. Augustine is an aggressive grass, crowding out most weeds. Particularly well adapted to soils of the Florida Everglades. Pests include brown patch, gray leafspot, chinch bugs and St. Augustine Decline (SAD) virus. The best defense against pests is to plant resistant varieties.

VARIETIES

'Bitter Blue'—Blue-green, medium density. Frost tolerant. Does not wear well.
Floratam'—Dark green, good density. Resists SAD virus and chinch bugs. Poor tolerance to cold.
'Floratine'—Dense, horizontal growth habit. Accepts low mowing—to 1/2 inch. Overall cold hardiness is fair. Low-temperature color retention is good.
'Seville'—Dark green, dense, more tolerant of shade and cold than other St. Augustines. Resists SAD virus and gray leafspot disease. Susceptible to chinch bugs.

St. Augustinegrass

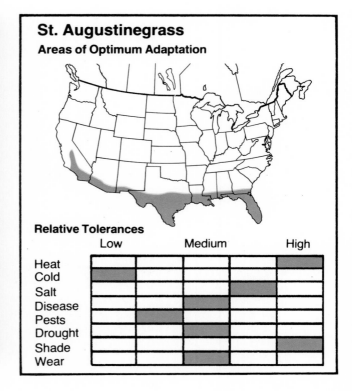

St. Augustinegrass
Areas of Optimum Adaptation

Relative Tolerances

	Low		Medium		High
Heat					■
Cold	■				
Salt				■	
Disease			■		
Pests		■			
Drought			■		
Shade					■
Wear			■		

242

ZOYSIAGRASS
Zoysia species

To Plant: Use sprigs, plugs or sod. Five cubic feet of sprigs will cover 1,000 square feet. Space 3-inch-diameter plugs on 12-inch centers.
Water: Little, once established.
Fertilizer: Apply 4 pounds actual nitrogen per 1,000 square feet per year.
Mowing: Mow 1-1/2 to 2 inches high with a reel or rotary mower.

Zoysiagrass is highly tolerant of drought and pests. Two disadvantages prevent it from being the most popular southern lawn grass: Winter dormant period is long and overseeding is difficult due to the turf density. Also, the rate of establishment is slow, sometimes requiring two full growing seasons.

VARIETIES

'Emerald'—Dark green, medium texture. Dense and slow growing. As attractive as hybrid Bermudagrass. Developed in Georgia and introduced in 1955.
'Jade'—Dark green, medium texture. Dense and slow growing. Developed in southern California and introduced in 1980. Establishes in one season from sprigs. Retains winter color in warmest areas of Southwest.
'Meyer' or *'Z-52'*—Dark green, relatively coarse texture. Poor winter color, but greater cold hardiness than 'Emerald' or 'Jade.' Introduced in 1951.

'Emerald' zoysiagrass

Zoysiagrass
Areas of Optimum Adaptation

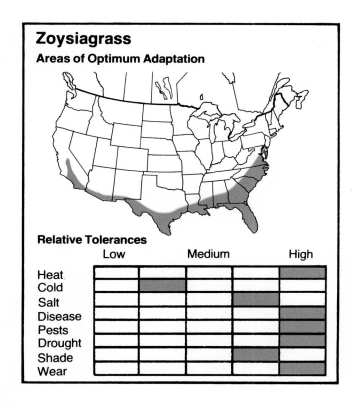

Relative Tolerances

	Low		Medium		High
Heat					▓
Cold		▓			
Salt				▓	
Disease					▓
Pests					▓
Drought					▓
Shade				▓	
Wear					▓

'Jade' zoysiagrass

Sowing Seed

1. Hand-held broadcast spreaders are inexpensive, lightweight and easy to use. They hold about 3 pounds of seed or fertilizers, and cover a 6- to 10-foot swath with each pass.

2. How vigorously you turn the crank of broadcast spreader determines distance seed is spread, but walking rows 4 feet apart is about right. Spread half the seed walking one direction and half walking the crisscross direction. Apply starter fertilizer and siduron pre-emergent weed control now if necessary.

3. Rent peat moss spreader, also called squirrel cage, from a nursery or rental agency. Some spilling is inevitable. Fill away from new lawn rather than directly over seeded area.

4. Apply mulch layer about 1/4 inch thick. Larger seeds, such as rye and fescue grasses, can be covered deeper. Cover small seeds—bermuda, bent and bluegrasses—slightly less deeply.

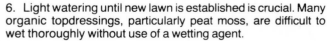

5. Firmly press seed into soil with final rolling. Rolling often makes the difference between good and poor seed germination. If more than half-filled with water, the roller's weight makes handling difficult and soil is needlessly compacted.

6. Light watering until new lawn is established is crucial. Many organic topdressings, particularly peat moss, are difficult to wet thoroughly without use of a wetting agent.

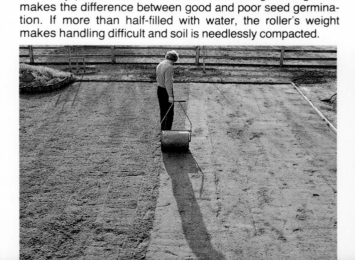

Installing Sod

1. Remove existing lawn with a *sod cutter,* available at rental agencies.

2. Level and firm soil with rake and roller half-filled with water. Finished grade should be 1/2 to 1 inch below walks, patios and driveway to accommodate sod thickness. Apply starter fertilizer now if necessary. Water thoroughly.

3. Start laying sod at longest straight boundary of area. If soil is soft or wet, work from a piece of plywood to distribute your weight. Tightly butt edges and ends together. Stagger strips as if laying a brick wall. Avoid overlapping edges.

4. Use a sharp knife to cut and fit sod around corners and irregular shapes. Work from bottom to top on steep slopes. Secure strips with wooden stakes if necessary.

5. If laying a large area, do not wait until installation is complete before watering. As soon as about 200 square feet are laid, sprinkle to prevent drying, especially during warm weather. Continue sprinkling until all sod is laid.

6. Roll with roller to ensure firm soil-to-root contact. Mound soil around exposed edges to prevent drying. Water until sod is spongy-wet to foot pressure. Soil should be moist to about 6 to 8 inches. Water frequently and heavily for 2 to 3 weeks until sod is firmly rooted.

Lawn Care Schedule
Warm-Season Grasses

Warm-season grasses dominate in southern regions and summer rainfall areas of the high plains. They grow vigorously in midsummer with temperatures between 80F and 95F (27C and 35C). Compared to cool-season grasses, they are more drought, heat and wear tolerant. Many have a low, creeping growth habit, usually with above-ground runners. Most tolerate low mowing and brown during winter dormancy.

Illustrations below show basic timing of most important lawn chores utilizing simple hand tools.

Spring

PLANTING—Sow seed of bermudagrass, bahiagrass or centipedegrass after soil has warmed thoroughly in spring. Late spring is also best time to plant sprigs or stolons of improved bermudagrass and St. Augustinegrass. Lay sod of warm-season grasses in late spring through summer.

Seed

Sod

WATERING—The rule of 1 inch of water per week holds true for warm-season grasses. Growing season and distribution of rainfall are important variables. Best time to water is just before dawn. Check to be sure water soaks into soil.

MOWING—Mow frequently to maintain proper height. Try to reduce grass height by one-third or less with each mowing. Mowing frequency is determined by growth rate. Increase mowing frequency during late spring and summer—periods when the lawn grows fast.

FERTILIZING—Bahiagrass and centipedegrass can be fed with one spring and one fall application. Heavy feeders such as bermudagrass and St. Augustinegrass need regular applications every 30 to 60 days. Make last fall application 1 month before lawn goes dormant.

DETHATCHING—Best time to dethatch warm-season grasses is 2 to 3 weeks after spring green-up. This timing favors fast recovery of lawn. Bermudagrass and zoysiagrass accept heavy dethatching. Dethatch centipedegrass, bahiagrass and St. Augustinegrass lightly.

AERATING—Aerate any time to reduce soil compaction and improve penetration of air, water, fertilizer and insecticide. Aerate prior to overseeding to improve germination of winter lawn. Aeration will also reduce water runoff and increase water penetration.

WEEDS—Control summer annual weeds with early spring pre-emergent herbicide. Control winter annual weeds with fall application of a similar product. Spray winter weeds in dormant lawns with post-emergent herbicide.

Crabgrass

Annual bluegrass

Clover

INSECTS—Chinch bugs favor St. Augustinegrass. Spray early summer and again 2 to 3 weeks later to limit damage. Check for grubs spring and summer. Combat with insecticides midsummer and fall.

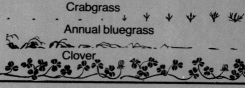

Sod webworm larva and adult

Grubs

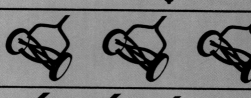

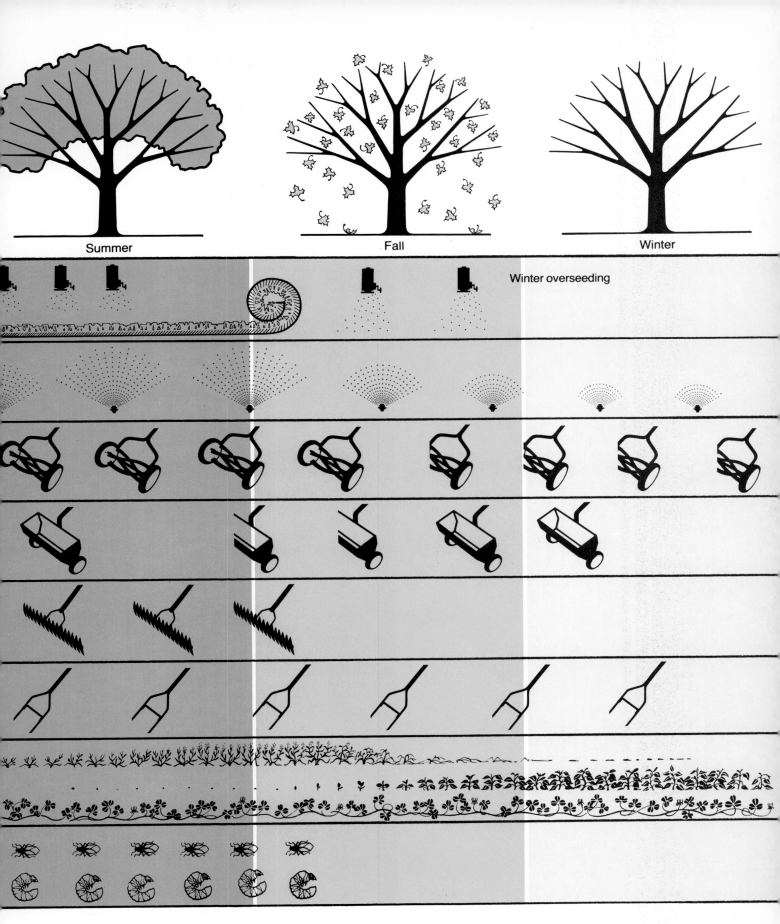

Summer   Fall   Winter

Winter overseeding

Lawn Care Schedule
Cool-Season Grasses

Cool-season grasses are the most important lawn grasses. They thrive throughout northern regions. They prefer brisk spring and fall temperatures between 60F and 75F (16C and 24C). Their growth habit is more upright, so they are cut higher than warm-season grasses. Essentially dormant through midsummer, they remain green if irrigated.

Illustrations below show basic timing of most important lawn chores utilizing simple hand tools.

Spring

PLANTING—Sow seed of Kentucky bluegrass, fescue and ryegrass in fall, while soil is still warm from summer but air is cool. Early spring is second-best planting time. Lay sod anytime or when available. Plant bentgrass sprigs in fall.

Seed

Sod

WATERING—Lawns need approximately 1 inch of water per week. In a few locations, annual rainfall is adequate, but most lawns need additional water from sprinklers. Water during early morning, before dawn if possible. Always water thoroughly.

MOWING—Healthy and vigorous lawns need frequent mowings spring and fall. Reduce height of tall lawn gradually. Never cut more than one-third at once unless renovating. Raise cutting height and reduce frequency during summer to improve heat and drought tolerance.

FERTILIZING—Apply 75 percent of the lawn's yearly allotment of fertilizer in fall months, the remainder in spring. Limit single applications of fast-release fertilizers to 1 pound and slow-release fertilizers to 2 pounds actual nitrogen per 1,000 square feet.

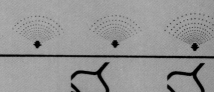

DETHATCHING—Dethatch in early spring or early fall, just before peak growth periods. Kentucky bluegrass requires regular thatch removal. Of the cool-season grasses, turf-type ryegrasses and tall frescues are least prone to development of thatch.

AERATING—Aerate to reduce soil compaction and improve penetration of air, water, fertilizer and insecticide. Aerate sloping lawn to reduce water runoff and increase water penetration rate.

WEEDS—Use a pre-emergent herbicide in spring for crabgrass and similar summer annual weeds. Use pre-emergent herbicide in fall for annual bluegrass and similar winter annual weeds. Combine pre-emergent and post-emergent herbicides to eliminate perennial weeds such as oxalis.

Crabgrass

Annual bluegrass

Clover

INSECTS—Sod webworm infests just about every type of lawn. Check for these night feeders with pyrethrum test. Manage Japanese beetle grubs with milky spore disease. Midsummer and fall insecticide treatments are necessary to control all other kinds of grubs.

Chinch bugs

Grubs

248

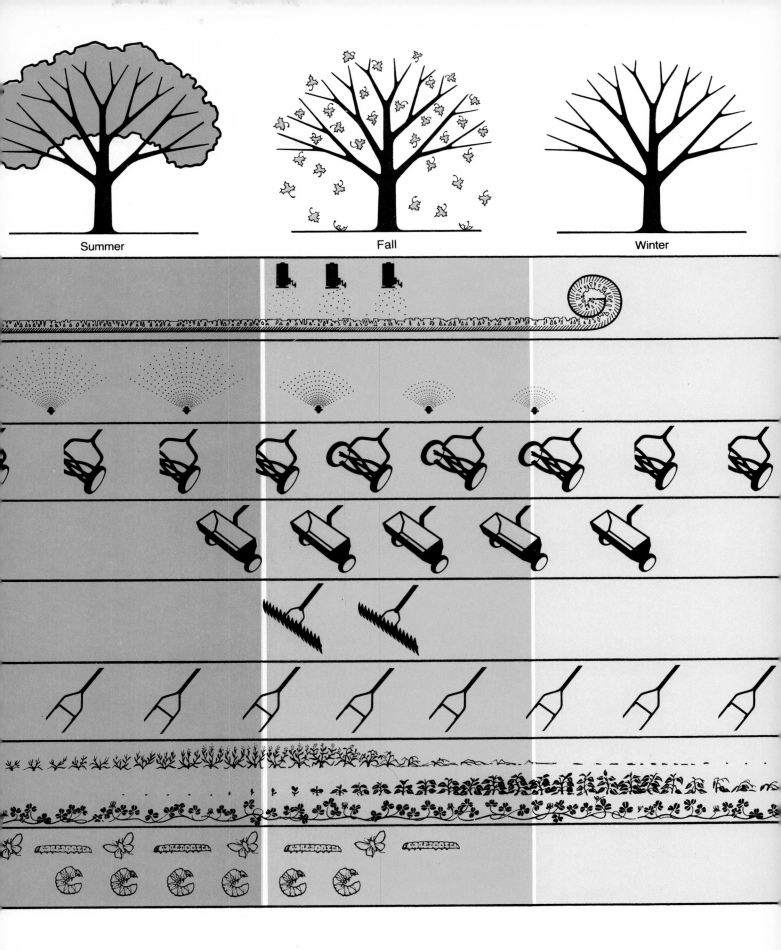

Summer   Fall   Winter

249

TREES AND SHRUBS

Although trees and shrubs perform different functions in the landscape, their planting and care have much in common, so there is good reason to combine them into a single book. Both belong to a distinct group within the plant kingdom, known collectively as *woody plants,* because they have the ability to form a tough, durable cell structure called *wood.* Wood forms the sturdy framework that permits trees and shrubs to grow larger and live longer than other plants. In fact, there is no botanical difference between a tree and a shrub. These are simply common terms that make a distinction on the basis of appearance, or *growth habit.*

The accepted definition of a *tree* is a woody plant that tends to form a single main trunk and is capable of growing 15 feet or higher. *Shrubs* are generally defined as woody plants under 15 feet high that form multiple stems and a thicket of twiggy branches.

However, these definitions have no scientific recognition because there are too many anomalies to make any hard and fast rules. For example, in its juvenile stage, *Euonymus alatus*—known as burning bush for its red fall coloring—grows shrubby with a cluster of main stems and a thicket of branchlets. But with the passing of time, it produces a thick main trunk and spreading canopy to become a handsome 15- to 20-foot tree.

Conversely, many trees can be kept shrublike by pruning to control size and encourage multiple stems. There are also dwarf forms of many standard-size tree species.

From a design standpoint, trees and shrubs perform different functions. Shrubs are usually used as low, decorative highlights. They are often used as *understory* plants to landscape areas beneath tall trees in woodland and garden settings. Trees, on the other hand, tend to be planted for skyline effects, tall windbreaks, making wooded lots and creating shade. They are the most dominant plants in the landscape. Trees and shrubs become perfect companions when the trees provide a backdrop and the shrubs are used at eye level in the foreground for ornamental accents. H. Thomas Hallowell Jr., the owner of the large estate garden of Deerfield, near Philadelphia, typified the attitude of most home gardeners when he said of his garden, "For me, trees and shrubs exist for one purpose—to make a pretty picture."

For the most part, shrubs are expected to be more ornamental and functional than trees. Their ornamental impact comes mostly from flowers, fruits and leaves—the more colorful their appearance, the more highly rated they tend to be among home gardeners. At the other extreme, when shrubs are needed for practical reasons, such as for hedges and screens, we want them to be as unobtrusive as possible so that other plantings and design elements can be accentuated. An example is a tall hedge of yew or privet that provides a solid green backdrop for a colorful flower bed.

Shrubs are not expected to be as long-lived as trees, so the loss of a shrub is little cause for tears because they are usually replaced easily at modest cost. Trees, however, are valued more for their stature, shape and form. If a tree provides good color, we tend to look on it as a bonus. Furthermore, the loss of a large, mature tree can be distressing, for it can take many years to replace.

Without question, some of the world's most impressive tree plantings have been established by the British. At Chatsworth, a large estate garden in England, the value of old trees was so acutely appreciated that wide avenues were planted to look their best 300 years into the future!

Trees and shrubs represent a vast group of plants from many climates. It is impossible to cover every aspect of their uses and needs in a single book. Some tree books are *nature* books, primarily intended for identification of individual wayside or forest trees. This is a *garden* book, and its intent is to satisfy three essential gardening needs:

● *Ideas*—suggestions for using various kinds of trees and shrubs in the landscape.

● *Planting and care*—practical information on how to grow and care for trees and shrubs.

● *Recommendations*—an encyclopedic listing of garden-worthy trees and shrubs, giving specific descriptions and growing information.

Left: Suburban backyard garden owes its spectacular beauty to a profusion of flowering trees and shrubs underplanted with perennials and woodland wildflowers. Dogwoods and azaleas are the dominant woody plants. Use of evergreen conifers is limited to mature Canadian hemlock and juniper at upper left.

TREES AND SHRUBS FOR DIFFERENT USES

AUTUMN COLOR

Following are some of the best trees and shrubs for autumn color.

Asterisk (*) denotes shrubs.

Botanical Name	Common Name
Acer species	Maples
Amelanchier arborea	Sarvistree
Betula species	Birches
Carya species	Hickories
Cercidiphyllum japonicum	Katsura
Cornus florida	Common Dogwood
Cotinus coggygria	Smoke Tree
*Euonymus alatus	Burning Bush
Franklinia alatamaha	Franklinia
Fraxinus species	Ashes
Ginkgo biloba	Ginkgo
Lagerstroemia indica	Crape Myrtle
Larix species	Larches
Liquidambar styraciflua	Sweetgum
Liriodendron tulipifera	Tulip Tree
Nyssa sylvatica	Tupelo
Oxydendrum arboreum	Sourwood
Pistacia chinensis	Chinese Pistacio
Populus species	Poplars
Pyrus calleryana	Callery Pear
Quercus coccinia	Scarlet Oak
Rhus typhina	Staghorn Sumac
Sassafras albidum	Sassafras
*Viburnum species	Viburnum
Zelkova serrata	Japanese Zelkova

DECORATIVE BERRIES OR FRUIT

Asterisk (*) denotes shrubs.

Botanical Name	Common Name
Aralia spinosa	Devil's Walking Stick
Arbutus unedo	Strawberry Tree
*Berberis thunbergii	Japanese Barberry
*Callicarpa japonica	Beautyberry
*Carissa grandiflora	Natal Plum
Castanea mollissima	Chinese Chestnut
*Chaenomeles speciosa	Flowering Quince
Citrus species	Ornamental Citrus
Cornus kousa	Korean Dogwood
*Cotoneaster horizontalis	Rockspray Cotoneaster
Crataegus species	Hawthorns
Diospyros kaki	Japanese Persimmon
*Ilex species	Hollies
Koelreuteria paniculata	Golden Rain Tree
*Mahonia bealei	Leatherleaf Mahonia
Malus species	Crabapples
*Nandina domestica	Heavenly Bamboo
*Poncirus trifoliata	Hardy Orange
Prunus species	Cherries, Peaches, Plums
*Pyracantha coccinea	Firethorn
*Rosa rugosa	Rugosa Rose
*Skimmia japonica	Japanese Skimmia
Sorbus aucuparia	Mountain Ash
*Viburnum species	Viburnums

DECORATIVE BARK

Asterisk (*) denotes shrubs.

Botanical Name	Common Name
Acer griseum	Paperbark Maple
*Acer palmatum 'Senkaki'	Red-twig Maple
Alsophila cooperi	Australian Tree Fern
Betula papyrifera	White Birch
*Cornus sanguinea	Red-twig Dogwood
*Cornus sericea 'Flaviramea'	Yellow-twig Dogwood
Cryptomeria japonica	Japanese Cedar
Eucalyptus species	Eucalyptus
Lagerstroemia indica	Crepe Myrtle
Pinus nigra	Austrian Pine
Platanus occidentalis	Buttonwood
Prunus serrula	Shiny Bark Cherry
Salix × chrysocoma 'Niobe'	Golden Weeping Willow
Stewartia sinensis	Chinese Stewartia

SKYLINE TREES

Asterisk (*) denotes evergreens.

Botanical Name	Common Name
*Abies species	Firs
Acer saccharum	Sugar Maple
Aesculus hippocastanum	Horse Chestnut
*Araucaria araucana	Monkey Puzzle Tree
*Araucaria heterophylla	Norfolk Island Pine
Carya species	Hickories
*Casuarina cunninghamiana	Australian Pine
Catalpa species	Catalpas
*Cedrus species	Cedars
Cercidiphyllum japonicum	Katsura Tree
*Chamaecyparis species	False Cypresses
Chorisa speciosa	Floss Silk Tree
*Cupressus species	Cypresses
*Eucalyptus species	Eucalyptus
Fagus species	Beech
Fraxinus species	Ashes
Ginkgo biloba	Maidenhair Tree
Gleditsia triacanthos inermis	Honeylocust
Jacaranda acutifolia	Jacaranda
Juglans nigra	Black Walnut
*Juniperus virginiana	Red Cedar
Larix	Larches
*Liriodendron tulipifera	Tulip Tree
*Metasequoia glyptostroboides	Dawn Redwood
Nyssa sylvatica	Black Tupelo
*Palmae	Palms
Paulownia tomentosa	Empress Tree
*Picea species	Spruces
*Pinus species	Pines
Platanus occidentalis	Buttonwood
Populus species	Poplars
Pseudolarix kaempferi	Golden Larch
Quercus species	Oaks
Robinia pseudoacacia	Black Locust
Salix babylonica	Weeping Willow
*Sciadopitys verticillata	Japanese Umbrella Pine
Taxodium distichum	Bald Cypress
Tilia species	Lindens
*Tsuga species	Hemlocks
Ulmus species	Elms
Zelkova serrata	Zelkova

WINDBREAK TREES AND SHRUBS

Asterisk (*) denotes shrubs.

EVERGREEN

Abies species	Firs
Casuarina cunninghamiana	Australian Pine
Chamaecyparis lawsoniana	Lawson False Cypress
Cupressocyparis leylandi	Leyland Cypress
Cupressus macrocarpa	Monterey Cypress
*Escallonia rubra	Escallonia
Eucalyptus species	Eucalyptus
*Ilex species	Hollies
Juniperus virginiana	Eastern Red Cedar
*Ligustrum species	Privets
*Nerium oleander	Oleander
Olea europa	European Olive
Picea abies	Norway Spruce
Pinus strobus	White Pine
Pinus sylvestris	Scotch Pine
Podocarpus macrophyllus	Yew Podocarpus
Taxus species	Yews
Thuja occidentalis	American Arbor-vitae
Tsuga canadensis	Canadian Hemlock

DECIDUOUS

Acer platanoides	Norway Maple
Carpinus species	Hornbeams
Crataegus species	Hawthorns
Nyssa sylvatica	Black Tupelo
Platanus acerifolia	London Plane Tree
Populus hybrids	Hybrid Poplars
Ulmus parvifolia	Chinese Elm

STREET AND CITY TREES

Asterisk (*) identifies plants noted for spectacular flowering displays.

Botanical Name	Common Name
*Acacia longifolia	Acacia
Acer species	Maples
*Aesculus species	Horsechestnuts
Ailanthus altissima	Tree of Heaven
Carpinus betula	European Hornbeam
Casuarina cunninghamiana	Australian Pine
*Chorisa speciosa	Floss Silk Tree
*Crataegus species	Hawthorns
*Elaeagnus angustifolia	Russian Olive
Eucalyptus ficifolia	Scarlet Gum
Fraxinus species	Ashes
Ginkgo biloba	Maidenhair Tree
Gleditsia triacanthos inermis	Honeylocust
*Koelreuteria paniculata	Golden Rain Tree
Liquidambar styraciflua	Sweetgum
Pinus sylvestris	Scotch Pine
Pinus thunbergiana	Japanese Black Pine
Pistacia chinensis	Chinese Pistacio
Platanus acerifolia	London Plane Tree
*Pyrus calleryana 'Bradford'	Bradford Pear
Quercus species	Oaks
*Sophora japonica	Japanese Pagoda Tree
Tilia cordata	Littleleaf Linden
Ulmus parvifolia	Chinese Elm
Zelkova serrata	Japanese Zelkova

SHADE-TOLERANT TREES AND SHRUBS
Asterisk (*) denotes shrubs.

Acer palmatum	Cutleaf Maple
*Aesculus parvifolia	Bottlebrush Buckeye
Alsophila cooperi	Australian Tree Fern
*Aucuba japonica	Gold Dust Plant
*Buxus species	Boxwood
*Camellia japonica	Camellia
Cercis canadensis	Eastern Redbud
Cornus florida	Flowering Dogwood
Cryptomeria japonica	Japanese Cedar
Enkianthus campanulatus	Red-Vein Enkianthus
*Euonymus alatus	Burning Bush
*Euonymus fortunei	Wintercreeper
Halesia carolina	Silverbell
*Hamamelis species	Witchhazels
*Hedera helix	English Ivy
*Hydrangea macrophylla	Hydrangea
*Ilex species	Hollies
*Kalmia latifolia	Mountain Laurel
*Kerria japonica	Japanese Kerria
*Leucothoe fontanesia	Drooping Leucothoe
*Mahonia species	Mahonias
*Nandina domestica	Heavenly Bamboo
*Pachysandra terminalis	Japanese Spurge
*Parthenocissus quinquefolia	Virginia Creeper
*Pieris japonica	Andromeda
*Pittosporum tobira	Fragrant Pittosporum
*Prunus laurocerasus	Cherry Laurel
*Rhododendron species	Azaleas, Rhododendrons
*Skimmia japonica	Japanese Skimmia
*Taxus species	Yews
Tsuga canadensis	Canadian Hemlock

TREES FOR WOODLAND & GROVES
Asterisk (*) denotes evergreens.

*Abies concolor	White Fir
Acer rubrum	Red Maple
Acer saccharum	Sugar Maple
Amelanchier arborea	Sarvistree
Betula papyrifera	White Birch
Carya species	Hickories
Cercis canadensis	Eastern Redbud
Cornus florida	Flowering Dogwood
Crataegus species	Hawthorns
*Cryptomeria japonica	Japanese Cedar
*Eucalyptus species	Eucalyptus
Fagus species	Beeches
Fraxinus species	Ashes
Gleditsia triacanthus inermis	Honeylocust
Halesia carolina	Silverbell
Juglans nigra	Black Walnut
*Juniperus virginiana	Eastern Red Cedar
Liquidambar styraciflua	Sweetgum
Liriodendron tulipifera	Tulip Tree
*Magnolia grandiflora	Southern Magnolia
*Metasequoia glyptostroboides	Dawn Redwood
Nyssa sylvatica	Black Tupelo
Oxydendrum arboreum	Sourwood
*Picea species	Spruces
*Pinus species	Pines
Platanus occidentalis	Buttonwood
Populus tremuloides	Quaking Aspen

*Pseudotsuga menziesii	Douglas Fir
Quercus species	Oaks
Robinia pseudoacacia	Black Locust
*Sequoia sempervirens	Coast Redwood
*Taxodium distichum	Bald Cypress
*Tsuga canadensis	Canadian Hemlock
Ulmus species	Elms
Zelkova serrata	Japanese Zelkova

HEDGES
Asterisk denotes evergreens.

Abelia × grandiflora	Glossy Abelia
Arundinaria species	Bamboo
Berberis thunbergii	Japanese Barberry
*Buxus sempervirens	English Boxwood
*Buxus microphylla	Japanese Boxwood
*Carissa grandiflora	Natal Plum
Chaenomeles speciosa	Flowering Quince
*Chamaecyparis lawsoniana	Lawson False Cypresses
Crataegus phaenopyrum	Washington Hawthorn
*Cupressus species	Cypress
Elaeagnus angustifolia	Russian Olive
*Escallonia rubra	Escallonia
Euonymus alatus	Burning Bush
Fagus sylvatica	European Beech
Forsythia × intermedia	Forsythia
Gardenia jasminoides	Gardenia
*Hibiscus rosa-sinensis	Chinese Hibiscus
Hibiscus syriacus	Rose of Sharon
*Ilex species	Hollies
*Juniperus species	Junipers
Ligustrum species	Privet
Lonicera species	Honeysuckles
*Myrica species	Wax Myrtles
*Nerium oleander	Oleander
*Osmanthus species	False Hollies
*Photinia × fraseri	Red Tip Photinia

Azalea 'Coral Bells' drapes its flowering branches over stone wall. Partial concealment of architectural structures is one of principal uses for flowering shrubs.

*Pinus mugo mugo	Mugo Pine
*Pinus strobus	White Pine
*Pittosporum species	Pittosporum
*Podocarpus macrophylla	Fern Pine
*Prunus laurocerasus	Cherry Laurel
Pyracantha species	Firethorn
*Raphiolepsis indica	Indian Hawthorn
*Rhododendron species and hybrids	Azaleas, Rhododendrons
Rosa species	Roses
Spiraea species	Spireas
Syringa vulgaris	Lilac
*Taxus species	Yews
*Thuja species	Arborvitaes
*Tsuga species	Hemlocks
Viburnum species	Viburnums
Weigela florida	Weigela

VINES AND CREEPERS

Bougainvillea spectabilis	Bougainvillea
Campsis radicans	Trumpet Creeper
Celastris scandens	Bittersweet
Euonymus fortunei	Wintercreeper
Ficus pumila	Creeping Fig
Hedera helix	English Ivy
Hydrangea anomala	Climbing Hydrangea
Jasminum nudiflorum	Yellow Jasmine
Lonicera hallii	Hall's Honeysuckle
Parthenocissus quinquefolia	Virginia Creeper
Polygonum aubertii	Silver Lace Vine
Rosa banksiae	Lady Banks Rose
Rosa laevigata	Cherokee Rose
Trachelospermum jasminoides	Confederate Jasmine
Wisteria floribunda	Wisteria

PLANTING

A moderate amount of care taken in planting is well worth the small amount of time and expense involved. This includes conditioning the soil, if needed, *before* you set the tree or shrub in the hole. The old maxim, "Dig a ten-dollar hole for a five-dollar tree," says it succinctly.

The actual method of planting depends on whether the plants are *bare-root, balled-and-burlapped* or *containerized.* General planting procedures common to all three types are covered here.

WHEN TO PLANT

Containerized and balled-and-burlapped plants can be planted virtually any time the soil can be worked and watered. For bare-root deciduous trees, the best planting times are early spring or late fall when the plants are dormant. Bare-root needleleaf evergreens in exposed situations are best planted in spring because of their high moisture needs and susceptibility to dehydration from winter conditions.

Though most home gardeners think in terms of spring planting, fall is actually a good planting season for many trees and shrubs. In the South, where winters are mild, fall planting makes especially good sense because it avoids the heat and drought stress of hot summers, and gives newly planted stock an extended cool, moist period in which to become well established.

Though deciduous trees enter a dormant period in winter when the top growth loses its leaves, the roots remain active until the ground actually freezes. Winter dormancy is also induced by day length, so that trees in frost-free sections of the country may lose their leaves and go dormant, even though temperatures are favorable for normal growth. Generally speaking, it is safe to plant hardy trees and shrubs up to 6 weeks before the ground freezes. This is not only true of broadleaf deciduous trees and shrubs, but also of certain deciduous needleleaf conifers, such as larches, dawn redwood and bald cypress. Only during the depths of winter will the roots stop growing, and they will revive at the return of a warm spell long before the top breaks dormancy and leafs out.

The success rate of evergreens can be improved by planting in spring in Northern states. Because they continue to transpire large amounts of moisture dur-

Balled-and-burlapped trees are waiting to be shipped to retail garden centers. Balled-and-burlapped is the safest way to buy trees and shrubs.

ing winter, they are more susceptible to dehydration during dry, windy or severely cold winters. However, if supplemental watering can be provided, and if the site is not too exposed, evergreens can safely be planted in fall.

A gardener once planted three new evergreen azaleas in spring on an exposed stream bank and lost them all from summer drought. A gardener planted three more on the same site in fall, and though some leaves were browned by a sudden early freeze, they all revived spectacularly in spring and he didn't lose one.

Also, he's had similar success with containerized and balled-and-burlapped needleleaf evergreens, especially live Christmas trees. Every year prior to the ground freezing, he digs a hole where he wants the tree to grow after it does its duty as a Christmas tree. He saves the soil in a wheelbarrow, keeping it in a garage area to prevent it from freezing. While the tree is in the house decorated with lights, the root ball remains in its burlap or container, but is placed in a plastic trash bag so it can be watered whenever the soil feels dry, without puddling onto the living room rug.

Three weeks after Christmas, he moves the tree from the living room to the garage for 2 weeks to acclimatize it, then moves it outdoors into the hole. It is

watered with at least 2 gallons of water whenever a week goes by without natural rainfall. He has never lost a tree yet. There was one year when a Douglas fir started to show severe browning on one side, but he doused it with a hose almost daily and sprayed its needles weekly with a liquid fertilizer and it greened up beautifully.

DIGGING THE HOLE

In the case of bare-root stock, you need to dig a hole 6 inches deeper than the roots extend. As you dig, separate the good soil (topsoil) from inferior soil (subsoil). After the hole is dug, break up the bottom with a spade, fork or crowbar. Then put about 6 inches of topsoil into the bottom so the new roots will have fertile soil in which to grow. Mixing an amendment such as peat moss or compost with the planting soil at the rate of 1 part amendment to 3 parts soil will improve soil structure, particularly if the soil is clay or sand.

In the case of stock that is balled-and-burlapped or containerized, the planting procedure is a little different. If the soil is good and well-suited to the particular plant—for example, planting azaleas or rhododendrons in a woodsy or high-humus soil—dig your hole the same size as the root ball and lower the root ball into the hole.

PLANTING A TREE

1. Dig hole twice the width of the root ball. To keep tree from settling in hole, do not dig hole deeper than height of root ball.

2. Add thin layer of good topsoil or compost to bottom of hole. Sprinkle fertilizer into bottom of hole and stir into soil.

3. Gently lower balled-and-burlapped tree into hole. Use a plank to slide heavy root ball to avoid straining yourself by lifting it.

4. Untie string from around trunk and loosen burlap flaps. Remove any nails.

5. Fill around sides of root ball with topsoil or compost. Pack soil to settle it.

6. Untie strings from around branches. Prune away any of the branches that are broken or appear dead.

7. Apply mulch of wood chips or similar organic material to deter weeds and conserve moisture.

8. Apply at least 5 gallons of water to roots. Water same amount weekly in the absence of rainfall.

9. Wrap trunk with tree wrap to avoid sun scorch and to deter pests such as rodents and deer.

BARE-ROOT PLANTING

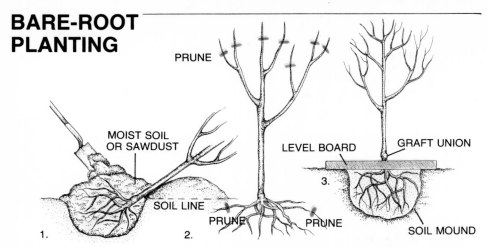

1. If you can't plant bare-root stock immediately, dig a shallow hole in a protected location and cover roots with sawdust or topsoil and keep moist. This is called *heeling-in*. 2. If top seems too large in relationship to roots, prune back excessive topgrowth. Also prune off any damaged roots or ones too long to fit into planting hole. 3. Use level board to position tree at correct level. With grafted trees, graft union should be above soil line. Spread out roots over soil mound in planting hole, then backfill hole.

If, however, the site has poor soil, it's better to improve soil over the whole site or at least dig a bigger-than-normal planting hole. For example, when planting azaleas and rhododendrons in a heavy clay or stony soil, it might be advisable to haul in leaf mold to thoroughly amend the soil structure before digging planting holes. Or, with larger shrubs and trees, dig a generous hole and backfill with leaf mold before planting. Determine whether or not your soil needs amending before planting. A light application of a general-purpose fertilizer may also be beneficial right after planting.

As the planting hole is filled, create a *catchment* or *catch basin* around the tree or shrub to hold water, by mounding soil to form a rim. Make the catch basin so the perimeter is positioned around the root mass. After 6 to 8 weeks, extend the perimeter directly below the plant's *drip line*, or outer edge of the leaf canopy.

Fill the basin with water and allow the soil to settle. If the plant settles too much, gently raise it back to the original planting depth, adding more soil, if necessary. Never plant more deeply than the level at which the plant grew originally. Next, cover the soil with an organic mulch to retain moisture and deter weeds. Wood chips or shredded leaves are ideal.

BARE-ROOT PLANTS

All bare-root trees and shrubs need to be planted as soon as possible after you receive them—preferably the same day. Bare-root evergreens have green leaves year-round and it's easy to determine the health of plants on arrival. Bare-root stock of deciduous trees is generally sold in *dormant* condition with no leaves showing, for spring or fall planting. As the plants enter their winter dormant period in autumn—and before they break dormancy in spring—many kinds can be efficiently shipped and planted. To prolong the dormant state in spring and extend the selling season for bare-root stock, some mail-order nurseries will hold deciduous trees in cold storage.

The roots of bare-root stock are generally wrapped in moist sphagnum moss or damp newspaper to prevent their drying out during transit. Before planting, remove this packing material carefully and immerse the roots in a bucket of water for 2 to 3 hours.

There are five *Don'ts* when planting bare-root stock:

1. *Don't* let plants dry out. Keep the roots moist.

2. *Don't* let the roots freeze. Store plants in a frost-free area.

3. *Don't* let plants mold in storage. If planting is delayed beyond 10 days, spray with Captan or Benlate to discourage mold.

4. *Don't* handle plants roughly. Roots and branches are usually brittle and will break easily.

5. *Don't* store plants too long. It is better to risk planting too early than storing too long.

Do not delay planting a day longer than absolutely necessary. If you cannot plant the same day bare-root stock is received, lay the plants down in a cool basement or other cool, sheltered, shaded place. Cover the roots with damp newspaper or a damp cloth to prevent drying out.

Pruning is sometimes desirable even before you plant. For example, with bare-root stock, if any roots are broken, the damaged portions should be pruned away. Similarly, if the leader or any side branches are broken, the damaged portions should be pruned clean.

Do not plant a bare-root tree on which the top growth is disproportionate to the bottom. If the tree is *top-heavy*, with more branches than the root system appears it can support, prune back the branch ends and allow the root system to produce new growth according to its own ability. As mentioned earlier, if bare-root plants have already started to leaf out, prune the top growth back by one third to avoid stressing the tree.

BALLED-AND-BURLAPPED PLANTS

These are generally field-grown in well-spaced planting rows. A machine is used to dig up the plant with a rounded or cone-shaped root ball. The root ball is wrapped in burlap to keep it from falling apart, and bound secure with string. This is a popular way for many nurseries, tree farms and garden centers to sell trees and shrubs, though it is the most expensive because considerable labor is needed to dig the trees, wrap and transport them. The ball should be intact and solid when purchased and should not show signs of breakage, which could damage the fine roots.

Balled-and-burlapped trees are often planted as is, with no attempt to remove the string or the burlap, because the theory is that these materials will quickly decompose once the root ball is covered with soil. However, some root balls are bound with plastic string which does *not* decompose, and may strangle the tree as the girth of the trunk expands. Even if the root ball is bound with natural fibers, it is best to cut or loosen the string from around the trunk.

There is wide disagreement over whether the burlap itself should be removed. The best policy is to simply loosen the top, but not until you have lowered the root ball into its hole. If you try to remove the burlap completely, the root ball will generally fall apart, breaking delicate root ends in the process, which destroys the advantage of paying a premium price for a balled tree. However, when you backfill the hole, make sure the edges of the burlap are well covered with soil. Any exposed burlap will act like a wick, drawing moisture away from the root ball.

CONTAINERIZED PLANTS

These are generally grown in metal or plastic containers, peach baskets or peat pots, usually varying in size from 1-gallon to 15-gallon capacity. This is a popular way for nurseries and garden centers to sell trees and shrubs. They are generally more expensive than bare-root stock, but less expensive than balled-and-burlapped plants. With peat containers and peach baskets, it is generally sufficient to cut away the bottom of the container and plant the whole package. The peat decomposes quickly once covered with soil, and the thin wood of the peach basket soon rots away to release the side roots.

With both metal and plastic containers that don't decompose, use a sharp knife or sheet-metal shears to cut away the sides and release the root ball. Alternatively, you can cut out the bottom and push the root ball up out of the container. In some cases, the container can be tipped upside-down and the plant will slip out easily. The whole idea is to keep as much soil as possible around the roots.

If the plastic container is large and heavy, cut out the bottom and slide the tree into its planting hole. Then, when the root ball is well seated in the hole, remove the sides of the container with a hatchet, heavy duty can opener or sheet-metal shears. In most cases, a tree or shrub in a 1- to 5-gallon plastic or corrugated-metal container will easily slip out, if you tap the container several times and upend it. Large plants are best handled by two people. In all cases, be careful not to shatter the root ball.

Sometimes, if the tree or shrub has been in the container too long, it will be *rootbound*, that is, the roots have become crowded and taken on the shape of the container. After the root ball is in the planting hole, loosen or cut any matted or encircling roots so they can spread out into the surrounding soil. Otherwise, severe problems with girdling roots may develop in future years.

AFTERCARE

The basics of tree and shrub care are

CONTAINER PLANTING

1. With metal and plastic containers, trim away any roots protruding through drainage holes to facilitate removal of container. 2. Tilt plastic container on its side and gently slide it off root ball, tapping container lightly to loosen, if necessary. 3. Cut metal container on opposite sides with shears and spread container apart. 4. Pull loose any encircling or matted roots and prune off broken or damaged ones. Plants in peach baskets (5.) and peat pots (6.) can be planted as-is. Peat pots and flimsy wood sides of peach basket quickly decompose in moist soil.

watering, mulching, fertilizing, pruning, protection from pests and diseases, and protection from weather extremes. Newly planted trees and shrubs are much more vulnerable than established ones, so some of these chores will have to be done on a more frequent basis until the plant is better able to fend for itself.

Most shrubs and bare-root trees are small and do not need staking. But large balled-and-burlapped and container-grown trees will require staking if they cannot stand on their own or will be exposed to high winds. This is especially true of trees that have grown tall and spindly because they have been crowded in the nursery row.

During the summer months, newly planted trees and shrubs generally require more frequent watering than established ones—at least weekly for most kinds. Young trees and shrubs are also susceptible to weather extremes, especially sunscald during summer and freezing during winter.

STAKING

Some trees need support to help get them established. This is particularly true of open-branched evergreens such as Atlas Cedars and any deciduous trees

with long, straight trunks. *Bare-root* stock is generally too small to stake, but trees that are *balled-and-burlapped* or *containerized* often require staking.

Even in sheltered locations where wind is unlikely to snap the trunk or blow a newly planted tree over, even slight winds can rock a newly planted root ball and either break feeder roots or tilt the tree out of alignment.

The best way to stake a tree to anchor the roots is with three sets of guy wires. Loop one end around a main branch where it meets the trunk, about two-thirds up the tree, cushioning the area of contact with strips of cloth or rubber hose. Extend the other wires out on opposite sides of the tree and secure to stakes driven into the ground, like tent pegs.

To stake a tall, spindly tree, use two tall stakes, positioned on opposite sides of the trunk, as shown in the drawing above. The trunk should be tied to the stakes with a non-abrasive material such as cloth or rubber strips. Tie strips loosely enough to allow some trunk movement in the wind, but not so loose that the trunk will be abraded by contact with the stakes. If the tree is staked too rigidly, it will develop a weak, thin trunk.

HOW TO STAKE A TREE

1.

2.

3.

4.

1. One-stake method for support of bare-root trees. Drive stake before planting tree to avoid damaging roots. 2. Two-stake method for support of tall, spindly balled-and-burlapped or container trees. Tie tree loosely to stake to allow some trunk movement. Use cloth strips or padding where ties contact trunk. 3. Guy wires are used to support larger trees and prevent movement of root ball. Use sections of flexible rubber hose or other padding to protect branches where wires contact them. 4. Wires woven through bent-wire pins driven in ground splay out tree branches to make a spreading outline and also to support tree. Pieces of flexible rubber hose or other padding is used where wires contact branches. This technique is used to direct branch growth on flowering and fruiting trees to allow maximum air circulation for improved blossom and fruit production.

Wire guys are used to stake tree. To prevent guys from cutting into bark, loops are cushioned with rubber hose.

WATERING

Newly planted trees and shrubs need to be watered generously. During the first 6 months of active growth, if a week goes by without natural rainfall, trees and shrubs should be watered. As a rule of thumb, water at least twice a week for first 2 months after planting.

Do not keep trees and shrubs constantly swamped with water. Unlike small plants such as annual flowers and vegetables that require almost daily watering during dry weather, trees and shrubs benefit more from a deep, thorough watering once or twice a week. This allows soil to dry out slightly between waterings so air can reach the roots. Only a few swamp plants—such as bald cypress—will tolerate constantly wet conditions. Adequate drainage is vital for most trees and shrubs.

Because sandy soils lose moisture more quickly than clay soils, adding large amounts of peat moss, leaf mold or similar organic amendment is recommended to help retain moisture.

Although most mature trees and shrubs can endure longer periods of drought than smaller plants, and need not be watered as frequently, they still require adequate moisture. If a tree or shrub goes too long without water, it will become stressed, making it vulnerable to diseases and pests.

Frequent shallow waterings during a dry spell in an attempt to save a tree will have little effect. This kind of emergency relief can work with small plants, which recover quickly, but once the ground is dry and a tree or large shrub has started to dehydrate, it requires copious amounts of water to save it.

MULCHING

A mulch is any type of soil covering used for the purpose of conserving moisture, suffocating weeds and stabilizing soil temperatures. Mulches can be organic—shredded bark or licorice root, for example—or inorganic, such as gravel, decorative rock or black plastic. Organic mulches are popular for placing around trees and shrubs because most tend to be highly decorative. Those made from wood and vegetable byproducts are especially desirable because they decompose and enrich the soil. Also, they tend to keep the soil cool for improved plant growth. However, some organic mulches deplete the soil of nitrogen while decomposing, so it is desirable to use them in conjunction with a nitrogen fertilizer.

Care should be taken when using landscape stone around acid-loving plants such as hemlocks, dogwoods, hollies, azaleas and camellias, because rain can leach alkaline salts from the stone into the soil and change the pH balance. Feeding these plants with fertilizers marked "for acid-loving plants" can help prevent this.

Black plastic has a tendency to overheat the soil if it is not covered with a layer of organic mulch. Also, it has an unnatural appearance that many people find objectionable. Black plastic of at least a 5-mil thickness is mostly used as a weed barrier under decorative mulches such as stone and bark chips.

Mulch materials should be chosen according to cost and local availability. At one time, licorice root was a popular mulch throughout North America, but in

Heavy mulch of shredded bark in azalea bed not only deters weeds, conserves moisture and keeps soil cool, but helps establish a *mowing strip* so grass can be cut without the mower touching branches.

MULCHING MATERIALS

Material	Thickness for Weed Control	Advantages	Disadvantages	Comments
Aluminum foil	1 layer.	Reflective surface increases light intensity in areas. Helps control aphids. They become disoriented by it.	Tears easily. Looks unnatural. Expensive for large areas. May reflect too much heat in warm-summer areas.	Cools soil. Allow soil to warm before using around new plantings. Best for short-season areas.
Bark chips and ground bark	2 to 3 inches.	Attractive, natural appearance.	Harbors ants, ticks and termites. Expensive for large areas.	Cools soil. Allow soil to warm before using around new plantings. Bark products available in a variety of sizes.
Compost	3 to 4 inches.	Adds nutrients to soil. Usually attractive, natural appearance. One of the best organic mulch materials.	If compost is not made properly, it may harbor weed seeds.	Cools soil. Allow soil to warm before using around new plantings.
Corncobs, ground	3 to 4 inches.	Attractive, natural appearance.	Takes nitrogen from soil as it decomposes. Compensate with high nitrogen fertilizer.	Cools soil. Allow soil to warm before using around new plantings.
Cottonseed hulls	3 to 4 inches.	Attractive, natural appearance. Adds some nutrients to soil.	Lightweight—blows away when dry. Possible contamination from chemical sprays.	Cools soil. Allow soil to warm before using around new plantings. Available in South and parts of Southwest.
Grass clippings	2 to 3 inches.	Commonly available. Decomposes quickly to add organic matter and nutrients to soil.	Sometimes contains weed seeds. May need additional application midseason to be effective as a weed control. Thick layers will mat.	Cools soil. Allow soil to warm before using around new plantings. Best applied when dry. Don't use clippings treated with weed-killers.
Hay and straw	6 to 8 inches.	Attractive, natural appearance. Adds nutrients to soil. Commonly available.	May contain seeds. May need additional applications midseason if used for weed control.	Cools soil. Allow soil to warm before using around new plantings.
Leaf mold	3 to 4 inches.	Attractive, natural appearance. Adds nutrients to soil. The best organic-mulching material.	Takes time to make. A lot of leaves are needed to make a small amount. Turns soil acid. Compensate with lime.	Cools soil. Allow soil to warm before using around new plantings. Good moisture-holding capacity.
Newspapers	1/4 inch.	Commonly available. Decomposes quickly.	Unnatural appearance, but can be covered with other, more attractive mulch.	Cools soil. Allow soil to warm before using around new plantings.
Peanut hulls	3 to 4 inches.	Adds nutrients to soil. Decomposes quickly to add organic matter to soil.	Lightweight. Blows away when dry. Not readily available outside Southern states.	Cools soil. Allow soil to warm before using around new plantings.
Peat moss	2 to 3 inches.	Attractive, natural appearance. Adds organic matter to soil.	Expensive for large areas. Better as soil amendment.	Cools soil. Allow soil to warm before using around new plantings. Good moisture-holding capacity.
Pine needles	3 to 4 inches.	Natural appearance. Readily available. Gradually adds organic matter to soil.	Slightly acidic, but no problem when lime is used prior to planting.	Cools soil. Allow soil to warm before using around new plantings.
Plastic, black	1 layer. Use 1-1/2 mil thickness.	Excellent for weed control. Maintains warm soil temperatures.	Unnatural appearance.	Warms soil. Use under other mulches, especially stone, for permanent weed barrier.
Plastic, clear	1 layer. Use 1-1/2 mil thickness.	Maintains higher soil temperature than black plastic, encouraging earlier establishment of sub-tropicals.	Unnatural appearance. Weeds grow underneath.	Warms soil. Best used in conjunction with an irrigation system.

recent years has become less available in many parts of the country and is somewhat high priced. Organic mulches of wood byproducts, such as wood chips and shredded bark are more-common, less expensive alternatives.

Extended use of organic mulch has the disadvantage of depleting nitrogen in the soil due to the accelerated activity of decay microorganisms. This condition can be corrected through periodic additions of a high-nitrogen fertilizer.

In the Southwest, gravel and rock are not as expensive as bark and other wood mulches, while on the West Coast cedar chips are becoming a popular choice for their ability to repel slugs and other pests. In agricultural areas, locally available agricultural byproducts are used as mulches. Examples are corncobs, cottonseed hulls, various nut hulls, grape pomace and mushroom compost.

FERTILIZING

There are many misconceptions about the need to fertilize trees and shrubs. Because trees in the wild are not given applications of commercial fertilizers, the general notion is that trees don't need feeding. But that is not the case.

In the wild, trees shed their leaves and the leaf litter is allowed to build up on the forest floor. It decays and forms leaf mold, which provides the tree with vital nutrients and trace elements as it breaks down further. This life-giving humus also acts as a mulch, covering the soil to conserve moisture, stabilize soil temperatures and discourage weeds. In most home landscapes, leaves are not allowed to remain on the ground. They are raked up and either burned or otherwise disposed of. For this reason, supplemental feedings of fertilizer is *essential* to healthy tree and shrub growth.

There is a great deal of conflicting information about fertilizing trees and shrubs. Some experts warn not to fertilize until after the first year of planting, others recommend applications immediately after planting. There is also disagreement as to whether high-nitrogen formulas or high-phosphorus formulas are best. However, without a soil test to determine the precise makeup of your soil, and an understanding of a particular plant's nutrient requirements, specific recommendations are difficult, but here are some general guidelines:

The first year a tree or shrub is in the ground, all we should ask of it is to survive through its first winter. At the time of planting, a mild application of a high-phosphorus fertilizer, such as 5-10-5, can be mixed in with the soil. High-phosphorus fertilizers are recommended for initial applications because they stimulate root development. The best time to make subsequent applications of fertilizer is in the fall. Tree roots continue to function in winter whenever the soil temperature is above 40F (4C). Limb and trunk development in the spring is largely derived from food stored in the roots during fall and winter. Commercial fertilizers applied in the spring do not generally benefit a tree that same spring. However, fertilizer applied to a tree in the fall as it slows down its metabolism will benefit the tree remarkably the following spring and summer.

Tree fertilizers are usually sold in granular form for applying to the soil. Fertilizer may be applied directly on the soil surface because most feeder roots are in the upper few inches of soil. According the the U.S. Forest Service, except where slow-release fertilizers are used and on sloping sites, there is little advantage to using fertilizer *tree spikes* or injecting other fertilizer formulations into the soil by boring holes in the ground or by other means.

Because trees and shrubs can also absorb nutrients through their leaves, liquid fertilizers can be applied to leaves in a fine spray. Called *foliar feeding,* this application method is usually used only as a quick "pick-me-up" or booster to stimulate growth at a particular time of need—such as when flower buds are forming on flowering shrubs, or when fruit is forming on fruiting trees.

There are three primary nutrients essential to healthy plant growth. *Nitrogen* is the most important of these, because it is responsible for healthy leaves. *Phosphorus* is the next most important nutrient because it promotes flowering, fruiting and healthy root development. The third major nutrient *potassium* (potash) promotes cold-hardiness, disease resistance and overall vigor.

The primary nutrients are sometimes abbreviated to N-P-K on the fertilizer package, with the amount of each nutrient given as a percentage, such as 20-10-10. In this case, the numbers mean that the formula is composed of a total of 40% nutrients—20% nitrogen, 10% phosphorus and 10% potassium. Usually, the rest of the formula is filler—water or sterile granules that serve as a distributing agent—though the fertilizer may also contain small amounts of other nutrients, depending on brand.

A good soil provides 13 of the 16 plant nutrients necessary for healthy growth. In addition to the three primary nutrients discussed above, plants require the others, called *trace elements*, in varying amounts. The three most important for healthy tree and shrub growth are *calcium, iron* and *boron.* Lack of calcium, for example, is evident in some species of *Prunus* when the trunk or branches crack and ooze a gummy resin. This condition, called *gummosis,* can also indicate the presence of borers. If the resin is clear, lack of calcium is usually the cause; if the gum is mixed with sawdust, then a borer is the culprit.

Lack of boron will cause new growth at branch tips to shrivel and die. Lack of iron is the most common cause of *chlorosis,* a condition indicated by yellowed leaves with predominately greener leaf veins. Chlorosis can also be caused by lack of copper. These and other trace elements are usually not applied on a regular basis, but only if the tree or shrub shows a specific deficiency in one of them. If you suspect a nutrient deficiency, describe the symptoms to a local nurseryman, tree specialist or extension agent. They are generally familiar with soil conditions and nutrient deficiencies common to your area. For instance, lack of iron is common in areas with alkaline soils.

However, the ability of a tree or shrub to use fertilizer depends on other factors besides nutrient content. Good soil texture—a crumbly loam soil, for example—helps a plant's roots penetrate freely and absorb the nutrients efficiently. The other vital factor is pH—a measurement of acidity and alkalinity. Some trees and shrubs demand a highly acid soil. Plants such as rhododendrons, azaleas, camellias, hollies and andromeda demand such high levels of acidity that special fertilizers are available, marked "for acid-loving plants." Miracid is a familiar example.

Though modifying soil pH is practical for flower beds and vegetable plots, it is much more difficult to accomplish for trees and shrubs. In areas of the country where a particular soil pH predominates—acid soils are prevalent in the Northeast, alkaline soils in the Southwest—the easiest solution is to create a raised bed, using landscape ties to form the sides, and filling the center with an appropriate soil mix. Smaller trees and shrubs can be grown in containers. Easier yet would be to grow species adapted to local conditions.

SCHEDULE FOR TREE AND SHRUB CARE

This chart shows the recommended times for the various basic tasks required to maintain healthy trees and shrubs. However, specific problems may arise that require immediate attention, such as storm damage to a tree or an untimely outbreak of a certain pest or disease. In some cases, you may have to call in a professional tree-care service to correct the problem. Appropriate timing for many of these tasks will depend on location and plant species. Check with local extension services for recommendations.

TYPE OF CARE	Jan	Feb	Mar	Apr	May	June	July	Aug	Sept	Oct	Nov	Dec
Transplanting Large Trees	■	■	■	■					▪	▪	▪	▪
Transplanting Small Trees and Shrubs		■	■	■					▪	▪	▪	
Pruning Flowering Trees and Shrubs		▪	▪		▪	▪	■	■		▪		
Pruning Foliage Trees (Shade Trees)	■	■	▪	▪	▪	▪	▪	▪	▪	▪	■	■
Fertilizing	▪	▪	■	■	■	■	■	■	■	■		
Aerating and Conditioning Soil	▪	▪	■	■	■	■	■	■	■	■		▪
Spraying For Control of Scale on Dormant Plants	▪	▪	■									
Spraying Evergreens (Pest and Disease Control)					■	■	■	■	■			
Spraying Fruit Trees (Pest and Disease Control)			▪	▪	■	■	■	■	▪	▪		
Spraying Shade Trees (Pest and Disease Control)				▪	■	■	■	■	▪			
Gassing Borers					▪	■	■	▪	▪	▪		
Irrigation				▪	■	■	■	■	▪			
Removing Undesirable Trees	■	■	▪					▪	▪	■	■	■
Winterizing Trees and Shrubs										▪	■	■

■ Most Important ▪ Also Recommended

Leaf Mold—Adding leaf mold in spring and fall will benefit mixed-shrub borders and trees with a circle of turf cleared around the base of the trunk. Mrs. Lena Caron, director of gardens at the famous Ladew Topiary Gardens, near Monkton, Maryland, feels that the value of leaf mold cannot be overrated in maintaining healthy plants. It wasn't until the garden's caretakers started stockpiling it to use around their trees and shrubs that they began to see a remarkable improvement in the general health and flowering ability of the plants.

Rich, black leaf mold is a kind of compost. It has long been valued as an amendment to improve soil texture, but it also makes an excellent fertilizer. Leaf mold can be dug up directly from the forest floor, but the best source of the material is from storing fallen leaves in special compost piles. Form a circular bin with chicken wire to hold the leaves together. The leaves will decompose much faster if they are shredded with a lawn mower before loading into the bin.

You can also speed up decomposition by adding nitrogen. The nitrogen provides food for the microorganisms responsible for decay. Nitrogen is available naturally in animal manure and in green plant parts such as fresh green leaves and fresh grass clippings.

A general compost is a good alternative to leaf mold. It is made from all kinds of general plant or vegetable waste, biodegradable kitchen scraps and other decomposable organic matter. Large scale composting is best done in square or rectangular wooden bins treated against rot.

The key to making good garden compost is to maintain a balance between *green material* and *dead material*. Technically, this is a nitrogen (green) to carbon (dead) ratio that must be maintained for efficient decomposition of organic materials in the pile. So when you add a batch of fresh grass clippings or hedge trimmings (green material) to the pile, cover it with a layer of sawdust or wood chips (dead material).

Although compost is excellent for im- proving texture and moisture retention, it does not always provide adequate amounts of soil nutrients. Periodic soil tests are recommended as a check on soil nutrient levels.

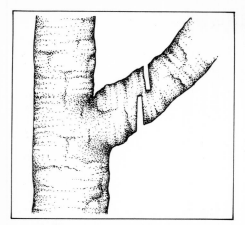

First, undercut branch until saw begins to bind. Make second cut from top, slightly to outside of undercut, to remove branch. Third cut close to tree eliminates stub. Make cut just outside bark collar. Cut may be sealed with orange shellac.

PRUNING

Pruning is considered by most tree experts to be the most important phase of tree care. Although there are trees and shrubs that require less pruning than others—particularly trees in a naturalized setting—some pruning is advisable, if only to remove dead or diseased branches and to keep pathways clear. Landscape trees are pruned mostly to improve their appearance and health. Correctly done, pruning is an invigorating process that channels the plant's energy into the remaining branches. Pruning also helps limit plants to a specific size, improves flowering and fruiting and eliminates wayward branches that might interfere with power lines or structures.

Pruning is mostly done to shape a tree or shrub to a particular form. Prune a tree along the sides and it will tend to grow spirelike or columnar. Prune out the leader and it will tend to grow outward until a new leader has a chance to grow, which in turn can be pruned out again, and so on, to keep the tree bushy.

There are two basic kinds of pruning techniques—*heading* and *thinning*. Heading involves cutting back branches to a side branch or lateral bud. This results in a denser, more compact form. Heading is most often done to control the overall size of a tree or shrub. Thinning interior branches increases the amount of light and air penetration to the crown, improving vigor and wind resistance.

Generally speaking, shrubs can take much heavier pruning than trees. Some shrubs benefit from pruning right down to the ground. For instance, when for-

BASIC PRUNING TECHNIQUES FOR TREES

TOPPING A TREE

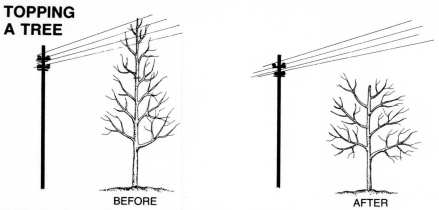

BEFORE   AFTER

Topping central leader of tree stimulates side branching.

LOWER-BRANCH PRUNING

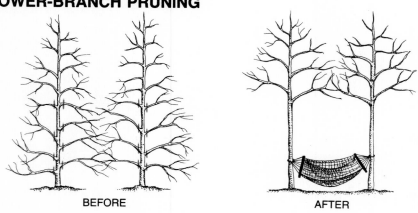

BEFORE   AFTER

Lower side branches are pruned away to leave slender, straight trunks and overhead leaf canopy.

SCULPTURAL PRUNING A CONIFER

BEFORE   AFTER

All branches except selected few are pruned back to main trunk. Stakes and wires are used to bend trunk and remaining branches, forcing tree to grow to desired form.

BASIC PRUNING TECHNIQUES FOR SHRUBS

REJUVENATING A SHRUB

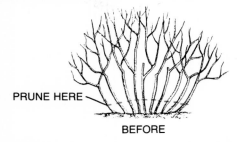

PRUNE HERE

BEFORE

AFTER

Heavy pruning to just above soil level stimulates bushy new growth.

THINNING

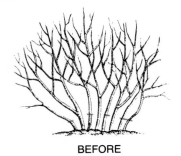

BEFORE

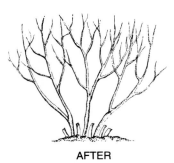

AFTER

Prune away suckers and intermediate stems on multi-stemmed shrub to open up interior. This allows more light penetration and air circulation.

LOWER-BRANCH PRUNING

BEFORE

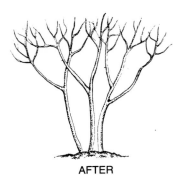

AFTER

Lower side branches are pruned away to leave only main, upright stems.

PRUNING CUTS

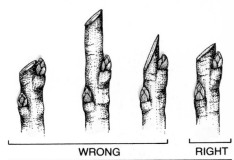

WRONG   RIGHT

Correct cut is made at a slight angle about 1/4 inch above bud.

Loppers allow you to cut through thick branches up to 3 inches in diameter.

Bow saw is suitable for cutting through thick branches.

Electric hedge shears make easy work of shaping shrubs.

sythia has established itself, it is often a good policy to prune it down to the ground immediately after flowering. This stimulates growth of new stems and a more vibrant flowering display the following spring on a compact plant.

If you want a tree with a trunk that's clear of limbs so you can walk under it, prune off undesirable lower limbs.

Some trees to send up sprouts at the soil line, called *suckers*. If you want a single-stemmed tree, remove these.

Always prune on a slant so cut ends of branches shed water, and make the cut at least 1/4 inch above a bud on shrubs and 1 inch above a bud on trees.

Avoid pruning flowering trees or flowering shrubs other than immediately after flowering. For example, pruning a rhododendron late in the year, such as fall or winter, will deprive the plant of flowers in spring. Pruning other deciduous trees and shrubs is best done in fall, winter or early spring while plants are dormant.

Boxwood shrub is protected from cold winter winds by a wood frame covered with burlap. In exposed situations in cold climates, boxwood leaves will turn brown unless protection is provided.

Plastic tree wrap helps protect a newly planted tree from *sunscald*. Wrap also protects bark from rodents and deer.

Fig tree is protected from freezing by wire cylinder filled with leaves. Tree has been pruned short so it is completely encased, or *mummified*.

The four most-useful pruning tools are: hand pruners for cutting small branches up to 1/4 inch in diameter; two-handled lopping pruners for cutting thick branches up to 2 inches in diameter; a curved pruning saw or bow saw for cutting through thicker branches, and electric hedge shears to trim shrubs to a smooth, clean outline. A chain saw can be used to cut very large limbs, but this work is best done by a tree surgeon.

When using a pruning saw on large branches, always make the initial cut on the underside of the branch before cutting through the branch from above. That way the branch will not tear on its underside, but come away clean.

WINTER PROTECTION

Many hardy trees and shrubs can survive freezing weather provided they stay dormant during the entire cold spell and have sufficient moisture in the root zone to prevent dehydration from cold winds and winter sun. A tree or shrub subjected to alternate thawing and freezing is easily damaged. One way to help keep a plant dormant is to pile mulch material over the root zone *after* the ground freezes. This helps *keep* the ground frozen until a definite spring warming trend has started.

Similarly, if a tree or shrub has insufficient moisture in autumn through lack of natural rainfall, it can die unless supplemental water is provided through irrigation. This is especially true of evergreens that continue to transpire large amounts of moisture during winter.

Burlap can be used to protect special plants—especially newly planted trees—in exposed locations. Trees can

be protected with burlap trunk wraps, shrubs by surrounding the entire plant with a burlap shelter. In addition to burlap, suitable screens can be made from reed matting and wire cylinders wrapped with tar paper. Anti-dessicants are sprays that apply a thin coating of wax or plastic to exposed leaves and branches to protect woody plants from moisture loss.

Heavy snowfall and freezing rain can cause tremendous damage. If snow is left to freeze on many kinds of evergreens—boxwood especially—ugly brown patches will result. In severe cases, this condition, known as *winterkill,* can kill the entire plant.

Freezing rain can be devastating, and there is not much that can be done after the fact. Usually the rain falls in the night and freezes as it touches limbs. It can be a beautiful sight the following morning, but if a sudden strong wind comes up, the sound of crashing limbs will fill the air within minutes. The best remedy is prevention.

Prior to the snow season, columnar trees should have their branches bound close to the trunk with twine. This prevents the snow or ice from pulling the branches out of alignment and snapping them. Immediately after snow falls and before it has a chance to freeze, use a broom to sweep off the snow covering from low shrubs and reachable tree branches.

Cracks or splits in bark can occur when the west or south side of a tree trunk is warmed excessively by winter sun. When the sun sets and the temperature drops drastically, the cells on the exposed side of the tree can be killed.

The bark then cracks or splits. If severe enough, this damage can kill the top, particularly in the case of young trees unprotected by tree wrap. To minimize the risk of bark cracks from frost, either wrap the trunk with a white reflecting tree wrap or paint the trunk with white latex paint.

Fruiting fig is a particularly vulnerable tree in Northern climates. Though the roots are reasonably hardy, the top is easily damaged by cold. The best way to get a fruiting fig—and other small, tender trees and shrubs—through the winter is to prune back excessive topgrowth and make what nurserymen call a *mummy.* Form a wire cylinder around the trunk and fill the air space between the trunk and the wire with leaves or straw, as shown in the photo above.

An alternative method for small shrubs is to prune the top to within 12 inches of the ground and cover the plant with a "Wall-O-Water" plastic cone. The cone is formed by cylinders of water that will freeze and create a warm microclimate around the plant.

In addition to figs, tender plants such as hibiscus, bamboos and jasmines can be nursed through the winter in regions where the plants are at the coldest limits of their recommended hardiness zones.

Another important technique for providing winter protection involves bareroot plants purchased in autumn. Sometimes you may find you have insufficient time to get them planted before winter arrives and must hold them over until spring. You can protect them using a technique called *heeling-in.* This is done by digging a shallow trench in a sheltered location, inserting the roots at an angle into the trench and covering them with loose soil. The trunks protrude at an angle to present a low profile to damaging winds. In spring, before active growth begins, the heeled-in plants can be easily dug up and moved to their permanent sites.

If a containerized or balled-and-burlapped plant is left above ground over winter, chances are it will die from freezing temperatures. To save these plants until spring planting, sink them into pits with loose soil or mulch piled to the top of the container or burlap. Alternatively, build up a raised area of landscape ties, set your plants in the center and mound loose soil or wood chips several inches above the container rim or burlap.

PESTS AND DISEASES

Trees and shrubs suffer much less from pests and diseases than other forms of cultivated plants, such as vegetables. Also, the evidence is clear that maintaining plants in vigorous condition is by far the best protection. Adequate amounts of fertilizer and moisture, and timely pruning are especially important. When trees are weakened from neglect, competition from other plants, or by a long summer drought, they become highly vulnerable to attack.

The common lawn mower and filament-line grass trimmers are also a major causes of pest and disease problems. Careless use of these and other garden implements can cause bark wounds that provide a point of entry for pests and disease organisms.

Most shrubs and small trees can be treated with many of the same pest controls used on other garden plants. Descriptions of specific pests and diseases, starting at right, include recommended controls. However, it is usually not practical for a homeowner to administer these and other cures for pest and disease problems of large trees. Cures rely heavily on chemical poisons and specialized equipment to reach the extremities of a tree. It's better to call in a tree-service company. Certain preventative measures can be taken by homeowners, including use of traps and biological controls, such as predatory insects and bacterial products. Also, the use of tree wraps on young trees can prevent sunscorch and rodent damage.

PESTS

The bigger the pest, the easier it is to control. Deer and rodents, for example, are easily discouraged from eating bark and girdling a tree simply by using protective plastic tree wraps. Infestations by sap-sucking scale insects, caterpillars and wood- eating borers are much more difficult to control, often requiring professional tree services to eliminate them.

Controls can be classified as *preventative* and *curative*. Many pests that can be prevented may be impossible to eradicate once they have a foothold. For example, oils sprayed on trees while dormant can kill eggs of overwintering insects, especially aphids and mites.

On the other hand, it simply isn't practical to take preventative measures against every potential tree pest. However, some problems can be pinpointed as potentially disastrous. Gypsy moth is an example. Most trees can survive defoliation through one season, but won't make it through two.

If you live in an area where a specific pest is a problem, it might be worth getting together with neighbors to take preventative action through a large-scale spray program. If you are new to an area, a good way to pinpoint potential pest problems is to check with your county extension agent.

Here are some of the most common pest problems afflicting trees and shrubs:

Aphids are tiny, soft-bodied insects about 1/8 inch long that form colonies on tender parts of trees and shrubs, sucking their juices. Though infestations are seldom serious enough to kill a tree or shrub, they are carriers of diseases. Also, they excrete a substance called *honeydew*, which attracts sooty-mold fungus that coats leaf surfaces with a black deposit.

Look for aphid colonies at the tips of branches and on newly sprouted leaves. They are usually green, but can vary in color from white to black. Viburnums and roses are especially vulnerable.

Control: Jets of water directed at the infested branch tips can dislodge them. Sprays of insecticidal soaps or a mild solution of dish detergent in water are also effective. Malathion, Sevin and pyrethrum-based insecticides are common chemical controls.

Bagworms are the caterpillar larvae of a night-flying moth, widely dispersed from New England to Texas. The larvae hatch from eggs and build around themselves cone-shaped bags made from pieces of leaf, particularly evergreen needles. Spruce, arborvitae and cedars are especially susceptible to attack. The pest can cause severe defoliation, stress and death.

Control: Bags can be hand-picked from infested trees. Winter is a good time to remove the bags because they contain the eggs of the next generation. The bacterial disease *Bacillis thuringiensis* is effective while larvae are small. Sprays of diazinon, malathion and Sevin are effective chemical controls, applied every 7 to 10 days during spring and whenever re-infestation occurs.

Borers include the larvae of a number of different kinds of beetles and moths. They are capable of burrowing through even the toughest wood, causing branches to wilt and trees to die. Eggs are deposited by the adult female on the bark of the trunk. These hatch, and the larvae immediately penetrate the bark. Once inside the wood, they are virtually impossible to control. Among many trees, such as flowering peach and cherry, the tree bleeds a gummy brown or white substance from holes made by the borers. A similar condition, caused by lack of calcium in the soil, is known as *gummosis*.

Control: Borer infestation is prevalent among newly transplanted trees. Any kind of barrier wrapped around the trunk will deter the pest, particularly a commercially available plastic tree wrap, which should remain in place for at least 2 years. Sprays of malathion and methoxychlor will kill the adult female moths before they have a chance to lay eggs. These sprays need to be applied at regular intervals to be effective, particularly from midsummer into autumn when the female is actively laying eggs. Moth balls heaped around the base of trunks during this period is an effective control practiced by organic gardeners. Pheromone traps designed to attract the adult moths of several borer species can be used to pinpoint mating and egg-laying periods.

For severe infestations, the services of a professional tree service should be considered. The commercial pesticide *Borerkil* is effective against small infestations. It is a paste that is squeezed into the holes to asphyxiate the borers.

Gypsy Moths were accidentally introduced into New England from Europe in the 1880's and have gradually spread throughout most of the Northeast. The female is a flightless moth that lays its eggs in elongated tan egg cases that are deposited in the fissures of bark. Oaks are particularly susceptible. The larvae

Peach-borer damage is evident by gummy sap oozing from holes made by the borers.

Japanese-beetle trap is one of the few non-chemical controls to combat pests. Sex attractant lures beetles into disposable bag.

hatch as tiny black worms that grow rapidly into 2-inch, long-haired caterpillars. In some years, they are so numerous they can completely defoliate trees. When defoliation occurs 2 years in a row, the tree usually dies.

Control: Sprays of Sevin are the most common chemical control, applied in spring after eggs have hatched. The bacterial disease *Bacillis thuringiensis* is an effective biological control. Once infected, the caterpillar stops eating and starves to death. *B.thuringiensis* is sold under the brand names Thuricide, Dipel and Biotrol.

Japanese Beetle is a widespread insect pest. In its adult stage, it is a serious problem of many trees and ornamental shrubs. These beetles feed on the upper leaf surfaces, leaving the leaves skeletonized. Trees most susceptible to Japanese beetles include linden, elm, maples, horsechestnut, birch, black walnut, apple, cherry, plum, and mountain ash. Trees in full sun are particularly prone to attack. From fall through spring the larvae—large, white grubs—live in the soil, feeding on the roots of lawn grasses.

Control: A bacterial spore disease *Bacillus popillae*—also known as milky spore—is effective in killing 70% to 80% of resident populations. Traps using sex attractants that lure adult beetles into disposable bags are less effective, even though they are capable of trapping large numbers. Most of the chemical controls recommended for Japanese beetles are only partially effective, owing to the ability of the pest to build up resistance rapidly. Sevin and diazinon offer partial control if applications are repeated at intervals of 7 to 10 days during periods of heavy infestation.

Leaf Miners are the larval stage of numerous insects, including flies, moths and beetles. Adults lay their eggs inside the leaves of specific trees and shrubs. When the young hatch, they begin burrowing through the leaf, leaving snaking patterns and blotches. Leaf miners are especially serious pests on birches, but also attack holly, beech, elm, boxwood and many conifers.

Control: Once the pest is inside the leaf, it can only be controlled by a systemic insecticide such as Orthene. In their adult stage, the insects are more easily controlled by spraying with malathion, diazinon or Sevin.

Mites are colonies of tiny spiderlike arachnids no bigger than grains of pepper. Usually colored red or brown, they build webs among leaves and stems and suck plant juices. Infestations can be so severe they will kill trees and shrubs—even tough plants such as junipers. On broadleaf plants mite feeding damage is most severe toward the interior of the tree. Symptoms include curling of leaf edges and a dusty appearance to the underside of the leaves. On evergreens, needles look dull and lack luster—ugly patches of brown needles disfigure the plants and eventually kill them. The presence of delicate white webs is a sure sign of mites.

Control: Once infestations are heavy, control may be impossible. Kelthane is an effective mite spray, applied on upper and lower leaf surfaces when mites first appear. Insecticidal soap is also effective.

Rodents and Deer can cause major damage to trees and shrubs, especially during winter. Mice and other rodents will gnaw the bark and cambium layer of young trees and shrubs, girdling the tree and killing it. Deer are also fond of stripping bark from young trees, and eating tender shoots as well. Male deer like to rub their horns on the trunk of a young tree, scraping off the bark and cambium layer and killing the tree.

Control: Use a commercial tree wrap on young trees to protect the trunk. Plastic tree guards are particularly effective. Forming flexible spiral cylinders, they expand freely as the tree grows. Keep fresh mulch away from base of tree to discourage mice from nesting around base of plant.

Scales are sucking insects that attach themselves to branches like limpets. Some are hard-bodied and well camouflaged to resemble lumps of bark. Others are soft bodied, white and quite conspicuous. Symptoms of scale injury are wilt, dieback and chlorosis. Some scales excrete *honeydew,* a moist sticky substance that can develop an ugly, destructive fungus disease called sootymold, which forms a black, powdery covering on leaf surfaces.

Control: Apply a dormant-oil spray in early spring, or a scalecide in early spring and summer. Remove and burn badly infested branches.

Webworms and Tent Caterpillars attack trees in spring and fall. The branches become covered in flosslike webs or tents containing colonies of voracious caterpillars. Tent caterpillars emerge from their tents in spring and can eat considerable quantities of leaves. The fall webworm lives on leaves encased in its tent and does little damage. The tents themselves are unsightly and are mostly attached to species of cherry, hawthorn and crabapple.

Control: The bacterial disease *Bacillis thuringiensis* is an effective biological control when applied as a spray. Effective chemical sprays include Sevin, diazinon and malathion.

DISEASES

Relatively few diseases of trees and shrubs are lethal. Exceptions such as *Dutch elm disease* and *oak wilt* can be both lethal and fast-acting. Diseases of trees and shrubs usually occur when the plant has become weakened by environmental conditions, such as pest attacks, strangulation by vines, dehydration from drought or lack of nutrients.

When diseases do occur, they can normally be diagnosed early and corrected. However, some symptoms, such as leaf spots and branch dieback, may need an expert to identify the particular disease organism responsible so that a suitable cure or control can be administered. Good sources for expert advice include the horticulture department of your state university, or the state or county extension service.

Diseases are generally classified as *infectious* and *non-infectious*.

Infectious diseases are commonly caused by fungus, bacteria or viruses. Fungus diseases cause the greatest amount of damage to trees and shrubs. Fungus organisms are unable to manufacture chlorophyll, so many obtain their nourishment from living plant tissue. They reproduce by means of microscopic spores that are dispersed by wind or rain, or carried on the bodies of insects.

Bacteria and viruses also obtain their nourishment from living plant tissue. They reproduce by cell division, and are easily transmitted from one plant to another by wind or insects.

Non-infectious diseases are mostly caused by environmental conditions such as nutrient deficiencies, but also by chemical or mechanical injury to plants. For example, mineral deficiencies in soil can cause *chlorosis,* or leaf yellowing. Lack of iron is one of the most common causes of chlorosis. Lack of calcium in the soil can cause *gummosis,* whereby the bark splits and bleeds a gummy sap. Excessive exposure to sun turns leaves brown, a condition referred to as *sunscorch.* On some trees, such as horse chestnut, sunscorch looks hideously lethal, turning leaf margins an ugly brown, but it rarely kills a tree.

Diseases of trees and shrubs can also be classified as *leaf diseases, stem diseases, vascular diseases* and *root diseases,* referring to the part of the tree that is mostly infected.

Leaf diseases include *powdery mildew, leaf spot, leaf blotch, leaf blight, leaf sunscorch, rust* and *chlorosis.* Of these, powdery mildew is probably the most common. Prevalent during periods of high humidity, it occurs mostly in mid-summer and fall, coating leaf surfaces with gray or powdery white patches. Though generally not lethal, it can weaken a tree or shrub and leave it vulnerable to attack by more serious diseases.

Stem diseases include *anthracnose, cankers, galls, dieback, witches broom*

Anthracnose disease on dogwood. This particularly destructive strain is known as *lower branch dieback.*

Orange spots with dark centers are evidence of cedar-apple rust on crabapples.

and *rot.* Cankers are dead areas on branches or trunks. They may be sunken or raised and show cracking or flaking. Fruiting bodies of fungi may frequently break through the diseased area. Cankers can completely girdle a branch, killing it.

Gall diseases appear as growths on branches or trunks caused by fungi, bacteria or viruses that enter the tree through wounds. The growths are exceedingly ugly, but rarely lethal. Some insects also cause galls.

Root diseases include *shoestring root rot,* a fungus that attacks tree roots of weakened trees, causing severe branch dieback and death.

Vascular diseases include *Dutch elm disease, verticillium wilt* and *oak wilt.* They attack the inner sapwood, causing branch dieback and death.

Here are some of the most common diseases that attacks trees and shrubs:

Anthracnose includes numerous strains of a fungus disease that attacks trees and shrubs. An especially destructive form is currently causing widespread death to dogwoods throughout North America. Also called *lower branch dieback,* it first shows itself when branch tips die, followed by dieback of entire lower branches. Leaves shrivel, turn brown and remain attached to the tree, even through winter.

Trees in shaded locations are especially susceptible. Death can occur within 3 years of infection. Other trees susceptible to special forms of anthracnose include sycamore, ash, elm and maple. With these trees, the disease is not lethal but causes some leaf drop

and scattered twig dieback. The severity of anthracnose is determined by the weather, with a cool, moist spring favoring disease development.

Control: Once a tree is heavily infected, controls are ineffective. Sprays of Benomyl or Maneb can control mild infections, if properly administered by a tree-service company. Infections generally follow a period of stress, such as drought. The best preventative method is to keep trees healthy by regular watering and fertilizing.

Cankers are stem diseases that affect the branches and trunk of many trees. They are caused by fungi and bacteria. Infected areas start to crack or flake away, turn dark and become sunken. Some will form a ridge of raised bark around the canker. When a canker girdles a branch, it cuts off the flow of sap and the branch dies. When the trunk is girdled by a canker, the tree will die. Some cankers produce colorful fruiting bodies of fungus—red and yellow slimy masses that emerge through a crack.

Control: Keep plants in good health. Prune away infected branches and burn. Between each cut, sterilize the cutting tool with rubbing alcohol. When cankers occur on trunks, they can be removed by routing out the diseased area back to living wood, then painting the wound with shellac.

Cedar Apple Rust is widespread throughout the Northeast wherever junipers and apples grow in close proximity. It needs two kinds of trees to complete its destructive life cycle. First it overwinters on species of junipers, forming corky brown galls. Then, in

Crown galls disfigure main trunk and branches of weeping willow.

Powdery mildew on lilac. Though it rarely kills plants, powdery mildew is unsightly and weakens them.

spring, the galls radiate slimy yellow fingers like the arms of an octopus. These produce spores that must land on species of apple trees, where they infect leaves, twigs, fruit and stems. This stage of the disease is called *rust*. It is first evident as yellow or orange spots on leaves, then as swollen lesions on new growth. The spots thicken to produce small, black fruiting bodies that disperse spores to infect junipers.

Control: Plant only disease-resistant varieties, or avoid planting crabapples in close proximity to junipers. Fungicidal sprays, such as Zineb, can be used on junipers or crabapples. On crabapples, make four to five applications of spray, spaced at 10-day intervals, after buds open in spring. On junipers, make four applications at 7-day intervals in mid-summer.

Chlorosis is a general term used to describe nutritional deficiencies of plants. Typical symptoms are a yellowing of leaves, usually leaving the veins deep green. Any imbalance of plant nutrients can cause chlorosis, but it is mostly associated with a deficiency of iron. It is especially common among acid-loving plants planted in alkaline or neutral soil.

Control: With acid-loving plants, the addition of organic matter to the soil will help. For more immediate results, the use of a fertilizer marked 'for acid-loving plants' is best. Or use an iron-chelate, either in the soil or sprayed on leaves. Sulfur added to soil is also an effective control.

Crown Galls are caused by bacteria that produce ugly, warty swellings on trunks, branches or roots, particularly on willows and poplars. Cherry, walnut and roses are also susceptible. Galls usually cause little damage, but can spoil the ornamental value of specimen plants.

Other kinds of galls—caused by fungi—commonly infect the leaves or twigs of oak trees and look like huge tumors.

Control: A common source of gall infection is through a trunk injury caused by a lawn mower or other implement.

Fireblight is common on crabapples, hawthorn, firethorn, cotoneaster and mountain ash. It is prevalent throughout all areas of North America with hot, humid summers—particularly the Northeast and Midwest. Blossoms, shoots, branch tips and fruit turn brown or black and appear scorched. Fireblight completely destroys a plant's ornamental value and will sometimes kill the plant. Infected branches are scarred by conspicuous cankers and rough, scaly areas of bark.

Control: Plant only disease-resistant varieties in areas where the disease is a problem—control is extremely difficult. Prune away all branches and twigs showing evidence of the disease, disinfecting the pruning tool *after every cut* by dipping in rubbing alcohol.

Powdery Mildew attacks the leaves of many ornamental trees and shrubs, particularly lilacs, crabapples, hawthorns and roses, and most broadleaf evergreens, such as rhododendrons and azaleas. It appears as a gray or dirty white powdery coating on leaf surfaces. On plants that are infected early in the season, severe growth distortions can result. Though it usually does not kill the plant, powdery mildew looks ugly and weakens it by inhibiting photosynthesis. High humidity favors the disease because the spores will only germinate in warm, saturated air.

Control: Spray leaf surfaces with benomyl whenever the fungus appears and at 10-day intervals as needed. Other fungicides such as sulfur, karathane, chlorothalonil and triflorine are also effective controls.

Scab is the most common disease among crabapples and hawthorns, prevalent in all areas of North America except desert regions. It also attacks mountain ash and pyracantha. The disease begins with olive-colored, velvety leaf spots that become larger and turn dark brown. The center of each spot bulges upward, giving the appearance of a scab. Severely infected trees can lose their leaves by midsummer, and any fruits that form generally shrivel up and turn black. The disease is prevalent during wet weather. Though scab is an unsightly disease and can severely weaken a tree or shrub, it does not kill it.

Control: Use scab-resistant varieties of crabapples and pyracantha. Chemical controls require four applications of benomyl or zineb at 14-day intervals from the time the buds open in spring.

Woodrot diseases are caused by fungi that gain a foothold in a wounded part of a tree and cause decay. The decay can produce a "hollow tree," destroying the heartwood, but will not infect actively growing layers of wood. The fungi responsible for woodrot are usually the *shelf fungus* type or *toadstools*.

Control: Wounds and pruning cuts should be shaped properly to facilitate rapid healing. Fertilizing and watering as needed can also encourage tree vigor and prompt wound closure. In severe cases the infected area can be routed out to living wood and filled with cement, like a tooth filling. However, the filling of cavities should be practiced only as a last resort because it often results in new pockets of rot underneath. Also, rigid columns of cement can cause trunks to snap off in a wind.

ENCYCLOPEDIA OF ORNAMENTAL TREES & SHRUBS

The following encyclopedia includes more than 15 separate species or distinct varieties of trees and shrubs. They are arranged alphabetically by botanical (Latin) name, with the exception of azaleas, bamboo and palms. Although azaleas belong to the genus *Rhododendron*, they are a large, distinct group of plants within that genus, so it seemed best to list them by their common name. Bamboo describes a large group of woody members of the grass family, also represented by several genera. These are described in this chapter.

In botanical nomenclature, plants are identified by the *genus* name and the *species* name. For instance, the genus name for all oaks is *Quercus*. The California live oak is identified by the botanical name *Quercus agrifolia*. Plants are further divided into varieties or cultivars within the species, such as *Aucuba japonica* 'Variegata'. Acuba japonica identifies the gold dust plant (species) and 'Variegata' describes a particular variety of gold dust plant that has smooth, green leaves with yellow spots. Botanical nomenclature and plant classification are discussed in more detail in this chapter.

Hardiness—This term refers to a plant's ability to survive cold temperatures—the lower the minimum winter temperature a plant can survive, the hardier it is. Generally speaking, a *hardy* plant is one that can survive temperatures below freezing (32F/0C), while a *tender* plant cannot.

Though most trees and shrubs listed in this encyclopedia are hardy, some of them are tender. These plants may tolerate light frosts, but generally grow well only in mild-winter climates such as coastal California and the South. A few are so tender they will survive only in frost-free areas, such as Southern California and the Gulf Coast, but they are such spectacular plants that they deserve to be featured in this book.

Height and Size—The size of a plant is determined by its height and spread at maturity. However, within important plant groups, especially conifers, there are many dwarf varieties that are suitable for small spaces. Also, the size of many trees and shrubs can be controlled by pruning. Soil type, rainfall and other climatic factors can have an influence on size. The sizes given in this encyclopedia are those attained under average growing conditions. Under ideal conditions, trees and shrubs may grow bigger than the sizes given here, and under adverse conditions—poor soil in particular—they may grow smaller.

Flowers of *Abelia* × *grandiflora*.

Growth Rate—General terms such as *fast growing*, *medium-fast growing* and *slow growing* are sometimes used for describing growth rates of trees and shrubs. Trees tend to be fast growing in their juvenile years (the first 3 or 4 years especially) then slow down and spread out. A tree that grows 4 feet or more a year during its juvenile years, such as tulip poplars and paulownias, would be considered fast growing. Trees that grow 2 to 4 feet a year are medium-fast growing, those that grow less than 2 feet a year are slow growing.

A different scale of reference applies to shrubs. Slow-growing shrubs are those that put on less than 1 foot of growth a year—boxwood is considered extremely slow-growing at only 1 inch a year. Medium-fast growing shrubs grow 1 to 2 feet a year, fast-growing shrubs 2 or more feet a year. Vining shrubs capable of growing 6 to 10 feet or more a year—such as trumpet creeper—are considered extra-fast growing.

Variety Recommendations—Some descriptions give specific variety recommendations, with an explanation for why they are considered superior for landscape use. The 'Bradford' form of Callery pear and 'Sargent's Weeping' form of hemlock are examples of trees that are so outstanding that they rate special mention.

It is impossible in a book of this scope to feature every species and variety deemed "garden worthy." The primary criteria used in the following selection is *ornamental value*—plants that are either attractive and useful as *shade* trees or ones that have decorative flowers, leaves or berries. However, you'll find a broad range of trees and shrubs for many landscape uses. The selection represents a cross-section of trees and shrubs suitable to a wide range of climates and soil conditions. In the following listing, symbols identify plants as trees or shrubs:

BOTANICAL NOMENCLATURE

Horticulturists identify plants by their scientific or botanical names. A plant is identified by both its genus and species name, set in italics. Cultivar names within a species are set off in single quotes. The system of identifying and classifying plants by botanical names is called *taxonomy*.

Genus (plural genera)—This term defines a large group of plants that share certain basic characteristics. For example, there are about 450 kinds of oak trees and all belong to the genus *Quercus*.

Species—This describes a distinct type of plant within a genus. For example, *Quercus robur* (English oak) is a species native to Europe, particularly England.

Variety—In the strict botanical sense, the term *variety* denotes a natural variation within a species. For example, the common white dogwood (species) is known botanically as *Cornus florida*, but the pink-flowering dogwood is considered a natural variation identified as *Cornus florida* var. *rubra*.

Cultivar—When a variety has resulted from selection among cultivated plants, then the term *cultivar*—meaning cultivated variety—

is sometimes used instead of the term *variety*. For example, the red-flowering dogwood 'Cherokee Chief'—a selection from the pink variety—is considered a *cultivar* and is written botanically as *Cornus florida* 'Cherokee Chief'. In this and other modern books, the term variety is used to mean both natural varieties and cultivars, although cultivars are readily identified by the name set off in single quotes, as in 'Cherokee Chief' above.

Hybrids—These are plants that result from crossing two distinctly different plants. They can be crosses between plants of different genera *(bigeneric hybrids)*, different species, between a species and a hybrid or between two hybrids. To denote a hybrid, the botanical name includes the symbol "×." For example, × *Cupressocyparis leylandi* denotes a cross between two genera, in this case between *Cupressus macrocarpa* (Monterey cypress) and *Chamaecyparis nootkatensis* (Nootka false cypress). When the × appears in the middle of a name, it denotes a hybrid within the same genera, usually between two species, cultivars or hybrids. For example, *Cytisus* × *praecox* denotes hybrid between two species of *Cytisus*, in this case a hybrid variety of Scotch broom.

Strain—A group of plants, usually within a species, with common lineage.

TREES SHRUBS

ABELIA GRANDIFLORA
Glossy Abelia

Reasonably hardy semi-evergreen flowering shrub hybridized from species native to Asia. Plants grow 3 to 6 feet high and equally wide, creating a spreading, dense rounded habit. The shiny green, oval leaves turn bronze by late summer, making a bold contrast to the pinkish-white, trumpet-shaped flowers that are 3/4 inches wide, held in clusters and persisting all summer.

How to Grow—Plant from containers. Propagated mostly from softwood cuttings. Prefers moist, well-drained, acid soil in full sun or partial shade.

Landscape Use—Excellent flowering hedge. Mass plantings good for erosion control on slopes.

ABIES CONCOLOR
White Fir

Firs consist of about 40 species of evergreen conifers, widely dispersed throughout the Northern Hemisphere, including North America. White fir is native to Colorado and high-elevation areas of California. Conical in habit, it is slow growing to 100 feet and spreads 40 feet. Numerous related species and varieties are popular as landscape plants, including prostrate and pendulous forms. Two widely planted species are Balsam fir *(A. balsamea)*, valued for its fragrant balsam odor, and Fraser fir *(A. fraseri)*, which is popular as a Christmas tree. Douglas fir belongs to a different genus *(Pseudotsuga menziesii)*.

How to Grow—Plant balled-and-burlapped or from bare-root stock. White fir tolerates summer heat and drought but must have some winter chill. Fraser and balsam firs prefer moist, well-drained, acid soil that is rich in humus.

Landscape Use—Lawn highlight, skyline tree and windbreak.

ACACIA LONGIFOLIA
Sydney Golden Wattle

Tender evergreen flowering shade trees native to Australia, popular in frost-free locations such as Florida and California. Trees grow to 25 feet high, spread 25 feet, have graceful willowlike blue-green leaves. Weeping branches erupt into a billowing mass of yellow pompon flowers in early spring. A related species, *A. baileyana*—known as Bailey acacia or Cootamondra Wattle—is very similar in appearance, but with greener, fernlike foliage. Plants are reasonably fast growing, shallow rooted and not long lived.

How to Grow—Plant from containers or balled-and-burlapped.

Propagated mostly from seeds and softwood cuttings taken in summer. Can be pruned after flowering to maintain a compact shape. Prefers sandy, moist soil. Tolerates salt spray. Susceptible to scale pests.

Abies concolor (white fir) growing as a grove.

Acacia longifolia (Sydney golden wattle tree) in flower under glass at Longwood Gardens, Pennsylvania.

Acer palmatum 'Dissectum Atropurpureum' (Japanese threadleaf maple) showing purple summer foliage.

Acer platanoides (Norway maple) in summer.

Landscape Use—Sensational street tree and lawn highlight. In Northern states often grown in tubs under glass for winter flowers.

ACER
Maples

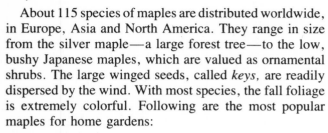

About 115 species of maples are distributed worldwide, in Europe, Asia and North America. They range in size from the silver maple—a large forest tree—to the low, bushy Japanese maples, which are valued as ornamental shrubs. The large winged seeds, called *keys,* are readily dispersed by the wind. With most species, the fall foliage is extremely colorful. Following are the most popular maples for home gardens:

JAPANESE MAPLE *(Acer palmatum* and *A. japonicum)*

Though two species of maple are commonly called Japanese maple, it is *A. palmatum*—also known as cut-leaf maple—that is familiar to most people and more widely planted. *A. japonicum,* also known as full-moon maple, generally has broader, less-indented leaves, and grows slightly higher. Culture is generally the same for both species. The following description applies to *A. palmatum.* The variety 'Senkaki' has red branches, excellent for winter color.

Reasonably hardy deciduous ornamental shrub or small tree native to Japan. Superb landscape plant for many situations. Very graceful foliage and plant habit. Grows to 20 feet, spreads 20 feet or more. Beautiful rounded shape, sharply indented leaves that are usually purple or lime-green in color, depending on the variety, changing to orange in fall. Small, purple, inconspicuous flowers are followed by small, paired winged seeds formed in clusters. Plant is slow growing, shallow rooted, long lived. Numerous varieties are available. 'Dissectum' is a strain known as lace-leaf and thread-leaf maples, for their finely cut, feathery leaves.

How to Grow—Best planted from containers or balled-and-burlapped. Propagated from seeds and from bud grafts. Prefers fertile, acid loam or sandy soil in full sun or filtered light, sheltered from wind.

Landscape Use—Superb lawn highlight. Popular for bonsai and sculptural pruning. Also widely used as container plants for decorating decks and patios.

NORWAY MAPLE *(Acer platanoides)*

Hardy deciduous shade tree native to Europe. Vigorous, pollution resistant, growing 50 to 60 feet high, spreading 35 to 45 feet. Five-lobed, dark green leaves have sharp tips, and change to yellow and orange in fall. Clusters of small, greenish-yellow flowers appear in spring as the leaves start to unfurl and are more conspicuous than those of most other maples. Large bunches

of winged seeds change color from green through pink to brown, dispersing by wind in fall. Billowing, rounded habit, medium-fast growth, shallow rooted, long lived.
How to Grow—Plant balled-and-burlapped or from bare-root stock. Propagated by seeds, which germinate at low soil temperatures (40F/4C). Does well in a wide range of soils, including alkaline soil. Tolerates dry conditions better than most maples. Needs full sun.
Landscape Use—Lawn highlight, street tree, windbreak. Good choice for creating a wooded lot, though it casts such dense shade few plants can grow under its canopy.

RED MAPLE *(Acer rubrum)*

Hardy deciduous shade tree native to eastern North America. Derives its name from the rich, red flowers that appear in early spring even before the leaves unfold. Also called swamp maple because of its natural distribution along stream banks and areas subjected to periodic flooding. Grows 50 to 80 feet high, spreads 40 to 60 feet. Attractive oval or rounded habit. Dark green leaves are typical maple-leaf shape, turning orange or scarlet-red in fall. Dull, red-winged seeds turn brown before dispersal by the wind. Medium-fast growth, fairly deep rooted, long lived.
How to Grow—Plant balled-and-burlapped or from bare-root stock. Propagated from seeds, cuttings and grafts. Prefers fertile, moist, acid soil that is rich in humus, but also thrives in many poor soils. Grows in sun or partial shade.
Landscape Use—Good lawn highlight and windbreak. Superb for lining vistas and driveways. Popular choice for creating a wooded lot. Not highly pollution tolerant.

SILVER MAPLE *(Acer saccharinum)*

Hardy deciduous shade tree native to eastern North America. Flexible branches sway in the wind, flashing the bright, silvery undersides of the otherwise medium-green leaves. Grows 60 to 90 feet, spreads 50 to 80 feet. Upright, oval habit. Small, inconspicuous, greenish-yellow flowers are borne before the leaves unfold in spring. Seeds are winged, but not showy. Fast growth, fairly deeply rooted, long lived.
How to Grow—Plant balled-and-burlapped or from bare-root stock. Propagated mostly from seeds, but also layering and cuttings. Prefers deep, moist, acid soil though it tolerates poor soils. Grows in sun or partial shade.
Landscape Use—Lawn highlight, windbreak. Some experts consider this a "weed tree" because of its greedy roots and ability to self-seed, but it is popular in suburban gardens and admired for its leaves that sway in the slightest breeze, reflecting sunlight off their silvery undersides.

SUGAR MAPLE *(Acer saccharum)*

Hardy deciduous shade tree native to eastern North America. Source of maple syrup, produced by tapping the

Acer rubrum (red maple) showing fall colors.

Acer saccharinum (silver maple) flashes silvery leaves when the wind blows.

Aesculus hippocastanum (European horsechestnut) in full flower.

Ailanthus altissima (tree of heaven) at Paso Robles, California, in 110F heat.

trees for their watery sap during winter months. Grows 70 to 80 feet, spreads 40 to 60 feet. Beautiful rounded or oval habit. Medium-green leaves are typical maple shape, sharply pointed, changing to yellow and orange- red in fall. Greenish-yellow flowers appear in early spring before the leaves unfold, followed by winged seeds. Fairly slow growing, fairly deeply rooted, long lived.

How to Grow—Plant balled-and-burlapped or from bare-root stock. Propagated mostly from seeds, budding and layering. Prefers fertile, moist, acid loam soil in sun or light shade. Leaf scorch is a problem in dry soils.

Landscape Use—Favorite choice for creating a wooded lot. Good lawn highlight and windbreak.

AESCULUS HIPPOCASTANUM
European Horsechestnut

Hardy deciduous flowering shade tree native to Greece and Albania. Grows 60 to 70 feet, spreads 40 to 60 feet. Beautiful upright, rounded habit. Oval, serrated leaflets are arranged in groups of five or six, splayed out like a hand. White flowers appear in spring, borne in long, conical clusters known as *candles,* up to 12 inches long. Red and pink flowering varieties are available. Flowers are followed by spiny, round nut cases that split open to release a single, shiny brown nut in fall. Grows moderately fast, deep rooted, long lived.

How to Grow—Best planted balled-and-burlapped. Propagated from seeds except for named varieties, which are budded or grafted. Thrives in any deep, fertile, moist soil in full sun. Bagworm and borers can be serious pests.

AILANTHUS ALTISSIMA
Tree of Heaven

Hardy deciduous shade tree native to China. Grows 40 to 60 feet high, spreads 30 to 50 feet. Compound dark green leaves resemble those of sumac. Yellowish-green flowers are borne in large clusters, males and females on separate trees. Female flowers are followed by reddish-brown winged seeds borne in clusters, persisting into fall. Rate of growth is very fast—up to 6 feet a year in its juvenile years. Roots run deep.

How to Grow—Plant from containers or from bare-root stock. Propagated from seeds and cuttings taken from female plants, because the odor from male flowers is unpleasant. Plants tolerate a wide range of soils, even poor soil, though they do best in light, moist, sandy soil. Prefers full sun.

Landscape Use—Extremely tolerant of industrial pollution. Widely used as a street tree. Takes heavy pruning. Some experts consider Tree of Heaven a "weed tree" because of its ability to naturalize on vacant city lots and come back even after being cut back to the ground. However, it does have its admirers, and is often planted for fast shade in extremely poor soils.

274

ALBIZIA JULIBRISSIN
Silk Tree

Reasonably hardy deciduous flowering shade tree native to Asia, where more than 100 related species are distributed from Iran to Japan. Also known as mimosa tree. Plants grow to 30 feet high, spread 40 feet, creating an airy canopy of feathery, fernlike leaves made up of small, oval, overlapping leaflets. The pink powderpuff flowers appear in midsummer, followed by long, slender seed pods filled with bean-size seeds.

'Tyron' (light pink) and 'Charlotte' (deep pink) are outstanding disease-resistant varieties.

How to Grow—Plant from containers. Propagated mostly from seeds. Prefers a sandy or loam soil in a sunny, open location. Tolerates drought and pollution.

Landscape Use—Light, airy tree for tropical effect. You can let grass grow right up to trunk. Excellent for shading lawns and patios. Good skyline tree.

Albizia julibrissin (silk tree) showing silky pink flower plumes.

ALSOPHILA COOPERI
Australian Tree Fern

Tender evergreen shade tree native to Australia. Plants grow to 20 feet high, with a slender, fibrous, palmlike trunk and a crown of light green fronds that cascade like a fountain. Similar widely grown species include West Indian tree fern *(Cyathea arborea)*, Hawaiian tree fern *(Cibotium glaucum)* and Tasmanian tree fern *(Dicksonia antarctica)*.

How to Grow—Best planted from containers. Propagated from spores or offsets. Plants need a humid atmosphere and acid, humus-rich soil in sun or light shade.

Landscape Use—Mostly grown in clumps in atriums and courtyards where irrigation is readily available to meet their high moisture requirements. Outdoors it is restricted mostly to coastal California and southern Florida. Popular container plant for conservatories in Northern climates.

AMELANCHIER LAEVIS
Sarvistree

Hardy deciduous flowering tree native to North America from Maine to South Carolina. Also called serviceberry, shadblow and Juneberry, it is among the first trees to flower in early spring, covering itself in snow-white blossoms resembling those of crabapples. These are followed by small, purple, edible fruits. Forms a rounded crown and multiple trunks, but can be pruned to a single trunk. Grows to 30 feet, spreads 20 feet. The oval, pointed leaves turn yellow, orange and red in fall.

How to Grow—Plant from containers or bare-root stock. Propagated from seeds, suckers and grafts. Plants tolerate poor soil and prefer sun or partial shade.

Landscape Use—Good lawn highlight. Looks attractive in mixed-shrub borders. Especially lovely planted as a grove of three or more trees at the edge of a lawn.

Amelanchier laevis (sarvistree) in full flower. Edible fruits resemble blueberries.

Aralia spinosa (devil's walking stick) has tropical-looking foliage.

Araucaria araucana (monkey puzzle tree) towers above a home near San Francisco.

ARALIA SPINOSA
Devil's Walking Stick

Small, hardy deciduous tree native to North America from Pennsylvania to Florida and east to Iowa. Also known as Hercules' club because the trunk and branches are armed with vicious spines. Plants grow 10 to 20 feet high. Leaves have a tropical appearance, growing from multiple slender trunks. Panicles of white flowers cover the topmost branches in summer, followed in fall by purple-black fruit clusters resembling huge bunches of elderberries, which are relished by birds. A taller-growing related species from Japan *(A. alata)* has variegated leaves.

How to Grow—Plant from containers. Mostly propagated from root division. Tolerates a wide variety of soils, even poor and alkaline soil in full sun or partial shade.

Landscape Use—Good background plant, forming an impenetrable thicket of tropical-looking foliage. Many experts consider it a "weed tree" too aggressive for most outdoor situations, but can be effective when confined to an atrium or bordering a patio.

ARAUCARIAS

Three kinds of *Araucarias* are popular in mild-climate areas of North America—mostly Southern California and Florida. They are the bunya-bunya tree, the monkey puzzle tree and Norfolk Island pine. All are tender, evergreen trees.

BUNYA-BUNYA *(A. bidwillii)*

Evergreen conifer native to Australia. Plants are moderately fast growing, with a dense, billowing, pyramidal shape, to 60 feet high, spreading 35 feet. Has upward-curving branches and coarse, dark green, scalelike needles. Produces very large cones (up to 20 pounds).

How to Grow—Plant from containers. Tolerates dry and alkaline soil, making it popular in desert areas. Prefers full sun.

Landscape Use—Good lawn highlight. Excellent windbreak.

MONKEY PUZZLE *(A. araucana)*

Slow-growing, evergreen conifer native to Chile. Plants are pyramidal-shaped in their juvenile stage, maturing into giant trees 60 to 70 feet high with a 30-foot-wide domed canopy. Female trees bear large coconut-size cones. Knifelike, dark green scales point upward so that animals—such as monkeys—can climb up but cannot shinny back down.

How to Grow—Plant from containers. Prefers moist, sandy or loam soil in a sunny location.

Landscape Use—Good lawn specimen. Not for confined spaces. Marvelous skyline silhouette.

NORFOLK ISLAND PINE (A. heterophylla)

Evergreen conifer native to Norfolk Island in the South Pacific. Popular throughout North America as house plants because of their low light tolerance. Popular outdoors in frost-free areas, particularly Southern California and Southern Florida but will take light frosts. Moderately fast growing to 80 feet high, spreading 20 feet. From a distance, mature plants look like slender feathers. Branches sweep upward, coming to a sharp point.

How to Grow—Plant from containers. Plants tolerate a wide range of soil conditions, including sandy and alkaline soil in sun or partial shade.

Landscape Use—Excellent lawn specimen. Popular container tree to decorate patios and atriums. Excellent for coastal gardens. Magnificent skyline silhouette.

ARBUTUS UNEDO
Strawberry Tree

Tender broadleaf evergreen bush capable of becoming a small tree. Native to Europe. Derives its common name from the clusters of strawberrylike fruits that ripen in summer. White flowers are decorative, small and urn-shaped. New growth of green leaves exhibits a reddish cast. Slow growing to 20 feet high, spreading 20 feet. 'Compacta' and 'Elfin King' are good dwarf forms. A related species, *A. menziesii,* (madrone) is native to the Pacific Northwest and California, and is noted for its attractive, peeling red bark.

How to Grow—Plant from containers. Propagated from seeds. Prefers sandy or loam soil in full sun, and regular moisture. Needs lower branch pruning to form an attractive tree. Does best in coastal gardens.

Landscape Use—Attractive lawn highlight. Good for mixed-shrub borders.

AUCUBA JAPONICA
Gold Dust Plant

Hardy slow-growing broadleaf evergreen shrub native to Japan. Derives its common name for the variegated leaves that are flecked with yellow. Grows to 10 feet high, spreads 8 feet, but generally kept shorter by shearing. Different varieties have different variegation but the common 'Variegata' has smooth, shiny green leaves covered with golden spots. 'Picturata' has golden yellow centers and green leaf margins.

How to Grow—Plant from containers. Cuttings root easily taken any time of year. Prefers moist, humus-rich, acid soil in a sheltered, lightly shaded location.

Landscape Use—Popular for foundation plantings, especially in shrub borders combined with rhododendrons and dwarf conifers. Beyond its hardiness range it can be grown indoors in containers.

Araucaria heterophylla (Norfolk Island pine) is a favorite spire-shaped evergreen for frost-free areas.

Arbutus unedo (strawberry tree) showing close-up of ripe, edible fruits, for which it gets its common name.

Aucuba japonica 'Variegata' (gold dust plant) is a hardy evergreen with broad, gold-flecked leaves.

Azalea stewartsonia has evergreen foliage, creates dome of brick-red flowers in spring. It is kept compact by shearing.

AZALEA
Rhododendron Species

At one time azaleas and rhododendrons were thought to belong to different plant genera, but botanists have decided azaleas are really a small-leafed, compact type of rhododendron. There are two basic kinds of azaleas—evergreen and deciduous. The evergreen species are mostly native to Asia, and the deciduous species mostly native to North America.

Azaleas are much more popular as landscape plants than true rhododendrons, chiefly because they are less demanding of cool temperatures and high rainfall. In the South and Southern California it is the evergreen *R. indicum* (Southern Indian azalea) that is most popular because of its large, showy flowers. In the North, the evergreen Kurume azaleas are preferred for their hardiness. Kaempferi hybrids, Gable hybrids and Glen Dale hybrids are other popular evergreen groups.

Hardy deciduous azaleas include the *R. mollis* types, Exbury hybrids and Knap Hill hybrids.

Flowers on evergreen azaleas are mostly star-shaped and come in white and shades of pink, red and purple. Many of the deciduous azaleas have funnel-shaped flowers, like honeysuckle, and the color range includes yellow. Height ranges from 1 foot to 10 feet high depending on variety, but most plants normally are kept pruned to 3 to 6 feet high.

How to Grow—Plant from containers. Propagated mostly from seeds and cuttings. Plants prefer acid, humus-rich soil in light shade. Should be protected from direct sun and drying winds.

The majority of azalea varieties have exacting climate requirements. Native azalea-growing areas include the mid-Atlantic coast, Pacific Northwest, Southern Appalachian Mountains and swampy areas of the South. The best way to choose varieties for your area is to visit a specialist azalea grower or check with your local university or county extension agent. Though no single variety is adaptable to all areas of North America, by careful selection, azaleas can be grown from Canada to southern Florida.

Landscape Use—Undoubtedly the most popular of all flowering shrubs for foundation plantings. Excellent for mass plantings on slopes, in island beds and mixed-shrub borders.

BAMBOO
Arundinaria and Phyllostachys Species

Native mostly to Asia, bamboos comprise a large number of genera, including *Arundinaria, Bambusa, Phyllostachys* and *Sasa*—the four most widely planted groups in North America. They are woody, evergreen members of the grass family, and though dwarf kinds suitable as ground covers are available, bamboos mostly form tall canes topped with willowy leaves. Some are *clump-forming* and stay within bounds. Others are *running,* using vigorous underground rhizomes to spread in all directions.

Most bamboos are tender plants, but a few are sufficiently hardy to withstand temperatures of -20F (-29C) and even lower in sheltered sites.

Arundinaria variegata (dwarf white-stripe bamboo) grows a low mounded clump of striped green and white leaves, 3 to 4 feet high. *Phyllostachys aureosulcata* (yellow groove bamboo) grows to 30 feet high, has beautiful green canes striped golden yellow. Both are hardy, and though tops may be damaged by freezing, they recover quickly.

How to Grow—Transplant from containers. Propagated by division. Bamboos grow in most soils, except heavy clay and waterlogged soil. All need full sun, tolerate high heat and humidity.

Landscape Use—*Arundinaria variegata* makes a fine specimen shrub for tubs and mixed-shrub borders. *Phyllostachys aureosulcata* forms runner-type clumps and is best used as a grove.

Yellow groove bamboo *(Phyllostachys aureosulcata)* is more cold-hardy than most other bamboos and grows up to 30 feet.

BAUHINIA BLAKEANA
Hong Kong Orchid Tree

Species of orchid trees are tender, semi-evergreen flowering trees native to India and China. The Hong Kong variety is a sterile hybrid of unknown parentage. It is undoubtedly the showiest of several kinds popular in frost-free areas, particularly Southern Florida and Southern California. The leaves are highly unusual—two-lobed like a cloven hoof. Plants grow to 30 feet, spread 20 feet, cover themselves with exotic 4-inch reddish-pink flowers in early spring, sometimes even before the leaves are completely unfurled. Other popular kinds include *B. variegata* (common orchid tree) displaying lavender flowers and *B. purpurea* (purple orchid tree) with reddish flowers.

How to Grow—Plant from containers. Propagated by cuttings, the species mostly from seeds. Tolerates a wide range of soils, particularly dry, sandy soil, in full sun or partial shade. Temperatures below 25F (4C) will kill the tree.

Landscape Use—Good lawn highlight and street tree.

In frost-free areas, *Bauhinia blakeana* (Hong Kong orchid tree) flaunts orchidlike flowers in early spring.

Calycanthus floridus (sweet shrub) showing fragrant, rusty red flowers.

CALYCANTHUS FLORIDUS
Sweetshrub

Also known as Carolina allspice, this hardy deciduous shrub is native to North America, from Virginia to Florida. Its best attribute is the delightfully fragrant, dusky, reddish-brown flowers that permeate the air with a strawberrylike scent in May and June. Though the flowers are small (up to 2 inches across) and rather inconspicuous, the fragrance is reason enough to grow it. Stems and branches are also aromatic when bruised or dried. Grows 6 to 9 feet high and up to 9 feet wide. Slow-growing, dense, bushy and rounded—though highly variable in habit and size of flowers. A rare, yellow-flowered form is available, called 'Katherine'.

How to Grow—Plant from containers. Propagated mostly from cuttings rooted in moist sand. Also from seed. Tolerates a wide range of soils, but prefers moist loam, in full sun or partial shade.

Landscape Use—Mostly grown near doorways and outdoor-living areas where the fragrant spring flowers can be best appreciated. Pick the flowers and crush the petals into a bowl for an especially heady fragrance indoors or out.

CAMELLIA JAPONICA
Camellia

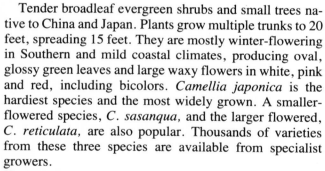

Tender broadleaf evergreen shrubs and small trees native to China and Japan. Plants grow multiple trunks to 20 feet, spreading 15 feet. They are mostly winter-flowering in Southern and mild coastal climates, producing oval, glossy green leaves and large waxy flowers in white, pink and red, including bicolors. *Camellia japonica* is the hardiest species and the most widely grown. A smaller-flowered species, *C. sasanqua,* and the larger flowered, *C. reticulata,* are also popular. Thousands of varieties from these three species are available from specialist growers.

How to Grow—Plant from containers. Propagated by seeds and cuttings, though most commercial varieties are the result of grafting onto 2 year-old rootstocks. Plants prefer a moist, fertile, well-drained humus-rich soil, in a sunny or semi-shady location. *C. japonica* can be grown outdoors as far north as Long Island, in a sheltered location, but frost damages the flowers. In Northern states camellias are best grown under glass where frost-exclusion is all that's necessary to ensure superb flowering. Although plants are cold-hardy to -10F/-24C, camellias are risky outside of relatively frost-free areas because late frosts frequently damage flowers.

Landscape Use—Widely used for foundation plantings in frost-free areas; also to line driveways. Branches are pliable and plants can be trained flat against a wall to create a beautiful evergreen espalier. Good container plant for atriums and courtyards. Oriental gardeners refer to the camellia as "living jade" and feature it extensively in their gardens.

Camellia japonica 'Victor Emmanuel' flowering at Cypress Gardens, Florida.

HIBISCUS SYRIACUS
Rose of Sharon

Hardy deciduous flowering shrubs native to China. Also known as *Althaea* from an earlier botanical name. Produces white, rose-red and violet-blue flowers in late summer, flowering continuously until frost. Grows 8 to 10 feet, spreads 6 to 8 feet. The 4-inch flowers can be double or single, usually with a contrasting 'eye'. 'Blue Bird' is a popular violet-blue variety. 'Red Heart' is an appealing white with a red eye.

Chinese or Hawaiian hibiscus *(Hibiscus rosea-sinensis)* is a popular flowering shrub in frost-free areas of coastal California, Florida, the Gulf Coast and Southwest desert. Upright, spreading shrub that grows 6 to 8 feet, but may reach 10 to 15 feet under ideal conditions. Many varieties available with flowers up to 10 inches across in white and shades of yellow, pink, orange and red. Extensively grown under glass in Northern states.

How to Grow—Plant from containers. Easily grown from seeds that germinate reliably if scarified. Cuttings taken in summer also root readily. Flowers best in moist, humus-rich soil in full sun. Benefits from heavy pruning after flowering.

Landscape Use—Good lawn highlight. Also makes an attractive hedge and windbreak.

HYDRANGEA MACROPHYLLA
Hydrangea

Hardy deciduous flowering shrub native to Japan. Fast growing to 8 feet with an equal spread. Cultivated varieties are grouped into two kinds—*hortensias* and *lacecaps*. The hortensias have mostly globular flowers, up to 10 inches in diameter, in white, pink, red and blue. The lacecaps have flat flower heads that splay out like a fan—a center of small flowers surrounded by larger ones. Though the lacecaps are less spectacular, they have a sophisticated appeal and are especially attractive in lightly shaded locations.

Two other hydrangea species are extremely popular for their late summer flowers—the peegee hydrangea *(H. paniculata* 'Grandiflora') and the oak leaf hydrangea *(H. quercifolia)*. Both are white-flowered with unusually large flower heads. The peegee hydrangea is easily trained into a tree form, pruned of lower side branches.

How to Grow—Plant from containers. Propagated mostly from softwood cuttings easily rooted in moist sand. Prefers acid soil, rich in leaf mold for blue flowers. In neutral and alkaline soil flowers turn pink and red. Likes sun or partial shade. Hardiness depends on variety.

Landscape Use—Foundation plantings, mixed-shrub borders, hedges and containers.

Hibiscus syriacus 'Red Heart' covers itself in beautiful flowers in late summer.

Hydrangea macrophylla planted to form an avenue at Filoli Garden, near San Francisco, California.

Picea pungens glauca (Colorado blue spruce) contrasts beautifully with a background of deciduous white ash trees.

Picea abies (Norway spruce) is a favorite evergreen conifer to plant as a lawn highlight and windbreak.

PICEA
Spruce

More than 40 species of spruce are widely distributed throughout the Northern Hemisphere—many of the best are native to North America. They are hardy evergreen conifers with sharp, short needles and a spirelike habit. The cones of most types are hanging and egg shaped. The Norway spruce and the Colorado spruce are popular as Christmas trees.

COLORADO SPRUCE *(Picea pungens)*

Native to Colorado. Grows to 60 feet, spreads 25 feet. Though the species is dark green, the most popular variety is 'Glauca', which has blue needles. Forms a dense, narrow pyramid with stiff, spreading branches reaching to the ground.

How to Grow—Plant balled-and-burlapped or from bare-root stock. Propagated from seeds and cuttings. Not fussy about soil provided it drains well. Needs full sun. Susceptible to spider mite infestations.

Landscape Use—Lawn highlight, windbreak.

NORWAY SPRUCE *(Picea abies)*

Native to Europe. Grows to 60 feet, spreads 30 feet. Makes a broad, dense, dark green pyramid. The extremely beautiful weeping form, 'Pendula', is prized as a lawn highlight.

How to Grow—Plant balled-and-burlapped, from containers or from bare-root stock. Not fussy about soil, provided drainage is good. Needs full sun.

Landscape Use—Excellent windbreak. Good for lining driveways.

WHITE SPRUCE *(Picea glauca)*

Native to Canada and Alaska. Grows to 60 feet, spreads 20 feet. Dense, spirelike habit and dark green leaves. A particularly fine form is the variety 'Conica', known as dwarf Alberta spruce. It is extremely slow growing—just 2 to 4 inches a year—quickly becoming the most widely planted of dwarf conifers for foundations. Popular for its extremely dense, symmetrical cone-shaped outline.

How to Grow—Plant balled-and-burlapped. Propagated from seeds and cuttings. Not fussy about soil. Needs full sun. Susceptible to spider mites.

Landscape Use—The species makes a good windbreak and a decent lawn highlight. 'Conica'—dwarf Alberta spruce—is excellent for rock gardens, dry walls, foundations and entryways.

THUJA OCCIDENTALIS
American Arborvitae

Hardy evergreen conifer native to North America from Canada to North Carolina. Though numerous dwarf and mutant forms have been introduced into cultivation, the species is fairly fast growing to 60 feet, spreading 15 feet, with a dense, upright spire-shaped habit. Scaly leaves resemble those of cedars—soft to touch and splayed out like a fan. Related species include the Western arborvitae (*T. plicata*)—widely planted in the Pacific Northwest—and the Oriental arborvitae (*T. orientalis*), which is mostly used in the southeastern and western states.

How to Grow—Plant balled-and-burlapped. Propagated mostly from cuttings taken in early spring. Tolerates a wide range of soils, including moist soil and alkaline soil, but needs good fertility to maintain an attractive, dense column. Susceptible to infestations of bagworms.

Landscape Use—Excellent tall hedge or screen. Also makes a good backdrop for flower beds and perennial borders. Good windbreak tree. Also popular for foundation plantings and as a matched pair at entryways.

Tilia americana (American linden) presents a towering outline over a spacious lawn.

TILIA CORDATA
Littleleaf Linden

Hardy deciduous shade tree native to Europe. Plants grow to 60 feet, spread 30 feet, have an attractive, rounded pyramidal habit. Leaves resemble those of poplars—heart-shaped, serrated and dark green in summer, changing to buttercup-yellow in fall. 'Greenspire' is a particularly fine form, developing a strong leader and distinctive pear shape. A native American species, the American linden (*T. americana*) does not have such good fall color.

How to Grow—Plant balled-and-burlapped. Propagated from seeds and budding onto seedling understocks. Prefers deep, moist, fertile loam soil in sun or partial shade.

Landscape Use—Good lawn highlight. Also widely planted as a street tree and to line driveways, though plants are susceptible to damage from de-icing salts.

TRACHELOSPERMUM JASMINOIDES
Confederate Jasmine

Tender evergreen flowering vine native to China. Also called star jasmine. Popular throughout the South and Southern California. Plants grow to 15 feet, spread 15 feet. Numerous fragrant, white flowers cover the vine in summer.

How to Grow—Plant from containers. Propagated from softwood cuttings taken in summer. Plants prefer moist, humus-rich, acid soil in full sun or partial shade. Takes heavy pruning to keep it within bounds.

Landscape Use—Mostly used to cover a trellis, wall or fence. Also planted where its pleasant fragrance can be enjoyed.

Trachelospermum jasminoides (star jasmine) is a fast-growing vine for covering arbors and trellises. Flowers are fragrant.

Tsuga canadensis 'Pendula' (Sargent's weeping hemlock) is considered among the finest of all weeping evergreen trees.

Ulmus parvifolia (Chinese elm) has leaves that grow directly from the trunk and main branches, giving the appearance of a tree covered with epiphytic ferns.

TSUGA
Hemlock

Hardy evergreen conifers native to North America and Asia. The most popular species is the Canadian hemlock *(T. canadensis)*, which grows slowly to 75 feet, spreading 35 feet. Pyramidal habit, with sweeping branches that touch the ground. Needles are small, medium green.

Sargent's weeping hemlock is a particularly fine weeping variety. Habit is wide-spreading and billowing, resembling a green waterfall. Exquisite when planted beside a lake and as a lawn highlight.

How to Grow—Widely planted from bare-root stock for hedges and windbreaks; otherwise planted balled-and-burlapped. Propagated from seeds and by layering. Prefers moist, well-drained, acid soil in sun or partial shade.

Landscape Use—Good lawn highlight, but most often used as a windbreak and formal hedge. At the Ladew Topiary Gardens, near Monkton, Maryland, some particularly fine hemlock hedges can be seen, their tops artistically sheared to create waves with topiary swans swimming along.

ULMUS
Elms

Hardy deciduous shade trees native to North America, Europe and Asia. The American elm *(U. americana)* was at one time a widely planted street tree, but as a result of the accidental introduction of Dutch elm disease from Europe, it is considered too risky to establish any new American elms for decorative value. Plant breeders at the U.S. National Arboretum, in Washington, D.C., recently announced the introduction of three new elm varieties that are highly resistant to this disease, each from a different genetic background. One of them, 'Dynasty', is a variety of Chinese elm *(U. parvifolia)* with an upright, fast-growing, rounded habit. The second, 'Pioneer', has Scotch elm *(U. glabra)* in its parentage and makes a spreading, globe-shaped shade tree. The third of the group, 'Homestead', has Siberian elm *(U. pumila)* in its background and develops a pyramidal crown and strong, stout central trunk.

Of the many species available to home gardeners, perhaps the most desirable substitute for American elm is the Chinese elm. It is an upright, spreading tree that grows to 50 feet and spreads 50 feet. It is often confused with Siberian elm, which is not as desirable for landscape use. Scotch elm *(U. glabra)* includes a beautiful weeping form known as the 'Camperdown' elm, valued as a lawn highlight. All elms have oval, pointed, serrated leaves with prominent leaf veins.

How to Grow—Plant balled-and-burlapped or from bare-root stock. Propagated from seeds and cuttings. Elms are not fussy about soil but prefer deep, moist loam.

Landscape Use—Chinese elm and the new National Arboretum varieties make good street trees and wooded lots.

VIBURNUM
Viburnum

Native to North America, Europe and Asia, there are more than 200 species of viburnum worldwide. They are broadly divided into deciduous and evergreen kinds. Plants grow bushy, with beautiful white flowers followed in most cases by ornamental berries. Here is a sampling of the best kinds:

BLACKHAW VIBURNUM *(V. prunifolium)*

Deciduous North American species distributed from New England south to Florida and Texas. It has many small, flattened, creamy white flower clusters in early spring. The most vigorous, durable and earliest-flowering of viburnums. Grows to 12 feet, spreads 12 feet, but usually kept 5 to 6 feet by pruning.

CHINESE SNOWBALL *(V. macrocephalum)*

Deciduous Chinese species with dense, upright habit. Grows to 15 feet, spreads 10 feet. The most spectacular of all viburnums because the size and quality of the flowers. Individual flowers are completely round, up to 8 inches across, and can completely cover the plant in spring. Does not produce berries because flowers are sterile.

DOUBLEFILE VIBURNUM
(V. plicatum 'Tomentosum'*)*

Deciduous Chinese species. Flower clusters are white, up to 4 inches across, resembling those of lacecap hydrangeas, and crowd the long, sweeping branches that appear to be arranged in tiers. Flowering in spring, these are followed by decorative, bright red fruits that are eagerly devoured by birds. Grows to 10 feet, spreads 12 feet. 'Shasta'—a recent introduction from the U.S. National Arboretum—has flower clusters up to 6 inches across.

KOREAN SPICE VIBURNUM *(V. carlesii)*

Deciduous Korean species. Rounded flower clusters are up to 3 inches across, extremely fragrant, white tinged with pink, appearing in spring. Grows 6 to 8 feet, spreads to 8 feet. Dense habit and upright, spreading branches.

LEATHERLEAF VIBURNUM
(V. rhytidophyllum)

Evergreen Chinese species. The shiny, dark green leaves are leathery and lance-shaped. They add a distinctive contrast and unusual texture to foundation plantings and mixed-shrub borders. Decorative, creamy white, flat flower clusters up to 4 inches across appear in spring, followed by blue-black ornamental berries. Upright, rounded, open habit. Grows to 15 feet, spreads 15 feet.

Viburnum macrocephalum (Chinese snowball bush) produces the largest flowers of any viburnum.

Viburnum tomentosum (doublefile viburnum) radiates long, sweeping branches crowded with lovely, flat flower clusters.

ROSES

The rose is by far the most popular flower in the world, and for good reasons. Some form of rose grows everywhere except for the most frigid and most tropical regions. There is a size and form of rose for virtually any size and kind of garden. Use them individually as specimen plants or massed as bedding plants. Most important, roses unquestionably belong among the most obliging and most responsive garden plants. They involve and then reward gardeners.

The intention of this chapter is to introduce you to a wide choice of roses then briefly explore the basics of care.

KINDS OF ROSES

There are seven important categories of roses: hybrid tea, grandiflora, floribunda, miniature, climber, shrub and antique roses. But keep in mind that these categories, particularly of the hybrids, were invented for the convenience of gardeners. They overlap in many instances—a hybrid tea can look more like a floribunda, or just the reverse.

Hybrid Tea—Roses of this group most nearly match the modern idea of what a rose should be. Flowers may range impressively from soft to brilliant colors. Some are very fragrant, others are scentless. Flowers are usually borne one to a long stem—perfect for cutting—and they come in waves all season. The first wave is in spring, then, conditions granting, every 6 weeks until fall.

Plant a hybrid tea if you have room for only one rose—or plant gardens of hybrid teas if you want to fill buckets with long-stemmed, perfect flowers.

These plants that produce such a prodigious display of intense flowers are vigorous beyond the usual understanding of the word. But for all their vigor, they are susceptible to pests and diseases—primarily aphids, spider mites, thrips, black spot, mildew and rust. Luckily, there are convenient and effective solutions available.

Grandiflora—This category was created in 1949 for a very special rose. It was vigorous and prolific like a floribunda, but produced beautiful flowers like a hybrid tea.

The first grandiflora variety was named 'Queen Elizabeth', in honor of the Queen of England, and to this day remains the standard of all grandiflora roses.

Use grandiflora roses as profusely flowering background shrubs, or if pruned somewhat more severely, as you would any hybrid tea.

Floribunda—Floribundas are better understood as low-growing, low-maintenance, flowering shrubs than as a "rose." You might hear them described as "the modern landscape rose." This is not to suggest that none have beautifully formed, colored and scented flowers. Some do.

Floribundas usually grow in the 3- to 4-foot range. The plants are more branched and more shrubby looking than hybrid teas. Flowers usually come in clusters of five to seven, are a little more flat and often have fewer petals than a hybrid tea or grandiflora. On the other hand, these roses flower steadily throughout the season, so bushes are virtually never out of bloom.

Plant floribundas for low borders, hedges and area dividers. Several vari-

Grandiflora 'Gold Medal'.

Floribunda 'Intrigue'.

Hybrid tea 'Dainty Bess' is beautiful example of single flower form.

eties are useful for cut flowers. Check descriptions that come with the plant or choose plants in flower. Plants are somewhat more hardy and pest resistant than hybrid teas or grandifloras.

Miniature Roses—A typical miniature rose plant is about 6 inches tall. Some are a little shorter, some are taller. The larger miniature roses are often referred to as *patio roses*. Flowers are abundant and identical to the familiar rose form in every way except size. Most miniatures are somewhat less fragrant than the larger roses.

Miniature roses are as versatile as they are variable. They make excellent edging plants, especially in front of a bed of larger roses. Or use them massed in beds. They also make excellent container plants, even indoors. If you want to grow miniature roses indoors, give them a bright windowsill or fluorescent light and they will grow and flower easily.

Species Roses—These are the natural, unhybridized roses. A typical example is *Rosa banksia,* one of the best-known and most-planted roses. It is a thornless, vining, climbing rose. Another is *Rosa rugosa,* a favorite of many herb gardeners for its excellent hips. Species roses always have single (five-petal) flowers that appear once each season in spring. They also reproduce true from seed.

Antique Roses—This huge group includes primarily the popular hybrids of previous generations—in other words,

they are the "modern" roses of yesterday.

There are two main groups of antique roses—the *Europeans* and the *Chinas.* The *cabbage* or *provence* roses and the *damask* roses are the fundamental European kinds. The *China* rose and the *tea* rose are the China types. These roses and their early hybrids are the classic old roses. The modern hybrid teas were developed from the tea roses.

Climbing Roses—The four main groups of climbing roses are *large-flowered climbers, climbing sports, ramblers* and *Kordessii climbers.*

Large-flowered climbers develop stout, 8- to 15-foot canes. Flowers are 2 to 6 inches in diameter and usually clustered. They usually bloom in spring. Unlike the climbing sports described at right, large-flowered climbers will produce flowers from vertically trained canes. Some offer varying degrees of repeat bloom throughout the season—check individual plant descriptions at the nursery. Large-flowered climbers are hardy to about 0F (-18 C).

You may occasionally hear the term *pillar roses.* These are actually large-flowered climbers that don't quite reach the proportions typical of a climber. About 8 to 10 feet is a standard height for pillar roses. They are important because they can be trained vertically, such as on a pillar, and still produce flowers.

Roses known as *climbing sports* are naturally occurring, extra-vigorous

Miniature roses grow well in containers. Left: 'Mary Marshall'; right 'Peaches 'n' Cream'.

mutations of bush roses. They are usually discovered in a field of a few thousand bush roses, all of the same type. The grower notices a bush that is typical except for one branch that keeps growing to a length well beyond the others. A climbing sport is the result of a bud taken from that extra-long branch and grafted to its own rootstock. Most popular bush roses are available in climbing-sport forms.

It is important to understand flowering habits of climbing sports. Unlike the large-flowered climbers, climbing sports usually develop flower-bearing spurs where a branch curves over. Once the canes reach near their full length, you need to arch and tie them over. They are well adapted to training along a post-and-rail fence or over an arbor. Trained up, pillarlike, their performance will likely disappoint you.

Climbing sports are cold hardy to about 20F (-7C). Where temperatures regularly drop below that, untie and low-er the canes to the ground. Then cover them with soil to protect them.

Ramblers develop long, soft, pendulous canes that will trail along the ground, climb up into and throughout a tree, or over a house. They're great for an informal cottage-garden look but not for smaller, more tailored gardens. Flowers come in spring, only on 2-year-old canes. Any canes older than that can always be removed. The best time to remove old canes is late spring, after flowering. Ramblers are hardy to -10F (-23C) and need only soil mounded over their crown to survive lower temperatures—mulches are not required to protect the plant.

Kordessii climbers are recent rose innovations, taking their class name from hybridizer Wilhelm Kordes. Compared to most climbers, they are of moderate size, have low maintenance requirements and are extremely hardy—to about -30F (-34 C). Several colors are available.

HOW TO BUY A ROSE

The best way to buy a rose is from a reputable nursery. A good nursery provides the highest quality plants of the finest varieties.

One of the most practical, up-to-date rose references is *The Handbook for Selecting Roses,* published each year by the American Rose Society, Box 30,000, Shreveport, LA 71130. Cost is 25 cents. The handbook lists all the available roses and their ratings.

ARS Ratings—The members of the American Rose Society (ARS) pool their rose-growing experience to rate most available roses. Roses are rated on a scale of 1 to 10, where 10 is an ideal specimen of its type. Ratings from society members throughout the country are averaged and the result is that rose's rating.

Local Rose Societies—Local rose groups are often the best source of advice about which rose variety to buy. Unlike the ARS ratings, the experience

Climbing rose 'Royal Sunset'.

Rambler roses have long, soft canes that trail along ground, or climb into and through trees, like the variety 'Evangeline' does here.

Well-planned rose garden allows plenty of room for roses to grow.

of local rosarians is not diluted by experiences of other growers in different climates. In short, they know which roses grow best where you live. You can find your local rose society by writing to the national coordinating office of the ARS at the address given above.

PLANTING ROSES

Roses will tolerate a wide range of soil and climatic conditions—they are tougher plants than you might expect. But to grow at their best, roses prefer full sun, good air circulation and fertile, well-draining soil.

Fill the planting hole with water before setting the rose in place. If a pool of water remains after 1 hour, bore through the bottom of the hole with a water jet or post-hole digger. Most of the time you will break through to a draining layer of soil. If you don't, and you need to plant at that location, build a raised bed at least 12 inches high.

Competing tree and shrub roots can sometimes be a problem. Root competition doesn't spell death for a rose, but it does guarantee less than optimum performance. It is possible to remove roots of nearby plants before planting, only to have them re-invade the area after a season or two. An underground barrier around plants will prevent this. Or, every few years, temporarily remove the roses during the dormant season and dig out competing roots.

Either clay soils or sandy soils are suitable, but both benefit from the addition of organic matter. Add organic matter approximately 1/3 by volume to original soil. Soil pH should be near neutral (7.0).

When to Plant—Dormant bare-root plants become available at nurseries at appropriate planting times for your area. Mail-order nurseries usually make shipments at the correct planting times for your region.

You can plant container-grown roses throughout the growing season. Beginning rose growers are encouraged to buy container-grown roses so they can see exactly what the flowers look like.

Spacing—The idea is to situate each bush far enough from its neighbor so that roots and tops have room to grow to their natural sizes. This also allows room for you to prune, spray, cut flowers and so forth.

Hybrid teas, floribundas and grandifloras—the modern bush roses—are usually positioned 3 to 4 feet apart. Old roses have a wider spread, so they need to be spaced as much 6 feet apart. But keep in mind these are guidelines for you to apply to your own situation. You can control the size of a mature rose to some extent by pruning.

Transplanting Roses—Roses can always be transplanted without difficulty. The best time is from late winter to very early spring while the plant is still dormant. First, make the plants easier to handle by pruning them back to their basic framework of three to six canes, each about 1 to 2 feet long. Carefully slice through roots with your shovel until the plant is largely free, then begin to lift. Once the plant is free, wash away clinging soil and trim away damaged or tangled roots. Replant as soon as possible, or pack in moist sawdust and store in a cool, shaded location.

HOW TO GROW ROSES

Deep, thorough watering is the first prerequisite of healthy roses. Because watering is so essential, it pays to take pains setting up the right kind of program from the beginning.

The basic rule is plenty of deep soaking, preferably without wetting the leaves. The frequency depends on your climate and weather, but a weekly watering is the general rule in most areas. Any convenient watering method is fine.

Drip systems are almost ideal because they deliver water to each rose at a rate the soil can absorb. Drip systems are most water-efficient, so they are the obvious choice in regions where water is especially precious. Where water is particularly high in salts, drip systems are beneficial because the salt in the water continually moves to the fringes of the wetted soil, away from the root system.

A hose-end bubbler is effective but can be a lot of work if you have several roses, or if the roses aren't near the hose. Keep in mind that water can come from a hose faster than the soil can absorb it, so make a good-size basin around each rose and fill each basin more than once each time you water.

Sprinklers do contribute to the spread of some rose diseases, but they have advantages too. Wetting leaves tends to keep the plants cleaner and so discourages spider mites. But if you plan to water roses with sprinklers, make an effort to water early in the morning so the plants have plenty of time to dry before evening. Also be prepared to conduct a regular spray program for pests and diseases, which is a good idea anyway.

Mulch—A layer of organic mulch, such as wood chips, compost or peat moss, encourages root growth, conserves water, and discourages weeds.

Make mulching an every-season practice, applying it around the first of June—or as soon as soil is fully warmed in your area. Remove mulch in fall to eliminate overwintering pests and diseases such as blackspot fungus and spider mites.

Feeding—Roses need regular and plentiful fertilizer to grow best. There are several fertilizers that will serve the need.

To begin with, you can rely on one of the several fertilizer products available at your nursery. Most are moderate to low in nitrogen (N), with slightly less phosphorus (P), and potassium (K). An example is a fertilizer such as 12-10-8. Many of these will also include various amounts of other essential nutrients, such as sulfur and iron. Equally important, fertilizers formulated especially for roses include helpful, specific directions on the package label.

PRUNING ROSES

There are basic principles you can apply when pruning any rose. The overall idea is to encourage new growth.

After some roses are several years old, new basal growth virtually stops. New canes are produced high on a few older canes instead of arising from below ground. Prune away old canes just beyond where new canes start.

Remove dead canes all the way to the base of the plant. Dead canes are brown and shriveled inside and out. Removing dead canes is the first step in pruning any rose. Use a saw if necessary.

Remove portions of frost-damaged canes after buds begin to swell. Winter-damaged wood can be determined by cutting through a cane. Healthy wood is white all the way through. Any brown discoloration indicates frost damage. Frost-damaged portions of canes should be removed.

Remove weak, thin, spindly growth that crowds the bush's center. Prune to spread branches out, opening the center. Remove crowding stems and twigs back to their point of origin. Never leave stubs. Where two branches cross, remove the one *below* the crossing point to prevent rubbing.

Suckers—vigorous shoots that grow from the rootstock below bud unions—should be removed. They are usually easy to identify—their color and character is different from the rest of the bush. Continued growth of suckers weakens preferred rose varieties.

Always cut at an angle about 1/4 inch above an outward-facing bud, as shown in the drawing on the next page. There is a bud at every leaf. The angle of the cut should slope away from the bud. A cut made at this point heals rapidly and water drains away from the bud. Stubs, a point of disease and pest entry, will not develop if you cut close to the bud.

When to Prune—The most important time to prune roses is in early spring, just before the first burst of growth. Roses are also pruned in fall, less hard than in spring, to thin and prepare them for the rigors of winter. Where winters are colder than 0F (-18C) roses are lightly pruned in fall, just enough so they can be wrapped or covered. Finally, roses are pruned all summer, with every flower you cut, or every wayward branch you remove.

Bark mulch keeps weeds down, looks neat and retains soil moisture.

Drip emitter is near ideal way to water roses.

Best fertilizers are those especially formulated for roses. Granular type shown here is easy to apply.

PRUNING ROSES

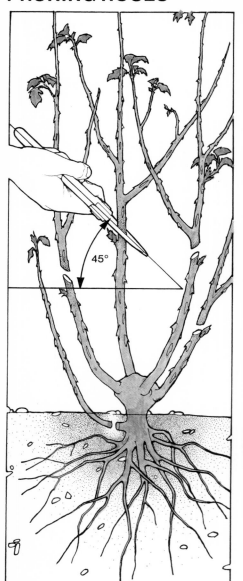

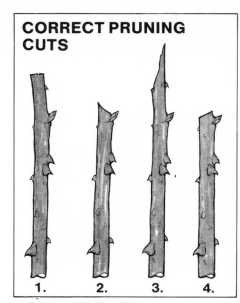

Left: Prune hybrid tea roses during the dormant season. Cut back vigorous canes to about half their length, but so they are all about the same height. Make cuts at a 45° angle about 1/4 inch above a bud. Remove suckers and any dead or crowded branches. Right: New growth from buds below pruning cuts will flower the following spring.

RECOMMENDED PLANTING AND PRUNING TIMES

Region	Planting and Pruning*
Pacific Northwest	February and March
Pacific Coast	January and February
Southwest	Late December into January
South Central	Late January into February
Mid South	February and March
Subtropical	December and January
North Central	April and May
Atlantic Coast	March and April
Northeast	April and May

*Heavy pruning is best done before buds open in spring. Most roses can be lightly pruned anytime. Dead-head faded flowers to encourage additional blooms.

How to Prune—Exactly how to begin varies with the situation you're facing, but the following instructions apply if you have an old, overgrown, tangled hybrid tea or grandiflora bush with lots of deadwood and, of course, wicked thorns.

Start with heavy gloves and a small folding saw to cut away the oldest, thickest canes as close to the ground as you can manage. These canes are usually brown and wrinkled. You will probably have to use loppers or strong pruning shears to reduce upper portions of these canes into smaller pieces that can be untangled. Canes you choose to keep should be the youngest, and they should be evenly arranged around the bush. As a rule, three to five canes are left to form the structural framework of the bush.

Damage from frost or pests causes a brown staining inside the canes. Cut away a little at a time until canes are a healthy white clear through.

Next, begin to thin and shape the remaining upper growth until the bush is as symmetrical as you can make it and roughly vase-shaped. To do this, remove branches pointing toward the center of the bush, along with most of the thinnest, twiggiest growth.

As mentioned, make pruning cuts at an angle just above an eye or bud. That way no stub remains to die back, ultimately into the main cane. Choose where to make cuts largely on the location of a bud headed the direction you want growth to take.

PESTS AND DISEASES

The first rule of pest protection is to water, feed and prune so that your plants are healthy. Insect pests are inevitable, and healthy plants are least set back by attacks and best able to recover.

292

Secondly, make a habit of frequent and close inspections of your plants. If you are a serious enthusiast, this hardly needs mentioning—you do it anyway. If your approach is more on the practical side—"I'll do what I have to do"—the habit will pay off. You will discover diseases and pest infestations sooner, while they are more susceptible to control measures.

Here is a listing of the major rose pests and diseases, and what to do about them:

Aphids—Common in spring, aphids are usually the first pest of the season to attack roses. You'll find them clustered on the tips of soft, new growth. First try a soap-type insecticide. Or use one of the granular systemics—often combined with a fertilizer—that you cultivate into the soil at the plant's base.

Spider Mites—These dot-size spiders thrive during hot weather. Their colonies first develop on the undersides of leaves. You can spot them with a magnifying glass. While the plants are dormant, use dormant sprays of horticultural oils and liquid lime-sulfur. That treatment destroys overwintering eggs, the main source of summer's mite problems. During the growing season, use the miticides that contain kelthane or plictran.

Thrips—These tiny insects live inside flowers, especially white ones, and chew on petals. Orthene is presently the most effective pesticide. Use it morning or evening, spraying flowers only. A fine mist of spray is most effective.

Powdery Mildew—Warm days followed by cool nights almost guarantee this mildew on rose leaves. A small amount of water, from dew for instance, is all that's needed to get it started. Powdery mildew is common in spring and fall. It won't kill the bush, but will ruin leaves, reducing the number of flowers produced. Water early in the morning so leaves can dry thoroughly before the cool part of the day. Various fungicides are useful for mildew control. Funginex is a widely available brand that also controls other important rose diseases. Actidione PM, benomyl, and Parnon are other recommended mildew-control fungicides.

Blackspot—Round, black spots appear on lower leaves first. The disease occurs in almost every climate, but is most common and most destructive in areas with frequent summer rains and high humidity. Here, regular spraying every 7 to 10 days is recommended. Use fungicides containing triforine, benomyl, folpet or maneb.

Rust—Rustlike spots on leaf undersides are sure signs of this disease. Rust is common to cool climates. Use Plantvax or fungicides containing triforine or zineb.

WINTER PROTECTION

Most roses will require protection to survive winters with temperatures below 0F (-18C). Soil heaped over the bud unions and crowns of bush roses is generally adequate. For more protection, various kinds of plastic, Styrofoam, paper or cardboard cones are available to set over pruned shrubs before covering with soil. Wait until after the early frosts but just before hard freezes—before Thanksgiving in most areas.

Unfasten canes of climbing roses from their trellis and pin to the ground with stakes or wire pins before covering with 4 inches of soil. Uncover them in spring only after the possibility of spring frosts is past.

Protect tree roses by severing roots on one side of the bush, laying it over, then covering it with soil. This protection method is called *heeling-in*.

CUT ROSES

Here are some tips for making cut roses last longer:
- Cut between 3 p.m. and 5 p.m. Leaves and flowers have most abundant food supply at this time.
- Use a sharp knife or scissors-type pruning shears to avoid mashing stems.
- Cut while still in the bud stage. Varieties with few petals should be cut "tight," even before green sepals unfold. Varieties with 40 or more petals should be cut after a few petals have unfolded.
- Immerse cut roses up to their necks in warm water for 20 minutes, as shown in photo below. This straightens necks and helps revive wilted roses. Then move to cool, dark place for 1 to 2 hours. Before arranging, wash leaves and stems in warm, soapy water, then trim about 1 inch off stem. Cut stems underwater, if possible.
- Every day or two, change water and cut stems back about 1/2 inch. Make slanting cuts with sharp knife or shears.
- Keep arrangement in cool spot at night.

Preservatives are available that make cut flowers last longer. Check with local florist shops.

293

The floribunda 'Simplicity' in three stages of bloom

BUDS AND FLOWERS

The American Rose Society has established groups of basic bud and flower shapes.

Technically, according to the ARS, a *bud* is "in full color and not more than one-fourth to one-third open." It becomes a *bloom* upon opening more than half-way.

BUDS MAY BE:

Slender or tapered—These gradually expand from the base to the center, then taper toward the top at about the same degree as toward the base. 'Blue Moon' is an example.

Pointed—More fully expanded at the base, the bud tapers to a distinct point at the top. 'Charlotte Armstrong' is an example.

Ovoid—Sometimes called *egg-shaped,* this bud has a full base that narrows to a basically rounded end. 'Peace' is an example.

Urn-shaped—The bud is rounded at the base, narrows near the top, then widens at the top. 'Pink Parfait' has this type bud.

Rounded—Also called *globular,* these are simply round. The lower half forms an almost perfect semi-circle. An example is 'Red Devil'.

FLOWERS MAY BE:

Pointed and high centered—This is the classic rose flower shape. It attracts the most attention and affection. 'Century Two' and 'Christian Dior' are good examples.

Globular and globular high centered—The shape of this flower is nearly round, particularly toward the base. Examples are 'Queen Elizabeth' or 'Peace'.

Cupped—The outer shape of the bloom is like a cup in profile. 'Gypsy' has this shape flower.

Flat or thin—This flower is not deep. Petals extend at nearly right angles from the flower base. 'Sterling Silver' is an example.

Camellia-like or imbricated—This form is characteristic only of fully open blooms. The petals are successively bent back over each other like a camellia.

Informal or cactus—The petals of such flowers are not uniform, giving the flower an irregular outline. Some of the older species roses have this type flower.

FLOWERS

All wild roses and some modern ones bear flowers that have only five petals. This is the rose's natural complement of petals and so it is called *single.* Roses that have as many as 15 petals are called *semidouble.* If more than 15, the flowers are called *fully double.* Rose books sound absolute: "35 to 40 petals: Fully double." But again, "It depends." Weather is the main influence. When temperatures are cool, buds grow for a long time before opening. Flowers then will have more than the average number of petals. During the hottest days of summer, buds grow fast and water and nutrients may be in short supply. Flowers then will frequently have fewer and perhaps many fewer petals than average. Conversely, cool weather often makes problems for many petaled flowers. Roses with 55 to 60 petals may clump-up or "ball" instead of opening properly. If your area frequently has cool and damp weather, such as along a coast, flowers with 50 or fewer petals will perform better.

Substance is the amount of moisture and starch in the petals. It is the quantity and quality of matter in the petals. It determines texture, crispness, firmness, thickness and toughness. Good substance improves the stability and durability of form and the keeping quality of the rose. Red roses with good substance appear velvety; pastels appear opalescent. Yellows and whites have a sparkle and sheen.

Remontant flowering is a term that means continual flowering, a quality much desired by hybridizers. All modern hybrid teas, grandifloras, floribundas and miniatures are remontant to greater and lesser degrees. Remontant roses produce a flower at the end of almost every new shoot.

Some climbers and most of the wild and old roses do not flower at shoot tips. They make flowers on laterals that develop from new shoots, and have only one blooming period a year, usually in spring.

ROSES BY MAIL

Mail order is often the only source of some hard-to-find roses. Many of the following nurseries are specialists. Their catalogs are in themselves an education. Telephone numbers are listed if the nursery takes calls.

Jackson & Perkins Co.
83A Rose Lane
Medford, OR 97501
(503) 776-2121
Largest rose grower in the world, more than 16 million roses growing at any one time. Official AARS demonstration garden open to public. Free, 32-page color catalog primarily lists roses, but also includes bulbs, vegetables, perennials, berries and dwarf fruit trees.

Kelly Bros. Nurseries, Inc.
650 Maple St.
Dansville, NY 14437
(716) 335-2211
Free, 70-page color catalog offers a wide range of nursery stock, including complete listings of miniatures, hybrid teas, floribundas and grandifloras.

McDaniel's Miniature Roses
7523 Zemco St.
Lemon Grove, CA 92045
(619) 469-4669
Free listing of many varieties of miniature roses includes cultural information. Plants shipped air mail year-round. Many unusual varieties can be supplied—write with your requests.

Miniature Plant Kingdom
Don and Becky Herzog
4125 Harrison Grade Road
Sebastopol, CA 95472
(707) 874-2233
Catalog $1 (refundable). Over 700 varieties. Open 9 a.m. to 4 p.m. Thursday through Sunday; Monday and Tuesday by appointment.

Mini-Roses
Ernest D. Williams
Box 4255, Station A
Dallas, TX 75208
Free, 16-page catalog; spring mailer sent May 1 announces new varieties. "Foremost breeder of hybrid tea form miniature roses."

Nor'East Miniature Roses, Inc.
Harm, Chip and John Saville
58 Hammond St.
Rowley, MA 01969
(617) 948-2408
also
Nor'East Miniature Roses, Inc.
P.O. Box 473
Ontario, CA 91762
(714) 988-7222
Beautiful, 18-page color catalog of many unusual varieties, including most Award of Excellence miniature roses. Official AARS demonstration garden.

Pixie Treasures
4121 Prospect Ave.
Yorba Linda, CA 92686
(714) 993-6780
Descriptive 15-page catalog ($1, refundable on first order) includes 200 of the "finest and latest varieties" of miniature roses. Company is family owned and operated. Plants are guaranteed healthy on arrival.

Rosehill Farm
Gregg Neck Road, Box 406
Galena, MD 21635
(301) 648-5538
Free color catalog features only miniature roses. Shipped year-round with 60-day guarantee. Retail and wholesale. Mastercard and Visa accepted.

Roses by Fred Edmunds, Inc.
6235 S. W. Kahle Road
Wilsonville, OR 97070
Color 32-page catalog free upon request. Many types and varieties of roses, including some of foreign introduction. All are guaranteed.

Roses of Yesterday and Today
(formerly Tillotson's Roses)
802 Brown Valley Road
Watsonville, CA 95076
(408) 724-3537
Informative 70-page catalog costs $2. Specialty is old, rare and unusual roses, many of historical importance. Also many new, hardy shrub roses. Visa and Mastercard accepted.

Sequoia Nursery
Moore Miniature Roses
2519 E. Noble
Visalia, CA 93277
Free color catalog in spring and fall features varieties hybridized by Ralph Moore. Wholesale and retail mail orders accepted. Many novelty miniatures, bush varieties, hanging baskets and miniature tree roses, some with lavender, orange and striped flowers.

Stocking Rose Nursery
785 N. Capitol Ave.
San Jose, CA 95133
(408) 258-3606
Free, 280 page color catalog offers good selection of hybrid teas, grandifloras, floribundas, climbing and tree roses. Many AARS award winners. Open 8:30 to 5 daily, 10 to 5 Sundays, closed Thursdays. Official AARS test garden.

Tate Rose Nursery
Route 20, Box 436
Tyler, TX 75708
Free listing includes 100 varieties of popular hybrid teas, floribundas, grandifloras and climbers. Many patented roses. Roses not shipped to California.

Thomasville Nurseries, Inc.
The Hjorts
P.O. Box 2 (ZIP) 31799
1842 Smith Ave.
Thomasville, GA 31792
(912) 226-5568
Good selection of many kinds of roses. Descriptive 24-page catalog free upon request. Also lists native and evergreen azaleas, liriope and daylilies. Official AARS test garden open to public from mid-April to mid-November.

Tiny Petals Miniature Roses
489 Minot Ave.
Chula Vista, CA 92010
(619) 422-0385
The largest selection of the 'Cream of the Crop' in miniatures. Open daily. Beautiful garden displays. Blooms year-round. Visitors and garden groups welcome. Free catalog. Plants guaranteed healthy on arrival. Visa and Mastercard accepted.

Rose Lists

The following lists are based on the recommendations of Consulting Rosarians from throughout the United States. In some cases, they recommend roses not included in this book. Please consult with your nurseryman, local rose society or the American Rose Society for additional information.

HIGH-RATED ROSES

Members of the American Rose Society rate roses on a scale ranging between 1 and 10. Here are the highest rated roses of various classes.

Hybrid teas
First Prize	9.0
Peace	9.0
Granada	8.9
Tiffany	8.8
Tropicana	8.8
Mister Lincoln	8.7
Garden Party	8.6
Double Delight	8.5
Paradise	8.5
Lady X	8.4

Grandifloras
Queen Elizabeth	9.0
Pink Parfait	8.4
Sonia	8.0
Montezuma	7.7
Olé	7.7
Camelot	7.7
Mount Shasta	7.7
Carrousel	7.6

Floribundas
Europeana	8.8
Little Darling	8.8
Iceberg	8.6
Walko	8.5
Gene Boerner	8.4
Sea Pearl	8.4
Betty Prior	8.3
Floradora	8.3

Miniatures
Starina	9.4
Beauty Secret	9.0
Cinderella	8.9
Toy Clown	8.9
Magic Carrousel	8.9
Judy Fischer	8.8
Mary Marshall	8.7
Simplex	8.6
Starglo	8.6
Chipper	8.5
Holy Toledo	8.5
Over the Rainbow	8.5

Climbers
Altissimo	8.8
Don Juan	8.6
Handel	8.6
Dortmund	8.6
May Queen	8.4
Royal Flush	8.3
Royal Sunset	8.1
America	8.0
Aurora	8.0
Climbing First Prize	8.0

Old roses
Mme Hardy—damask	9.0
Rosa rubrifolia	9.0
Rosa hugonis	9.0
Koenigin von Daenemark—alba	8.9
Sombreuil—tea	8.6
Mme Plantier—alba	8.6
Tuscany—gallica	8.4
Paul's Early Blush—hybrid perpetual	8.3
Rosa damascena bifera—damask	8.2
Vierge de Clery—centifolia	8.2

Shrub roses
Cornelia—hybrid moschata	9.0
Will Scarlet—hybrid moschata	8.8
Ruskin—hybrid rugosa	8.5
Pink Grootendorst—hybrid rugosa	8.5
Alchymist—shrub	8.4
Nevada—hybrid moyesii	8.4
Country Dancer—shrub	8.2
Rosa rugosa rubra	8.2
Sea Foam—shrub	8.1
Mermaid—hybrid bracteata	8.0

EXHIBITION ROSES

Medal winners of rose shows throughout the United States are reported to the ARS. They are scored according to best of the class, second best of their class, and so on. The following list includes the top 10 exhibition roses for 1973-1982 in four classes. Exhibition roses are also highly rated for use in the home garden.

Top 10 Exhibition Roses for 10-Year Period (1973-1982)

Hybrid Teas	Ranking
First Prize	1
Garden Party	2
Royal Highness	3
Pristine	4
Peace	5
Pascali	6
Double Delight	7
Granada	8
Swarthmore	9
Toro	10

Grandifloras	Ranking
Queen Elizabeth	1
Aquarius	2
Pink Parfait	3
Sonia	4
Montezuma	5
Mount Shasta	6
Camelot	7
Comanche	8
Scarlet Knight	9
Olé	10

Floribundas	Ranking
Europeana	1
Little Darling	2
Gene Boerner	3
Ivory Fashion	4
First Edition	5 (tie)
Iceberg	5 (tie)
Fire King	6
Angel Face	7
Redgold	8
Sea Pearl	9
Vogue	10

Miniatures	Ranking
Starina	1
Magic Carrousel	2
Toy Clown	3
Mary Marshall	4
Beauty Secret	5
Starglo	6
Judy Fischer	7
Rise 'n' Shine	8
Over the Rainbow	9
Cinderella	10

'Climbing Handel'

EASY-TO-GROW ROSES

All roses are easy to grow, but some will tolerate more neglect because of their greater vigor or disease resistance. It is a relative measure—many floribundas and shrub roses are very tough. All of these will perform well with a minimum of care.

Aquarius—grandiflora
Bewitched—hybrid tea
Charlotte Armstrong—hybrid tea
Double Delight—hybrid tea
Duet—hybrid tea
Fragrant Cloud—hybrid tea
Granada—hybrid tea
King's Ransom—hybrid tea
Lady X—hybrid tea
Lucky Lady—grandiflora
Peace—hybrid tea
Queen Elizabeth—glandiflora
Simplicity—floribunda

'Aquarius'

LONG-LASTING CUT ROSES

How long a rose will last after cutting depends primarily upon how it is treated. All things being equal, thick-petaled roses will last longest. A good rose for cutting should have long stems, so this list is restricted to hybrid teas and grandifloras.

Camelot
Christian Dior
Duet
Electron
Miss All-American Beauty
Montezuma
Olé
Peace
Prominent
Royal Highness
Swarthmore
Tiffany
Tropicana

HOT-WEATHER HYBRID TEAS

Hot weather affects roses two ways: They grow faster, sometimes too fast, and they are stressed. Rose flowers with 50 or more petals often will not open properly in cool weather and do best with plenty of heat. But many good roses just can't produce their full-sized flowers when weather is hot.

Heat-tolerant hybrid teas can be divided into two groups—those recommended for hot and dry climate and those recommended for hot and humid climates. Consultants are the Tucson Rose Society and Gulf Coast Consulting Rosarians Jim Miller and Dr. E. W. Lyle.

Reliable hybrid teas for hot and dry climates:
Charlotte Armstrong
Chrysler Imperial
Double Delight
First Prize
Granada
Miss All-American Beauty
Mister Lincoln
Oldtimer
Peace
Royal Highness
Sutter's Gold
Tropicana

Reliable hybrid teas for hot and humid climates:
Bewitched
Chrysler Imperial
Double Delight
Fragrant Cloud
Garden Party
Honor
Lady X
Mister Lincoln
Paradise
Pascali
Peace
Perfume Delight
Red Masterpiece
Tiffany
Toro
Tropicana

'Charlotte Armstrong'

COOL-WEATHER HYBRID TEAS

In cool weather growth and bud formation is slow. Flowers with 55 or more petals often cannot grow fast enough to open properly. Petals stick together or ball. Mildew is more of a problem. The following have all won the City of Portland Gold Medal.

Double Delight
Fragrant Cloud
Pascali
Peace
Princess Margret
Prominent
Red Devil

'Garden Party'

COLD WINTER HYBRID TEAS

Wherever winter temperatures drop below zero, most hybrid teas need some winter protection. Where subzero temperatures are the rule, substantial protection will be necessary. Many of the shrub roses are exceptionally hardy and will survive extreme cold with no protection. Floribundas and polyanthas tend to be slightly more cold-tolerant than hybrid teas. The following hybrid teas are recommended by the Northern Chicagoland Rose Society.

Big Ben
Double Delight
First Prize
Fragrant Cloud
Garden Party
Granada
Mister Lincoln
Paradise
Pascali
Peace
Pristine
Sunblest
Swarthmore
Tropicana

FRAGRANT ROSES

These are some of the strongly fragrant roses. Many of the old roses are fragrant. The gallicas are particularly good for *potpourri*. Modern roses that are dark red frequently have the long lasting, old-fashioned perfume. Winners of the James Alexander Gamble Award for Fragrant Roses are noted with an asterisk.

Hybrid teas and grandifloras
Arizona—grandiflora
Chrysler Imperial*—hybrid tea
Command Performance—hybrid tea
Crimson Glory*—hybrid tea
Electron—hybrid tea
Fragrant Cloud*—hybrid tea
Granada*—hybrid tea
Heirloom—hybrid tea
Mister Lincoln—hybrid tea
Oklahoma—hybrid tea
Olé—grandiflora
Papa Meilland*—hybrid tea
Perfume Delight—hybrid tea
Royal Highness-hybrid tea
Sterling Silver—hybrid tea
Sundowner—grandiflora
Sutter's Gold*—hybrid tea
Tiffany*—hybrid tea
Tropicana—hybrid tea
White Lightnin'—grandiflora

'Chrysler Imperial'

Floribundas
Angel Face
Apricot Nectar
Iceberg
Rose Parade
Saratoga
Spanish Sun
Sunsprite

Climbers
America
Blossomtime
Climbing Chrysler Imperial
Climbing Crimson Glory
Climbing Etoile de Hollande
Climbing Peace
Climbing Sutter's Gold
Climbing Tropicana
Don Juan
Red Fountain
Royal Sunset

GROUND COVER ROSES

Many kinds of roses can serve as ground covers. Low-growing floribundas or miniatures can be planted in masses. Some climbers can be "pegged," their long canes pulled back and attached to the ground. Roses classed as rambler and hybrids of *Rosa sempervirens* have supple, flexible canes and many make excellent ground covers.

Dorothy Perkins—rambler
Evangeline—rambler
Félicité et Perpetue—hybrid sempervirens
Max Graf—hybrid rugosa
May Queen—rambler
New Dawn—large-flowered climber
Red Cascade—miniature
Rosa laevigata or Cherokee Rose
Rosa wichuraiana or Memorial Rose
Sea Foam—shrub

'Evangeline' rambler

Pegged climber in bloom

LOW HEDGE ROSES

Floribundas and polyanthas are naturals here. Low-growing hybrid teas and shrub roses make outstanding low hedges.

Bon-Bon—floribunda
Cathedral—floribunda
Cherish—floribunda
China Doll—polyantha
Country Dancer—shrub
Escapade—floribunda
Europeana—floribunda
First Edition—floribunda
Ginger—floribunda
Iceberg—floribunda
Music Maker—shrub
Sally Holmes—shrub
Sarabande—floribunda
Simplicity—floribunda
Spartan—floribunda
Sunsprite—floribunda
The Fairy—polyantha
Trumpeter—floribunda
Virgo—hybrid tea
Yesterday—floribunda

'Europeana' in front, 'Cathedral' at rear

LOW EDGING ROSES

Neat, 10-inch edging borders are a particularly effective use for miniature roses. Here are several of the best.

Beauty Secret
Bo Peep
Cinderella
Cricri
Hula Girl
Judy Fischer
Popcorn
Puppy Love
Red Flush
Red Imp
Rise 'n Shine
Starina
White Angel
Yellow Doll

TALL SHRUB ROSES

There are several varieties to chose between. Many excellent shrubs have come from Kordes in Germany. Professor Buck of Iowa State has developed many low-maintenance shrub roses. Some are species from which our garden roses have derived.

Applejack—shrub
Berlin—shrub
Bonn—shrub
Carefree Beauty—shrub
Elmshorn—shrub
F. J. Grootendorst—hybrid *rugosa*
Fritz Nobis—shrub
Frühlingsgold—hybrid *spinosissima*
Golden Wings—shrub
Mermaid—hybrid *bracteata*
Montezuma—grandiflora
Phyllis Bide—rambler
Queen Elizabeth—grandiflora
Rosa banksiae (yellow or white)
  Lady Banks Rose
Rosa rugosa Japanese Rose
Rosa soulieana
Sitka—shrub
Sparrieshoop—shrub

'Sparrieshoop'

Rosa banksiae normalis

DISEASE-RESISTANT ROSES

No modern rose is immune to all diseases and there are many degrees of "resistance." Climate is the primary influence. Rust is a problem in California and the Southwest where blackspot is rare. Blackspot is a problem in climate with summer rain. A rose may successfully resist blackspot in Los Angeles but be devastated by it in Louisiana. Many of the shrub roses, species roses and polyanthas are more disease resistant than most of the modern roses. Fungicides will effectively control mildew, blackspot and rust.

The following lists are the results of a symposium conducted by Lincoln Atkiss of Newton Square, Pennsylvania. Representatives of public rose gardens throughout the U.S. were questioned and their responses tabulated. They were limited to the hybrid teas, grandifloras and floribundas. Roses are listed in descending order.

Most disease resistant
Tropicana*
Queen Elizabeth
Prominent
Miss All-American Beauty
Pristine
Peace
Tiffany
Cathedral
Fragrant Cloud
Pascali
Pink Peace
Europeana

Hybrid teas most resistant to blackspot
Tropicana*
First Prize
Miss All-American Beauty
Mister Lincoln
Tiffany
Portrait
Pink Peace
Pristine
Proud Land
Duet
Peace
Electron

'First Prize'

*'Tropicana' is very resistant to blackspot, and throughout most of the United States, mildew. In the western states, it is quite prone to mildew.

Grandifloras and floribundas most resistant to blackspot
Queen Elizabeth
Prominent
Rose Parade
Razzle Dazzle
Gene Boerner
Europeana
Montezuma
First Edition
Ivory Fashion
Sonia
Carrousel
Angel Face

Hybrid teas most resistant to mildew
Tiffany
Pristine
Miss All-American Beauty
Futura
Pascali
Peace
Seashell
Pink Peace
Proud Land
Mister Lincoln
Tropicana*
Chicago Peace

Grandifloras and floribundas most resistant to mildew
Queen Elizabeth
Europeana
Rose Parade
Charisma
Sarabande
Saratoga
Cathedral
Sunsprite
Prominent
Razzle Dazzle
First Edition
Evening Star

'Chicago Peace'

HEDGES AND SCREENS

Hedges, screens and espaliers are plants that can serve you. Before you buy plants to grow into one of these forms, you should decide on the function you want them to perform. Use this chapter for planning. After you know your landscape needs, choose plants to suit your purposes from the lists included in the following pages.

Be realistic about the amount of care you want to give plants. All require various levels of maintenance, from low to high. Most screens require only occasional shaping and care. Hedges require anything from yearly shaping to weekly shearing. The faster the growth, the more often shearing is required. Espaliers need intensive care for three years and regular care thereafter.

A plan is important. Shrubs and trees planted at random have little impact except as clutter. Grouped into screens and hedges, the same plants define spaces and create visual lines. There is no reason why these lines must be straight. A curved hedge softens the corners at a square lot.

Use plants to solve functional problems before you concentrate on aesthetics or style. The Planning Process on the following page will help you arrive at logical and pleasing designs. It is best to start with a basic framework of plants that are chosen for screening, privacy and definition of functional areas.

Informal landscape styles depend on *contrasts* for their qualities. Lines are loose. Formal styles depend on symmetry, order and restraint for their qualities. Lines are tailored. You can strive for an architectural, sculptural, natural, classic, picturesque or Oriental effect. Or you may create your own style. Keep it simple in the beginning.

Hedges of dark-green, fine-textured foliage are the most basic of these plants.

The more tightly they are sheared, the less space they require.

Homeowners are often advised to envision their property as outdoor rooms, with hedges for walls, ground covers for floors and trees for ceilings. Outdoor rooms can transform flat, open sites into interesting spaces that appear larger, and have a direct connection to the existing architecture. But avoid limiting the use of hedges and screens to the role of a living wall. Use them to break up small, roomlike yards by rounding out corners, or position them to "borrow scenery."

DIRECT MOVEMENT AND ADD INTEREST

Using hedges and screens to direct movement is a useful design technique. Lines of plants, combined with human curiosity, tend to draw people through outdoor spaces.

Left: Branches of canopy-shaped trees interweave to make a solid, overhead screen. This kind of planting is useful to create privacy if tall buildings stand over your lot. Hedge in background further encloses area, helping to complete the feeling of an outdoor room. Above: Windbreak of tall, evergreen trees produces a sheltered microclimate and serves as backdrop for small, sunny terrace.

A path leads the eye. Borders, hedges and screens create a sense of movement by turning flat paths into channels. Tall screens or crisply sheared hedges of any size heighten this effect. Lower hedges define areas without blocking vision. Use them to separate pedestrian and vehicular traffic. Thorny material discourages wandering and shortcuts across lawn and planting areas.

Curve a path behind a hedge or screen, and curiosity will motivate people to explore. Turn flat, open space into interesting areas with hedges. As people move through the garden, spaces are concealed then revealed to create a sense of anticipation. Contrast bright, large expanses with shady, narrow corridors. Allow a glimpse of view, then force people to follow an indirect route to make the objective or vista seem more worthwhile.

SCREEN AND DIRECT VIEWS

One of the most important functions of a hedge or screen is to selectively block objects from view. Use either to screen a tennis court, a distant view of a smoke-belching factory, a single, local eyesore or the small corner where the garbage cans are stored.

Canopy-shaped trees screen views from above and below. Short baffle sections of hedge can be positioned to screen front windows from headlight glare and neighbors' eyes.

Hedges and screens are also used to direct views. One or two bold lines of plants call attention to the feature to which they point. A great vista may be overwhelming or lost without proper framing. If a feature in the landscape is worth noticing but is surrounded by distractions, frame the feature and screen the rest.

BORROWED SCENERY

This is an ancient design principle attributed to the Japanese. Hedges and screens are artfully arranged to obliterate every trace of straight property lines and surrounding neighbors. Attention is directed to a feature in the distance—a tree, mountain or temple. The garden, however small, becomes part of a greater landscape picture, and the feature is "borrowed" to become part of the garden. The result is a feeling of spaciousness and a connection to nature. Straight, square, property lines disappear so the garden seems to expand.

Home entry is designed to intrigue. After visitors enter wrought-iron gate, green passageway and walk disappear behind leafy screen. This creates an urge to find out "what's around the corner?" See photos opposite.

The Planning Process

Go outside and take a long look at your property. Divide it into areas by asking yourself these questions:

1. *What needs to be screened?*
2. *What edges need definition for a visual line or a boundary barrier?*
3. *Which views should be accentuated or hidden?*
4. *Is privacy needed?*
5. *Who will use the space or spaces, and what are their activities?*
6. *Should microclimates be modified?*
7. *Are there winds to block, breezes to capture, windows to shield from glare or sun?*
7. *Will various areas be unified in a design? Should they be?*
8. *How will people move through the garden or property? Where will paths lead?*

The answers to these eight questions will help you determine what spaces you need and their size. Next, ask yourself some practical questions that will affect your choice of plants and the form they will take: hedge, screen or espalier.

1. *Should plants have dense foliage to block a view or ensure privacy?*
2. *Is fast cover a necessity?*
3. *How much maintenance and pruning time do you have on a weekly, monthly or yearly basis? Be realistic.*
4. *How much space is available?*

Are there limits on the height and width of plants? Will shearing be required?
5. *Should corner intersections or driveways be kept clear so drivers will have unobstructed views of oncoming traffic?*
6. *Is snow-removal equipment used in your neighborhood? If so, place hedges or screen 3 or 4 feet back from sidewalks to allow snow banks to form.*
7. *Will neighbors cooperate in trimming property-line hedges? It is best to include two or three feet of path behind a hedge for ease in pruning.*
8. *Do you live where plants should be fire retardant or drought tolerant?*
9. *Do you want to attract birds or bees with fruit, flowers, seasonal color or berries?*

Keep the cultural requirements of plants in mind. Consider the following:

1. *Is climate particularly harsh? Are winters severe? Is the area subject to high winds or coastal salt spray?*
2. *Is it sunny or shady?*
3. *What is the soil like?*
4. *How is the soil drainage? Is the soil soggy or dry?*
5. *Are tree roots nearby that will compete with hedge, screen and espalier plants?*
6. *Do you have any microclimates that can be used to your plant's advantage?*

Simple turn in the path is crucial to create interesting sequence between entry gate and front door. The hedges enclose and screen house from view, while creating the green passageway effect.

Path turns then continues to front door. Contrast of closed-in entry walk and open, spacious garden makes walkway sequence from gate seem longer and more interesting than a straight line.

Here are some other classic tricks for using hedges and screens for design effects. But do not try them all at once.

● Create several small gardens in one by enclosing areas with hedges. Fill each area with colorful, seasonal plants—spring-flowering bulbs in one, summer perennials in another. For maximum color impact, plant color plants with framework and backdrop hedges.

● Use color to create effects. Dark, cool hues seem to retreat into the background. Light, warm hues seem to advance.

● Experiment with forcing perspective. The eye moves quickly along sheared hedge lines. To create an illusion of greater distance, make two apparently parallel hedges converge slightly at one end. A similar effect can be created by slanting the tops of sheared hedges slightly up or down a few inches at one end.

● Create interesting contrasts by combining crisply sheared hedges with loose, flowery screens or borders.

● Use light-green or yellow-green foliage plants or variegated varieties with white or yellow leaf markings to brighten dark corners. Screens with white flowers accomplish the same

thing. Or use any dark-green hedge or screen as a backdrop for a low, white-flowering border.

● Several species of plants growing together and sheared into one multi-patterned and multicolored unit create a striking *mosaic hedge.* Choose plants with similar growth habits and growth rates.

● Arrange hedges or screens in a labyrinth pattern to create a maze.

PRIVACY

Wherever you might need a fence, plant a hedge or screen. They are cheaper and their use is rarely restricted by ordinances. Screens, hedges, short baffle sections of hedge or aerial hedges can be used if your front windows look directly onto the street, but local codes prohibit fences more than three feet high. Canopy trees provide privacy to city dwellers whose gardens are situated below tall buildings.

An *aerial hedge* stretches a fence. This is when lower branches are gradually pruned from the trunks over several growing seasons until the leaves begin clearing the fence top. Regular hedge forms can then be created, with the screening effect extended to the height

desired.

Six feet is the typical maximum fence height allowed by zoning regulations in area yards and side yards. But six feet is just above eye level and creates an awkward visual line. It is also inadequate when second-story windows look down into your property. An aerial hedge can solve problems of privacy and aesthetics. Use them in conjunction with low fences or walls.

Another privacy solution for low walls is to place planter boxes along the wall top. Let plants grow as high as necessary. A strong, architectural effect is obtained by constructing boxes the width of the wall, painting them the same color and then shearing plants to the same width. Select species recommended for container planting. Installation can be permanent. Or remove the boxes in winter to allow more sun to shine on the area or to protect cold-tender plants, like citrus, from frost.

Le Corbusier and Pierre Jeanneret devised what is probably the ultimate use of movable screens in their 1931 design of the De Beistegui penthouse roof garden. Clipped hedges were set into electrically operated sliding boxes. One had only to flip a switch for complete privacy or a fabulous view of Paris.

FAST PLANTS FOR PRIVACY

A fast-growing screen or hedge has advantages and disadvantages. The more rapid the growth rate, the more you have to shear. Plants that grow quickly tend to be short-lived. A fast variety is useful planted behind a slow-growing, permanent variety. Remove the fast plant when it has passed its prime or when the permanent planting has matured.

Acacia longifolia ....Sydney golden wattle
Acer ginnala ....Amur maple
Bambusa .... Bamboo species
Berberis koreana ....Korean barberry
Berberis thunbergii .... Japanese barberry
Carissa grandiflora ....Natal plum
Chamaecyparis lawsoniana ....Port Orford cedar
Cornus stolonifera .... Red-osier dogwood
Cupressocyparis leylandii Cupressocyparis
Cupressus glabra .... Arizona cypress

Dodonea viscosa ....Hopbush
Escallonia rubra .... Escallonia
Eucalyptus ....Eucalyptus species
Euonymus fortunei .... Wintercreeper
Hibiscus rosa-sinensis ..... Tropical hibiscus
Ilex cassine ....Dahoon holly
Ilex 'Nellie R. Stevens' .... Holly
Ilex opaca .... American holly
Ligustrum ....Deciduous privets
Lonicera korolkowii 'Zabeli' ....Zabel's honeysuckle
Lonicera tatarica .... Tatarian honeysuckle
Malus baccata 'Columnaris' .... Columnar Siberian crabapple
Nerium oleander ....Oleander
Philadelphus x virginalis ....Mock orange
Photinia x fraseri ....Photinia
Picea abies ....Norway spruce
Picea glauca ....White spruce
Pinus eldarica ....Mondell pine
Pittosporum crassifolium ....Karo
Pittosporum undulatum .... Victorian box

Plumbago auriculata ....Plumbago
Populus alba 'Bolleana' ....Bolleana poplar
Populus nigra 'Italica' ....Lombardy poplar
Populus simonii 'Fastigiata' ....Pyramidal Simon's poplar
Potentilla fruticosa ....Potentilla
Prunus caroliniana .... Cherry laurel
Prunus ilicifolia ....Hollyleaf cherry
Prunus laurocerasus ....Laurel cherry
Pseudotsuga menziesii .... Douglas fir
Pyracantha .... Pyracantha
Raphiolepis indica .... Indian hawthorn
Rhamnus alaternus ....Italian buckthorn
Rhamnus cathartica ......Common buckthorn
Rhamnus frangula 'Columnaris' .... Tallhedge buckthorn
Salix purpurea ....Purple-osier willow
Sequoia sempervirens ....Coast redwood
Spiraea .... Spiraea species
Syzygium paniculatum ....Eugenia
Tamarix aphylla ....Tamarisk
Tsuga heterophylla ....Western hemlock

Prunus laurocerasus, English laurel, is a fast-growing hedge or screen.

Syzygium paniculatum is a fast-growing, narrow hedge plant. It requires frequent clipping to keep it neat and narrow.

PROTECTION FROM OUTSIDE ANNOYANCES

Hedges and screens can protect you from many other nuisances besides wind or inquisitive eyes. Position hedges to shield your yard and windows from headlight glare or the glare from streetlights. Locate movable screens according to season to block sunlight and glare reflected from paved surfaces, swimming pools, glass or light-colored walls. This strategy also reduces heat gain indoors.

Hedges and screens reduce dust more than fences or walls. In addition to deflecting dust, leaf surfaces capture and trap dust as it adheres. This principle applies equally well to salty ocean spray.

A dense, wide, evergreen hedge also reduces noise levels slightly. Hedges and screens composed of certain plant species can act as firebreaks in combination with bare soil or fire-retardant ground covers.

NOISE BUFFERS

Plants absorb and refract sound. Hedges and screens reduce noise slightly. You may not even be able to notice a difference in noise levels. If the source of the noise is blocked from view, the sound *seems* to be reduced. It also helps to plant noise buffers with lawns or ground covers adjacent to noise source.

Earth mounds called *berms* are effective noise buffers. A hedge or screen on top of an earth mound is more effective than berms alone. Broadleaf evergreens may be the most sound-absorbing plants.

Calocedrus decurrens .... California incense cedar
Carpinus betulus .... Hornbeam
Ceratonia siliqua .... Carob
Chamaecyparis lawsoniana .... Port Orford cedar
Citrus .... Citrus
Cupressocyparis leylandii Cupressocyparis
Cupressus .... Cypress species
Eucalyptus globulus 'Compacta' .... Dwarf blue gum
Eucalyptus lehmannii .... Bushy yate
Euonymus kiautschovica 'Manhattan' .... Euonymus
Fagus sylvatica .... Beech
Ilex .... Holly
Juniperus .... Juniper species
Ligustrum lucidum .... Glossy privet
Picea abies .... Norway spruce
Picea glauca .... White spruce
Pinus eldarica .... Mondell pine
Pinus nigra .... Austrian pine
Pinus strobus .... White pine
Pittosporum eugenioides .... Lemonwood
Pittosporum undulatum .... Victorian box
Podocarpus gracilior ..Podocarpus fern pine
Podocarpus macrophyllus .... Yew pine
Prunus caroliniana .... Cherry laurel
Prunus ilicifolia ....Hollyleaf cherry
Pseudotsuga menziesii .... Douglas fir
Sequoia sempervirens ....Coast redwood
Syzygium paniculatum .... Eugenia
Tamarix aphylla .... Tamarisk
Taxus .... Yew
Thuja occidentalis ....American arborvitae
Tsuga canadensis ....Canadian hemlock
Tsuga heterophylla ....Western hemlock

Bird's-eye view shows hedge-enclosed yard. Busy intersection is just outside. Inside, view of city street is eliminated. Lawn and other plantings create a relaxing retreat. Fence with low planting breaks wall effect of hedge and helps reduce noise.

INCREASE LIVABLE OUTDOOR SPACE

The front yard of most homes is often a patch of lawn and some driveway. This useful outdoor area is much more inviting for adults and safer for children when it is enclosed. Where zoning ordinances prohibit fences in front, plant a hedge. Neighbors find walls of living greenery much less objectionable than wooden fences or walls of masonry.

Another way to increase outdoor space is to make an outdoor "closet" by planting double walls of plants around the periphery of your property. These double walls might be two hedges or screens spaced 5 to 10 feet apart, a screen and hedge combination or two rows of edible fruit espaliers on fence supports. Into this closet place barbeque grills, the dog house, compost pile, extra garden furniture, pool equipment and metal storage sheds. The same area could also serve as a dog run or children's play area. An illusion of greater space in the garden outside the screen is achieved by removing clutter. Noise from outside is slightly reduced, and one sees only fresh greenery. This added quiet and simplicity expand the perception of space, even though actual outdoor space has been slightly reduced.

MOVABLE SCREENS

A line of boxed plants makes a movable screen. Because of their shape, sheared hedges or certain espaliers grown in boxes are especially suited to narrow spaces. They can be used where paved surfaces or balconies make it impossible to grow plants in the earth.

Container plants make terrific temporary screens. They are inexpensive and versatile, and the results are almost instant. They create privacy on roof gardens, and it is simple to move them aside if views are desired. Boxed canopy trees produce instant shade and screening. Use deciduous species or move canopies in winter if shade is not wanted.

Plants can be grown in containers if the soil is not suitable. Use a special soil mix that allows for good drainage. Many commercial potting soil mixes are available. Generally, plants require more water and fertilizer when grown in containers. Check soil moisture content frequently, and apply weak, liquid fertilizer regularly during the growing season.

Evergreen screens block view of city street, and enable these homeowners to expand their living space by installing a pool in the front yard.

Small-lot jumble of fruit trees, vegetables and odd shrubs is concealed and protected in outdoor "closet" formed by patio wall and streetside hedge.

MOVABLE SCREENS AND CONTAINER ESPALIERS

Almost any plant will grow in a container. The plants listed here are particularly well suited because of their compact size, or ability to thrive without elaborate care. For minimum maintenance, select a plant with a loose, screen form. Sheared hedges, espaliers and topiary in containers should be given the same pruning as their free-growing counterparts. However, plants in containers can move when you do, which means your efforts will not be wasted should you relocate.

A container built as a short section of hollow, free-standing fence with planting pockets is called a *fedge.* Plant strawberries, ivy or trailing annuals in these fence-hedge combination screens for quicker results than provided by newly planted boxed shrubs. Position fedges wherever movable screens are needed. Or use them as a permanent garden feature like a baffle. They are easy to build. You can buy them prefabricated from nurseries and by special order under the brand name Living Wall. Built-in drip-irrigation systems save time and water.

Abelia x grandiflora ....Glossy abelia
Arbutus unedo 'Compacta' ..Strawberry tree
Bambusa .... Bamboo species
Buxus .... Boxwood
Camellia japonica ....Camellia
Camellia sasanqua ....Sasanqua camellia
Carissa grandiflora ....Natal plum
Citrus ....Citrus—most species
Eriobotrya japonica .... Loquat
Euonymus fortunei ....Wintercreeper
Feijoa sellowiana .... Pineapple guava
Gardenia jasminoides ....Gardenia
Hibiscus rosa-sinensis ..... Tropical hibiscus
Ilex ....Holly—dwarf cultivars
Ilex crenata ....Japanese holly
Ilex vomitoria .... Yaupon holly
Juniperus .... Juniper species
Laurus nobilis .... Grecian laurel
Ligustrum japonicum .... Japanese privet
Ligustrum lucidum .... Glossy privet
Ligustrum texanum .... Waxleaf privet
Malus pumila .... Apple
Myrtus communis .... Myrtle
Nandina domestica ....Nandina
Nerium oleander .... Oleander

Osmanthus heterophyllus ....False holly
Osmanthus fragrans .... Sweet osmanthus
Photinia x fraseri .... Photinia
Pinus mugo mugo .... Mugo pine
Pittosporum crassifolium 'Nana' .... Dwarf karo
Pittosporum tobira .... Tobira mock orange
Pittosporum undulatum .... Victorian box
Plumbago auriculata .... Plumbago
Podocarpus gracilior ..Podocarpus fern pine
Podocarpus macrophyllus .... Yew pine
Prunus ....European plum
Prunus ....Japanese plum
Prunus caroliniana .... Cherry laurel
Psidium .... Strawberry guava
Punica granatum 'Chico' .... Dwarf pomegranate
Pyrus communis .... Pear
Pyrus hybrid ....Pear-apple
Raphiolepis indica .... Indian hawthorn
Rosa .... Rose
Rosmarinus officinalis ....Rosemary
Syzygium paniculatum ....Eugenia
Taxus ....Yew
Viburnum tinus .... Laurustinus

Screens in containers can be moved wherever needed to create privacy. Here they soften the starkness of solid masonry walls and paving, and divide space into more usable sections.

Movable screens can be created with espaliers in containers. This is *Citrus reticulata,* mandarin, supported by a simple wire-and-wood frame.

PLANTS TO PLEACH

Pleach means to weave and interlace branches. In pleached hedges, the branches of individual plants are grafted together to form an impenetrable living fence that may be sheared. *Crataegus* and *Tilia* are classic subjects for pleaching.

Carpinus betulus .... Hornbeam
Crataegus .... Hawthorn
Fagus sylvatica .... Beech
Malus pumila .... Apple
Pyrus communis .... Pear
Pyrus hybrid ....Pear-apple or Asian pear
Pyrus kawakamii .... Evergreen pear
Tilia cordata .... Littleleaf linden

BARRIERS FOR SECURITY

Thorny or prickly shrubs or trees planted closely together make an impenetrable barrier. Osage orange, *Maclura pomifera,* was used on American rangeland before the invention of barbed wire. In the Middle Ages, hedgerows made stock-proof fences in Great Britain.

Space any of the following plants 6 inches apart to keep children and dogs in or out. Spacing 12 inches apart keeps adults and larger animals out. If deer are a problem, hedge or screen should reach at *least* 8 feet high. Be sure to choose plants that deer do not like to eat.

Low, thorny hedges beneath windows may discourage burglars, but few plant barriers can keep out a determined professional. The ultimate barrier is a secured metal or barbed-wire fence hidden within a thorny hedge.

Slow-growing barrier plants normally last decades longer than wood fences. Weave chicken wire through stems as a temporary barrier. The wire need not be removed after plants are mature.

Berberis .... Barberry
Carissa grandiflora .... Natal plum
Carpinus betulus .... Hornbeam
Chaenomeles speciosa .... Flowering quince
Citrus .... Citrus
Crataegus .... Hawthorn
Elaeagnus angustifolia .... Russian olive
Elaeagnus pungens .... Silverberry
Escallonia rubra .... Escallonia
Ilex .... Holly
Mahonia aquifolium .... Oregon grape
Pseudotsuga menziesii .... Douglas fir
Punica granatum .... Pomegranate
Pyracantha .... Pyracantha
Rhamnus cathartica .... Common buckthorn
Rosa .... Rose
Taxus .... Yew

Berberis thunbergii, 'Atropurpurea', Japanese barberry, for barrier.

Leaves of *Ilex cornuta* 'Rotunda' are spiny, good for barriers.

Cratageus phaenopyrum, Washington thorn, has sharp thorns.

THE RIGHT SIZE

Border plants, low, medium and high hedges, screens and large-scale hedge-walls serve various purposes in the landscape. One of the easiest ways to reduce maintenance chores is to use plants that do not exceed a specific, desired height.

Classics, as indicated in the following, are plants that have proved their popularity and value for a century or more. Many classics live for 100 years or more. It is best to choose plants that last for generations if stately effects are desired.

BORDERS

Border plants are those that stay in the below-the-knee range. Artemisia, dwarf box, apple and pear horizontal cordons, Japanese holly, rosemary, lavender and myrtle are classics. Those marked with an asterisk * require little shaping. Others need pinching or shearing to keep them dense, neat and border-size.

*Artemisia abrotanum .... Southernwood
Baccharis pilularis .... Dwarf coyote brush
*Berberis thunbergii .... Dwarf Japanese barberry
*Buxus .... Dwarf boxwood
*Caragana pygmaea .... Dwarf pea shrub
*Carissa grandiflora 'Boxwood Beauty' .... Dwarf natal plum
*Chaenomeles japonica 'Alpina' .... Dwarf quince
Euonymus fortunei .... Wintercreeper
Euonymus japonica ...... Evergreen euonymus
*Forsythia x intermedia 'Arnold Dwarf' .... Forsythia
Ilex cornuta .... Dwarf Chinese holly cultivars
Ilex crenata .... Japanese holly
Ilex vomitoria .... Yaupon holly
*Ilex vomitoria 'Nana', 'Stokes' .... Dwarf yaupon cultivars
Lagerstroemia indica .... Dwarf crape myrtle
*Lavandula .... Lavender

Ligustrum japonicum .... Japanese privet
Ligustrum ovalifolium .... California privet
*Ligustrum 'Suwanee River' .... Privet
Ligustrum texanum .... Waxleaf privet
*Lonicera xylosteum .... Dwarf honeysuckle
Malus pumila .... Apple—single horizontal cordon
*Myrtus communis .... Dwarf myrtle
*Nandina domestica .... Dwarf nandina
Nerium oleander .... Dwarf oleander
Physocarpus opulifolius .... Dwarf ninebark
*Pinus mugo mugo .... Mugo pine
Pittosporum crassifolium .... Dwarf karo
*Pittosporum tobira 'Wheeler's Dwarf' .... Dwarf tobira
Potentilla fruticosa .... Potentilla
Punica granatum 'Chico' .... Dwarf pomegranate
*Pyracantha .... Dwarf pyracantha
*Raphiolepis indica 'Ballerina' .... Ballerina Indian hawthorn
Pyrus communis .... Pear—shaped horizontal cordon
Pyrus hybrid .... Apple-pear—single horizontal cordon
Ribes alpinum .... Alpine currant
*Rosa .... Rose
Rosmarinus officinalis 'Collingwood Ingram' .... Rosemary
Salix purpurea .... Dwarf blue arctic willow
Spiraea japonica 'Alpina' .... Daphne spiraea
*Viburnum opulus .... Dwarf cranberry bush

A border of unclipped, dwarf *Ilex cornuta,* Chinese holly, accentuates a graceful curve adjacent to walk.

Border planting of *Ilex vomitoria,* yaupon, helps guide pedestrian traffic around turn in sidewalk.

LOW HEDGES

A low hedge—from knee to waist high—is one of the most versatile landscape forms. Here are some of the best. Many of these are held low by pruning. Those marked with an asterisk * stay low on their own and require little pruning.

Berberis buxifolia .... Magellan barberry
*Buxus .... Dwarf boxwood
Buxus microphylla
    var. japonica .... Japanese boxwood
*Buxus microphylla
    var. koreana .... Korean littleleaf box
*Caragana pygmaea .... Dwarf peashrub
*Carissa grandiflora .... Natal plum
Chaenomeles speciosa .... Flowering quince
Cornus mas .... Cornealian cherry dogwood
Cotoneaster lucidus .... Hedge cotoneaster
*Escallonia .... Escallonia
*Euonymus fortunei .... Wintercreeper
*Euonymus japonica ..... Evergreen euonymus
                              cultivars
*Forsythia x intermedia
    'Arnold Dwarf' .... Forsythia
*Forsythia ovata 'Ottawa' ...... Ottawa forsythia
*Ilex cornuta .... Chinese holly
*Ilex crenata .... Japanese holly
Lagerstroemia indica .... Dwarf crape myrtle
*Lavandula .... Lavender
Ligustrum japonicum .... Japanese privet
Ligustrum ovalifolium .... California privet
Ligustrum texanum .... Waxleaf privet
Mahonia aquifolium
    'Compacta' .... Compact Oregon grape

Matus pumila .... Apple—horizontal cordon
*Myrtus communis .... Myrtle
*Nandina domestica 'Nana' ..... Dwarf nandina
*Nerium oleander .... Dwarf oleander
*Physocarpus opulifolius 'Nanus',
    'Dart's Gold' .... Dwarf ninebark
*Pinus mugo mugo .... Mugo pine
*Pittosporum crassifolium .... Dwarf karo
Pittosporum tobira
    'Wheeler's Dwarf' .... Dwarf pittosporum
Plumbago auriculata .... Plumbago
Podocarpus macrophyllus .... Yew pine
Potentilla fruticosa .... Potentilla
Prunus caroliniana .... Cherry laurel
Prunus laurocerasus .... Laurel cherry
Prunus lusitanica .... Portugal laurel
*Punica granatum .... Dwarf pomegranate
Pyracantha .... Pyracantha
Pyrus communis .... Pear horizontal cordons
Pyrus hybrid .... Pear-apple horizontal cordons
Rhododendron .... Southern indica and
                  kurume hybrid azaleas
*Ribes alpinum .... Alpine currant
*Rosa .... Rose
Rosmarinus officinalis .... Rosemary
Salix purpurea .... Dwarf blue arctic willow
Spiraea x bumalda .... Bumalda spiraea
Spiraea japonica .... Japanese spiraea
Syringa patula .... Dwarf Korean lilac
Syzygium paniculatum .... Eugenia
Taxus cuspidata .... Japanese yew
*Viburnum opulus
    'Nanum' .... Dwarf cranberry bush
Xylosma congestum .... Shiny xylosma

MEDIUM HEDGES

Waist-high to chest-high hedges define and enclose space without blocking vision, so they are rarely categorized as screens. Not all have to be sheared, although many can be held to the desired height by pruning. Those marked with an asterisk * stay at medium height without clipping.

*Abelia x grandiflora
    'Edward Goucher' .... Glossy abelia
*Arbutus unedo 'Compacta' .... Compact
                          strawberry tree
*Arctostaphylos densiflora
    'Howard McMinn' .... Manzanita
*Atriplex lentiformis 'Breweri' .... Brewer
                            saltbush
Berberis buxifolia .... Magellan barberry
Berberis darwinii .... Darwin barberry
Berberis koreana .... Korean barberry
Berberis x mentorensis .... Mentor barberry
Berberis thunbergii .... Japanese barberry
*Buxus microphylla
    var. japonica .... Japanese boxwood
*Buxus microphylla
    var. koreana .... Korean littleleaf box
Buxus sempervirens .... English box
Camellia japonica .... Camellia
Camellia sasanqua .... Sasanqua camellia
Caragana arborescens .... Siberian pea tree
Carissa grandiflora .... Natal plum
Carpinus betulus .... Hornbeam
Chaenomeles speciosa .... Flowering quince
Chamaecyparis lawsoniana .... Port
                           Orford cedar

Podocarpus macrophyllus, yew pine, separates path from lawn. It is held to this size by pruning.

Ilex crenata 'Helleri', Japanese holly, combines with azaleas in background.

MEDIUM HEDGES, CONTINUED

Citrus .... Citrus
Cornus mas .... Cornelian cherry dogwood
Cotoneaster lucidus .... Hedge cotoneaster
Cupressocyparis leylandii
  Cupressocyparis
Dodonea viscosa .... Hopbush
Elaeagnus angustifolia .... Russian olive
Elaeagnus pungens .... Silverberry
Escallonia rubra .... Escallonia
Euonymus alata .... Winged burning bush
Euonymus fortunei .... Wintercreeper
Euonymus japonica ..... Evergreen euonymus
Feijoa sellowiana .... Pineapple guava
Fontanesia fortunei .... Fontanesia
Forsythia ovata 'Ottawa' .... Forsythia
Gardenia jasminoides .... Gardenia
Hibiscus syriacus .... Rose of Sharon
Ilex .... Holly cultivars
Lagerstroemia indica .... Crape myrtle
Laurus nobilis .... Grecian laurel
Ligustrum .... Deciduous privet
Ligustrum japonicum .... Japanese privet
Ligustrum lucidum .... Glossy privet
Ligustrum obtusifolium
  regelianum .... Regal privet
Ligustrum texanum .... Waxleaf privet
Lonicera x xylosteum
  'Clavey's Dwarf' .... Lonicera
Mahonia aquifolium .... Oregon grape
Malus pumila .... Apple cordon fence
Malus sargentii .... Sargent crabapple
Myrica californica .... Pacific wax myrtle

Myrtus communis .... Myrtle
Nandina domestica .... Nandina
Nerium oleander .... Oleander
Osmanthus fragrans .... Sweet osmanthus
Osmanthus heterophyllus .... False holly
Photinia x fraseri .... Photinia
Pinus strobus .... White pine
Pittosporum crassifolium .... Karo
Pittosporum eugenioides .... Lemonwood
Pittosporum tenuifolium .... Black-
  stemmed pittosporum
Pittosporum tobira .... Tobira mock orange
Pittosporum undulatum .... Victorian box
Plumbago auriculata .... Plumbago
Podocarpus gracilior .... Podocarpus fern pine
Podocarpus macrophyllus .... Yew pine
Potentilla fruticosa
  'Jackmanii' .... Potentilla Jackman's variety
Prunus .... European plum
Prunus .... Japanese plum
Prunus caroliniana .... Cherry laurel
Prunus ilicifolia .... Hollyleaf cherry
Prunus laurocerasus .... 'Otto Luykens'
Prunus lusitanica .... Portugal laurel
Prunus maritima .... Beach plum
Punica granatum .... Pomegranate
Pyracantha coccinea .... Pyracantha
Pyrus communis .... Pear—cordon fence
Pyrus hybrid .... Pear-apple—cordon fence
Raphiolepis indica .... Indian hawthorn
Rhamnus alaternus .... Italian buckthorn
Rhamnus cathartica .... Common buckthorn
Rhamnus frangula
  'Columnaris' .... Tallhedge buckthorn

Rhododendron .... Southern indica
  hybrid azaleas
Rhododendron maximum .... Rosebay
  rhododendron
Rhododendron obtusum ..... Kurume azalea—
  a Classic
Rhododendron PJM .... Hybrid
  rhododendrons
Rosa .... Rose
Rosmarinus officinalis .... Rosemary
Sequois sempervirens .... Coast redwood
Spiraea prunifolia plena .... Bridal-wreath
  spiraea
Syringa x chinensis .... Chinese lilac
Syringa patula .... Dwarf Korean lilac
Syringa vulgaris .... Lilac
Syzygium paniculatum .... Eugenia
Tamarix aphylla .... Tamarisk
Taxus .... Yew
Thuja occidentalis .... American arborvitae
Tsuga canadensis .... Canadian hemlock
Tsuga heterophylla .... Western hemlock
Vaccinium ashei .... Rabbiteye blueberry
Vaccinium corymbosum .... Blueberry
Viburnum dentatum .... Arrowwood
Viburnum japonicum .... Viburnum
Viburnum lantana .... Wayfaring tree
Viburnum
  opulus .... European highbush cranberry
Viburnum suspensum .... Sandankwa
Viburnum tinus .... Laurustinus
Xylosma congestum .... Shiny xylosma

Natural form of *Nandina domestica*, nandina, works well as an easy-care, medium-size hedge.

Taxus species make some of the finest clipped hedges. Form and maximum height vary with the cultivar. Medium height is ideal for separating and defining an area without producing a closed-in feeling.

HIGH HEDGES AND SCREENS

Many of the most popular, classic hedge and screen plants are listed under Large-Scale Hedges and Screens, but they can be held to eye level or lower by pruning. The plants listed here rarely exceed 6 to 8 feet. Shape them into hedges or leave them natural as screens where space allows. Those marked with an asterisk * should not be sheared.

Abelia x grandiflora .... Glossy abelia
Acer circinatum .... Vine maple
Atriplex lentiformis
  'Breweri' .... Brewer saltbush
*Bambusa glaucescens
  riviereorum .... Chinese goddess bamboo
Berberis buxifolia .... Magellan barberry
Berberis darwinii .... Darwin barberry
Berberis koreana .... Korean barberry
Berberis x mentorensis .... Mentor barberry
Berberis thunbergii .... Japanese barberry
Buxus microphylla
  var. japonica .... Japanese boxwood
Buxus sempervirens .... English box
*Camellia japonica .... Camellia cultivars
Camellia sasanqua .... Sasanqua camellia
Caragana arborescens .... Siberian pea tree
Carissa grandiflora .... Natal plum
Chaenomeles speciosa .... Flowering quince
Citrus .... Citrus
*Cornus stolonifera .... Red-osier dogwood
Cotoneaster lucidus .... Hedge cotoneaster
Escallonia .... Escallonia
*Eucalyptus spathulata .... Swamp malee
Euonymus alata .... Winged burning bush
Euonymus fortunei 'Sarcoxie' .... Sarcoxie
  wintercreeper
Euonymus kiautschovica
  'Manhattan' .... Euonymus
*Forsythia x intermedia .... Forsythia
*Gardenia jasminoides
  'Mystery' .... Mystery gardenia

Hibiscus rosa-sinensis .... Tropical hibiscus
Ilex .... Holly
Juniperus .... Juniper
*Lagerstroemia indica .... Crape myrtle
Ligustrum japonicum .... Japanese privet
Ligustrum texanum .... Waxleaf privet
Ligustrum x vicaryi .... Vicary golden privet
Malus sargentii .... Sargent crabapple
Mahonia aquifolium .... Oregon grape
Myrtus communis .... Myrtle—a Classic
*Nandina domestica .... Nandina
Nerium oleander .... Oleander
*Philadelphus x virginalis .... Mock orange
Plumbago auriculata .... Plumbago
Prunus laurocerasus .... Laurel cherry
Punica granatum .... Pomegranate
Pyracantha .... Pyracantha
Raphiolepis indica .... Indian hawthorn
Rhododendron .... Rhododendron hybrids
*Rhododendron maximum .... Rosebay
  rhododendron
Rosa .... Rose
Rosmarinus officinalis
  'Tuscan Blue' .... Rosemary
Spiraea prunifolia plena .... Bridal-wreath
  spiraea
Syringa x chinensis .... Chinese lilac
Syringa vulgaris .... Lilac—some cultivars
*Vaccinium ashei .... Rabbiteye blueberry
*Vaccinium corymbosum .... Blueberry
Viburnum japonicum .... Viburnum
*Viburnum lantana .... Wayfaring tree
*Viburnum opulus 'Compactum' .... Compact
  European highbush cranberry
Viburnus tinus
  'Spring Bouquet' .... Spring bouquet
  laurustinus
*Weigela .... Weigela
Xylosma congestum 'Compacta' ...... Compact
  shiny xylosma

LARGE-SCALE HEDGES AND SCREENS

Large screens and hedgewalls from 8 feet to 50 feet high are useful for privacy, noise control and definition of space on a grand scale. Those marked with an asterisk * should not be sheared. Most can be clipped and held to a much lower height. Classics are time-honored plants that will live for a century or more.

Acacia longifolia .... Sydney golden wattle
Acer campestre .... Hedge maple—a Classic
Acer ginnala .... Amur maple
Arbutus unedo .... Strawberry tree—a Classic
Bambusa .... Bamboo—a Classic
Buxus sempervirens . English box—a Classic
Calocedrus decurrens .... California
  incense cedar
Camellia japonica .... Camellia—a Classic
Camellia sasanqua .... Sasanqua
  camellia—a Classic
Caragana arborescens .... Siberian pea tree
Carissa grandiflora .... Natal plum
Carpinus betulus .... Hornbeam—a Classic
Ceratonia siliqua .... Carob
Chamaecyparis lawsoniana .... Port
  Orford cedar
Citrus .... Citrus Classics
Cocculus laurifolius .... Cocculus
Cornus mas .... Cornelian cherry dogwood
*Cornus stolonifera .... Red-osier
  dogwood
Corylus avellana .... Filbert—a Classic
Crataegus .... Hawthorn—a Classic
Cupressocyparis leylandii
Cupressocyparis
*Cupressus glabra .... Arizona cypress
*Cupressus sempervirens
  'Stricta' .... Italian cypress—a Classic
Dodonea viscosa .... Hopbush
Elaeagnus angustifolia .... Russian olive
Elaeagnus pungens .... Silverberry

'Heitzii' juniper, with its blue-gray color and interesting texture, makes an imposing high screen.

LARGE-SCALE HEDGES AND SCREENS, CONTINUED

Eriobotrya japonica .... Loquat
Escallonia rubra .... Escallonia
Eucalyptus .... Eucalyptus
Euonymus alata .... Winged burning bush
Euonymus japonica ...... Evergreen euonymus
Fagus sylvatica .... Beech—a Classic
Feijoa sellowiana .... Pineapple guava
Fontanesia fortunei .... Fontanesia
Forsythia x intermedia .... Forsythia
Hibiscus rosa-sinensis .... Tropical hibiscus
Ilex .... Holly—a Classic
Juniperus chinensis .... Chinese
juniper—a Classic
Juniperus scopulorum .... Rocky
Mountain juniper
Juniperus virginiana .... Eastern red cedar
Lagerstroemia indica .... Crape myrtle
Laurus nobilis .... Grecian laurel—a Classic
Ligustrum amurense .... Amur privet
Ligustrum x ibolium .... Ibolium privet
Ligustrum japonicum .... Japanese
privet—a Classic
Ligustrum lucidum ... Glossy privet—a Classic
Ligustrum ovalifolium .... California privet
Lonicera korolkowii
'Zabeli' .... Zabel's honeysuckle
Lonicera tatarica .... Tatarian honeysuckle
Malus baccata 'Columnaris' .... Columnar
Siberian crabapple
Malus pumila .... Apple espalier—a Classic
Malus sargentii .... Sargent crabapple
Nerium oleander .... Oleander—a Classic
Osmanthus fragrans .... Sweet osmanthus
Osmanthus heterophyllus .... False holly—
a Classic
Photinia x fraseri .... Photinia
Picea abies .... Norway spruce
Picea glauca .... White spruce
Pinus eldarica .... Mondell pine

Pinus nigra .... Austrian pine
Pinus strobus .... White pine
Pittosporum crassifolium .... Karo
Pittosporum eugenioides .... Lemonwood
Pittosporum tenuifolium .... Black-
stemmed pittosporum
Pittosporum tobira .... Tobira mock orange
Pittosporum undulatum .... Victorian box—
a Classic
Prunus .... European plum
Prunus .... Japanese plum
Podocarpus gracilior .... Podocarpus
fern pine—a Classic
Podocarpus macrophyllus .... Yew pine—
a Classic
Pyrus communis .... Pear espalier—
a Classic
Pyrus hybrid .... Pear-apple espalier
Populus alba 'Bolleana' .... Bolleana poplar
Populus nigra 'Italica' .... Lombardy
poplar—a Classic
Prunus caroliniana .... Cherry laurel
Prunus ilicifolia .... Hollyleaf cherry
Prunus laurocerasus .... Laurel cherry—
a Classic
Prunus lusitanica .... Portugal laurel—
a Classic
Prunus maritima .... Beach plum
Prunus serrulata
'Amanogawa' .... Columnar Japanese
flowering cherry
Pseudotsuga menziesii .... Douglas fir
Punica granatum ..... Pomegranate—a Classic
Pyracantha .... Pyracantha
Raphiolepis indica .... Indian hawthorn
Rhamnus alaternus .... Italian buckthorn
Rhamnus cathartica .... Common buckthorn
Rhamnus frangula
'Columnaris' .... Tallhedge buckthorn
Rhododendron .... Southern indica
hybrid azaleas

Rhododendron maximum .... Rosebay
rhododendron
Rosa .... Rose Classics
Salix purpurea .... Purple-osier willow
Sequoia sempervirens .... Coast redwood
Spirea x vanhouttei .... Vanhoutte spiraea
Syringa x chinensis .... Chinese lilac
Syringa vulgaris .... Lilac
Syzygium paniculatum .... Eugenia—a Classic
Tamarix aphylla .... Tamarisk
Taxus .... Yew—Classics
Thuja occidentalis .... American
arborvitae—a Classic
Tilia cordata .... Littleleaf linden—
a Classic
Tsuga canadensis .... Canadian hemlock—
a Classic
Tsuga heterophylla .... Western hemlock
Viburnum dentatum .... Arrowwood
Viburnum lantana .... Wayfaring tree
Viburnum lentago .... Nannyberry
Viburnum opulus .... European
highbush cranberry
Viburnum tinus .... Laurustinus
Weigela florida .... Weigela
Xylosma congestum .... Shiny xylosma

Pittosporum eugenioides, lemonwood, grows to 40 feet high but can be kept much lower by pruning.

Podocarpus macrophyllus, yew pine, is excellent as a large-scale hedge for narrow spaces.

Pruning After Planting

Fast-Growing Deciduous or Broadleaf Evergreen Plants

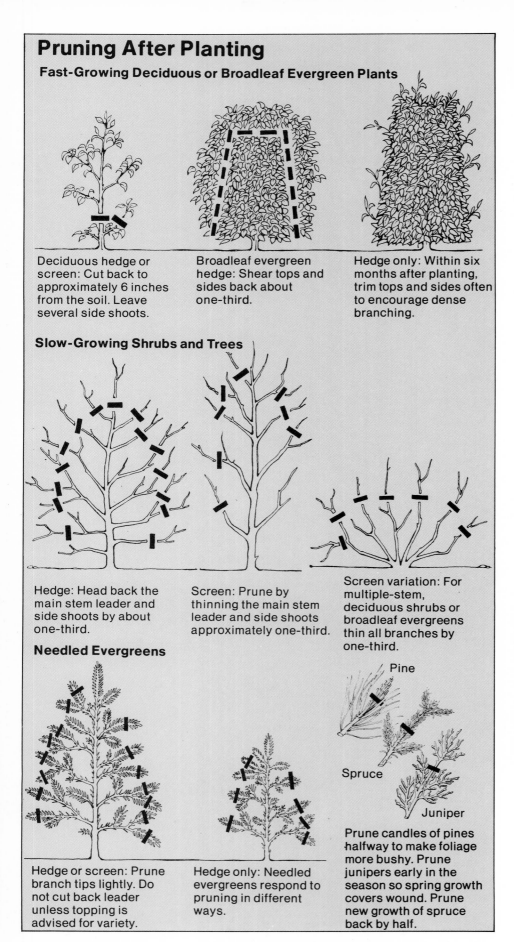

Deciduous hedge or screen: Cut back to approximately 6 inches from the soil. Leave several side shoots.

Broadleaf evergreen hedge: Shear tops and sides back about one-third.

Hedge only: Within six months after planting, trim tops and sides often to encourage dense branching.

Slow-Growing Shrubs and Trees

Hedge: Head back the main stem leader and side shoots by about one-third.

Screen: Prune by thinning the main stem leader and side shoots approximately one-third.

Screen variation: For multiple-stem, deciduous shrubs or broadleaf evergreens thin all branches by one-third.

Needled Evergreens

Hedge or screen: Prune branch tips lightly. Do not cut back leader unless topping is advised for variety.

Hedge only: Needled evergreens respond to pruning in different ways.

Pine

Spruce

Juniper

Prune candles of pines halfway to make foliage more bushy. Prune junipers early in the season so spring growth covers wound. Prune new growth of spruce back by half.

FIRST-YEAR MAINTENANCE

Both hedges and screens require deep, regular watering during their first year. Watering deeply encourages deep rooting. Fertilizing speeds growth, but if slow-release fertilizer is applied at planting, further applications are not necessary.

Hedges and screens require some pruning the day they are planted, but pruning requirements are different after plants become more established. Screens require little if any pruning after their first pruning.

Hedges require careful shaping the first year or two following planting to develop dense branching and strong form. The most important part of shaping is keeping the top of the hedge narrower than the base. This allows for more even growth and exposure to the sun. Start pruning from the bottom and work up. Keep cutting the top back until the sides and base are dense, gradually permitting the hedge to reach the desired height.

In most cases, do not cut back the tops of needled evergreen conifer hedges.

Fine-textured, broadleaf evergreens and deciduous plants with small leaves should be sheared. Shoots on plants with large leaves should be cut back one by one to prevent a ragged look. Another method for pruning plants with large leaves is to shear just before the spring burst of new growth. The ragged cut leaves are quickly covered with fresh new foliage.

Hedge and border plants are planted closely together. This crowding forces roots to compete for moisture and nutrients. Regular clipping stimulates the plants to produce new leaves. Root competition and continually stimulated growth means that these forms should receive at *least* one annual application of slow-release fertilizer. Remove weeds as soon as they are noticed to eliminate competition. After hedges have grown to become dense, weeds are usually eliminated naturally by the shade created under the hedge plants.

Pruning Hedges the Second and Third Year

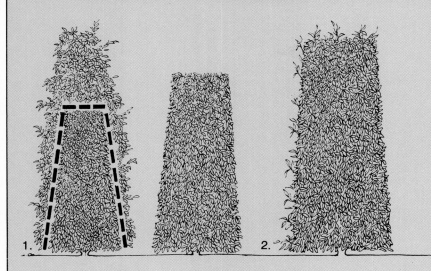

Fast-Growing, Deciduous or Broadleaf Evergreen Plants

1. Second year: In the spring, cut back severely, removing about half of the new growth. Every month or so, shear sides and top to maintain the desired form. In cold-winter climates, do not prune at the end of summer—it will promote new, cold-tender growth. Shape deciduous hedges during their dormant season. In mild-winter climates, shear sides and top as necessary to maintain desired form.

2. Third year: Every month or so, shear sides and top to maintain the desired form. In cold-winter climates, do not prune at the end of summer—it will promote new, cold-tender growth. Shape deciduous hedges during their dormant season. In mild-winter climates, shear as necessary to maintain desired form. Follow these pruning techniques each year.

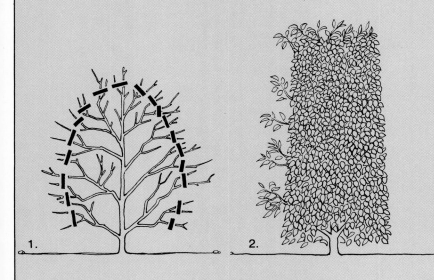

Slow-Growing Shrubs and Trees

1. Second year: With slow-growing plants, pruning is necessary only once or twice a year. Remove about one-third of new growth, keeping base of plant wider than the top. Shape deciduous hedges—except *Fagus* and *Carpinus* species—during their dormant season.

2. Third year: Pruning is necessary only once or twice a year. Plants are now large enough to be given their shaped form. Cut to the outline desired. Do not cut back the top until hedge reaches its ultimate height. Follow these pruning techniques each year.

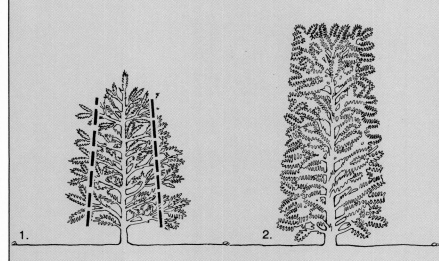

Needled Evergreens

1. Second year: Trim and top at the appropriate time for particular conifer species. Shape to the desired form. Do not let conifers get out of bounds, or it may be difficult to reclaim plantings. Pruning back below young, green needles usually leaves stubby, unattractive growth.

2. Third year: Follow second-year pruning techniques the third year, and each subsequent year.

SHEARING

There are many methods for attaining crisp, sheared, hedge lines. No matter what method you choose to follow, it is important to shear sides of the hedge first, then the top. Start at the bottom and work up, maintaining a slight, inward taper. This taper keeps the base foliage dense because sunlight penetrates all the way down to the bottom of the plant. This taper is often referred to as *batter*, a word that evolved from the connection between architecture and hedges. Tall hedgewalls sometimes have steep batter to accentuate their image of stability.

Choosing a hedge form is basically a matter of personal taste. Slightly tapering sides prevent sparse bottoms. Triangular tops shed snow more readily and help prevent branch breakage in severe winters. Some people give their hedge tops graceful curves or create decorative accents. Some shear one side and prune the foliage on the other to expose the trunks.

TOPIARY

Topiary means to shape a plant into a dense, unnatural form, usually an animal or geometric shape. Topiary has been popular through the centuries. Many plants listed in the encyclopedia may be sheared into topiary forms. Traditional species for this treatment include *Taxus, Buxus, Laurus, Myrtus, Ligustrum japonicum, Syzygium* and *Tsuga*. Consider planting topiary in containers. They can move when you do.

MAINTENANCE OF SCREENS AND SHAPED HEDGES

Taking care of screens or lightly shaped hedges is simple during the years after planting. Maintenance normally consists of one annual pruning and fertilizing with slow-release commercial fertilizer. Cut out diseased or dead wood and remove branches that detract from beauty or form. Suckers may be removed, left to contribute to the density of the hedge or screen or replanted to extend the line.

Topiary is the art of sculpting plants with pruning shears. Animal shapes and geometric forms are popular.

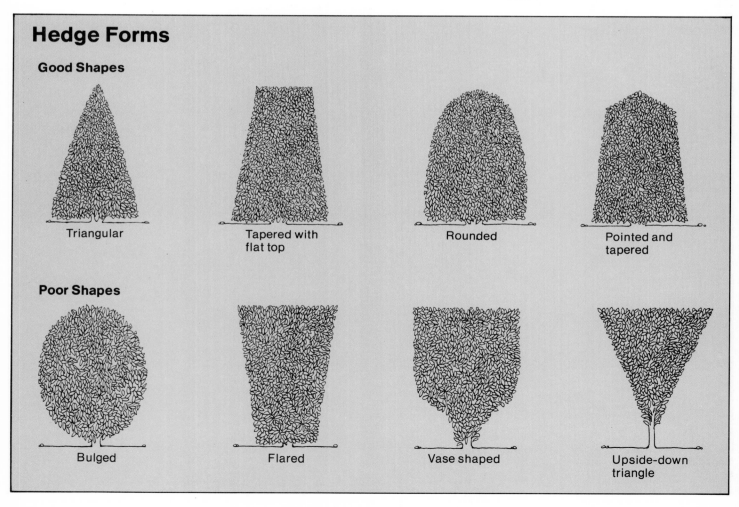

Hedge Forms

Good Shapes

Triangular

Tapered with flat top

Rounded

Pointed and tapered

Poor Shapes

Bulged

Flared

Vase shaped

Upside-down triangle

Crisply sheared edges are essential for an elegant, formal hedge. This professional gardener clips the sides first, then the top. He does it all by eye—experience is his guideline.

Many gardeners shear one section of hedge at a time. Platform on sturdy sawhorses makes a safe support for each section of work.

Electric hedge shears speed up trimming, but a steady hand is needed to avoid overclipping.

Lightly shaped or informal hedges and screens can be pruned in various ways to control size or stimulate new growth or flowers. Shoots are usually cut back one by one. The timing depends on several factors. Most deciduous species are lightly shaped in their dormant season—winter—by thinning. Plants that bloom in spring on shoots developed during the previous year should be pruned right after their flowers fade. Plants that bloom in summer or fall on shoots that develop the same year should be pruned in early spring.

In general, prune plants that produce berries or fruit after the berries or fruit have disappeared or after they have been harvested.

Many people prune shrubby screens every three or five years to revitalize them or to control their size. The same method is used for deciduous and broadleaf evergreen plants. Remove weak, dead or diseased growth. Cut about one-third of the oldest shoots to ground level. Prune deciduous species during the dormant season. Prune broadleaf evergreens in mild-winter climates during winter. In cold-winter climates, prune broadleafs in spring.

PROTECTING AGAINST COLD

Elaborate coverings to protect plants against cold are expensive, time consuming and unattractive. The best protection is to plant species adapted to your climate conditions.

Broadleaf evergreen species need the most care to make it through snowy weather in cold-winter climates. Certain site conditions favor their survival. A windbreak sometimes makes it possible to grow broadleafs where they are not adapted. They need shelter from harsh winter winds that dry and damage their foliage. A partially shady or fully shaded site also favors their survival.

Never prune late in the summer in cold-winter climates. Pruning stimulates new growth. Young, cold-tender leaves are quickly killed by frosts.

Water deeply and well in late fall before the soil freezes. An *antidesiccant* is a protective film that can be sprayed on leaves at this time. It reduces moisture loss by inhibiting the natural process of *evapo-transpiration* that continues through winter.

Broadleaf evergreens adapted to mild-winter climates have different requirements to protect them from cold. A plant growing in Zone 9 that is not reliable out of Zone 10 needs a special approach. Pruning, watering or fertilizing toward the end of summer encourages undesirable, new, cold-tender growth that is easily damaged by frost. Taper off watering as the end of summer nears to harden new tissue and make it woody.

Do not remove plants that have been killed to the ground by severe winter weather. Wait until all danger of frost has past, then cut out dead wood, water deeply, fertilize and mulch. New shoots usually appear in spring. Follow the correct pruning procedures for newly planted hedge or screen forms.

RENOVATION

Most overgrown and neglected hedges and screens may be revitalized and restored by forcing new growth. Bare spots can be filled in by replacing dead plants. Cut out poorly placed, dead

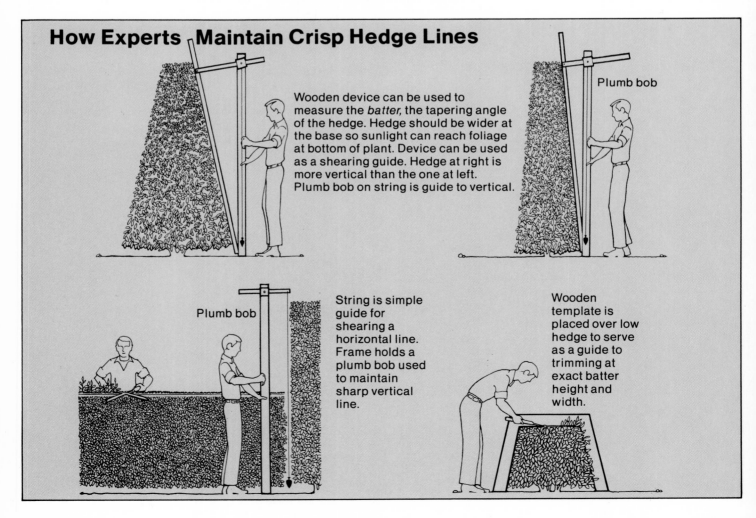

How Experts Maintain Crisp Hedge Lines

Wooden device can be used to measure the *batter*, the tapering angle of the hedge. Hedge should be wider at the base so sunlight can reach foliage at bottom of plant. Device can be used as a shearing guide. Hedge at right is more vertical than the one at left. Plumb bob on string is guide to vertical.

Plumb bob

Plumb bob

String is simple guide for shearing a horizontal line. Frame holds a plumb bob used to maintain sharp vertical line.

Wooden template is placed over low hedge to serve as a guide to trimming at exact batter height and width.

or diseased branches. Try renovation before taking the drastic step of replacing an entire hedge or screen.

Broadleaf evergreens should be renovated in early spring. Deciduous species should be renovated during the dormant season.

Few coniferous needled evergreens respond to severe pruning. Once they become overgrown, they are often replaced. Cutting back below current growth leaves stubs that will not resprout.

When you renovate, give your plants a healthy dose of the basics—*remove weeds, water deeply, fertilize and add a mulch.* For slow-growing screens, follow basic pruning techniques. Remove poorly placed, dead or diseased branches, thin overly long or weak branches. Lightly thin to stimulate new growth.

Cutting an overgrown screen down to size usually stimulates new growth. New height will be maintained slightly above ladder top.

Renovation

Cut and Come Again Method

Twiggy Shrubs with Basal Shoots
Cut back to within a few inches of ground level in the appropriate season.

Shrubs with Stout Stems on a Basal Clump
Cut back to within 1 foot of the ground in the appropriate season. Remove poorly placed branches and stems entirely.

Fast-Growing Hedges that Tolerate Heavy Pruning
1. Cut deciduous plants back to a few inches. Cut evergreens back to within 1 foot of ground level.
2. Within the next six months, trim tops and sides of new growth often to encourage dense branching. Allow hedge to reach desired height gradually. Keep base wider than top. Resume regular pruning schedule after form is attained.

ESPALIERS

Most pliable trees and shrubs make fine espaliers, but edible espaliers have obvious advantages. Training fruit against walls is a practice that began in Western culture with the Romans, and reached a state of high art in medieval castle and monastery gardens. Apples and pears benefited from the heat that radiated from the garden walls. Herbs laid out nearby in intricate beds flourished in full sun— free from the shade of trees. In warm, Mediterranean climates, rosemary and grapes were the favored espalier subjects.

Espalier methods range in complexity from planting pre-trained forms available from nurseries to complicated techniques that are more like botanic architecture. Low-maintenance espaliers in simple, free-form patterns are composed of relatively slow-growing plants that do not require constant pruning.

Every espalier needs some support and attention for at least three growing seasons. Shapes are attained gradually. After the desired pattern is formed, maintenance consists of checking and retying supports, snipping out unwanted growth and rubbing off buds before they develop into unwanted branches. Some espaliers mature into large plants with stout trunks and branches. Supports may be removed when plants reach this size.

PATTERNS

Informal patterns are attractive arrangements of branches that do not conform to a traditional shape. Minimum training is necessary. You simply follow your imagination and the plant's natural branching character.

Formal patterns conform to traditional designs. Branches are trained to follow defined lines. Because the requirements are strict, few plants can be manipulated into formal patterns. Those that are adapted to formal training are the most versatile plants to espalier. Apples and pears are included in this group. These can take on any shape, from horizontal, French-style, garden borders only one foot high to elaborate, lattice patterns known as the *Belgian fence*.

PLACEMENT GUIDELINES

Many fruit and flower espaliers benefit from the protection of windbreaks. But espaliers placed too close to windbreak plants will be forced to compete with them for nutrients and light. This may slow plant growth, which is an advantage in some cases. Consider the particulars of your situation before you plant.

Be aware of the sun's exposure when selecting a wall support for an espalier. Some plants thrive in cool shade; others prefer sunny heat. Fruit trees need about six hours of sunlight daily. South-facing walls receive the most sun and heat. East-facing walls receive morning sun and afternoon shade. West-facing walls

Left: Container espaliers take up little space, can be positioned wherever growing conditions are most favorable and move when you do. Pruning is easy during the deciduous dormant period, when the form is clearly visible. Above: 'Golden Delicious' apple, trained on post-and-wire supports, is a heavy producer of fruit.

get morning shade and intense afternoon sun. Shade from nearby trees or buildings may alter amounts of sunshine available to espaliers.

Heat from the sun is radiated off exposed walls and paving. This is an advantage or a liability. In mild-climate regions, heat-loving plants thrive when placed directly against south- or west-facing walls. A site out of the wind with an overhang usually provides protection from frost. This permits you to grow varieties slightly out of their normal range.

In hot-summer climates, heat from south- and west-facing walls may cook fruit and scorch espaliers. To avoid this, train on a wire or wood frame positioned about 6 inches from the wall. In cold-winter climates, place cold-tender plants subject to frost damage out of the wind in a shady or partly shady location.

Fruit-producing espaliers trained on post-and-wire fences will be exposed to the greatest amount of sunlight if fences run north to south.

CHOOSING THE PATTERN AND THE PLANT

Pay close attention to shaping and pruning espaliers started from scratch during the first several seasons. Single cordons and informal fan patterns are the easiest. Complicated forms in three dimensions are for dedicated, experienced gardeners only.

Pick a plant variety to suit the pattern, or vice versa. Many species are not suited to formal, symmetrical shapes. Generally, slow-growing plants make good espaliers. It is also necessary to know the mature size of plants. Plan spacing and supports when you select a pattern to determine the number of plants to buy. A single cordon hedge effect requires spacing plants 1 to 3 feet apart. Dwarf fruit are spaced about 6 to 8 feet apart. Full-size trees and shrubs spread 10 to 20 feet or more.

Plants with arching branches, notably *Pyracantha* and *Forsythia* species, can be trained to spread much greater than their branches normally grow.

If you are planting more than one espalier, choose one variety for a uniform appearance, or several varieties for a mosaic effect. A selection of varieties with different fruit maturity dates—early, midseason and late—will extend the harvest season.

ROOTSTOCKS

Dwarfs are recommended for apple and pear espaliers. They begin to bear fruit at a young age, and their growth is more restrained than full-size trees.

A wide variety of apple rootstocks are available. Many are labeled simply as "dwarf" or "semidwarf" with no further explanation. However, some labels give more specific details. For example, you might see the initials M and M.M. M

Espalier Supports for Cold Locations

At night, cold air flows down hillsides and slopes. It can be trapped by solid plantings or walls, freezing espaliers and nearby plants. Espaliers trained against open fences or on post-and-wire supports allow air to pass through.

stands for *Malling*. **M.M.** stands for *Merton-Malling*. These names designate the origin of the rootstock. M.7 and M.M.106 are both semidwarf. M.M.106 is slightly larger. M.9 and M.4 are more dwarf. These trees will always require support, and are excellent if 6 feet is the maximum desired height. They produce more fruit than non-dwarfs for the space occupied. M.26 is a dwarf with a faster growth rate than most other dwarfs. M.2 and M.M.111 produce large, vigorous trees adapted to poor soil conditions.

ERECTING SUPPORTS

Materials for the espalier frame should be sturdy and built to last. Nails, screws, angle irons, pipe, bars, nipples, turnbuckles and wires should be galvanized to resist rust. Use 8- to 16-gage wire, depending on the ultimate size of the plant variety selected. The smaller the gage number, the thicker the wire. Vinyl-clad wire is rust resistant. Black wire is practically invisible on free-standing supports. Choose colors to blend with wall surfaces.

Bamboo poles or lightweight wood stakes are often used for additional support between wires. It is not necessary to treat them with a preservative to resist rotting, but other wood, especially fence posts, should be treated. Or, use pressure-treated lumber.

Fasten espalier branches loosely with plastic plant ties or plain cord. If fasteners are tied too tight, they girdle and kill branches. Check ties regularly—at least once a year.

Take advantage of existing surfaces when you build the support. Espaliers can be tied directly to chain-link fences. Wood fences do not absorb and release as much heat as block walls, and are easy to nail. Trace patterns directly on the support with wire. The method of wall support that you choose depends on whether plants can grow directly against walls in your climate.

Nail or drill into walls or into the mortar joints between bricks or blocks. Insert expansion bolts to hold hardware securely. For more securely structured frames, attach wooden posts or angle irons with holes to accept screws and support wires. Space supports to allow plants to spread.

Substantial frames placed 6 inches or more from the wall surface should be held in place with threaded pipe. Drill into walls, force in a lead collar and screw in threaded pipe. Attach a wire,

Chain-link fence provides support for many kinds of espaliers. 'Comice' pear greatly improves the appearance of the fence and creates privacy.

Post-and-wire framework supports apple espalier. It is important to build supports to last: They will be in use for many years.

welded rebar or wood frame. If desired, finish off threaded pipe ends with flanges.

It is possible to train branches directly around pipes, as long as they are placed at predetermined distances for formal patterns, and training is done in gradual stages.

POST CONSTRUCTION FOR FREE-STANDING SUPPORTS

Most free-standing supports utilize post-construction techniques used in fencing. After posts are set, a wire or wood trellis is installed. Posts may be positioned close to walls or included in the landscape like a fence.

Use wooden 2x4 or 4x4 posts or 1-1/2-inch-diameter metal pipe fence posts. Posts must be buried *at least* 2 feet deep in the ground. A poured concrete collar will hold posts more securely than tamped earth.

Space posts according to espalier pattern and plant size. Place one plant between posts set 6 to 10 feet apart, or position two plants 6 feet apart between 4x4 posts set 12 feet apart.

String wire at regular, 12- to 36-inch intervals, depending on espalier pattern.

Some people position plants first to determine the height of the lowest wire. No matter what interval is chosen, wire courses should be parallel. Choose a wire gage that can support the plant's mature weight and the distance spanned. Eight gage is best for posts spaced farther than 6 feet apart.

Position screw eyes on end posts. Drill holes through middle posts in alignment with screw eyes. String wire between posts, and place a turnbuckle at one end of each wire to hold them taut. Variation: Use 4x4 end posts with screw eyes and turnbuckles. String wires and pull taut. Attach wire to 2x4 middle posts with staples.

You can build wooden trellises or buy them prefabricated. Install trellises against walls or on free-standing supports. It is helpful to devise a way to remove the trellis if painting or other maintenance is necessary. You can also nail trellises to fence posts. Do not force the trellis to span large distances that will produce sagging. Eight feet is the recommended maximum span for a 2x4.

Espaliers in containers can be supported by small poles or posts inserted directly into the soil, or nail them onto the sides of the container. String wire at intervals on this framework. Frames of welded *rebar*, steel construction rod, are also useful. The simplest framework consists of a few stakes nailed to the back of the container or poked into the soil.

LUMBER PRESERVATIVES

Wooden posts placed in direct contact with the ground are susceptible to rot. Decay can be delayed by using *pressure-treated wood*. This is lumber treated with preservatives forced deep into the cells of the wood. Pressure-treated lumber may have a greenish or brownish color. Many types are safe to use around plants. Use wood designated as *LP-22* for ground-contact applications. Use *LP-2* for above-ground use.

You can apply a preservative yourself. Use copper or zinc naphthenate, trade name Cuprinol. It is not toxic to plants, but it turns wood greenish. This is rarely a problem because espalier limbs usually cover their framework. If green wood is objectionable, paint it, or treat only the portion that will be in contact with the soil.

Preservatives can be brushed or rolled

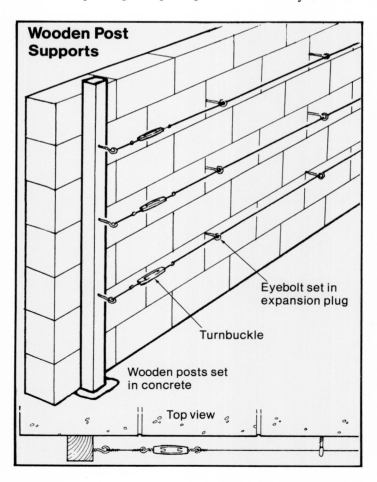

Wooden Post Supports

Eyebolt set in expansion plug

Turnbuckle

Wooden posts set in concrete

Top view

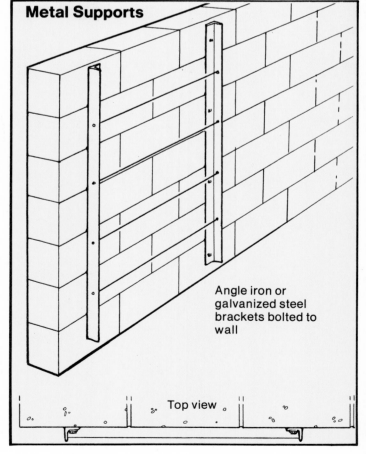

Metal Supports

Angle iron or galvanized steel brackets bolted to wall

Top view

Apple espaliers on a small balcony are located high above a city street. Plants are exposed to strong winds, so they require heavy-duty supports.

Metal bracing is bolted to wooden framework and railing to support espaliers in winds.

Espalier pattern is a formal Verrier palmette. Wooden framework and plant produce a light, screening effect.

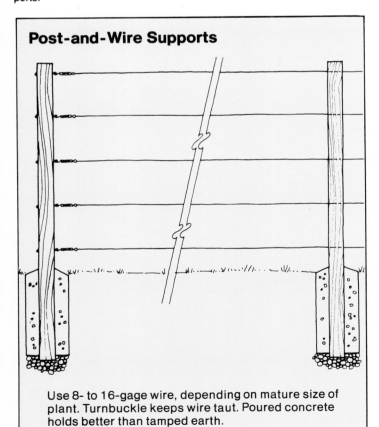

Post-and-Wire Supports

Use 8- to 16-gage wire, depending on mature size of plant. Turnbuckle keeps wire taut. Poured concrete holds better than tamped earth.

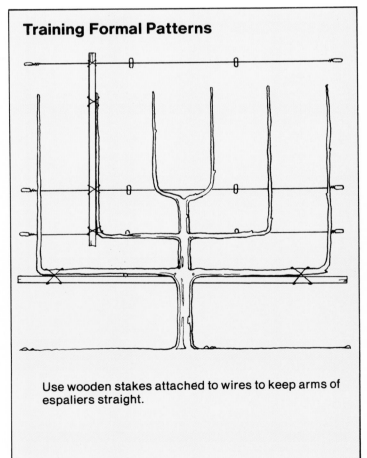

Training Formal Patterns

Use wooden stakes attached to wires to keep arms of espaliers straight.

on. But for best penetration, soak lumber in a large container or trough full of preservative. Make a trough of concrete blocks or 4x4's, and line it with plastic.

Whenever you saw through treated lumber, including pressure-treated lumber, paint preservative on the freshly cut ends. Do not burn wood scraps of treated lumber: Toxic fumes can be released.

Avoid using creosote and *penta*, pentachlorophenol, as preservatives. They are toxic to plants and humans.

BUYING PLANTS

Before planting, take a sketch of your espalier pattern to the nursery and ask a knowledgeable clerk for help. If you do not buy pre-trained espaliers, choose young, vigorous plants. They respond well to training. Deciduous varieties purchased bare root are inexpensive and ready to prune. Deciduous fruit trees should be one- or two-year-old *whips*—straight stems.

If you are planting fruit-producing plants, ask about pollination requirements. Some require a pollinator nearby to produce fruit. Ask about the rootstock if the plant is not labeled. Keep in mind that apple and pear dwarfs or semidwarfs bear fruit earlier than full-size trees.

PLANTING

Review basic information on soil preparation, heeling in and other planning procedures. In addition, here are some special pointers for planting espaliers.

If you are planting fruit trees, be sure the graft union, if present, is at least 2 inches above the ground *after* the soil has been watered and tamped down. The union is a bulge just above the roots where the *scion*—the trunk of the tree—was grafted.

Cordons are often grown at a 30° to 45° angle to increase the number of fruiting spurs. These trained forms are called *oblique* cordons. They grow more slowly so they are easy to control, and require less height than the same-size vertical cordon. This means they are more productive. For the most effective results, plant oblique cordons at an angle or lower them gradually later on. Position the scion so it will be on the top side of oblique cordons.

Place plants at least 6 inches from walls or fences to permit trunks to expand. Space plants according to their ultimate size or the size you plan to prune them. Space single upright or oblique cordons 1 foot or more apart. Space dwarf fruit trees 6 to 8 feet apart. Apples on M.27 rootstock should be planted 4 feet apart; M.9 rootstock 10 feet apart; M.26 rootstock 10 to 12 feet apart; M.106 rootstock 12 to 15 feet apart; M.2, M.7 and M.111 rootstock 15 to 18 feet apart.

Wall footings often extend below ground into the area where you might

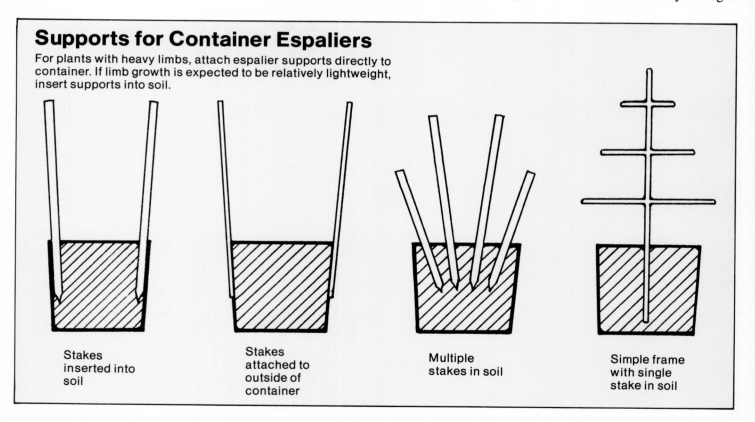

Supports for Container Espaliers

For plants with heavy limbs, attach espalier supports directly to container. If limb growth is expected to be relatively lightweight, insert supports into soil.

Stakes inserted into soil

Stakes attached to outside of container

Multiple stakes in soil

Simple frame with single stake in soil

want to place your espalier rootball. If this is the case, bend the roots carefully to get as close to the wall as possible. Or, place the plant at an angle, pointing the trunk toward the wall. You can gradually train the trunk back and up against the wall.

Espaliers trained against a wall often blossom earlier than free-standing trees. This can create a problem if another tree is needed to bloom at the same time as a pollinator. Plant an additional espalier on the same wall, or graft on a pollinator branch.

Organic or inorganic fertilizers supply necessary plant nutrients. High-nitrogen fertilizers stimulate fruit trees to produce fast, undesirable, woody growth. Be conservative in applying fertilizer to fruit trees. Too little is better than too much. Wait for the second growing season before fertilizing and then apply a conservative amount of a slow-release type.

Both productive and functional, edible espalier of sweet oranges requires infrequent but careful pruning.

INFORMAL ESPALIERS

Acer circinatum .... Vine maple
Berberis .... Barberry
Camellia japonica .... Camellia
Camellia sasanqua .... Sasanqua camellia
Caragana arborescens lorbergi .... Ferny caragana
Carissa grandiflora .... Natal plum
Chaenomeles speciosa .... Flowering quince
Citrus .... Citrus—all varieties
Cocculus laurifolius .... Cocculus
Cornus mas .... Cornelian cherry dogwood
Cotoneaster .... Cotoneaster
Crataegus .... Hawthorn
Cydonia oblonga .... Fruiting quince
Dodonaea viscosa 'Green' .. Green hopbush
Dodonaea viscosa 'Purpurea' and 'Saratoga' .... Purple hopbush
Elaeagnus pungens .... Silverberry
Eriobotrya japonica .... Loquat
Escallonia 'Balfouri' .... Escallonia
Eucalyptus caesia .... Eucalyptus
Eucalyptus erythrocorys .... Red-cap gum
Eucalyptus orbifolia .... Round-leafed mallee
Euonymus alata .... Winged burning bush
Euonymus fortunei .... Wintercreeper
Euonymus japonica .... Evergreen euonymus
Euonymus kiautschovica 'Manhattan' .... Euonymus
Feijoa sellowiana .... Pineapple guava
Forsythia x intermedia .... Forsythia
Gardenia jasminoides .... Gardenia
Hibiscus syriacus .... Rose of Sharon
Ilex .... Holly
Juniperus .... Juniper
Lagerstroemia indica .... Crape myrtle
Ligustrum japonicum .... Japanese privet
Ligustrum texanum .... Waxleaf privet
Magnolia grandiflora ...... Southern magnolia
Malus pumila .... Apple
Malus sargentii .... Sargent crabapple
Nerium oleander .... Oleander
Osmanthus fragrans .... Sweet osmanthus
Osmanthus heterophyllus .... False holly
Philadelphus x virginalis .... Mock orange
Photinia x fraseri .... Photinia
Plumbago auriculata .... Plumbago
Podocarpus gracilior ..Podocarpus fern pine
Podocarpus macrophyllus .... Yew pine
Prunus ..... European and Japanese varieties
Prunus caroliniana .... Cherry laurel
Prunus laurocerasus 'Zabeliana' ...... English laurel
Prunus serrulata 'Amanogawa' ..... Japanese flowering cherry
Punica granatum .... Pomegranate
Pyracantha fortuneana 'Graberi' Pyracantha
Pyracantha coccinea 'Government Red' .... Pyracantha
Pyrus communis .... Pear
Pyrus hybrid .... Pear-apple
Pyrus kawakamii .... Evergreen pear
Raphiolepis indica 'Majestic Beauty' ....Indian hawthorn
Rhododendron ....Some rhododendron varieties
Rosa .... Rose
Rosmarinus officinalis .... Rosemary
Taxus .... Yew species
Viburnum tinus .... Viburnum
Weigela florida .... Weigela
Xylosma congestum ....Shiny xylosma

FORMAL ESPALIERS

Camellia japonica .... Camellia
Camellia sasanqua .... Sasanqua camellia
Forsythia x intermedia .... Forsythia
Ilex cornuta 'Burfordii' ....Burford holly
Ilex crenata .... Japanese holly
Citrus limon .... Lemon—see Citrus
Magnolia grandiflora ...... Southern magnolia
Malus pumila .... Apple
Prunus serrulata 'Amanogawa' ..... Columnar Japanese flowering cherry
Pyracantha 'Graberi' .... Pyracantha
Pyrus communis .... Pear
Pyrus hybrid .... Pear-apple
Pyrus kawakamii .... Evergreen pear
Taxus cuspidata .... Japanese yew
Taxus x media .... Intermediate yew

Pyrus kawakamii, evergreen pear, as informal espalier.

Long-lived spur common to apples, above, and pears is a type of branch that lives for years, producing the flowering buds that develop into the fruit.

Short-lived spur found on apricots, above, also produces flower buds. Spur dies within two to five years and must be pruned periodically so that it will be replaced with new growth.

Peaches and nectarines bear fruit on shoots that must be replaced yearly. For this reason, a continual supply of new, young wood is essential. Severe pruning each year helps ensure optimum fruiting.

CLASSIC PATTERNS

Forcing plants into patterns goes against their nature, but is a challenge that produces lovely, lacy structures. Classic, time-honored espalier patterns were not devised simply to make use of small spaces or to be purely ornamental. They evolved as early horticulturists learned to control the vigor of major branches, referred to as *limbs* or *arms,* to avoid excess woody growth. This in turn increased the yield of fruit.

Apples and pears are traditional espalier subjects. They form *spurs*—short, stubby, modified branches— that bear the flower buds that produce flowers and fruit. Because fruit tree branches are generally more vigorous when allowed to grow upright, training them to grow at a more horizontal angle forces energy into the spurs, accelerating their development. Branches can be trained to the desired angle from the start, or gradually lowered. Begin lowering branches in the dormant season after one season of fast, vertical growth. The latter approach produces the pattern in less time.

Slow, diligent training is the key to success with formal espaliers. The word "formal" in garden history has come to mean *symmetrical, ordered, somewhat geometric and neat.* Espalier specialist Dr. Robert Stebbins of Oregon State University has this comment on formal espaliers: "The formal patterns were designed to achieve an equilibrium between growth and fruiting throughout the tree without excessive amounts of pruning. Informal patterns are easier than formal types, but production and fruit quality may be less."

Most classic patterns have retained their French names. There are many variations of the patterns and their names. The word "espalier" has been applied to at least one specific pattern. The French use it to describe a tree that has branches attached directly to a wall. In this book, any plant trained to a flat plane is an espalier.

In the past, skilled gardeners used espaliers of various plants to form the walls of three-dimensional garden structures, grafting branches together where they crossed. You can use versatile, single cordons to form arches or pattern edges. Try to cover your support framework with espalier limbs and single cordons.

PRUNING

Prune espaliers as often as necessary during the growing and dormant seasons to maintain the pattern. Pinching out buds you know you do not want to develop is an effective control method. Remove watersprouts and suckers whenever they appear.

Summer pruning of apples and pears is recommended to promote greater spur formation. Spurs that form may be much longer than their slow-growing counterparts on deciduous fruit trees pruned during the dormant season.

Start pruning in late spring or early summer after the first flush of growth. Cut back side shoots to three buds 4 to 6 inches long from the main limb. New shoots will sprout from the cuts. Whenever new shoot growth is longer than 10 or 12 inches, cut back to one or two buds from the last cut.

Usually a minimum of two summer prunings are necessary. One pruning each month in summer is better.

In cold climates, avoid pruning in late summer. Early fall frosts can damage the new, cold-tender growth stimulated by pruning. Wait until the dormant season to remove unwanted growth.

Avoid pruning the *main leader,* the central trunk or stem, until it has reached the desired length. Pruning this limb stimulates a new, vigorous extension leader to form. This new leader is often bare of spurs and is usually not as easy to hold to a pattern as other branches.

Tying vigorous shoots so their tips face down may force them to form flower buds. Shoots that never attain a length greater than 9 inches often have fruiting buds at their tips. Do not cut these back. Some experts recommend pinching out flower buds in the first spring after planting to prevent fruit formation. If you do this, be very careful not to damage spurs. Thin excess fruit from spurs when they are thumbnail size. Again, be careful not to damage spurs. As trees mature, their spurs can become crowded with buds. Thin spurs of weak and excess buds, leaving about two or three buds per spur.

The classic patterns shown on the following pages are for people who like to clip and prune. Others should not avoid espaliers, but they should let the plant determine its own informal pattern.

ESPALIER, TIER OR HORIZONTAL T

This popular pattern is called *espalier* in Europe. It is known in the United States as a *tier espalier* or *horizontal T* to distinguish it from other espalier patterns.

Cut back a leader to just above three buds. This stimulates buds to produce several new shoots. Train new shoots to the pattern. These beginning steps are the same steps that are necessary to start the *palmette oblique, Belgian fence, Verrier palmette* and *U-shaped* espaliers, described in the following pages. You can also start a horizontal T using a young, branched tree. To do this, make the cut, and lower the best remaining one or two branches gradually, using stakes tied to the wires.

This pattern with a first level approximately 12 inches above the soil makes a classic garden border. It is often called a *single horizontal cordon*. A double tier maintained at the second-wire level produces a low-hedge effect. Several tiers create a full-hedge effect.

The disadvantage of the horizontal T is sporadic limb vigor. Watersprouts tend to form on vigorous, low limbs close to the central leader. The ends of these lower limbs tend to lose vigor. Cut out watersprouts, but don't prune excessively or it can disrupt the balance between shoot growth and fruiting. Train limbs straight to avoid excessive watersprout formation. Tie or tape as much as necessary.

Develop only three tiers on dwarf fruit. Develop more tiers on full-size trees.

Ancient apple in a horizontal T covers a lathhouse wall. This is the formal pattern that most people associate with the word *espalier*.

Tier or Horizontal T

1. Head bare-root whip or young branched tree at or near first wire. Leave at least three buds or branches below cut. Tie branches to wire below cut.

2. During first growing season, permit buds to develop into shoots.

3. Choose three best shoots and remove others. Train two horizontally along wires and one vertically. Shorten long branches so all are approximately equal in length.

4. During the growing season, prune or pinch plant regularly to maintain the pattern. Shorten side shoots and subshoots to spurs.

5. In second dormant season, head plant at or near second wire. Repeat process of training new shoots and central leader from buds that develop next season.

6. A minimum of four years is required to obtain an espalier this height. Each dormant season, repeat steps 1 through 4 as necessary to hold pattern and develop spurs.

SINGLE CORDONS

The name *cordon* means *rope, ribbon* or *cord*. Single cordons are the simplest espalier form. They are straight stems with severely shortened branches. On fruit trees, these shortened branches are loaded with fruit buds, making the cordon one of the most efficient fruit-producing forms. Many varieties can be grown in a space no taller or wider than most fences. Choose plants from the *formal* list only.

Vertical cordons are versatile. They are often combined with other espalier patterns to form edges at the end of a row. They are easy to train up end posts to conceal framework. For a hedge effect, space 1 to 3 feet apart and train on post-and-wire frames. Or, stake plants individually without a framework. The farther apart cordons are spaced, the more open their screening effect. Use them as fences or as dividers to separate different sections of the garden. Vertical cordons can also be trained like vines into arches or over pergolas.

Oblique cordons are trained at a 30° to 60° angle from the ground. Plant at the desired angle or lower plants gradually as they grow. Training at an angle permits the cordon to grow longer yet still be within arm's reach. It also encourages increased fruit production.

Oblique cordons grow more slowly than vertical cordons so more energy is forced into *fruiting* buds instead of into *leaf* and *shoot* buds. For rows running north to south, point tops toward the north. For rows running east to west, point tops toward the east. Oblique cordons also make an attractive screen.

Horizontal cordons are the classic French kitchen-garden border. Apple or pear whips are bent down gradually and trained horizontally 12 to 18 inches above the soil. It is actually easier to achieve the look of a horizontal cordon by pruning in the horizontal-T.

The *Braided* and *Arcure* variations produce lovely, light screening effects. Both begin as single cordons, then one branch is trained to a pattern. Maintaining them requires constant pinching.

Vertical Cordon

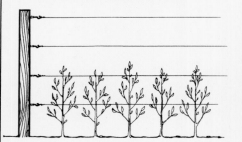

1. Select high-headed or unpruned trees. Stake individual plants or train on wire framework. Cut back side shoots to spurs. Do not cut back leader.

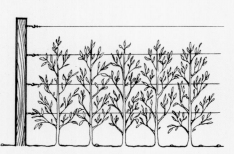

2. Maintain dominant central leader. Prune new side shoots to spurs. Prune old side shoots, permitting subshoots to develop, then cut back to spurs.

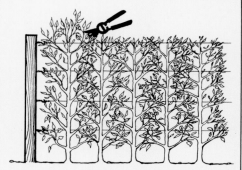

3. Continue to shorten side shoots and subshoots. Prune leader only when it reaches desired height.

Oblique Cordon

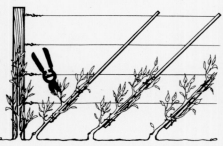

1. Select high-headed or unpruned trees. Space 2 to 3 feet apart at a 60° to 45° angle with bud union on top. Tie to stakes that are attached to wires. Cut back side shoots to spurs. Keep them at this length. Do not cut back leader. Plant a single, vertical cordon at end of row.

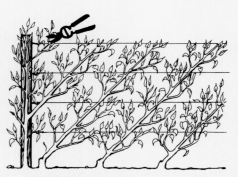

2. Do not prune leader until desired height is reached. Prune new side shoots to spurs. Keep old side shoots shortened to spurs, permitting spurs to form. Remove stakes when trunks are stout enough to stand alone. Tie trunks to wires.

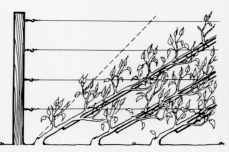

3. Optional: Lower cordons gradually to 30° angle. This allows branches to grow longer, controls vigorous growth and forces more fruit. Do not cut back leaders if you plan to lower cordons.

Single, vertical cordons of apples planted approximately 1-1/2 feet apart look like a hedge and produce an abundant crop.

Horizontal and Braided Variations

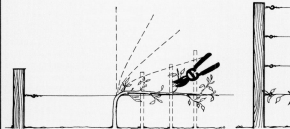

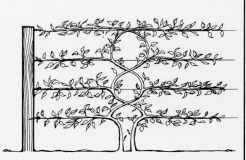

1. Horizontal: Plant whips and bend trunk gradually down, using stakes as necessary. Shorten all side shoots to spurs. Train leader as long as desired along wire.

1. Braided: Plant two whips and bend trunks gradually down. Allow two side shoots to develop. Train upright. Shorten all other shoots.

2. Braided: Train original two shoots to braided pattern over the seasons. Train single side shoots as horizontals along wires. Shorten all others to spurs.

Arcure Variation

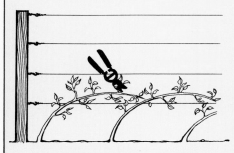

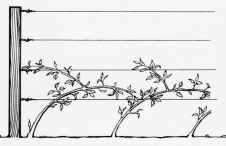

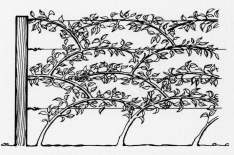

1. Arcure: Select whips that are 3 to 4 feet tall. Plant at a slight angle. Allow new growth to begin, then bend and tie whips to form arches. Leave only one new shoot for each plant at top center of arch.

2. At end of first growing season, bend top center shoot down in opposite direction of arch and tie in place. Remove all but one of its top center shoots.

3. Repeat process to develop successive arched branches. Shorten all side shoots to spurs. Prune regularly to maintain pattern. There will be little increase in length of oldest shoots growing at an angle.

PALMETTE OBLIQUE

Traditionally, this pattern has all tiers of branches trained at the same angle—narrow, broad or 45°, depending on available space. The pattern is formed much like the horizontal T, so choose plants from the *formal* list only.

The training technique illustrated here does not produce as stylized a palmette as the traditional method. Branch angles are chosen to regulate fruiting. The bottom tier is trained at 45°, the middle tiers spread more obliquely and the top tier is horizontal. Permit the branches to grow as far as possible for greatest fruit yield. You can regulate the angle of each individual branch to control branch vigor. Gradually lower over-vigorous branches by training to almost-horizontal. This forces energy into the fruit buds. Train weak branches at an upright angle until the desired length is obtained. Gradually lower them to the chosen angle.

Arms—limbs or branches—of palmette oblique can be raised or lowered to control fruiting.

Palmette Oblique

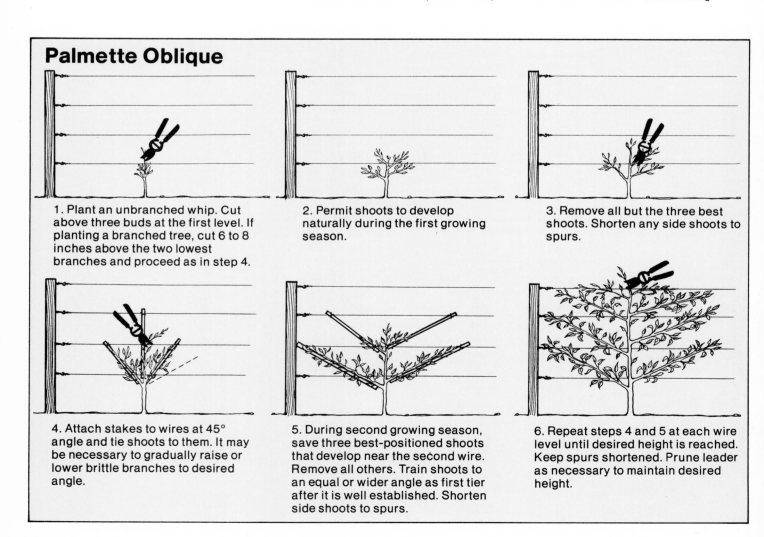

1. Plant an unbranched whip. Cut above three buds at the first level. If planting a branched tree, cut 6 to 8 inches above the two lowest branches and proceed as in step 4.

2. Permit shoots to develop naturally during the first growing season.

3. Remove all but the three best shoots. Shorten any side shoots to spurs.

4. Attach stakes to wires at 45° angle and tie shoots to them. It may be necessary to gradually raise or lower brittle branches to desired angle.

5. During second growing season, save three best-positioned shoots that develop near the second wire. Remove all others. Train shoots to an equal or wider angle as first tier after it is well established. Shorten side shoots to spurs.

6. Repeat steps 4 and 5 at each wire level until desired height is reached. Keep spurs shortened. Prune leader as necessary to maintain desired height.

BELGIAN FENCE

The charm of this pattern is due to its elegant, open, lattice effect that is especially apparent when deciduous trees are out of leaf. A dramatic, finished appearance requires exact spacing in a straight line, training all arms to the same angle and positioning all crotches, or Y's, at the same level. At least three trees plus two single cordons at the ends are necessary to complete the pattern edges.

The longer a Belgian fence is extended, the greater its visual impact. Five feet is the recommended minimum height. An angle of 45° is traditional for the Y's. The illustrations on this page have 60° angles.

This is a formal pattern, devised specifically for apples or pears. It is possible to use mixed varieties of apples and pears within the same fence. Advanced horticulturists can also train lemons, apricots, plums, cherries, peaches or nectarines to this pattern if trees are spaced farther apart. Other trees with large leaves from the formal list require greater spacing to display the pattern. Spacing farther than 2 feet produces a more oblique diamond shape.

Oblique cordons planted alternately left and right in a row at 45° also produce a Belgian fence effect.

The *losange variation,* illustrated below, also requires wider spacing to display the finished pattern. This method permits side branches to develop, which quickly produces a dense effect. For these reasons, the losange is well suited to large-scale uses where space is not a limitation.

Beautiful lattice pattern of Belgian fence is most noticeable on deciduous plants when they drop their leaves.

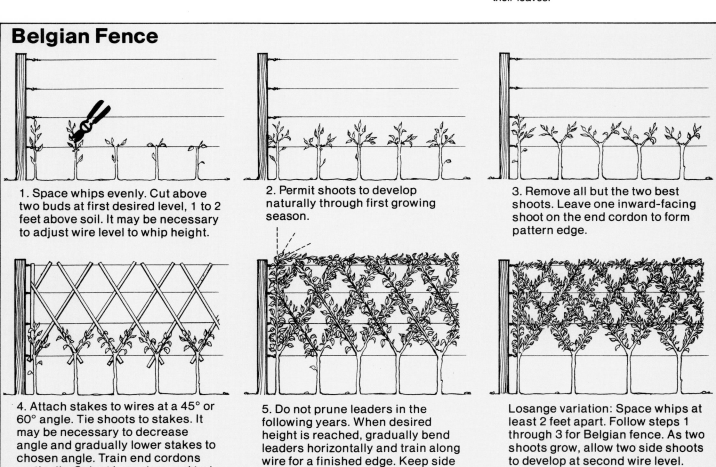

Belgian Fence

1. Space whips evenly. Cut above two buds at first desired level, 1 to 2 feet above soil. It may be necessary to adjust wire level to whip height.

2. Permit shoots to develop naturally through first growing season.

3. Remove all but the two best shoots. Leave one inward-facing shoot on the end cordon to form pattern edge.

4. Attach stakes to wires at a 45° or 60° angle. Tie shoots to stakes. It may be necessary to decrease angle and gradually lower stakes to chosen angle. Train end cordons vertically. Select branches and train at chosen angle to complete pattern. Shorten side shoots to spurs.

5. Do not prune leaders in the following years. When desired height is reached, gradually bend leaders horizontally and train along wire for a finished edge. Keep side shoots shortened to spurs.

Losange variation: Space whips at least 2 feet apart. Follow steps 1 through 3 for Belgian fence. As two shoots grow, allow two side shoots to develop at second wire level. Train them at a 45° angle to pattern on stakes.

VERRIER PALMETTE

This popular, formal palmette pattern was named for Louis Verrier, a French horticulturist who taught the art of espalier in the middle part of the 19th century. Choose plants from the *formal* list only for this pattern.

There are many ways to train plants to the Verrier palmette. Use a post-and-wire framework and strong stakes tied securely to the wires to support the vertical arms. They require a rigid frame to keep them straight. Henry Leuthardt Nursery in New York state recommends that eyebolts be set into the wall behind the arms at the exact position where they will be bent. Arms are then tied to hori-

zontal or vertical wires strung between the eyebolts. Stakes are used to supplement the framework.

The pattern starts in the same way as a tiered espalier. When branches have reached a length of at least 12 inches they are gradually bent up in 5° to 10° increments. Space tiers about 12 inches apart. Keep the distance equal between vertical arms.

If the branches are too stiff to turn up at a sharp angle, make fine saw cuts halfway through the limbs 1 to 2 inches apart on the outer sides of the bend. This permits a sharp bend to be made. Cuts usually heal in a season.

Old pear in a six-arm Verrier palmette pattern is sturdy enough to stand with no support. Few espaliers hold their pattern when supports are removed.

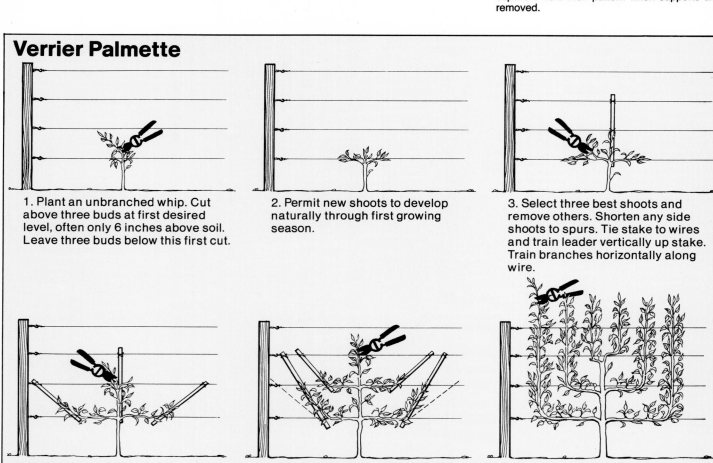

Verrier Palmette

1. Plant an unbranched whip. Cut above three buds at first desired level, often only 6 inches above soil. Leave three buds below this first cut.

2. Permit new shoots to develop naturally through first growing season.

3. Select three best shoots and remove others. Shorten any side shoots to spurs. Tie stake to wires and train leader vertically up stake. Train branches horizontally along wire.

4. During dormant season, tie stakes to wires. If branches are the desired length, gradually bend branches up first tier. Cut leader at height of second wire.

5. New shoots will develop below cut, as in step 2. Select three best shoots as in step 3. Continue bending first branches as necessary to upright position. Bend second tier when branches reach desired length. Cut leader at height of third wire in dormant season.

6. Repeat previous steps to develop third tier. Finish bending second tier to pattern. Train arms as high as desired, then maintain at that level. Some plants will hold pattern without support when they are mature. Remove frames if desired.

U-SHAPES

Most of the general remarks about Verrier palmette espaliers apply to formal U-shapes, including the necessity of choosing plants from the *formal* list only. The single U and U with a center vertical limb are also called *multiple vertical cordons.* They may be grown obliquely like cordons, but they are formed in a manner similar to a Verrier palmette. The distance between each vertical arm should be equal. Some people train short horizontal branches off the U's at even distances along the wires to increase the amount of fruiting wood.

Verrier palmette is easier to train than double and triple U-shapes, and is more productive. The triple U is sometimes called a *candelabra.* It is difficult to form and the training takes a lot of time. The double and triple U prevents excess vigor of limbs close to the trunk. All limbs are equally balanced in vigor.

Four-armed Verrier palmette pears add visual relief to a blank wall.

U-Shapes

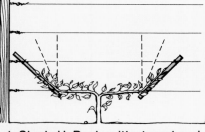

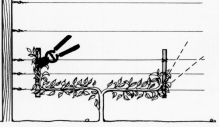

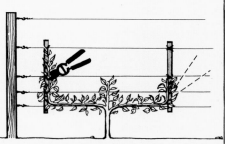

1. Single U: Begin with steps 1 and 2 of Verrier palmette . Cut out all but two best shoots. Train these horizontally along wires until desired length is obtained. Bend tips up gradually, using stakes tied to wires.

1. Double U: Follow steps 1 and 2 of Verrier palmette. Save two shoots and train horizontally along wires. Bend up as shown for Single U. In dormant season, cut branches at height of second wire above two buds.

1. Triple U: Begin with steps 1 and 2 of Verrier palmette, but save *three* shoots. Train one up and two horizontally along wires. Bend up two outer branch tips like single U. Then cut all three at height of second wire above two buds.

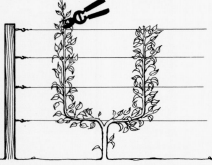

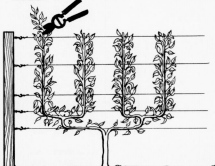

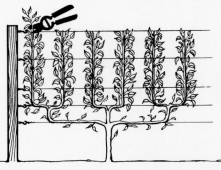

2. Permit branches to grow as high as desired and maintain them at that length.

2. Permit shoots to develop below cut. Save two best shoots and remove all others. Train shoots horizontally along wires, bending them up, using stakes tied to wires. Maintain at desired height.

2. Allow new shoots to develop at second cut. Select best two and remove all others. Train these shoots horizontally along wires and bend up, using stakes. Maintain at desired height.

DRAPEAU MARCHAND

Early fruit production is the benefit of this training method originating in Anjou, France. Drapeau Marchand is an informal pattern, but maximum fruiting on apples, pears and figs is still possible. Other fruit to try with this method include peach, nectarine, plum, citrus and apricot.

Some people train the bottom branch on the downward side of the trunk up to the lowest wire. This creates a fuller appearance.

To make the pruning and training steps for this pattern easy to follow, the plants in the illustrations appear more formal than they actually are. In the garden, the effect is more loose and casual. Many commercial orchards use this method and it is well suited to windy sites.

Drapeau Marchand is an informal pattern that is usually easy to maintain. Maximum fruiting on many kinds of plants, including apples, pears and figs is possible when grown in this form.

Drapeau Marchand

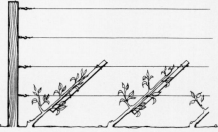

1. Plant whips or branched trees at 40° to 60° angle. Tie plant to first wire, or tie to stakes attached to wires if length exceeds wire. Space trees by size, approximately 8 to 12 feet apart for many dwarfs. Do not prune leader.

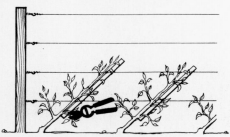

2. At planting time, tie any existing branches to wires at 45° angle at opposite direction. Do not prune except to shorten branches growing outward and on downward side of trunk to spurs.

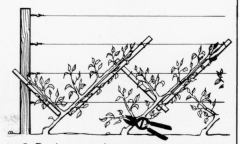

3. During growing season, continue training leader at chosen angle. Train branches at 45° in opposite direction. Tie to wires or use supplemental stakes. Shorten branches growing outward and downward. In summer, shorten side shoots on major branches to spurs.

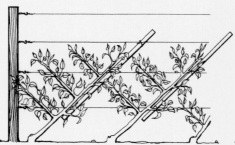

4. Avoid major pruning the following dormant season. Remove dead or poorly spaced spurs and branches.

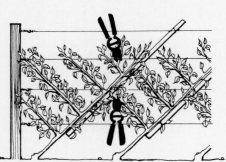

5. Continue training leader and branches. Shorten side shoots through the growing season. Cut back branches that cross adjacent trees.

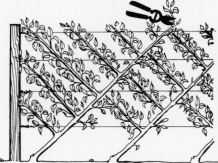

6. Each dormant season, follow process in step 4. Train major limbs in summer and shorten other shoots to spurs as in step 3. Maintain branches at desired length and leader at desired height. Remove stakes and hold pattern by tying loosely to wires.

FAN SHAPES

This informal pattern was designed for fruit trees. It is suited to peaches and nectarines that are pruned heavily each year to renew fruit-bearing wood. The fan is popular for figs, plums, apricots, cherries and other trees that are difficult to train formally. It is also a favorite pattern for apples and pears because it is easy and it looks natural. Fans are traditionally trained against walls to take advantage of heat that is radiated back toward the plant. A post-and-wire framework is shown, but a variety of framing systems may be used. Training a fan on a wooden trellis is particularly popular.

The basic objective with this pattern is to create a permanent structure of major limbs that fan over an allotted space. Spurs or shoots along the major limbs produce fruit. Short spurs may grow in any direction. Remove outward-growing shoots or those that point toward the wall.

Peaches and nectarines that need a continual supply of new wood are pruned every year just after new spring growth, when shoots are about 12 inches long. Prune each new shoot back to two buds. Two new shoots will develop from these buds. The following spring, permit one of these shoots to bloom and prune the other shoot back to two buds.

Every year the shoot permitted to bloom will produce fruit. The shoot that was pruned back will produce the new shoots needed the following year. This ensures a continual supply of new wood. Allow new shoots to grow about 15 inches long before tying them to the flat surface support.

Fan

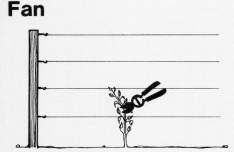

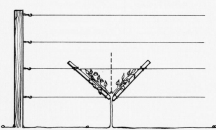

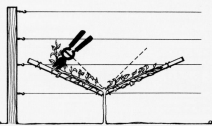

1. Plant an unbranched whip and cut above three buds. Or plant a branched tree and shorten side shoots to spurs.

2. Several shoots will appear in spring. Save two of the best. Tie these shoots to stakes attached to wires. Train at 45° angle. Remove backup shoots (dotted lines), when major shoots are established.

3. Shorten two major branches to about half their length. Lower to a 30° angle. Do this gradually to prevent breakage. Remove any side shoots.

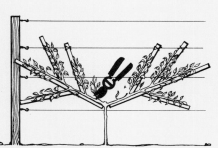

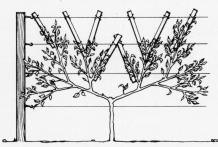

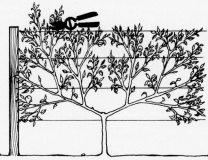

4. Permit shoots to develop naturally through the second growing season. Choose four shoots—two on the upper side of each major branch, one on its end to extend its length, and one on the downward side. Tie these shoots to stakes and remove all others.

5. During the dormant season, cut back each of the major and secondary branches by one-third. In the third growing season, permit shoots to develop on secondary branches. Choose four best as in step 4, removing others. Use stakes as necessary. During fourth growing season, shorten framework arms by one-fourth.

6. Permit new shoots to develop every 4 inches along framework arms. Pinch their tips in late summer. Do not remove them in the dormant season. They will bear fruit the following year. Remove first shoots after harvest for varieties requiring annual removal of wood. Permit framework arms to grow to desired length. Prune them in dormant season by one-fourth if they are not growing vigorously.

FRUITS, BERRIES, AND NUTS

Gardeners grow fruit for many of the same reasons they grow fresh vegetables. Home-grown fruit can be allowed to ripen on the plant until it reaches flavor perfection. If you have ever compared a store-bought peach or apple with one just picked from the tree, you know what a difference this can make. If you haven't made such a comparison, you have some very pleasant experiences ahead. The flavor and quality of home-grown fruit can't be matched.

There are a number of reasons why home-grown fruit tastes so good. First, there is only one place where most fruit is meant to ripen and that's on the tree. Only there will sugar content build to a peak and important texture changes take place. Once the fruit reaches this stage, it can't be shipped long distances. Supermarket fruit is usually picked slightly hard and unripe so it can be shipped.

Home-grown fruit is also better be-cause you can choose the best-tasting varieties—ones that are hard to find in a supermarket. Most commercial fruit varieties are developed for appearance, shipping qualities and shelf life, rather than flavor. For instance, the most important commercial apple variety, 'Red Delicious', is popular primarily because of its excellent exterior color. Ask any apple expert how its flavor compares to such varieties as 'Cox's Orange' 'Pippin' or 'Jonagold'. There's no comparison in flavor—and 'Red Delicious' is not a good cooking apple.

When you choose fruit varieties, select the ones that best satisfy your objectives. Many fruit, nut and berry plants are beautiful additions to the garden. A number of the characteristics that you would use to choose ornamental plants can also be found in fruiting plants—fragrant flowers, and brightly colored fruit and autumn foliage, to name a few. Fruiting plants can also be versatile in the landscape. Blueberries can be used as a hedge. Many fruits, including apples and pears, can be trained as espaliers. Kiwifruit or grape vines can cover an arbor. Large nut trees, such as pecans, make excellent shade or lawn trees.

No matter which fruit you want to grow or how the plants will function in your yard, the first thing to determine is whether or not a particular fruit, nut or berry is adapted to your area. Climate adaptation is one of the most important factors in ease of care, quality of harvest, and even plant survival.

ADAPTATION

The following climate factors greatly influence which fruit you can grow:
Hardiness—Each fruit-bearing plant has a *minimum temperature* below

Left: Raspberries are closely related to blackberries but differ in that fruit readily separates from the core. Raspberry 'Meeker' is shown here.

Above: Trees in backyard fruit orchard are pruned to make picking easy.

LOW-CHILL FRUITS

This is a list of deciduous fruit varieties developed especially for mild-winter climates. All deciduous fruits require a certain number of *chilling hours* to produce fruit, as discussed on the following page. The varieties listed here require fewer chilling hours than standard fruit varieties. If you live in a mild-winter area, check with a local nursery or your university or county extension agent to find out the number of chilling hours for your area. If you can't get this information, use the conversion chart at right to figure chilling hours. To use the chart, you'll need to find out the mean (average) temperature of the coldest month of the year—usually January—from your local weather service. Then choose a variety that requires the *same or fewer* number of chilling hours in your area.

*In climates where winter days are generally sunny, a 10% to 20% reduction in the number of chilling hours should be made.

Mean Temperature Coldest Month (January)	Chilling Hours Accumulated for Season*
46F (8C)	988
48F (9C)	883
50F (10C)	778
52F (11C)	675
54F (12C)	575
56F (13C)	475
58F (14C)	355
60F (15C)	288
62F (17C)	200
64F (18C)	118
66F (19C)	58
68F (20C)	0

APPLES

Variety	Chilling Hours	Ripening Date	Remarks
'Anna'	350	L. June	Crisp, juicy, sweet-tart flavor. Green with red blush. Self-fruitful but does better with 'Dorsett Golden' as pollenizer.
'Beverly Hills'	600	September	Best in areas with mild summers. Good flavor.
'Dorsett Golden'	250	L. June	Crisp, juicy, sweet. Yellow with 10% pink blush. Self-fruitful.
'Ein Shemer'	450	July	Similar to 'Golden Delicious'. Best in areas with mild summers. Good flavor and texture.

NECTARINES

Variety	Chilling Hours	Ripening Date	Remarks
'Panamint'	400	L. June	Semifree, medium fruit. Very good flavor, widely available.
'Sunfre'	500	M. June	Semifree, very good flavor, large fruit.
'Sunred'	250	E. May	Semifree, small fruit. Excellent flavor, red color.
'Sunripe'	350	M. May	Semifree, medium fruit. Excellent flavor.

PEACHES

Variety	Chilling Hours	Ripening Date	Remarks
'Babcock'	450	E. July	White flesh, good texture, poor flavor.
'Desert Gold'	350	E. May	Semicling, good flavor, small fruit, widely available.
'Earligrand'	200	E. May	Semicling, good flavor, medium fruit.
'Flordabelle'	150	M. May	Freestone, good flavor and texture, very large fruit.
'Flordagold'	325	L. May	Semifree, very good flavor and texture, medium fruit.
'Flordaking'	400	M. May	Semicling, good flavor, large fruit.
'Flordaprince'	150	L. April	Semicling, good flavor and texture, excellent color.
'Flordared'	100	M. May	Freestone, good flavor, small fruit, lacks firmness.
'Gold Dust'	550	M. June	Semifree, very good flavor and texture.
'June Gold'	650	M. June	Semicling, large fruit, good flavor and texture. Very showy blooms.
'Rio Grande'	450	E. June	Freestone, large fruit, excellent flavor and texture.

PEARS

Variety	Chilling Hours	Ripening Date	Remarks
'Baldwin'	500	August	Good texture and flavor. Moderate resistance to fire blight.
'Flordahome'	400	M. July	Sweet, buttery textured flesh when ripe. Plant with 'Hood' or 'Pineapple' for cross-pollination.
'Hood'	400	M. July	Sweet, buttery textured flesh when ripe. Very good flavor, self-fruitful, resistant to fire blight.
'Pineapple'	500	L. July	Tart flavor, good for canning. Highly resistant to fire blight.
'Shinseiki'	400 est.	L. July	Excellent Asian pear, which seems to have a low chilling requirement. Self-fruitful.
'20th Century'	400 est.	E. August	Crisp, sweet, juicy Asian pear, which seems to have low chilling requirement.

Chart developed by Mike Burraston, Bountiful Nursery, Tucson, AZ.

which its tissues will be killed. However, this is not as clear-cut as it sounds. The time of year when the cold weather occurs and the duration of cold are two climatic factors that influence whether or not the plant will be injured. Most plants are less hardy in fall than they are in the dead of winter.

The location of the tree in the garden, soil-moisture content, wind and sunlight also influence the plant's susceptibility to injury. Local nurseries and extension agents can also help you judge whether or not a fruit, berry or nut is hardy enough for your area.

Spring Frosts—Even if the type of fruit you want to grow is hardy enough for your area, its blossoms and small developing fruit may be susceptible to damage from spring frosts. Blossoms and fruit are much less hardy that the tree itself. Most will be damaged if temperatures fall just a few degrees below freezing. Early-blooming fruits and nuts, such as apricots, almonds and Japanese plums, are most susceptible to damage from spring frosts. If you live in an area with late-spring frosts, choose late-blooming varieties.

Chilling Requirements—Most deciduous fruits require a certain number of hours near 45F (7C) during winter or they will not correctly break dormancy in spring. This number of hours is called a *chilling requirement*. Whereas cold hardiness is a major limiting factor for growing fruit in cold climates, chilling requirements restrict the varieties of deciduous fruits that can be grown in mild-winter climates. In many areas of the South and West, selecting varieties with a low chilling requirement (low-chill varieties) is critical to success with most deciduous fruit.

Low-Chill Varieties—Recent interest in low-chill deciduous fruits has fostered the development of many new varieties, with more being introduced each year.

If you live in a mild-winter climate and want to grow deciduous fruits, you'll first have to find out the number of *chilling hours* in your area. For information on chilling hours, contact your county extension service or university extension agent, or use the conversion chart on the facing page. Then choose varieties that have a chilling requirement equal to or less than that amount of hours. Visit nurseries that specialize in low-chill varieties. Also refer to the list of low-chill varieties and their chilling requirements on the facing page.

Heat and Humidity—Some fruits re-

quire more summer heat than others to ripen their crop. Peaches, many types of citrus, almonds, some grapes, and pecans like long, hot summers. On the other hand, some fruits are generally intolerant of high summer temperatures and prefer cooler climates. These include raspberries, many blackberries, highbush blueberries, and some apple varieties.

When high summer temperatures are combined with high humidity, many fruits are subject to severe disease problems. This is why many stone fruits, and European and American grapes, are rarely successful in the Deep South. Humidity and cool temperatures can cause problems as well. In coastal areas of the Pacific Northwest where summer fog or long, rainy periods are common, many varieties of apricots and cherries are especially susceptible to disease. In such areas, selecting disease-resistant varieties or maintaining a preventative spraying program is critical to success with some fruit.

CULTURAL REMINDERS

Standard gardening practices will play an important role in the quality of your harvest. Planting in a sunny spot where the soil is well drained, applying water regularly and, if necessary, feeding regularly with fertilizer, will help ensure healthy plants and the best possible harvest. Pollination needs are important for many tree fruits, nuts and berries. Other specific factors that must be considered for fruit trees are discussed at right.

Pollination—Most fruiting plants are either *self-fruitful* or *self-unfruitful*. Self-fruitful plants provide their own pollen for pollination and can produce fruit without any other plants present. Self-unfruitful plants require another plant nearby to provide for cross-pollination. The plant should be of the same type and bloom about the same time. Bees, insects or wind act as pollinators and carry pollen from one tree to the other. So with self-unfruitful plants you have to grow more than one plant to produce fruit. With some self-unfruitful plants, such as Japanese plums, the second plant must be a specific variety.

GROWING FRUIT TREES

Fruit that is borne on trees, such as apples, pears and cherries, have some specific requirements not shared with berries or nuts. Because each tree has a different bearing habit, correct pruning

and training is important. Some trees, including peaches and nectarines, must be pruned heavily to remain productive. Others, such as apples and pears, should be pruned more selectively. Apples, apricots, peaches, nectarines and Japanese plums overproduce, meaning they will set more fruit than they can actually ripen to perfection. To correct this problem, you should reduce the number of fruit by thinning. Otherwise, you'll have a lot of small, low-quality fruit.

The best time to thin fruit is right after *June drop*, a period when most trees naturally thin themselves by dropping some of their fruit. Although called June drop, this may happen as early as April in some areas. It is often hard to notice exactly when June drop occurs, if it occurs at all. As general rule, thin fruits as soon as spring frost danger is over or when fruits reach 1/2 to 1 inch in diameter. Leave 6 to 8 inches between fruit or, with apples and Japanese plums, thin to one fruit per cluster. Thin carefully, making sure you don't damage fruiting spurs.

GROWING BERRIES

Berries are remarkably productive plants. Under ideal conditions, 25 mature strawberry plants can produce up to 30 quarts of fruit per season, six mature blueberry plants can produce up to 15 quarts of fruit, 12 mature blackberry plants can produce up to 15 quarts of fruit and 24 mature raspberry plants can produce up to 30 quarts of fruit. These amounts are enough to supply a family of five with fresh fruit. If you plan to do any preserving, you may want to plant more.

Most fruits and some nuts, like almonds shown here, are thinned so remaining fruit will be larger.

Carefully trained apple trees are good example of using fruit trees for landscaping.

Most blackberries and some grapes require a trellis for support and easy harvesting. Erect-type blackberries and raspberries need little support. Usually only a light wire or string suspended between stakes is needed to keep them upright.

When you build a trellis, make it strong. Any wood that will be in contact with soil should be pressure treated with a wood preservative. Otherwise, it will eventually rot. Pressure-treated lumber is available at lumber yards. Specify wood treated with a preservative that is non-toxic to plants.

Soil preparation prior to planting is particularly important with many berry plants. Work in ample amounts of organic matter to a depth of 6 to 12 inches.

GROWING NUTS
Most nut trees grow quite large. Avoid planting too close to the house or where the trees will eventually shade out other areas of the garden. Give nut trees plenty of room.

Most nuts must be dried in the sun several days before they can be stored. Always remove the husk first. A nut has been dried long enough if the kernel snaps in two rather than bending.

Nut trees generally do not have to be

pruned as severely as fruit trees to produce quality fruit, but they do require some pruning.

VARIETY SELECTION
Fruit breeding is an advanced science. Most types of fruits, nuts and berries are available in many varieties. Often, it may appear as if a certain type of fruit is not adapted to your climate. It may not be hardy enough, it may need more chilling, or it may have disease problems. However, by doing a little homework you may find an exceptional variety that can be grown in your area. Many fruits are available in extra-hardy varieties, low-chill varieties or disease-resistant varieties. A little bit of searching through mail-order catalogs or a few short phone calls with local extension agents and nurseries that specialize in fruit trees may greatly increase your gardening enjoyment.

Adaptation is not the only factor that should influence variety selection. Plant early, midseason, and late-ripening varieties to extend the harvest period. Also, don't forget how productive most fruiting plants can be. Select varieties of fruit that can be used in a number of ways or those that store well. Otherwise, you may have to give away or waste a lot of fruit.

Dwarf Trees—Many types of fruit and nut trees are available in dwarf varieties. The term *dwarf* refers to the size of the tree—dwarf trees bear full-size fruit. Dwarf trees are ideal where space is limited, and many are excellent choices for large containers (15-gallon size or larger). Dwarf trees are also easier to harvest, spray and prune.

There are two basic types of dwarf trees—those in which the *scion,* or fruiting part of the tree, is grown on a dwarf rootstock, and those in which the scion itself is genetically dwarf. Scions from most varieties of fruits can be grafted to a dwarf rootstock of a closely related tree. With genetic dwarfs, it is the scion that is dwarf, grafted onto standard-size rootstock. Compared to trees with dwarf rootstocks, genetic dwarfs offer fewer varieties because they must be specially bred. Many have a tendency to overbear, so they require special attention to fruit thinning.

FRUIT
This section gives basic cultural information for growing popular deciduous fruits, citrus and tropical fruit.

APPLES
Apples are by far America's favorite fruit. One variety or another can be grown almost anywhere in the United States. They are relatively easy to grow, are available in almost any size tree—thanks to the Malling dwarf rootstocks—and can be used to make some of America's favorite recipes, including apple pies, applesauce and ciders.

Important Numbers—Standard apple trees may reach over 25 feet high and usually take 4 to 8 years after planting to bear fruit. Dwarf varieties grow smaller—size depends on the rootstock—and take 3 to 4 years to bear a crop. Plant standard-size trees at least 20 feet apart. Dwarf varieties can be planted much closer.

Adaptation—Apples can be grown almost anywhere, but variety selection is important. Chilling requirements average about 900 hours, but low-chill varieties have chilling requirements as low as 250 hours. Most apple trees can withstand temperatures as low as -30F (-34C) if properly hardened-off. *Apple scab,* a fungal disease that thrives in humid areas, limits adaptation in many parts of the East.

Pollination—Most apple varieties are only partially self-fruitful, so it's best to

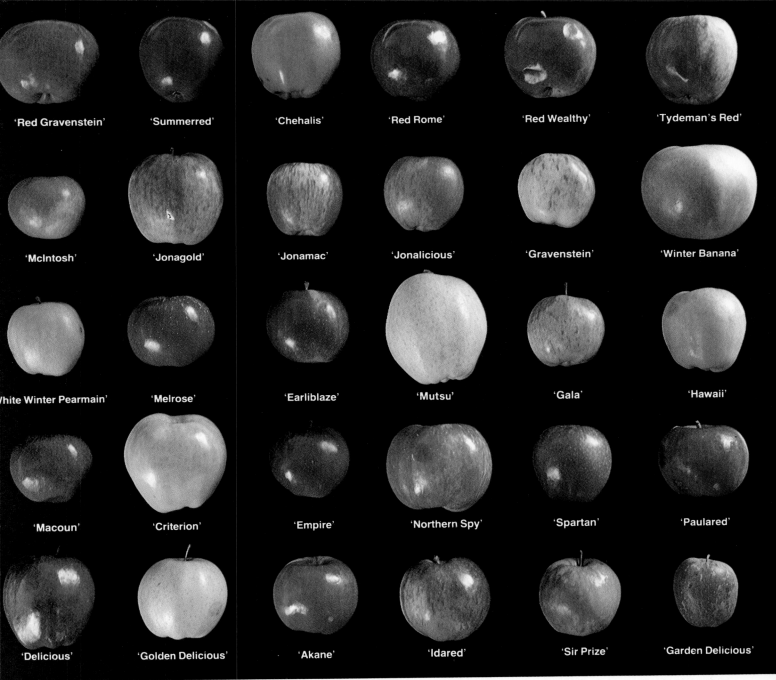

'Red Gravenstein' 'Summerred' 'Chehalis' 'Red Rome' 'Red Wealthy' 'Tydeman's Red'

'McIntosh' 'Jonagold' 'Jonamac' 'Jonalicious' 'Gravenstein' 'Winter Banana'

'White Winter Pearmain' 'Melrose' 'Earliblaze' 'Mutsu' 'Gala' 'Hawaii'

'Macoun' 'Criterion' 'Empire' 'Northern Spy' 'Spartan' 'Paulared'

'Delicious' 'Golden Delicious' 'Akane' 'Idared' 'Sir Prize' 'Garden Delicious'

Shown here are some of the many apple varieties available to gardeners. The difference in color and form may be surprising to those used to the two or three commercial varieties sold at the local supermarket.

have another variety nearby that is blooming at the same time. Because it's likely some of your neighbors have apple trees—or crabapple trees, which are also good pollinizers—you probably won't have to plant more than one tree. If there are no apple trees nearby, you can graft a scion of a good pollinator variety onto a branch of your apple tree.

Pruning—Just after planting, trees should be headed to 18 to 24 inches tall. Training main scaffold limbs begins the first summer.

Train dwarf and semidwarf apple trees to a central leader. Use a stake or wire to support espaliers. Use a temporary support only if the tree is exposed to strong wind. Spread side limbs, if necessary.

Train standard-size trees to develop three or four leaders at 20° to 30° from vertical. Head leaders annually and remove competing shoots. Spread secondary scaffolds, if necessary.

The main apple varieties differ as much in growth habits as in fruit. Each

typical growth habit requires slightly different training and pruning. The many varieties of apples have been categorized into four main groups according to similarities in growth habits—Type I, Type II, Type III and Type IV. If you don't know which type you have, follow general recommendations for pruning and observe the growth habit. Within a season or two, you'll probably be able to place your tree in one of the four groups described above.

Type I Apples: These are spur-types such as 'Starkrimson Red Delicious' and 'Jonagold'. They tend to be upright, develop narrow crotches and branch sparsely. Fruiting occurs on many short, long-lived spurs. Most fruit develops near the main trunk.

Head primary scaffolds to stimulate branching, or retain a large number of primary scaffold limbs from the central leader without heading. Dormant-season heading must be followed by thinning branch ends to single shoots after new growth begins.

Type I varieties require little pruning once trained. Spurs remain productive for 10 or more years. Because spurs are long-lived, they are sometimes susceptible to a disease known, appropriately enough, as dead-spur disease. It is a drastic problem because it destroys most old spurs within a short time. The only recourse is to remove stricken limbs entirely, then renew them using an available water sprout (sucker).

Type II Apples: These are non-spur varieties typified by most standard non-spur strains of 'Delicious'. They branch frequently and the fruiting zone tends to migrate away from the trunk.

Train Type IIs with few major limbs. Use spreaders on scaffold limbs to develop wide-angle crotches. Mature trees require moderate to heavy annual pruning to renew fruiting buds. Thin relatively upright replacement shoots. Head nearly horizontal branches back to 2-year-old wood so they won't break once loaded with fruit.

Type III Apples: These are spreading trees as typified by standard-size 'Golden Delicious' and 'Mutsu'. Branch angles are naturally wide, and branching is frequent. They bear on 1- to 3-year-old spurs, and the fruiting zone tends to migrate rapidly from the trunk to the outside of the tree.

Train trees to develop no more than three primary scaffold limbs. After the first fruit crop, head secondary scaffold limbs to stiffen them.

Mature Type IIIs require extensive annual thinning. To renew fruiting wood, thin upright shoots that develop from 2- or 3-year-old wood. Lighten branch ends each year by thinning to single, upright shoots.

Type IV Apples: These are tip-bearers such as 'Red Rome', 'Granny Smith' and 'Tydeman's Early Worcester'. They have upright main scaffolds, narrow crotches and extensive branching. Fruit is borne on the end of last season's shoots. The lower half of shoots may be without leaves or fruit. Fruiting wood develops at branch ends, causing the tree to spread.

Train Type IVs to no more than three leaders. To promote secondary branching and to stiffen the main branch, head leaders annually to about 2 feet from their previous head. Midsummer heading also helps in this training.

Mature Type IVs require heavy annual thinning in order to replace fruiting wood. Make all thinning cuts to upright shoots in 2- to 3-year-old wood around the outside of the tree canopy.

Varieties—There are hundreds of apple varieties, differing in climate adaptation, fruit color and shape, ripening period and how the fruit can be used. 'Anna' and 'Dorsett Golden' are favorite

Heavy crops, especially on small trees, often must be supported with props to avoid breaking branches.

low-chill varieties for areas with mild winters. 'Red Melba', 'Haralson' and 'McIntosh' are excellent varieties known for their hardiness. 'Chehalis', 'Liberty' and 'Prima' are disease-resistant varieties that are useful in areas where apple scab is a problem. 'Golden Delicious', 'Jonagold' and 'Jonathan' are delicious multipurpose apples that can be eaten fresh or cooked, or used to make cider.

Any variety can be dwarfed using the Malling (M) and Merton-Malling (MM) dwarf rootstocks. *MM-106 stock* dwarfs trees by 30% less than standard size; *M-26 stock*, by 50%; *M-9 stock*, by 60% and *M-27 stock*, by 70% to 75%. 'Garden Delicious' and 'Compact McIntosh' are genetic dwarfs. Spur varieties are also more compact, and lower growing than standard varieties.

Harvesting—Apples are ready to harvest when they reach their characteristic color and when a gentle upward twist easily separates them from the tree. When a few apples have already fallen, the rest of the crop is ready to harvest. Pick apples carefully so you do not damage the fruiting spurs.

APRICOTS

Apricots are one of the prettiest fruit trees you can grow—soft green, heart-shaped leaves fluttering in the wind, and bright pink flowers clothing branches in spring. However, apricots also have the most limited range of adaptation. They bloom early in spring, and in cold climates their blossoms and young fruit are often destroyed by spring frosts. In warm, humid areas, fungal and bacterial diseases further limit their adaptation.

Important Numbers—Standard apricot trees are large, sometimes growing as much as 25 feet high and 20 feet wide. They should be spaced at least 20 feet apart. Trees usually begin bearing 3 to 4 years after planting. No fully dwarfing rootstocks have been developed but many varieties are available as semi-dwarf trees that grow 12 to 25 feet high. There is also at least one genetic dwarf variety that maintains a height of 6 to 8 feet.

Adaptation—Early-blooming characteristics and susceptibility to disease limit adaptation in many areas, even though most trees are hardy to -15F (-26C). Average chilling requirements are between 600 and 800 hours, but many low-chill varieties are available. Ideal climates for growing apricots are found in dry areas of the West, Pacific

Apricots 'Blenheim' (top) and 'King Cot' (bottom) illustrate size difference of largest and smallest varieties.

Northwest, and Southwest. In other areas, fruit production will be unreliable or disease problems will be severe.

Pollination—Most apricots are self-fruitful. Varieties that are self-unfruitful can be pollinated by any other variety blooming at the same time.

Pruning—Apricot trees too often tend to spread excessively. Cutting away horizontal limbs helps direct upward growth. Head scaffold limbs to maintain desired tree height. Keep fruiting wood thinned.

Varieties—The varieties 'Moorpark' and 'Blenheim' are excellent for the correct climate. 'Moongold' and 'Sungold'

were developed for cold climates. 'Goldcot' is widely adapted and is a good choice wherever growing conditions are less than ideal. 'Goldenglo' is a beautiful genetic dwarf variety. Low-chill selections include 'Katy', 'Goldkist', 'Earligold', 'Perfection' and 'Flora Gold'.

'Plum Parfait' is a hybrid between a plum and an apricot that bears apricot-like fruit on a small tree.

Harvesting—Harvest apricots when they reach full color and begin to soften slightly. Fruit won't ripen all at once but over a period of 2 to 3 weeks.

Fruit of sweet cherry 'Jubilee' are borne in clusters. These are ready for picking.

CHERRIES

There are two types of cherries commonly grown in home gardens—*sweet cherries* and *sour cherries*. Most people are familiar with sweet cherries because these are the type grown commercially and sold in supermarkets. Sour cherries, or pie cherries as they are often called, are grown primarily in cold-winter climates and are used to make pies, pastries and juice. Sweet cherries and sour cherries also differ in the size of tree they are borne on and the areas in which they can be grown.

Important Numbers—Sweet cherries are borne on large, spreading trees that can reach 40 feet high and 30 feet wide. They should be spaced at least 35 to 40 feet apart. Sour cherries are borne on smaller trees that rarely exceed 15 feet in height but can become twice as wide. They should be spaced 15 to 20 feet apart. Both sweet and sour cherries are available as dwarfs that grow about 6 to 8 feet high. Both kinds take about 5 to 6 years to begin bearing.

Adaptation—Although sweet cherries and sour cherries differ substantially in climate adaptation, both share high chilling requirements of over 800 hours. This excludes them from much of the southern and southwestern United States. Sweet cherries also bloom relatively early and are subject to damage from spring frosts. In addition, rain close to harvest time causes the fruit to crack, and temperatures over 100F (38C) inhibit fruit development. Trees are hardy to -20F (-29C). Parts of Northern California, the Northwest and Northeast are considered the best cherry-growing regions.

Sour cherries can be grown almost anywhere they receive adequate chilling. They are extremely hardy, withstanding temperatures of -35F (-38C).

Pollination—Most sweet cherries require another cherry variety nearby to provide pollen. Almost any variety will do, however, 'Bing', 'Royal Ann', and 'Lambert' will not pollinate each other. All sour cherries are self-fruitful.

Pruning—Cherries are borne on long-lived spurs. Sweet cherries are usually trained to a central leader and are pruned heavily to keep them within bounds. Train sour cherries to a vase shape. Once mature, they require very little pruning.

Cherry, Sour: The weight of a crop of sour cherries can easily break trees because of their brittle wood and weak crotches. To help prevent such damage, head nursery trees at 18 to 24 inches. Select three or four shoots with wide crotch angles and train to a multiple leader. After the first dormant heading of scaffold limbs, further heading will not be required because of the free-branching pattern of the tree. Contain height and spread of mature trees by thinning.

Cherry, Sweet: Normally, sweet cherry trees branch only at the beginning of the growing season, if at all. Unless you prune them, these trees can rapidly become leggy.

Head nursery trees about 18 to 24 inches after planting. Head all shoots to 24 to 36 inches after the first and second year's growth. Removing terminal buds of shorter shoots promotes branching. Head only the vigorous shoots during the third and fourth year. Once fruiting begins, gradually remove a few scaffold branches until only seven or eight remain. Head all shoots annually in dormant season to encourage low, spreading trees that are easily picked.

Thin tops of mature trees as necessary to let in more light and keep upper limbs within reach. Vigor of old trees can be increased by harder pruning, using both heading and thinning.

Varieties—'Lambert', 'Royal Ann', 'Van', 'Bing' and 'Rainier' are popular sweet cherry varieties. 'Hedelfigen' and 'Ulster' are good for cold areas or those with frequent summer rain. 'Stella' is a self-fruitful variety. 'Compact Stella', 'Compact Lambert' and 'Starkcrimson' are genetic dwarf sweet cherries. 'North Star' and 'Montmorency' are popular sour cherries. 'North Star' is a small, compact tree.

Harvesting—The best way to tell if cherries are ripe is to pick a few and taste them. Pick with the stems attached if you intend to store the fruit or eat it fresh. Cherries can be picked without stems attached if you plan to use them for canning or cooking.

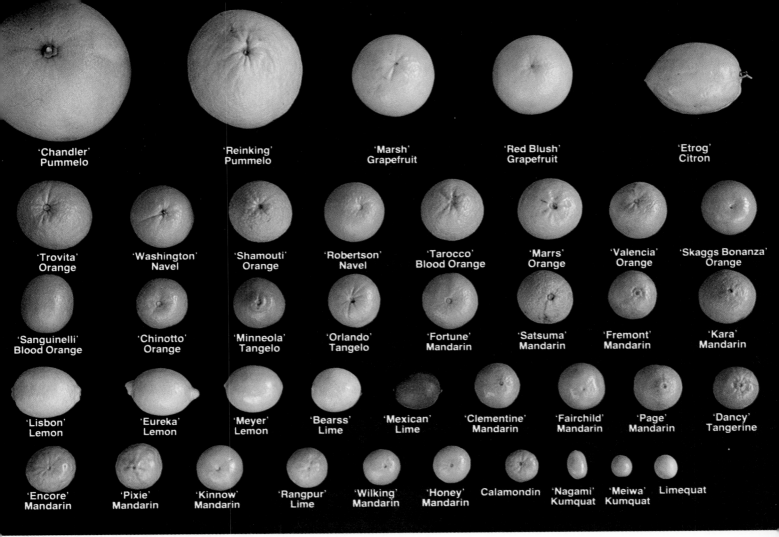

'Chandler' Pummelo   'Reinking' Pummelo   'Marsh' Grapefruit   'Red Blush' Grapefruit   'Etrog' Citron

'Trovita' Orange   'Washington' Navel   'Shamouti' Orange   'Robertson' Navel   'Tarocco' Blood Orange   'Marrs' Orange   'Valencia' Orange   'Skaggs Bonanza' Orange

'Sanguinelli' Blood Orange   'Chinotto' Orange   'Minneola' Tangelo   'Orlando' Tangelo   'Fortune' Mandarin   'Satsuma' Mandarin   'Fremont' Mandarin   'Kara' Mandarin

'Lisbon' Lemon   'Eureka' Lemon   'Meyer' Lemon   'Bearss' Lime   'Mexican' Lime   'Clementine' Mandarin   'Fairchild' Mandarin   'Page' Mandarin   'Dancy' Tangerine

'Encore' Mandarin   'Pixie' Mandarin   'Kinnow' Mandarin   'Rangpur' Lime   'Wilking' Mandarin   'Honey' Mandarin   Calamondin   'Nagami' Kumquat   'Meiwa' Kumquat   Limequat

The citrus family is a large one, from giant pummelos to tiny kumquats and limequats.

CITRUS

Citrus are evergreen fruit trees that offer tremendous rewards for gardeners in mild climates of the South, Southwest and West. They are among the easiest fruit to grow and are exceedingly handsome plants with fragrant white flowers, clean green leaves, and brightly colored fruit. In many areas where they are adapted they double as ornamentals, lining the avenues as street trees or providing privacy as hedges.

Important Numbers—Types of citrus vary greatly in height. Lemons are most vigorous and can reach over 20 feet high. Grapefruit, pummelos, 'Valencia' and navel oranges, and 'Dancy' tangerines are also large trees that can reach 18 to 20 feet. Mandarins and blood oranges are smaller, reaching 12 to 15 feet. Kumquats, kumquat hybrids, and 'Meyer' lemon are naturally smaller trees that usually grow between 8 to 12 feet high.

Even within groups of citrus, varieties will differ in size and tree shape. Spacing between trees will differ according to height, but there should be at least as much distance between trees as the trees are tall. Dwarf varieties of citrus will be about 50% smaller than standard trees. Exceptions are varieties grafted to 'Flying Dragon' rootstock, which will maintain a height of 5 to 7 feet.

Adaptation—Few fruit trees are as dramatically affected by climate variations. Winter cold, heat, humidity, fluctuations between day and night temperatures, and light intensity all have strong influences on adaptation, fruit color and fruit flavor. Some varieties are only adapted to the humid South, others grow best in the coastal areas of California. Checking with your local nurserymen or university extension agent is one of the best ways to determine which types of citrus you can grow.

Hardiness is one of the most important

factors in determining adaptation. Limes are the most sensitive to cold. They will usually be damaged if temperatures fall below freezing (32F, 0C). Lemons are slightly more hardy, being able to withstand temperatures as low as 28F to 30F (12C to -1C). Kumquats are the hardiest, able to withstand temperatures as cold as 18F (-8C). Hardiness of other citrus types falls somewhere between these extremes, with oranges at a midpoint of 26F (-3C). However, hardiness is a difficult factor to determine exactly. Duration of cold is also important. Also, mature fruit is often less hardy than foliage.

How warm it is where you live is also important in determining which type of citrus you can grow. Grapefruits need a lot of heat to sweeten their fruit and are best adapted to desert areas of the Southwest and to Florida. Lemons can withstand cooler temperatures and can be grown in cool coastal areas of California. Citrus is usually sweeter but less brightly colored when grown in the humid Southeast. Arid climates promote more acid in citrus and more brightly colored rinds.

Pollination—Most citrus varieties are self-fruitful. Exceptions are some varieties of mandarin that produce larger crops when other mandarin varieties are planted nearby.

Pruning—Citrus species grow, bloom and fruit at any time the weather is favorable, eliminating the need to prune for fruit renewal. They are pruned for appearance, size control, or to allow light and chemical sprays into the center of the tree.

Pruning the tops keeps trees from becoming too tall for easy picking. Do not prune lower, outer limbs because they produce most of the fruit. Thin to maintain a compact shape and ensure that early fruiting takes place on wood strong enough to support fruit weight. Thin to strong laterals or to main branches at any time in frost-free climates or after frost danger in cold climates.

Orange and grapefruit trees should be trained to develop a strong central leader. Gradually remove lower side limbs to raise the head. Train until trees are high so lower limbs can spread out and downward. Mature trees require only removal of dead, twiggy growth.

Due to their rangy nature, lemon trees require more training than other citrus trees. Head young trees at about 3 feet and select three or four main leaders. Head leaders severely to balance the top, if necessary. Thin and head as required to develop compact growth.

Lemon trees produce vigorous water sprouts that run through the center of the tree. When correctly spread, they can be used to fill gaps in the canopy of the tree. Spread apart water sprouts before they are too stiff. Tie them in place, if necessary.

Varieties—There are many types of citrus and many more varieties of each type. Popular orange varieties in the West include 'Washington' and 'Roberton' navel oranges, 'Valencia', and 'Trovita'. 'Valencia' is also grown in Florida, as are 'Hamlin', 'Parson's Brown' and 'Pineapple'. 'Eureka' and 'Lisbon' are lemon varieties grown in the West. 'Meyer' lemon grows well in all citrus areas. 'Redblush' and 'Marsh Seedless' are red and white grapefruit varieties for the hottest climates. 'Duncan' and 'Tarocco' grapefruit are grown in Florida. 'Moro' and 'Sanguinelli' are varieties of blood orange for western

'Mission' is a popular fig variety in the West.

gardeners. The coloration of blood oranges is less predictable in the Southeast. 'Dancy', 'Clementine' and 'Satsuma' are three of many popular mandarin varieties.

Harvesting—Most citrus varieties ripen between November and March depending on type and where they are grown. Fruit grown in warm areas will ripen before the same variety grown in cooler ones. The best way to test ripeness is to pick a sample and taste it. Fruit color is a poor indicator of ripeness. Ripe fruit of most citrus types can be left on the tree for at least 3 to 4 weeks without deteriorating.

FIGS

A mature fig tree can be a stunning sight. The branches are twisted and gnarled. They appear almost muscular. The leaves are huge with deeply cut lobes, adding a definite tropical appearance to the spreading canopy. The fruit is deliciously sweet and soft textured. Few fruit trees can have such a dramatic presence and provide such a bountiful harvest with a minimum of care.

Important Numbers—Mature fig trees can fairly quickly reach 40 feet high and up to 60 feet wide. However, they can be kept much smaller by pruning. In orchardlike conditions, space trees at least 20 feet apart.

Adaptation—Lack of winter hardiness is the most important limiting factor that determines where figs can be grown.

Most varieties are severely damaged or killed if temperatures reach 0F (-18C). Temperatures of 10F (-12C) can injure some varieties. Figs have a very low chilling requirement of less than 300 hours, which is seldom a limiting factor.

Pollination—All popular fig varieties are self-fruitful.

Pruning—Edible figs can be pruned to grow as trees or as bushes with multiple trunks. Bushes regenerate faster after freezes than trees do, thus are preferable for cold regions.

For bushes, plant in a depression and head 12 inches above the ground. After several branches have formed, fill in the depression, and mound soil so that the bases of the shoots are below ground. Head shoots annually at 2- or 3-foot intervals to stimulate branching pattern and ensure fruiting close to the ground.

Trees should be trained to the multiple leader system with three or four main scaffold limbs and two or three secondary scaffolds on each main scaffold. Remove suckers and sprouts at the base of tree each year.

Some fig varieties produce their first of two annual crops on wood of the previous season. Heading would remove most of this wood, so mature figs should be pruned by thinning. Varieties that produce fruit on the current-season's shoots should have all of the previous-season's shoots headed to one or two buds during the dormant season. The remaining buds produce long shoots that bear 10 to 15 figs.

Varieties—'Mission' and 'Brown Turkey' are popular varieties in the West. 'Celeste' and 'Texas Everbearing' are popular in the South. Check with your local nurserymen for other locally adapted varieties.

Harvesting—Figs usually produce two crops. The first ripens in early summer, the second in fall. In some climates, only the first crop matures. Figs are ready to pick when the *neck* of the fruit softens, causing it to droop from the branch. If any milky latex drips from the branch after the fruit is picked, its not quite ripe.

PEACHES AND NECTARINES

Peaches and nectarines are the juicy fruits of summer. Many varieties are available. With careful selection, you can begin harvesting peaches and nectarines in late spring and continue throughout summer, never experiencing a day without fresh fruit.

Peaches and nectarines have identical cultural and climatic requirements. In fact, a nectarine is simply a fuzzless peach.

Important Numbers—Peaches and nectarines are borne on relatively small trees that are easily maintained below 15 feet high. Under orchard conditions, they should be spaced 15 to 20 feet apart. Many varieties are available on partially dwarfing rootstocks that restrict growth to about 10 to 12 feet. Genetic dwarf varieties that seldom grow over 8 feet high are also available. Most peaches and nectarines will begin bearing fruit 2 to 3 years after planting.

Adaptation—Peaches and nectarines have chilling requirements that average between 600 and 900 hours. However, there are many low-chill varieties that allow these delicious fruits to be grown in even the warmest climates of the United States. Trees are hardy to about -15F (-26C) The best quality fruit is produced in hot-summer climates. Fungal and bacterial diseases, such as brown rot and bacterial canker, can be serious problems in humid areas. Peach leaf curl requires control in most areas of the country.

Pollination—Almost all peach and nectarine varieties are self-fruitful.

Pruning—These two trees require more pruning than any other fruiting tree. Those left with a central leader may grow too much at the top, losing lower limbs due to shading. Two-leader, Y-shaped trees fit into small spaces better than trees with more limbs. Three-leader trees are strong and easy to care for. More leaders are not desirable. Genetic dwarfs only require thinning to four or five scaffolds.

At planting time, head young trees 6 inches above the ground for short trees,

There are literally hundreds of peach varieties. 'Cardinal' is shown here.

2 feet above the ground for gardening space underneath. Shorten side shoots to 2 or 3 inches where you want a scaffold branch, spacing branches evenly around the trunk and several inches apart vertically to help prevent weak crotches. Remove all other shoots. If you want a central-leader tree, remove all side limbs and do not head leader.

During summer, pinch unwanted shoots to direct cane growth into scaffolds. Head scaffold limbs at 24 to 30 inches from the trunk during the first dormant season to strengthen secondary limbs and scaffold. Remove vigorous shoots that compete with secondary scaffolds.

In the second dormant season, thin shoots again. During the third dormant season, thin fruiting wood to prepare for next season's fruiting.

Peaches and nectarines bear only on the previous season's wood, so bearing trees must be pruned annually. Head the upper, outer shoots in midsummer to late summer to bring sunlight to lower limbs and prevent dieback from shading. Remove fruiting shoots when dormant and cut back shoots of medium vigor. Prune to counteract the strong tendency of fruiting wood to move upward and out-ward away from the trunk.

Thin these back to more upright shoots. Upper, outside branches tend to spread too much. Thin weakest spots, leaving shoots of about pencil-thickness spaced far enough apart for good light distribution and fruit production.

Varieties—There are hundreds of varieties. Peaches and nectarines come in white-fleshed and yellow-fleshed varieties, and with flesh that either clings to the pit (clingstone) or separates from the pit easily (freestone). Freestone varieties are best for canning or preserves. Excellent flavored midseason peach varieties include 'Fay Elberta', 'Halehaven' and 'Flavorcrest'. Outstanding midseason nectarines include 'Sunglo' and 'Flavortop'. 'Flordagold', 'Flordaking', 'Desertgold' and 'Mid-pride' are a few of many low-chill peaches. 'Fantasia' and 'Sunrise' are low-chill nectarines. 'Fantasia' has a sweet-kernel pit that can be cracked and eaten like an almond. 'Honey Babe' and 'Sensation' are popular genetic dwarf peaches. 'Honeyglo', 'Nectar Babe' and 'Sweet Melody' are excellent genetic dwarf nectarines.

Harvesting—Let peaches and nectarines ripen completely on the tree. Pick when they begin to soften slightly.

Pear in bottle makes unique gift. Attach bottle to branch as soon as tiny fruit forms.

PEARS

There are basically two types of pears—*European* and *Asian*. European pears are familiar to most people. They are picked green and ripened off the tree. They have delicious, soft-textured flesh and the classic pear shape. Asian pears are round and can be eaten right after they are picked. However, the most important difference between Asian and European pears is that Asian pears have a crisp texture that resembles an apple. In fact, Asian pears are often called apple pears. Asian pears are gaining rapidly in popularity because of their delicious flavor and unique texture.

A third group of pears called *hybrid pears* are, as the name suggests, hybrids between Asian and European varieties. They are particularly popular in the southern United States because of their low chilling requirements and greater resistance to fire blight. Their fruit resembles European varieties.

Important Numbers—All pears are borne on handsome, glossy foliaged trees that are easily maintained below 20 feet tall. At least one fully dwarfing rootstock is available—Old Homex Farmingdale No. 51—that dwarfs trees to 6 feet in height. There are also some varieties available as semidwarfs that reach 12 to 15 feet high. Space pears 18 to 25 feet apart. Trees begin bearing 4 to 8 years after planting.

Adaptation—Most pears have chilling requirements between 600 and 900 hours. However, varieties with lower chilling requirements are available. The greatest limiting factor to where pears can be grown is susceptibility to the bacterial disease *fire blight*. The disease is common almost everywhere east of the Rocky Mountains and in many areas of the West. Planting disease-resistant varieties is the best preventative measure. Most pear varieties are hardy to about -20F (-29C).

Pollination—Pears require another variety in bloom nearby to produce the biggest possible crop.

Pruning—When planting, head pear trees 24 to 30 inches above the ground. Select three well-spaced scaffold limbs and remove any shoots between them, leaving any shoots below scaffold limbs to fill in the bottom of trees. Keep central leader for 1 or 2 years to help spread permanent scaffolds before removing it completely.

Each year, head scaffolds at 2-1/2 to 3 feet above the previous year's heading. Do not head side shoots. Summer pinching of rapidly growing leaders stimulates branching. To prevent breaking young, flexible limbs, tie scaffold limbs together.

Pear trees usually require heavy pruning to stimulate fruit-set, especially when there's no cross-pollination. Pears bear on long-lived spurs. On 2- or 3-year-old wood, head only those shoots that are over 2 feet long, back to flower buds at about 18 inches. Remove wood that fruited heavily during the previous year, leaving a well-positioned, 1-year-old shoot as a replacement. Remove water sprouts and suckers to help replace fruiting wood.

Varieties—'Fan Stil', 'Moonglow', 'Orient' and 'Sure Crop' are popular hybrid or European pears with resistance to fire blight. 'Bartlett' and 'Seckel' are widely available summer pears. 'Anjou' and 'Comice' are excellent winter pears. 'Chojoro' is a good Asian pear variety. Low-chill varieties include 'Flordahome', 'Hood' and the Asian variety 'Shinseikei'.

Harvesting—European and hybrid pears must be harvested green and ripened off the tree. If left to ripen on the tree, fruit will not reach peak flavor. Summer pears ripen in about 1 week at room temperature. Winter pears must be stored in a cold place for 6 to 8 weeks before they will ripen at room temperature. Asian pears are ready to pick when they reach an even yellow color and break easily from the fruiting spur. They can be eaten immediately.

PERSIMMONS

Two types of persimmons are grown in the United States—the *Oriental persimmon* and *American persimmon*. Both require minimum care and are extremely ornamental trees with glossy, green leaves that turn colorful shades of yellow, orange or red in fall. Oriental persimmons are grown most often but the American persimmons are much hardier and can be grown in climates where Oriental types cannot.

Important Numbers—Under ideal conditions, persimmon trees grow up to 40 feet tall and 30 feet wide. They are often much smaller. Trees should be spaced about 25 feet apart. They will usually begin bearing at 3 years of age.

Adaptation—Lack of hardiness is the only factor that determines whether or not you can grow persimmons. Oriental persimmons are hardy to 0F (-18C). American persimmons are hardy to about -20F (-29C).

Pollination—American persimmons are self-unfruitful; Oriental persimmons generally self-fruitful.

Pruning—Nursery trees should be headed to 2-1/2 to 3 feet at planting time. Choose five or six shoots, spaced over a foot or more apart along the trunk, to form scaffold limbs. Prune other growth below scaffolds. After the first season's growth, head scaffolds from 1/3 to 1/2 their original length. Avoid any more pruning until the tree begins to bear fruit.

Remove occasional crossing or poorly placed limbs on mature trees. Thin to more upright shoots to lighten ends of branches. Thin out tops of old trees to stimulate growth and allow sunshine in.

Varieties—There two types of persimmon varieties—*astringent* and *nonastringent*. Astringent varieties must be allowed to soften to an almost mush-like consistency before they can be eaten. Non-astringent types can be eaten firm-ripe like an apple. Most American persimmons are grown from seedlings and all bear astringent fruit. Astringent varieties of Oriental persimmon include 'Hachiya' and 'Tamopan'. 'Fuyu' is the most popular nonastringent variety.

Harvesting—Astringent persimmons can be left on the tree until they soften, but they may be damaged by birds. You can also pick when they are still slightly hard and ripen them off the tree. Nonastringent persimmons are picked when they reach full color. Use pruning shears to harvest persimmons, leaving 1 to 2 inches of stem attached to the fruit.

PLUMS

You can probably grow at least one of the three basic plum types. In cold climates, plant *hybrid plums,* which are known for their hardiness. In most other areas of the United States you can choose between *Japanese plums* or *European plums*. Japanese plums have red-skinned fruit and are the ones commonly sold in supermarkets. European plums have deep purple, freestone fruit. Some varieties with high sugar content are often dried and called prunes. In mild-winter climates, plant low-chill varieties of Japanese plums. A fourth group, called *cherry plums,* are hybrids between an American native plum and Japanese plum. They are small trees with plumlike fruit and are widely adapted.

Important Numbers—All plums are borne on relatively small trees that are easily maintained below 15 feet. While no fully dwarfing rootstocks are available, many varieties are sold as semidwarf trees that grow between 10 and 12 feet high. Space standard plums 18 to 20 feet apart. Semidwarf trees can be planted as close as 12 feet apart. Most plums will begin bearing at 3 to 4 years old.

'Stanley' is a popular European plum.

Adaptation—Each type of plum has its own climate requirements. Japanese plums bloom early, along with apricots, and are subject to damage from late spring frosts in many areas of the country. However, many varieties have low enough chilling requirements to be grown in the mildest winter climates. European plums bloom later but have higher chilling requirements, excluding them from many southern areas. Both Japanese and European plums are hardy to about -20F (-29C). Hybrid plums are trees for northern regions. Trees are hardy to at least -30F (-35C).

Pollination—European plums are self-fruitful, but most varieties do better if cross-pollinated. Japanese and hybrid plums need another variety to provide pollen.

Pruning—Train to a multiple leader with three or four main scaffold limbs. At planting time, head to 18 to 24 inches, selecting those shoots that will be leaders. Upright shoots with narrow crotches should be held in a spread position by spring-type clothespins during the first growing season.

European plums or prunes require only one light heading of scaffold limbs about 2 to 2-1/2 feet from the crotch to stimulate branching. Light pruning results in heavier and earlier fruit.

Prune bearing European plums to lighten branch ends, thus preventing

breakage. Renewal of fruiting wood comes from long water sprouts that grow from the upper side of arched, fruiting limbs. Cut back to the arch of these limbs to reduce tree height and renew fruiting wood.

Japanese plums need more severe heading of scaffold limbs to strengthen them and encourage branching. Thin to retain the outside spreading limbs. To stimulate branching, keep well-positioned secondary branches and head primary scaffolds just above secondary branches about 24 to 36 inches from the crotch.

Thin third-year scaffolds during the third dormant season to one or two per secondary branch. Thinning interior shoots helps the tree to spread.

Bearing Japanese plums should have 1-year-old shoots thinned, leaving some of them to renew fruiting wood. Also remove some branches carrying old, weak spurs.

Varieties—'Pipestone', 'Tonka' and 'Superior' are popular hybrid plums. Each will pollinate the other. 'Burbank', 'Eldorado', 'Queen Ann' and 'Satsuma' are among many popular Japanese plums. 'Santa Rosa' and 'Methely' are excellent low-chill Japanese plum varieties. Both are also excellent pollinizers for most other varieties. 'Brooks', 'French Prune' and 'Stanley' are popular European plums. 'Sprite' and 'Delight' are excellent cherry plum varieties.

Harvesting—European plums ripen over a period of several weeks. They should be picked when they begin to soften. Japanese and hybrid plums are picked at a slightly firmer stage. As soon as you notice a few fruit softening, the rest of the crop is ready to pick.

TROPICAL AND SUBTROPICAL FRUIT

Areas of the Southeast and Southwest where winter temperatures rarely drop below freezing present the interesting possibility of growing tropical and subtropical fruit. Some of these fruits, such as avocados and bananas, are familiar to American palates. Others, including papayas and mangos, are less familiar but are staples in the diets of millions of people in tropical countries around the world.

Growing these fruits often means making concessions. In climates that are less than ideal, they may need special nurturing to get them to bear fruit. Being able to situate these plants in the best possible microclimate is also highly important. Also, you must always be ready to provide protection if the weather threatens to get too cold. You might even want to grow them in containers and move them to a protected spot or a greenhouse during the cold season. But if you go to the trouble of giving these plants what they need, you can be rewarded with exciting and exotic-flavored tropical fruit.

Here are brief descriptions of some of the most popular tropical and subtropical fruit:

Avocados—These large, evergreen trees can reach over 40 feet high. There are two types—Guatamalan varieties and Mexican varieties. Guatamalan avocados include the varieties 'Hass' and 'Reed', and are generally more sensitive to cold than Mexican avocados. The foliage of Mexican avocados is hardy to about 24F (-4C). Fruit and flowers are more sensitive and may be damaged if temperatures fall below freezing. Varieties include 'Mexicola', 'Bacon' and 'Zutano'. Both types of avocado will fail to set fruit if temperatures are cool during blossoming. Both must have extremely well-drained soil.

Dwarf varieties include 'Whitsell' and 'Glenn', both 16 to 20 feet in height. Together, these trees provide fruit year-round.

Bananas—These trees provide large, tropical-looking leaves on tall, erect,

fast-growing trunks that can grow as high as 20 feet. Plants must be protected from wind and frost. Soil should be rich and well drained. Good choice for containers. Many varieties are available, including dwarf types that only grow 5 to 6 feet high.

Guavas—There are several types of guavas, but the easiest and most attractive are *strawberry guavas* and *lemon guavas*. Both have glossy green leaves, pretty white flowers and brightly colored red or yellow fruit with a sweet, aromatic flavor. Plants are hardy to 20F to 25F (-7C to -4C).

Loquat—These are round-headed evergreen trees with heavy-textured, sharply toothed, deep green leaves. Grows 15 to 25 feet high. Foliage is hardy to 20F (-7C) but blossoms, which open in late fall to midwinter, are damaged at about 28F (-2C). Yellow fruit are juicy and sweet, and have three large seeds. Excellent for making jams and jellies.

Macadamia Nut—These glossy-foliaged evergreen trees reach 25 to 30 feet high. They produce a rich-flavored nut with an extremely hard shell. Grows best in Hawaii and coastal areas of Southern California. Hardy to about 25F (-4C).

Mango—These large, compact evergreen trees bear long sprays of yellow to red flowers. Sensitive to cold. Temperatures below 25F (-4C) may kill the tree entirely. Warm days and nights are necessary for fruit to set. Select locally adapted varieties.

Natal Plum—Widely grown as an ornamental shrub for its glossy green leaves, fragrant, white flowers and brightly colored fruit. Easy to grow. Hardy to 26F (-3C). Many varieties are available, but only 'Fancy' is recommended for fruiting quality. Plant two different varieties for cross-pollination.

Papaya—This large herbaceous plant with huge, deeply lobed, fanlike leaves can reach 25 feet high. Grows fast and may bear fruit as soon as 8 months after planting seed. Rather difficult to grow except in Hawaii. Requires exceptional soil drainage and warm weather year round. Frost sensitive. Plant male and female plants to ensure pollination. The hybrid 'Babaco' from Ecuador shows great promise for cooler climates—it is hardy to 26F (-3C).

Pineapple Guava—Not a true guava. Handsome shrub with silvery green leaves and unusual red and white flowers. Used as an ornamental in many areas of California. Fruit is pear-shaped

with delicious minty flavor and drops from the plant when ripe. Shrub is easy to grow and can be trained as a hedge. Varieties selected for good fruit quality are 'Coolidge', 'Nazemetz' and 'Trask', all hardy to about 15F (-10C). Some varieties produce better when cross-pollinated with another variety.

Avocado trees can reach over 40 feet high. Because avocados bruise easily, special long-handle picking device is used.

BERRIES

BLACKBERRIES

Blackberries are known by many names—loganberries, boysenberries, olallieberries and youngberries. Actually, each of these berries is a variety of blackberry. Loganberries are a hybrid blackberry variety known as 'Logan'. Boysenberries are a hybrid variety called 'Boysen', and so on. The parentage of these hybrids is rather confusing because there are many species of blackberry native to almost every part of the United States. This means that one blackberry variety or another can probably be grown in your area.

Planting—Blackberries are borne on vigorous, thorny canes that are either erect or spreading. Both types are usually planted bare root. They are planted in trenches or individual holes, set an inch deeper than they were in the nursery. Plant erect blackberry varieties 24 to 30 inches apart in rows spaced 6 to 10 feet. Trailing blackberries require a trellis for support. The most common type is a two-wire trellis with the first wire about 30 inches above the ground and the second 5 feet above the ground. Plant trailing varieties 5 to 8 feet apart in rows spaced 8 to 10 feet. After planting, cut back canes to 8 to 10 inches above the ground.

Adaptation—Blackberries produce the best-tasting fruit in areas with mild winters and cool summers. Varieties differ dramatically in adaptation. Chilling requirements range from 100 to 1000 hours. Hardiness varies from -20F (-29C) in some erect types to 5F (-15C) in boysenberries and other varieties. To determine the best varieties for your area, consult your local nurserymen or university extension agent.

Pollination—All blackberries are self-fruitful.

Pruning—Blackberries are borne on 2-year-old canes. Pruning consists of removing canes that have fruited and tying to the trellis young canes that will fruit the following spring. Young canes grow from the base of fruited canes. Erect blackberries can be grown without a trellis by heading unfruiting canes from 4 to 6 feet above the ground.

Varieties—'Bailey', 'Darrow' and 'El Dorado' are erect varieties for cold climates. 'Dallas', 'Brazos' and 'Flordagrand' are low-chill varieties commonly grown in the Southeast. 'Olallie', 'Young' and 'Logan' are low-chill vari-

'Olallie' is a popular low-chill blackberry grown in the Southwest.

eties commonly grown in the Southwest. Other popular varieties include 'Marion', 'Chehalem', 'Lucretia' and 'Boysen'.

Harvesting—Blackberries should be picked every 2 or 3 days for a period of 1 or 2 weeks. Pick berries when they reach full size and color and when they separate easily from the cluster.

BLUEBERRIES

Blueberries have one cultural requirement that sets them apart from most other fruits that are grown in the home garden—they must be grown in acid soil. If you can meet this requirement and if you choose varieties that are adapted to your climate, you'll be rewarded not only with a delicious crop, but also with the visual delights of what is perhaps America's most beautiful native fruit.

Blueberries are borne on clean-foliaged shrubs that bear dainty clusters of white flowers in spring and turn stunning shades of red and orange before dropping their leaves in fall.

There are two types of blueberries grown in North America. Highbush blueberries are the type seen in supermarkets. Most varieties are best adapted to northern, cold-winter climates, but low-chill varieties are available. Rabbit-eye blueberries are grown in warmer climates of the South and West.

Planting—Set bare-root plants 4 to 6 feet apart in rows spaced about 10 feet apart. Blueberries can double as ornamentals and be worked into shrub borders or planted as hedges.

Adaptation—Most highbush blueberries have chilling requirements of over 800 hours and are hardy to -20F (-29C). They grow best in areas with cold winters and mild summers. Rabbit-eye blueberries have only slight chilling requirements but are only hardy to about 0F (-18C). They are more tolerant to warm summers and are widely grown in the Southeastern United States.

Pollination—Rabbit-eye blueberries are self-unfruitful. Some highbush blueberries are self-fruitful, but usually benefit by cross-pollination. To ensure adequate pollination plant at least three different varieties.

Pruning—Pruning is relatively simple. Thin plants to keep the center open and remove criss-crossing branches, especially near the base. Remove branches that are over 4 years old. If fruit is small, shorten branches that have abundant flower buds.

Varieties—There are many blueberry varieties. 'Berkeley', 'Bluecrop', 'Collins' and 'Herbert' are a few of many popular highbush blueberries. Low-chill highbush blueberry varieties include 'Sharpebule' (under 200 hours), 'Avonblue' (400 hours) and Flordablue (200-300 hours). Popular rabbit-eye blueberries include 'Bonita', 'Woodard

KNIFFEN SYSTEM

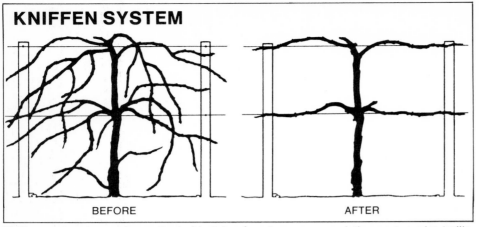

BEFORE   AFTER

Kniffen system is popular method of training American grape varieties on two-wire trellis. Each year, old fruited canes are removed and young, vigorous growth, which will produce fruit the following year, is cut back to six to ten buds and tied to trellis wires (left). From base of old fruiting cane, select two or three strong canes and cut back to two to three buds each (right). Growth from these buds will supply next year's fruiting canes.

Delight', 'Southland' and 'Tifblue'.

Harvesting—Blueberries are ready to pick when they turn deep blue, usually in midsummer. You can pick every few days, but because ripe blueberries will last on the vine for 8 to 10 days, you can do one picking, if desired.

GRAPES

There are four types of grapes commonly grown in North America: *American, European, French hybrids* and *muscadines*. Each type has different fruit characteristics and climate adaptation. American grapes bear strong-flavored fruit with tough skins that separate easily from the flesh. Fruit color ranges from greenish yellow to red to purplish red. American grapes can be eaten fresh or used to make jelly or juice. European grapes are more delicately flavored and have thin skins. They come in white or red varieties and are used to make some of the world's finest wines. Many are also excellent table grapes.

Hybrid grapes share qualities of each parent—European and American. They make excellent wine and have greatly expanded wine-grape growing into areas where European grapes cannot be grown. Muscadine grapes are a strong-flavored, slip-skinned fruit that come in white, red or purple varieties.

Planting—Grapes are usually planted bare root. Set American, European and hybrid grapes 8 to 10 feet apart in rows spaced 10 to 12 feet apart. Muscadine grapes should be spaced 12 to 15 feet apart in rows 18 to 20 feet apart.

Adaptation—Each type of grape has different climate requirements. American grapes are primarily grown in areas with cold winters and mild summers. They are hardy to 0F (-18C) and usually require a growing season of at least 160 days to ripen their fruit. Chilling requirements vary from 400 to 1200 hours but disease problems exclude them from the Southeast. European grapes require a long, hot, dry growing season to ripen their crop. They have chilling requirements of at least 800 hours and are only hardy to 10F (-12C). European grapes are most popular in the dry-summer areas of the western United States. Hybrid grapes are adapted to most of the same areas where American grapes can be grown. Muscadine grapes are best adapted to the hot, humid climates of the Southeast. They are hardy to 10F (-12C) and have only a slight chilling requirement. All grape varieties are susceptible to damage from late spring frosts.

Pollination—All grapes are self-fruitful, with the exception of some older varieties of muscadine grapes, which bear only female flowers and must have a male variety nearby to set fruit.

Pruning—European grapes *(Vitis vinifera),* grown primarily for wine making, produce fruitful basal buds on the previous season's wood, while the basal buds of American species (*V. labrusca* and *V. rotundifolia*) are not fruitful. Thus, *V. vinifera* can be pruned back to two to four basal buds on each cane annually. The American natives need much longer canes.

When planting grapes, head cuttings to three buds and prune roots to about 6 inches long. Plant top buds level with the soil surface and mound loose soil over the plant to protect it from sunburn. Insert a stake to support plants as the canes grow.

During the first dormant season, remove all but one cane from each vine. Cut back single canes to two or three buds. During the second summer, save the strongest and best-positioned shoots and remove the rest. Tie shoots loosely to the stake and remove suckers from roots and old stems. Tied branches should be allowed to branch freely.

European grapes that are confined to small spaces are usually *head-pruned*. Cut off canes at the node above where the head forms, cutting through the node to destroy the bud. Tie canes securely to the top of supporting stakes and loosely about halfway to the ground.

Remove all laterals below the middle of the trunk, as well as any weak laterals in the upper half of the vine. Head two to four of the stronger laterals back to two or three basal buds each.

Mature head-trained vines are spur-pruned to restrict their size. Remove all but three to six of the strongest canes that developed in the third summer after planting vine. Head remaining cane to two, three or four basal buds—the greater the diameter of the vine, the more buds that can be left. Leave more of these fruiting spurs each year as vines mature.

A similar method of pruning that often makes European grapes more productive is *cane-pruning*. Head remaining canes to six to 18 buds depending on the vigor or diameter of the canes. Select canes to form a fan-shaped vine, rather than leaving canes spaced evenly around the trunk.

During the third dormant season, select two canes and tie them to a support. Head two other canes at basal buds. Basal bud growth produces the next season's fruiting canes. Leave more canes as vines mature.

American grapes are usually pruned by the *Kniffen system,* which is similar to cane-pruning except that a second, higher pair of canes is selected and tied to a higher support. Keep the central leader straight by tying it to a cane. Head canes just above top vines. See drawing on the facing page.

Remove all but two canes at each level following the next season's growth.

Head canes to four to eight buds and fasten canes to the support. As vines mature, remove all canes that have fruited and select vigorous new canes for the next year's fruit. Tie canes to the support and head the canes back to six to 10 buds, according to cane diameter and vigor. Choose two or three strong canes from the base of the old fruiting canes (arms) near the trunk and head each to two or three buds. Their growth produces the next season's fruiting cane.

A variation of head-pruning is *cordon-training,* in which two permanent laterals stretch in opposite directions along a support such as a wire, fence or wall. Select two strong laterals, one on the main shoot, at a point 8 to 10 inches below the support to serve as the cordon arms. Pinch back all other laterals and the main shoot, then fasten the arms to the support at least 1 foot back from their growing tips.

Varieties—There are many varieties of each type of grape. Choosing the right varieties for your area is important. Consult with your local nurseryman or university extension agent to find out which varieties do best where you live.

Harvesting—The best way to tell if grapes are ripe is to taste a few once they have reached full color. Harvest clusters with pruning shears or a sharp knife.

RASPBERRIES

Raspberries are closely related to blackberries but differ in that their fruit separates easily from its core, while blackberries are picked core and all. Raspberries also have a narrower range of adaptation, being best adapted to areas with cool summers and mild winters. Raspberries are available in varieties that produce red, yellow, purple or black fruit.

Planting—Raspberries are usually planted bare root. Plant red- and yellow-fruited varieties 30 to 36 inches apart in 6-inch-deep trenches spaced 6 to 10 feet apart. Plants will spread to form a solid row. Black and purple raspberry plants do not spread. Plant in individual holes 2 to 3 feet apart in rows spaced 6 to 8 feet apart. Cut back all raspberry plants to 5 to 6 inches above the ground after planting.

'Brandywine' is a good purple raspberry—mature berries are slightly darker than immature ones shown here.

Adaptation—Raspberries are hardy to between -20F and -30F (-29C and -34C) and have a chilling requirement of 200 hours or more. They are best adapted to areas with cool, moist summers such as the Pacific Northwest and parts of the Midwest and Northeast. Recently developed low-chill varieties include 'San Diego', 'Oregon No. 1030' and 'Dorman'.

Pollination—All raspberries are self-fruitful.

Pruning—The easiest way to grow raspberries is to train them between a four-wire trellis with two parallel wires, spaced about 2 feet apart at a height of 3-1/2 feet, and two more parallel wires at a height of 2 feet. Pruning involves removing canes that have fruited and selecting the most vigorous 1-year-old canes to train between the parallel wires of the trellis, for fruiting the following year.

Varieties—There are many raspberry varieties. They vary in fruit color, ripening period and climate adaptation. Most varieties bear one large crop sometime near midsummer. Everbearing varieties bear two major crops—one in spring and then another in fall. Popular red raspberry varieties for the Midwest and Northeast include 'Boyne', 'Latham' and 'Newburgh'. In the Northwest 'Puyallup', 'Sumner', 'Meeker' and 'Willamette' are popular varieties. 'September' and 'Heritage' are widely grown everbearing raspberries. 'Amber' and 'Fallgold' are popular yellow raspberries. 'Brandywine' is a good purple raspberry. 'Allen', 'Black Hawk' and 'Cumberland' are a few of many black raspberries.

Harvesting—Raspberries are ripe when a gentle pull separates them from their core. Pick every few days during the harvest period.

Bird netting protects backyard strawberry patch. Loose mulch keeps weeds down.

STRAWBERRIES

Strawberries are one of the least demanding and most adaptable fruits you can grow. One variety or another can be grown almost anywhere in North America. Their low, clumping habit allows them to fit in the smallest available spot, making strawberries perfect for containers. When given room, they will spread and form an attractive mat or ground cover.

There are two types of strawberries: *spring-bearing strawberries* and *everbearing strawberries*. Spring-bearing strawberries bear one large crop in spring. Everbearing varieties produce fruit over the entire growing season, although it doesn't amount to a lot of fruit at any one time.

Strawberries spread by *runners,* small vinelike arms that produce another plant at their tip. Often referred to as *babies,* these small plants will root and grow wherever they settle. The original plant that produced the runner is called the *mother plant.* If strawberry plants are left to send out runners at will, they will eventually create a dense mat of plants, often called a *strawberry patch.* However, strawberry plants sometimes produce runners at the expense of fruit. So by cutting off runners whenever they occur, you may get more or larger fruit per plant. These factors will influence how you plant strawberries.

Planting—Start with plants certified to be disease free. This will ensure that they are not contaminated with hard-to-detect viruses, which can be a problem if you start with babies from your neighbor's patch. Plants are usually sold bare root. They are planted in fall in mild-winter areas, spring in cold-winter areas. In some areas of the Southeast, strawberries are grown as annuals, planted in midsummer for a spring crop.

There are basically two planting schemes to follow. The first is called the *matted row,* in which plants are placed 18 to 24 inches apart in rows spaced 48 inches apart. Runners are allowed to fill in at will until rows are about 2 feet wide and solid with strawberry plants. Each year, thin out older plants and allow new babies to become established. If you don't thin, plants will loose productivity. The *hedgerow* system of planting strawberries produces the biggest fruit. Plants are grown 12 inches apart on 6-inch-high soil ridges spaced 24 to 30 inches apart. All runners are cut off as soon as they are noticed. A variation of this method is called the *selective hedgerow,* in which plants are set 24 inches apart in rows spaced 48 inches apart. Each plant is allowed to set two evenly spaced runners; all others are removed.

The hedgerow and selective hedgerow methods make it easier to use a mulch to keep berries clean and provide winter protection. Planting depth is important—not so shallow that roots are subject to drying, and not so deep that the crown is covered. To establish strong plants, remove all blossoms and runners the first growing season. Most experts also recommend replanting after the third or fourth season.

Adaptation—Varieties have been developed for almost every region of the United States and Canada. Mulching is important in cold-winter climates. In areas where late spring frosts are common, plant everbearing varieties. If frost destroys the first blossoms, everbearing strawberries will continue blooming and produce fruit. Spring-bearers may not bloom again once their flowers are destroyed.

Pollination—All strawberries are self-fruitful.

Pruning—Strawberries do not require any pruning other than to remove runners, if necessary. Replace old plants every 3 or 4 years.

Varieties—A number of varieties are available. Local adaptation is often important. Consult your local nurseryman or university extension agent to find out which varieties are best adapted to your area.

Harvesting—Pick strawberries when they reach full color. You'll have to pick every few days in spring. Leave stems attached if you plan to store the fruit in the refrigerator.

NUTS

ALMONDS

The narrow range of adaptation of almonds eliminates them from most gardens in the United States. However, if you like a challenge, select your planting spot carefully and provide protection from spring frosts, or plant a dwarf variety in a container and move it to a protected spot in spring.

Important Numbers—Almonds are medium-size trees that are easily maintained below 25 feet in height with an equal spread. They are commonly spaced 25 to 30 feet apart in orchard conditions. A few dwarf varieties can be maintained below 10 feet in height. Most almond trees will begin bearing at 3 to 4 years of age.

Adaptation—Although almonds are fairly hardy and have a relatively low chilling requirement, their early-blooming characteristics and need for long, dry summers generally limit successful nut production to warm-summer areas of California.

Pollination—With a few exceptions, all almonds are self-unfruitful and require another variety nearby to provide pollen.

Pruning—Once a sturdy, vase-shaped framework is established, little pruning is necessary.

Varieties—'Nonpareil', 'Jordanola', 'Ne Plus Ultra' and 'Hall's Hardy' are popular varieties. 'All-In-One' and 'Legrand' are self-fruitful varieties. 'Garden Prince' is a self-fruitful dwarf variety.

Harvesting—Almonds should be harvested when the hulls split open and are partially dry. Shake the tree or knock the nuts off with a stick. Remove the hulls and sun-dry for at least 2 days. When the kernels rattle in the shell the nuts are ready for storage. Stored in a cool, dry, well-ventilated place, almonds will keep up to 6 months.

Filberts are ripe when husk dries out and nuts fall to the ground. To avoid deterioration, gather nuts frequently.

FILBERTS (HAZELNUTS)

There are several species of filberts, or hazelnuts as they are often called, that can be grown in North America as ornamentals. The European filbert is the only one grown extensively for edible nuts. It is adapted primarily to the Pacific Northwest and parts of California. But some hybrid filberts—crosses between native American species and the European filbert—do produce acceptable nuts and extend filbert growing into the Midwest and Northeast.

Important Numbers—Filberts are shrubby plants that are usually maintained under 20 feet tall. Space plants 18 to 20 feet apart. Most filberts will begin bearing at 4 years of age.

Adaptation—European filberts have high chilling requirements—at least 800 hours—which excludes them from most southern climates. In addition, they flower in late winter or early spring, making them susceptible to spring frost damage. These facts, and susceptibility to a fungal blight in the East, limits their culture primarily to portions of the Pacific Northwest and California. Hybrid filberts have disease resistance and hardiness that extend their range into to parts of the Midwest and Northeast.

Pollination—Most filberts are self-unfruitful and require another variety nearby to provide pollen.

Pruning—Little pruning is necessary if they are allowed to grow in their natural shrublike form.

Varieties—'Barcelona', 'Du Chilly', 'Royal', 'Daviana' and 'Hall's Giant' are common European filbert varieties. 'Bixby', 'Buchanan', 'Potomac' and 'Reed' are common hybrid filberts.

Harvesting—Filberts are harvested when they fall to the ground. Gather nuts as often as possible to avoid deterioration. Dry in the sun and store in a cool place.

PECANS

Pecans are borne on large, beautiful trees with bright green, compound leaves that turn bright yellow before dropping in fall. They are grown as shade trees in many areas where the climate prevents the production of edible nuts.

Important Numbers—Pecans require a lot of space. At maturity, some can reach over 80 feet high and about half as wide. They should be planted no closer than 40 to 50 feet apart. Most trees will begin bearing at 4 years of age.

Adaptation—Pecans require long, warm summers of at least 200 frost-free days to produce an edible nut. The deep South and the Southwest desert are ideal climates, but pecans can also be grown in warmer areas of central and northern California and in parts of the upper South. There is little known about the chilling requirements of pecans, but trees have been known to provide good crops with as low as 100 hours. Trees are hardy to about 0F (-18C). Pecan trees are susceptible to zinc deficiency. Affected trees respond well to foliar applications of chelated zinc.

Pollination—Solitary pecan trees will produce a crop, but for maximum production, plant two varieties for cross-pollination.

Pruning—Once an initial sturdy framework is established, pecans require little pruning.

Varieties—'Choctaw', 'Cheyenne' and 'Mohawk' are widely adapted varieties. 'Western Schley' is popular in the West.

Harvesting—Pecans are knocked from the tree with poles or long sticks. They are ready to harvest when the hulls begin to split and the shells are well filled with meat.

WALNUTS

There are two types of walnuts commonly grown in the United States: the *English or Persian walnut* and the *Eastern black walnut*. Both are large, stately trees that can double as lawn or shade trees. The widely grown English walnut is the type found in supermarkets and known for its thin shell and large, sweet meat. The Eastern black walnut has a harder shell but is an equally delicious nut. In fact, many people consider it more flavorful than English walnuts. A close relative of the walnuts, the butternut, is a similarly beautiful tree, grown in many cold-winter climates.

Important Numbers—All walnuts are borne on large trees that need a lot of room to grow. English walnuts can grow over 60 feet high with an equal spread. The Eastern black walnut can grow over 100 feet high with about half the spread. Neither should be planted closer than 50 feet apart. Grafted varieties of either type will begin bearing at about 5 years of age.

Adaptation—Choosing the right variety is one of the most important factors when growing English walnuts. In many areas, early-blooming varieties are subject to frost damage and severe disease or insect problems. Most have chilling requirements of between 500 and 1000 hours, but low-chill varieties, such as 'Placentia', are available. However, severe disease problems prevent success in most areas of the Southeast. English walnuts are hardy to at least -35F (-37C).

The Eastern black walnut is widely adapted and can be grown over most of the United States and Canada. It has a relatively low chilling requirement and is hardy to at least -20F (-29C).

Pollination—Most walnuts will produce larger crops if a different variety that blooms at the same time is planted nearby. However, many gardeners harvest sufficient crops with only one tree.

Pruning—Head nursery trees at planting time to four or five buds and tie leader to a 6-foot-tall stake. Pinch back all shoots that compete with the central leader.

At the end of the first growing season, head the leader about three buds above the stake and remove all side limbs. Break off buds on short stems to encourage strong scaffold limbs from secondary buds below. If the leader failed to grow enough, head it back to last season's growth. Continue training and staking the leader through the second summer.

During the second dormant season, select four to six wide-angled crotched scaffold limbs about 5 to 7 feet above ground, avoiding those that are horizontal. Remove lateral branches below the lowest scaffold limb and cut lower branches on the trunk to short stubs.

For newer varieties that bear laterally, prune and head scaffolds each dormant season.

Most young bearing trees do not need pruning. However, some new, heavy-bearing varieties stop growing or break apart if shoots aren't headed 25% to 50% each year. All mature trees benefit from thinning to let light into the canopy. You'll probably need to call in tree or landscape service to prune large trees.

Varieties—The best advice on variety selection is to consult your local nurseryman or university extension agent. Some of the popular varieties of English walnuts grown in the western United States include 'Payne', 'Franquette', 'Placentia' and 'Spurgeon'. 'Hansen' and 'Adams' are popular in the eastern United States. 'Thomas' is a widely planted variety of black walnut.

Harvesting—Walnuts are ready to harvest when the hulls split and the nuts begin to fall from the tree. When a few start to fall, knock the rest off with a pole or long stick, being careful not to break branches. Remove the hulls and wash the nuts with water to remove tannins, which will stain the shells. Dry in the sun as you do almonds. Walnuts will keep many months if stored in a cool, dry place.

Immature English walnuts have bright green hulls. Walnuts are ready to harvest when hulls split open and nuts begin to fall to ground. If hulls of some ripe nuts are not easily removed, soak nuts in water overnight, then use pocketknife to remove hull.

English walnut makes a beautiful shade tree.

VEGETABLES

No matter how vegetable gardening is described—hobby, pastime, hedge against inflation—it is blessed with benefits. Few experiences in life are more pleasurable and satisfying than planting seeds, being responsible for their growth and reaping a bountiful harvest. Consider the following:

☐ Vegetable gardening teaches self-help and instills a sense of accomplishment. The Chinese have a saying: *To be happy all your life, become a gardener*.

☐ Vegetable gardening is a pleasant escape from everyday stress and anxiety. Problems seem to dissipate as soon as you get your hands in the soil.

☐ Vegetable gardening teaches children responsibility and provides an opportunity for families to do something together. Exercise and learning derived from gardening stimulate the body and the mind.

☐ Vegetable gardening requires no expensive investment. Seeds are among the biggest bargains today, capable of returning a value more than 100 times

their initial cost.

☐ Growing vegetables reduces your food bill. Don't expect to get rich from the savings, but a garden can fulfill the fresh-vegetable requirements of your family during the summer months. If you are lucky to live in a mild climate, you may be able to grow fresh vegetables year-round. In addition, many vegetables can be stored or preserved for use out of season.

☐ Garden-fresh vegetables are one of the best sources of vitamins. No other food group—milk, meat, eggs or fish—can match the balanced nutrition vegetables bring to a diet.

☐ The flavor of home-grown vegetables is reason enough to have a garden. Compare the taste of tomatoes from the supermarket produce counter to those picked at peak freshness from your own back yard. What a difference!

Just as there are many reasons to grow vegetables, there are many ways to grow them. As you read this chapter and talk

with other gardeners, you'll receive an assortment of advice, some of it conflicting. Don't become confused trying to follow every expert's "fool-proof" techniques. Growing vegetables is not a pure science, and there are no exact formulas for success. Popular methods such as *mulch gardening, organic gardening, raised-bed gardening, French-intensive gardening, wide-row planting* and *square-foot gardening* are not applicable for all people and situations. The best way to garden is to borrow a little from each to suit you, the location and the vegetables you are growing.

Keep in mind that a vegetable garden can take on many forms. For example, many gardeners integrate vegetables into their landscape. Vegetables can be part of a foundation planting on one side of the house. They can be planted in terraces along a slope, or in a raised bed of railroad ties. Clusters of tomatoes, peppers and eggplant in containers along a redwood deck are attractive and productive.

Left: Vegetable gardens are not limited in design to rectangular lots—this one is part of a backyard landscape. The hand-carved sign in the background sums up the feelings of its keeper. Above: Probably the greatest pleasure of growing vegetables is the payoff—a wheelbarrow brimming with a day's harvest.

CLIMATE AND PLANTING DATES

It is early spring and the sun is shining brightly. The soil has been prepared for planting. It is not frozen or soggy. The time seems right to plant the first cold-hardy vegetables. But how can you be sure you are planting at the right time?

It pays to be concerned with planting dates. A major cause of garden failure is planting too soon or too late. To be successful, a good gardener must plant in harmony with the season, considering different cultural and climatic requirements of the vegetable plants. As a guide, vegetables are classified as *cool season* or *warm season,* according to season when they grow best.

Cool-season vegetables tolerate mild frosts and are usually planted just before the last frost in spring. In mild-winter areas, they are often planted in fall to mature in the cool winter months. Most require cool temperatures or their growth and flavor are adversely affected. Some, such as lettuce and cabbage, will *bolt*—go to seed—as soon as warm temperatures arrive.

Warm-season vegetables are damaged by below-freezing temperatures, so they are planted after the last frost in spring. Some are slightly more cold tender and are planted two to three weeks later. Many, such as melons, corn and peppers, require a long, hot growing season to mature.

Refer to the heading *Cold Hardy or Tender* in the following chart to determine a vegetable's tolerance to cold. *Cold-hardy* plants accept slight frosts. *Cold-tender* plants are damaged or killed by frosts.

CLIMATE INGREDIENTS

The climate of your area determines which vegetables you can grow successfully and their best planting dates. Many factors make up the unique climate of your garden. The most important include spring and fall frosts, winter and summer temperatures, elevation and large bodies of water.

Frost dates. The number of days between the last spring frost and the first fall frost is the length of your *growing season.* In certain northern and high elevation areas of the United States and Canada, the growing season can be fewer than 100 days. In coastal areas of southern California and southern Florida, the growing season is 365 days.

Temperature extremes. Summer high and winter low temperatures affect climate. Lack of sunshine and heat can cause problems with warm-season vegetables. For example, in areas of western Washington and western Oregon, fog reduces the amount of sunshine. Summer temperatures are too low for full ripening of fruit-producing vegetables: eggplant and peppers. At the other extreme, high summer heat in the Southwestern deserts prevents fruit set of tomatoes, peppers and eggplant.

Winter lows determine the growing season of cool-season crops. If temperatures do not drop much below freezing, cool-season vegetables can be grown through winter.

Bodies of water. Large areas of water such as the oceans or the Great Lakes temper climate. Because water is one of the best heat reservoirs, lakes and oceans warm and cool slowly. In summer, water evaporates and cools the surrounding air. In winter, water acts as a buffer against cold temperatures. An example of this is the area around the Great Lakes. Gardeners living here have a growing season longer than that of regions more than 100 miles south.

MICROCLIMATES

Microclimates are small climates within a larger surrounding climate. Exposure to the sun, changes in elevation, bodies of water and slope of the land create microclimates.

On a large scale, a mountainous region in a low-elevation climate is a microclimate. The higher elevation causes temperatures to be cooler. Last spring frosts come later and first fall frosts come earlier to shorten the growing season. If you live in such an area, your planting dates will generally be later than those of the lower elevation area.

On a small scale, your own home lot has microclimates. If you take a walk around your house you can feel subtle differences. The northern exposure does not receive afternoon sunshine, so it is cooler and more moist. The southern and western exposures receive afternoon sun, so are warmer. Slope of your lot and surrounding terrain influences air flow. Cold air flows down valleys and canyons—as well as your lot—taking the path of least resistance, much like a stream or river. The cold air lowers temperatures, which can damage tender crops.

Locate microclimates before you choose your garden site. This is especially important for short-season climates. In these areas, a site that warms early in spring is necessary to grow warm-season vegetables to maturity.

FROST PROTECTION

Protection against frost is necessary in most areas at the beginning and end of the growing season. Some gardeners use commercially available products. Others recycle household products normally thrown away in the trash. Whatever method of frost protection you choose, *don't leave coverings over plants during warm or sunny days.* Otherwise, the heat will dehydrate tender seedlings.

Hot caps. These are clear paper or clear plastic cones used to cover individual plants. They have a lip that is covered with soil to hold them in place. Their use is usually confined to protecting the transplant stage of bushy plants such as cucumbers, tomatoes, peppers and eggplant.

A suitable hot cap can be made from plastic, 1-gallon milk jugs. Simply cut out the bottom with scissors. On windy days a narrow stake can be used to hold the jug in place.

Cloches. This French word (pronounced *klo'-sh)* means *bell jar.* Its name is derived from the bell-shaped, glass jars traditionally used to protect tender plants from frost. They are made from clear plastic rather than glass, and are usually shaped like a tent to cover a short, wide row of plants.

Plastic tunnels. These kits have metal supports to support a length of clear plastic sheeting with ventilation holes. They are designed to protect a long, wide row of plants.

Early planting of tomatoes are protected from frost with wire cylinders wrapped in plastic. Black plastic over the ground will help increase soil temperature.

Sprinklers. Watering with a lawn sprinkler in the middle of the garden overnight helps prevent mild frosts. Air movement and the heat released by the water as it cools help to increase temperatures.

CLIMATES OF NORTH AMERICA

The following is a broad overview of North American climates. For more specific information on your area, contact your state university extension service or local cooperative extension agent.

Midwest, Northeast and Canada. This area has two distinct climates. In areas with growing seasons of 190 days or more, two plantings of cool-season crops can be made—early spring for early summer harvests, and midsummer for fall harvests. A single planting of warm-season vegetables generally remains productive until frost. Wait until the soil warms in spring before planting melon crops, squash, lima beans, cucumbers, eggplant, peppers and tomatoes.

In northern parts of the United States and parts of Canada, cool-season crops do well. In areas with cool summers, they can be grown through the season. In areas that have warm summers, planting dates for a fall harvest must be timed properly. The growing season for warm-season vegetables is short. Early maturing varieties are necessary, as are season-stretching techniques. The techniques described in the following on short-season areas apply here.

Regions with short growing seasons. A short growing season is generally de-

Glass cloche covers new crop of peas. Similar units made of clear plastic are also available. Be sure to remove coverings during sunny days or plants may be injured.

fined as having less than 100 frost-free days, as in zone 7 on the climate map. The cool summers of these areas allow cool-season crops to do well, but growing fruit-producing warm-season vegetables presents special challenges.

Early maturing varieties are necessary, and should be planted as soon as the weather allows. Be prepared to protect plants from frost when they are first set out. A raised-bed garden gives you a jump on the season. The raised soil warms faster than soil at ground level. Planting through clear plastic mulch warms the soil faster in spring, and keeps it warm through the season. Melons and squash especially prefer the warm soil.

South. In this section of the United States, the ground does not usually freeze, but heavy frosts are common in many areas. Prolonged cold spells occur occasionally when arctic air pushes back warm air from the Gulf of Mexico.

The South has three basic vegetable climates. The upper South is much like the adjacent Midwest. Cool-season crops have two planting times— early spring and midsummer. Warm-season crops do well here, with some having two planting seasons.

In the central South, spring planting can begin as early as February for cool-season crops. Warm-season plantings can begin in mid-March.

In areas near the Gulf of Mexico, cool-season crops are best planted in early September to mature throughout fall. Warm-season crops can be planted as soon as mid-February.

In many areas of the South, a combination of high humidity and high temperature interferes with fruit set of tomatoes and peppers. Plant these and other warm-season crops as early as possible so they will mature before the onset of high heat. In long growing-season areas, some warm-season crops can be planted in late summer to mature in early fall.

The South is also notorious for being home to insect pests, notably armyworms, corn earworms, nematodes and mole crickets. Select disease-resistant varieties, and implement a regular pest control schedule soon after planting.

The South has many microclimates—mostly high elevation locations with cool summers. If you live in one of these areas, it is best to check locally for planting dates.

Tropical Florida. This region extends far out into the warm Gulf Stream. Frosts are rare and the area generally

enjoys year-round growing conditions. Warm-season crops can be grown during winter, although ripening may not occur until February or March.

Busiest planting times are October for cool-season crops and January to February for warm-season crops.

During the tropical summer heat, most fruiting vegetables stop bearing. Diseases also take a heavy toll of plants. It is best to plant two crops of warm-season vegetables—one to mature in early spring and the other to mature in fall.

Certain perennial vegetables—especially asparagus and rhubarb—cannot tolerate the high summer temperatures, or experience insufficient low winter temperatures to provide roots with the necessary dormancy.

Southwest. This area has long growing conditions for both cool- and warm-season crops, allowing two harvesting periods for each.

Frosts occur, but usually only from December to February. Cool-season crops should be planted in fall to mature during winter. Warm-season crops are planted early in the year to take advantage of pleasant spring weather.

In the lower sections of the Gila River Valley and Colorado River Valley of Arizona, a few favored locations escape killing frosts for two or three years at a time. Tomatoes and other warm-season crops can be grown unprotected all year, although fruit ripening may be inhibited during December, January and February.

Southwestern summers are exceedingly hot. Timing of plantings is critical, especially in the low and intermediate deserts. Cool-season crops must mature in late fall to early spring. Warm-season crops should be planted as early as possible to mature before midsummer. High temperatures, especially at night, prevent fruit set of tomatoes, peppers and eggplant.

High desert areas are often plagued by early fall frosts, so fall planting is not possible in these areas. Using a cold frame to extend the growing season is helpful. Because late spring frosts are common, be prepared to protect plants.

California. This state features a collection of climates prevalent elsewhere in the United States—from year-round subtropical growing areas to short-season, high-elevation regions. Because its climate is so complex, climate maps and descriptions can be considered only in general terms.

The southern half of California has several distinct climates. The coastal area—from Santa Barbara south to the Mexican border—has 300 or more frost-free days of mild weather each year. This allows cool-season crops to be grown year-round. Summer fog is a factor where the warm interior air draws in cool Pacific air. The fog reduces the amount of sunshine, which slows development of many warm-season crops. Inland climates vary greatly, depending on elevation and proximity to the coast and desert.

Northern California also has microclimates too complex to show on a map. Much of this area is influenced by the Pacific Ocean and summer fog. The immediate coastal area experiences moderate temperatures. Conditions are excellent for growing cool-season crops year-round.

In the interior valleys, summers are sunny and warm, creating exceptional growing conditions for warm-season crops, especially melons, sweet corn and tomatoes. Tropical vegetables such as jicama, chayote, winged bean and casaba melon do well in the valleys away from fog.

In many parts of these inland valleys, winters are mild enough to grow cool-season crops through winter. Otherwise, planting occurs mostly in February and March and again in August to September. April is the busiest month for planting warm-season crops. Because the season is long, a second planting can be made in June for a fall harvest.

Pacific Northwest. The climate of this area is unique. Western Washington and western Oregon have a long growing season—up to 250 days—with last spring frosts occurring in mid-March. But cool, cloudy summer weather reduces sunshine, and the soil warms slowly in spring. These cool conditions are excellent for cool-season vegetables, but warm-season vegetables require heat and sunshine to mature. Growing melons here is difficult. Tomatoes, peppers and sweet corn must be confined to early maturing varieties. Plant in raised beds to warm the soil early in spring, and take advantage of warm microclimates.

In eastern Washington there is enough summer sun to ripen long-maturing, warm-season varieties. In eastern Oregon the growing season is short. Cool-season crops are recommended. Grow early varieties and use season-stretching techniques.

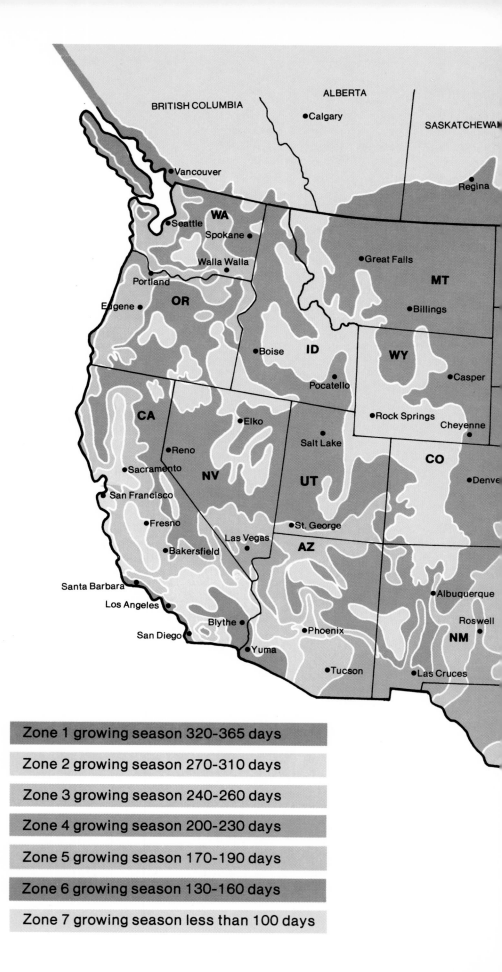

Zone 1 growing season 320-365 days

Zone 2 growing season 270-310 days

Zone 3 growing season 240-260 days

Zone 4 growing season 200-230 days

Zone 5 growing season 170-190 days

Zone 6 growing season 130-160 days

Zone 7 growing season less than 100 days

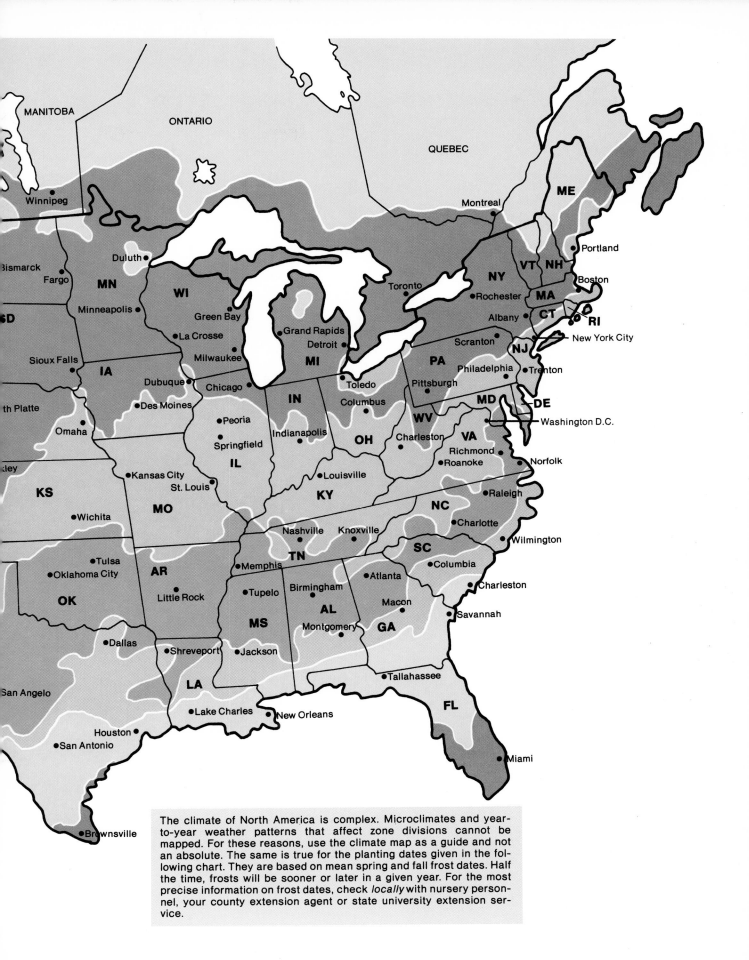

The climate of North America is complex. Microclimates and year-to-year weather patterns that affect zone divisions cannot be mapped. For these reasons, use the climate map as a guide and not an absolute. The same is true for the planting dates given in the following chart. They are based on mean spring and fall frost dates. Half the time, frosts will be sooner or later in a given year. For the most precise information on frost dates, check *locally* with nursery personnel, your county extension agent or state university extension service.

When to Plant

Vegetable	Zone 1	Zone 2	Zone 3	Zone 4	Zone 5	Zone 6	Zone 7
Amaranth	Feb 10-Apr 1	Mar 1-Apr 1	Mar 15-Apr 15	Apr 5-May 1	May 1-Jun 1	May 15-Jun 15	Jun 15-Jul 15
Artichoke, Globe	not recommended	Feb 5-Apr 1	Mar 20-Apr 1	Apr 5-May 1	Apr 20-May 15	May 10-Jun 10	May 15
Asparagus	not recommended	not recommended	Feb 1-Mar 10	Mar 1-Apr 10 Nov 15-Jan 1	Mar 15-Apr 15 Oct 20-Nov 20	Mar 10-May 15	May 1-Jun 1
Asparagus Pea	Feb 10-Apr 1 Oct 1-Dec 1	Mar 1-Apr 1 Sep 1	Mar 15-Apr 1 Sep 1	Apr 5-May 1 Aug 1-Sep 1	May 1-Jun 1	May 15-Jun 15	Jun 15-Jul 15
Bean, Broad	Jan 1-Feb 1 Oct 1-Dec 1	Jan 15-Mar 1 Sep 1	Feb 15-Mar 15 Sep 1	Mar 1-Apr 1 Aug 1-Sep 1	Mar 15-Jul 1 Aug 1-Sep 1	Apr 1-Jul 1	Apr 15-Jul 15
Bean, Cowpea	Feb 10-May 1	Mar 1-May 15 Jul 1-Aug 1	Mar 15-May 25 Sep 1	Apr 5-Jun 30 Jul 1	May 1-Jun 15	May 25-Jun 15	**
Bean, Garbanzo	Feb 10-May 1 Sep 1	Mar 1-Apr 1 Aug 15-Sep 30	Mar 15-Apr 1 Aug 15-Sep 30	Apr 10-May 1	May 1-Jun 1	May 15-Jun 15	**
Bean, Lima	Feb 20-May 1 Sep 1-Oct 1	Mar 15-Jun 1 Aug 15-Sep 30	Apr 1-Jun 15 Jul 15-Sep 1	May 1-May 10 Jul 1-Aug 15	May 15-Jun 30	Jun 1-Jun 15	not recommended
Bean, Scarlet Runner	Feb 1 Oct 1-Dec 1	Feb 5 Aug 1	Mar 1- Aug 1	Mar 15-Aug	May 1-Aug 1	May 15-Aug 1	Jun 1-Aug 15
Bean, Shelling	Feb 10-May 1 Sep 1	Mar 1-May 15 Jul 1-Aug 1	Mar 15-May 25 Aug 1	Apr 10-Jun 30	May 1-Jun 15	May 25-Jun 15	**
Bean, Snap	Feb 10-May 1 Sep 1	Mar 1-May 15 Jul 1-Aug 1	Mar 15-May 25 Jul 1-Sep 1	Apr 10-Jun 30 Jul 1-Aug 15	May 1-Jun 30	May 25-Jul 1	Jun 1-Jun 15
Bean, Soy	Feb 10-May 1 Sep 1	Mar 1-May 15 Jul 1-Aug 1	Apr 1-May 25 Jul 1-Sep 1	May 1-Jun 30	May 15-Jun 15	Jun 1-Jun 15	Jun 10-Jun 15
Bean, Winged	Feb 20-Jun 1 Jul 1-Aug 1	Mar 15-May 15	Apr 1-May 25 Jul 1-Sep 1	May 1-Jun 30	May 15-Jun 15	May 25	not recommended
Beet	Jan 10-Mar 15 Sep 1-Nov 1	Feb 5-Apr 15 Sep 1	Feb 15-May 15 Sep 1-Dec 1	Mar 15-Jun 1 Aug 1-Sep 15	Apr 1-Jun 15 Jul 15-Aug 1	Apr 15-Aug 1	May 1-Jun 15
Broccoli	Jan 1-Jan 30 Aug 1-Oct 1	Jan 15-Mar 1 Sep 1	Feb 15-Mar 15 Aug 1-Sep 15	Mar 1-Apr 15 Aug 1-Sep 15	Mar 25-May 1 Aug 1-Sep 15	Apr 15-Jun 1	May 10-Jun 10
Brussels Sprouts	Jan 1-Jan 30 Aug 1-Oct 1	Jan 15-Mar 1 Sep 1	Feb 15-Mar 15 Aug 1-Sep 15	Mar 1-Apr 15 Aug 1-Sep 1	Mar 25-May 1 Aug 1-Sep 15	Apr 15-Jun 1	May 1-Jun 10
Burdock	Jan 10 Sep 1-Dec 1	Feb 5-Mar 1 Sep 1	Feb 15-Mar 15 Aug 1-Sep 15	Mar 15-Apr 15 Aug 1-Sep 15	Mar 25-May 1 Aug 1-Sep 15	Apr 15-Aug 15	May 1-Jun 10
Cabbage	Jan 10-Feb 10 Sep 1-Dec 1	Jan 15-Feb 25 Sep 1	Feb 5-Mar 1 Sep 1-Dec 1	Mar 15-Apr 1 Aug 1-Sep 15	Mar 10-Apr 10 Aug 1-Sep 15	Apr 15-Jun 15	May 10-Jun 1
Cabbage, Chinese	Jan 1-Mar 1 Sep 1-Dec 1	Feb 1-Feb 25 Sep 1-Nov 1	Sep 1-Oct 15	Aug 1-Oct 1	Jun 15-Aug 15	Jun 1-Jul 15	May 15-Jun 15
Cantaloupe	Feb 20-Apr 1	Mar 15-May 15	Apr 1-May 30	May 1-Jun 1	May 15-Jun 15	Jun 1-Jul 1	**
Cardoon	Feb 10-May 1	Mar 1-Apr 1	Mar 15-Apr 1	Apr 10	May 1	May 15	Jun 1
Carrot	Jan 10-Mar 1 Sep 1-Dec 1	Feb 5-Mar 1 Sep 1-Oct 1	Feb 15-Mar 20 Sep 1-Nov 1	Mar 15-Apr 20 Jul 1-Sep 1	Apr 5-Jul 1	Apr 5-Jun 1	May 10-Jun 1
Cauliflower	Jan 10-Feb 1 Sep 1-Oct 1	Feb 5-Feb 20 Sep 1	Feb 15-Mar 10 Aug 1-Sep 15	Mar 1-Mar 20 Aug 1-Sep 15	Apr 1-May 10 Aug 1-Sep 15	Apr 15-Jun 15	May 20-Jun 15
Celeriac	Feb 10 Sep 1-Dec 1	Mar 1-Apr 1 Sep 1	Mar 20 Jul 15-Sep 1	Apr 10 Jul 1-Aug 15	May 1 Jun 1-Jul 15	May 15	Jun 1
Celery	Jan 10-Feb 10	Feb 5-Mar 1 Sep 1	Mar 1-Apr 1 Jul 15-Sep 1	Mar 15-Apr 20 Jul 1-Aug 15	Apr 10-May 1	Apr 10-Jun 1	May 20-Jun 15
Celtuce	Jan 10 Oct 1-Dec 1	Jan 15-Mar 1 Sep 1	Mar 1-Apr 1 Sep 1-Oct 1	Mar 15-Apr 15 Aug 1-Sep 15	Mar 25-Apr 30 Aug 1-Sep 15	Apr 15-May 1	Apr 15-May 15
Chard, Swiss	Jan 10-Apr 1 Jun 1-Nov 1	Feb 5-May 1	Mar 1-May 15 Jun 1-Oct 1	Mar 15-Jun 15 Jun 1-Sep 15	Apr 1-Jun 15 Aug 1-Sep 15	Apr 15-Jun 15	May 20-Jun 15
Chayote	Feb 10-Mar 1	Mar 5-Apr 15	Apr 1	Apr 15-May 1	May 1	not recommended	not recommended
Chicory, Leaf	Jan 10 Oct 1-Dec 1	Feb 5-Mar 1 Sep 1-Oct 1	Mar 1-Mar 15 Sep 1	Mar 15-Apr 1 Aug 1	Apr 5 Aug 1-Sep 15	Apr 20	May 15
Collards	Jan 1-Feb 1 Sep 1-Dec 1	Feb 5-Apr 1 Sep 1	Feb 15-Apr 1 Aug 1-Sep 1	Mar 1-May 1 Aug 1-Sep 1	Mar 15-Apr 15 Aug 1-Sep 15	Apr 1-Apr 15	May 1 Jul 1
Corn, Sweet	Feb 10-Apr 1	Mar 1-Apr 15	Mar 15-May 1	Apr 10-Jun 1	May 1-Jul 10	May 15-Jun 1	**
Cress, Pepper	Indoors all year	Indoors all year	Indoors all year	Indoors all year	Indoors all year	Indoors all year	Indoors all year
Cress, Upland	Jan 10-Feb 15	Jan 15-Mar 1 Sep 1	Feb 15-Mar 15 Oct 1-Dec 1	Mar 1-Apr 15 Sep 1	Mar 20-May 10 Aug 15-Oct 1	Apr 20-Jun 1	May 15-Jun 15
Cress, Water	Feb 10-Mar 1 Oct 1-Dec 1	Mar 15 Sep 1	Mar 15 Sep 15-Nov 15	Apr 10 Sep 1	May 1 Aug 1-Sep 1	May 15	May 30 Aug 1-Sep 1
Cucumber	Feb 20-Apr 1 Sep 1	Feb 15-Apr 15	Apr 1-May 1 Jun 1-Aug 15	May 1-Jun 1	May 15-Jul 1	Jun 1-Jun 15	**
Dandelion	Jan 10 Oct 1-Dec 1	Jan 15-Mar 1 Sep 1-Oct 1	Feb 15-Mar 15 Sep 1-Oct 1	Mar 1-Mar 15 Sep 1	Mar 15-Apr 1 Aug 1-Sep 15	Mar 15-Apr 1	Apr 1 Aug 1
Eggplant	Feb 20-Mar 15	Mar 15-Apr 15	Mar 15-May 1 Jun 1-Aug 1	May 1-Jun 1	May 15-Jun 10	Jun 1-Jun 15	**
Endive	Jan 10-Mar 1 Oct 1-Dec 1	Feb 5-Mar 1	Mar 1-Apr 1 Sep 1-Oct 1	Mar 15-Apr 15 Aug 1	Apr 1-May 1 Aug 1-Sep 15	Apr 15-May 15	May 1-Jun 1

**Difficult to grow in this zone.

366

How to Plant

Vegetable	Method of Growing	Cold Hardy or Tender	Depth to Plant Seed	Days to Germination	Weeks to Transplant	Spacing (in inches) Plants	Rows	Days to Harvest	Plants per Person	Comments
Amaranth	seeds	tender	1/4 inch	10-15 at 70F		16-20	20-24	60-70	15	Tolerates hot summers.
*Artichoke, Globe	seeds or roots	tender	1/2 inch	12 to 15 at 70F	8-10	36	36-48	180	5	Perennial in mild-winter areas.
*Asparagus	seeds or roots	hardy	1/2 inch	14-21 at 75F	10	12-18	36	2 years	10	
Asparagus Pea	seeds	tender	1/2 inch	7-14		4-6	12-24	70	30	Provide short trellis for support.
Bean, Broad	seeds	hardy	2 inches	7-14 at 55F		6-10	9-24	70	30	Plants must mature during cool weather.
Bean, Cowpea	seeds	tender	1-1/2 inches	6-10 at 70F		6-12	18-48	75	15	Young pods are edible as snaps.
Bean, Garbanzo	seeds	tender	1-1/2 inches	7-14 at 70F		12	24-30	105	15	Seeds susceptible to rot during cool, rainy conditions.
Bean, Lima	seeds	very tender	2 inches	7-10 at 70F		3-6	18-36	70-90	30	Seeds susceptible to rot.
Bean, Scarlet Runner	seeds	hardy	1-1/2 inches	5-10 at 70F		6	5 feet	70	6	Provide poles for support.
Bean, Shelling	seeds	tender	1-1/2 inches	6-10 at 70F		6	24-36	80	15	Bush and pole varieties available.
Bean, Snap	seeds	tender	1 inch	6-10 at 70F		2-6	18-36	50-60	30	Pick beans frequently.
Bean, Soy	seeds	tender	1 inch	10-14 at 70F		4-6	24-36	70	30	Pods shell easily if boiled.
Bean, Winged	seeds or plants	very tender	1-1/2 inches	7-14 at 70F	3	6-12	36	70-100	15	Provide poles for support.
Beet	seeds	hardy	1/4 inch	6-10 at 70F		3-4	12-18	50-60	45	Provide continuous moisture.
*Broccoli	seeds or plants	hardy	1/4 inch	5-10 at 70F	6	18	24-36	50-70	10	Heavy feeder, especially nitrogen.
Brussels Sprouts	seeds or plants	hardy	1/4 inch	8-10 at 70F	6	18-24	24-36	80-90	10	Usually best as a fall crop.
Burdock	seeds	hardy	1/4 inch	7-14 at 70F		24	36	100	30	Also known as gobo.
*Cabbage	seeds or plants	hardy	1/4 inch	5-10 at 70F	6	12-24	24-36	60-90	10	Protect transplants against cutworms.
*Cabbage, Chinese	seeds or plants	hardy	1/4 inch	3-5 at 70F	6-8	18-24	24-36	45	10	Pak choy, a nonheading cabbage, tolerates crowding.
Cantaloupe	seeds or plants	tender	1/2 inch	5-10 at 75F		12	4-6 feet	75-100	4	Protect from cucumber beetles.
Cardoon	seeds or plants	tender	1/4 inch	10-14 at 75F	6	24-36	36	120	3-6	Blanch stems before harvesting.
Carrot	seeds	hardy	1/8 inch	7-10 at 60-70F		1-1/2 to 2	12-18	55-80	90	Plant in short, wide rows.
*Cauliflower	seeds or plants	hardy	1/4 inch	4-10 at 70F	6-8	24	18-36	65-80	10	Bolts to seed with warm weather.
*Celeriac	seeds or plants	hardy	1/8 inch	10-20 at 65F	10	12	24	100	15	Grow for its edible roots.
*Celery	seeds or plants	hardy	1/8 inch	10-14 at 65F	10-12	12	24-36	95-150	15	Blanching stems improves flavor.
Celtuce	seeds	hardy	1/8 inch	7-14 at 55F		6-12	12-24	70	30	Harvest young leaves.
Chard, Swiss	seeds	hardy	1/2 inch	4-10 at 70F		12	18-36	45-55	15	Pay close attention to thinning.
Chayote	seeds	tender	bury fruit	7-10 at 75F		36	36	200	1	Plant whole fruit with top end exposed slightly.
Chicory, Leaf	seeds	hardy	1/4 inch	7-14 at 70F		6-12	18-24	90	15	Best grown as a fall crop.
Collards	seeds or plants	hardy	1/4 inch	4-10 at 70F	5-6	12-24	24-36	60-70	10	Slight frost improves flavor.
Corn, Sweet	seeds	tender	1 inch	6-10 at 70F		8-12	36	55-95	15	Plant rows in blocks for best pollination.
Cress, Pepper	seeds	hardy	surface-sow	1-2 at 70F		1/8	1/8	10	1 packet	Use as sprouting seeds.
Cress, Upland	seeds	hardy	1/4 inch	3-7 at 70F		6	12	60	30	Plants will survive cold winters.
Cress, Water	seeds or plants	hardy	1/4 inch	7-10 at 55F	6	4-6	12	70	30	Grows best in clear, running water.
Cucumber	seeds or plants	very tender	1 inch	6-10 at 70F	4-6	8-12	36-48	50-79	5	Protect from cucumber beetles.
Dandelion	seeds	hardy	1/4 inch	7-14 at 55F		6-9	12	95	30	Blanch leaves for best flavor.
*Eggplant	plants	very tender	1/4 inch	7-14 at 80F	6-8	18-24	36	70-90	6	Protect from flea beetles.
Endive	seeds	hardy	1/4 inch	7-14 at 70F		9-12	18	70-80	15	Bunch leaves over heart to sweeten.

*Transplants are preferred instead of seed.
Row spacings are based on single, straight rows.

Plants per Person indicates approximate amount of plants for fresh use.
Adjust according to personal preference or if you plan to store produce.

Vegetable	Zone 1	Zone 2	Zone 3	Zone 4	Zone 5	Zone 6	Zone 7
Garlic	Oct 1-Dec 1	not recommended	Feb 1-Mar 1 Aug 15-Oct 1	Feb 20-Mar 20 Sep 1	Mar 10-Apr 15	Apr 1-May 15	May 1-Jun 1
Ginseng	not recommended	not recommended	Feb 15-Apr 1	Mar 1-Apr 1	Mar 15-May 1	Apr 1-May 1	Apr 15-Jun 1
Gourd	Feb 20-Apr 1 Aug 1-Sep 1	Mar 15-Apr 1	Apr 1-May 1	May 1-May 15	May 15	Jun 1	**
Huckleberry, Garden	Feb 10-Apr 1 Sep 1	Mar 1-Apr 1	Apr 1-May 1	Apr 10-May 15	May 1	May 15	Jun 5
Husk Tomato	Feb 10-Apr 1 Sep 1	Mar 1-Apr 1	Apr 1-May 1	Apr 10-May 15	May 1	May 15	Jun 5
Jerusalem Artichoke	Feb 15 Jun 1-Dec 1	Mar 15-Apr 15	Apr 1-May 1	Apr 15-May 30	May 15	May 20	Jun 5
Jicama	Feb 20	Mar 15	Apr 1	**	not recommended	not recommended	not recommended
Kale	Jan 1-Feb 1 Sep 1-Dec 1	Jan 15-Feb 20 Sep 1-Oct 1	Feb 15-Mar 10 Aug 15-Oct 15	Mar 1-Apr 1 Aug 1-Sep 1	Mar 20-Apr 20 Aug 1-Sep 15	Apr 10-May 10	May 1-Jun 1
Kohlrabi	Jan 1-Feb 1 Sep 1-Dec 1	Jan 15-Feb 20 Sep 1-Oct 1	Feb 15-Mar 10 Sep 1-Oct 15	Mar 1-Apr 10 Aug 1-Sep 1	Mar 20-May 10 Aug 1-Sep 15	Apr 10-Jun 30	May 1-Jun 1
Leek	Jan 1-Feb 1 Oct 1-Dec 1	Jan 15-Feb 15 Sep 1	Feb 1-Mar 1 Sep 1-Nov 1	Feb 20-Apr 1	Mar 15-May 1	Apr 15-May 20	May 1-May 15
Lettuce	Jan 10-Feb 1 Sep 1-Dec 1	Feb 5-Feb 15 Sep 1	Feb 15-Mar 10 Sep 1-Nov 1	Mar 15-Apr 1 Aug 1-Oct 1	Apr 1-May 1 Aug 1-Sep 15	Apr 20-Jun 30	May 10-Jun 30
Mustard	Jan 1-Mar 1 Sep 1-Nov 1	Jan 20-Mar 1 Sep 1-Oct 1	Feb 15-Apr 1 Sep 1-Dec 1	Mar 1-Apr 20 Aug 15-Nov 1	Mar 20-May 10 Aug 1-Sep 15	Apr 15-Jun 30	May 10-Jun 30
Okra	Feb 20-Apr 15 Aug 1-Sep 1	Mar 15-Jun 1	Apr 1-Jun 15 Jun 1-Sep 10	May 1-Jun 15 Jun 1-Aug 10	May 15-Jun 1 Jun 1-Jul 15	Jun 1	**
Onion	Jan 1-Jan 15 Oct 1-Dec 1	Jan 1-Feb 15 Sep 1	Feb 5-Mar 10 Oct 1-Dec 31	Mar 1-Apr 1 Sep 1-Oct 1	Mar 15-Apr 15	Apr 10-May 15	May 1-Jun 10
Parsley	Jan 1-Jan 30 Sep 1-Dec 1	Feb 5-Mar 1 Sep 1	Feb 15-Mar 15 Sep 1-Jan 1	Mar 1-Apr 10 Aug 15-Nov 1	Mar 20-May 1 Aug 1-Sep 15	Apr 15-May 15	May 10-Jun 10
Parsnip	Jan 10 Sep 1-Dec 1	Feb 5-Mar 1 Aug 1-Sep 1	Feb 20-Mar 15 Aug 1-Sep 1	Mar 15-Apr 10 Jul 1-Aug 1	Apr 1-May 1 Aug 1-Sep 15	Apr 20-May 20	May 10-Jun 10
Pea	Jan 1-Feb 15 Sep 1-Dec 1	Jan 15-Mar 1 Sep 1	Feb 1-Mar 15 Sep 1-Nov 1	Feb 20-Mar 20 Aug 15-Oct 1	Mar 10-May 1 Aug 1-Sep 15	Apr 1-Jun 1	May 1-Jun 15
Peanut	Feb 10-Apr 1	Mar 15-Apr 15	Apr 1-May 1	Apr 10-May 15	May 1	May 15	not recommended
Pepper	Feb 20-Apr 15 Jun 1-Sep 1	Mar 15-May 1	Apr 1-Jun 1 Jun 1-Jul 1	May 1-Jun 1 Jun 1-Aug 1	May 15-Jun 10 Jun 1-Jul 1	Jun 1-Jun 15	Jun 15-Jun 30
Potato	Jan 10-Feb 15 Aug 1-Sep 1	Feb 5-Mar 1 Aug 1	Feb 15-Mar 15 Aug 10-Sep 15	Mar 1-Apr 1 Aug 1	Apr 1-May 10 May 15-Jun 15	May 1-Jun 15	May 1-Jun 1
Pumpkin	Feb 20-Apr 1 Aug 1	Mar 15-Apr 15	Apr 1-May 1	May 1-May 15	May 15-Jun 10	Jun 1	Jun 1-Jun 30
Radish	Jan 1-Apr 1 Aug 1-Sep 1	Jan 1-Apr 1 Sep 1-Nov 1	Jan 15-May 1 Sep 1-Oct 1	Mar 1-May 1 Sep 1-Oct 1	Mar 10-May 10 Aug 15-Sep 15	Apr 1-Jun 15	May 1-Jun 1
Rhubarb	not recommended	not recommended	Mar 1	Apr 1	Mar 25	May 1	Jun 1
Rutabaga	not recommended	Jan 15-Feb 1	Feb 1-Mar 1 Aug 1-Sep 1	Mar 1-Apr 1 Jul 15-Aug 15	May 1-Jun 1 Aug 1-Sep 15	May 1-May 20	May 10-Jun 1
Salsify	Jan 10-Feb 10 Sep 1-Nov 1	Feb 5-Mar 1	Mar 1-Apr 1 Jul 15-Aug 15	Mar 15-Apr 15 Jun 10-Jul 10	Apr 1-May 15 Jun 1-Jul 1	Apr 15-Jun 1	May 10-Jun 1
Scorzonera	Jan 10-Feb 1 Sep 1-Nov 1	Feb 5 Aug 1	Mar 1-Mar 15 Aug 1	Mar 15-Apr 1	Apr 1-Apr 15	Apr 15	May 10
Shallot	Jan 1-Feb 10 Oct 1-Dec 1	Jan 1-Mar 1	Feb 15-Mar 15 Aug 15-Oct 1	Feb 15-Apr 1	Mar 15-May 1	Apr 10-May 10	May 1-Jun 1
Spinach	Jan 1-Feb 15 Oct 1-Dec 1	Jan 1-Mar 1 Sep 1	Jan 20-Mar 15 Oct 1-Dec 1	Feb 15-Apr 1 Sep 1-Oct 15	Mar 15-Apr 20 Aug 1-Sep 15	Apr 1-Jun 15	Apr 20-Jun 15
Spinach, Malabar	Feb 20-Apr 1	Mar 15-Apr 15	Apr 1-Apr 15 Jun 1-Aug 15	Apr 20-May 1 Jun 1-Aug 1	May 1	Jun 1-Jul 1	Jun 10
Spinach, New Zealand	Feb 10-Apr 15	Mar 10-May 15	Apr 1-May 15 Jun 1-Aug 15	Apr 10-Jun 1	May 1-Jun 15 Jun 1-Jul 15	May 15-Jun 15	Jun 1-Jun 15
Squash, Summer	Feb 20-Apr 15 Jun 1-Sep 1	Mar 10-May 15	Apr 1-May 15 Jun 1-Aug 10	Apr 10-Jun 1 Jun 1-Aug 1	May 1-Jun 15 Jun 1-Jul 15	May 15-Jun 15	Jun 1-Jun 20
Squash, Winter	Feb 20-Apr 15 Aug 1	Mar 10-May 15	Apr 1-May 1 Jun 20-Aug 20	Apr 10-Jun 1 Jun 10-Jul 10	May 1-Jun 15 Jun 1-Jul 1	May 15-Jun 15	Jun 1-Jun 20
Strawberry, Alpine	Feb 1 Sep 1-Dec 1	Mar 1-Apr 1 Sep 1	Mar 15-Apr 15 Sep 1	Apr 10	May 1	May 15	May 15
Sunflower	Feb 10-Mar 1 Aug 1	Mar 1-Apr 1	Mar 15-Apr 15	Apr 10-May 15	May 1-Jun 15	May 15-Jun 20	Jun 1
Sweet Potato	Feb 20-Mar 1	Nov 15-Apr 1	Mar 15-Apr 15	Apr 10-May 15	May 15-Jun 15	**	**
Tomato	Feb 15-Apr 10 Aug 1-Sep 1	Mar 5-May 1	Mar 20-May 20 Jun 1-Jul 15	Apr 15-Jun 1	May 5-Jul 15 Jun 1-Jul 1	May 20-Jun 15	Jun 5-Jun 30
Turnip	Jan 1-Feb 15 Oct 1-Nov 1	Jan 15-Mar 1 Sep 1	Feb 1-Mar 15 Sep 1-Oct 15	Mar 1-May 1 Aug 1-Sep 15	Mar 10-May 1 Aug 1-Sep 15	Apr 1-Jun 15	May 1-Jun 15
Watermelon	Feb 20-Apr 1	Mar 15-Apr 15	Apr 1-May 1	May 1-Jun 1	May 15-Jun 15	Jun 1-Jul 1	**
Yam, Chinese	Feb 20-Apr 1	Mar 15-Apr 1	Apr 1-Apr 15	May 1-May 15	May 15-Jun 15	Jun 1-Jun 20	**

**Difficult to grow in this zone. See Climate text.

Vegetable	Method of Growing	Cold Hardy or Tender	Depth to Plant Seed	Days to Germination	Weeks to Transplant	Spacing (in inches) Plants	Rows	Days to Harvest	Plants per Person	Comments
Garlic	bulbs (cloves)	hardy	2 inches	10 at 55-70F		4	12	90	6 cloves	Each clove segment produces a new plant.
Ginseng	seeds or roots	hardy	surface-sow	400-680 at 70F	10	6	12	5 years	10	Roots develop slowly.
Gourd	seeds or plants	very tender	1 inch	6-14 at 70F	4	24-36	36	120	6	Provide vines with strong supports.
*Huckleberry, Garden	plants	tender	1/4 inch	7-14 at 70F	6-8	24-36	24-36	70-80	6	Boil berries briefly to remove bitterness.
*Husk Tomato	plants	tender	1/4 inch	7-14 at 70F	8	36	36	70	5	Also known as ground cherry and cape gooseberry.
Jerusalem Artichoke	roots	hardy	2-4 inches	14 days at 70F		15-24	36	110	15	Productive and hardy perennial.
Jicama	seeds or plants	very tender	1 inch	7-14 at 70F	8-10	24	6 feet	240	15	Tubers taste like water chestnuts.
Kale	seeds or plants	hardy	1/4 inch	3-10 at 70F	4	18	24-36	50-65	10	Hardy enough for winter greens.
Kohlrabi	seeds or plants	hardy	1/2 inch	3-10 at 70F	4-6	4-6	18	50-70	30	Turniplike bulbs form above the soil.
Leek	seeds or plants	hardy	1/2 inch	7-14 at 70F	4-6	2-4	12-24	140	45	Leave in garden until ground freezes.
Lettuce	seeds or plants	hardy	1/4 inch	4-10 at 55-65F	4	12	18	60-70	15	Space leaf types 6-8 inches apart.
Mustard	seeds or plants	hardy	1/2 inch	3-5 at 70F	4	12	18-24	35-60	20	Grow as a fall crop.
Okra	seeds	very tender	1/2 inch	7-14 at 70F		12-24	36	50-55	15	Harvest pods regularly.
*Onion	seeds, plants, sets	hardy	1/4 inch	7-12 at 70F	6	4	6-12	75	45	Space green bunching types 2 inches apart.
*Parsley	seeds or plants	hardy	1/8 inch	7-28 at 70F	6-8	6-12	12	50	2	Outdoor sowings are slow to germinate.
Parsnip	seeds	hardy	1/4 inch	15-20 at 70F		4-6	12-18	120	60	Leave in garden until ground freezes.
Pea	seeds	hardy	1-2 inches	6-15 at 60F		2-4	24-36	50-80	60	Bush types do not need staking.
Peanut	seeds	tender	1-1/2 inches	18-21 at 70F		18	36	110	15	Shell seeds before sowing.
*Pepper	plants	very tender	1/4 inch	10-15 at 70F	8	18-24	24	70-100	5	Harvest fruit regularly.
*Potato	tubers or seeds	hardy	1/4 inch	5-10 at 70F	8	12	30	90-105	15	Potato seed has recently become available.
Pumpkin	seeds or plants	very tender	1 inch	6-10 at 70F	4	4-6 feet	6-8 feet	85-120	1	Grow bush types to save space.
Radish	seeds	hardy	1/2 inch	4-6 at 60F		1	12	25-35	80	Provide with constant moisture.
Rhubarb	roots (crowns)	hardy	4 inches			36	36	2 years	2	Easy to grow from seed.
Rutabaga	seeds	hardy	1/2 inch	3-10 at 70F		6-8	18-24	80-90	30	Turnips are easier to grow.
Salsify	seeds	hardy	1/2 inch	7-14 at 60F		4-6	12-18	110	60	Leave in garden until ground freezes.
Scorzonera	seeds	hardy	1/4 inch	7-14 at 70F		3-6	6-12	90-100	30	Provide with regular moisture.
Shallot	bulbs	hardy	surface-sow	7-10 at 55F		8	12	100	25	Bulbs form in clusters.
Spinach	seeds	hardy	1/2 inch	7-12 at 50-60F		4-6	12-18	40-50	30	Grow spinach substitutes during warm weather months.
Spinach, Malabar	seeds or plants	tender	1/4 inch	7-10 at 70F	6-8	6-8	36	70	15	Grow on trellis to save space.
Spinach, New Zealand	seeds	tender	1/2 inch	7-14 at 55F		12	24-36	70	15	Warm-weather substitute for spinach.
Squash, Summer	seeds or plants	very tender	1 inch	6-12 at 70F	4	36	36	50-70	3	Protect from cucumber beetles.
Squash, Winter	seeds or plants	very tender	1 inch	6-12 at 70F	4	36-56	6-8 feet	85-120	3	Plant bush types to save space.
*Strawberry, Alpine	plants	hardy	surface-sow	14-21 at 70F	8-10	12	18-24	90	15	Seeds need light to germinate.
Sunflower	seeds	hardy	1 inch	7-12 at 70F		12	36	80-90	7	Roots emit a toxin that can affect nearby plants.
Sweet Potato	plants	very tender	3-4 inches	10 days at 70F	6	12	4 feet	120	15	One root produces many sprouts for planting.
*Tomato	plants	tender	1/4 inch	6-14 at 70F	6-8	24-36	36-48	55-90	3-5	Use wire cages for supports.
Turnip	seeds	hardy	1/2 inch	7-10 at 70F		3-4	12-18	40-60	30	Tops make delicious greens.
Watermelon	seeds or plants	very tender	1 inch	5-7 at 75F	4	5-6 feet	5-6 feet	75-100	3	Requires long, hot summer.
*Yam, Chinese	seeds or tubers	very tender	1/2 inch	10 at 70F	4-6	12	36	120	15	Grow on trellis for support.

*Transplants are preferred instead of seed.
Row spacings are based on single, straight rows.

Plants per Person indicates approximate amount of plants for fresh use.
Adjust according to personal preference or if you plan to store produce.

TRANSPLANTING

Plants grown indoors and transplanted to the garden need to be handled with care. Treat them like eggs. Transplant shock can cause plants to grow slowly, and can sometimes result in death.

Hardening-off. Before a transplant is taken from a warm, comfortable indoor environment to the cool or sunny outdoors, it should be *hardened-off,* gradually acclimated to its new home. Even cold-hardy plants such as cabbage and broccoli should be given a gradual transition from an indoor environment to the outdoors. Hardening-off is most important with tender plants such as tomatoes, eggplant and peppers. A simple way to harden-off plants is to expose them to increasing amounts of cold or sunlight, depending on the weather situation. For example, place plants in the sun for an hour the first day, and gradually increase the exposure over a 10-day period until plants accept a full day of sun.

Placing transplants in a *cold frame* is a good way to get them adjusted to the outdoors. A cold frame is usually a wooden compartment that has a covering of glass or plastic. See photograph at right. It is often placed partially in the ground for insulation. The frame is left open during the day and closed at night. Normally, transplants are placed in a cold frame for about 10 days to ready them for transplanting.

Wood or aluminum cold frames can be purchased ready-made. The best of these are fitted with an automatic vent opener that is activated by the sun. For information on solar-powered vent openers write: Bramen Co., Inc., Box 70, Salem, MA 01970; or Dalen Products Inc., 201 Sherlake Drive, Knoxville, TN 37922.

If you don't have a cold frame, improvise with a wooden crate covered with a sheet of glass. Or place plants outdoors during the day and cover with plastic during the night. Anchor the plastic around the sides with bricks or stones, and keep the plastic from touching the plants.

Transplants should be planted when conditions are cool, such as on cloudy days or in late afternoon. After planting, do not let the soil dry out. You will probably have to water every day, maybe twice a day in warm weather. Place water directly in the root area. Protect seedlings with some sort of shade the first few days after planting if sunlight is intense.

Shop around for high-quality transplants. Choose plants that are sturdy, compact and healthy green.

Do not plant seedlings directly in the garden from a greenhouse or the warm, sheltered indoors. Placing them in a cold frame for several days helps seedlings acclimate before being planted in the garden.

Even after plants are *hardened-off,* some frost protection may be needed. A plastic milk jug with the bottom removed is perfect for individual plants.

TRANSPLANTING TIPS

● Buy sturdy, compact plants that have healthy green color. Avoid tall, lanky specimens that have yellow leaves and appear to be stretched. Their spindly growth may be caused by crowded roots. Or they may not have received enough light and tried in vain to grow toward the sun or light source.

● Ask nursery personnel if the plants have been *hardened-off*—gradually acclimated from greenhouse to the outdoors. If they have come straight from a greenhouse without being exposed to the outdoors for 10 days, they may sustain severe shock when transplanted to your garden.

● Examine the underside of leaves for signs of pests. If you find a cucumber beetle already on a cucumber transplant, chances are the plant will die from the wilt disease the beetles transmit. Eggplant with flea beetles and tomatoes with whiteflies should also be avoided.

● Do not buy transplants in flower or with fruit unless they are growing in a large container. The root system is simply inadequate to support the plant's advanced top growth. A tomato plant flowering in a 2-1/2-inch pot will probably die when transplanted.

● Water transplants in containers just before you plant them. It helps ease the rootball out of the container and lessens shock. If the transplant is in a plastic pot, take a knife and gently run it around the rim between the soil and the pot. The rootball can be pulled free without breaking roots and disturbing soil particles. The more original potting soil you can plant, the better transplants will grow.

● Cucumber and tomato plants form roots along their stems, so plant them deep to encourage extra roots to form. Plants that form edible parts at the soil surface such as leeks, celery and onions should be planted shallowly.

● Plants subject to cutworm damage should be protected with cutworm collars. If you have slug problems, take precautions to control them. It is not uncommon to set out a row of transplants in the afternoon and find them eaten by morning.

PLANTING

The most common method of planting vegetables is in a single row. For the sake of simplicity, it is the system described on seed packets to give spacing distances.

Block planting and *wide-row* planting are other common planting methods. These are new names to describe planting systems that have long been practiced in China and Europe. No single system of planting is ideal for all vegetables. Use the system that suits you, the available space and the growth requirements of the particular vegetable.

THREE EFFICIENT PLANTING METHODS

Single row. This is best for vegetables that require ample space, such as tomatoes, peppers, eggplant, squash, cucumbers and cabbage. Sometimes the single row is mounded into "hills" instead of continuous raised rows. The extra soil depth created by the hills benefits large plants with vigorous root systems, such as squash, melons, cucumbers and potatoes.

Wide row. Sometimes called *matted-row* planting and *French intensive*. Rows are generally 2 to 3 feet wide and raised 4 to 6 inches off the ground. It is efficient with vegetables that grow in a small space and tolerate crowding or close spacing. Looseleaf lettuce, parsley, dwarf peas, radishes, chives, thyme and mint can be planted this way.

Block planting. Sometimes called *square-foot* gardening. This system is efficient with vegetables that grow in a compact area but do not tolerate crowding—head lettuce, beets, carrots, turnips and onions. Block planting differs from a matted row in that plants are spaced uniformly, usually in a diamond pattern. The wide rows are usually 2 to 3 feet wide and mounded 4 to 6 inches high.

THINNING PLANTING BEDS

Some vegetables tolerate crowded conditions but require thinning to achieve adequate spacing of individual vegetables. Unfortunately, it is psychologically unpleasant to destroy healthy, useful seedlings. Keep in mind that it pays to be ruthless because crowded plants produce poor results.

Seed tapes and pelleted seeds also save thinning. Or mix fine seeds with sand or compost and broadcast in a wide row.

Single row is the traditional way to lay out a vegetable garden. Large vegetables such as tomatoes and potatoes are best grown this way. Other vegetables can often be grown more efficiently in a wide row or block planting.

Wide-row planting is best for vegetables that will tolerate some crowding. Shown here are two rows of dwarf peas at left and a row of radishes at right.

Block-row planting is similar to wide row, but only certain kinds of vegetables can be grown this way. *Heading* vegetables such as lettuce and cabbage are especially adapted to this method.

Many gardeners hate to thin seedlings, but consider it is a necessary evil. When plants compete for water, nutrients and space, they *all* suffer.

Succession planting, planting crops to mature at different times, extends the harvest period. Here, radish seeds are sown to replace a harvested crop.

This interplanting of low-growing parsley and upright-growing Swiss chard uses garden space efficiently.

When thinning, take care not to disturb adjacent seedlings. Thin when the soil is moist, such as after a rain or watering, so roots pull up with least resistance. Or take a pair of sharp-pointed scissors and snip off the seedlings at the soil line.

Thinning may be necessary in several stages of plant growth. With carrots and beets, some gardeners like to make a superficial thinning as soon as the seedlings are up, then do a more thorough job after the plants are well established.

DOUBLE CROPPING AND SUCCESSION PLANTING

To get full value from a vegetable plot, practice *double cropping*. This means clearing a crop that has been harvested or has exhausted itself, and replanting with the same crop or a different crop.

For example, snap beans produce a flush of pods over 2 to 3 weeks, then deteriorate rapidly. By pulling out vines as soon as production dwindles, you can replant and obtain a second crop the same season. In most areas of the United States, you can obtain a third crop before fall frosts end the growing season. Similarly, two or three crops of lettuce can be harvested from the same garden space by double cropping.

Some vegetables cannot be replanted immediately because of the change in season. For example, English peas are grown in spring, and cannot be replanted because plants will not tolerate summer heat. Remove spent vines and plant a fast-growing summer vegetable in its place.

Succession planting is similar to double cropping. You sow vegetables at intervals during the season to provide a continuous harvest. One planting will come into harvest as another finishes bearing. Lettuce, snap beans, sweet corn and radishes should be planted at two-week intervals to maintain a long harvesting period.

An additional way to extend harvests is to plant vegetables with *different maturity dates*. Certain vegetables are classified as "early," "midseason" or "late." This is particularly true of tomatoes and sweet corn. By checking the "days to maturity" in this book, on a seed packet or catalog description, you can plan an extended harvest. For example, by planting 'Early Girl' hybrid (54 days), 'Better Boy VF' hybrid (72 days) and 'Supersteak VFN' hybrid (80 days), you can harvest tomatoes over several

months. With sweet corn, by planting 'Earliglo EH' hybrid (65 days), 'Honey & Cream' hybrid (78 days) and 'Silver Queen' hybrid (92 days), you will enjoy sweet corn through the summer.

COMPANION PLANTING AND INTERCROPPING

Most vegetables seem to get along fine together. If rows are spaced properly, you should never have to worry about the carrots getting along with the cucumbers or the beans preferring to be near broccoli.

Many herbs possess exotic flavors and fragrances for repellent reasons—usually to repel certain insects and foraging animals. These repellent properties can sometimes be used to good advantage in the garden. Chives, parsley and garlic are often recommended for planting near vegetable crops for this reason. However, many horticulturists point out that there is too much speculation and not enough scientific evidence to support claims for repellent properties. Many herbs such as garlic and chives must be bruised before the repellent odor is released. They repel best when juice is extracted from them for spraying directly onto plants.

In some gardeners' opinions, the claims made for companion planting of herbs are exaggerated. Indeed, gardeners have seen many vegetables ravaged by insects in spite of being close to "repellent" herbs.

Intercropping saves space in the vegetable garden. This is done by planting two vegetables close together, one to be harvested quickly before the other vegetable has matured and filled out. For example, lettuce and spinach can be grown between tomato plants. They can be harvested long before the tomato plants have grown to full-bearing size and begin to block out light. Similarly, tall, slender vegetables such as onions can be interplanted with compact vegetables such as beans and lettuce without being crowded.

Planting a Garden

1. Lay out site according to plan, using stakes and string to mark the boundaries. Choose a site in a sunny, well-drained location.

2. Remove sod or weeds if they are present. Shake valuable topsoil from roots. After removing sod, take soil from several areas of the plot for a soil test.

3. Most garden soil requires addition of organic matter to improve the soil structure. Spread 3 to 6 inches of amendment such as compost over the area to be planted.

4. Using a spade or power tiller, thoroughly mix topsoil and amendment. Dig down to the depth of the spade—approximately 12 inches.

5. Rake the soil surface to make it level. Remove stones and weed or grass roots. Keep a sharp eye out for larvae of harmful insects.

6. Scatter fertilizer over the soil. Lime or sulfur may also be needed to adjust soil pH. Rake into soil at root zone area. Wait 10 days before planting.

7. Using a trowel or similar tool, prepare furrow for seeds. Use string as a guide to keep planting rows and beds straight.

8. Sow large seeds in straight, evenly spaced rows. Cover and firm with soil. Many small-seed vegetables can be scattered over the soil surface.

9. Set out transplants according to their cold hardiness. Tomatoes, shown above, should be planted only after danger of frost has passed.

WATER, WEEDS AND MULCH

Water is the key to growth of all plants. In addition to supplying life-giving moisture, water dissolves nutrients so they can be absorbed by plant roots. Plants grow rapidly when moisture is plentiful, but become subject to both moisture and nutrient stress when water is scarce. Water is also the key to seed germination. It softens the seed coat and swells the seed embryo to stimulate growth. Because vegetables are composed mostly of moisture, their flavor is greatly affected by the water supply. Even the sugars responsible for sweetness move into the fruit from the leaves in soluble form.

The most common mistake when watering vegetables is failing to provide enough on a regular basis. Many gardeners wait until lack of moisture is noticed, then desperately try to water plants back to life. Vegetables need to be watered regularly to grow. Without continuous growth, many vegetables produce off-flavors or will not set fruit.

Too much moisture can have a negative effect on vegetables. Waterlogged soil prevents air from reaching the root zone. Except for aquatic vegetables such as watercress, plants will die or suffer from root rot when deprived of air. Melons can crack open and rot. Vining crops such as cucumbers are more likely to get mildew diseases. Slugs and snails, which thrive in a moist environment, can cause complete destruction. Nutrients, especially nitrogen, can be leached from the plant root zone.

Good soil drainage is essential. If your proposed site for a vegetable plot has poor drainage, you have two alternatives: Put in a drainage system to take the water away or build a raised bed. A raised bed brings the garden soil up above the surrounding soil level so water drains freely. You may want to build up the sides with railroad ties, lumber or stones.

Supplying vegetables with proper amounts of water is an art, particularly with respect to timing. Vegetables have critical periods when they should be watered for greatest yields. Some prefer watering in regular amounts at every stage of their growth cycle. Others need it more at certain critical stages such as flowering and fruiting.

All vegetables grow well with moderate, regular amounts of water throughout the season. But if you fine-tune your watering schedule to supply an abundance of water at the period of greatest need, you can expect better-than-normal yield and fruit size.

The period of "greatest need" varies with the different types of vegetables. For example, vegetables that produce fruit or set pods—beans, peas, corn, tomatoes, peppers and eggplant—need more water when they are flowering and setting fruit or pods. Leaf crops—cabbage, lettuce and spinach—need water on a steady, continuous basis to keep growing and produce largest weight gains. Root crops—turnips, potatoes, beets, carrots and parsnips—also need water on a steady, continuous basis to gain weight and size. If subjected to a dry spell, they simply stop growing.

Irrigation methods that supply water in steady, regular amounts, such as drip irrigation, are desirable. Lacking that, you should time waterings so that each vegetable benefits from it the most.

WHEN TO WATER
Seeds and transplants. When small seeds such as carrots and lettuce are planted directly into the garden, water every day if it doesn't rain. These seeds are planted close to the soil surface and are more susceptible to drying out than seeds of peas, beans and corn, which are

Left: Droplets of water serve as a visual reminder that vegetables need *continuous* moisture.
Above: Straw mulch around zucchini plant helps simplify garden care. It reduces weed growth and cools the soil during the warm summer months.

planted deeper. Moisture is also important immediately following germination, especially for root crops. When a good rain or watering follows germination, carrot roots grow straight down, helping to produce finely shaped carrots. If the root growth is slowed by lack of moisture, the carrot root can become distorted by harvest time.

When transplants are set into the garden, water immediately and keep soil moist until they are established. Transplanted seedlings often sustain root damage and need regular amounts of moisture for a couple of weeks to recover from transplant shock. If the temperature is warm when you set out your transplants, it is helpful to supply some kind of temporary shade until they become adapted.

Established plants. As soon as a plant begins to wilt, it needs water immediately or it will die. Lack of moisture shows itself in different ways, depending on the plant and its sensitivity to moisture stress. Beets stop growing and take on a fibrous quality. Radishes grow hollow and stringy. Melons will not set fruit. Sweet corn will not fill each ear to the tip. Leafy vegetables sometimes take on a bitter flavor. Snap beans grow distorted. Tomatoes suffer physical disorders such as blossom-end rot. Squash and cucumbers wilt.

Do not wait until plants show symptoms of water need. Check the garden soil regularly—every day if temperatures are warm—and supply plants with water in their root zone. An easy way to check moisture content of garden soil is to grab a handful of topsoil and squeeze it. If the particles cling together, the soil has adequate moisture. If the particles separate and feel dry, like sand, the soil needs moisture.

A frequent question asked about watering is, "What time of day is best?" Watering is best done in early morning. Watering at this time means less loss through evaporation and from wind.

MOISTURE-HOLDING CAPACITY OF SOIL

Different types of soil have varied capacities for holding moisture in the plant's root zone. Clay soils are prone to waterlogging, while sandy soils allow moisture to drain away too rapidly. The best kind of garden soil is a loam soil. Its composition is somewhere between sand and clay. A loam soil drains well, yet the spaces between soil particles retain enough water to supply plant roots.

WAYS TO WATER

The big problem with watering is getting it to your plants in sufficient quantities when Mother Nature proves uncooperative. If you live in an area that does not receive regular rainfall, irrigation will be necessary. The simplest source of water is from an outdoor faucet, whether it is attached to a city water supply or a well system.

Common methods of irrigation are furrow irrigation, hand-held garden hoses, lawn sprinklers set in the middle of the garden and drip irrigation systems that apply water to the root zone of plants.

Furrow irrigation is one of the most common methods of watering vegetables. Furrows or channels are created with a hoe or shovel and water is applied to the rows, which reaches the plant's root zone. Allow for dry pathways, or rows will be muddy after you water. This can be a mess when you walk between rows to harvest.

Any form of hand irrigation is generally the least-effective method. It seems as if you are applying more water than you actually are, and only the top few inches of soil are moistened. But if you have the time and the patience to wet the soil thoroughly to the root zone, it is still an acceptable way to water. Using an extension wand, which attaches to the end of the hose, makes hand watering easier and faster.

Lawn sprinklers are a big improvement over hand watering. They can be set in place to water as long as necessary to soak soil in the root zone. The biggest drawback with sprinklers is that they can waste water through evaporation on hot days.

DRIP IRRIGATION

When first raising vegetables, some gardeners irrigate with a lawn sprinkler in the garden, or apply water with a garden hose. These watering methods usually do the job, but they are more *corrective* than *preventative*. During warm periods, plants can come under stress before you use the hose or sprink-

Water Correctly

The illustration at right shows what happens when a plant is given frequent, shallow waterings. Roots grow where there is water—in the upper soil surface. During periods of warm, windy weather or if an irrigation is missed, the plant is unable to absorb the water it needs. The plant at far right is given deep, regular waterings. The roots penetrate deeply into the soil so they have a greater reservoir of water and nutrients to draw upon.

ler. Gardeners using *drip irrigation* sometimes say that they will never again water any other way. The difference in plant performance is incredible, especially because the system *prevents* plant stress due to lack of water.

Drip irrigation is a system of hoses that lie across the soil close to plant roots, either on top of the soil or buried out of sight. Depending on design, drip hoses ooze moisture through pores along the hose wall, or drip moisture from *emitters,* tiny holes spaced at regular intervals along a hose. Drip irrigation is especially effective when installed under black plastic. This not only protects the hoses from damage, it reduces evaporation.

Spaghetti emitters have long, flexible tubes coming from a main hose. At the end of each flexible tube is a type of valve that does a fine job of dripping moisture. They are probably best suited for watering individual plants such as fruit trees or plants in containers.

The biggest benefit of drip irrigation is that you can water the whole garden regularly by a single turn of the faucet. Plants receive regular moisture, and are not subjected to water stress. The basics of watering correctly still apply— putting sufficient amounts of water in the root zone.

Economically, drip irrigation systems also make sense. They save water due to less waste—as much as 30%. Because plants make continuous, rapid growth, they produce early and bountiful yields.

Usually, the bigger your vegetable garden, the more complex the drip system. For a small area, it is sufficient to place drip hose up and down the rows with one end connected to a water spigot. With 1/2-inch diameter hose and emitters spaced 2 feet apart, and with average water pressure, water should be able to travel about 250 feet on level ground from your water spigot. This can be doubled to 500 feet if two hoses are connected to the spigot by a Y valve.

To irrigate large gardens, you may have to consider a more sophisticated set-up. Such a system might involve lateral hoses connected to a larger line, called a *header* line, fitted with a water-pressure regulator. Some systems can incorporate a special fertilizer tank that injects soluble fertilizer into the water. Plants are fed automatically while they are being irrigated. Some drip-irrigation companies will help you design a system if you send them a plan of your garden with your order. Many have a specifica-

tion sheet at the front of their supply catalog.

Drip systems vary in cost and quality. To decide which system is best for you, look for drip-irrigation advertisements in garden magazines. Send for their descriptive material and study it. Many retail garden-center outlets also carry drip-irrigation supplies that you can examine in the store.

One of the least-expensive systems is *Irrigro.* It consists of a white plastic hose with tiny pores. The pores allow water droplets to ooze through the sides of the hose, watering the soil all along its length. A source for Irrigro hose is International Irrigation Systems, 1555 Third Avenue, Niagara Falls, NY 14304.

Polyflex hose has emitters spaced at 18-inch or 24-inch intervals. Water drips from the emitters and saturates the soil in a wide circle until the soil is moistened along the length of the hose. If you are interested in more information on polyflex hose, write Submatic Irrigation Systems, Box 246, Lubbock, TX 79408.

Beads of water ooze slowly from tiny pores in drip irrigation hose. Water is supplied slowly and directly to the root zone of plants so there is less waste through evaporation. Other kinds of drip systems are available, including those with *emitters* or tiny valves set at regular spaces along the hose.

Drip irrigation hose is being laid to supply small garden with water needs. In this case, hose is placed up and down a series of narrow, raised planting beds.

Simple Drip System Layout

This drip system layout for a small garden is simple and effective. Y-valve connection—shown in circle—joins two sections of drip hose, each 100 feet long, to cover approximately 500 square feet of garden space. A design of this type works well with raised planting rows, designated by the color tint.

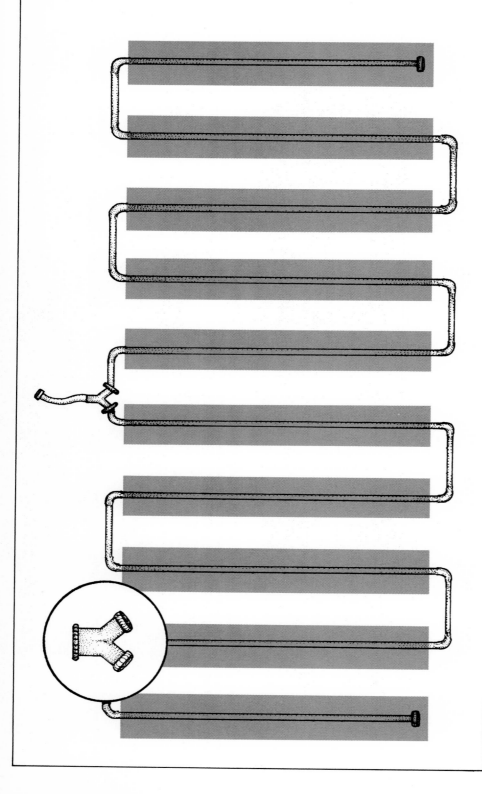

WEEDING

The most frequent cause of vegetable garden failure is weeds. In a short time, unchecked weed growth can turn a neatly planted vegetable plot into a jungle. Weeds not only compete with vegetables for moisture and nutrients, they also block sunlight. It is easy to become discouraged when weeds claim your garden. The best way to combat them is to keep them from getting ahead.

A few minutes spent pulling young weeds at the end of each day is far more sensible than trying to catch up on a week of neglect. This is especially true in midsummer when weeds grow fast. Some gardeners use every good rain as a signal. They go outside immediately after the rain has ceased. Weeds are easy to pull while the ground is wet and yielding.

When you do the initial soil preparation of your garden, remove all pieces of weed roots that you see. The smallest piece of plantain or dandelion root can grow into a full-size weed. Avoid walking on a newly cultivated garden. The surface compaction helps many weed seeds to germinate.

Use a mulch between rows to suffocate weeds. If installed correctly at the beginning of the gardening season, a mulch is actually the easiest way to control weeds. You may want to grow your vegetables through black plastic so weeds cannot grow up between plants. Some gardeners eliminate weeds in my garden rows by laying down thick layers of newspapers, then covering them with a thick layer of dry pine needles. If you can't use a mulch, cultivate with a hoe or hand weeder.

When using straw or hay as a mulch, make sure it is clean and not full of dried weeds or grass seeds. These seeds will be in weed heaven in your garden, and can create havoc the next year or later the same season when the mulch decomposes.

HAND WEEDING

Even when you use a mulch, some weeds are persistent enough to break through. Two tools are excellent for hand weeding—a hoe for weeding between the rows, and a hand fork for scratching out weeds close to the row.

Wear gloves when removing weeds by hand. Some cause skin irriations. Try to remove weeds with roots intact. If the stem breaks above ground and the root remains in the soil, the weed will grow back.

When using a hoe or hand cultivator, take care not to disturb adjacent vegetable roots. For example, dandelion roots are long and tapering and come up without too much disturbance to the adjacent soil area. But plantain roots spread, and yanking them out can unseat nearby plants. This is especially true for root vegetables, which are bothered by any kind of soil disturbance.

HERBICIDAL WEED KILLERS

Use of chemical herbicides used to be confined to ornamental gardens, but now a few herbicidal weed killers are available for vegetables. You should read the label carefully and make absolutely certain the product *is* approved for vegetables.

Herbicidal weed killers are effective in keeping pathways clear of weeds. The most convenient kinds are available in dry granular form in a shaker box.

Usually, weed killers work by preventing the germination of weed seeds, so are best used as "weed preventers." If you have a weedy patch that you want to plant, it still must be cleared by hand. There is generally a waiting period before you can plant. Follow label directions carefully.

MECHANICAL CULTIVATORS

By planting rows of vegetables wide enough to accommodate a power tiller, you can use these ground-breaking machines as weeders to keep pathways clear. Mechanical cultivators that you push are effective if the rows are spaced wide enough. Be careful that the cultivator or tiller doesn't snag the roots of vegetables as you pass down the row. Proper spacing of plants and operating power cultivators in low gear helps prevent this kind of accident. You still need to weed by hand near the vegetable plants, but this is usually a minor chore compared to clearing long rows of weeds from pathways.

POSITIVE ATTITUDE

It helps to take a positive attitude toward weeding. Just think of all the exercise you are getting, and all the nutrient-rich compost you can make with each wheelbarrow-load! Most of all, consider how much water and nutrients those weeds are stealing from your vegetable plants. You are helping increase your harvests by eliminating the competition.

Keeping up with weed-pulling chores is the best offense against weeds taking over your garden. This wheelbarrow-full is destined for the compost pile.

Mulching prevents many weeds from reaching the surface. Those that do grow through this pine-needle mulch are easy to pull.

The common garden hoe gets almost daily use during peak periods of weed growth. Hoe with caution around shallow-rooted vegetable plants.

MULCHING

Mulching is a term used in gardening to describe a covering over the soil. A mulch performs three important functions:

1. It conserves moisture by reducing evaporation.

2. It prevents weed growth by cutting off light to germinating weed seeds, and prevents most weed seedlings from breaking through the soil surface.

3. It modifies soil temperatures by cooling or warming the soil, depending on the mulch and the time of year it is applied.

A mulch can be *organic*, such as straw, compost, leaf mold, bark chips, shredded leaves or lawn clippings. Or it can be *inorganic*, such as plastic, gravel, rock and strips of discarded carpeting. Each has advantages and disadvantages.

Before applying any mulch, organic or inorganic, the soil should be moist so the mulch will help keep it that way.

Organic mulches are *biodegradable*, meaning they eventually break down and add their matter to the soil. This improves the soil texture, which in turn increases the moisture- and nutrient-holding capacity of the soil. Organic mulches also tend to have a cooling effect on the soil. This is beneficial in summer when temperatures are high, but it is a deterrent in spring when warm temperatures are desired to germinate seeds and promote seedling growth. For this reason, organic mulches are usually applied after seeds and transplants are up and growing.

If you have access to a continuous supply, decomposed compost is an excellent mulch. Apply it up to 6 inches deep. Properly made, it is weed-free, disease-free and full of nutrients.

Black plastic is one of the best inorganic mulches. It has the advantage of being inexpensive and easy to install. It is best set in place before planting. It warms the soil early in spring, which helps crops grow faster.

In warm-summer areas, black plastic may overheat the soil when temperatures rise. If this is true for your location, it is best to cover the plastic with an organic mulch to decrease the soil temperature. The organic mulch also looks better and more natural than the black plastic.

Black plastic is an effective mulch, shown here with block planting of onions.

Bark chips are decorative and functional between rows of radishes.

Grass clippings are normally available free. When they decompose, they add their nutrients to the soil.

Pine needles are attractive and easy to apply, but are not available in all areas.

Vegetable garden features a combination of black plastic film and wood chips. The plastic *warms* the soil in spring to help seedlings grow faster. When temperatures rise in the summer, bark can be placed over the plastic to *cool* the soil. This allows better root growth in the upper soil layer.

Pest Control for Common Insect Pests

APHIDS. Numerous species of aphids are common in vegetable gardens, including green, red, black and white kinds. They form large colonies around tender parts of plant stems and on leaf undersides. They suck sap from plants and produce a sticky substance called *honeydew,* formed from their excrement. Infested plants turn yellow, lose leaves and become stunted. Aphids are also carriers of disease.
Chemical control: Early in the season, begin a spray program of malathion or diazinon. Once they become numerous, aphids are difficult to control.
Organic control: Inspect plants frequently and blast colonies with a jet of water from a garden hose. Soap and water spray—1 teaspoon dishsoap to 1 gallon of water—can be effective. Add a layer of aluminum foil around base of plants. This reflects light onto the underside of leaves, making them an undesirable habitat. Ladybugs are natural enemies. Sprays of nicotine sulfate are also effective.

COLORADO POTATO BEETLE. Mature beetle resembles a ladybug, but is slightly larger—3/8 inch long. Body is yellow with black stripes. Eggs are yellow-orange, laid in clusters on eggplant, potato and tomato leaves. Larvae are hump-backed and red with black spots along the sides.
Chemical control: Spray infested plants with Sevin, malathion, methoxychlor or diazinon.
Organic control: Hand-pick egg clusters from plant leaves, checking undersides. Dust plants with rotenone and pyrethrum combination or diatomaceous earth.

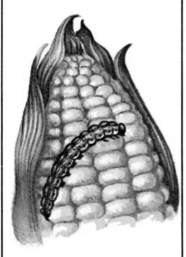

CORN EARWORM. Also known as *fruit worm.* The most common sweet corn pest. Corn earworm is the larva stage of a moth that lays its eggs on corn silks. Tiny larvae eat their way into the ear where they live on tender kernels. Worms are yellowish green, to 1-1/2 inches long. They cannot be detected unless the husk is peeled back. When corn is not available, these pests eat into tomato fruit, okra pods, pea pods and squash fruit.
Chemical control: When corn silks appear, apply 4 or 5 treatments of Sevin at 4-day intervals.
Organic control: Apply rotenone, pyrethrum or diatomaceous earth at 4-day intervals after silks appear and until they turn brown and brittle. Or fill an eye dropper with clear mineral oil and apply it to silks after the ear has started to fill out. Trim silks close with scissors once pollination has been achieved. Egg-laying moths prefer long, trailing silks.

CUCUMBER BEETLE. Striped and spotted cucumber beetles are yellow and 1/4 inch long. Spotted species is shown. They damage melons, cucumbers, squash, beans and potatoes by chewing stems, flowers, leaves and fruit. They usually cluster around the crowns of young plants and among blossoms. Look for brown scars along stems. Adult striped cucumber beetle spreads bacterial wilt to cucumbers, squash and melons, causing vine death.
Chemical control: Apply Sevin or diazinon when seedlings emerge and every 5 days until vines are established.
Organic control: Sprinkle leaves with wood ashes, pyrethrum, rotenone or garlic spray. Applying a thick mulch around plants also seems to help. For serious infestations, make an organic spray by mixing a handful of wood ashes and a handful of lime in 2 gallons of water. Helpful to apply sprays of rotenone-pyrethrum when you set out transplants, or when seedlings first appear.

CUTWORMS. Black, brown or gray, 1/2 to 1-1/2 inches long. Normally spend the day curled up in a C-shape, just below the soil surface. Often found in garden soil when digging or tilling. At night they chew on plant stems. Damaged plants keel over at soil level.
Chemical control: Drench soil with diazinon prior to planting. Or use Sevin by mixing 2 level teaspoons in 1 gallon of water. Spray plant bases and surrounding soil in late afternoon to early evening.

Organic control: Protect transplants with a paper or metal collar. Use bottomless paper cups slit along one side so they can be wrapped around the plant stem. Bury lip of cup in the soil.

FLEA BEETLES. Tiny black beetles, 1/16 inch long, cluster on leaf surfaces and jump when disturbed, like animal fleas. They are particularly fond of eggplant. Look for small holes in leaves, as though peppered with gunshot. Crops of secondary preference are radishes, turnips, beets, corn, potatoes and tomatoes.
Chemical control: Dust or spray with Sevin, diazinon or malathion.
Organic control: Dust with wood ashes, rotenone, pyrethrum or apply garlic spray. Remove all debris from garden in fall to discourage overwintering of pests. Till and rake garden soil after harvest to make it less sheltered for egg-laying females.

HORNWORM. The green hornworm is a large caterpillar 3 to 4 inches long. Eight diagonal stripes run along each side. A spike or horn emerges at the end of its tail. It is the larva of the hawk moth and feeds largely on leaves of tomatoes, peppers and eggplant. Look for bare branches and black droppings beneath plants.
Chemical control: Sevin, diazinon and malathion are effective.
Organic control: Hand-picking is the best control method. Inspect plants often and remove worms with a gloved hand. *Bacillus thuringiensis* is also effective.

IMPORTED CABBAGE WORM. Larvae of the cabbage white butterfly. Lays eggs on cabbage plants and other members of the cabbage family. Caterpillars are green, about 1 inch long, with a slender, orange stripe down the middle of the back. They eat ragged holes in leaves and chew channels into cabbage heads.
Chemical control: Sevin and methoxychlor are effective.
Organic control: Use *Bacillus thuringiensis,* a bacterial disease affecting caterpillars.

JAPANESE BEETLES. Beetles are usually 1/2 inch long, shiny, coppery brown, with metallic green shoulders. They can be seen feeding on plants. When disturbed, they fly off suddenly, emitting a whirring sound. Larvae look like white cutworms. They overwinter in soil under sod, living on a favorite diet of grass roots. Adults devastate leaves and flowers of many plants, including corn, beans, okra and rhubarb.
Chemical control: Although malathion or Sevin controls them, a better control is a beetle trap.
Organic control: Hang a Japanese beetle trap on a pole near the vegetable garden. Sex hormone attracts male beetles to trap. Effective and capable of trapping thousands of beetles in one season. Wear gloves and hand-pick colonies.

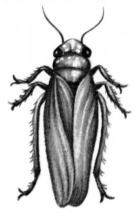

LEAFHOPPERS. These grasshopperlike insects are tiny, usually green and 1/8 inch long. They sit still on leaves, then hop abruptly into the air. Many different species attack different plants. They suck plant juices, causing leaf distortions. Leaf edges curl and appear burned. The biggest potential danger is introduction of virus diseases. Especially troublesome in fall.
Chemical control: Apply Sevin, diazinon, malathion or methoxychlor.
Organic control: Destroy garden debris to prevent pests from overwintering. Dust plants with rotenone, pyrethrum or diatomaceous earth.

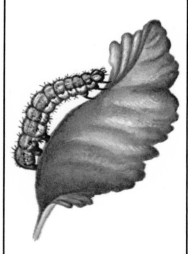

LOOPERS. These bright green caterpillars are the larvae of a moth. They measure 1-1/2 inches long and crawl by hunching the middle part of their back into a loop. They eat leaves, particularly members of the cabbage family. Inspect plants in spring for signs of looper droppings, which look like black pinheads. Holes and ragged leaf edges also indicate their presence.
Chemical control: Sevin and diazinon are highly effective.

Organic control: *Bacillus thuringiensis,* a bacterial disease affecting only caterpillars, is an effective control.

MEXICAN BEAN BEETLES AND BEAN LEAF BEETLES. Larvae of Mexican bean beetle cause serious problems with beans. Adult beetles overwinter in dead vegetation. They are yellow, about 1/3 inch long, covered with spines resembling a pincushion. Examine undersides of leaves for egg clusters and for larvae. Damaged leaves often resemble fine lace because all but the leaf vein is eaten. Bean leaf beetles are most common in the southeastern United States, but are also found in midwestern and eastern states.
Chemical control: Spray with Sevin or malathion.
Organic control: Hand-pick colonies when small. Dust with rotenone, pyrethrum or diatomaceous earth. A spray using garlic concentrate or garlic-pepper may be effective. Destroy all bean stalks and garden debris in fall so beetles do not overwinter. Praying mantis is an insect predator.

MITES. Common spider mites are small, measuring only 1/50 of an inch. They are oval, and yellow, green or red. They suck plant juices, and are most prolific in dry weather, undergoing a complete life cycle in less than a week. Look for fine webbing over and under the foliage. Mottled, speckled, curling and wilting foliage is an indication of mite activity.

Chemical control: The miticide Kelthane is most effective. Treatment must be administered early in the season. Once these pests are established, they are difficult to bring under control. Diazinon and malathion sprays used at weekly intervals offer some measure of control.
Organic control: Destroy garden debris so mites cannot overwinter. Ladybugs are natural predators of mites.

NEMATODES. Microscopic worms live in soil and attack plant roots. Roots become shriveled, with swellings called *galls* ranging in size from a pinhead to 1 inch in diameter. Galls cut off flow of nutrients to the plant. Plants may become stunted, turn yellow and produce undersized, distorted fruit.
Chemical control: Soil drenches of insecticide are usually ineffective. Soil fumigation is effective, but requires the knowledge of a professional. Contact your county extension agent.
Organic control: Grow plants resistant to nematode attack. Certain varieties of tomatoes, for example, have the letter "N" after their name, such as 'Supersteak VFN'. These initials indicate resistance to *verticillium, fusarium wilt* and *nematodes.* You might try planting the garden one year with French marigolds instead of vegetables. Studies indicate that these marigolds repel nematodes.

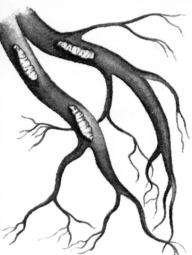

ROOT MAGGOTS. These fly larvae resemble common house fly maggots. They are white, peg-shaped, 1/4 inch long. Several species exist. These include the cabbage maggot, which also attacks radishes; onion maggot; and carrot maggot, which also infests celery and parsnips. Fly lays its eggs at the plant base. Maggots crawl into the soil where they feed on the roots. Look for wilted leaves and stunted growth.
Chemical control: Use a soil drench of diazinon prior to planting. For onion maggots, dust or spray with malathion.
Organic control: Dusting with wood ashes, rotenone, pyrethrum and diatomaceous earth offers some measure of control. Spray with garlic concentrate or garlic-pepper spray. Covering soil with black plastic mulch and planting through the plastic helps prevent adult flies from laying eggs near crops.

SLUGS AND SNAILS. Slugs are basically snails without shells. Most active during wet weather and in early evening and early morning. Look for them under boards, stones or mulch during the day. They leave slimy, silvery trails that can be seen in early morning. Both pests do great damage by chewing leaves.
Chemical control: Use slug pellets marked "safe for fruits and vegetables." Scatter pellets on pans to prevent soil contamination. Using 4 tablespoons of Sevin 50% wettable powder to 1 gallon of water is also effective.
Organic control: Keep area around garden clean of trash, boards and other potential hiding places. Apply diatomaceous earth or wood ashes between rows and around plants. Beer in shallow pans lures some slugs and snails. They crawl into the pans and drown.

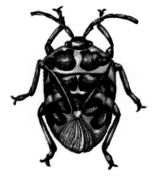

SQUASH BUGS, STINK BUGS AND RELATED SPECIES. Squash bugs and related pests such as the harlequin bug (shown above), stink bug and tarnished plant bug injure plants by sucking their juices. Each type of bug attacks a different vegetable. Harlequin bugs destroy cabbage, radishes and turnips. Stink bugs seek peas and beans. Tarnished plant bugs are partial to beets, celery and about 50 other vegetable crops. Squash bugs harm pumpkins, cucumbers and melon vines, as well as squash. Bugs vary in color, depending on species. Most are broad-shouldered and shaped like a shield. Injured plants show brown blotches or stunted, distorted growth.
Chemical control: Malathion, Sevin and diazinon sprays are effective.
Organic control: Place boards along rows for squash bugs to hide under. Hand-pick and destroy them each morning. Dust plants with rotenone, pyrethrum or diatomaceous earth. Remove debris from garden so bugs cannot overwinter. Check leaves frequently.

SQUASH VINE BORER. This is the caterpillar of a moth that lays its eggs at the base of plants. Larvae bore their way into stems. Borers are white, about 1 inch long. They are difficult to control because they work hidden inside stems. In addition to squash, they attack pumpkins, cucumbers and melons. Look for small, round holes along squash stems and a small pile of sawdustlike material. Plants wilt as larvae bore inside of vines.
Chemical control: Some control is possible by using sprays of malathion and methoxychlor. The most effective chemical control is Thiodan. As vines grow, treat them 3 times at 7-day intervals.
Organic control: Use rotenone, pyrethrum or diatomaceous earth to obtain partial control. Inspect vines for infestation. If you locate entry hole, insert a wire to determine location of the borer. Slit vine above the borer and destroy it. Bind slit shut again with twist-tie. Effective preventative control is to apply garlic spray to the base of each squash vine. Pungent odor helps repel the egg-laying moth.

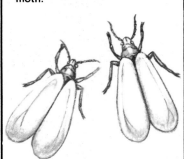

WHITEFLIES. These small, sucking insects have white bodies covered with powder. They resemble miniature moths. When disturbed, they fly up in a cloud like flakes of snow. They often hide underneath leaves, sucking plant juices. They are particularly fond of peppers and tomatoes. As many as four generations can be born during a warm, dry season. The young, called *crawlers,* are yellow and hatch from eggs laid under leaves. Plants are stunted and fruit yields are reduced.
Chemical control: Spray with malathion every 2 days for a 10-day period. Cover undersides of leaves. Diazinon is also effective.
Organic control: Whiteflies are attracted to the color yellow. Hang yellow boards covered with a sticky substance between plants. An aluminum mulch is also an effective control. It reflects light onto leaf undersides and disorients the insects. Ladybugs are a natural predator of whiteflies.

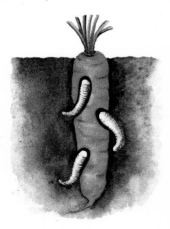

WIREWORMS. Yellowish brown insects measure up to 1-1/2 inches long. They feed below the ground on seeds and seedlings, and bore holes in root crops. You may see them when tilling garden soil. Harvest a few carrots or radishes and inspect for irregular holes where wireworms may be feeding.
Chemical control: Drench soil with diazinon. Do not use near pumpkins, eggplant or rutabaga. Read label for other precautions.
Organic control: Hand-pick wireworms from soil at time of cultivation. Good soil drainage reduces wireworm populations. Regular use of compost or wood ashes helps keep wireworms under control.

DISEASE CONTROL

Plant diseases can be divided into two general groups: *parasitic* and *nonparhahsithic*. The parasitic group includes diseases caused by fungi, bacteria, viruses, mycoplasmas and nematodes. Parasitic organisms are microscopic and live off plant tissue, putting the plant under stress. In severe cases, they may cause the plant to die. The presence of these parasites is recognized as a disease.

The nonparasitic group includes diseases caused by physical disorders. These include injuries from sprays and unfavorable growing conditions—nutrient deficiencies or an improper balance of elements essential to plant growth.

THE IMPORTANCE OF PREVENTION

Prevention is more important with diseases than with insect pests. Insects can usually be eradicated when they become a problem, but most plant diseases cannot be destroyed after a plant is infected. Instead, the infected part has to be removed. Often, by the time a disease is noticed, it is too late. The plant must be sacrificed to prevent the disease from spreading. A preventative program aimed at controlling disease also helps control insect pests. Good gardening practices as outlined in this section will help keep diseases out of your garden.

Keep the garden clean. Many disease organisms overwinter in plant wastes. All plant debris including spent vines, roots, stems and leaves should be raked and burned or put on a compost pile. Well-made compost usually kills weed seeds and plant diseases, and neutralizes plant poisons.

Rotate crops. Diseases that cause slight damage one year could overwinter and devastate crops the next. By *rotating crops* each year—moving specific vegetables from one location of the garden to another—you help prevent diseases from gaining a foothold.

Buy virus-free plants. Do not purchase any vegetable plants for your garden unless they are certified "virus- and disease-free." This is particularly important with tubers such as potatoes, and roots such as asparagus. Before buying vegetable transplants, inspect leaves and stems carefully for any signs of disease or damage.

Plant disease-resistant varieties. Many vegetable varieties have been developed with resistance to a particular disease or group of diseases. Look for plants with the initials V, F, N or all three. This indicates that the plant is resistant to verticillium wilt, fusarium wilt and nematodes.

Destroy infected plants. Cut out infected plant parts. If serious, remove and destroy diseased plants so the disease is not spread to healthy plants. Certain parasites such as powdery mildew that live on the surface of plants can be eradicated by dusting or spraying with a fungicide.

Protect plants with preventative controls. Certain diseases such as powdery

Common Plant Diseases and Their Control

ANTHRACNOSE. Fungus disease that causes wilting of affected plant parts. White areas appear on leaves, causing them to wither. Infects members of the cucumber family, including melons, pumpkins and squash. Sometimes a problem on tomatoes.
Control. Clear garden of all plant wastes in fall. Don't save seeds from pods infected by the disease. Plant disease-resistant varieties.

BACTERIAL WILT. When cucumber plants suddenly collapse from the top down, chances are they are infected by bacterial wilt disease.
Control. Because this disease is spread by cucumber beetles, control of these pests is essential. Plant disease-resistant varieties. Clean up garden in winter and burn or dispose of spent cucumber vines. Avoid growing cucumbers in same location the following year.

BLACK ROT. Cabbages are highly susceptible to rotting, especially during wet weather and when planted too close together. Heads become soft and yellow on one side then turn black and mushy.
Control. Choose varieties described as being resistant to rot disease. Use sterile potting soil when growing transplants. Treat seeds with a fungicide such as benomyl.

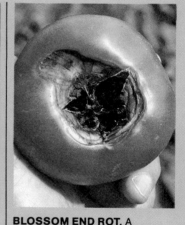

BLOSSOM END ROT. A nonparasitic disease that usually occurs because of irregular or inadequate watering. Such watering causes the trace element calcium to be deficient. Tips of fruit such as tomatoes and peppers turn black.
Control. Water transplants regularly until they are established. Use a mulch to conserve moisture. Mix lime or wood ashes into soil to provide plants with adequate amounts of calcium.

mildew can be prevented by using fungicides *before* they occur. Complete coverage of plant parts is normally necessary, plus repeated applications. Fungicides are more effective when applied prior to rains because infection usually occurs during periods of high moisture.

Follow proper cultural practices. Healthy, vigorous growth allows plants to avoid many diseases. The plant nutrient potash helps plants fight diseases. Well-draining soil enriched with compost helps encourage healthy growth. Use of drip-irrigation systems that water plants only in the root zone reduces disease. Most diseases enter plants when they are wet.

Plant treated seeds. Seeds treated with mild organic fungicides can prevent seed decay and damping-off disease. Seed companies offering treated seed normally do so at no extra cost. In the case of bulbs and tubers such as onions and potatoes, plant *certified* virus-free stock.

Use disease controls. Fungicides are products that are toxic to *fungi*, which cause many diseases. They are applied as dusts or sprays. The most popular is a copper-based fungicide called a *Bordeaux* mixture. You can make your own Bordeaux mix. Mix 2 ounces of copper sulfate in 1 gallon of water. Add 2 ounces of hydrated lime to 2 gallons of water. Combine both to make 3 gallons of Bordeaux mixture.

FUNGICIDES

Although dozens of chemical and organic disease controls have been produced to combat specific diseases, a home gardener is not like a farmer who specializes in just one or two crops. A home gardener often has a dozen or more crops to care for, and would soon be overwhelmed trying to protect the garden from every disease. Gardeners generally want a broad-spectrum control that works against most of the diseases most of the time.

Here are brief descriptions of widely available, general-purpose disease controls.

Copper-containing fungicides. Bordeaux mixture is the best known, composed of copper sulfate, lime and water. See formula at left. The mixture is sprayed over foliage.

Sulfur-containing fungicides. Sulfur is one of the oldest, general-purpose fungicides. Wettable sulfurs, containing a wetting agent, allow the sulfur to be mixed easily with water to form an easy-to-apply spray.

Organic fungicides. Many organic fungicides are available. In many cases, they have replaced the older fungicides. Use them with caution, because some are toxic to fish, animals and people. *Captan, maneb* and *zineb* are examples. They are usually available as wettable powders for use as all-purpose fungicides. Captan is also used as a seed treatment to control damping-off disease.

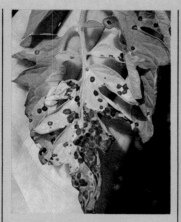

FUSARIUM AND VERTICILLIUM WILTS. These are fungus diseases affecting tomatoes, peas, eggplant, peppers, potatoes, melons, pumpkins and squash. Vines turn brown, then wilt and die. Part of a plant may wilt then recover briefly, but soon the entire plant will perish.
Control. Do not plant in the same spot where either disease has occurred in a previous year. Plant disease-resistant varieties such as 'Supersteak VFN' tomato or any other variety with the initials "VF" after its name.

LEAF BLIGHT AND LEAF SPOTS. Several fungi cause leaf spots. Brown, circular spots with light-colored centers cover leaves, which eventually wither and die. Prevalent on beans, beets, cucumbers, eggplant, potatoes, melons and tomatoes.
Control. Disease organism overwinters in soil and on seeds. Rotate crops so plants won't be grown in soil contaminated from previous year's growth. Do not save seeds from your own garden for replanting—they may harbor the disease.

POWDERY MILDEW. This fungus disease thrives in wet conditions. Powdery white patches appear on leaf and stem surfaces. They reduce the light that reaches the plants and cause leaves to shrivel. Susceptible plants include beans, melons, cucumbers, pumpkins, squash and watermelon.
Control. Plant disease-resistant varieties such as 'Marketmore 76' cucumber. Irrigate carefully so leaves and stems do not get excessively wet, which encourages the disease. Spray with a preventative fungicide such as Karathane.

RUST. Red or dark brown, powdery pustules on leaves, stems and seed pods. Most abundant on lower leaves, causing severe injury and death. Prevalent on asparagus and beans.
Control. The fungicide zineb prevents infections. Planting resistant varieties is best. Pruning infected plant parts helps bring disease under control. Disinfect pruning shears after each cut in a 50% bleach and water solution. Burn or dispose of infected branches.

GALLERY OF GARDEN VEGETABLES

The following common and not-so-common vegetables are organized alphabetically for easy reference. Descriptions for most vegetables give background and cultural information, pest control and harvesting tips. Vegetable varieties are recommended, with reasons why they are superior.

Many vegetables have a section entitled "Inside Report." Most were compiled by interviewing the plant breeder responsible for creating a particularly outstanding vegetable variety.

Special emphasis has been placed on illustrating each vegetable as realistically and naturally as possible. The majority of vegetables pictured were grown in home gardens, using the growing techniques described in this section.

A special effort has been made to recommend varieties known to be widely adaptable. But some vegetables are better adapted to certain regions and these have also been noted. An additional source of variety recommendation is your local cooperative extension service. This agency is listed in the phone book under different names. Look under the "County" or "State University" headings for *Agricultural Extension Service, Cooperative Extension Service, County Extension Service,* or *County* or *Agricultural Agent.*

A way to obtain regional favorites is through catalogs of seed companies located in your area. For example, certain cold-tolerant varieties are better for cool-season areas of the Pacific Northwest and short-season areas of Canada. Seeds for such varieties are normally offered by seed companies located in Washington State, Maine and Canada. Similarly, there are varieties adapted to warm climates of the South and Southwest, offered by seed companies located in these areas.

In addition to regional varieties, you need to consider regional planting dates. In the North, cool-season crops can be planted approximately three weeks before your last frost date in spring. In areas with mild frosts or *no* frosts, such as Florida, the Gulf States, southern California and southern Arizona, cool-season crops are best planted in fall—usually September and October. This way, crops can be harvested during winter and early spring before the onset of hot weather. Check locally among experienced gardeners or with your cooperative extension service.

Problems with pests and diseases also occur on a regional level. If you are a new gardener or new to an area, ask your neighbors which pests are known to bother certain crops in your area. You can then implement a specific control program to combat pests and diseases before they become established.

Left: A vine loaded with sun-ripened, 'Supersteak VFN' tomatoes. Above: Nothing else says freshness like just-picked vegetables from a backyard garden.

Seedhead of grain amaranth.

Artichoke 'Grande Beurre', grown from seed.

AMARANTH

Two kinds of amaranth are commonly grown in home gardens. Leaf amaranth produces leafy greens that are excellent, hot-weather substitutes for spinach. Grain amaranth, popular in Aztec civilizations, produces large seedheads prized for their nutritive content.

Tampala (*Amaranthus* species) is the most widely grown leaf amaranth. It produces edible greens within 6 to 8 weeks after seeds are sown. Leaves can be used raw in salads or cooked like spinach. Young leaves are tender and require only a few minutes to cook. Stems can be braised, imparting a flavor similar to artichokes.

Tampala freezes better than spinach or Swiss chard. It retains a more appetizing color, shrinks very little and has a better flavor.

Grain amaranths have edible leaves, but they are mostly grown for their huge, yellow, bronze and red flower plumes. They produce thousands of nutty seeds that contain high-quality protein.

How to grow: Sow seeds 1/4 inch deep directly in the garden after all danger of frost has passed. Seeds need darkness and 70F (21C) temperature to germinate. Thin seedlings so plants stand 16 to 20 inches apart in rows 20 inches apart.

Pest and disease control: Insect damage is normally minor, usually caused by chewing insects such as Japanese beetle. These can be easily controlled by rotenone organic dust or Sevin chemical spray.

Harvesting and use: Begin by picking young leaves, which are cooked like spinach. A large, decorative seedhead develops about midsummer. When seeds have turned brown, cut flowerhead and shake or thrash over a newspaper to collect seeds.

A favorite way to eat the seeds is to cook them like popcorn. Heat a metal skillet until hot, and pour in 1 tablespoon of amaranth seeds. Move the skillet constantly to keep seeds from burning while they pop. When popping subsides, seeds are ready to eat.

Recommended varieties: Tampala or 'Fordhook Spinach' (50 days) is an excellent spinach substitute. Available from Burpee.

ARTICHOKE

Globe artichoke (*Cynara scolymus*) is an edible thistle, producing flower buds that are delicious to eat. Cardoon (*Cynara cardunculus*) is a close relative grown for its edible leaf stalks. Both of these vegetables originate in the Mediterranean.

The edible part of globe artichoke is the flower bud, which consists of a cluster of overlapping fleshy scales. Flower buds must be picked young, before the purple flower blossoms begin to show. A large, healthy plant will produce up to 50 edible buds.

When flowers are allowed to open they resemble a giant thistle head. They are greatly admired by floral designers who dry them for use in arrangements. Leaves of globe artichoke are large and deeply serrated—very striking in the landscape. Well-grown specimens can reach a height of 6 feet and are sometimes used in perennial flower borders as a dramatic highlight.

Artichokes have strict temperature and moisture requirements. Most commercial varieties produce poorly when the temperature falls below 65F (19C) during the May to September growing period. For this reason, over 90% of commercial artichoke production in the United States is confined to a small area of central, coastal California. Here winters are mild and coastal breezes keep summers cool.

Selecting the right variety for home use is important. Maturity dates range from 24 months for California artichokes grown from roots, to less than 8 months for certain European varieties grown from seed. Because of variety differences, traditional growing instructions for artichokes are misleading. The time-honored theory that artichokes can be grown only in the coastal valleys of California or in mild-winter areas of the South is now outdated.

The secret to growing artichokes in regions with snow cover and freezing temperatures is to start from seed. Choose a fast-maturing variety like 'Grande Beurre' (160 days) and grow it as an annual. Areas of the country with 100 frost-free days should be able to produce worthwhile crops of artichokes the first season.

How to grow: Start seeds indoors at the same time you start tomatoes. This is about 8 to 10 weeks before outdoor planting, which should not occur until all danger of frost has passed. Highest germination is assured if seeds are stored in the refrigerator for two weeks to help break dormancy. Plant seeds in individual pots and provide bottom heat to encourage faster germination.

When seedlings are about 4 to 6 inches tall, set them 3 feet apart in rows spaced 3 feet apart in fertile soil. Artichokes are extremely heavy feeders and do best in soils enriched with garden compost, manure or leaf mold. If soil is lacking in fertility, rake into the soil an application of general-purpose fertilizer before planting. Read the package label for amounts. A booster application should be given to plants in midsummer.

Once planted, artichokes demand large amounts of water. Soil should always be kept moist. During hot, humid weather, plants may wilt but usually recover during the night.

If the ground freezes in winter in your area, it is best to dig up roots in fall. Brush soil from roots and store them in a cool, dark, sheltered place, preferably with an air temperature of 33F to 40F (1C to 5C)). If this is not possible, store roots in pots of soil in a cool, bright location such as in a cold frame. They will remain in a semidormant state until spring.

In areas free from snow cover and where winter temperatures stay above 20F (−7C), artichokes can be left in the ground. In spring, roots normally send up a mass of shoots called *suckers*. To make plants most productive the second season and thereafter, prune away all but four of the strongest shoots. These will use all of the plant's energy and produce heavy crops.

Pest and disease control: Aphids are the most serious pest. They congregate in groups along tips of new shoots and infest developing buds. Aphid colonies are usually green or black. The safest control is to blast them with jets of water from a garden hose. You can also rub aphids off stems with a gloved hand before colonies become numerous.

Slugs and snails can cause serious damage in the early stages of growth. Place slug bait in shallow pans so the poison does not contaminate soil. Be sure to use bait labeled "safe for vegetables."

Harvesting and use: Buds can be harvested when they are the size of a tennis ball or larger, before the purple part of the flower begins to show. Small buds are more tender to eat. Cut the bud from the plant using a sharp knife. See How To Cook And Eat An Artichoke for instructions on preparing the bud.

Recommended varieties: 'Grande Beurre' (160 days) produces a harvest the first year from seed. Available from Thompson & Morgan. 'Green Globe' (180 days), a widely available variety, will also produce edible buds the first year.

HOW TO COOK AND EAT AN ARTICHOKE

As much confusion surrounds how to eat artichokes as how to grow them. First, cut the artichoke from the flower stem immediately below the globe or *bud,* with about 1 inch of stem attached. Remove about 1 inch of the tip and hard, spiny leaves from around the base of the bud. Rinse the artichoke. Put salt, lemon juice and the artichoke in a pan of water and bring to a boil. Cook for 30 minutes or until the base is soft to the touch of a fork. After cooking, turn upside down to drain away water.

Prepare a dish of melted butter. To eat, pull away leaf sections of the artichoke, starting from the outside and working toward the center. Dip the base of each leaf section in butter and pull it between your teeth. The tender portion easily parts from the inedible, fibrous portion, which you discard. Each leaf toward the middle of the artichoke becomes more tender. Eventually you will reach the *choke,* or the immature flower head. Scoop this out with a spoon, leaving the *heart,* the tastiest part of all. Eat the heart and stem section with fingers or fork. Garnish with a squeeze of lemon juice if you desire.

Remove artichoke from plant with a knife. Leave 1 inch of stem attached.

Cut away sharp tips of bud scales. Peel away tough, lower leaf scales.

Cut off spiny top with sharp knife. Artichoke is ready to cook. See above.

'Jade Pagoda' hybrid is the earliest heading variety of Chinese cabbage.

PAK CHOY

This fast-maturing, nonheading variety of Chinese cabbage is grown in the Orient as fresh greens.

How to grow: Because plants tolerate crowding, they are generally grown in short, wide rows about 5 feet long. Sow seeds 1/4 inch deep directly in the garden. Thin each plant to stand 2 inches apart. Space rows 12 inches apart. Make first sowings 3 weeks before your last frost date and continue until night temperatures exceed 70F (21C). Successive sowings should be made at 2-week intervals to ensure a continuous supply. Pak choy tolerates poor soil, but needs a continuous supply of moisture to ensure rapid growth during cool weather. Also grows well as a fall crop.

Pest and disease control: Flea beetles are the plant's worst enemy. Control with Sevin chemical spray or rotenone organic insecticide.

Harvesting and use: Harvesting can begin within 20 days of sowing seeds, and continue until the plant produces a flowerhead. Tip of the flowerstalk is tender and delicious until the buds open and display yellow flowers similar to broccoli. Cook by boiling or stir-fry.

CHINESE CABBAGE

Two kinds of Chinese cabbage are popular in home gardens—*heading* and *nonheading*. Heading kinds are oval shaped, with light green, crinkled leaves that are yellow inside. Heads mature within 70 days after sowing seeds under cool conditions. They usually do best as a fall crop, transplanted to the garden in midsummer.

Nonheading kinds are sometimes called *bok choy* or *pai tsai*. They are loose-leafed and much easier to grow than heading types. Leaves are dark green and have thick, succulent, white stems. Plants mature in only 45 days after sowing seeds. They can be grown as a spring or fall crop.

How to grow: Chinese cabbage will tolerate mild frosts and can be sown directly in the garden several weeks before the last frost date. It is better to sow seeds in peat pots or peat pellets for transplanting. Plant seeds 1/4 inch deep. Bok choy plants can be set into single rows or block planted in wide, raised beds, spaced at least 1 foot apart with 2 feet between rows. Space heading types 1-1/2 to 2 feet apart. Light soils enriched with garden compost or well-decomposed animal manure are best.

Pest and disease control: Broad-spectrum chemicals like Sevin and malathion are widely used by commercial growers and are effective against most cabbage pests. To guard against diseases, your best control is to plant disease-resistant varieties.

Harvesting and use: Bok choy can be picked as soon as leaves and stems are large enough. Stems can be harvested from several plants, or an entire plant can be picked at one time. Heading Chinese cabbage is harvested as a whole plant. Use the same as regular spring cabbage.

Recommended varieties: Among heading varieties, try 'Jade Pagoda' hybrid (60 days). It is the earliest, largest, most heat-resistant variety. Handsomely savoyed leaves are highly ornamental. George W. Park is a source for seed. 'Crispy Choy' is the earliest of the nonheading varieties. It matures in 45 days, growing crisp, succulent, snow-white stalks edible raw or cooked. Burpee is a source for seed.

Chinese cabbage bok choy shows its crisp, succulent, white leaf stalks. These plants were ready to harvest in 45 days from sowing seeds.

Pak choy is a nonheading type of Chinese cabbage. If allowed to grow quickly during periods of cool weather, it produces tips that are delicious to eat as greens.

Celery 'Golden Self-Blanching' is an early, heavy producer.

CELERY

Wild forms of celery are distributed throughout southern Europe. Prized for crisp, crunchy leaf stalks that are eaten raw or cooked, cultivated kinds derived from wild species have been grown in gardens for hundreds of years.

Edible leaf stalks grow as a clump from the soil line. Many gardeners prefer to *blanch*—whiten the stems— to improve the flavor. This is accomplished by wrapping stems with brown paper collars to exclude light. Heaping loose soil or shredded leaves against the stalks will also do the job. Be aware that blanching reduces nutritional value.

How to grow: Although seeds can be sown directly in the garden three weeks before the last frost date, it's best to start seeds indoors. Sow seeds in trays filled with a peat-based potting soil such as Jiffy-Mix. Plant 10 to 12 weeks before last spring frost date. Seeds are tiny and require light for best germination. Lightly press them into soil and spray with water. Cover tray with a plastic bag and place in indirect light. Fluid seed sowing is also a good way of sowing celery. It allows pregerminated seeds to be sown in the garden. Seeds germinate in 10 to 14 days at a soil temperature of 65F (19C). Space plants 6 inches apart in rows 2 feet apart, or plant in wide rows. Transplant seedlings after last frost.

Celery's most vital need is regular moisture. Soil for celery should have good moisture-holding capacity, so an organically rich soil is important. Garden compost, leaf mold and decomposed stable manure are acceptable soil conditioners for a celery bed. Use drip irrigation or a lawn sprinkler set in the middle of the planting. Soak soil thoroughly when you water.

Celery is a heavy feeder and requires a fertile soil. Supply with booster applications of fertilizer during the growing season.

Pest and disease control: Watch for celery worms. They chew leaf stalks at the soil line, causing discoloring and rot. Remove by hand or dislodge with a jet of water from a garden hose. Sevin is the chemical spray to use. It will also control aphids. Organic gardeners use pyrethrum or rote-none to control insect pests.

Harvesting and use: Begin as soon as edible stalks are large enough to pull. Early pickings can be taken by pulling outer stalks of several plants and allowing plants to continue to grow more stalks from the center. Celery is hardy, and will tolerate mild frosts. It can be left in the garden well into fall. Heaping fallen leaves or similar insulating material against stems will help protect plants. For long periods of storage, celery can be moved to a root cellar or cold frame. Pull entire plant, roots and all, and stand upright in moist sand. Push roots in sand and leave tops uncovered. Celery is best when used with other vegetables in cooked dishes. For example, try them cooked with tomatoes or in vegetable soup.

Recommended varieties: Two kinds of celery are popular—green celery and golden or self-blanching celery. Most gardeners tend to prefer green varieties over golden kinds. 'Tendercrisp' (105 days) is considered best, combining earliness with heavy stalk production. 'Golden Self-Blanching' (115 days) is a popular pale-stalked variety.

Close-up view of 'Tendercrisp'. It is the best home garden celery, growing crisp, juicy stalks 10 to 14 days earlier than other varieties.

Left, leaves of celtuce. Right, mature stalks.

'Fordhook Giant' Swiss chard.

CELTUCE

Celtuce is native to China and is closely related to lettuce. Because of its thick, central stalk it combines the uses of both celery and lettuce, hence the name *celtuce*. It is easy to grow and deserves to be more widely planted in home gardens.

How to grow: Plant and cultivate exactly as you would lettuce, either as a spring or fall crop. Sow seeds 1/8 inch deep. Space plants 9 to 12 inches apart in rows 1 to 2 feet apart, or block-plant in raised beds. Celtuce grows quickly. It produces greens within 60 days and stalks within 90 days of sowing seeds directly in the garden. Young leaves have four times the vitamin C content of regular lettuce.

Pest and disease control: The most troublesome pests are slugs and snails, which can devour young seedlings before they have a chance to become established. When the stalks start to mature, these pests also eat the skin, causing the stalk to split open and discolor. Control with slug bait placed in shallow pans so poison does not wash into soil. Rabbits and other foraging animals can be kept away by enclosing the garden with a fence.

Harvesting and use: When celtuce leaves are young they may be used as lettuce, either fresh in salads or boiled as greens. The most tasty part of celtuce is the heart of the stalk, which can be eaten raw or cooked once skin has been peeled away and discarded. The pale green hearts have a crisp and succulent texture. The flavor is hard to describe—something similar to the heart of an artichoke.

This is a good winter crop in areas with mild winters. It is excellent for growing in cold frames where winters are more severe.

Recommended varieties: Celtuce is not available in different varieties. Offered by Burpee, which first introduced it to the United States.

SWISS CHARD

This extremely hardy, drought-tolerant leaf crop is grown primarily for its dark green, "blistered" leaves and crisp, crunchy leaf stalks. Because of its heat tolerance, Swiss chard, also known as spinach beet, makes an excellent substitute for spinach when cooked.

The more you harvest outside leaves, the more new leaves grow from the middle. The first picking of leaves can usually be made within 60 days of sowing seeds. Individual leaves can reach 3 feet in length.

How to grow: Sow seeds directly in garden 2 weeks before the last frost date in your area. Plant seeds 1/2 inch deep in rows spaced 18 inches apart. Thin seedlings so plants are spaced 12 inches apart, 2 feet between rows. Seeds germinate in 4 to 10 days at 50F to 70F (10C to 21C) soil temperature. Like beet seed, chard seed is a cluster of several individual seeds. Careful thinning will be necessary to space seedlings for good growth. Although plants will grow in poor, infertile soils, they do best in soil enriched with high nitrogen fertilizer.

Pest and disease control: Normally not bothered by pests. A few chewing insects may nibble holes in some of the leaves, but damage is rarely extensive enough to warrant control.

Harvesting and use: Begin as soon as the plants are established, pulling outer leaves from several plants so that more new leaves will grow from the center. Chard withstands frosts in fall, and usually remains productive until a hard freeze. Leaf stalks are highly nutritious, and can be cut away from the leaf and braised. Serve with buttered breadcrumbs as an excellent substitute for asparagus.

Recommended varieties: 'Fordhook Giant' (55 days) has large leaves and pearly white leaf stalks. 'Ruby' (55 days) is highly ornamental with red midribs and red leaf veins. 'Ruby' has such attractive, brilliant red stalks, it is often used in borders as an ornamental plant, or in containers for a dramatic highlight. Both are widely available from leading seed catalogs.

Chayote fruit hang from vines that require support.

'Sugarhat' chicory in the garden prior to harvesting.

CHAYOTE

Chayote (pronounced *cha-yo-tay*) is a member of the gourd family, native to Mexico. Green, pear-shaped fruit are produced on vigorous vines that require a strong trellis or overhead structure for support. A single vine will cover 25 feet in a season, up to 50 feet in warm-climate areas. Fruit is solid. When mature, it drops from the vine like a bomb, burying its base in the soil so that it will sprout.

How to grow: Plant the entire fruit. Roots grow from the base and a shoot sprouts from the center. This sometimes occurs while fruit is on the vine. In mild areas that receive some frosts, plant in spring after danger of frost has passed, or start in 5-gallon container in a protected area.

Vines need 6 to 9 months of warm, frost-free weather to produce worthwhile crops. For this reason, chayote is grown mostly in Florida and southern California. In frost-free locations it grows as a perennial, yielding fruit for several years. In areas with mild frosts and where no freezing of the ground occurs, vines will die back to roots. At the onset of warmer weather, roots normally produce new shoots. Plants are highly productive. One vine will produce up to 100 fruit, weighing 1 pound or more each.

Pest and disease control: Protect young plants from cucumber beetles by using rotenone or Sevin.

Harvesting and use: Pick fruit when they have grown to the size of a large pear. Although fruit are best eaten fresh and boiled until tender, they will store for a month in the vegetable bin of a refrigerator.

To eat chayote, slice mature fruit into sections and boil for about 10 to 15 minutes. Chayote can also be sliced thin for eating raw. Flavor is similar to water chestnuts. Roots form swollen tubers and are also edible. They can be harvested the second season.

Recommended varieties: 'Perlita' (200 days), little pearl or chestnut chayote, comes from Guatemala. Fruit are about the size of a lemon. Its cooked texture is like a baked potato. It and a larger Mexican variety are available from Exotica Seed.

CHICORY

Chicory has been a popular salad vegetable and medicinal plant since early Roman times. It is a common sight along the roadsides of America, producing beautiful blue flowers the size of cornflowers. Because it is so widespread, many people believe chicory is a native American wildflower. Actually, wild chicory is an escapee from cultivation, brought to the United States from the Mediterranean by immigrants.

Two forms of chicory are popular in home gardens. *Witloof chicory* is grown mostly for *forcing* during winter to produce golden yellow *chicons,* cone-shaped shoots popular in salads. See the following for forcing instructions. *Leaf chicory* produces a head of salad greens somewhat like lettuce.

How to grow: Witloof chicory is started from seed as an outdoor vegetable. The objective is to produce a healthy root system for storage during winter. Although seedlings will tolerate mild frosts, it is better to delay planting until season is well advanced. Three months of growing will produce the right size of root for top-quality chicons. Sow seeds 1/4 inch deep directly in the garden. Space plants 6 inches apart with 2 feet between rows. Plant in an open, sunny location in a well-drained soil rich in organic matter. Avoid adding coarse manure or coarse compost to the soil. They often contain obstructions that cause roots to split.

Dig roots before the ground freezes. Trim leaves back to within an inch of the root. Discard any roots that are less than 1/2 inch in diameter. Store roots in sawdust or moist sand at about 30F to 40F (− 1C to 5C) for 6 to 8 weeks. To force, place roots in wooden crates deep enough to accommodate them. Roots can be trimmed from the bottom to form uniform lengths of 8 to 9 inches. Line crates with drainage material such as gravel. Add 3 inches of fine topsoil and push roots into soil so they stand straight up. Fill in around sides to top of roots with more fine soil until roots are covered. On top of this, add an 8-inch layer of sawdust or peat moss. Store in a cool, moist place.

For the forcing, crates must be stored at 50F to 60F (10C to 16C). Soil must be kept moist. In four weeks chicons (shoots) should begin to appear. As the top of each chicon shows through the sawdust covering, dig down to the base and cut off chicon at the root. Chicons should measure about 5 inches long and 3 inches across. Once the main chicon has been harvested, several more smaller chicons will grow from root.

To grow leaf chicory, sow seeds directly in the garden as soon as the ground can be worked in spring. Seeds will germinate at low temperatures, like lettuce, and seedlings are frost hardy. Plant seeds 1/4 inch deep and thin to stand 12 inches apart, in rows 12 inches apart. Leaf chicory is also good to grow as a fall crop. Sow seeds in midsummer. Plants are hardy so they will normally survive in the garden until a hard freeze.

Pest and disease control: Slugs and snails may be a problem, even in greenhouses. Place slug bait in shallow pans near the plantings.

Harvesting and use: Leaf chicory is harvested like lettuce. Roots of chicory make an excellent substitute for coffee. Wash and peel, then cut into small diced pieces. Roast in an oven at 300F (114C) until crisp and brown. Grind and add one part chicory to one part coffee for a strong, dark brew.

Recommended varieties: With most varieties of witloof chicory, the sawdust covering over roots is essential to keep heads tight. Without a cover—just darkness—heads will be loose. Several new hybrid varieties are now available that can produce tight heads without the covering. Developed in Europe, the most popular varieties are 'Normato', early; 'Mitado', midseason; and 'Tardivo', late. Try growing them in a tub or pot. Cover with another upturned pot to provide the required darkness. Available from Thompson & Morgan.

A cross between chicory and endive results in 'Sugarhat' (90 days), usually listed in seed catalogs under chicory. It is a salad green like lettuce but hardier. Because of its hardiness, it is useful to grow as a fall vegetable. Available from Burpee and Twilley.

Collards are nonheading cabbages with tasty leaves.

COLLARDS

These nonheading members of the cabbage family produce nutritious leaves popular in the South as a cooked vegetable green. They not only tolerate hot weather, but survive temperatures down to 15F (−9C).

Plants are taller than cabbage, standing 2 to 3 feet high at maturity. They tolerate poor soils, but respond well to high-nitrogen fertilizers and side dressings of stable manure.

How to grow: Seeds can be sown directly in the garden several weeks before your last frost date in spring. A midsummer planting is preferred because it allows plants to reach peak maturity by fall. Sow 1/4 inch deep in rows spaced 2 feet apart. Allow 1-1/2 feet of space between plants. Although seedlings tolerate mild frosts, seeds need high temperatures to germinate. To gain earliest crops, you can start seeds indoors in peat pots or peat pellets 5 to 6 weeks before outdoor planting. Seeds germinate in about 5 days at 70F (21C) soil temperature. Because young seedlings are susceptible to damage from damping-off disease, consider treating soil with captan.

Pest and disease control: Collards attract the same insect pests as cabbage. Rotenone organic vegetable dust or Sevin chemical spray will protect plants from most chewing insects. Dipel and Thuricide are good organic controls against caterpillars. Aphids are occasionally a problem. Blast them off plants with a water hose, or rub them off with a gloved hand while colonies are still small.

Harvesting and use: Pick leaves as soon as plants are established. If grown as a fall crop, pick leaves after frost—cold tends to improve their flavor.

Recommended varieties: 'Georgia' (80 days) produces juicy, blue-green leaves.

Witloof chicory produces *chicons*—young shoots from roots stored indoors in a dark area.

Jicama tubers taste like water chestnuts.

Kale 'Dwarf Blue Curled Vates'.

JICAMA

Also known as Mexican potato, jicama (pronounced *hik-ama*) is a vigorous, vining plant that produces edible tubers. They taste like water chestnuts without the starchiness. To grow full-size tubers as large as a grapefruit, plant needs 9 months of warm, frost-free weather. It will produce small, usable tubers with 4 months of warm weather. It has been grown with great success in a Pennsylvania garden.

Jicama is also grown as an ornamental to cover arbors and chain-link fences. The plants are spectacular, with large, shiny, heart-shaped leaves. Vines grow to 20 feet long in one season, bearing attractive, purple, pealike blossoms.

How to grow: In northern states and short-season areas, start seeds indoors at 70F to 80F (21C to 27C) soil temperature 8 to 10 weeks before outdoor planting. Because plants are damaged by frost, transplant only after all danger of frost has passed. In areas with a growing season of 250 days or more, seeds can be sown 1 inch deep directly in the garden. Plant in mounded rows spaced 2 feet apart and water during dry spells. Vines can be allowed to sprawl over the ground, but need at least 6 feet of space. To save space, they may be trained on a trellis. Large, heart-shaped leaves are highly ornamental.

Pest and disease control: Plant has its own built-in pesticide. Leaves, flowers and seeds are toxic to pests as well as to humans.

Harvesting and use: Dig tubers carefully from soil prior to frost. When the outside skin is peeled, the sweet, crisp inside flesh can be eaten raw or cooked.

Recommended varieties: Generally not sold by variety name. Gurney and Thompson & Morgan are sources for seed.

KALE

Kale is a cool-season plant originating from Europe and closely related to cabbage. It is valued for its nutritional content. It contains more Vitamin A, ascorbic acid and iron by weight than snap beans, corn or peppers. Kale is an extremely hardy plant, often surviving freezes and producing fresh greens during winter months. Several varieties are popular in home gardens, including plain-leaf and curly kinds. Colors range from light green to blue-green.

How to grow: Seeds can be sown directly in the garden in spring, or midsummer for a fall crop. Plant 1/4 inch deep in rows spaced 2 feet apart. Thin resulting seedlings so individual plants stand 1-1/2 feet apart. Do not allow the soil to form a crust because this will inhibit germination. Crusting can be avoided by frequent watering until seeds sprout, or cover soil with a thin layer of mulch.

Kale tolerates a wide pH range, from 5.5 to 6.5. Soil enriched with garden compost or well-decomposed animal manure is preferred.

Pest and disease control: Spraying with Sevin or dusting with rotenone organic pesticide helps to control flea beetles. Organic controls such as Dipel or Thuricide will reduce damage from cabbage worms. Planting through black plastic normally prevents entrance of root maggots into the soil. Kale shows some natural tolerance to attack from root maggots.

Harvesting and use: Plants that grow quickly have better flavor than those that grow slowly. Avoid eating older leaves because they are often bitter. Younger shoots and leaves have a sweet flavor. Frost also helps to improve flavor of leaves. Kale freezes well. Because it is so hardy, it may be better to maintain a few plants through the winter for greens out of season.

Recommended varieties: 'Dwarf Blue Curled Vates' (55 days), has low, compact growth habit and attractive, curly leaves.

Close-up of the popular 'Sugar Snap' pea.

PEAS

Peas have been cultivated for thousands of years, and have been discovered buried in the tombs of Egyptian pharoahs. The original wild species has never been found, although evidence points to eastern Africa and western Asia as possible origins.

Three kinds of peas are grown in home gardens: *English peas,* which require shelling; *edible-pod peas,* which have tiny peas but edible pods; and *snap peas,* which produce plump, sweet peas and thick, edible pods. Snap peas are the newest of the three, developed from a breeding program in Idaho.

All three kinds prefer cool growing conditions. They are hardy and tolerate mild frosts. In the South and southern California they are grown as a winter crop.

Seed catalogs often classify peas as *smooth seeded* or *wrinkle seeded.* This describes the appearance of the peas when dried. It is an important flavor consideration. Wrinkle-seeded peas are considered much sweeter than smooth-seeded kinds, but smooth-seeded peas produce an extra-early crop.

Peas stop bearing at the onset of hot weather. In some instances, they can be cut to the ground and encouraged to sprout a second crop in fall. It is possible to plant a crop in summer for fall harvests.

How to grow: Because seeds are easy to handle and will germinate at 45F (7C) soil temperature, they are best sown directly in the garden early in spring. Plant 1 to 2 inches deep in double rows spaced 3 to 6 inches apart, 2 feet between the next double row. They tolerate crowding and can be spaced 2 inches apart in the row. Most pea varieties are climbers, requiring a trellis for support. Dwarf types are available and they help to support each other without a trellis if planted in double rows. Even dwarf varieties are more productive and resist rot if planted along a short trellis.

Pea flowers are self-pollinating. They set pods automatically once they start flowering. They prefer sandy soil with plenty of organic matter. Add a general-purpose fertilizer to the soil a few weeks before planting because seedlings are sensitive to fertilizer burn.

Pest and disease control: Usually not a serious problem. Deer love the young vines and may need to be fenced out. Occasionally, pea aphids are a nuisance. They can be controlled by a dousing from the garden hose, or by using a vegetable dust such as rotenone. Slugs and cutworms sometimes cause damage. The pea weevil is a pest that enters the developing pods. It bores a hole and lays eggs inside the pea without leaving a noticeable mark. The larvae hatches while the pea is in storage and eats its way out. Sevin and rotenone control the adults. Peas are more susceptible to diseases than any other natural hazard. Seeds can be lost to rotting, which is why many seed houses offer seeds treated with a mild organic fungicide. Choose disease-resistant varieties, especially kinds that resist fusarium wilt, downy mildew and leaf curl virus.

Harvesting and use: Peas should be picked on a regular basis. Once vines start to flower, pods grow quickly, especially after rainfall. The more you pick, the more peas the vine will be able to produce. In addition to eating fresh

English pea 'Burpeeana Early' can be grown without supports. Pick at this stage.

English pea 'Novella' is a dwarf. Because it has extra tendrils, it is self-supporting when grown in double rows.

'Oregon Sugar Pod' grows to only 28 inches tall, but is best grown on a trellis of chicken wire.

from the vine, peas are excellent for freezing. English peas are favored for storing dry and for canning.

EDIBLE-POD PEAS

The Chinese prize these peas and use them extensively. Sometimes called *snow peas* or *sugar peas,* they must be picked young before peas start to swell the pod. If allowed to mature, the pod takes on a fibrous quality. The current favorite variety is 'Oregon Sugar Pod' (68 days).

'Dwarf Gray Sugar' (65 days) is earlier than 'Oregon Sugar Pod' and can be grown without supports. A short trellis of chicken wire will encourage greater production and keep vines clean.

ENGLISH PEAS

These peas have two drawbacks. They must be shelled, which is tedious, and they require a lot of space to produce a sizeable crop. Some new varieties with extra-long pods have come onto the market. The best of these seems to be the disease-resistant variety 'Maestro' (61 days), developed by Cornell University. 'Maestro' yields up to 11 peas in each pod.

'Novella' (70 days) is a reliable, self-supporting pea. The unique quality of 'Novella' is its unusual number of tendrils, which intermingle with other pea plants to make a self-supporting row. The peas are small and sweet. Vines are high yielding. The tendrils can be eaten cooked, imparting a flavor similar to broccoli.

Other favorites include 'Burpeeana Early' (63 days), and 'Wando' (68 days). 'Wando' is one of the best for hot-summer areas.

SNAP PEAS

This variety makes pea growing worthwhile for space-conscious gardeners. Plump, sweet peas with thick, edible-pods ensure twice the amount of produce by weight compared to other pea types. 'Sugar Snap' (70 days) won an All-America Award for its many virtues.

This 15-foot row of 'Sugar Snap' peas produced over 1,000 pods at one picking. Vines were so heavy with peas they bent over the chicken wire fence used for support.

INSIDE REPORT: 'SUGAR SNAP' PEA

When gardener and author Derek Fell was director of All-America Selections, the national seed trials, he discussed the possibility of entering a new type of pea called a *snap pea* with Calvin Lamborn, a plant breeder from Idaho. The more Lamborn described its unique qualities—fat edible pods, plump sweet peas—the more Fell urged him to enter it.

The pea was duly entered, tested throughout the United States, and promptly carried off a Gold Medal—the highest award for any vegetable. It took three years for the breeder to grow sufficient seed to supply the anticipated demand. 'Sugar Snap' pea gained instant acceptance with gardeners in a blaze of publicity never before given a new vegetable.

Let Calvin Lamborn tell you about it in his own words:

"In 1969, during my first year with Gallatin Valley Seed Co., Dr. M.C. Parker, then research director, explained to me his many research projects. Among these projects was a plant-breeding program to reduce parchment and strings in edible-pod peas. He had nearly abandoned the project because the pods with less parchment or strings were more distorted and therefore less desirable.

"Dr. Parker later showed me a mutant found in peas, called a *tight pod.* I examined this mutant form to learn why the pods were tight. I was surprised to find its pod walls were twice as thick as other peas. If the pod walls of edible-pod peas were twice as thick, perhaps, they wouldn't become distorted when the parchment and strings were reduced.

"This tight-podded mutation also had good-quality shelled peas. It appeared feasible that a cross between this rogue and a standard edible-pod pea might produce a thick pod without distortion and having good-quality peas.

"The cross was made and the result proved different enough from the standard edible pods and shelled peas to be considered a new vegetable. It has thick, crisp pod walls without parchment. Pods are tight and free from distortion. When the pod is bent, it will snap like a fresh, snap-bean pod, hence we call them *snap peas.* These peas can be used as a multipurpose vegetable. Pods and peas together are exceptional. Peas can be shelled out and used alone. One pod wall is as thick or thicker than the whole standard edible pod. They also can be cooked like standard edible pods.

"These snap peas are good either fresh or cooked. They are excellent for freezing, but not for canning. A good way to cook them is to stir-fry them in hot oil just a few minutes—long enough for the pods to change to a dark green color."

Dwarf varieties of snap peas are also becoming available. 'Sugar Bon', 'Sugar Mel' and 'Sugar Rae' grow 18 to 30 inches high. 'Sugar Bon' is said to be earlier and more heat resistant than 'Sugar Snap'. Available from Park and Henry Field's.

Rhubarb can be grown from roots or seeds.

RHUBARB

Wild varieties of rhubarb are widely dispersed throughout Asia, particularly in Turkey, India and China. But it wasn't until the 18th century that European gardeners began cultivating it in any quantity.

A hardy perennial, rhubarb is grown for its tart, succulent leaf stalks, which are usually boiled to produce a delicious sauce or pie filling. Stems are light green or red, depending on variety. The dark green leaf area itself is not edible. It contains poisonous amounts of oxalic acid.

Rhubarb is a cool-weather plant. It will not do well wherever temperatures are consistantly above 75F (24C) during summer, or above 40F (5C) during winter.

The coloring of rhubarb stalks is greatly affected by weather conditions. In cool climates such as the Pacific Northwest, the red coloring is intensified. Plants are larger in cool areas, with leaves reaching up to 10 feet high. The same variety in a warmer climate may grow no more than 3 feet high.

How to grow: Rhubarb is most often grown from roots or *crowns,* purchased through mail order catalogs or from local garden centers. These roots are usually planted in spring, allowing some pickings the second season. Rhubarb can also be grown from seed. If plants receive adequate moisture and nutrients, seed-grown rhubarb will also produce pickings the following season.

Planting from roots: When planting roots, the biggest danger is rot. Plant in full sun in well-drained soil. Do not bury the crown—place it level with the soil surface. Space roots 3 feet apart in rows 3 feet wide. If soil is poor quality, dig a trench or individual planting holes 2 feet wide. Fill with a mixture of equal parts garden topsoil, sand, and garden compost or decomposed stable manure. A fairly acid soil—pH 5.0 to 6.0—is best. Water regularly during dry spells. The importance of regular moisture cannot be overemphasized. In addition to soil quality, it is the most important requirement for rhubarb. Waterlogging should be avoided because it can cause rot. Planting in raised beds helps prevent rotting. In areas where winter temperatures fall to 10F to 20F (−12C to −7C), heap some protective mulch over the crowns after soil has frozen. Straw or shredded leaves will form a protective blanket that can be removed after the spring thaw.

Planting from seed: Seeds are large and easy to handle. Plant them directly in the garden 1 inch deep in groups spaced 3 feet apart. Thin seedlings in each group to the most healthy plant. If flower stems appear, cut them back. Seed production can drain the plant of energy. After plants have reached three years of age, roots can be divided to create more plants.

Pest and disease control: Concentrate on repelling the rhubarb curculio, also known as snout beetle. It bores into the stalks, crowns and roots, causing rot. It is usually found around wild dock, a common garden weed. Dusting plants with rotenone or spraying with Sevin will help keep this pest under control. Destroy plantings of wild dock around your garden, which can harbor the pest.

Harvesting and use: Do not harvest the first year after planting, and harvest only 2 or 3 weeks of the second year. Once plants are established the third year, begin as soon as leaf stalks are large enough. Once the ground thaws, growth is rapid. Rhubarb is one of the first vegetables to be harvested in spring. Harvest can continue until hot weather sets in, after which the stalks deteriorate in quality. To remove stalks from the plant, grasp a stalk firmly near its base and pull away from the plant. Stalk should come off cleanly, resulting in a "spoon" shape at its end. Do not cut stalks from the plant, as this can damage root and induce rot. Rhubarb freezes well for eating out of season.

FORCING RHUBARB

Roots can be *forced* into producing early yields. To force, follow these steps:

Outdoors. In areas of the country with severe winters, wait until daffodil leaves start to poke through the soil. At this time, cover the dormant rhubarb roots with a garbage can, bucket or barrel. Heap straw or shredded leaves around the container for insulation. Check under the container in about five weeks. Stalks should be ready for harvesting.

Indoors. Before the ground freezes, dig up roots and plant in tubs. Leave them exposed to frosty weather for several weeks, then bring inside to a warm basement or greenhouse. Cover with a box or anything that will exclude light, and water to keep moist. Edible stalks should be ready for harvesting in 4 to 5 weeks.

Recommended varieties: Most gardeners prefer red-stemmed rhubarb to green-stemmed varieties. 'MacDonald' or 'Valentine' are most popular. 'Victoria' is a popular green-stemmed variety.

Alpine strawberry 'Baron Solemacher'.

Sunflower 'Sunbird' hybrid grows large seedheads.

ALPINE STRAWBERRY

Alpine strawberry, *Fragaria vesca,* is similar to the common cultivated strawberry, *Fragaria x ananassa.* But many gardeners consider alpine strawberry a berry fruit rather than a vegetable fruit. Because it grows from seeds rather than roots, it is usually listed in the vegetable section of seed catalogs. The vegetable garden is only one place to grow the bushy, compact plants. They also make an attractive ground cover in the landscape. Berries are sweet and appear the first season if seeds are started early indoors.

How to grow: Start seeds indoors 8 to 10 weeks before planting outdoors. Seeds are tiny and need light to germinate, so do not cover them completely with soil. Press seeds into moist soil to anchor them. Germination can be erratic, but seedlings will make an appearance after 14 to 21 days. Plant outdoors after all danger of frost has passed, although alpine strawberry will tolerate mild frost. Space plants 8 to 12 inches apart in rows spaced 1-1/2 to 2 feet apart.

Never allow the soil surface to dry out after planting. Maintain moisture by misting soil surface with a spray bottle. Water flowing from a watering can or hose will disturb the seeds.

Pest and disease control: Generally pest and disease-free until plants begin bearing fruit. When fruit appear, cover rows with plastic netting to protect against birds and mice. If berries come in contact with soil they will rot. Prevent rot by applying a mulch of straw or other organic material over the soil.

Harvesting and use: Start picking fruit as soon as they are ripe—midsummer to fall—on a continuous basis. Eat fresh as a dessert fruit or serve with fresh cream. Berries can also be frozen and made into delicious jam.

Recommended varieties: 'Alexandria' (100 days), available from Park and Thompson & Morgan, produces the largest fruit. Plant breeders are in the process of creating varieties with even larger fruit. Seed of 'Alexandria' is sometimes in short supply. If unavailable, 'Baron Solemacher' (105 days) is a good substitute.

SUNFLOWER

Giant sunflowers are native to the American continent. They are grown mainly for their highly nutritious seeds, which are edible when shelled. They grow quickly, producing beautiful flowers that mature into heavy seedheads measuring up to 24 inches across. In a single season, a sunflower can grow to 20 feet high. They are best confined to a special area of the vegetable garden, where they will not shade other vegetables. Sunflowers also emit a toxin from their roots that inhibits growth of nearby plants. This will affect vegetable plants if they are planted within 3 feet.

How to grow: Sow seeds directly in the garden in a sunny location after all danger of frost has passed. Seeds are large and easy to handle. Plant 1 inch deep, 1 foot apart in rows spaced 3 feet apart. Germination occurs in 10 days at 70F (21C) soil temperature. Soil should be fertile for largest heads and meatiest seeds. Plants respond to a general-purpose fertilizer worked into the soil at the start of the season. Follow with a booster application when flower heads appear.

Pest and disease control: The biggest pest problem is birds that strip seeds from the mature flowerheads. Many gardeners like to plant sunflowers around the home specifically to attract birds. If *you* want the seeds, tie cheesecloth or clear plastic bags with air holes around the heads when they are nearly ripe.

Harvesting and use: Begin when the seedhead becomes so heavy it appears ready to bend over and spill its seeds on the ground. Cut heads and hang in a warm, dry place. When heads have dried, rub the surface with your hand and seeds will fall out. Seeds are high in protein and can be roasted, shelled and eaten as snacks. Health food stores sell machines that will dehull seeds. Sunflowers are also rich in oil.

Recommended varieties: 'Sunbird' (68 days) is a dwarf variety, producing large heads on stems that grow half the height of regular giant sunflowers. Burpee is a source. The variety to grow for the largest seedheads is 'Mammoth Russian' (80 days), available from most mail order sources.

HERBS

Herbs have played an important part in the history of civilization. Ancient cultures such as the Chinese, Abyssinians, Greeks, Romans, Egyptians and Aztecs took advantage of the culinary and medicinal properties associated with herbs. Many herbs became valued as cosmetics, fumigants, deodorants, insect repellents and dyes. Some were thought to possess supernatural properties and were used in religious ceremonies. Herbs were also associated with witchcraft and sorcery in ancient times—probably due to their potency. With most herbs, a little goes a long way.

Early settlers brought European herbs to America, mostly for use as kitchen flavorings and medicines. In colonial times, an herb garden by the kitchen door was regarded as a necessity. As cities became larger and stores made herbal products and substitutes more available, herb gardening declined.

Today, there is a renewed interest in growing herbs. People are discovering that herbs fresh from the garden are much more flavorful than dried, packaged products.

GROWING HERBS OUTDOORS

The most surprising fact about herbs is how easy most are to grow. In the wild, they exist in some of the most inhospitable places, sprouting and growing like weeds after every rainfall. The biggest problem with herbs in the home garden is keeping them tidy and within bounds. Sinking a container planted with herbs into the soil is a good way to keep some of the aggressive kinds from becoming invasive.

With most culinary herbs, a single, healthy planting is sufficient for a year's supply for an average family. Instead of planting herbs in rows as you would vegetables, tuck them into odd corners of the garden. Or create a special area where you can grow one or two plants, or many different kinds. If you are interested in an ornamental effect, herbs work well as borders, ground covers and low hedges. You may want to plant a traditional *knot garden.*

Herbs generally require an open, sunny location and good soil drainage. Soil fertility is not always necessary, but the majority of popular herbs prefer a light, sandy soil amended with plenty of organic matter.

Planting and propagation. Many popular herbs can be grown easily from seeds, and are started the same way as vegetables. Most herbs are *biennials,* plants that live for two years, or *perennials,* plants that live for more than two years. Perennials are easily propagated by dividing established clumps. This is done by digging into an established planting with a hand trowel or shovel. You can then separate a clump complete with roots and soil for transplanting. Chives, mint, lavender and tarragon are easily divided.

In some cases, a stem cutting can be taken. Roots will sprout by immersing the cutting in water or moist potting soil. Mint can be propagated this way.

Left: Knot garden is created from low hedges of herbs at Filoli Estate, Woodland, California. Gentle curves produce a pleasing, informal atmosphere. Above: Chives in bloom create a beautiful border against picket fence.

Hardy annual herbs such as basil are usually grown from seeds. They die down after the first season but usually reseed freely. Hardy biennial herbs such as parsley generally survive the winter and go to seed the second season. Hardy perennial herbs such as chives, mint and lavender sometimes become permanently established, growing thicker and wider each year.

Although many perennial herbs are hardy to cold, a protective mulch of straw, pine needles or shredded leaves is advisable where freezing temperatures occur. Place over and around plants to a depth of 3 inches.

GROWING HERBS IN CONTAINERS

Many herbs grow well in containers indoors on a sunny windowsill. Some may not have as rich a flavor when grown indoors, but still provide zest to meals. Clay pots 6 inches in diameter are best if you have the room, but even 4-inch pots produce useful plants.

Container herbs should be grown in a soil mix composed of two parts sterile potting soil and one part course sand or perlite. When plants get too tall and "leggy," prune them back to a compact, dome shape. Position plants in a south- or east-facing window. Although most herbs tolerate warm, dry conditions, summer sun streaming through the window can burn plants. Mist plants in summer and keep soil moist but not water-logged.

Although herbs generally do well in poor soil, give them a weak, liquid fertilizer once every two weeks at time of watering.

USING AND PRESERVING HERBS

With the exception of herbs grown for their aromatic seeds, pick *young* leaves and stems for culinary use. The top whorl of leaves of a basil plant, for example, is much more flavorful than older, lower leaves.

Drying is the most popular way to store herbs for extended periods. To dry herbs, harvest plant parts early in the day. This is when they are most flavorful. Rinse plants with cold water and hang them by their stems. Air-dry in a dry, dark, well-ventilated place, such as a garage or storage shed. Or spread herbs on cookie sheets lined with wax paper. Drying is complete when leaves feel crumbly, which takes about 7 to 10 days. Oven drying is the quickest method, but most volatile oils are lost and flavor is reduced. Low, gentle heat with good air circulation is preferred. If you choose to dry in an oven, spread on a baking sheet and set oven to 200F (76C). Drying times vary but usually an hour or less is sufficient. Store dried herbs out of direct sun to preserve their oil content.

Certain herbs freeze well. Parsley, mint, basil and burnet are just a few. Harvest young leaves. Wash and blanch in boiling water for 50 seconds. Cool quickly in ice water, drain, then package and freeze. Basil, chives and dill can be frozen without blanching.

COOKING WITH HERBS

Some of the most basic foods take on gourmet flavors with the addition of a simple herb. Taste the difference in scrambled eggs with a sprinkling of chives. Add chopped parsley to mashed potatoes. Sprinkle finely chopped chervil leaves over a green salad. Crush a sprig of mint into a glass of iced tea. Sprinkle some flakes of chopped basil leaves over stewed tomatoes.

Use herbs sparingly until you learn how a given amount affects the flavor of a dish. Aromatic oils of herbs are often strong, and too much of any flavor can be objectionable.

Following is a selection of the most useful and easy-to-grow *edible herbs*. They have been chosen for their value as flavorings or herbal teas, rather than for medicinal or cosmetic uses.

A fine example of a formal herb garden can be seen at the Royal Horticultural Society Garden, Wisley, England. Bronze urn serves as a focal point.

Herbs don't have to be planted in a formal garden or in a specific pattern. Casual grouping of assorted herbs combines well with stone walkway.

Mrs. Phyllis Shaudys, herb specialist, dries herbs on trays supported on frames used for drying laundry. Dehumidifier in room helps keep air dry.

ANISE

Pimpinella anisum

An annual growing 1-1/2 to 2 feet high, anise has bright green, finely serrated leaves and small, whitish flowers in flat clusters. Leaves and seeds have a cool, sweet flavor suggestive of licorice.

How to grow: Plants grow rapidly from seeds sown directly into the garden. Sow seeds 1/4 inch deep after all danger of frost has passed. Plant in full sun and in light, well-drained soil. Water regularly. If planted in rows, thin 6 to 8 inches apart in rows 2 feet apart.

Pest and disease control: Generally free of pests and diseases.

Harvesting and use: Green leaves can be cut whenever plants are large enough. Use leaves to make an herbal tea, in salads or as a garnish. Gather seeds about 1 month after flowers bloom. Seeds are good to chew as a breath freshener. Use seeds to flavor confections such as cakes and cookies. Oil from anise seeds is used in medicines.

Recommended varieties: Not sold by variety name. A separate herb, *hyssop,* is sometimes sold as anise.

Pure white flowers of anise appear at top of plants in midsummer. Seeds are usually ready to harvest in fall.

Whole anise seeds can be used as a licorice flavoring in cakes and cookies. Harvest when they are gray-green.

BASIL

Ocimum basilicum

Sweet basil is an attractive annual that grows to about 18 inches tall. It produces light green, broad-pointed leaves and small, white, spikelike flowers.

How to grow: Plants grow easily from seeds sown directly in the garden. Sow seeds 1/4 inch deep after all danger of frost has passed. Thin plants to stand 12 inches apart. Basil likes full sun and moist, well-drained soil. Pinch stems to promote bushy, compact growth.

Pest and disease control: Basil is considered by some to be an insect repellent, but slugs and snails love it and will strip leaves from plants. Control with slug bait. Place bait in shallow dishes so the poison does not contaminate the soil. Japanese beetles are also attracted to basil. Use beetle traps or pyrethrum insecticide as organic controls. Use Sevin as a chemical control.

Harvesting and use: Green leaves can be picked about 6 weeks following planting. Harvest leaves for drying just before flowers open. Spicy-scented basil leaves, fresh or dried, are one of the most popular of all kitchen herbs. Cooks favor basil for all kinds of tomato dishes. Add it to soups, vegetables and Italian dishes.

Recommended varieties: 'Dark Opal' is highly ornamental with glossy purple leaves and purple flower spikes. Use it as a background planting in contrast to brightly colored flowers such as yellow marigolds. Other varieties include 'Lettuce Leaf', 'Lemon' and 'Well-Sweep Miniature'.

Rows of sweet basil are at peak maturity, just prior to flowering. Top whorl of new leaves is the most flavorful.

The bright blue, star-shaped flowers of borage are decorative as well as useful. Their cucumberlike flavor is refreshing in summer drinks.

Burnet has a cucumber flavor like borage. Add the fresh leaves to salads or cold drinks. Use dried leaves in salad dressings and soups.

Caraway is grown for its seeds, which appear soon after flowering. Add them to meat stews, fish casseroles, coleslaw and cheese spreads.

BORAGE
Borago officinalis

This decorative annual has beautiful, sky-blue, star-shaped flowers. Gray-green leaves grow to 5 inches long. Plants grow 2 to 3 feet tall with an equal spread.

How to grow: Borage is best grown from seeds sown directly in the garden. It is difficult to transplant. Sow seeds 1/4 inch deep after all danger of frost has passed. Thin plants to stand 2 feet apart. Borage does best in dry, sunny places.

Pest and disease control: Chewing insects such as Japanese beetles may attack the leaves. Pyrethrum or Sevin will control them. Also consider beetle traps.

Harvesting and use: Sprays of borage flowers and leaves are used to give a cool, cucumberlike flavor to summer drinks. Pick blossoms as they open. Use young, fresh leaves—they are not as flavorful when dried.

BURNET
Poterium sanguisorba

This vigorous perennial herb forms dense, mound-shaped clumps. Leaves are dark green and toothed, and unfold like an accordion. Plant grows 2 feet high and spreads 2 feet wide.

How to grow: Plant in full sun. Burnet is best sown directly in the garden. Its long taproot makes transplanting difficult. Sow seeds 1/4 inch deep and thin plants to stand 12 inches apart. Burnet tolerates poor soil but does best in sandy, well-drained soil. Propagate by dividing roots of a healthy, established clump.

Pest and disease control: Relatively pest- and disease-free.

Harvesting and use: Pick leaves as soon as they are large enough to handle. Burnet lends a cucumber flavor to cold drinks and wines. Leaves can also be chopped fine and sprinkled over salads. Drying destroys the flavor, so store leaves by freezing.

CARAWAY
Carum carvi

Caraway is a biennial plant that grows in a mound to about 30 inches high. Flowers appear in flat, white clusters. Finely cut, bright green leaves resemble carrots.

How to grow: Caraway is easily grown from seeds. Plants do not usually bear seeds the first year. If planted in fall, they produce seeds the following year. Caraway is not easily transplanted. Sow directly in the garden 3 weeks before last frost date. If planted in rows, thin 8 to 12 inches apart in rows 3 feet apart. Plant prefers loose, well-drained soil. Protect roots with a mulch in winter.

Pest and disease control: Relatively free of pests and diseases.

Harvesting and use: Seeds should be harvested when ripe. This is usually a month after flowering when seeds turn grayish brown. Seeds have a distinctive, aromatic odor and flavor. Oil of caraway seeds is an important ingredient in liqueurs. Use seeds in Hungarian-type dishes, coleslaw, cheese spreads, meat stews and fish casseroles.

CATNIP
Nepeta cataria

Catnip is a hardy perennial plant that grows 3 to 4 feet high. Heart-shaped leaves are gray-green. Flowers are usually white or blue.

How to grow: Plant seeds or propagate by division. Sow seeds 1/4 inch deep. Thin plants to stand 2 feet apart. Catnip is best planted in spring or late fall. Prefers fertile, sandy soil. When young, plants are decorative and compact. As they grow older, they become straggly. Use catnip as an ornamental background plant.

Pest and disease control: Generally free of pests and disease, but *cats* can be pests. They can destroy new plantings. Protect plants with netting or a wooden frame covered with chicken wire until they become established, and are better able to withstand "attention" from cats.

Harvesting and use: Cut and dry mature leafy tops and leaves at any stage of development. Catnip leaves are used for tea and seasoning.

Recommended varieties: Normally not sold by variety name. Two ornamental kinds listed in mail order catalogs and sold by variety or species name are *Nepeta mussinii* and 'Six Hills Giant'.

CHERVIL
Anthriscus cerefolium

This is a hardy annual that grows up to 2 feet high and spreads 1 foot wide. Lacy leaves resemble parsley but are a lighter shade of green. Small, delicate, white flowers appear in flat clusters.

How to grow: Sow seeds directly in the garden 3 weeks before last frost date. Seedlings are difficult to transplant. Thin plants 3 to 4 inches apart. Plant in fertile soil in a sunny site. Keep soil moist. For denser foliage, cut flower stems before they bloom.

Pest and disease control: Generally free of pests and disease.

Harvesting and use: Leaves are best used fresh. Pick them just before buds open for maximum flavor. Cut, dry and store the green, tender leaves. Use as a garnish on salads, soups and egg dishes. Add it to melted butter for a fish or chicken baste.

CHIVES
Allium schoenoprasum

Chives are small, dainty, onionlike plants. They grow in clumps that reach about 10 inches high. These hardy perennials with decorative, bright pink flowers make attractive border plants.

Garlic chives, *Allium tuberosum,* are similar in appearance to regular chives but leaves have a slight garlic flavor. Plants are a little larger and produce clusters of beautiful white flowers on tall stems. They are perennials, and are harvested and used like chives.

How to grow: Seeds can be sown directly in the garden 3 weeks before last frost date. However, it is better to start them indoors. Sow seeds 1/4 inch deep in a tray filled with potting soil. Transplant small clumps of seedlings 12 inches apart in rows spaced 2 feet apart. Chives thrive in poor soil, but perform best in an organically rich soil high in phosphorus. They require little care, other than dividing

Catnip is often grown in perennial borders as an ornamental. It is also valued for its aromatic leaves, which make a refreshing tea.

Chervil is best grown in a clump planting rather than a row. Harvest the leaves like parsley. Chervil gives a mild, anise flavor to soups, salads and egg dishes.

This is a 2-year-old clump of chives. Leaves add a zesty, onionlike flavor to foods. Flowers are edible and highly ornamental.

Comfrey plants grow in a neat mound. Chop the vitamin-rich leaves very fine and add to salads, or cook small amounts to eat like spinach.

Coriander in full bloom. The seeds that follow are valued for their perfume scent and flavor. Use them as a condiment in confections.

plants when overcrowded. Easily propagated by division.

Pest and disease control: Remarkably pest- and disease-free. Chives are regarded as an effective insect repellent. They are often used around other vegetables for natural insect control. Chives do attract greenfly on rare occasions. They can be washed off plants with a soap and water solution.

Harvesting and use: Use chives to impart a delicious, subtle, onionlike flavor to foods. Grow them in containers on a sunny windowsill and cut fresh leaves whenever you need them.

COMFREY
Symphytum officinale

More curative powers are claimed for comfrey than any other herb. The name is a corruption of *con firma*, alluding to its reputation for healing broken bones and wounds.

A popular catalog describes comfrey as follows: "This is one of the key plants in herbal remedies. Up to 33% protein is contained in the leaves and it is high in vitamins and minerals. Probably the only plant known to man that contains vitamin B12, normally found only in raw liver and raw egg yolk. It also contains vitamins A, C, E and the B complex. It has a case history of benefits to the kidneys and urinary tract. Herbalists claim it is one of the only herbs that help prevent cataracts of the eyes in middle age."

Comfrey is a hardy perennial. It grows as a vigorous clump of large, pointed, dark green leaves to 3 feet high and 2-1/2 feet wide.

How to grow: Plants are easily grown from seeds, but are easier to cultivate from root cuttings. Roots are brittle. A small piece of root will sprout a new plant. If you start from seeds, sow 1/4 inch deep directly in the garden 3 weeks before last frost date. Thin seedlings to stand 2-1/2 to 3 feet apart. Comfrey is not particular as to soil quality, but grows best in soil rich in organic matter. Requires regular amounts of water.

Pest and disease control: Relatively pest- and disease-free. Snails may eat holes in leaves, but damage is rarely extensive enough to worry about.

Harvesting and use: Harvest leaves selectively, choosing some from each plant. Leaves can be chopped fine and sprinkled on salads or cooked like spinach. Use comfrey sparingly.

Recommended varieties: In addition to green varieties, there are pink, red and green-and-white variegated types.

CORIANDER
Coriandrum sativum

Coriander is a dainty annual that grows to 2 feet tall. Aromatic seeds are known as *coriander*. Leaves are known as *Chinese parsley* or *cilantro*. White or purplish-tinged flowers appear in small, flat heads.

How to grow: Easily grown from seeds. Sow directly in the garden after all danger of frost has passed. Long taproot makes transplanting difficult. Plant seeds 1/4 inch deep and thin plants 6 to 10 inches apart. Does best in well-prepared garden soil that has good drainage. Requires regular amounts of water.

Pest and disease control: Generally free of pests and diseases.

Harvesting and use: Gather seeds as they ripen in mid-summer. They are round, about 1/8 inch in diameter, and have a delicious taste and perfume smell. Coriander seeds are used as a condiment in confections. Freshly chopped leaves can be added sparingly to soups, salads and stir-fried dishes.

DILL
Anethum graveolens

This popular annual herb has bluish green stems that contrast with finely divided, yellow-green, plumelike leaves and yellowish flowers. Plants grow about 2 to 3 feet high and 1 foot wide.

How to grow: Seedlings do not transplant well, so grow from seeds sown directly in the garden. Sow 1/4 inch deep 3 weeks before last frost date. Thin plants to stand 9 to 18 inches apart. Plants may need staking in rich, loose soils.

Pest and disease control: Generally free of pests and diseases. Rabbits sometimes eat young dill plants. Keep rabbits out with fencing. Aphids and greenfly are occasionally attracted to young stems. Wash them off with spray from a garden hose, or rub them away with a gloved hand. Sevin is an effective chemical spray. Dill becomes a pest itself unless confined to a special area of the garden. Seeds scatter and come up like weeds the following year.

Harvesting and use: For best results, pick leaves just as flowers open. Pick seeds when they are flat and brown. Leaves and seeds are popular for flavoring pickles, sauerkraut and beet dishes. Dill can be combined with garlic and pepper to produce a highly flavored, Mediterranean or East European pork roast.

FENNEL
Foeniculum vulgare azoricum

Two kinds of fennel are frequently listed in seed catalogs. *Florence fennel,* the more popular type, is grown for its stems and succulent, bulbous base. *Wild fennel* is grown for its anise-flavored leaves.

Fennel is a tender perennial but is usually grown as an annual. It looks similar to dill and grows 2 to 3 feet high, spreading 2 to 3 feet wide. Leaves are feathery and light green. Small yellow flowers are formed in flat clusters in late summer and early fall. Where leaf stalks meet the soil a fleshy, white bulb is formed. Bulb is crisp, crunchy and has a flavor like licorice. Sometimes listed in catalogs as "Finocchio."

How to grow: Fennel grows easily from seeds. Sow seeds 1/4 inch deep directly in the garden 3 weeks before last frost date. Thin plants to stand 10 to 12 inches apart. Plants like full sun but produce larger bulbs under cool conditions. Supply with fertile soil high in organic matter for best results. Space rows 3 feet apart and thin plants 10 to 12 inches apart.

Pest and disease control: Concentrate on eliminating infestations of wireworms and other soil insects. They can chew bulbs, causing discoloration and poor flavor. Compost and wood ashes mixed into the soil may discourage them. Recommended chemical treatment for soil pests is diazinon. Greenfly occasionally attacks young stems. Wash off with soap and water solution.

Dill in full bloom. All parts—flowers, seeds, stems and leaves—are edible but should be used sparingly. Use to flavor meats, pickles and vegetable dishes.

Florence fennel forms a cluster of fleshy stems close to the soil. Cooked or raw, these crisp, succulent stalks have a delicious licorice flavor.

Horehound leaves are the source of a distinctive flavor used in confections and candies. When steeped in hot water they make a refreshing herbal tea.

Harvesting and use: To use as a condiment, pick seeds when dry but before they fall from plant. Stems for eating should be picked before the flower stalks bloom, and before the onset of hot weather. Leaves have an aniselike, licorice flavor. Lower part of the stems can be eaten like celery. Seeds can be used to add flavor to cheese spreads and vegetable dishes.

HOREHOUND
Marrubium vulgare

This tender perennial resembles mint, except plants are covered with a velvety down. Grayish green leaves are crinkled and tend to turn downward. Flowers are white and appear in clusters on stems of plants at least 2 years old. Plants form dense clumps up to 2 feet high with an equal spread. Because of its weedy growth habit, horehound is best placed in the background. Or plant in a sunken container to keep it from becoming invasive.

How to grow: Horehound can be propagated from seeds, cuttings or by division. Sow seeds 1/4 inch deep directly in the garden 3 weeks before last frost date. Thin seedlings to stand 1 to 2 feet apart. Plants grow well in light, sandy soil and withstand full sun and intense heat. Horehound survives mild winters but needs protection in cold-winter areas.

Pest and disease control: Generally free of pests and diseases. It can become a pest itself if allowed to reseed continually.

Harvesting and use: Leaves and small stems can be cut for use before plants bloom. Horehound is the source of the familiar, old-fashioned candy of the same name. It is also used to make an herbal tea.

Recommended varieties: 'Black', 'White', 'Silver' and 'Variegated' are available from herb catalogs.

HYSSOP
Hyssopus officinalis

Hyssop is an evergreen perennial that grows to no more than 2 feet high, spreading to 3 feet wide. It has woody stems, small, pointed green leaves and spikes of small, blue, white or pink flowers. If pruned, it makes an attractive border or small hedge.

How to grow: Hyssop is easily grown from seeds. Sow directly in the garden after all danger of frost has passed. Sow 1/4 inch deep and thin seedlings to stand 2 to 3 feet apart. After hyssop is established, it is a hardy plant. Tolerant of poor soil.

Pest and disease control: Generally free of pests and diseases.

Harvesting and use: Pick leaves just prior to flowering. Pungent leaves are used to flavor liqueurs and as a garnish with meat and fish. Use sparingly to flavor soups and stews. Oil obtained from leaves is used in making perfume. Store by freezing or drying.

Recommended varieties: Common hyssop is the most widely available variety. Some herb specialists also offer 'Anise' hyssop and 'Camphor' hyssop. These names describe the fragrance of their aromatic leaves.

Hyssop is an attractive, compact-growing plant that does best in partial shade. Leaves have a strong, bitter flavor but can be used sparingly to flavor meat dishes.

LEMON BALM
Melissa officinalis

Closely resembling mint in appearance and growth habit, lemon balm spreads like a weed. Confine it to a small planting. Plants grow 2-1/2 feet high, spreading to 2 feet wide. Light green leaves are heavily veined. A variegated type is also available.

How to grow: Plants are easy to grow from seeds. Start them indoors for transplanting or sow directly in the garden. Sow seeds 1/4 inch deep 3 weeks before last spring frost date. Thin plants 2 to 3 feet apart. Tolerates poor soils. Plants die down in winter, but roots are perennial and new growth appears in spring.

Pest and disease control: Generally free of pests and diseases. Sometimes attracts greenfly, which can be washed off plant stems with soap and water solution.

Harvesting and use: As the name suggests, this plant imparts a wonderful lemon fragrance and flavor. Leaves make a delicious herbal tea and can be used as a flavor enhancer in place of lemon. Try it on fish, salads or fruit dishes. When added to iced tea or alcoholic beverages, a crushed sprig of leaves has the same flavoring effect as a slice of lemon.

Fresh leaves of lemon balm add appealing color and flavor to summer drinks. Use dried leaves to make tea, but don't steep too long or flavor will be overpowering.

MARJORAM
Origanum majorana

Marjoram is one of the most fragrant and popular of all herbs, usually grown as an annual. Its growth habit is low, reaching about 1-1/2 feet high spreading up to 2 feet wide. It makes an attractive border plant. Small, oval, gray-green leaves are velvety to the touch. Sweet marjoram is preferred by most gardeners over the similar wild or pot marjoram.

How to grow: Marjoram is easily grown from seeds or cuttings. In cold climates, it is best treated as an annual, or grown in a container and brought inside during cold weather. Sow seeds 1/4 inch deep directly in the garden after all danger of frost has passed. Thin seedlings 1 to 2 feet apart. Plant in an open, sunny location in a well-drained soil.

Pest and disease control: Generally free of pests and diseases.

Harvesting and use: Use leaves fresh anytime or dried as a flavoring in cooking. To dry, cut leafy stems when plant is flowering. Oil derived from leaves is often an ingredient in perfume.

Marjoram, also known as *sweet marjoram,* is a popular herb that can be used fresh or dried. Add it to omelets and vegetable and meat dishes.

OREGANO
Origanum vulgare

Also called *wild marjoram,* this plant is much coarser than sweet marjoram, *Origanum majorana,* and has a scent more like thyme. It is a hardy perennial with sprawling stems that can reach up to 3 feet high. Small flowers are pink or white.

How to grow: Plant seeds 1/4 inch deep 3 weeks before last frost date. Thin plants to stand 10 to 12 inches apart. Plants can also be propagated by division. Tolerates poor soil. Stimulate foliage growth by cutting back flowers. Replant in three or four years when plants become woody.

Pest and disease control: Generally free of pests and diseases.

Oregano is often used in Italian cooking. It is similar to marjoram except it is a cold-hardy perennial; marjoram is an annual.

Peppermint displays its dainty flower clusters and deep purple stems. Use leaves to make a fragrant tea, but don't steep too long or the flavor becomes too strong.

PEPPERMINT
Mentha piperita

Peppermint has an interesting history. It was introduced in England in 1676, a hybrid of watermint and spearmint. It was the first commercial crop grown in England, beginning in 1750. A botanist of the time coined the name "peppermint" to describe it. Today all peppermint crops are derived from those 17th century English hybrids.

Plants are hardy perennials. They produce many upright stems to 2 feet or more high, spreading 1 foot wide in a single season. Dark green leaves and reddish-tinged stems have a pleasant, minty fragrance. Tiny, purplish flowers appear in thick, terminal spikes 1 to 3 inches long.

How to grow: Peppermint grows best in a rich, moist soil, in sun or shade. Propagate by seeds, division or cuttings. Cutting sprigs frequently promotes fast growth.

Mint cuttings root easily in water. This is the preferred method of propagation. Plants can be divided by their roots. If you want to grow from seeds, sow 1/4 inch deep directly in the garden 3 weeks before last frost date. Thin plants to stand 6 inches apart, and allow them to form clumps or matted rows.

Pest and disease control: Mint leaves are susceptible to rust disease. Prune and destroy infected foliage. Winter clean-up of dead plants helps control the disease.

Harvesting and use: Use leaves anytime. To dry for storage, leaves are best harvested just as flowers begin to appear. Leaves are used to make an herbal tea and for other flavorings. Oil from the plant is used in products such as chewing gum, confections, toilet water, soap and liqueur.

Recommended varieties: There are two main varieties— black peppermint and white peppermint. Black peppermint is the variety grown commercially in the United States as a source of peppermint oil. It can be identified by its deep purple stems. White peppermint is less vigorous, less flavorful and has light green leaves and stems.

Rosemary is an attractive plant in the landscape, and a popular flavoring for stews and meat dishes such as pork and veal. Use leaves fresh or dried.

ROSEMARY
Rosmarinus officinalis

Rosemary is an evergreen shrub in areas where winter temperatures stay above 5F (−15C). Plants have dark green, needlelike leaves, woody stems, and tiny, pale blue blossoms. Flowers appear in spring and attract bees. Fragrance is suggestive of nutmeg and pine needles. In colder areas, this perennial should be brought indoors and kept as a pot plant during winter. Varieties vary in form and size. Most are dense, spreading shrubs up to 3 feet wide.

How to grow: Rosemary grows best in well-drained, sunny locations in soil containing lime. Lime should be added each year in acid-soil areas. Plants can be propagated by cuttings or grown from seeds. Sow seeds 1/4 inch deep directly in the garden 3 weeks before last frost date. They require up to 3 weeks or more to germinate. You may also start seeds indoors and transplant. Thin seedlings to stand 1 to 2 inches apart for a dense, hedgelike effect. Plants grow slowly, adding about 6 inches of height each season. Keep moist and mist often during hot weather. Otherwise, plants may drop their leaves. Pinch tops of plants to keep compact.

Pest and disease control: Plants sometimes become infested with red spider mites. They are difficult to control once established. Malathion and dicofol are common chemical sprays used to control mites. Frequent dousing with a soap and water solution is an organic control.

Harvesting and use: Narrow leaves have a spicy fragrance. Use fresh leaves as needed any time of the year. Rosemary is a popular flavoring for meats and dressings, or as a garnish on roasts. Oil from leaves is used in medicines.

Recommended varieties: Over 20 varieties are sold by herb specialists. Different flower colors are available, from deep blue to pink. 'Prostrate' grows to 2 feet high and spreads to 5 feet wide. 'Tuscan Blue' grows upright to 5 feet high.

Sage can be grown as a border plant. Leaves are strongly flavored and can be added to poultry stuffing and meat, egg and vegetable dishes.

SAGE
Salvia officinalis

This is a woody, hardy, perennial plant with oblong, woolly, gray-green leaves. Sage grows 2 to 3 feet or more high, sprawling 2 to 3 feet wide.

How to grow: Start from seeds or cuttings. Sage is slow to begin growth. Sow seeds indoors 8 weeks before outdoor planting date. Plant in garden in full sun 3 weeks before last frost date. Space plants 2 to 2-1/2 feet apart. If a hedge effect is desired, space plants 6 to 12 inches apart. Plants eventually become woody and should be renewed every 3 to 4 years. Pick leaves before or at blooming. Cut stems back after blooming to encourage new growth.

Pest and disease control: Nematodes can be highly destructive. French marigolds are said to help repel these soil pests. Soil may require fumigation for complete eradication.

Harvesting and use: This aromatic and slightly bitter herb is often included in stuffings for poultry, rabbit, pork and baked fish. It is also used to flavor sausage and meat loaf.

Recommended varieties: Over 25 varieties are available. Mail order herb catalogs are the best sources. Pineapple sage, *Salvia elegans,* has a pineapple fragrance. Garden sage, *Salvia officinalis,* has an anise fragrance. It is the most common variety. It grows 2 to 2-1/2 feet high. Oval leaves are gray-green. Purple sage is a gray-leafed variety. Young leaves have a purple cast.

Sage is adapted to growing in containers, as shown by this healthy specimen. Purple basil and thyme are growing in containers in background.

SUMMER SAVORY
Satureja hortensis

This is a tender annual that grows up to 18 inches high and spreads 12 inches wide. It has small, bronze-green leaves, and small, lavender or white flowers. Leaves are pungent and spicy.

How to grow: Summer savory grows best in a well-prepared, loam-type soil. Seeds can be sown directly in the garden after all danger of frost has passed. Sow 1/4 inch deep and thin plants to stand 10 inches apart.

Pest and disease control: Generally free of pests and diseases.

Harvesting and use: Harvest leafy tops when plants are in bud. Hang in an airy, shady place until crisp and dry. Use as a condiment with meats and vegetables. Summer savory is generally more sweetly flavored than winter savory.

Summer savory adds a peppery taste to salads, soups and stews. It has a milder flavor and is preferred over the similar winter savory.

WINTER SAVORY
Satureja montana

This woody, perennial plant has dark green, shiny, pointed leaves. It grows to 2 feet high and spreads as wide. Flowers are small, in shades of white and lavender. It is a perennial plant, whereas summer savory is an annual. It has a stronger flavor and is normally used sparingly with other herbs.

How to grow: Propagate by cuttings or grow from seeds. Sow seeds 1/4 inch deep directly in the garden 3 weeks before last frost date. Thin seedlings to stand 12 inches apart. Prefers a light, sandy soil. Keep dead wood trimmed out of plant. Leaves are evergreen in mild-winter areas.

Pest and disease control: Generally free of pests and diseases.

Harvesting and use: Pick young shoots and leaves anytime. Leaves are best dried for winter use. Winter savory is a condiment, often used as a flavoring in liqueurs. It can also be used in small quantities with other herbs to flavor soups and stews.

Recommended varieties: Several named varieties are available. 'Nana' is a dwarf variety.

Close-up view of winter savory shows its dainty white flowers. Culinary use is the same as for summer savory. Its flavor is more potent, so add to dishes sparingly.

SPEARMINT
Mentha spicata

Spearmint is a hardy perennial. Pointed, slightly crinkled leaves are lighter green than peppermint. Plants grow 1-1/2 to 2 feet tall, spreading 12 inches the first season. They form thick clumps each season by sending out underground runners. Plant has a sweet, minty fragrance.

How to grow: Cuttings and root division are the most common forms of propagation. Plants can also be started from seeds. Sow seeds directly in the garden 3 weeks before last frost date. Plant 1/4 inch deep and thin seedlings to stand 6 inches apart. Spearmint grows best in moist, fertile soil. Growth is more vigorous with frequent harvesting.

Pest and disease control: Susceptible to rust disease. Prune away and destroy infected foliage. Cleaning garden in winter helps prevent rust. Mealybugs sometimes form colonies on spearmint. Dab them off with cotton swabs dipped in rubbing alcohol.

Spearmint is one of the most popular garden herbs. Top whorl of leaves can be used to flavor cold drinks, make mint sauce and create a refreshing herb tea.

Harvesting and use: Pick fresh leaves and leafy stem tips for use anytime. To dry leaves for later use, harvest just as flowering begins. Leaves are used to flavor cold drinks and teas and to make mint sauce. Oil from leaves is used in confections.

Recommended varieties: Spearmint is the most popular home garden mint. In addition, there are dozens of other varieties available. 'Apple' mint, 'Ginger' mint, 'Orange' mint and 'Pineapple' mint are just a few.

Flowers of sweet cicely appear in spring. Clusters of pods that follow contain black, aromatic seeds flavored like licorice. Leaves are sweet and make a tasty tea.

SWEET CICELY
Myrrhis odorata

Every part of this plant is edible and has a sweet, licorice flavor. Plants grow to 3 feet tall and spread to 2 feet wide. They produce lacy leaves and beautiful white flower clusters. A hardy perennial, sweet cicely is one of the first herbs to flower in spring.

How to grow: Jet-black seeds take up to a month to germinate. Sow directly in the garden 3 weeks before last frost date. Or sow in early fall so plants can grow during cool weather and go dormant after a hard frost. Mild-winter climates do not have enough cold for dormancy. Plants will grow vigorously the following spring. Plant seeds 1/4 inch deep in fertile soil enriched with plenty of organic matter. Space plants 2 feet apart. Soil should be kept moist. Plants can tolerate light shade.

Pest and disease control: Generally free of pests and diseases. Young stems occasionally attract aphids, which can be rubbed or washed off.

Harvesting and use: Finely chopped leaves are useful as a garnish for salads, egg dishes and seafood. Immature seeds taste like licorice, and are delicious to chew before they become hard.

SWEET WOODRUFF
Galium odoratum

A low, spreading, perennial plant, sweet woodruff grows in clumps about 8 inches high. Slender leaves are borne in star-shaped whorls. Tiny, white flowers are formed in loose clusters. When plant leaves are crushed, they have a sweet scent similar to vanilla and fresh-mown hay.

How to grow: Sweet woodruff is a hardy perennial and usually survives through winter if grown in sheltered areas. Plants thrive in semishade. They make an attractive ground cover under taller plants and around bases of trees. Sow seeds directly in the garden 3 weeks before last frost date. Thickly broadcast seeds over the soil surface and rake into soil. Plants tolerate crowding, and grow in dense, spreading, matlike clumps. Soil should be fertile, preferably mixed with plenty of organic matter such as peat moss, leaf mold or garden compost.

Pest and disease control: Generally free of pests and diseases.

Harvesting and use: To store, harvest and dry plants in spring when flavor is the strongest. Leaves can also be frozen. Sweet woodruff is used most often to lend its distinctive flavor to German May wine.

Sweet woodruff makes an excellent, ornamental ground cover in partial shade. Leaves, fresh or dried, can be added to drinks or used to make tea.

CONTAINER GARDENING

Plant breeders have recognized the great appeal of container gardening. Many varieties of flowering annuals specially suited to container culture have been developed. 'Cascade' petunias and cascade lobelias are popular annuals because of their beauty in hanging baskets, tubs and window boxes.

Many gardeners grow annuals in containers because they have little garden space. Others with acres of gardening room enjoy having colorful container plantings close to the house—on decks, patios, terraces and in entryways.

CONTAINER CHOICES: ANNUALS

A large assortment of containers is available at garden centers. But part of the fun of container gardening is hunting for offbeat pots, tubs and other containers at junk shops, auctions and garage sales.

Be sure the mature size of the plant is in scale with the size of the container. Annuals that grow to 10 inches high will look good in an 8-inch pot. But if plants grow to 3 feet high at maturity, they will look tall and gangly. Most popular annuals are available in dwarf and full-size varieties.

When choosing containers for your flowering annuals, keep in mind the two conditions that often cause failure with container gardening—*rapid moisture loss* and *overheating*. The more insulation against heat and cold, the longer the flowering display. A container with a double wall has better insulation than one with a single wall. If you make your own containers out of wood, it is a good idea to construct double walls. Air space between the two walls supplies insulation.

Moisture loss is avoided by choosing a roomy container in relation to size of the plants, and by watering regularly. A soil mix that drains well yet *retains* moisture in the root zone long enough for roots to absorb it is important.

Overheating of the container soil, which causes root damage, can be avoided by choosing the right kind of container. Wood and clay containers are best because they insulate the soil, helping to keep it cool. Steel and plastic are least desirable because they offer little insulation and overheat quickly.

All containers—wood, plastic, clay, ceramic or steel—should have drainage holes in the bottom. Place stones, screens or pieces of broken clay pot over drainage holes to keep soil mix from being washed out with waterings. Window boxes used as floor units around patio areas or on balconies should have trays or pans placed under them to collect water. Otherwise water will run out of pots to spill on your neighbor's patio below.

If it is not possible to punch holes, such as with steel cauldrons and certain window-box containers, create a drainage area within the container. Line the bottom with several inches of horticultural charcoal or volcanic rock.

Wooden barrels and tubs make excellent planters. They not only have a natural appearance, they are well insulated. Heartwood of redwood and red cedar resist rot and last longer than other woods. It is still best to line them with a sheet of plastic such as a garbage bag to prevent rot.

A coat of asphalt emulsion can also be used as a rot-resistant barrier. Raise wooden containers several inches above ground to prevent the base from rotting.

Whiskey half-barrels make particularly good planters. These can be purchased cut in half, sometimes fitted with rope handles, and with drainage holes already drilled. If you use a plastic liner be sure plastic has holes punched to correspond with the barrel's drainage holes.

Unglazed clay pots and concrete urns generally make excellent planters. Because the containers are porous, water, air and carbon dioxide move through the sides of the container. Because moisture evaporates through the sides of the pot, more-frequent watering is required.

A particularly attractive clay container is the strawberry pot. It is shaped like a small barrel with pockets around the sides for holding plants.

Plastic pots are prone to overheating.

Glazed ceramic pots do not heat up as rapidly as plastic. Because the sides of pots are sealed, evaporation of moisture and movement of air in container soil is restricted. Some plastic containers have a liner that creates a humid air space between potting soil and plastic pot. These are better than regular plastic pots.

Steel cauldrons and other metal containers are prone to overheating but are popular for ornamental reasons. These are best used in areas out of intense sun, planted with shade-loving plants. Few steel containers have drainage holes. Be sure to add drainage material.

Wire baskets lined with sphagnum moss are readily available from garden-supply centers. These hanging baskets make striking displays in entryways and on patios—anywhere plants can be seen close-up.

Exposure to wind and sun is a problem, causing dehydration and overheating. If sphagnum moss is kept moist, it helps create a humid air space around the root zone.

Plants that drape and trail are naturals for hanging baskets. Plants that do not have a natural, cascading effect can be used by planting them around the sides

of basket through the moss. Pansies and petunias are especially attractive planted this way.

Baskets should be at least 9 inches in diameter, but bigger is better—up to 16 inches. To fill a wire basket, place it on a flower pot or bucket to hold it in place. Line bottom and sides with moistened sphagnum moss to a thickness of 1 inch. This creates a planting nest. Fill center area of basket with potting soil. Or make a mix of equal parts peat, sifted garden topsoil and sand. Place plants in position. Create planting holes in the side by poking holes through moss with a pencil or other sharp instrument. Water plants daily. Feed with diluted liquid fertilizer at least once a week when you water.

SOIL FOR ANNUALS

Container soil should provide plants with three primary functions: *adequate anchorage, moisture- and nutrient-holding capacity* and *drainage*. Brands of specially formulated soilless mixes are available from garden centers. They are called *soilless* because they do not contain garden soil. They are made up of materials such as peat moss, ground bark and other organic products. Usually materials are sterilized and fertilizer and

Wooden window boxes serve as planters for blue lobelia and white alyssum. These two annuals are among the best for a cascading effect.

trace elements are added to the mix.

Two ingredients commonly included in potting soils are *vermiculite*—lightweight, expanded mica, and *perlite*—porous, volcanic rock. Both are granular materials capable of holding many times their own weight in moisture. Because of their structure they also add valuable air space to the mix.

Although these mixes can be used as-is from the bag, they are expensive. In some instances they are too light and plants can be toppled by gusts of wind. Many gardeners prefer to add some garden loam to the mix. This gives plants better anchorage and reduces evaporation of moisture. It also makes the mixes go farther.

Be aware that by adding garden loam the mix is no longer sterile. In addition, soil drainage is reduced. Consider the plant's requirements for soil drainage and water requirements before adding garden loam. Amount of loam to add depends on its condition, but in most situations 1/3 loam to 2/3 soilless mix is a good ratio.

MAKING YOUR OWN SOIL MIX

The most popular container mixes are available in two basic formulations. One has been developed for the East, where peat moss is available and relatively inexpensive. The other is more common in the South and West, where ground pine, fir bark or redwood sawdust is more available.

Cornell Mixes—for the East: After many years of research, Cornell University developed several lightweight soil mixes, primarily for professional growers. Many planter mixes available to gardeners today are based on the Cornell formula. A typical Cornell mix contains by volume:
- 1/2 sphagnum peat moss, coarse
- 1/2 vermiculite No. 2, 3 or 4 size
- Add *chelated* micronutrients to the water used for moistening the mix. Micronutrients contain elements needed in trace amounts by plants. Lightly moisten ingredients and mix thoroughly. It helps if water is warm. Allow to stand in a pile for 24 to 48 hours so the dry peat will soak up moisture. To a cubic yard add:
- 1/8 coarse sphagnum peat moss
- 1/8 graded, 30-mesh, fine, sharp sand. Do not use sand from beaches. Omit sand or substitute perlite if weight of mix will be a problem.
- To a cubic yard of the above, add chelated micronutrients and the same starter ingredients as for the Cornell mix.

Wood half-barrels make excellent containers for annuals. These are 'Showboat' triploid-hybrid marigolds.

Hanging baskets and tubs filled with grandiflora petunias decorate entrance to swimming-pool bathhouse.

• 5 pounds ground limestone, preferably *dolomitic lime,* which contains both calcium and magnesium
• 2 pounds single superphosphate fertilizer
• 1 pound calcium nitrate or 1/2 pound ammonium-nitrate fertilizer

U.C. Mixes—for the South and West: The University of California developed this family of mixes for growers in the West, primarily for containers. A typical U.C. mix contains by volume:
• 1/4 small particles of fir or pine bark—1/2 inch or less diameter.
• 1/2 aged or composted redwood sawdust, or "forest compost"—a sawmill mix of fine and coarse sawdust composted with a little nitrogen fertilizer. Or pulverized pine bark.
• 1/8 coarse sphagnum peat moss
• 1/8 graded, 30-mesh, fine, sharp sand. Do not use sand from beaches. Omit sand or substitute perlite if weight of mix will be a problem.
• To a cubic yard of the above, add chelated micronutrients and the same starter ingredients as for the Cornell mix.

Mixing Tips—For small lots, keep in mind that a *cubic foot* fills about 7 to 10 1-gallon cans. Count on about a 15% to 20% loss of volume when you mix ingredients. The small particles simply fill in between the larger ones.

To keep the soil mix sterile, blend materials on a plastic sheet or concrete pad that has been washed with a solution of 1 part bleach and 10 parts water. Use clean, sterile tools for mixing. To mix thoroughly, shovel ingredients into cone-shape piles. Drop material on top of pile so it cascades evenly down sides of cone. Build cone three times to ensure a complete mix. Store unused mix in plastic garbage cans or heavy-duty plastic bags to prevent contamination.

Moisten soil mix before adding it to container so it is thoroughly saturated. Dry potting soil is difficult to moisten after it's in the container. Don't rely on available fertilizer to last through the season. After plants begin to flower, feed regularly with diluted liquid fertilizer every 2 weeks.

WATERING

Watering may be necessary every day, depending on the size of the container. Test for soil moisture by taking a pinch of topsoil and rubbing it between your fingers. Hanging-basket plants, because they are more exposed than container plants to heat and wind, are es-

pecially susceptible to drying out. They may need watering as often as three times a day to keep plants from wilting.

Viterra Hydrogel is a product that can be added to soil mixes to prevent rapid drying out and dehydration. It is a granular material that is capable of absorbing up to 20 times its own weight in moisture. This product is useful when added to hanging-basket soils and seed flats, which tend to dry out rapidly.

Drip-irrigation systems are well adapted to container gardening. Systems with "spaghetti" hoses work well. These have small, numerous hoses projecting from a main hose. Each small hose supplies water to individual containers or hanging baskets. Emitters at the end of each small tube supply water slowly to soil around root area.

FERTILIZING CONTAINER PLANTS

Most annuals in containers require regular amounts of fertilizer. Nutrients, especially nitrogen, are continually being washed out of the soil. A timed-

release fertilizer distributes plant nutrients for an extended period. But you will probably have better results by adding a diluted liquid fertilizer about once a week when you water. Plant foods designed to be mixed with water can be purchased in concentrated form as liquid or crystals.

Premium-quality soil mixes are fortified with starter fertilizer and minor elements such as iron. If you use such mixes, do not feed plants for 3 to 4 weeks after seeding or transplanting. If you feed right away, the extra dose could injure your plants.

Long-handle watering wand makes it easy to water hanging baskets. These are 'Grande' and 'Twinkles' impatiens.

BULBS IN CONTAINERS

For the most dramatic way to display a small number of bulbs, grow them in containers. On a grand scale, you might want to try three or four lilies in a large tub. Or perhaps an eye-catching display of miniature snowdrops in a bonsai pot is more your style. Both approaches are colorful and create their own special effect.

Bulbs in containers emphasize a focal point such as a doorway, or frame a scenic view. They can direct traffic along a path, or call attention to a pool or piece of garden sculpture. One of their best uses is indoors, brightening a room or a table setting.

Container bulbs have a great advantage over in-ground plants because they can be moved to a protected area in adverse weather or during heavy winds. If the pots are rotated regularly, the bulbs grow more evenly and with straight stems. When bulbs are grown in pots, they can be moved out of view after bloom and replaced with other seasonal color.

It is generally more pleasing to use containers in groups rather than lining them up like soldiers. The bulbs do not have to be the same color, size or shape. Pots of tall, light-blue 'Wedgewood' Dutch iris are striking when combined with pots of golden trumpet daffodils. Low pots of purple or white *Crocus* work well in front of these.

Similarly, different colors of the same type of flower can also be used together. Pots of pink tulips combined with pots of lilac and white tulips of the same variety make an impressive display. A pot of lilies can steal the scene when placed at an entryway. A bonus is the lilies' nighttime fragrance. Potted bulbs also combine well with low pots of spring-blooming annuals such as pansies, violas or forget-me-nots.

Mixing different kinds of bulbs in a single container is not desirable. Chances are that one bulb will bloom and decline before the others bloom. The spent flowers and fading foliage detract from the beauty of the planting. It is much better to plant a single variety in each pot so bulbs in each pot bloom simultaneously.

There is no better way of displaying a small bulb than in a bonsai pot. Small species of *Narcissus* and *Crocus* are particular favorites in these containers. Placing a piece of lava rock or driftwood in the background of the container adds a natural touch.

When grouping bulbs in containers, it is not necessary to have pots that are the same size, height or shape. It helps to have them of the same material and color. If simplicity is your style, one beautiful pot of daffodils by a front door gives a feeling of warmth and welcome to arriving guests.

A fun way to grow small bulbs is to use them as a colorful ground cover in large containers. Try them beneath plants such as dwarf citrus, dwarf fruit trees, tree roses and tree wisteria. In mild climates, *Freesia*, 'Grand Duchess' *Oxalis*, *Ipheon*, *Lapeirousia* and *Tritonia* accept the restricted root space. In colder climates, try dwarf varieties of *Anemone*, species *Cyclamen*, *Eranthis*, *Ipheion*, *Muscari* or *Oxalis adenophylla*.

Above: Wine carafes are perfectly suited to house Dutch hyacinth bulbs, grown in water indoors.

Pots of tulips, hyacinths, daffodils and *Ipheion* make a striking springtime display.

Flowers of paper-white *Narcissus* enhance outdoor living areas with their beauty and their fragrance.

'February Gold' daffodils in foreground are spaced as closely as possible to produce this compact planting. In the background are gold *Freesias* and white *Azaleas*.

A container grouping on a terrace: Clockwise from front is *Ipheion, Anemone coronaria,* two-toned Picotee hybrid *Ranunculus, Tritonia crocata* with lime tree in clay container, 'Temple of Beauty' tulips, 'Mt. Hood' large cup *Narcissus,* 'Thalia' *Triandrus Narcissus,* 'Lady Derby' pink hyacinth and a red Darwin tulip.

Tight, "shoehorn" planting of 'Pink Pearl' hyacinths in a terra-cotta pot makes a striking display.

Haemanthus kathariniae makes an outstanding display at a terrace door. This rare and exotic South-African native is attractive in any setting.

CHOOSING CONTAINERS

Containers for bulbs are available in many sizes, shapes and kinds. You can choose from brightly glazed clay pots, plastic pots, wooden boxes and tubs, Japanese bonsai pots, metal pots and glass jars.

Each type of container has advantages and disadvantages.

Glazed and plastic pots do not allow water to evaporate through the sides. This means that less moisture is lost, and watering is less frequent than with unglazed containers. But because evaporation is reduced, the pots tend to heat up with warm weather. Too much heat can damage or kill the roots of plants.

Glazed and plastic pots are often available only in bright colors. You notice the pot and not the plant. However, a plastic pot with an attached saucer, no matter what the color, works well placed inside a basket, metal pot or urn.

Clay pots "breathe," which allows air circulation. This also allows water to evaporate from the sides, providing good drainage. But this means that watering has to be more frequent. In warm-summer areas, watering may be necessary every day. In addition, when the water evaporates, soil salts are left behind on the pot, which can be detrimental to the plant. This does not occur with plastic pots.

Wooden tubs and boxes have a natural look that lends itself well to informal settings. Wood is a good insulator that helps keep the soil cool in warm weather. Redwood and cedar are best because of their natural resistance to moisture and decay. To prevent rot and to increase the longevity of wooden containers, raise them off the ground with small blocks.

Tops of containers should not have holes or spaces in the seams. These allow water to run off without going to where it is needed—the plant's root zone. Plug spaces with sphagnum moss to prevent moisture loss.

No matter what kind of container you choose for your bulbs, be sure that it allows for good drainage. All containers should have one or more holes in the bottom to allow excess water to drain away after each watering. Many pots are manufactured with a removable plug.

SOIL FOR CONTAINERS

Drainage is the most important consideration when choosing soil for containers. Most garden soils are too heavy, especially clay soils, and do not allow for fast drainage. Therefore, it is best to plant bulbs in a prepared soil mix. Ingredients such as sand, *perlite,* a porous volcanic rock, and *vermiculite,* expanded mica, are excellent for providing drainage. Perlite and vermiculite are lightweight so pots are easy to move. The standard mix of one-third leaf mold, one-third peat moss and one-third sand is one of the best combinations for potting.

Several brand names of soil mixes are available at retail outlets. Many are based on mixes developed by the University of California and Cornell University. These mixes are free of soil-borne diseases.

Before filling the containers with soil, moisten the mix slightly before putting it into the pots. Bone-dry soil often resists water penetration. Also mix in some superphosphate, which supplies phosphorus. Follow directions on the package label as to amount. Bulbs use more phosphorus than other nutrients, so it is a good idea to have sufficient amounts in the mix for use when the bulb needs it.

Most bulbs are satisfied with a standard soil mix, as described previously. A few tropical bulbs prefer a more water-retentive mix, so add in some sphagnum peat moss. Among these are tuberous begonia, *Gloxinia, Eucharis* and *Achimenes.* Others, such as the many South-African bulbs that grow in sand or gravel in the wild, prefer faster drainage. With these bulbs, it is helpful to add a little sand to the soil mix.

POTTING BULBS

Before putting soil into containers, place a piece of broken clay pot, screening or other material over the drainage hole in the bottom. This allows the water to drain freely yet prevents the soil from washing out. A handful or two of sand over the broken piece ensures even drainage.

Fill the pot with soil to the desired depth. In containers, bulbs are planted closer to the surface than in the ground so roots will have the most room. They are also planted closer together than in the ground to make a full, attractive display, but not so close that they touch sides. When planting tulips, face the flat side of the bulb toward the outside of the pot. The leaves will then grow in a way that makes a prettier display.

After the first shoots appear, keep the soil damp. Watering every day will do no harm if soil drainage is adequate.

Apply water at low pressure so it trickles onto the soil. High-pressure watering washes out the soil and pushes over the foliage when it appears.

HANGING-BASKET BULBS

Certain bulbs have a trailing growth habit and pendulous flowers, such as the hanging varieties of tuberous begonias and *Achimines.* Bulbs of this type look best displayed in a hanging basket. These are wire baskets lined with sphagnum moss. The moss remains moist after watering and increases the humidity around the plant. The wire forms and moss are available at nurseries.

When you make hanging baskets, don't skimp on the moss. Moisten the moss before placing it in between the spaces of the wire basket. Fill it in until the moss is about 1 inch thick. It helps to add extra moss in the bottom of the basket to prevent the soil from washing out. Fill the basket with a house-plant soil mix, and you are ready to plant the bulbs.

Because they are highly exposed to wind and sunlight, hanging baskets dry out rapidly. They require water on a regular basis. If you plan to display several containers, consider installing a drip-irrigation system to water the baskets.

Bulbs in a fanciful container make a unique gift. Ingredients are few: bulbs, planter mix, milled sphagnum peat moss, planter, wrapping paper and ribbon.

You have an option as to when to give your gift of bulbs. You can either present the preplanted container . . .

. . . or time your planting so that bulbs will be in full bloom for that special occasion.

VEGETABLES AND HERBS IN CONTAINERS

If you don't have space for a garden plot, many kinds of vegetables and herbs can be grown in containers. If you live in an apartment, condominium or mobile home, this may be the only way you can garden. Perhaps you simply want to grow a few vegetables like tomatoes and peppers, or maybe a salad garden. Containers offer a suitable alternative to growing them directly in the soil.

Mobility is an advantage with container gardening. You can get an early start on the season by placing vegetables outdoors during warm daylight hours. When cool evenings approach, you can move containers inside or under a sheltered area. If containers are heavy, you may have to install caster wheels to move them about.

Vegetables in containers can also be ornamental. Try planting vegetables in half whiskey barrels or terra-cotta pots.

Make them part of your patio, porch or landscape.

CHOICES OF CONTAINERS

Containers are available in a wide range of sizes, shapes and materials. One of the best materials is wood. Containers made of redwood and cedar are best, because both types of wood resist rotting. Avoid growing vegetables in plastic pots. They have a tendency to heat up quickly in the sun. Too much heat damages plant roots and dries out the soil rapidly. Ceramic containers offer better insulation qualities but have a tendency to lose moisture through absorption and evaporation, especially clay pots.

When choosing containers for your vegetable plants, keep in mind the two conditions that often cause failure with container gardening—*rapid moisture loss* and *overheating*. A container with a double wall has better insulation than one with a single wall. If you make your own containers out of wood, it is a good idea to construct dual walls. The air space between the two walls supplies insulation. You can fill the space with moist, crumbled newspapers for additional cooling. Double-walled plastic containers are also available.

To make wooden containers rot-resistant, line the inside with plastic sheeting such as a garbage bag. Or apply a coat of asphalt emulsion for more permanent protection. If you use the plastic, be sure to punch holes in the bottom for drainage.

Some plastic containers have a liner that creates a humid air space between the potting soil and the plastic pot. This system also offers additional insulation.

Most fruiting plants such as cucumbers, tomatoes and peppers require pots that hold at least one gallon of soil. They may also require at least a quart of water every day.

All containers—wood, plastic, clay or ceramic—should have drainage holes in the bottom. Place stones, screens or broken clay pots over them to prevent the soil from washing away with each watering.

Above: Narrow side yard has enough space for a productive garden, featuring lettuce, carrots and beans.

SOIL FOR VEGETABLES

The objective of any soil mix is to create a growth medium that supports plants and holds moisture and nutrients in the root zone. Soil should also allow for sufficient drainage—air spaces between the soil particles are necessary for the roots to breathe. A soil that is made mostly of sand or peat drains too rapidly. Nutrients are washed from the root zone, and plants tend to dry out quickly. A soil composed mostly of clay is too dense in structure and does not have enough air space for plant roots. Topsoil from the garden is also too heavy and dense for most container plants.

The best choice of planting medium for containers is a "soil-less" potting mix. Such mixes are termed "soil-less" because they do not contain soil or earth. Rather, all ingredients are sterile materials, such as peat moss, vermiculite, perlite, sand and ground bark, blended with a small amount of fertilizer.

Mixes are available under many different brand names, and can be purchased from garden-supply stores and home centers. As a rule, buy a bagged soil mix if you are going to fill containers that total up to 20 gallons capacity. Beyond that point, the economics begins to favor making your own.

Some prepared mixes are based on sand, which is heavy; Sand weighs about 100 pounds per cubic foot. Others are based on peat moss or fir bark and are so light that you can easily carry a 2-1/2 cubic-foot bale.

Two ingredients commonly included in potting soils are vermiculite, which is lightweight expanded mica, and *perlite*, porous volcanic rock. Both are granular materials capable of holding many times their own weight in moisture. Because of their structure, they also add air spaces to the mix.

MAKING YOUR OWN SOIL MIX

The most popular container mixes are available in two basic formulations. One has been developed for the East, where peat moss is available and relatively inexpensive. The other is more common in the South and West, where ground pine, fir bark or redwood sawdust is more available.

Cornell Mixes—for the East: After many years of research, Cornell University developed several lightweight soil mixes, primarily for professional growers. Many planter mixes available to gardeners today are based on the Cornell formula. A typical Cornell mix contains by volume:

- 1/2 sphagnum peat moss, coarse
- 1/2 vermiculite No. 2, 3, or 4 size
- Add *chelated* micronutrients to the water used for moistening the mix. Micronutrients contain elements needed in trace amounts by plants. Lightly moisten ingredients and mix thoroughly. It helps if water is warm. Allow to stand in a pile for 24 to 48 hours so the dry peat will soak up moisture. To a cubic yard of such a mix, add:

- 5 pounds ground limestone, preferably *dolomitic lime*, which contains both calcium and magnesium
- 2 pounds single superphosphate fertilizer
- 1 pound calcium nitrate or 1/2 pound ammonium-nitrate fertilizer

U.C. Mixes—for the South and West: The University of California developed this family of mixes for growers in the West, primarily for containers. A typical U. C. mix contains by volume:

- 1/4 small particles of fir or pine bark—diameter of 1/2 inch or less
- 1/2 aged or composted redwood sawdust, or "forest compost"—a sawmill mix of fine and coarse sawdust composted with a little nitrogen fertilizer. Or pulverized pine bark
- 1/8 coarse spagnum peat moss
- 1/8 graded, 30-mesh, fine, sharp sand. Do not use sand from beaches. Omit sand or substitute perlite if weight of mix will be a problem.
- To a cubic yard of the above, add chelated micronutrients and the same starter ingredients as the Cornell mix.

Mixing tips. For small lots, keep in mind that a *cubic yard* contains 27 cubic feet. A *cubic foot* fills about 7 to 10 1-gallon cans. Count on about a 15% to 20% loss of volume when you mix ingredients. The small particles simply fill in between the larger ones.

To keep the soil mix sterile, blend materials on a plastic sheet or concrete

Redwood raised bed serves as a large container near a brick patio. Wide end piece is a handy seat when watering or weeding.

'Pixie' hybrid tomatoes are growing in pots inside a greenhouse. Compact growth habit of vine makes 'Pixie' ideal for containers.

Most herbs grow well in containers, such as lavender, left, and thyme, right. Containers are decorated coffee cans, with holes punched in the bottoms for drainage.

pad that has been washed with a solution of 1 part bleach and 10 parts water. Use clean tools for mixing. To mix thoroughly, shovel the ingredients into cone-shaped piles. Drop material on top of pile so it cascades evenly down the sides of the cone. Build cone three times to ensure a complete mix. Store unused mix in plastic garbage cans or heavy-duty plastic bags to prevent contamination.

FERTILIZING CONTAINER PLANTS

Container plants require regular amounts of fertilizer. Nutrients, especially nitrogen, are continually being washed out of the soil. A slow-release fertilizer distributes plant nutrients over an extended period. But you will probably have better results by adding a diluted liquid fertilizer about once a week when you water. Plant foods designed to be mixed with water can be purchased in concentrated form as liquid or crystals.

For fruit-producing vegetables such as peppers and tomatoes, fertilizer should have a high phosphorus content, the middle number in a fertilizer analysis. Look for formulations such as 5-10-10.

Premium-quality soil mixes are fortified with starter fertilizer and micronutrients such as iron. If you use such mixes, do not feed plants for three to four weeks after seeding or transplanting. If you feed right away, the extra dose could injure your plants.

WATERING

Vegetables in containers generally require constant attention to water needs. Some may need watering every day, depending on the size of the container, the weather and the vegetable. Cucumbers, peppers and tomatoes require as much as a quart of water for every two quarts of soil. Hanging basket plants, because they are more exposed than container plants to heat and wind, are especially susceptible to drying out. They may need watering as often as three times a day to keep plants from wilting.

Viterra Hydrogel is a product that can be added to soil mixes to prevent rapid drying out and dehydration. In granular form, it is capable of absorbing up to 20 times its own weight in moisture. This product is useful when added to hanging basket soils and seed flats, which tend to dry out rapidly, especially in summer.

Drip irrigation is well-adapted to container gardening. Those with "spaghetti" hoses—numerous small tubes projecting from a main hose—are efficient in supplying individual containers and hanging baskets with water. Emitters at the end of each small tube slowly supply water to the soil.

RECOMMENDED VARIETIES FOR CONTAINERS

Given sufficient soil depth, any vegetable can be grown in a container. Some varieties within plant groups are more successful than others. Here are some common vegetables that can be grown in containers. When a recommendation is given that a vegetable be grown in a "windowbox container," this means a container with at least 8 inches soil depth and 5 gallons soil capacity.

Artichokes. 'Grande Beurre' usually produces artichokes the first year. Grow in 15-gallon tubs.

Beans. 'Bush Roma' is a compact, heavy producer of fine-flavored romano beans. Grow in windowbox containers. Space each plant 6 inches apart.

Beets. 'Pacemaker II' is an early, uniform and sweet-flavored hybrid. Grow in windowbox container. Space each plant 6 inches apart.

Broccoli. 'Green Comet' is early and compact. Grow in 5-gallon pots, or 15-gallon tubs, 3 plants per tub.

Brussels sprouts. 'Jade Cross' is early and heavy yielding. Grow in 5-gallon pots or 15-gallon tubs, 2 plants per tub.

Cabbages. 'Stonehead' is early and compact. Forms a solid ball with few outer leaves. Can be spaced 15 inches

'Salad Bowl' lettuce is a good choice as an edible ornamental, growing in this narrow space between path and garden.

Half whiskey barrels are used to grow vegetables at the edge of this patio. Barrels are attractive as well as long lasting.

'Salad Bowl' lettuce grows in a hanging basket. Basket is made of wire and filled with sphagnum moss to create a mounded effect.

apart, half as much space as other hybrids. Grow in 15-gallon tubs, 3 plants per tub.

Carrots. 'Short 'n Sweet' is early and sweet with small central core. Grows in windowbox containers. Space each plant 1 inch apart.

Cauliflower. 'Snow Crown' hybrid is early. Grow in 5-gallon pots or in 15-gallon tubs, 3 plants per tub.

Cucumbers. 'Pot Luck' hybrid and 'Spacemaster' hybrid are compact varieties that grow in hanging baskets as well as containers. 'Fembaby' hybrid is the best variety for containers, especially indoors. It is an all-female variety that sets fruit without cross-pollination. 'Fembaby' requires a short trellis for support and must not be allowed to cross-pollinate with other cucumbers. Grow in 1-gallon pots.

Eggplant. 'Oriental Egg' produces small, white fruit. 'Jersey King' hybrid produces black, medium-size fruit. 'Slim Jim' hybrid produces small, black fruit. All have a compact habit suitable for containers. Grow in 1-gallon pots.

Herbs. Containers are the best way to keep many invasive varieties within bounds. Parsley, chives, garlic, thyme, catnip, sage, lavender, sweet basil and chervil are adapted to containers. One plant is sufficient for most family's needs. Grow in quart-size pots or larger.

Lettuce. 'Tom Thumb' is a compact head lettuce that produces more heads per square foot than any other heading variety. Loose-leaf varieties tolerate crowding. 'Ruby' and 'Salad Bowl' are decorative with frilly leaves. Grow in windowbox containers.

Onions. Giant-size kinds such as 'Giant Walla Walla', and bunching kinds such as 'Evergreen Long White Bunching', are worthwhile to grow in windowbox containers.

Peppers. Sweet varieties such as 'Sweet Banana' and 'Early Prolific' hybrid are heavy yielding and early. Grow in 2-gallon pots or 15-gallon tubs, 4 plants per tub.

Potatoes. All varieties grow well in barrels. Sweet potatoes make excellent hanging baskets. Grow in 15-gallon tubs, 4 plants per tub.

Radishes. 'Cherry Belle' is earliest and has short tops, which allows for greater productivity. Grow in windowbox containers, each plant spaced 1 inch apart.

Rhubarb. 'Valentine' has brilliant red stalks. Grow in 5-gallon containers.

Spinach. 'Melody' hybrid is early and disease resistant. New Zealand spinach is a vining spinach substitute with heat resistance. Grow in windowbox containers. Space plants 4 inches apart.

Swiss chard. 'Ruby' has brilliant red stalks, making it highly ornamental. Grow in windowbox containers or 15-gallon tubs, 5 plants per tub.

Squash. Bush-type varieties of zucchini such as 'Gold Rush' hybrid and 'Early Golden' crookneck are excellent for growing in 2-gallon pots.

Turnips. 'Tokyo Cross' hybrid is a sweet-flavored, white variety. It is early and has good disease resistance. Grow in windowbox containers. Space each plant 3 inches apart.

Tomatoes. Many varieties are suitable for containers, but 'Pixie' hybrid is best of all. Vines are short and compact. Fruit are medium size. 'Tiny Tim' and 'Patio' are other common container tomatoes, but not as good as 'Pixie'. A hanging-basket variety is 'Tumblin' Tom'. Grow these compact vine types in 1-gallon pots or larger. For large-fruited, indeterminate types, use 15-gallon tubs.

Watermelons. 'Sugar Bush' has short vines requiring 6 square feet of space. It is the only variety suitable for containers, averaging 3, ice-box size, red-fleshed fruit. Grow in 15-gallon tubs, 1 plant per tub.

VEGETABLES IN HANGING BASKETS

Growing vegetables in hanging baskets is a very difficult method, but the ornamental effect can be dramatic. If gardening space is not available, hanging plants may be the only way you can garden. The problem with growing in hanging baskets is keeping plants watered. The soil in hanging baskets has a tendency to dry out much faster due to exposure to sun and wind. Using a drip irrigation system is one way to provide hanging basket plants with regular moisture.

You can make your own hanging containers from wire framework baskets and spagnum peat moss. The baskets are lined around the sides and bottom with the moss to form a "nest." This is filled with potting mix, and planted the same as any other container. The spagnum moss absorbs moisture and helps keep the soil cool. Plants can also be planted through the sides of the basket so that the entire basket becomes a "globe" of plants.

Watering is necessary at least once a day. Add a diluted liquid fertilizer to water once a week.

Raised beds are efficient, neat and attractive. Because soil is above ground level, it warms earlier in spring compared to conventional gardens.

RAISED BEDS

Raised beds are planting areas raised above the normal soil level. Many are bordered by wood, brick or stone. They are in a sense large, bottomless containers. Because they are above ground level, the soil warms faster in the spring and draining is improved. Raised beds help to create a neat, tidy appearance in the home landscape.

Rot-resistant redwood and cedar are good materials for building raised beds. Sturdy railroad ties are also popular. For extra-long raised beds, use telephone poles laid on their sides. These can be island beds or butted against a fence or wall.

The width of a raised bed should not be more than 6 feet, representing the total distance a person can comfortably stretch out with his hands from either side of the bed. If beds are butted against a wall, width should be reduced to 3 feet or less.

SPACE-SAVING TRAINING

Where space is limited, you may want to consider growing vegetables that can be trained up stakes, trellises and other forms of support.

Staking. There are several methods of staking tall-growing vegetables. Tomatoes, cucumbers and peppers can be trained to a single wood, metal or plastic stake, using string or twist-ties to secure stems to the supports.

Pole beans and tall varieties of peas can be trained up tripods and tepees. Use three or more poles set in a circle at the bottom, and tie poles together at the top.

Towers. The most efficient and easiest vertical-training method is growing plants inside cylinders of inexpensive wire *towers,* or cages. Tomato towers should be at least 5 feet high and 1-1/2 feet to 2 feet across. Concrete reinforcing wire with 6-inch mesh openings works exceptionally well. The wide mesh is necessary so you can harvest fruit by reaching through the wire, rather than trying to reach in from the top. Plant one tomato plant in the middle of each cylinder, and do not prune branches. As the plant grows, the branches push through the wire spaces so the plant becomes self-supporting.

Cucumber towers should be 3 feet in diameter and 3 feet high. Leave a gap about 1-1/2 feet wide along one side so you can reach inside to pick cucumbers from the middle of the tower. Plant several vines spaced 1 foot apart around inside and outside of the tower.

Squash towers can be made the same size as cucumber towers. Allow vines to climb up the middle and spill over the sides.

A-frames. These are short sections of trellis, usually 6 feet long. Frames are set over the soil like an "A" to support vining crops. They are usually constructed of wood and can be covered with chicken wire or plastic netting. They are useful for growing cucumbers, peas, vining squash, melons and similar vines. As melons gain weight, they should be supported with cloth or slings made of pantyhose or similar material. Without support, they may slip from the vine and burst when they hit the ground.

Netting and chicken wire. Use these attached between tall, wooden stakes to support many vining crops. Either can be draped against a wall to form a trellis.

Bamboo poles. Strong, long lasting and decorative, these can be used in countless ways to support beans, peas and other vining crops. For beans, it's best to erect them in a tripod or as an A-frame.

Recycled supports. Use your imagination to utilize throwaway materials for the garden. One of the most original trellising ideas was a collection of bicycle wheels randomly mounted against a wall. They supported cucumbers, balsam apples and spaghetti squash.

INTENSIVE GARDENING

Making every inch of space count is a good definition of intensive gardening. This can be done by growing vegetables in wide, raised rows—as matted rows with vegetables that tolerate crowded conditions, or in a block planting with vegetables that require more precise spacing.

An effective way of saving space in a vegetable garden is to plant vegetables with compact growth habits. When making vegetable selections among squash, avoid the *vining* varieties and try the newer *bush* varieties. Similarly, there are bush varieties of cucumbers, cantaloupes, watermelons, snap beans and other popular vegetables.

Intensive gardening also makes use of *interplanting.* For example, tall-stemmed chard can be interplanted among low-growing parsley. Quick-maturing lettuce can be planted among slow-growing brussels sprouts. The lettuce will be harvested and cleared from the bed by the time the brussels sprouts have spread to cut off the light. Pole beans can be grown with corn, using the corn stalks as supports.

Wire cage is set in place after tomato is planted. 'Pixie' grows to only 3 feet high. Large, indeterminate tomatoes require a cylinder 5 feet or more high.

Cucumber vine has been trained to a single pole to save space. An A-frame trellis is more efficient for numerous vines.

Gardeners with little room are among the most imaginative. Discarded bicycle wheels support balsam apple vine.

Genetic dwarf fruit trees, such as 'Southern Sweet' peach above, produce abundant crops of delicious, full-size fruit in a small area.

GROWING FRUIT IN SMALL SPACES

Growing fruit no longer brings to mind large orchards with trees in long, straight rows. Instead, the modern fruit gardener turns a small back yard, patio or even tiny balcony into a remarkably productive area.

Advances have been made primarily in the areas of growth-controlling rootstocks and compact varieties—*genetic dwarfs*. A better understanding of how tree growth is regulated has also helped fruit growers develop training and pruning practices for small trees. Summer pruning has been revived as a method of growth control. Growing trees in con-

tainers is becoming more popular as a method of controlling tree size. Special training systems such as espalier also keep trees small and use growing space efficiently.

DWARF FRUIT TREES

There are two types of dwarf fruit trees: those in which the fruiting part of the tree, or *scion*, is dwarfed by its rootstock or interstem; and those in which the fruiting part is genetically dwarf. Either way, the advantages are impressive. Controlled size eases pruning, thinning, spraying and harvesting and better adapts the tree to container culture. In general, dwarf trees have versatile use, fit in the smallest landscape and tend to fruit at an earlier age.

DWARFING ROOTSTOCKS

Dwarfing through rootstocks involves budding or grafting a desired variety to the root system of a closely related plant. The rootstock restricts growth of the tree because of one or more characteristics, such as slower nutrient uptake or a smaller root system. These factors are then passed on to dwarf the desired variety.

Vigor of the variety grafted on the dwarfing rootstock influences the eventual size of tree. Even when grown on the same rootstock, a vigorous apple variety such as 'Rhode Island Greening' produces a larger tree than a more restrained variety such as 'Macoun'. A similar comparison could be made between the more vigorous 'Dancy' tangerine and the smaller kumquat.

Dwarfing can also be achieved through use of an *interstem*. A small section of dwarfing rootstock is inserted as an interstem between a standard rootstock and a branchlet (top part) of the desired variety by means of a double graft. This takes advantage of the best qualities of three trees. The result: a dwarf tree with strong roots that produces desirable fruit.

Unfortunately, doing your own grafting is sometimes the only way to be sure which rootstock a variety is grown on. Fruit trees are often labeled and sold simply as "dwarfs" or "semidwarfs." The rootstock is not specified. This gives you no indication of the tree's eventual mature size.

GENETIC DWARFS

The second type of dwarf fruit tree is called a *genetic dwarf*. Here, the actual fruiting part of the tree, the scion, is dwarfed in size. It is grafted onto a standard-size rootstock and special care is taken to remove vigorous suckers. Many genetic dwarfs have tightly spaced fruit buds, resulting in a huskier-looking tree and a spectacular spring bloom. Spur-type apple varieties also have closely spaced fruiting buds, but they are not nearly as tightly packed as those of a genetic dwarf.

Genetic dwarfs require little pruning but need special attention to fruit thinning—many have a tendency to overbear. Most reach a height of 6 to 10 feet, depending on fruit type.

Genetic dwarfs have one distinct disadvantage compared to fruit types that are grafted onto dwarf rootstocks: a limited choice of varieties. You can graft any variety you like onto dwarfing rootstocks. Genetic dwarf varieties are limited to those that have been specially bred that way.

THREE IN ONE?

Many nurseries offer trees with two or more varieties of fruit on one tree. Grafting a twig of another variety onto a tree with the same bloom period is also a good way to provide cross-pollination. In certain cases, several species may be combined into one. See compatibility chart below.

Although this is a good way to grow several types of fruit in a small area, you must match variety vigor carefully. A combination of vigorous-growing 'Rhode Island Greening' apple and the less-vigorous 'Macoun' apple would probably end up with 'Rhode Island Greening' taking over, strangling the 'Macoun'. Careful pruning practices must balance varieties.

Another method that yields good results is to plant several varieties in one hole. Choose varieties of matching vigor and climate adaptation. Each tree is trained as a scaffold limb. They are slanted slightly outward and often tied together to support each other.

DWARFING METHODS

Following is a summary of the methods used to control various fruit and nut trees.

Apples—Any desired tree size can be obtained by choice of rootstock alone. This is fortunate, because some of the highest quality scion varieties are not available as genetic dwarfs. 'Garden Delicious' is the only *widely* available variety. The most-dwarfing rootstock, 'M-27,' (M stands for Malling) produces a tree 3 to 5 feet tall. On 'M-9' rootstock, some varieties may reach a height of 12 feet if supported. They can be held to 5 or 6 feet high by pruning. 'M-26,' 'M-7,' 'M-106' and 'M-111' rootstocks produce trees of increasing size in the order listed. On these rootstocks, trees can be pruned hard for growth control without being forced out of production. With

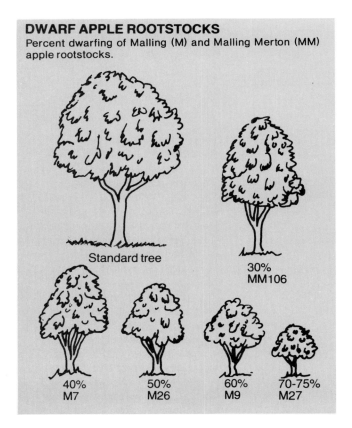

DWARF APPLE ROOTSTOCKS
Percent dwarfing of Malling (M) and Malling Merton (MM) apple rootstocks.

Standard tree

30% MM106

40% M7

50% M26

60% M9

70-75% M27

TREE FRUIT COMPATIBILITY

STOCK	ALMOND	APPLE	APRICOT	CHERRY, SOUR	CHERRY, SWEET	PEACH	PEAR	PLUM, EUROPEAN	PLUM, JAPANESE	QUINCE
ALMOND	X					X				
APPLE		X								
APRICOT			X			*		X	X	
CHERRY, SOUR				X	X					
CHERRY, SWEET				X	X					
PEACH	X		X			X		X	X	
PEAR							X			
PLUM, EUROPEAN	X		X			*		X	X	
PLUM, JAPANESE			X			*		*	X	
QUINCE							*			X

Trees bearing multiple types of fruit can be created by grafting or budding wood from one fruit type, or the scion, on to a tree, or the stock, of another fruit type. The chart above indicates compatibility between fruit types. The symbol * indicates that the combination is possible but may be short-lived or weak.

This 'Jonwin' apple on Malling 9 dwarf rootstock is 27 years old.

Citrus in containers are attractive landscape plants, and produce worthwhile crops as well.

some scion varieties, spur-type *mutants*, explained in the chapter on apples, are also available. When spur-type mutant varieties are grafted on growth-controlling rootstocks, remarkable productive and compact trees are obtained.

Apricots—Dwarfing techniques for apricots are not very advanced. A few scion varieties with genetically dwarfed growth habits such as 'Garden Annie' are available.

Almonds—The variety 'All-in-One' is a semidwarf tree with a dense habit and good productivity that does not require cross-pollination. 'Garden Prince' is a fully dwarf almond that grows to 8 feet tall and is very productive. It also produces good crops without cross-pollination.

Cherries—A few, compact scion varieties of sweet cherry—'Compact Lambert', 'Compact Stella', 'Garden Bing' —are available through some nurseries. Semidwarf trees are obtained by use of 'North Star' cherry rootstock. *Prunus mahaleb* rootstocks are often said to be dwarfing, but are not. Newer dwarfing rootstocks, such as 'Colt' from England and 'MxM 14', may prove to be better than existing rootstocks but have not yet been widely tested.

Figs—Figs are generally grown from cuttings and thus have no rootstock. No compact scion varieties are known. Figs are well adapted to growing in containers and can also be trained as a multi-trunk bush. Bush forms can be controlled by heavy pruning.

Filberts—The size of filbert trees can be limited by growing plants as multi-trunked bushes and periodically thinning large branches.

Nectarines and peaches—Genetic dwarfs of nectarine and peach have been developed by hybridization with such Chinese dwarf peaches as 'Flory' and 'Swatow'. These trees are very compact and can be grown easily in containers.

Size of standard nectarine and peach varieties can be controlled by central leader training, plus summer and dormant-season pruning. Rootstocks of *Prunus besseyi* and *Prunus tomentosa* are used to dwarf peaches but trees sucker profusely and are often short-lived. No doubt these rootstocks have been the source of disappointment for many home fruit growers.

Pears—Pear varieties with compact growth habits have not yet been developed . No fully dwarfing rootstocks are available. Quince roots are often used to provide semidwarf trees. Trees on quince rootstock sometime become sick and die in hot climates. Some quince roots provide very little dwarfing. 'Malling Quince A' is the most dwarfing. Provence types, such as 'BA 29', dwarf the tree very little. Quince roots also lack hardiness. The hybrid 'Old Home' × 'Farmingdale 333' is semivigorous but stimulates early production. Espalier training is a well-proven way to grow pears in a small space.

Plums and prunes—Rootstocks such as *Prunus besseyi* and *Prunus tomentosa* have been used to dwarf plums but the trees usually don't live long. 'St. Julian A' gives some but not much dwarfing. A

rootstock from England called 'Pixie' promises to produce a more satisfactory dwarf plum tree. Espalier training can be used very successfully to grow plums in small spaces. Container culture is also used for growth control.

Walnuts—There are no growth-controlling rootstocks for walnuts. Certain varieties such as 'Chico' set so profusely that they cease growth and stop bearing if not pruned heavily every year. Heavy pruning tends to dwarf them. These trees can be grown with multiple trunks to divide and reduce the vigor from a single root system.

GROWING FRUIT IN CONTAINERS

Restricting root growth of a fruit tree by growing it in a container usually results in dwarfing. Successful container growing requires the use of a soil with excellent drainage and a high percentage of air space. The best loam garden soil will rarely work when placed in a container, even if amended. It doesn't have the necessary amount of air space.

Therefore, a *synthetic soil* is recommended. It is frequently sold as a potting mix. In most cases potting soils shoud be used just as they come from the bag. These soils are lightweight, easy to handle, uniform in texture and free of disease organisms. Standard container mixes are sold under a variety of names, such as Jiffy Mix, Jiffy Mix Plus, Supersoil, Good Earth and Redi-Earth.

Synthetic soils are composed of an organic portion and an inorganic portion. If you mix your own soil, the

This Oregon State University experiment is visual proof that apples can be trained along wires. Result is a productive, fruiting fence in minimum space.

Many fruits grown in containers have restricted growth, as shown by fig above.

organic portion may be peat moss, pine bark, hardwood bark or fir bark. The inorganic portion may be vermiculite, perlite or fine sand. Potting soils in the West are often patterned after the University of California soil-less mixes. A typical example follows.

To make one cubic yard of container mix, combine:

    1/3 cubic yard peat moss
    1/3 cubic yard fine sand
    1/3 cubic yard ground pine or
       fir bark
    1-1/2 pounds urea-formaldehyde
       (38-0-0)
    3 pounds single superphospate
       (0-20-0)
    1 pound potassium nitrate
       (13-0-44)
    8 pounds calcium carbonate lime
    5 pounds dolomite lime
    1 pound iron sulfate

The urea formaldehyde (38-0-0) compensates for the nitrogen used as the bark and peat moss decay. Four pounds of blood meal or four pounds of hoof and horn meal serve the same purpose.

The calcium carbonate and dolomite are finely ground limes and their amounts are typical for most areas. In areas of high calcium-magnesium bicarbonate waters, lower rates should be used. Check with your water department to find out the mineral composition of your water.

All of the ingredients of a potting mix need to be thoroughly blended. Mix the components by shoveling them into a cone-shaped pile. Rebuild the pile three times to mix the ingredients thoroughly.

Trees grown in containers dry out faster than those grown in the ground. Water more frequently according to the needs of the tree during warm weather. Watering also leaches many nutrients, especially nitrogen, iron, zinc and manganese from the container soil. Apply nutrients more frequently but in smaller doses than with in-ground trees.

GLOSSARY

This glossary defines many of the botanical and horticultural terms used in this book, along with some that you may encounter in other gardening literature, and in conversations with nursery personnel, extension agents and other gardeners.

A

Acaricide (miticide): Pesticide that kills mites and ticks.

Accent plant: A plant that attracts attention to itself, usually because its form, foliage, texture or color is in contrast to its surroundings.

Acid soil: A soil with a pH less than 7.0. In practice, slightly acid soils are desirable for most plants, and only soils with a pH less than 6.5 are too acid for most plants. Rhododendrons and azaleas are notable exceptions, preferring soils with a pH of 4.5 to 5.5. Acid soils tend to be more spongy and open but less fertile than alkaline soils.

Active ingredient: In pesticides, the portion of the material that has the pesticidal effect.

Actual nitrogen: The actual amount of nitrogen in a bag of fertilizer. For instance, a 100 pound bag of fertilizer that is 10% nitrogen—as in 10-0-0— contains 10 pounds of nitrogen, as does a 50 pound bag of 20% fertilizer. Fertilizer recommendations in pounds of actual nitrogen are useful because they are independent of the brand and concentration of fertilizer you use.

Adobe soil: Heavy clay soil.

Adventitious growth: Bud, shoot, or root produced in an abnormal position or at an unusual time of development. An example is suckers or water sprouts at the trunk of a shrub or tree.

Aeration: The condition of plentiful oxygen supply on which roots and soil microorganisms thrive. Accomplished by cultivating or turning soil, *coring* lawns, turning compost and so forth. Air in well-aerated soils is very similar in composition to air above the soil. Air in poorly aerated soils contains more carbon dioxide and less oxygen.

Aerial bulb: See *Bulbil.*

Aerobic bacteria: Bacteria living or active only in the presence of oxygen. *See Anaerobic bacteria.*

Agricultural Extension Service: A government organization that provides information and consultation on gardening, as well as home economics and agriculture. Usually based at the Land Grant University of each state. Most counties in the United States also have an agricultural extension service or agent.

Air layering: Method of propagation by which aboveground stems develop roots while they remain attached to the mother plant.

Alkali soil: Soil with a pH of 8.5 or higher, and containing enough sodium to interfere with plant growth. High-sodium soils may be reclaimed by applications of gypsum followed by heavy leaching with water.

Alkaline soil: A soil with a pH higher than 7.0. Common in low-rainfall areas where mineral elements such as calcium and magnesium are not washed from soil. See *Acid soil.*

Alkalinity: A condition in which *basic elements* (hydroxyl or OH-ions) in a solution are more abundant than *acid elements* (Hydrogen or H + ions).

Alpine garden: A garden of plants that are native to alpine or high-elevation areas.

Alternate leaves: Leaves arranged singly at different heights and on different sides of the stem.

Alternate bearing: Production of heavier and lighter crops of flowers or fruits in successive years.

Ammonia: A colorless, pungent gas composed of one nitrogen atom and three hydrogen atoms. A primary component of many nitrogen fertilizers.

Ammoniacal: Containing ammonia. On fertilizer labels, the term indicates the nitrogen component based on ammonia. Ammoniacal fertilizers are acid-forming.

Ammonium: A crystalline salt containing one atom of nitrogen and four atoms of hydrogen. A basic component of many fertilizers, such as ammonium sulfate, which is used to acidify soil.

Anaerobic bacteria: Bacteria living or active in the absence of free oxygen. Gardeners encounter anaerobic bacteria in smelly compost piles and sulfurous, waterlogged soils. The smell of anaerobic bacteria is the gardener's warning to change conditions—whether in compost pile or soil—so air can circulate more freely.

Angiosperm: One of two main divisions of all seed-producing plants. These produce seeds in an enclosed ovary (carpel) within a flower. Includes all flowering plants. See *Gymnosperm.*

Annual: A plant whose entire life cycle is completed in a single growing season—germinating from seed, producing seed and dying.

Anther: The upper portion of a stamen that contains the pollen of a flower.

Anthracnose: A fungus disease that creates dead areas on leaves, stems or fruit.

Antidesiccant: A material that prevents or retards water loss in plants.

Antitranspirant: A plasticlike spray that coats leaves, thus slowing transpiration, or the loss of water vapor through leaves. Used on established plants that must endure a period of extreme drought, also on recently transplanted plants.

Apical dominance: Hormonal influence exerted by terminal bud in suppressing growth of lateral buds.

Arbor: An open structure, usually a horizontal framework supported by upright posts or columns, on which vines or other plants are trained.

Arborescent: Treelike or tending to become a tree.

Arboriculture: The practice of growing and caring of trees for ornamental purposes.

Arborist: Individual practiced in art of arboriculture—pruning, limb and tree removal, prevention and cure of tree diseases.

Arcure: A single cordon espalier in which whips are planted at slight angle, then new growth bent over to center of adjoining whip to form arches.

Aroid: A plant of the Araceae family such as Lords-and-Ladies.

Asexual propagation: Propagation by utilizing a part of the body tissue of the parent plant as opposed to growing a plant from seed. Same as *vegetative propagation.*

Atrium: Generally a small, roofless, planted courtyard within a building.

Auxin: Natural plant hormone (indole-3-acetic acid) that promotes plant growth by cell enlargement when used in extremely low concentrations.

Available moisture: Amount of water in soil that can be absorbed by plant roots.

Available nutrient: The portion of total nutrient in the soil that is in a form plant roots can absorb.

Avenue tree: A relatively large evergreen or deciduous tree planted along wide avenues. Larger than a street tree, it should be tolerant of pests, dust and smog, have deep roots and be nonfruiting.

B

Backfill soil: The soil used to fill a planting hole; sometimes amended with organic material.

Background plant: A large shrub or small tree with attractive, evergreen foliage. It should not require frequent attention and usually does not have showy flowers or fruit.

Balanced crotch: Two branches of a tree growing from the same point at the same rate. Undesirable because balanced crotches are weak and break easily.

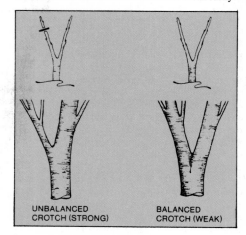

UNBALANCED CROTCH (STRONG)   BALANCED CROTCH (WEAK)

Balled-and-burlapped (B&B): Plant with a wrapped, compact mass of earth left around the roots. Larger nursery trees are often sold this way.

Bare-root transplanting: Usually dormant plants moved from one location to another with no soil around roots. Many nursery trees and shrubs are sold bare-root during their dormant period.

Bark graft: Grafting method in which a scion is inserted between the bark and xylem of stock.

Basal: Refers to the base or the lowest part of a plant or plant part.

Bedding plant: Flowering plants planted for seasonal color; commonly planted in masses or flower beds.

Berm: An elongated mound of earth.

Biennial: A plant that requires two growing seasons to complete its life cycle. Vegetative growth occurs the first season, flowering and seed production the second. Plant dies after flowering.

Biological pest control: The use of living organisms, such as bacteria or predatory insects, to control plant-destructive insects, mites or fungus.

Blanching: Covering a plant or part of a plant from light so that chlorophyll and associated cellular changes do not develop and tissues are more tender.

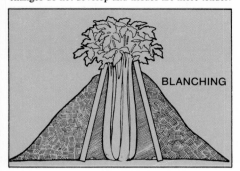

BLANCHING

Blind shoot: A shoot that fails to produce flowers, fruit or seeds as expected.

Blossom-end rot: Common disease of tomato fruit believed to be caused by calcium deficiency, drought or both. The flower end of the fruit cracks and develops a dry rot.

Bole: A strong, unbranched trunk.

Bolting: Premature flower and seedstalk growth. Often affects annual vegetables, such as lettuce or cabbage, and biennial herbs such as parsley or coriander (cilantro). Exposed to temperatures too cool or warm at critical stages of growth, these plants may produce flowers and seeds before useful vegetative growth.

Bone meal: Crushed or finely ground bones used as a fertilizer. The most common natural source of phosphorus.

Bonsai: Mature, even ancient-looking, miniature trees or shrubs. Size and growth are controlled by container size, pruning and feeding.

Border plant: Generally synonymous with herbaceous or flowering perennials. Usually annuals and perennials grouped for their colorful effect. Lower plants are situated to the front and taller ones to the rear of the border.

Botanical pesticide: Pesticides such as pyrethrum, nicotine, rotenone and ryania that occur naturally in certain plants.

Botanical variety: In botanical nomenclature, the category of plant classification after species. Example: *Juniper chinensis* var. *chinensis*. See *Cultivar.*

Boundary plant: A dense, compact, often thorny plant used to define boundaries or direct pedestrian traffic.

Bottom heat: Heat applied to the bottom of hot beds, benches or flats to speed or aid germination of seeds, or rooting of cuttings.

Bracts: Modified leaves at the base of some flowers. Also, leaves that serve as flower petals. Poinsettia and bougainvillea "flowers" are actually brightly colored bracts surrounding a small, insignificant flower.

Bramble: Usually wild relatives of blackberry, raspberry or dewberry, though the term sometimes refers to all plants of that genus *(Rubus).*

Bridge graft: A graft utilizing long scions to bridge a severe wound, such as girdling in the lower trunk of a tree. Scions are inserted into healthy bark above and below the wound.

Broadcast: To scatter seed or fertilizer uniformly over an area rather than in rows.

Broadleaf: Generally, any plant with wide leaves. More specifically, any plant with two cotyledon seed leaves (dicots). Characterized by netted rather than parallel leaf veins. Generally includes all trees except conifers and most flowering plants except grasses.

Broad-spectrum pesticide: Pesticides such as diazinon, malathion and sevin that are effective on a wide variety of plant pests.

Bud: Growing point or protrusion on a stem where a leaf, shoot or flower arises.

Budding: Method of grafting using a single bud as a scion, placed under the bark of the stock.

Bud sport: A cultivar arising from a natural bud mutation. A bud sport may differ in shoot length, leaves, flowers or fruit from other shoots of the same plant.

Bulb: A general term describing the underground storage parts of various plants. See *Corm, Rhizome, Tuber* and *Tuberous roots.* True bulbs, including daffodils, onions, lilies and tulips, resemble enlarged buds with many overlapping, fleshy leaf bases.

Bulbil: A small bulb produced above ground in the flower head or leaf axil of some bulbous plants. Small bulbs produced on the underground portion of plants are called *bulblets.*

C

Caliche: An essentially cemented layer of calcium carbonate (lime) at or just beneath soil surface. One of the many forms of hardpan. Often a problem in arid regions with alkaline, calcareous soils.

Caliper: The diameter of a nursery tree measured 6 inches above the soil level. Trees larger than 4 inches are measured 12 inches above the soil. In forestry, large trees are measured 4-1/2 feet above the soil. Also referred to as *diameter breast height*, abbreviated *DBH.*

Callus: Healing growth that covers plant wounds.

Calyx: The lowest or most outer flower parts. Usually green and leaflike, sometimes colored and petallike.

Cambium: Microscopic layer of living, dividing cells beneath bark from which new wood and bark develops. Best visualized as a thin cylinder just under the bark of trees.

Cane: Any hollow or pithy jointed stem, including the stems of reeds, bamboos, large grasses and small palms. Commonly refers to stems of raspberry, blackberry, grape and rose.

Cane fruit: Fruit of blackberry, raspberry, dewberry, boysenberry, gooseberry and currant.

Canker: Disease-caused trunk or stem lesion in which bark and sometimes cambium and wood are killed.

Canopy: The overhanging part of a tree which shades the ground.

Catkin: The drooping flower cluster, which looks something like a cat's tail, that appears in spring on walnut, pistache, hickory, oak and other windpollinated trees.

Caution: As relates to pesticides, the "signal" word on a pesticide label that indicates a slight toxicity.

Cell: Basic structural unit of plants and animals. Plant cells are surrounded by rigid cell walls.

Cellulose: Principal component of cell walls or fiber of plant tissue. Used to make paper, cellophane, explosives and other products.

Central leader: Dominant central branch of a tree. Also a method of training fruit and ornamental trees whereby pruning encourages a dominant central leader to develop.

Chelate: An organic molecule that binds to certain plant nutrients (in metal ion form) and prevents their conversion to an insoluble form, maintaining their availability to plant roots. The micronutrients iron, manganese and zinc are readily "locked up" in soil with an alkaline pH. This lock-up is prevented by chelates.

Chilling requirement: The minimum exposure to cold weather required by many deciduous plants to grow and develop correctly in spring. In general, 600 to 1,000 hours of temperatures between 32F and 45F (0C and 7C) are necessary to fully break a plant's dormancy. Chilling requirements are especially important in selecting deciduous fruit and nut trees.

Chimera: A plant composed of two genetically distinct tissues as a result of mutation, irregular cell division or grafting.

Chlorophyll: Green pigment within plant cells responsible for photosynthesis.

Chloroplast: Organ in plant cell that contains chlorophyll.

Chlorosis: Lack of chlorophyll, indicated by yellowing between veins of leaves. Chlorophyll does not develop because of a nutritional imbalance or deficiency, such as iron or manganese for example, or because of disease.

Chromosome: Microscopic structures that carry genetic information in the nucleus of all living cells. See *Diploid, Polyploid, Tetraploid,* and *Triploid.*

Clay: Microscopic-sized mineral particles. Clay soils contain 40% or more clay particles, less than 45% sand and less than 40% silt. Soils high in clay are noted for plasticity when wet, and for water and nutrient-holding capacity.

Cleft graft: A large tree serves as the stock. One or more main branches are sawed squarely, then split. Scions are inserted into the split or cleft.

Climber: A plant with long, usually thin and flexible branches that grow upwards, using tendrils, aerial roots or other means to hold onto a trellis, stake or other plant. Includes many vines.

Cloche: A temporary protective cover for young, delicate plants set outdoors early in the season. It is removed when danger of late frosts passes.

Clone: One of a group of asexually propagated plants all from one "mother" plant.

Cold frame: A low, unheated greenhouselike box used to propagate or acclimatize plants. Helps protect plants from climate extremes.

Cole crop: Any of the vegetables of the cabbage family, including broccoli, cabbage, kohlrabi and cauliflower.

Companion planting: Growing crops in the same area at the same time. Also, growing certain plants together because they are thought to benefit each other in some manner. Examples are squash with dill, tomatoes with basil and corn with beans.

Complete fertilizer: Any fertilizer than contains all three primary plant nutrients absorbed by roots— nitrogen, phosphorus and potassium.

Compost: Soil-improving and nutrient-rich material resulting from decomposition of organic materials.

Cone: A mass of scales or bracts bearing pollen or ovules; the seed-bearing fruit of pines and cycads. See *Gymnosperm.*

Conifer: Generally, plants that bear seeds in a cone. Conifers are usually evergreen, with the exception of bald cypress and larches and have needle-shaped or scalelike leaves. Wood of conifer trees is referred to as *softwood.*

Contact herbicide: Herbicides that kill only those portions of plants contacted by the spray. The herbicide is not systemic. Many perennial weeds will easily recover from such a spray, while annual weeds will not.

Container plant: Usually a shrub or tree of modest size that tolerates container conditions for many years. Also any plant—vegetable, herb, annual or perennial—grown in a pot or container.

Cool-season plants: Annual plants that grow best in cool, moderate temperatures of spring and fall, or winter in mild-winter climates. Examples are primroses, cole crops, calendulas, stocks, and pansies.

Cordon: A tree, usually a fruit tree such as an apple, with all branches removed so that only one main stem remains.

Corm: Flattened, underground plant part that stores plant food (carbohydrate). A type of bulb. Corms develop from the swollen base of a main stem. Gladiolus are an example.

Cormel: A small corm that forms at the base of a larger corm. Shallowly planted corms tend to develop a number of cormels.

Cornell mix: Artificial container-soil mix based on peat moss and vermiculite. Similar to but lighter weight than U.C. mix.

Corolla: Second series of floral parts, counting from the bottom of the flower.

Cotyledons: The first one or two leaves of a seedling, also called seed leaves, that store food during early growth. See *Dicotyledons* and *Monocotyledons*.

Cover crop: Grass or legume crop grown to improve soil by adding organic matter or to protect soil from erosion.

Cross-pollination: The exchange of pollen from the pollen-producing anthers of one flower to the pollen-receptive stigma of another. Occurs naturally via wind, bees or other insects, or is done intentionally by gardeners to produce a new hybrid or to increase fruit set of some crops, such as squash.

Crown: The point on a plant at soil level where stem tissue becomes root tissue. Also, the topmost portions of the leafy canopy of a tree.

Crucifer: Any plant belonging to the cabbage family (*Cruciferae*).

Cucurbit: Any plant of the squash family (Cucurbitaceae), including cucumbers, melons, squash and gourds.

Cultivar: Abbreviation of *cultivated variety*. A group of plants within a species that are of horticultural origin. Cultivars are distinguished by certain significant characteristics that are retained when the plant is reproduced, either sexually or asexually. The same as horticultural or agricultural varieties, but distinct from botanical varieties. In botanical nomenclature, the cultivar name is capitalized and set off by single quotes. Example: *Hemerocallis multiflora* 'Golden Chimes'.

Cultivate: Loosening soil surface around plants to destroy competing weeds and promote air circulation around roots.

Cut flower: Any flower that remains attractive long after being removed from the plant. Also a flower useful in arrangements.

Cutting: A section of plant—leaf, stem or root—that can be cut off and grown into a new plant.

D

Damping-off: A disease of emerging or newly emerged seedlings. The cause is one or more of several soil-borne fungi, all of them encouraged by excessive moisture. Sterilized soils are free of these fungi. Prevented with fungicides such as captan.

Danger-Poison: As relates to pesticides, a *signal word* on pesticide labels indicating a highly toxic compound.

Day-neutral plants: Plants whose development, flowering or fruiting are not influenced by relative lengths of light and dark periods.

Dead-heading: Removing flowers as soon as they fade to improve plant appearance and to redirect plant energy spent on seed development into encouraging additional blooms. Also done to prevent self-sowing of potentially invasive plants.

Deciduous: Trees or shrubs that drop their leaves at the end of the growing season and remain leafless during the winter or dormant period. Also occasionally applied to herbaceous plants that die to the ground in winter and return in spring.

Deflocculated soil: Soil lacking a well-aggregated structure. Caused by soft water (from sodium conditioning).

Dispersed soil: Soil in which clumped aggregates are separated into individual components. If caused by excessive sodium salts, dispersed soil can be recovered by gypsum. See *Flocculate*.

Defoliation: Unnatural loss of a plant's leaves, caused by weather, pests or herbicides.

Degree-day: A unit of heat energy representing one degree of temperature above a certain average daily temperature. Average daily temperatures are based on requirements of the plant being grown.

Delayed foliation: When leaf buds of deciduous trees grow slowly in spring. Fruit set from spring flowers may drop due to lack of leaf-supplied energy. Usually caused by a winter too warm to fully chill and break dormancy of leaf buds. See *Chilling Requirement*.

Determinate: Fixed or self-limiting growth habit that results in a plant of a definite maximum size. In many determinate plants, stem growth is terminated by a flower or fruit at outermost growing tips. Example: Determinate tomato plants only grow to a certain height and are usually short and bushy. They bear all their fruit at one time, then die. Indeterminate tomato plants continue to grow in size and produce fruit until killed by frost or old age.

Diatomaceous Earth (DE): Earthy deposit formed by skeletal remains of microscopic marine organisms called *diatoms*. When ingested by insects in pulverized form, DE punctures the insect's stomach, causing dehydration and death. Safe but relatively expensive nonchemical control for a number of insects.

Dibble: A pointed implement of wood, metal or plastic used to make holes for seeds or small plants.

Dicotyledon (dicot): Any plant with two cotyledon leaves. See drawing below.

Dieback: When branches die from tips downward toward the trunk or main branch.

Dioecious: Plants with male and female flowers on separate plants. Female individuals bear pistillate (fruiting) flowers and fruit, and male individuals bear staminate (pollinating) flowers.

Diploid: Cells with two sets of chromosomes ($2n$).

Disbudding: Snipping or pinching off flower buds or shoot buds.

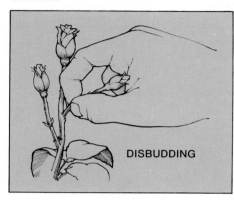

DISBUDDING

Diurnal: A plant with flowers that open during the day and close at night.

Division: A method of propagating clumping perennial plants by physically separating the crown of the plant to form two or more separate plants.

Dormant: Seeds, bulbs, buds, whole plants or plant parts in a period of inactivity, but capable of growth once conditions become favorable. Winter dormancy is triggered by cold weather, summer dormancy by hot weather.

Dormant spray: Pesticide applied during a plant's dormant period, usually "horticultural" or superior oil or lime-sulfur.

Double digging: Method of preparing soil whereby subsoil is replaced with topsoil. A process of deep cultivation, usually accomplished by digging and amending soil to a depth of two shovel blades (about 18 inches.)

Double flowers: Flowers with more than the natural number of petals common to the species found in the wild. Wild roses have five petals while modern garden roses have 25 to 60 petals. Additional petals are usually encouraged mutations that cause stamens or other flower parts to become petal-like.

Double nose: Bulbs capable of producing more than one flower.

Drip line: The imaginary line on the soil directly underneath the outermost leaves of a plant.

LEAF

SEEDLING

DICOT

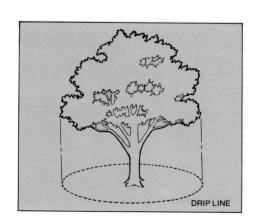

DRIP LINE

Dust: An extremely fine powder used as a pesticide carrier. Applied with squeeze bottles or one of a variety of special applicators.

Dwarf: A plant smaller at maturity than others of the same kind. Usually produced by grafting.

E

Edging plant: Low, compact, herbaceous or woody plant planted along walks or lawn borders.

Epiphyte: Nonparasitic plant, such as some orchids and bromeliads, that grows on another plant.

Ericaceous: Plants of the *Ericaceae* family, including the heathers, azaleas and rhododendrons, manzanitas and many others.

Espalier: A tree or shrub, ornamental or edible, trained to grow on a single plane, such as against a wall or fence.

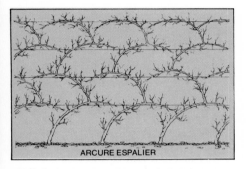

ARCURE ESPALIER

Established plant: A plant that is fully adjusted to its environment and rooted into the soil.

Etiolation: Result of growing plants in darkness, preventing the development of chlorophyll. Seedlings grown in low light are often pale in color and excessively tall.

Evapotranspiration: Total loss of water from plant and surrounding area, including both evaporation from soil surface and transpiration through leaves.

Everbearing: Fruit plants, such as many strawberry varieties, that produce fruit throughout the growing season rather than only in spring or fall.

Evergreen: Any plant that retains leaves year-round. Individual leaves may or may not last longer than one growing season. Leaves drop and are replaced intermittently rather than all at once. See *Deciduous*.

Everlasting flower: A flower that maintains its character and color after cut and dried. Strawflowers and sedums are examples.

Eye: A visible bud or growing tip, usually in a modified root or tuber. The term is often applied to potatoes and peony divisions.

F

F hybrids: Refers to the generations of hybrids following a cross-pollination. F1 hybrids are the first generation of breeding from a cross between parents of two different true-breeding cultivars within a species. F1 hybrids are commonly more vigorous and productive than their parents. F2 hybrids are produced by interbreeding the F1 hybrids and are less vigorous than their parents. Neither F1 nor F2 hybrids reproduce true from seed (true to type). F3 hybrids are the third generation from a cross.

Facer plant: A low plant positioned in front of taller plants or structures.

Fairy ring: Conspicuous, generally circular group of mushrooms common in lawns. Caused by several kinds of fungus, they live on decaying organic matter in the soil, such as dead tree roots, and do not directly damage the lawn.

Family: A botanical classification that is one step more broad than genus.

Fasciation: A growth abnormality in which two or more stems fuse forming one enlarged, flattened, often curved stem.

Fastigiate: A narrow, erect growth habit due to closely positioned vertical branches.

Fence plant: A plant well adapted to growing against, along, or on top of a fence.

Fertilize: To apply materials that contain essential plant nutrients to soil or plant foliage. Also used to mean *pollinize*.

Fertilizer: Any material that contains one or more essential plant nutrients. A commercial fertilizer must contain at least 5% plant nutrients, such as a 3-1-1.

Fertilizer burn: Damage to or death of plant tissues, resulting from the direct or excessive application of concentrated dry fertilizer to plant foliage or roots.

Fertilizer grade (analysis): The guaranteed analysis expressed in whole numbers as percent nitrogen (N), percent phosphorus oxide (P_2O0_5), and percent potassium oxide (K_2). These percentages are always shown on fertilizer labels in the order given above. Usually abbreviated N-P-K. For example, 10-5-5 fertilizer contains 10% nitrogen, 5% phosphorus and 5% potassium.

Fibrous roots: Many-divided root systems that branch hundreds of times near the crown. Azaleas and rhododendrons, ferns and other plants adapted to loose, forest humus soil, have fibrous roots. Fibrous-rooted plants are generally easier to transplant than plants with taproots.

Filament: Stalklike part of stamen that supports anther in flower.

Flat: Shallow plastic, metal or wood box for sowing seeds or rooting cuttings. Flats of ground-cover plants contain 64 to 100 plants each, depending upon the size and growth rate of the ground cover.

Flocculate, soil: To cause soil particles, especially clay particles, to clump together. See *Deflocculated soil*.

Flower: The reproductive organ of seed-bearing plants. Usually colorful. Because flowers are uniquely characteristic, they are used as the most important basis of distinction between plants.

Flowering, new wood: Flowers develop on growth that occurs the same season as the flowers. These are mostly summer- to fall-flowering plants and should be pruned in late winter or early spring before growth begins.

Flowering, old wood: Flowers develop on wood formed during the previous growing season. These are usually spring-flowering plants and should be pruned immediately after the period of bloom.

Foliar feeding: Spray applications of nutrients that have a low burn potential and can be absorbed through leaves.

Foot-candle: A measure of light energy. 1 foot-candle equals the amount of light falling on an object placed 1 foot from a standard, 1-candlepower light source.

Forcing: Reproducing natural conditions of day length, temperature or both, to initiate a plant's natural flowering process.

Foundation plant: A shrub or small tree used to soften the right angles where the house or other structure meets the soil surface.

Friable soil: Soil with good structure. Loose, well-aggregated soil that is easy to work, usually indicating plentiful organic matter.

Frond: Foliage of ferns and palms.

Fruit: Botanically, a fruit is a distinct organ that develops from the ovary of a flower—and sometimes nearby tissues—and encloses or includes the maturing seeds. In this sense, a green bean is as much a fruit as a peach. Horticulturally, a fruit is a sweet, fleshy, ripened ovary of a woody plant, used as food.

Full slip: Vernacular description of the easy separation of a melon fruit from the vine. Harvest melons when they are at "full slip".

Fumigation: Exposing soil, any enclosed area and sometimes plants to a volatile and poisonous gas to eliminate pests.

Fungi: An order of plants that have no chlorophyll, roots, stems or leaves. Because they lack chlorophyll for photosynthesis, fungi must derive energy from other plant and animal tissue, living or dead. Fungi that parasitize living plants cause *disease* conditions in that plant. Mushrooms and toadstools are fungi that typically derive energy from decaying organic matter.

Fungicide: A pesticide that kills fungi.

Furrow: A trench in soil for planting, carrying water or reducing erosion.

G

Gall: An abnormal growth on a plant, usually in response to a bacteria such as crown gall or an insect egg or larva in the stem or root.

Genus: A grouping of related plants including at least one species. One category more general than species in the system of plant classification. It is the first part of the two-part (binomial) Latin plant name used to identify a plant. The genus and species names are written in italics, with the first letter of the genus name capitalized. Example: *Ilex aquifolium*.

Germination: Sprouting of a seed and beginning of active growth.

Gibberellic acid (GA_3): A substance used to regulate or modify growth characteristics of some plants. Gibberellin makes bush peas or beans into pole peas or beans. Also, camellia growers "gib" flower buds to induce larger blooms.

Girdling: Cutting around a plant through the bark and cambium. Girdling completely around a plant eventually kills it. Partial girdling is sometimes done intentionally to promote flowering and fruiting of certain trees. Often occurs accidentally as a result of rodents or wood-boring insects.

Graft: Connecting part of one plant to part of another so that both will unite and grow as one plant. Successful grafts are usually between closely related plants. With trees, a branch or growing shoot, called a *scion*, is taken from one variety and grafted to the *stock* (branch or trunk) of another.

Graft hybrid: A grafted plant that shares characteristics of both stock and scion.

Granule: A particle of fertilizer or pesticide.

Greenhouse: A building with translucent sides and roof in which temperature and humidity are made more beneficial to certain plants. Used for growing delicate or out-of-season plants.

Greenhouse plant: A tender plant that requires protection from temperatures below 50F (11C) and from temperatures above 90F (32C).

Green manure: Usually a legume crop, such as clover, grown to be incorporated into the soil for its nutrient and organic matter benefits.

Grex: A collective term for cultivars of the exact same hybrid origin.

Ground cover: Turf grasses and hundreds of other low-growing plants of all types that cover and protect the soil from weed invasion and erosion. Nonliving ground covers include stone, mulch, paving and decking.

Growth regulator: Any natural or synthetic plant hormone that affects plant growth when used in extremely small amounts. See *Gibberellic acid (GA₃)*, *Indole-3-acetic acid (IAA)* and *Indole-3-butyric acid (IBA)*.

Gymnosperm: One of two main divisions of all seed-producing plants. These produce seeds on open scales, usually in cones. Includes cone-bearing trees such as pine, fir and spruce. See *Angiosperm*.

Gynoecious: Plants that produce female flowers only. Gynoecious plants require a nearby male plant of the same species for pollination in order to set seed or fruit. See *Monoecious*.

H

Half-hardy plant: A plant that is marginally cold-hardy in a given area. It is tolerant of average minimum winter temperatures, but must be protected during periods of extreme cold.

Hardening off: Gradual adjustment of tender plants recently moved from a greenhouse or indoors to a more rigorous outdoor environment. Cold frames or other protective devices are often used to harden-off such plants.

Hardiness: Generally refers to a plant's ability to survive low temperatures. As an example, a plant that is hardy to Zone 6 will survive minimum temperatures between -10F to 0F (-24C to -18C).

Hardpan: A hardened layer of soil that does not allow water drainage or root penetration. Caused by a number of factors, including mineral buildup at a certain soil level (see Caliche), soil compaction by heavy equipment—common in new housing developments—and cultivating to the same depth over a long period of time (plowpan).

Hard water: Water with abundant to excessive dissolved calcium and magnesium salts. Hard water improves soil structure but tends to increase the work plant roots must perform to absorb water. "Hard water makes soil soft; soft water makes soil hard" goes an old farmer's truism.

Hardwood: Dicot trees that include a certain cell structure conifers lack. Includes all broadleaf deciduous trees. Term does not refer to hardness or density of wood, though hardwoods usually have denser wood than softwoods. An exception is balsa (a hardwood) being "softer" than fir, a softwood. Ash, birch, hickory, oak and walnut are familiar North American hardwood trees.

Hardwood cutting: Mature, hardened section of stem removed in fall or winter to be used for propagation.

Hardy: A plant that needs no protection from cold during winter. Term is sometimes used to describe certain plants that can survive extremely cold winters, but is more often used in relative sense, as in *hardy to -25F (-32C)*. See *Hardiness*.

Heading back: A basic pruning cut, opposite of *thinning*. Shortening a branch by cutting back to a bud or side branch. Useful for changing direction of growth or for promoting more dense growth.

Heaving (frost heaving): Lifting of plants (or stones) out of the ground, caused by alternate freezing and thawing of water in the soil. Often responsible for the springtime death of shallow-rooted plants.

Heavy soil: A dense soil composed primarily of clay.

Hedge: Shrubs or other plants growing close to each other in a row to form a continuous mass of foliage. A "formal" hedge is pruned to a definite geometrical shape. An "informal" hedge is kept within certain bounds but allowed to assume a more-or-less natural or freeform shape.

Hedgerow: A large hedge, usually of several kinds of plants. Used in Great Britain since the Middle Ages to define field ownership and contain livestock. Hawthorn *(Crataegus monohgyna)*, field maple *(Acer campestre)* and beech *(Fagus sylvatica)* are three traditional hedgerow plants.

Heel cutting: A stem cutting taken with a piece or *heel* of 2-year-old wood attached.

Heeling-in: Storing bare-root plants in a favorable location, packed in soil or sawdust, until planting time.

HEELING-IN

Herb: Commonly any plant valued for flavor, aroma or medicinal qualities.

Herbaceous plant: Generally, any plant with soft, nonwoody stems, such as annuals, perennials and bulbs. Specifically, any perennial plant that dies back to the roots in winter and regrows in spring.

Herbicide: Pesticide that kills plants. Some herbicides are formulated to kill certain undesirable plants without harming desirable plants, provided they are used correctly. Others kill all vegetation.

Honeydew: Sweet substance exuded by aphids, scale and related insects. It attracts ants and supports growth of black sooty mold.

Horticulture: Cultivation of fruits, vegetables, ornamental trees, shrubs and herbaceous plants.

Horticultural variety: A variety or cultivar originating as a result of controlled pollination, selective breeding or hybridization.

Hose-in-hose flower: A type of double flower, common to azaleas and primroses, that seems to include a tubular-shaped flower within another flower.

HOSE-IN-HOSE FLOWER

Host: Any organism, such as a plant, on which other organisms live. A rose plant is a frequent host of aphids.

House plant: Any plant that can adapt to indoor environmental conditions, notably light and humidity. Many plants can be raised as house plants, but certain kinds, usually tropicals, are used especially for this purpose.

Humus: Dark colored, relatively stable remains of soil organic matter after most of it has decomposed.

Hybrid: Offspring of an intentional or natural cross between two plants with different genetic makeups. A primary or interspecific hybrid is the result of crossing plants of two different species. Although rare, hybrids have been developed by crossing two plants of different genera. Hybrids are often sterile and never reproduce true from seed. In botanical nomenclature, hybrids are indicated by the symbol "×," as in *Photinia × fraseri*.

Hybrid tea rose: The most favored modern rose. These moderate-size plants produce large, usually double flowers on long stems.

Hybrid vigor: Certain plants (corn, tomatoes) display significantly extra vigor in the F1 generation when certain specific parent varieties are crossed. Hybrid vigor tends to diminish in succeeding hybrid generations. See *F hybrids*.

Hydroponics: Growing plants without soil, utilizing a carefully controlled, nutrient-rich solution. One method uses a sterile medium, such as vermiculite, to hold roots and nutrient solution, in other cases, the roots are growing directly in the liquid nutrient solution. Can be done in a greenhouse or outdoors.

I

Inarching: Grafting method in which a plant is attached to another while still attached to its own roots.

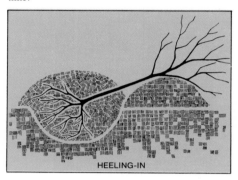
INARCHING

Indeterminate: Plants with a continuous growth pattern, or no fixed maximum size. Plant will continue to grow or bear fruit until killed by pests, disease, frost or other adverse conditions. See *Determinate*.

Indole-3-acetic acid (IAA): Plant hormone that promotes cell elongation.

Indole-3-butyric acid (IBA): Synthetic plant hormone used to promote root formation.

Inorganic: Any chemical or substance composed of matter that is not animal or vegetable, usually derived from mineral sources. Used in gardening vernacular to identify soil amendments, fertilizers and other garden chemicals not derived from plants or animals, also those that are synthetic in nature.

Insecticide: Pesticide that kills insects.

Integrated pest management: System of pest management (insects, weeds, diseases) that utilizes all methods of control—cultural techniques, predators, parasites and pesticides. The goal is to maintain pest populations below the level that causes unacceptable damage. Favored pesticides are narrow-spectrum, killing only specific pests.

Internode: Space on a stem between nodes or growing points.

Interstock: Section of stock grafted between a rootstock and scion.

J

June drop (fruit drop): Natural shedding of immature fruit in early summer.

Jute netting: A woven net made of jute fibers. Used for erosion control and seedling establishment on slopes. Biodegradable.

Juvenile growth: Growth of different character that occurs in immature (not capable of flowering) plants of a species. Some mature plants may produce juvenile growth near their bases (eucalyptus, acacia). Juvenile growth of English and Algerian ivy are more common than flowering, mature growth.

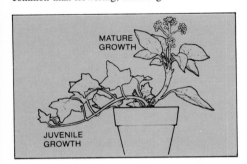

K

Kitchen garden: Any garden—indoors or out—producing herbs, salad greens, fruits, or cut flowers for home use.

Kniffen system: A two-wire support system for training grape vines.

Knot garden: English term for a garden design based on patterns used by weavers and lacemakers. Popular from 16th Century to late 18th Century. Knot gardens were made on level ground, usually in front of a house, with low hedge plants such as germander, dwarf lavenders, common thyme and lavender cotton.

L

Landscape: Surrounding terrain and its features. Used as a verb, the process of improving, personalizing, or making more attractive the property surrounding a residence or other building.

Landscape architecture: Designing and planning the arrangement of land, and the plants and objects upon it for the use and pleasure of people.

Landscape construction: The practice of installing landscape elements, usually according to a landscape plan or drawing. Physically creating the changes in the landscape envisioned and planned by others.

Lawn tree: A tree adapted to high moisture of a lawn and able to compete with grass roots for nutrients. Also, a lawn tree should be deep-rooted, have an attractive, clean habit and cast a light shade that permits grass to grow underneath.

Layering: Propagation method whereby stems still attached to plant are covered with moist soil, encouraging root formation. See *Air layering* and *Mound layering.*

LC50: The "lethal concentration" of active ingredient in a pesticide that kills 50% of the organisms being tested.

LD50: The "lethal dose" that kills 50% of the test organisms when testing a pesticide. Always measured in terms of milligrams of "technical" or undiluted material per kilogram of body weight (mg/kg). Rates vary for source of dose, oral (through the mouth) and dermal (through the skin). For example: malathion has an LD50 of 885mg/kg. An "average" lethal dose for a 150-pound person would be 66,375 milligrams (66.375 grams or 2.34 ounces).

Leaching: Applying up to 10 times the amount of water normally required to wet soil, to wash excessive amounts of soluble salts from the root zone.

Leader: Main stem or trunk. See *Central leader.*

Leaf cutting: A leaf or portion of a leaf removed from the parent plant and inserted in soil mix to grow a new plant. See page 102 for directions. To grow a *leaf bud cutting,* the leaf, its petiole and bud are removed from the plant and the bud is covered with moist soil until roots form.

Leaflet: An apparently separate, leaflike division of a leaf. It is not attached to a stem with a petiole and bud.

Leaf mold: A mulch or soil amendment composed of partially decayed leaves.

Leaf scar: Distinct part of a stem where a leaf and petiole were attached.

Leggy: The condition of plants with little foliage at their base or excessively long, thin stems. Usually caused by insufficient light. See *Etiolation.*

Legume: Any plant included in the family Leguminosae—acacia, peas, wisteria, alfalfa and clover.

Limestone: Sedimentary rock of calcite (mostly calcium carbonate), sometimes with significant quantities of magnesium carbonate (dolomite). Ground limestone is sometimes used to make soil more alkaline.

Loam: Technically, a textural class of soil that represents a compromise between characteristics of clay and sand soils. Loam contains less than 27% clay, 28% to 50% silt, and less than 52% sand.

Long-day plant: A plant that begins to flower when days are longer (nights shorter) than a minimum number of hours. Chrysanthemums are an example.

Loppers: Long-handled pruning shears used for branches 3/4 to 1-1/2 inches in diameter.

M

Macroclimate: Average weather patterns or climate conditions over a wide area. See *Microclimate.*

Manure: Composted animal excreta used to fertilize, enrich or improve soil.

Mellow soil: A soft, friable soil.

Meristem: Undifferentiated tissue at growing tips.

Microclimate: Small areas with a climate distinctly different than the surrounding climate, or macroclimate. Microclimates of various sizes are caused by slight differences in elevation, slopes and the direction they face (north, south, east, west) and proximity to large bodies of water. On an even smaller scale, a house, tree, wall, patio overhead, or even the type of soil mulch can influence temperature, humidity and exposure to sun and wind, creating several distinct microclimates within a single yard.

Micronutrient: A mineral element that plants require in only minute quantities. Also called *trace elements.* Although extremely small amounts are used, their absence will prevent proper plant growth.

Mildew: A surface-growing fungus, visible to the naked eye.

Miscible oil: An oil combined with an *emulsifier,* a material that allows it to mix with water and be applied as a spray. Used as an insecticide to control mites, scale, mealybugs and other insects. Kills by suffocation.

Mist propagation: Method of germinating seeds or rooting cuttings utilizing periodic fine-mist sprays over the area.

Mite: Tiny spider-like arachnids, several of which are common plant pests. Many are beneficial predators.

Miticide: Pesticide that kills mites.

Modified central leader: A training system preferred for upright and closed-center trees, which include apples, pears and some stone fruits. Develop a leader from a central axis and keep it in place until the basic tree framework is established—usually for 5 to 6 years. Then head back the central leader. This temporary central leader helps develop well-spaced, wide-angle scaffold limbs.

Molluscicide: A pesticide that kills snails and slugs.

Monocotyledon (monocot): A plant with one cotyledon in seedling stage. Grasses and conifers are monocots.

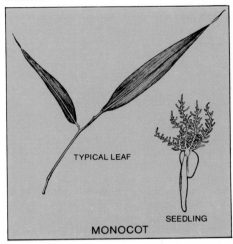

Monoecious: Plants that have separate male and female flowers but on the same individual plant. Plants of the cucumber family are usually monoecious.

Mosaic: A virus disease that causes mottling of leaves. One type, tobacco mosaic, affects tomatoes and some other food crops.

Mound layering: Similar to layering, but branches are left upright and moist soil or rooting media is mounded around them. Once roots form, branches are cut away from parent plant and transplanted.

Mulch: Any of a large number of materials, organic or inorganic, that are used to make a protective layer over soil to prevent weed growth, control erosion, maintain an even soil temperature or conserve moisture.

Mycorrhiza: The association of a fungus with the roots of a higher plant for mutual (symbiotic) benefit.

N

Native: A plant that is natural to an area or region.

Naturalized: An introduced plant that has established itself in a region or area but is not native. For instance, Bermudagrass has naturalized in many gardens, much to the dismay of their owners.

Nematocide: Pesticide that kills nematodes.

Nematode: Mostly microscopic worms, several of which parasitize plant roots. Beneficial nematodes are a part of integrated pest-control programs.

Nitrification: Conversion of ammonia ions to nitrate ions, accomplished by soil bacteria known as *Nitrosomonas* and *Nitrobacter*.

Nitrogen-fixing bacteria: Bacteria of the genus *Rhizobium* inhabit roots of legumes, consume atmospheric nitrogen and convert it to a form usable to plants.

N-P-K: The nutrient ingredients of common complete fertilizers. N is nitrogen, P is phosphorus, and K is potassium or potash. Where these letters appear on a fertilizer package, they are always followed by a number indicating the percentage of those nutrients in the fertilizer.

Node: The areas along a stem where a bud is present and a leaf or secondary stem may develop.

Nomenclature: A system of names. *Botanical nomenclature* refers to the usually two Latin names (genus name first, species name second) given to identify plants.

Nonselective herbicide: Chemicals that kill plants regardless of type. Used in areas where no plant growth is desired.

Nut: Hard-shelled fruit with one, usually edible, seed or kernel.

O

Offset: A short, lateral growth from the base of a plant, either as a scaly bud or with a rosette of terminal leaves. Most offsets readily form roots so are a convenient means of propagation.

Offshoot: A branch or lateral shoot arising from a main stem that is used for propagation.

Open-pollinated: Plant varieties produced by uncontrolled, natural cross-pollination in seed fields of parent varieties. Open-pollinated vegetable varieties are generally less expensive than hybrids and they produce true-to-type seeds.

Opposite leaves: Leaves that occur in matched pairs at each bud.

Orangery: Earliest "greenhouse" created by Romans and later Europeans to protect citrus through cold winters.

Organic: Any material of plant or animal origin. In gardening, many organic materials are used as fertilizer, mulch, or pesticides.

Organic gardening: A gardening technique that allows use of only natural or organic, rather than synthetic, fertilizers and pesticides.

Osmotic pressure: The negative pressure that influences the rate of diffusion of water through a semipermeable membrane such as a cell wall. High levels of salt in soil (from fertilizers or water) increases the soil's osmotic pressure, causing water to diffuse from roots into the soil. Plant shows drought symptoms even though soil is moist (physiological drought).

Ovicide: Pesticide that kills eggs of pests.

P

Parasite: Any organism (plant, insect, mite, fungus, nematode) that lives part or all of its life cycle at the expense of a host organism. Beneficial parasites are used to control many kinds of insect pests.

Parthenocarpic fruit: Fruit that develops without pollination (fertilization).

Pathogen: An organism or virus capable of causing disease in a host plant or animal. Beneficial pathogens, such as *Bacillus thuringiensis,* are used to control insect pests.

Pathology, plant: A special area of study within botany concerned with plant diseases and disorders.

Peat moss: Slightly decomposed remains of plants found in existing or former lakes, swamps, or marshes. Extremely water retentive and generally acid pH.

Peat pellet: A pellet of dried, compressed peat moss that expands with moisture and is used for starting seeds or cuttings. These and peat pots can be placed directly in the ground at planting time, reducing transplant shock.

Perennial: In the broadest sense, any plant that commonly lives 3 years of more. Perennial plants do not naturally die after flowering, as do annuals and biennials. Though all trees and shrubs are perennial, the term is commonly used to describe herbaceous (soft-stemmed) plants that die back to the roots in winter and regrow the following spring. Some perennials do remain evergreen in mild-winter climates.

Perfect flower: A flower that includes both male (stamens) and female (pistil) parts.

Perlite: Heat-treated volcanic material that is light and porous. Used as a component of artificial soil mixes and as a rooting medium.

Petiole: Stem that connects a leaf blade to a branch.

pH: A scale indicating relative acidity and alkalinity of a substance or solution. The symbol "pH" is the abbreviation of *potential hydrogen* and represents the negative logarithm of the concentration of hydrogen ions in gram atoms per liter. The scale ranges between 0 and 14. Midpoint 7 represents a neutral condition, neither acid nor alkaline. Below 7 is acidic, above 7 is alkaline. Most plants prefer a slightly acidic soil, around pH 6.5.

Pheromone: Sex attractant produced by insects. Synthetic pheromones are sometimes used in pest-control systems, such as Japanese beetle traps.

Phloem: Special cells in plants that carry food manufactured in leaves throughout the plant. Phloem is just under the bark.

Photoperiodism: The response of some plants to light exposure, natural or artificial, or specific lengths of time. Length of light and dark periods trigger plants to begin flowering or form tubers, bulbs or runners.

Photosynthesis: The name of the process occurring in plant chlorophyll that begins with simple minerals and gases and, in the presence of sunlight, produces a carbohydrate that plants use for food.

Phototropism: The characteristic of plants to grow toward a light source. The part of the plant exposed directly to light grows more slowly and the shaded part grows faster, thus the plant curves toward the light.

Physiological drought: This occurs when a plant suffers from drought although plenty of water is available in the soil. It happens if the water in the soil is frozen, or if the roots are unable for some reason to absorb the water. See *Osmotic pressure.*

Pistil: Principle female organ of a flower including the ovary in which seeds develop.

Pistillate: Flowers with only female parts. Also called *imperfect flowers.*

Pith: The center tissues of a stem.

Pleach: Training tops of usually small trees to interlace.

PLEACHED TREES

Plugging: Vegetative propagation of turf by planting small blocks or plugs of sod at certain intervals.

Poisonous plants: Poisons and toxins are widely distributed throughout nature, including many plants. Most ominous are the fruits of castor bean (*Ricinus*) or precatory bean (*Abrus*). One or two of either type, when chewed and swallowed, can be fatal to a child. The fruits and berries of some ornamental shrubs and trees are poisonous. Poison hemlock (*Conium maculatum*)—popularized by Socrates—is as deadly as its reputation. Ornamental plants with toxic properties include: bulbs— *Colchicum, Convallaria, Galanthus, Hyacinthus, Narcissus, Ornithogalum;* perennials and shrubs; *Aconitum, Aleurites, Atropa, Buxus, Celastrus, Daphne, Datura, Delphinium, Dicentra, Digitalis, Hypericum, Hyoscyamus, Iris, Kalmia, Leucothoe, Ligustrum, Lupinus, Nerium, Pieris, Rhododendron, Solanum, Taxus and Wisteria.* In some plants, toxic properties are in specific locations only, such as the leaves of rhubarb but not the stems, which are edible. Cassava (*Manihot*) becomes nontoxic after cooking. Poison ivy, poison oak and nettles produce allergic skin reactions as do *Primula obconica,* some of the spurges (*Euphorbia*) and dumbcanae (*Dieffenbachia*). There are many more plants with poisonous properties than those listed here. Children are the usual victims of these plants. Learn about native poisonous plants in your area. Teach children not to eat anything but real food. Find out from the nursery if the plants you're buying (or parts thereof) have poisonous properties.

Pollard: A tree whose scaffold branches are repeatedly cut back to points near the main trunk to form a crown of many small, dense branches. Pollarding is severe pruning treatment for most trees—sycamore is one of the most tolerant.

Pollen: Dustlike grains containing male sex cells produced by anthers in flowers.

Pollination: The transfer of pollen from anthers of one flower to the receptive stigma of the same or different flower.

Pollinator: A variety of a plant grown only as a source of pollen.

Polyploid: A plant with more than the normal number of chromosomes.

Pome: The botanical term for a fleshy fruit with thin, leathery skin such as apple.

Pomology: The study of growing and handling fruit plants.

Postemergence herbicide: Herbicides applied after weeds appear.

Predator: In gardening terms, an insect or mite that consumes another insect. Predators that kill garden pests are important components of integrated pest-control systems.

Preemergence herbicide: An herbicide applied to soil before weeds germinate.

Preplant herbicide: An herbicide applied to soil months or days before planting.

Pruning: Pinching, thinning, heading or shearing plants to direct growth, promote flowering or fruiting, improve health or appearance or avoid obstructions.

Pseudobulb: Bulblike base of some orchids and other plants in which moisture and food is stored.

Q

Quiescence: Plant dormancy imposed by external conditions, such as low temperatures.

R

Relative humidity: The amount of water vapor in the air compared to the amount required to saturate the air at a given temperature.

Remontant: Blooming a second time in one season, also called *repeat bloom*.

Repellent: Any material that repels but does not kill insects or other pests. Garlic is a natural insect repellent.

Reproductive phase: The stage of plant growth dedicated to producing flowers, fruit and seeds.

Respiration: In plants, the metabolic process in which stored carbohydrate is oxidized to produce energy and compounds necessary for growth. Opposite of photosynthesis, the process that creates carbohydrate or "food" for plant growth.

Rhizome: Spreading underground stem or runner.

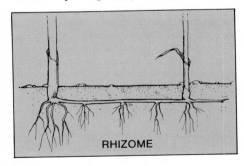

RHIZOME

Rock garden: Gardens established on slopes around natural or man-made rock outcroppings. Rock-garden plants are usually low growing, drought tolerant, and dependant upon fast drainage.

Roguing: Physically pulling or otherwise destroying undesirable individuals from plantings raised for seed. Usually done to obtain disease-free stock or true-to-type stock.

Roof garden: A garden of any size or description situated on a rooftop.

Root: Underground portion of plant that serves to anchor it and absorb water and minerals necessary for growth.

Rootbound: A condition with container-grown plants when roots have become crowded and establish a pattern conforming to the shape of the container. Rootbound nursery plants are not desirable because roots may never adjust to new growing environment. When planting rootbound plants, gently separate roots, cutting some if necessary, and redirecting them.

Root hair: Minute branches just behind growing tip of root, which are thin and permeable enough to allow water and mineral ions to pass through.

Root hardy: Plants with roots hardy enough to survive a rigorous winter although top portion of plant may be destroyed.

Root sucker: A branch that sprouts from a root, usually just around the base of the trunk, but sometimes several feet away from it.

Rooting hormone: A fine powder containing a plant hormone, such as a-Naphthalene-acetic acid (NAA), that aids in rooting of cuttings. Very little is needed—lightly dust the cut end of the cutting before inserting it in soil mix.

Runner: Horizontal shoot or branch that roots at tips.

Russeting: Roughened, brown areas on skins of fruit and commonly on potatoes.

S

Saline soil: A soil so saturated with soluble salts that most plants are unable to survive in it. See *Alkali soils*.

Sand: All mineral particles in a soil that are finer than gravel but larger than silt particles. A "sand" soil contains at least 85% sand and less than 10% clay.

Sapwood: Younger, outer layer of tissues in a trunk or stem that conducts and stores plant food.

Scalping: Mowing a lawn so low that green foliage is removed and only brown lower stems remain.

Scaly bulb: Bulbs with overlapping leaves that resemble scales.

Scarification: Conditioning a hard seed coat by scratching or sanding so that it will more readily absorb water and begin germination.

Scion: A branch or shoot of a woody plant used for grafting to a rootstock, sometimes to an interstock. Scions are chosen for desirable top growth, flowers, fruit, leaf color or pest resistance.

Screen, plant: A single plant or grouping of plants used to exclude the view of certain parts of the landscape.

Secateurs: Scissor- or anvil-type hand pruning shears.

Secondary pest: A potential pest of usually little importance that becomes a serious pest because predators and parasites that normally keep it in check are destroyed. Spider mites are a frequent secondary pest after use of the pesticide Sevin.

Seed: Embryonic plant in dormant state with food supply and protective covering. Swelling and then growth begin with favorable conditions of soil, moisture and temperature.

Selective pesticide: A pesticide that destroys specific kinds of insect pests while not interfering with beneficial insects.

Self-branching: Plants, usually annuals, that naturally develop side branches, becoming dense and compact. Self-branching plants usually do not require pinching.

Self-fruitful: A plant able to set and mature fruit without pollen from another plant.

Self-unfruitful: A plant unable to set and mature fruit without pollen from another plant. Self-unfruitful trees can be made self-fruitful by adding a graft of a variety that will pollinate it.

Semidouble flower: A flower with more than the minimum number of petals common to the species, but with fewer than a fully double flower.

SEMIDOUBLE

DOUBLE

Sexual propagation: Propagation by seed.

Shade tree: An evergreen or deciduous tree, fairly large in size, with dense foliage.

Shelter belt: Large-scale windbreaks of several rows designed to reduce wind velocity and protect plants and people from wind.

Shield budding: Grafting by inserting a bud or scion into a T-shaped opening in rootstock bark. Also called T-budding.

Short-day plant: A plant that begins flowering when daylight periods are shorter (nights longer) than a specific minimum.

Short-season plant: A plant such as radish that begins growth and matures over a relatively short time.

Shrub: A woody perennial plant, usually smaller than a tree, with several stems arising from the base (multiple trunk).

Sidedressing: An application of fertilizer applied just to the side of a row of plants, usually when plants reach a certain stage of growth, such as knee-high stage of corn.

Side graft: This type of graft is used when topworking a tree or whenever the stock is much larger in diameter than the scion. The scion is inserted into the side of the stock, not the cut end.

Silt: A mineral particle of soil midway in size between smaller clay particles and larger sand particles. Silt soils contain 80% or more silt and less than 12% clay.

Single flower: A flower with the minimum number of petals for its type. Usually found in the species, or the plant, as it grows in the wild. See *Double and Semidouble flowers*.

Slip: Cutting of a soft-stemmed plant (African violet or geranium) that readily roots, perhaps in a cup of water.

Sludge: Organic solid remains after sewage treatment. When composted into manure, it is often useful as soil amendment and sometimes as a fertilizer.

Sodding: Planting by rolling or setting out sod that was recently cut.

Sodic soil: A soil that contains enough sodium to prevent proper plant growth.

Softwood: Immature soft stem of a woody plant. Term also applied to wood of conifers.

Soil: A complex mixture of weathered minerals, decomposing organic matter, air spaces and a multitude of living organisms.

Soil texture: Relative proportions of the mineral components of soil—sand, silt and clay.

Solanaceous: Any plant of the family Solanaceae, including nightshade, pepper, potato, tomato and eggplant.

Sphagnum moss: A type of bog moss used by gardeners for packing plants, lining wire baskets, and occasionally as a rooting medium and soil amendment.

Sphagnum moss fibers: Stems and leaves of sphagnum moss with characteristic fibrous structure.

Sphagnum peat moss: Oven-dried peat containing at least 67% sphagnum peat fibers by weight.

Species: A group of plants that resemble each other in minute details and interbreed freely. Usually the most specific category of plant classification, although some species are further divided into subspecies and varieties or cultivars. A hybrid is a cross between two species.

Specimen plant: A plant with a particularly attractive habit of growth, suitable for displaying alone.

Sport: A mutation, a suddenly appearing marked deviation from type, also a bud or seed variation.

Spreader-sticker: A soapy, plastic material added to sprays to improve spreading and adhesion of sprays to plant surface.

Sprig: Small shoot or twig.

Sprigging: Method of planting lawns using cuttings or stolons of desired grass.

Spur: Short, fruit-bearing branch of some fruit trees, especially apples and cherries.

Spur-type fruit tree: A tree that forms more fruit-bearing spurs than nonspur trees, spaced more closely together.

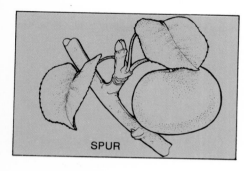
SPUR

Stamen: Male component of a flower consisting usually of a stalk or *filiment* and the anther where pollen is produced.

Staminate: A flower that has male stamen parts but not female or pistillate parts. An imperfect flower.

Standard: A naturally shrubby plant trained to a single, erect, treelike trunk. Also, the erect, inner petals of an iris flower.

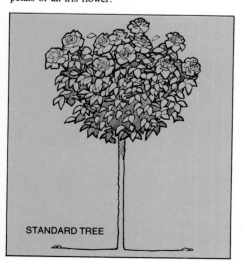
STANDARD TREE

Stele: The central vascular tissue in root and stem of a plant.

Stem: Basic aboveground part of plants, sometimes becoming woody, bearing buds from which leaves or secondary shoots arise.

Stem cutting: Part of a stem used for propagation.

Sterile soil: Usually a potting soil rendered free of plant-damaging organisms and weeds by heat treatment.

Stigma: The uppermost part of a pistil on which pollen grains settle and germinate.

Stipule: One of the pair of appendages at the base of the leaf in many plants.

Stolon: An underground stem that develops roots at nodes. Stoloniferous grasses such as Bermudagrass spread by means of stolons.

Stone fruit: A fruit whose single seed (kernel) is surrounded by a large, hard shell (pit) and is covered by fleshy pulp. Examples are plums, peaches and cherries.

Strain: A group of plants of one species that may not be technically distinct from other members of the species but are distinguishable on the basis of physical characteristics or environment.

Stratification: Storing seeds at cool temperatures—between 35F and 45F (2C and 7C) to overcome natural dormancy.

Street tree: A tree of modest height and clean appearance that is adapted to growth along streets under city conditions. Should have a high-heading habit and deep root system, and be pest free and non-fruiting.

Stress, plant: Pests, drought, heat, cold or other condition that slows or retards plant growth. Plant death often occurs when several stress factors add up to more than the plant can tolerate. Stress signs are the gardener's clue to specific plant needs.

Strip sodding: Planting 2- to 4-inch-wide strips of sod in rows 12 inches apart. Firm contact with surrounding soil is essential.

Style: Stalk connecting the stigma to the ovary in flowers.

Suberization: Conversion of cell walls into cork tissue by development of *suberin,* as when callus forms over a wound.

Subshrub: Term occasionally used to denote partially woody perennials.

Subsoil: Soil below usual depth of cultivation, usually more dense than topsoil and containing little or no organic matter.

Subspecies: Group of plants within a species that differs from other members of the same species by subtle characteristics.

Subtropical plant: Plant that tolerates more cold than a tropical plant but not as much as a hardy plant. Approximate minimum temperature tolerance of about 25F (4C).

Succession planting: Planting short-season crops such as radishes so plants mature at different times, extending harvest period.

Succulent plant: Usually drought-tolerant plant with leaves or stems that store considerable water.

Sucker: A fast-growing, upright secondary branch arising from roots, crown or main branches.

Summer-deciduous: Plant that loses leaves in summer to survive drought, rather than in winter to survive cold.

Surfactant: A spray additive that enhances spreading and effectiveness of sprays.

Sward: Turf. A dense ground cover of short grasses.

Systemic: A material that is absorbed by and moves throughout the vascular system of a plant. Several pesticides are systemic.

T

T-budding: Method of grafting, also called *shield budding.*

Taproot: Large, deep-growing main root from which lateral roots develop.

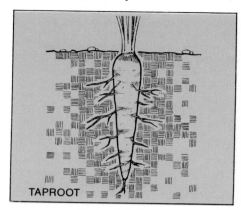
TAPROOT

Taxonomy, plant: Specialty within botany dealing with describing, naming and classifying plants.

Tender plant: A plant that most likely will not survive the expected winter of the climate where it is being grown.

Tensiometer: An instrument that measures moisture tension in soil. A plastic tube with a ceramic, porous cap at one end and a pressure gauge at the other end. Sometimes called an "artificial root."

Terminal bud: The bud at the end of a branch or stem.

Terrace: A level or defined, usually raised, paved or planted area that is a part of the garden, often the central part.

Terrarium: Miniature garden enclosed by glass.

Tetraploid: A plant with cells that contain four sets of chromosomes. Double the normal number of chromosomes. Tetraploid plants are frequently more vigorous than diploid plants with larger or more dramatic flowers or other features.

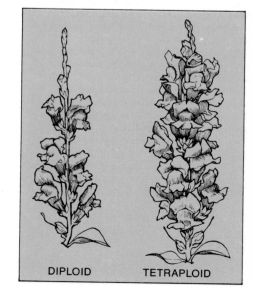
DIPLOID TETRAPLOID

Texture, soil: Relative amounts of mineral particles—sand, silt, and clay—in a soil.

Thatch: Spongy layer of dead stems and runners at soil level of lawn.

Thinning: Method of pruning that involves removing an entire branch to its point of origin. Also the selective removal of buds, flowers or immature fruit to encourage remaining fruit to grow healthier or larger.

Thorn: A special type of twig plants use as defense from grazing animals.

Tiller: A sprout or stalk, usually from a root or underground stem.

Tilth: The physical condition of a soil related to the ease with which it is worked and ease with which seedlings emerge and roots penetrate.

Tip layering: Method of propagation whereby growing tip is bent to the ground and covered with soil until it roots. Used with bramble fruits.

Top dressing: Soil amendment such as manure, sand or compost—applied to the soil surface and not incorporated. Used to cover seeds as when planting a lawn.

Topiary: Specialized pruning whereby shrubs are pruned or vines trained into specific, recognizable geometric forms.

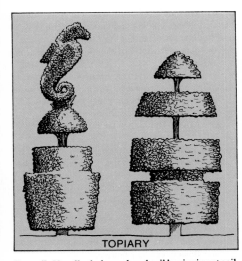

TOPIARY

Topsoil: Usually darker colored soil beginning at soil surface and extending downward a few inches to several feet. Usually a fertile soil rich in organic matter and conducive to plant growth.

Topworking: Changing the variety of a mature tree, especially a fruit tree, by grafting the new variety into scaffold branches of stock.

Trace element: Essential mineral nutrients needed in minute amounts. See *Micronutrient.*

Transpiration: Movement of vaporized water from plant leaves into surrounding air.

Transplant: To move a plant from one growing area to another.

Tree: Tall, woody plant with a single trunk, generally 10 feet or taller.

Triploid: Plant with cells that contain one and one-half the normal number of chromosomes. Vigorous but usually sterile.

Tropicals (tropical plants): Plants native to tropical regions of the earth. Generally requiring high humidity, they are damaged by temperatures that approach freezing.

True from seed: Plants whose seeds grow into plants identical to the parent. Also called *true to type.*

Tuber: Enlarged portion of underground stem (rhizome) such as a potato.

Tuberous root: Enlarged portion of a root such as dahlia or sweet potato.

Tunicate bulb: Bulbs with fleshy scales in series of concentric layers.

Turf: A lawn. Dense growth of lawn grasses that forms a living carpet.

U

U.C. mix: A container soil mix of peat moss and fine sand, devised by University of California (and other) researchers in the 1940s. U.C. mix consistently approximates characteristics of ideal loam soil without complications and variability of field soils.

Urea: A soluble, high-nitrogen (45%N) fertilizer.

V

Variegated leaves: Leaves that are naturally edged, splotched, spotted or colored. Usually caused by harmless virus.

Variety: A group of plants of one species with particular characteristics in common not shared by other plants of the same species.

Vase shape: Plants with shape spread outward toward the top.

Vase system: Method of training trees, especially fruit trees. The tree is headed at 18 to 30 inches above the ground at planting. Scaffold limbs originate 1 to 2 feet above ground level, are evenly spaced around the trunk, and are about 7 inches apart vertically. Apricots and peaches are commonly trained to the vase system.

Vegetable: Mostly annual plants cultivated for succulent, edible leaves, roots, flowers or fruits.

Vegetative propagation: Method of propagating plants using any part of the parent plant except seeds. Includes root, stem or leaf cuttings, division and grafting. Asexual propagation.

Vein: Grouping of cells in a leaf that carries water and food, as well as provides structural support for leaf tissue.

Vermiculite: Micalike mineral that expands like an accordion when exposed to extremely high temperatures. In gardening, vermiculite is useful as a seed-germination medium, rooting medium or soil-mix component because it is sterile and holds water and nutrients.

Vernal: Occurs in spring.

Vernalization: Exposing seeds or plants to low temperatures to imitate their natural dormant period, then warming plants to initiate flower development. An important process in forcing bulbs.

Vine: A woody or herbaceous plant that requires support of a trellis or other plants to grow upright.

Virus: In gardening terms, a common parasitic organism smaller than bacteria that retards growth of host plant, sometimes causing death.

Viticulture: Practice of growing grapes.

Volatile: Vaporizing or evaporating quickly, such as alcohol.

W

Warm-season plant: Plant of subtropical or tropical origin that requires high temperatures to grow and is killed by low temperatures. Warm-season vegetables are those usually grown during summer months.

Water sprout: A fast-growing shoot arising from an adventitious bud on the trunk of one of the main branches.

Weed: Usually a fast-growing volunteer plant competing with desirable plants. Any undesirable plant.

Wettable powder: Extremely fine powder that mixes with water and can be sprayed on plants.

Wetting agent: A soaplike material that modifies water, increasing its ability to wet a surface. Reduces surface tension of water.

Whip: A young, unbranched, flexible tree shoot usually growing from a recently budded or grafted rootstock.

Wilting: When leaves and soft stems lose stiffness and hang in limp fashion. Usually due to lack of water but also caused by pests, diseases or poor root function.

Windbreak: Anything that slows or redirects the wind, such as a row of trees or shrubs.

Winter annual: Plant that begins growth in cool weather of fall, survives winter, then sets and spreads seeds the following spring.

Witches broom: Tree or shrub branches that are unusually tufted, dwarfed, and closely set. Usually caused by a fungus disease recurring at the same location during the same stage in the plant's growth cycle.

X

Xerophyte: Plant adapted to growing in a region of extreme drought.

Xylem: Special plant cells that conduct water and dissolved mineral ions from roots to leaves.

Y

Yellows: Virus disease that stunts growth and yellows leaves. Aster yellows is a common example.

Conversion Tables

LENGTH

1 foot	12 inches
1 yard	3 feet
1 mile	5,280 feet
	1,760 yards

AREA

1 square foot	144 square inches
1 square yard	1,296 square inches
	9 square feet
1 acre	43,560 square feet
	4,840 square yards

VOLUME

1 tablespoon	3 teaspoons
	1/2 fluid ounce
	1/16 cup
1 fluid ounce	6 teaspoons
	2 tablespoons
	1/128 gallon
	1.805 cubic inches
	1/8 cup
	0.0625 fluid pint
1 cup	16 tablespoons
	48 teaspoons
	8 fluid ounces
	0.237 liter
1 pint	32 tablespoons
	2 cups
	16 fluid ounces
	67.2206 cubic inches
	appx. 1 pound water
1 quart (liquid)	64 tablespoons
	32 ounces
	4 cups
	2 pints
	57.75 cubic inches
	1/4 gallon
1 quart (dry)	1.1012 liters
	67.2 cubic inches
	0.125 peck
	1/32 bushel
1 gallon	128 fluid ounces
	16 cups
	8 pints
	4 quarts
	268 cubic inches
	231 cubic inches water
	.155 cubic foot
	.134 cubic foot water
	8.35 pounds water
1 peck	8 quarts
	2 gallons
	16 pints

1 bushel	2 pecks
	32 quarts
	64 pints
	8 gallons
1 cubic foot	0.8036 bushel
	7.5 gallons
	1,728 cubic inches
	62.4 pounds of water
2 cubic feet	1.61 bushels
	15 gallons
1 cubic yard	27 cubic feet
	22 bushels

To Find:

Volume of cube:	Multiply side by side by side.
Volume of cylinder:	Multiply squared radius by height by 3.141.

FLOW RATE

1 gallon per minute	0.134 cubic foot per minute.
1 cubic foot per second	450 gallons per minute
	1 acre-inch per hour
1 cubic foot per minute	7.5 gallons per minute
10.4 gallons per minute	1,000 square-foot-inch per hour

FLOW VOLUME

1 acre-inch	3,630 cubic feet
	27,154 gallons
1 acre-foot	43,560 cubic feet
	325,851 gallons
1000 square-foot-inch	624 gallons

WEIGHT

1 ounce	1/16 pound
1 pound	16 ounces
1 ton	2,000 pounds
1 cubic-foot soil	92 pounds
1 acre-foot soil	2,000 tons

Conversion to Metric Measure

When You Know	Symbol	Multiply By	To Find	Symbol
VOLUME				
teaspoons	tsp.	4.93	milliliters	ml
tablespoons	tbsp.	14.79	milliliters	ml
fluid ounces	fl. oz.	29.57	milliliters	ml
cups	c.	0.24	liters	l
pints	pt.	0.47	liters	l
quarts	qt.	0.95	liters	l
gallons	gal.	3.79	liters	l
LENGTH				
inches	in.	25.4	millimeters	mm
inches	in.	2.54	centimeters	cm
feet	ft.	30.48	centimeters	cm
yards	yd.	0.91	meters	m
TEMPERATURE				
Fahrenheit	F	0.56 (after subtracting 32)	Celsius	C

INDEX